A STUDY OF
HISTORY

*Issued under the auspices of the
Royal Institute of International Affairs*

A STUDY OF HISTORY

BY

ARNOLD J. TOYNBEE

Doloris
Sopitam recreant volnera viva animam.
Anon.

ABRIDGEMENT
OF VOLUMES I–VI
BY
D. C. SOMERVELL

1947
OXFORD UNIVERSITY PRESS
New York & London

PLAN OF THE BOOK

(The present volume is an abridgement of Parts I–V)

PREFACE BY THE AUTHOR

M^{R. D. C. SOMERVELL} explains in his own following prefatory note how he came to make this abridgement of the first six volumes of my book. Before I knew anything about it, a number of inquiries had been reaching me, particularly from the United States, as to whether there was any likelihood of an abridgement of these volumes being published pending the time—now inevitably postponed far beyond all original expectations owing to the war—when I should be able to publish the rest of the work. I had been feeling the force of this demand, but had not seen how to meet it (being, as I was, very fully occupied with war-work) until the problem was solved in a most happy way by a letter from Mr. Somervell telling me that an abridgement, made by him, was now in existence.

When Mr. Somervell sent me his manuscript, more than four years had already passed since the publication of volumes IV–VI and more than nine years since that of volumes I–III. For a writer the act of publication always, I suppose, has the effect of turning into a foreign body the work that, so long as it was in the making, was a part of its maker's life; and in this case the war of 1939–1945, with the changes of circumstance and occupation that it brought with it, had also intervened between my book and me (volumes IV–VI were published forty-one days before the war broke out). In working over Mr. Somervell's manuscript, I have therefore been able—notwithstanding his skill in retaining my own words—to read the abridgement almost as though it were a new book from another hand than mine. I have now made it fully my own by here and there recasting the language (with Mr. Somervell's good-natured acquiescence) as I have gone along, but I have not compared the abridgement with the original line by line, and I have made a point of never reinserting any passage that Mr. Somervell had left out—believing, as I do, that the author himself is unlikely to be the best judge of what is and is not an indispensable part of his work.

The maker of a skilful abridgement does an author a most valuable service which his own hand cannot readily do for him, and readers of the present volume who are acquainted with the original text will, I am sure, agree with me that Mr. Somervell's literary craftsmanship has been skilful indeed. He has managed to preserve the argument of the book, to present it for the most part in the original words and at the same time to abridge six volumes into one volume. If I had been set this task myself, I doubt whether I could have accomplished it.

Though Mr. Somervell has made the lesser task of working over his abridgement as light a one for the author as it could well be, two further years have passed since I first set to work on it. For periods of weeks and months on end I have had to let it lie untouched at my elbow. These delays have been due to the exigencies of war-work; but the notes for the rest of the book are intact, in the safe keeping of the Council on Foreign Relations in New York (I posted them in Munich week to the Executive Secretary of the Council, Mr. Mallory, who kindly undertook to look after them), and while there is life there is hope of finishing one's work. Not the least of my reasons for being grateful to Mr. Somervell is that the process of working on his abridgement of those volumes of the book that have already been published has helped me to begin to turn my mind again to those that I have still to write.

It is also a happy thing for me that this volume is being published, like the full version of the book, by the Oxford University Press, and that the Index is being made by Miss V. M. Boulter, to whom readers of the full version are already indebted for the two indexes to Volumes I–III and Volumes IV–VI.

ARNOLD J. TOYNBEE

1946

NOTE

BY THE EDITOR OF THE ABRIDGEMENT

M R. TOYNBEE'S *Study of History* presents a single continuous argument as to the nature and pattern of the historical experience of the human race since the first appearance of the species of societies called civilizations, and that argument is illustrated and, so far as the nature of the material allows, 'proved' at every stage by a diversity of illustrations drawn from the whole length and breadth of human history, so far as human history is known to the historians of our day. Some of these illustrations are worked out in great detail. That being the nature of the book, the task of the editor of an abridgement is in essentials perfectly simple, namely to preserve the argument intact, though in an abbreviated statement, and to reduce in some degree the number of illustrations and, in a much greater degree, the detail of their exposition.

I think that this volume makes an adequate presentation of Mr. Toynbee's philosophy of history in so far as it is set forth in the six published volumes of his yet unfinished work. If it did not do so Mr. Toynbee would obviously not have approved its publication. But I should be very sorry if it came to be regarded as an entirely satisfactory substitute for the original work. For 'business purposes' it is perhaps an adequate substitute: for pleasure surely not; for a large part of the charm of the original resides in the leisured amplitude of its illustrations. Only the big book, one feels, is aesthetically worthy of the bigness of its subject. I have been able to use to such a very large extent the actual sentences and paragraphs of the original that I have no fear that this abridgement will be found dull, but I am equally certain that the original will be found much more entrancing.

I made this abridgement for my own amusement, without Mr. Toynbee's knowledge and without any idea of publication. It seemed to me an agreeable way of passing the time. Only when it was finished did I tell Mr. Toynbee of its existence and place it at his disposal if at any time he cared to make any use of it. Such being its origin I allowed myself occasionally to interpolate a little illustration of my own not found in the original work. After all, it is written 'Thou shalt not muzzle the ox which treadeth out his master's corn'. These intrusions of mine are small in extent and smaller in importance. As the whole of my manuscript has been carefully revised by Mr. Toynbee and they have received his *imprimatur* along with all the rest, there is no need to indicate them either here or by means of footnotes to the text. I mention them merely because a careful reader who discovered them by comparing this book with the original might feel that, in respect of them, the game of abridgement was not being played according to the strictest rules. There are also one or two places where a few sentences have been interpolated, either by Mr. Toynbee or by myself, in view of events that have occurred since the original work was published. But on the whole, seeing that the first three volumes were published in 1933 and the others in 1939, it is amazing how little work of that kind was called for.

The 'Argument' which appears as an Appendix to the work is in effect an abridgement of an abridgement. Whereas this work presents an original of over 3,000 pages in 565, the 'Argument' presents the same in a mere 25. Read as a 'thing in itself' it would prove extremely indigestible, but it may prove useful for purposes of reference all the way through. It is, in fact, a kind of 'Table of Contents', and the only reason for not putting it at the beginning is that it would constitute a rather large and ugly object in the foreground of the picture.

For readers who wish to refer from this book to the original volumes the following equations will be useful.

Pages   1–79   represent Volume I of the original work.
  „   80–164   „   II   „
  „   165–243   „   III   „
  „   244–359   „   IV   „
  „   360–494   „   V   „
  „   495–565   „   VI   „

D. C. SOMERVELL

TABLE OF CONTENTS

I. INTRODUCTION

I

INTRODUCTION

I. THE UNIT OF HISTORICAL STUDY

HISTORIANS generally illustrate rather than correct the ideas of the communities within which they live and work, and the development in the last few centuries, and more particularly in the last few generations, of the would-be self-sufficient national sovereign state has led historians to choose nations as the normal fields of historical study. But no single nation or national state of Europe can show a history which is in itself self-explanatory. If any state could do so it would be Great Britain. In fact, if Great Britain (or, in the earlier periods, England) is not found to constitute in herself an intelligible field of historical study, we may confidently infer that no other modern European national state will pass the test.

Is English history, then, intelligible when taken by itself? Can we abstract an internal history of England from her external relations? If we can, shall we find that these residual external relations are of secondary importance? And in analysing these, again, shall we find that the foreign influences upon England are slight in comparison with the English influences upon other parts of the world? If all these questions receive affirmative answers we may be justified in concluding that, while it may not be possible to understand other histories without reference to England, it is possible, more or less, to understand English history without reference to other parts of the world. The best way to approach these questions is to direct our thought backwards over the course of English history and recall the principal chapters. In inverse order we may take these chapters to be:

(*a*) the establishment of the Industrial System of economy (since the last quarter of the eighteenth century);

(*b*) the establishment of Responsible Parliamentary Government (since the last quarter of the seventeenth century);

(*c*) the expansion overseas (beginning in the third quarter of the sixteenth century with piracy and developing gradually into a world-wide foreign trade, the acquisition of tropical dependencies, and the establishment of new English-speaking communities in overseas countries with temperate climates);

(*d*) the Reformation (since the second quarter of the sixteenth century);

(*e*) the Renaissance, including the political and economic as well as the artistic and intellectual aspects of the movement (since the last quarter of the fifteenth century);

(*f*) the establishment of the Feudal System (since the eleventh century);

(*g*) the conversion of the English from the religion of the so-called Heroic Age to Western Christianity (since the last years of the sixth century).

This glance backwards from the present day over the general course of English history would appear to show that the farther back we look the less evidence do we find of self-sufficiency or isolation. The conversion, which was really the beginning of all things in English history, was the direct antithesis of that; it was an act which merged half a dozen isolated communities of barbarians in the common weal of a nascent Western Society. As for the Feudal System, Vinogradoff has brilliantly demonstrated that the seeds of it had already sprouted on English soil before the Norman Conquest. Yet, even so, the sprouting was stimulated by an external factor, the Danish invasions; these invasions were part of the Scandinavian *Völkerwanderung* which was stimulating simultaneously a similar growth in France, and the Norman Conquest undoubtedly brought the harvest to rapid maturity. As for the Renaissance, in both its cultural and its political aspect it is universally admitted to have been a breath of life from Northern Italy. If in Northern Italy Humanism, Absolutism and the Balance of Power had not been cultivated in miniature, like seedlings in a sheltered nursery garden, during two centuries that fall approximately between 1275 and 1475, they could never have been bedded out north of the Alps from about 1475 onwards. The Reformation, again, was not a specifically English phenomenon, but a general movement of North-Western Europe for emancipation from the South, where the Western Mediterranean held the eye fixed upon worlds that were dead and gone. In the Reformation, England did not take the initiative, nor did she take it in the competition between the European nations of the Atlantic seaboard for the prize of the new worlds overseas. She won that prize as a comparatively late comer, in a series of struggles with Powers that were before her in the field.

It remains to consider the two latest chapters: the geneses of the Parliamentary System and the Industrial System—institutions which are commonly regarded as having been evolved locally on English soil and afterwards propagated from England into other parts of the world. But the authorities do not entirely support this view. With reference to the parliamentary system Lord Acton says: 'General history naturally depends on the action of forces

which are not national but proceed from wider causes. The rise
of modern kingship in France is part of a similar movement in
England. Bourbons and Stuarts obeyed the same law though with
different results.' In other words the Parliamentary System, which
was the local result in England, was the product of a force which
was not peculiar to England but was operating simultaneously in
England and France.

On the genesis of the Industrial Revolution in England no
higher authorities could be cited than Mr. and Mrs. Hammond.
In the preface to their book *The Rise of Modern Industry* they
take the view that the factor which goes farthest towards account-
ing for the genesis of the Industrial Revolution in England rather
than elsewhere is England's general position in the eighteenth-
century world—her geographical position in relation to the
Atlantic and her political position in respect of the European
balance of power. It seems, then, that British national history
never has been, and almost certainly never will be, an 'intelligible
field of historical study' in isolation; and if that is true of Great
Britain it surely must be true of any other national state *a
fortiori*.

Our brief examination of English history, though its result has
been negative, has given us a clue. The chapters which caught our
eye in our glance backward over the course of English history were
real chapters in some story or other, but that story was the history
of some society of which Great Britain was only a part, and the
experiences were experiences in which other nations besides Great
Britain were participants. The 'intelligible field of study', in fact,
appears to be a society containing a number of communities of the
species represented by Great Britain—not only Great Britain herself but also France and Spain, the Netherlands, the Scandinavian
countries and so on—and the passage quoted from Acton indicates the relation between these parts and that whole.

The forces in action are not national but proceed from wider
causes, which operate upon each of the parts and are not intelligible in their partial operation unless a comprehensive view is
taken of their operation throughout the society. Different parts
are differently affected by an identical general cause, because they
each react, and each contribute, in a different way to the forces
which that same cause sets in motion. A society, we may say, is
confronted in the course of its life by a succession of problems
which each member has to solve for itself as best it may. The
presentation of each problem is a challenge to undergo an ordeal,
and through this series of ordeals the members of the society progressively differentiate themselves from one another. Throughout,

it is impossible to grasp the significance of any particular member's behaviour under a particular ordeal without taking some account of the similar or dissimilar behaviour of its fellows and without viewing the successive ordeals as a series of events in the life of the whole society.

This method of interpreting historical facts may, perhaps, be made clearer by a concrete example, which may be taken from the history of the city states of Ancient Greece during the four centuries falling between 725 and 325 B.C.

Soon after the beginning of that period the society of which these numerous states were all members was confronted with the problem of the pressure of population upon the means of subsistence—means which the Hellenic peoples at that time were apparently obtaining almost entirely by raising in their territories a varied agricultural produce for home consumption. When the crisis came, different states contended with it in different ways.

Some, like Corinth and Chalcis, disposed of their surplus population by seizing and colonizing agricultural territories overseas—in Sicily, Southern Italy, Thrace and elsewhere. The Greek colonies thus founded simply extended the geographical area of the Hellenic Society without altering its character. On the other hand certain states sought solutions which entailed a variation of their way of life.

Sparta, for instance, satisfied the land-hunger of her citizens by attacking and conquering her nearest Greek neighbours. The consequence was that Sparta only obtained her additional lands at the cost of obstinate and repeated wars with neighbouring peoples of her own calibre. In order to meet this situation Spartan statesmen were compelled to militarize Spartan life from top to bottom, which they did by re-invigorating and adapting certain primitive social institutions, common to a number of Greek communities, at a moment when, at Sparta as elsewhere, these institutions were on the point of disappearance.

Athens reacted to the population problem in a different way again. She specialized her agricultural production for export, started manufactures also for export and then developed her political institutions so as to give a fair share of political power to the new classes which had been called into being by these economic innovations. In other words, Athenian statesmen averted a social revolution by successfully carrying through an economic and political revolution; and, discovering this solution of the common problem in so far as it affected themselves, they incidentally opened up a new avenue of advance for the whole of the Hellenic Society. This is what Pericles meant when, in the crisis of his own city's material fortunes, he claimed that she was 'the education of Hellas'.

From this angle of vision, which takes not Athens or Sparta or Corinth or Chalcis but the whole of the Hellenic Society as its field, we are able to understand both the significance of the histories of the several communities during the period 725–325 B.C. and the significance of the transition from this period to that which followed. Questions are answered to which no intelligible answer could be found so long as we looked for an intelligible field of study in Chalcidian, Corinthian, Spartan or Athenian history examined in isolation. From this point of view it was merely possible to observe that Chalcidian and Corinthian history was in some sense normal whereas Spartan and Athenian history departed from the norm in different directions. It was not possible to explain the way in which this departure took place, and historians were reduced to suggesting that the Spartans and Athenians were already differentiated from the other Greeks by the possession of special innate qualities at the dawn of Hellenic history. This was equivalent to explaining Spartan and Athenian development by postulating that there had been no development at all and that these two Greek peoples were as peculiar at the beginning of the story as at the end of it. That hypothesis, however, is in contradiction with established facts. In regard to Sparta, for example, the excavations conducted by the British Archaeological School at Athens have produced striking evidence that down to about the middle of the sixth century B.C. Spartan life was not markedly different from that of other Greek communities. The special characteristics of Athens also, which she communicated to the whole Hellenic World in the so-called Hellenistic Age (in contrast to Sparta, whose peculiar turning proved to be a blind alley), were likewise acquired characteristics, the genesis of which can only be apprehended from a general standpoint. It is the same with the differentiation between Venice, Milan, Genoa and other cities of Northern Italy in the so-called Middle Ages and with the differentiation between France, Spain, the Netherlands, Great Britain and other national states of the West in more recent times. In order to understand the parts we must first focus our attention upon the whole, because this whole is the field of study that is intelligible in itself.

But what are these 'wholes', which form intelligible fields of study, and how shall we discover their spatial and temporal boundaries? Let us turn again to our summary of the principal chapters of English history, and see what larger whole is found to constitute the intelligible field of which English history is a part.

If we start with our latest chapter—the establishment of the Industrial System—we find that the geographical extension of the intelligible field of study which it presupposes is world-wide. In order to explain the Industrial Revolution in England we have to take account of economic conditions not only in Western Europe but in Tropical Africa, America, Russia, India and the Far East. When, however, we go back to the Parliamentary System and pass, in so doing, from the economic to the political plane, our horizon contracts. 'The law' which (in Lord Acton's phrase) 'Bourbons and Stuarts obeyed' in France and England was not in force for Romanovs in Russia or 'Osmanlis in Turkey or Timurids in Hindustan or Manchus in China or Tokugawas in Japan. The political histories of these other countries cannot be explained in the same terms. We here come up against a frontier. The operation of 'the law' which 'Bourbons and Stuarts obeyed' extended to the other countries of Western Europe and to the new communities planted overseas by West-European colonists, but its writ did not run beyond the western frontiers of Russia and Turkey. East of that line other political laws were being obeyed at that time with other consequences.

If we pass back to the earlier chapters of English history on our list, we find that the expansion overseas was confined not merely to Western Europe but almost entirely to the countries with seaboards on the Atlantic. In studying the history of the Reformation and the Renaissance we may ignore without loss the religious and cultural developments in Russia and Turkey. The feudal system of Western Europe was not causally connected with such feudal phenomena as were to be found in contemporary Byzantine and Islamic communities.

Finally, the conversion of the English to Western Christianity admitted us to one society at the cost of excluding us from the possibility of membership in others. Down to the Synod of Whitby in 664 the English might have become converts to the 'Far Western Christianity' of 'the Celtic Fringe'; and, had Augustine's mission ultimately proved a failure, the English might have joined the Welsh and Irish in founding a new Christian church out of communion with Rome—as veritable an *alter orbis* as the world of the Nestorians on the Far Eastern fringe of Christendom. Later on, when the Muslim Arabs appeared on the Atlantic seaboard, these Far Western Christians of the British Isles might have lost touch as completely as the Christians of Abyssinia or Central Asia with their co-religionists on the European Continent. They might conceivably have become converts to Islam, as so many Monophysites and Nestorians actually did when the Middle

East passed under Arab rule. These suggested alternatives might be dismissed as fantastic, but the contemplation of them serves to remind us that while the conversion of 597 has made us one with Western Christendom it has not made us one with all mankind, but has simultaneously made a sharp line of division between ourselves as Western Christians and the adherents of other religious communions.

This second review of our chapters of English history has given us a means for taking spatial cross-sections, at several different dates, of that society which includes Great Britain and which is 'the intelligible field of historical study' as far as Great Britain is concerned. In taking these cross-sections we shall have to distinguish between certain different planes of social life—the economic, the political and the cultural—because it is already evident that the spatial extension of this society differs perceptibly according to the plane on which we focus our attention. At the present day and on the economic plane the society which includes Great Britain is undoubtedly co-extensive with the whole inhabitable and navigable surface of the Earth. On the political plane, again, the world-wide character of this society at the present day is almost equally apparent. When, however, we pass to the cultural plane the present geographical extension of the society to which Great Britain belongs appears to be very much smaller. Substantially, it is confined to the countries occupied by Catholic and Protestant peoples in Western Europe, America and the South Seas. In spite of certain exotic influences exercised on this society by such cultural elements as Russian literature, Chinese painting and Indian religion, and in spite of the much stronger cultural influences exercised by our own society on other societies, such as those of the Orthodox and Oriental Christians, the Muslims, the Hindus and the peoples of the Far East, it remains true that all of these are outside the cultural world to which we belong.

As we take further cross-sections at earlier dates we find that, on all three planes, the geographical limits of the society which we are examining progressively contract. In a cross-section taken about the year 1675, while the contraction is not perhaps very great on the economic plane (at least if we confine ourselves to the extension of trade and ignore its volume and content), the boundaries on the political plane shrink until they coincide approximately with those on the cultural plane at the present day. In a cross-section taken about 1475 the overseas portions of the area disappear on all three planes alike, and even on the economic plane the boundaries contract until they, too, coincide approximately with those on the cultural plane, now confined to Western

and Central Europe—except for a fast dissolving chain of outposts
on the eastern shores of the Mediterranean. In a primitive cross-
section, taken about the year 775, the boundaries shrink still
further on all three planes. At that date the area of our society is
almost restricted to what were then the dominions of Charlemagne together with the English 'successor states' of the Roman
Empire in Britain. Outside these limits, almost all the Iberian
Peninsula belongs at this date to the domain of the Muslim Arab
Caliphate; Northern and North-Eastern Europe is in the hands of
unconverted barbarians; the north-western fringes of the British
Isles are held by the 'Far Western' Christians; and Southern Italy
is under the rule of the Byzantines.

Let us call this society, whose spatial limits we have been studying, Western Christendom; and, as soon as we bring our mental
image of it into focus by finding a name for it, the images and
names of its counterparts in the contemporary world come into
focus side by side with it, especially if we keep our attention fixed
upon the cultural plane. On this plane we can distinguish unmistakably the presence in the world to-day of at least four other
living societies of the same species as ours:

(i) an Orthodox Christian Society in South-Eastern Europe and
Russia;

(ii) an Islamic Society with its focus in the arid zone which
stretches diagonally across North Africa and the Middle East from
the Atlantic to the outer face of the Great Wall of China;

(iii) a Hindu Society in the tropical sub-continent of India;

(iv) a Far-Eastern Society in the sub-tropical and temperate
regions between the arid zone and the Pacific.

On closer inspection we can also discern two sets of what appear
to be fossilized relics of similar societies now extinct, namely: one set
including the Monophysite Christians of Armenia, Mesopotamia,
Egypt and Abyssinia and the Nestorian Christians of Kurdistan and
ex-Nestorians in Malabar, as well as the Jews and the Parsees; and
a second set including the Lamaistic Mahayanian Buddhists of
Tibet and Mongolia and the Hinayanian Buddhists of Ceylon,
Burma, Siam and Cambodia, as well as the Jains of India.

It is interesting to notice that when we turn back to the cross-
section at A.D. 775 we find that the number and identity of the
societies on the world map are nearly the same as at the present
time. Substantially the world map of societies of this species has
remained constant since the first emergence of our Western Society.
In the struggle for existence the West has driven its contemporaries to the wall and entangled them in the meshes of its economic
and political ascendancy, but it has not yet disarmed them of their

distinctive cultures. Hard pressed though they are, they can still call their souls their own.

The conclusion of the argument, as far as we have carried it at present, is that we should draw a sharp distinction between relations of two kinds: those between communities within the same society and those of different societies with one another.

And now, having explored the extension of our Western Society in space, we have to consider its extension in time; and we are at once confronted with the fact that we cannot know its future—a limitation which greatly restricts the amount of light that the study of this particular society, or of any of the still extant societies, can throw on the nature of the species to which these societies belong. We must content ourselves with the exploration of our Western Society's beginnings.

When Charlemagne's dominions were partitioned between his three grandsons by the treaty of Verdun in A.D. 843, Lothaire, as the eldest, established his claim to possess his grandfather's two capitals of Aachen and Rome; and, in order that these might be connected by a continuous belt of territory, Lothaire was assigned a portion which straggled across the face of Western Europe from the mouths of the Tiber and Po to the mouth of the Rhine. Lothaire's portion is commonly regarded as one of the curiosities of historical geography; none the less the three Carolingian brothers were right in believing that it was a zone of particular importance in our Western World. Whatever its future might be, it had a great past behind it.

Both Lothaire and his grandfather ruled from Aachen to Rome under the title of Roman Emperor, and the line stretching from Rome across the Alps to Aachen (and onwards from Aachen across the Channel to the Roman Wall) had once been one of the principal bulwarks of the then extinct Roman Empire. By running a line of communications north-westwards from Rome across the Alps, establishing a military frontier on the left bank of the Rhine, and covering the left flank of that frontier by the annexation of Southern Britain, the Romans had cut off the western extremity of Transalpine Continental Europe and annexed it to an empire which, except in this quarter, was substantially confined to the Mediterranean Basin. Thus the line embedded in Lotharingia entered into the geographical structure of the Roman Empire before Lothaire's time as well as into that of the Western Society after it, but the structural function of this line for the Roman Empire and for the subsequent Western Society were not the same. In the Roman Empire it had been a frontier; in our Western Society it was to be a base-line for lateral expansion on either side and in all directions. During the deep sleep of the interval (*circa* A.D. 375–675) which intervened between the break-up of the Roman Empire and the gradual emergence of our Western Society out of the chaos, a rib was taken from the side of the older society and was fashioned into the backbone of a new creature of the same species.

It is now plain that in tracing the life of our Western Society backwards behind 775 we begin to find it presented to us in terms of something other than itself—in terms of the Roman Empire and of the society to which that empire belonged. It can also be shown that any elements which we can trace back from Western history into the history of that earlier society may have quite different functions in these two different associations.

Lothaire's portion became the base-line of the Western Society because the Church, pushing up towards the Roman frontier, here encountered the Barbarians pressing down upon the frontier from the no-man's-land outside, and eventually gave birth to a new society. Accordingly, the historian of the Western Society, in tracing its roots down into the past from this point, will concentrate his attention on the histories of the Church and the Barbarians, and he will find it possible to follow both these histories backwards as far as the economic, social and political revolutions of the last two centuries B.C., into which the Graeco-Roman Society was thrown by the vast shock of the Hannibalic War. Why did Rome stretch out a long arm towards the north-west and gather into her empire the western corner of Transalpine Europe? Because she was drawn in that direction by the life-and-death struggle with Carthage. Why, having once crossed the Alps, did she stop at the Rhine? Because in the Augustan Age her vitality gave out after two centuries of exhausting wars and revolutions. Why did the Barbarians ultimately break through? Because, when a frontier between a more highly and a less highly civilized society ceases to advance, the balance does not settle down to a stable equilibrium but inclines, with the passage of time, in the more backward society's favour. Why, when the Barbarians broke through the frontier, did they encounter the Church on the other side? Materially, because the economic and social revolutions following the Hannibalic War had brought multitudes of slaves from the Oriental World to work on the devastated areas of the West, and this forced migration of Oriental labour had been followed by a peaceful penetration of Oriental religions into the Graeco-Roman Society. Spiritually, because these religions, with their promise of an 'other-worldly' personal salvation, found fallow fields to cultivate in the souls of a 'dominant minority' which had failed, in This World, to save the fortunes of the Graeco-Roman Society.

To the student of Graeco-Roman history, on the other hand, both the Christians and the Barbarians would present themselves as creatures of an alien underworld—the internal and the external proletariat,[1] as he might call them, of that Graeco-Roman (or, to use a better term, Hellenic) Society in its last phase. He would point out that the great masters of Hellenic culture, down to and including Marcus Aurelius, almost ignore their existence. He would diagnose both the Christian Church and the Barbarian war-bands as morbid affections which only appeared in the body of the Hellenic Society after its physique had been permanently undermined by the Hannibalic War.

This investigation has enabled us to draw a positive conclusion regarding the backward extension in time of our Western Society. The life of that society, though somewhat longer than that of any single nation belonging to it, has not been so long as the span of time during which the species of which it is a representative has been in existence. In tracing its history back to its origins we strike upon the last phase of another society, the origins of which obviously lie much farther back in the past. The continuity of history, to use an accepted phrase, is not a continuity such as is exemplified in the life of a single individual. It is rather a continuity made up of the lives of successive generations, our Western Society being related to the Hellenic Society in a manner comparable (to use a convenient though imperfect simile) with the relationship of a child to its parent.

If the argument of this chapter is accepted it will be agreed that the intelligible unit of historical study is neither a nation state nor (at the other end of the scale) mankind as a whole but a certain grouping of humanity which we have called a society. We have discovered five such societies in existence to-day, together with sundry fossilized evidences of societies dead and gone; and, while exploring the circumstances of the birth of one of these living societies, namely our own, we have stumbled upon the death-bed of another very notable society to which our own stands in something like the relation of offspring—to which, in a single word, our own society is 'affiliated'. In the next chapter we shall attempt to make a complete list of the societies of this kind that are known to have existed on this planet and to indicate the relations in which they stand to each other.

[1] The word 'proletariat' is here and hereafter used to mean any social element or group which in some way is *in* but not *of* any given society at any period of that society's history.

II. THE COMPARATIVE STUDY OF
CIVILIZATIONS

WE have already found that our own Western Society (or Civilization) is affiliated to a predecessor. The obvious method of pursuing our search for further societies of the same species will be to take the other existing examples, the Orthodox Christian, the Islamic, the Hindu and the Far Eastern, and see if we can discover 'parents' for them also. But before we set out on this search we must be clear what we are looking for: in other words, what are the tokens of apparentation-and-affiliation which we are to accept as valid evidence. What tokens of such relationship did we, in fact, find in the case of our own society's affiliation to the Hellenic Society?

The first of these phenomena was *a universal state*[1] (the Roman Empire), incorporating the whole Hellenic Society in a single political community in the last phase of Hellenic history. This phenomenon is striking because it stands out in sharp contrast to the multiplicity of local states into which the Hellenic Society had been divided before the Roman Empire arose, and in equally sharp contrast to the multiplicity of local states into which our own Western Society has been divided hitherto. We found, further, that the Roman Empire was immediately preceded by a *time of troubles*, going back at least as far as the Hannibalic War, in which the Hellenic Society was no longer creative and was indeed patently in decline, a decline which the establishment of the Roman Empire arrested for a time but which proved in the end to be the symptom of an incurable disease destroying the Hellenic Society and the Roman Empire with it. Again, the Roman Empire's fall was followed by a kind of *interregnum* between the disappearance of the Hellenic and the emergence of the Western Society.

This interregnum is filled with the activities of two institutions: the Christian *Church*, established within and surviving the Roman Empire, and a number of ephemeral successor states arising on the former territory of the Empire out of the so-called *Völkerwanderung* of the Barbarians from the no-man's-land beyond the Imperial frontiers. We have already described these two forces as the *internal proletariat* and *external proletariat* of the Hellenic Society. Though differing in all else they agreed in their alienation from the *dominant minority* of the Hellenic Society, the leading classes of

---

[1] The words and phrases here *italicized* will be in constant use henceforth as technical terms of this Study.

the old society who had lost their way and ceased to lead. In fact the Empire fell and the Church survived just because the Church gave leadership and enlisted loyalty whereas the Empire had long failed to do either the one or the other. Thus the Church, a survival from the dying society, became the womb from which in due course the new one was born.

What was the part played in the affiliation of our society by the other feature of the interregnum, the Völkerwanderung, in which the external proletariat came down in spate from beyond the frontiers of the old society—Germans and Slavs from the forests of Northern Europe, Sarmatians and Huns from the Eurasian Steppe, Saracens from the Arabian Peninsula, Berbers from the Atlas and the Sahara, whose ephemeral successor states shared with the Church the stage of history during an interregnum or *heroic age*? In comparison with the Church their contribution was negative and insignificant. Almost all of them perished by violence before the interregnum came to an end. The Vandals and Ostrogoths were overthrown by counter-attacks on the part of the Roman Empire itself. The last convulsive flicker of the Roman flame sufficed to burn these poor moths to cinders. Others were overthrown in fratricidal warfare: the Visigoths, for example, received the first blow from the Franks and the *coup de grâce* from the Arabs. The few survivors of this Ishmaelitish struggle for existence incontinently degenerated and then vegetated as fainéants till extinguished by new political forces which possessed the indispensable germ of creative power. Thus the Merovingian and the Lombard dynasties were brushed aside by the architects of the Empire of Charlemagne. There are only two out of all the Barbarian 'successor states' of the Roman Empire that can be shown to have any lineal descendants among the nation states of Modern Europe, Charlemagne's Frankish Austrasia and Alfred's Wessex.

Thus the Völkerwanderung and its ephemeral products are tokens, like the Church and the Empire, of the affiliation of the Western Society to the Hellenic; but, like the Empire and unlike the Church, they are tokens and nothing more. When we turn from the study of symptoms to the study of causes we find that, whereas the Church belonged to the future as well as the past, the Barbarian successor states, as well as the Empire, belonged wholly to the past. Their rise was merely the obverse of the Empire's fall, and that fall inexorably portended theirs.

This low estimate of the contribution of the Barbarians to our Western Society would have shocked our Western historians of the last generation (such as Freeman), who regarded the institution of responsible parliamentary government as a development of certain institutions of self-government which the Teutonic tribes were supposed to have brought with them from no-man's-land. But these primitive Teutonic institutions, if they existed at all, were rudimentary institutions characteristic of primitive man at almost all times and places, and, such as they were, they did not survive the Völkerwanderung. The leaders of the barbarian war-bands were military adventurers and the constitution of the successor states, as of the Roman Empire itself at the time, was despotism tempered by revolution. The last of these barbaric despotisms was extinguished many centuries before the real beginning of the new growth which gradually produced what we call parliamentary institutions.

The prevalent over-estimate of the Barbarians' contribution to the life of our Western Society can also be traced in part to the false belief that social progress is to be explained by the presence of certain inborn qualities of race. A false analogy from the phenomena that were being brought to light by physical science led our Western historians of the last generation to picture races as chemical 'elements' and their miscegenation as a chemical 'reaction' which released latent energies and produced effervescence and change where, before, there had been immobility and stagnation. Historians deluded themselves into supposing that the 'infusion of new blood', as they metaphorically described the racial effect of the Barbarian intrusion, could account for those long-subsequent manifestations of life and growth which constitute the history of the Western Society. It was suggested that these Barbarians were 'pure races' of conquerors whose blood still invigorated and ennobled the bodies of their supposed descendants.

In reality the Barbarians were not the authors of our spiritual being. They made their passage felt by being in at the death of the Hellenic Society, but they cannot even claim the distinction of having delivered the death-blow. By the time when they arrived on the scene the Hellenic Society was already dying of wounds self-inflicted in the time of troubles centuries before. They were merely the vultures feeding on the carrion or the maggots crawling on the carcass. Their heroic age is the epilogue to Hellenic history, not the prelude to ours.

Thus three factors mark the transition from the old to the new society: a universal state as the final stage of the old society; a church developed in the old society and in turn developing the new; and the chaotic intrusion of a barbarian heroic age. Of these factors the second is the most, and the third the least, significant.

One more symptom in the 'apparentation-and-affiliation' between the Hellenic and the Western Society may be noted before we proceed with our attempt to discover other apparented societies, namely the displacement of the cradle or original home of the new society from the original home of its predecessor. We have found that a frontier of the old society became, in the instance already examined, the centre of the new one; and we must be prepared for similar displacements in other cases.

The Orthodox Christian Society. A study of the origins of this society will not add to our list of specimens of the species, for it is clearly twin offspring, with our Western Society, of the Hellenic Society, its geographical displacement being north-eastwards instead of north-westwards. With its cradle or original home in Byzantine Anatolia, much cramped for many centuries by the rival expansion of the Islamic Society, it ultimately secured a vast expansion northwards and eastwards through Russia and Siberia, outflanking the Islamic World and impinging upon the Far East. The differentiation of Western and Orthodox Christendom into two separate societies can be traced in the schism of their common chrysalis, the Catholic Church, into two bodies, the Roman Catholic Church and the Orthodox Church. The schism took rather more than three centuries to work itself out, beginning with the Iconoclastic controversy of the eighth century and ending with the final rupture on a point of theology in 1054. Meanwhile the churches of the rapidly differentiating societies had assumed sharply contrasted political characters. The Catholic Church in the West was being centralized under the independent authority of the medieval Papacy, whereas the Orthodox Church had become a docile department of the Byzantine state.

The Iranic and Arabic Societies and the Syriac Society. The next living society that we have to examine is Islam; and when we scan the background of the Islamic Society we discern there a universal state, a universal church and a Völkerwanderung which are not identical with those in the common background of Western and Orthodox Christendom but are unmistakably analogous to them. The Islamic universal state is the 'Abbasid Caliphate of Baghdad.[1] The universal church is, of course, Islam itself. The Völkerwanderung which overran the domain of the Caliphate at its fall proceeded from the Turkish and Mongol nomads of the Eurasian Steppe, the Berber nomads of Northern Africa and the Arab

---

[1] The subsequent 'Abbasid Caliphate of Cairo was an evocation of a 'ghost' of the Baghdad Caliphate, i.e. a phenomenon of the same kind as the 'Eastern Roman Empire' and the 'Holy Roman Empire'. In all three cases an affiliated society produced or preserved a 'ghost' of the universal state of its parent society.

nomads of the Arabian Peninsula. The interregnum occupied by this Völkerwanderung covers roughly the three centuries between A.D. 975 and A.D. 1275, and the latter date can be taken as that of the beginning of the Islamic Society as we find it in the world to-day.

So far all is plain, but further search brings us up against complications. The first is that the predecessor of the Islamic Society (not yet identified) proves to be the parent not of a single offspring but of twins, in this respect resembling the parental achievement of the Hellenic Society. The conduct of the pairs of twins has been, however, strikingly dissimilar; for, whereas the Western and the Orthodox Society have survived for over a thousand years side by side, one of the offspring of the parent society which we are seeking to identify swallowed up and incorporated the other. We shall call these twin Islamic societies the Iranic and the Arabic.

The differentiation among the offspring of the unidentified society was not, as was the schism among the offspring of the Hellenic Society, a matter of religion; for, though Islam bifurcated into the sects of the Sunnis and the Shi'is as the Christian Church bifurcated into the Catholic and Orthodox Churches, this religious schism in Islam never at any stage coincided with the division between the Iranic-Islamic and the Arabic-Islamic societies— though schism did eventually disrupt the Iranic-Islamic Society when the Shi'i sect of Islam became predominant in Persia in the first quarter of the sixteenth century of the Christian Era. Shi'ism thereby established itself in the very centre of the main axis of the Iranic-Islamic Society (which runs east and west from Afghanistan to Anatolia), leaving Sunnism predominant on either side of it in the two extremities of the Iranic World as well as in the Arabic countries to the south and west.

When we compare the pair of Islamic with our pair of Christian societies we see that the Islamic Society which emerged in what we may call the Perso-Turkish or Iranian zone bears a certain resemblance to our Western Society, while the other society which emerged in what we may call the Arabic zone bears a certain resemblance to Orthodox Christendom. For example, the ghost of the Baghdad Caliphate which was evoked by the Mamluks at Cairo in the thirteenth century of the Christian Era reminds us of the ghost of the Roman Empire which was evoked by Leo the Syrian at Constantinople in the eighth century. The Mamluks' political construction, like Leo's, was relatively modest, effective and durable by contrast with the empire of Timur in the neighbouring Iranian zone—a vast, vague, ephemeral shape which appeared and disappeared like the Empire of Charlemagne in the

West. Again, the classical language which was the vehicle of culture in the Arabic zone was Arabic itself, which had been the language of culture in the 'Abbasid Caliphate of Baghdad. In the Iranian zone the new culture found a new vehicle for itself in Persian—a language which had been cultivated by grafting it on to Arabic as Latin had been cultivated by grafting it on to Greek. Finally, the conquest and absorption of the Islamic Society of the Arabic zone by the Islamic Society of the Iranian zone, which occurred in the sixteenth century, had its parallel in the aggression of Western Christendom against Orthodox Christendom during the Crusades. When this aggression culminated in A.D. 1204 in the diversion of the Fourth Crusade against Constantinople, it looked for a moment as though Orthodox Christendom would be permanently conquered and absorbed by her sister society—a fate which overtook the Arabic Society some three centuries later, when the Mamluk power was overthrown and the 'Abbasid Caliphate of Cairo was extinguished by the Ottoman Padishah Selim I in A.D. 1517.

We must now take up the question—what was the unidentified society in which the 'Abbasid Caliphate of Baghdad marked the final stage, analogous to that marked by the Roman Empire in the Hellenic Society? If we trace history backwards from the 'Abbasid Caliphate, do we find phenomena analogous to the time of troubles which we found to be the penultimate stage of the Hellenic Society?

The answer is that we do not. Behind the 'Abbasid Caliphate of Baghdad we find the Ummayad Caliphate of Damascus, and behind that a thousand years of Hellenic intrusion, beginning with the career of Alexander of Macedon in the latter half of the fourth century B.C., followed by the Greek Seleucid monarchy in Syria, Pompey's campaigns and the Roman conquest, and only ending with the Oriental *revanche* of the warriors of early Islam in the seventh century after Christ. The cataclysmic conquests of the primitive Muslim Arabs seem to respond antistrophically, in the rhythm of history, to the cataclysmic conquests of Alexander. Like these, they changed the face of the world in half a dozen years; but instead of changing it out of recognition, *more Macedonico*, they changed it back to a recognizable likeness of what it had been once before. As the Macedonian conquest, by breaking up the Achaemenian Empire (i.e. the Persian Empire of Cyrus and his successors), prepared the soil for the seed of Hellenism, so the Arab conquest opened the way for the Umayyads, and after them the 'Abbasids, to reconstruct a universal state which was the equivalent of the Achaemenian Empire. If we superimpose

the map of either empire upon the other we shall be struck by the
closeness with which the outlines correspond; and we shall find
that the correspondence is not simply geographical but extends to
methods of administration and even to the more intimate phenomena of social and spiritual life. We may express the historical
function of the 'Abbasid Caliphate by describing it as a reintegration and resumption of the Achaemenian Empire—a reintegration
of a political structure which had been broken up by the impact
of an external force and the resumption of a phase of social life
which had been interrupted by an alien intrusion. The 'Abbasid
Caliphate is to be regarded as a resumption of the universal state
which was the last phase of the existence of our still unidentified
society, the search for which is thus shifted back a thousand years.

We must now inspect the immediate antecedents of the Achaemenian Empire in search for the phenomenon which we failed to
find in the antecedents of the 'Abbasid Caliphate: namely a
time of troubles resembling the time which in Hellenic history
immediately preceded the establishment of the Roman Empire.

The general similarity between the genesis of the Achaemenian
Empire and the genesis of the Roman Empire is unmistakable.
The chief difference of detail is that the Hellenic universal state
grew out of the very state which had been the principal agent of
destruction in the foregoing time of troubles, whereas in the
genesis of the Achaemenian Empire the successive destructive
and constructive roles of Rome were played by different states.
The destructive role was played by Assyria; but, just when Assyria
was on the point of completing her work by establishing a universal state in the society of which she was the scourge, she brought
destruction on herself by the excess of her own militarism. Just
before the grand finale the protagonist was dramatically struck
down (610 B.C.) and his role was unexpectedly assumed by an
actor who had hitherto played a minor part. The Achaemenidae
reaped where the Assyrians had sown; yet this substitution of one
performer for another did not change the character of the plot.

Having thus discerned our time of troubles we can now perhaps at last identify the society we are seeking. Negatively, we
can make out that it was not identical with that to which the
Assyrians belonged. The Assyrians, like the Macedonians at a
later stage of this long tangled history, played their part as intruders who came and went. In our unidentified society when it
was united under the Achaemenian Empire we can trace the
process of the peaceful ejection of the elements of culture intruded
by Assyria in the gradual replacement of the Akkadian language
and cuneiform script by the Aramaic language and Alphabet.

The Assyrians themselves, in their latter days, employed the Aramaic Alphabet for writing on parchment as a supplement to their traditional cuneiform script which they impressed on clay tablets or inscribed on stone. When they employed the Aramaic Alphabet they may be presumed to have used the Aramaic language. At any rate, after the destruction of the Assyrian state and of the short-lived neo-Babylonian Empire (i.e. Nebuchadnezzar's empire) which followed it, the Aramaic Alphabet and language continuously gained ground until, in the last century B.C., the Akkadian language and cuneiform script had become extinct throughout their Mesopotamian homeland.

A corresponding change can be traced in the history of the Iranian language, which emerged suddenly from obscurity as the language of the 'Medes and Persians', the ruling peoples of the Achaemenian Empire. Confronted with the problem of making records in a language (the Iranian or Old Persian) which had evolved no script of its own, the Persians adopted the cuneiform script for inscriptions on stone and the Aramaic for records on parchment, but it was the Aramaic script that survived as the vehicle of the Persian language.

In fact two elements of culture, one from Syria and one from Iran, were asserting themselves contemporaneously and at the same time entering into closer association with one another. From the latter end of the time of troubles preceding the establishment of the Achaemenian Empire, when the conquered Aramaeans were beginning to captivate their Assyrian conquerors, the process was continuous. If we wish to discern it at an earlier stage we may look into the mirror of religion and perceive how the same time of troubles breathed the same inspiration into Zarathustra, the Prophet of Iran, and into the contemporary Prophets of Israel and Judah. On the whole the Aramaean or Syrian element, rather than the Iranian, may be regarded as the deeper influence, and, if we peer back behind the time of troubles, the Iranian element fades out and we catch a glimpse of a society in Syria, in the generation of King Solomon and his contemporary King Hiram, which was just discovering the Atlantic and Indian Oceans and had already discovered the Alphabet. Here at last we have identified the society to which the twin Islamic societies (subsequently combined in one) were affiliated, and we will call it the Syriac Society.

In the light of this identification let us look again at Islam, the universal church through which our Syriac Society came at long last to be apparented to the Iranic and Arabic societies. We can now observe an interesting difference between the development

of Islam and that of Christianity. We have observed that the germ
of creative power in Christianity was not of Hellenic but of alien
origin (in fact of Syriac origin, as we can now identify it). By
contrast we can observe that the creative germ of Islam was
not alien from, but native to, the Syriac Society. The founder,
Muhammad, drew his inspiration primarily from Judaism, a
purely Syriac religion, and secondarily from Nestorianism, a form
of Christianity in which the Syriac element had recovered its
preponderance over the Hellenic. Of course a great institution like
a universal church is never 'pure bred' from a single society. In
Christianity we are aware of Hellenic elements, drawn from
Hellenic mystery religions and Hellenic philosophy. Similarly,
but to a much slighter extent, we can detect Hellenic influences
in Islam. Broadly speaking, however, Christianity is a universal
church originating in a germ that was alien to the society in
which it played its part, while Islam originated in a germ that was
indigenous.

Finally, we may measure the respective degrees of displacement of the original homes of the affiliated Iranic and Arabic
societies from the original home of the apparented Syriac Society.
The base line of the Iranic-Islamic Society, from Anatolia to
India, shows a big displacement. On the other hand the homeland
of the Arabic-Islamic Society in Syria and Egypt covers the whole
area of the Syriac Society, and the displacement is relatively small.

The Indic Society. The next living society we have to examine
is the Hindu, and here again we discern in the background our
standard tokens of the existence of an earlier society beyond the
horizon. The universal state in this case is the Empire of the
Guptas (*circa* A.D. 375–475). The universal church is Hinduism,
which attained supremacy in India in the Gupta Age, expelling and
supplanting Buddhism after Buddhism had been dominant for
about seven centuries in the sub-continent which was the common
cradle of both religions. The Völkerwanderung which overran
the Gupta Empire at its fall proceeded from the Huns of the
Eurasian Steppe, who were assailing the Roman Empire at the same
time. The interregnum occupied by their activities and by the
lives of the successor states of the Gupta Empire lies approximately within the dates A.D. 475–775. Thereafter there began to
emerge that Hindu Society which is still alive. Šankara, the father
of Hindu philosophy, flourished about A.D. 800.

When we push farther back in our search for the older society
to which the Hindu Society is affiliated we find, on a smaller scale,
the same phenomenon that complicated our search for the Syriac
Society, namely a Hellenic intrusion. In India this Hellenic in-

trusion did not begin as early as Alexander's campaign, which, so far as influence on Indian culture is concerned, had no lasting consequences. The real Hellenic intrusion upon India begins with the invasion of Demetrius, the Greek king of Bactria, about 183–182 B.C., and ends with the destruction of the last of the partially Hellenized intruders in A.D. 390, which may be taken as the approximate date of the establishment of the Gupta Empire. Following the lines that put us on the track of the Syriac Society we must look in India, as we looked in South-Western Asia, for a pre-Hellenic universal state, of which the Gupta Empire can be regarded as a post-Hellenic resumption, and we find this here in the Empire of the Mauryas, established by Chandragupta in 323 B.C., made illustrious by the reign of the Emperor Açoka in the following century and extinguished by the usurper Pushyamitra in 185 B.C. Behind this empire we find a time of troubles, full of destructive wars between local states, and covering in its span the lifetime of Siddhartha Gautama the Buddha. Gautama's life, and attitude towards life, are the best evidence that the society of which he was a member was in a bad way in his time; and this evidence is corroborated by the life and outlook of his contemporary Mahavira the founder of Jainism, and by the lives of others of the same generation in India who were turning away from This World and seeking to find the way to another through asceticism. In the farthest background of all, behind this time of troubles, we can make out a time of growth which has left its record in the Vedas. And so we have identified the society apparented to the Hindu Society; let us call it the Indic. The original home of the Indic Society lay in the Indus and Upper Ganges valleys, from which it spread over the whole sub-continent. Its geographical position is therefore virtually identical with that of its successor.

The Sinic Society. It remains to explore the background of the only remaining living society, which has its home in the Far East. Here the universal state is the empire, established in 221 B.C., of the successive Ts'in and Han dynasties. The universal church is the Mahāyāna, the variety of Buddhism which made its way into the Han Empire and so became the chrysalis of the present Far Eastern Society. The Völkerwanderung after the fall of the universal state proceeded from the nomads of the Eurasian Steppe who invaded the territory of the Han Empire round about A.D. 300, though the Han Empire itself had actually given way to an interregnum more than a hundred years earlier. When we turn to the antecedents of the Han Empire we find a clearly marked time of troubles, known in Chinese history as *chan kwo*, 'the (period of) contending states', and covering the two-and-a-half centuries following the death of Confucius in 479 B.C. The two marks of this age, suicidal statecraft and intellectual vitality directed towards the philosophy of practical life, recall the period of Hellenic history between the time of Zeno, the founder of Stoicism, and the battle of Actium which terminated the Hellenic time of troubles. Moreover in this case, as in that, these last centuries of the time of troubles were only the climax of a disorganization which had begun some time earlier. The flame of militarism which burnt itself out in the post-Confucian age was already alight before Confucius took his measure of human affairs. The mundane wisdom of that philosopher and the other-worldly quietism of his contemporary, Lao-tse, are proof that both realized that, in the history of their society, the age of growth already lay behind them. What name shall we give to the society upon whose past Confucius looked back with reverence, while Lao-tse turned his back on it like Christian leaving the City of Destruction? We may perhaps conveniently call this society the Sinic.

The Mahāyāna—the church through which this Sinic Society came to be apparented to the Far Eastern Society of to-day— resembles the Christian Church and differs from Islam and Hinduism inasmuch as the germ of life in which it originated was not indigenous to the society in which it played its part but was derived from elsewhere. The Mahāyāna appears to have been begotten in Indic territories which were subject to the Greek kings of Bactria and their semi-Hellenic successors, the Kushans, and it had undoubtedly taken root in the Kushan provinces in the Tarim Basin, where the Kushans were successors of the Prior Han dynasty, before these provinces were reconquered and re-annexed by the Posterior Han dynasty. Through this door the Mahāyāna entered the Sinic World and was then adapted by the Sinic proletariat to its own needs.

The original home of the Sinic Society was the basin of the Yellow River, from which it expanded to the basin of the Yangtse. Both basins were included in the original home of the Far Eastern Society, which expanded south-westwards along the Chinese coast and also north-eastward into Korea and Japan.

'*The Fossils*' (see p. 8). The information so far obtained by investigating the affiliations of the living societies will enable us to sort out the 'fossils' and assign them to the extinct societies to which they originally belonged. The Jews and Parsees are fossils of the Syriac Society as it was before the Hellenic intrusion upon the Syriac World. The Monophysite and Nestorian Christians are relics of the reaction of the Syriac Society against the Hellenic intrusion, successive and alternative protests against the Hellenization of what had been in origin a Syriac religion. The Jains of India and the Hinayanian Buddhists of Ceylon, Burma, Siam and Cambodia are fossils of the Indic Society of the period of the Mauryan Empire, before the Hellenic intrusion upon the Indic World. The Lamaistic Mahayanian Buddhists of Tibet and Mongolia correspond to the Nestorians. They represent an unsuccessful reaction against the metamorphosis of Mahayanian Buddhism from its original Indic form to the later shape—moulded by Hellenic and Syriac influences—in which it was eventually adopted by the Sinic Society.

None of these fossils gives us a clue to making any further additions to our list of societies, but our resources are not exhausted. We may push farther back into the past and find 'parents' for some of the societies which we have identified as being themselves parents of living specimens.

The Minoan Society. In the background of the Hellenic Society certain tokens of the pre-existence of an earlier society stand out quite clearly. The universal state is the maritime empire, maintained by command of the Aegean Sea from a base in Crete, which left a name in Greek tradition as the thalassocracy (sea-power) of Minos, and a mark on the face of the earth in the topmost strata of the palaces recently excavated at Cnossos and Phaestus. The Völkerwanderung after this universal state can be viewed, much transmuted by the alchemy of traditional poetry, in the oldest monuments of Greek literature, the *Iliad* and the *Odyssey*, and we also catch a glimpse of it, which no doubt shows us something more like the historical facts, in the contemporary official records of the eighteenth, nineteenth and twentieth dynasties of Egypt. This Völkerwanderung seems to have begun with an irruption of barbarians—Achaeans and the like—from the European hinterland of the Aegean, who took to the sea and overcame the Cretan thalassocracy on its own element. The archaeological evidence of their handiwork is the destruction of the Cretan palaces at the end of the age which archaeologists call 'Late Minoan II'. The movement culminated in a kind of human avalanche in which the Aegean peoples, victors and vanquished alike, overwhelmed the Empire of Khatti (the Hittites) in Anatolia and assailed, but failed to destroy, the 'New Empire' of Egypt. Scholars date the destruction of Cnossos at about 1400 B.C. and Egyptian records enable us to place the 'human avalanche' between 1230 and 1190 B.C. We may thus take 1425–1125 B.C. as the period within which this interregnum falls.

When we seek to trace the history of this older society we are handicapped by our inability to read the Cretan script, but archaeological evidence suggests that a material civilization evolved in Crete was suddenly propagated across the Aegean into the Argolid in the seventeenth century B.C. and from that point spread gradually into other parts of Continental Greece during the next two centuries. There is also evidence for the existence of the Cretan civilization extending backward to the Neolithic Age. We may call this society the Minoan.

But are we justified in treating the Minoan and the Hellenic societies as being related to one another in the same way as the Hellenic and Western or the other apparented-and-affiliated societies that we have identified? In these other cases the social link between two societies has been a universal church, which has been created by the internal proletariat of the old society and has afterwards served as a chrysalis within which the new society has taken shape. But there is nothing Minoan about the principal expression of Pan-Hellenism, namely the Olympian pantheon. This pantheon took its classical form in the Homeric epics, and here we see gods made in the image of the barbarians who descended upon the Minoan World in the Völkerwanderung which destroyed it. Zeus is an Achaean war-lord reigning on Olympus as a usurper who has supplanted his predecessor Cronos by force and has divided the spoils of the Universe, giving the waters and the earth to his brothers, Poseidon and Hades, and keeping the sky for himself. This pantheon is Achaean and post-Minoan through and through. We cannot even see a reflection of the Minoan religion in the dispossessed deities, for Cronos and the Titans are of the same order of being as Zeus and his war-band. We are reminded of the religion which had been abandoned by the majority of the Teutonic barbarians before their incursions into the Roman Empire began: a religion which was retained and refined by their kinsfolk in Scandinavia—to be abandoned by these in their turn in the course of their own Völkerwanderung (the raids of the 'Northmen') five or six centuries later. If anything in the nature of a universal church existed in the Minoan Society at the time when the barbarian avalanche descended upon it, it must have been something as different from the worship of the Olympians as Christianity was from the worship of Odin and Thor.

Did such a thing exist? There are faint indications that it did in the judgement of the greatest authority on the subject:

'So far as it has been possible to read the evidences of the old Cretan worship we seem to discern not only a prevailing spiritual essence but something in its followers akin to the faith that for the last two millennia has moved the adherents of successive Oriental religions,

Iranian, Christian and Islamic. It involves a dogmatic spirit in the worshipper far removed from the Hellenic standpoint. . . . Broadly comparing it with the religion of the Ancient Greeks, it may be said that it had a more spiritual essence. From another aspect, it had a more personal bearing. On the "Ring of Nestor", where the symbols of resurgence are seen above her head in chrysalis and butterfly shape, she [the Goddess] has clearly the power of giving life beyond the grave to her worshippers. She is very near to her votaries. . . . She guarded her children even beyond the grave. . . . Greek religion had its Mysteries, but the Greek Gods of both sexes, more or less on a par, by no means stood in such a close personal relation as is indicated by the evidences of the Minoan cult. Their disunion, marked by family and clannish feuds, was as conspicuous as their multiplicity of forms and attributes. In contrast to this, throughout the Minoan World, what appears to be the same paramount goddess constantly reappears. . . . The general conclusion is that we are in the presence of a largely monotheistic cult, in which the female form of the deity held the supreme place.'[1]

There is also some evidence on the subject in Hellenic tradition. The Greeks preserved the legend of a 'Zeus' in Crete who really cannot be the same deity as the Zeus of Olympus. This Cretan Zeus is not the leader of a war-band who comes on the scene full grown and fully armed, to take his kingdom by force. He appears as a new-born babe. Perhaps he is identical with the child represented in Minoan art as held up for adoration by the Divine Mother. And he is not only born—he dies! Were his birth and death reproduced in the birth and death of Dionysus, the Thracian deity with whom the God of the Eleusinian Mysteries became identified? Were the Mysteries in Classical Greece, like witchcraft in Modern Europe, a survival from the religion of a submerged society?

If Christendom had succumbed to the Vikings—falling under their dominion and failing to convert them to its faith—we can imagine the Mass being celebrated mysteriously for centuries in the underworld of a new society in which the prevailing religion was the worship of the Aesir. We can imagine this new society, as it grew to full stature, failing to find satisfaction in the religion of the Scandinavian barbarians and seeking the bread of spiritual life in the soil on which the new society had come to rest. In such a spiritual famine the remnant of an older religion, instead of being stamped out as our Western Society stamped out witchcraft when it caught the attention of the Church, might have been rediscovered as a hidden treasure; and some religious genius might

[1] Evans, Sir Arthur: *The Earlier Religion of Greece in the Light of Cretan Discoveries*, pp. 37–41.

have met the needs of his age by an exotic combination of the
submerged Christian rite with latter-day barbarian orgies derived
from the Finns or the Magyars.

On this analogy we might reconstruct the actual religious history
of the Hellenic World: the revival of the ancient and traditional
Mysteries of Eleusis and the invention of Orphism—'a speculative
religion, created by a religious genius', according to Nilsson—out
of a syncretism between the orgies of the Thracian Dionysus and
the Minoan mysteries of the birth and death of the Cretan Zeus.
Undoubtedly both the Eleusinian Mysteries and the Orphic
Church did provide the Hellenic Society in the Classical Age with
a spiritual sustenance which it needed but could not find in the
worship of the Olympians, an other-worldly spirit such as we
should expect to find in a time of troubles, a spirit which we
recognize as characteristic of the universal churches created by
internal proletariats in their decline.

On these analogies it is not altogether fantastic to espy, in the
Mysteries and Orphism, the ghost of a Minoan universal church.
Yet even if this speculation hit the truth (and this is questioned in
a later passage in this book in which the origins of Orphism are
examined),[1] that would hardly warrant us in regarding the
Hellenic Society as truly affiliated to its predecessor. For why
should this church require raising from the dead unless it had been
slain? And who will have been its slayers unless the barbarians
who had overrun the Minoan World? In taking the pantheon of
these murderous Achaeans, 'sackers of cities', for its own, the
Hellenic Society proclaimed them its parents by adoption. It could
not affiliate itself to the Minoan Society without taking the blood-
guiltiness of the Achaeans upon its head and proclaiming itself a
parricide.

If we now turn to the background of the Syriac Society we shall
find what we have found in the background of the Hellenic, a
universal state and a Völkerwanderung which turn out to be the
same as those which appear in the last chapters of Minoan history.
The final convulsion of the post-Minoan Völkerwanderung was
a human avalanche of uprooted wanderers in search of new homes,
driven pell-mell by the impetus of the last wave of barbarians from
the north, the so-called Dorians. Repulsed from Egypt, some of
these refugees settled on the north-eastern coast of the Egyptian
Empire and are familiar to us as the Philistines of the Old Testament narratives. Here the Philistine refugees from the Minoan
World encountered the Hebrew nomads who had been drifting
into the Syrian dependencies of Egypt out of the no-man's-land

¹ See p. 381.

of Arabia. Farther north the mountain-range of Lebanon set a limit to the simultaneous infiltration of Aramaean nomads and gave shelter to the Phoenicians of the coast who had managed to survive the impact of the Philistines. Out of these elements a new society, the Syriac, emerged as the convulsion subsided.

So far as the Syriac Society was related to any older member of the species it was related to the Minoan, and this in the same degree as the Hellenic was related to the Minoan—neither more nor less. One heritage of the Syriac Society from the Minoan may have been the Alphabet (but this is uncertain); another may have been the taste for long-distance seafaring.

It is at first sight surprising that the Syriac Society should be derived from the Minoan. One would rather have expected to discover that the universal state in the background of the Syriac Society was the 'New Empire' of Egypt and that the monotheism of the Jews was a resurrection of the monotheism of Ikhnaton; but the evidence is against it. Nor is there any evidence to suggest the affiliation of the Syriac Society to either of the societies respectively represented by the Empire of Khatti (the Hittites) in Anatolia and by the Sumerian dynasty of Ur and its successor the Amorite dynasty of Babylon, societies which we shall now proceed to examine.

The Sumeric Society. When we turn to the background of the Indic Society, the first thing that strikes us is that the religion of the Vedas, like the worship of the Olympians, shows evidence of having arisen among barbarians in the course of a Völkerwanderung and bears none of the distinguishing marks of a religion that has been created during a time of troubles by the internal proletariat of a society in decline.

In this case the barbarians were the Aryas who appear in North-Western India at the dawn of Indic history, just as at the dawn of Hellenic history the Achaeans appear in the Aegean. On the analogy of the relation in which we have found the Hellenic Society standing to the Minoan, we should expect to discover in the background of the Indic Society some universal state with a no-man's-land beyond its frontier in which the ancestors of the Aryas were living as an external proletariat until the breakdown of the universal state let them in. Can that universal state be identified and that no-man's-land located? We may perhaps obtain answers to these questions by first asking two others: Whence did the Aryas find their way to India? And did any of them, starting from the same centre, arrive at a different destination?

The Aryas spoke an Indo-European language; and the historical distribution of this group of languages—one group in Europe and the other in India and Iran—shows that the Aryas must have entered India from the Eurasian Steppe, along the routes followed by many successors down to the Turkish invaders, Mahmud of Ghaznah in the eleventh and Babur, the founder of the Mughal (Mogul) Empire, in the sixteenth century of our era. Now when we study the dispersion of the Turks we find some of them going south-east into India and others south-west into Anatolia and Syria. Contemporary, for example, with Mahmud of Ghaznah were the invasions of the Saljuq Turks which provoked the crusading counter-attack of our Western Society. The records of Ancient Egypt give evidence that within the period 2000–1500 B.C. the Aryas, breaking out of the Eurasian Steppe in the quarter where the Turks broke out three thousand years later, anticipated the Turks in their subsequent dispersion. While some, as we know from Indian sources, entered India, others overran Iran, 'Iraq, Syria and finally Egypt, where they established in the seventeenth century B.C. a rule of barbarian war-lords known to Egyptian history as the Hyksos.

What caused the Völkerwanderung of the Aryas? We may reply by asking: What caused the Völkerwanderung of the Turks? The answer to this latter question is supplied by historical record: it was the breakdown of the 'Abbasid Caliphate, and the Turks dispersed in both directions because the dying body of the 'Abbasid Empire furnished prey both in its homelands and in its outlying dependency in the Indus Valley. Does this explanation give us a clue to the corresponding dispersion of the Aryas? It does; for, when we look at the political map of South-Western Asia about 2000–1900 B.C., we find it occupied by a universal state which, like the Caliphate of Baghdad, was governed from a capital in 'Iraq, and whose territories extended in the same directions from the same centre.

This universal state was the Empire of Sumer and Akkad established *circa* 2298 B.C. by the Sumerian Ur-Engur of Ur and restored *circa* 1947 B.C. by the Amorite Hammurabi. The break-up of the empire after the death of Hammurabi ushered in the period of the Aryan Völkerwanderung. There is no direct evidence that the Empire of Sumer and Akkad extended to India, but the possibility is suggested by the recent unearthing, in the Indus Valley, of a culture (dating, on the two sites first explored, from *circa* 3250 to *circa* 2750 B.C.) which was very closely related to that of the Sumerians in 'Iraq.

Can we identify the society in whose history the Empire of Sumer and Akkad was the universal state? Examining the antecedents of this empire we find evidence of a time of troubles in which the Akkadian militarist, Sargon of Agade, was a conspicuous figure. Farther back we find an age of growth and creation on which recent excavations at Ur have thrown light. How far back into or beyond the fourth millennium B.C. this age extended we do not know. The society now identified may be called the Sumeric.

The Hittite and Babylonic Societies. Having identified the Sumeric Society we can go on to identify two others by proceeding, this time, not from the later to the earlier but in the reverse order.

The Sumeric Civilization extended into the eastern part of the Anatolian Peninsula, later called Cappadocia. Clay tablets, impressed with business documents in cuneiform, which have been found by archaeologists in Cappadocia, are evidence for this fact. When, after the death of Hammurabi, the Sumeric universal state broke down, its Cappadocian provinces were occupied by barbarians from the north-west, and in about 1750 B.C. the ruler of the principal successor state in this quarter, King Mursil I of Khatti, raided and sacked Babylon itself. The raiders withdrew with their booty and other barbarians, the Kassites from Iran, established an ascendancy in 'Iraq which lasted for six centuries. The Khatti Empire became the nucleus of a Hittite Society our fragmentary knowledge of which is mostly derived from the records of Egypt, with which the Hittites were constantly at war after Thothmes III (1480–1450 B.C.) had extended Egyptian rule into Syria. The destruction of the Hittite Empire by the same Völkerwanderung as overwhelmed the Cretan Empire has already been mentioned. The Hittites seem to have taken over the Sumerian system of divination, but they had a religion of their own and also a pictographic script in which at least five different Hittite languages were recorded.

Another society, also related to the Sumeric, comes to light, through the Egyptian records of the fifteenth century B.C., in the Sumeric Society's homelands: Babylonia, where the Kassite ascendancy lingered on into the twelfth century B.C., Assyria and Elam. The institutions of this latter-day society on Sumeric ground resemble so closely in most respects those of the antecedent Sumeric Society itself that it is doubtful whether it ought to be regarded as a separate society or as an epilogue of the Sumeric. We will, however, give it the benefit of the doubt and call it the Babylonic Society. In its last phase, during the seventh century B.C., this society suffered grievously in a hundred years' war, within its own bosom, between Babylonia and the military power of the Assyrians. The Babylonic Society survived the destruction of Assyria by seventy years and was finally swallowed up in the universal state of the Achaemenian Empire of Cyrus. These seventy years included the reign of Nebuchadnezzar and the 'Babylonian Captivity' of the Jews, to whom Cyrus appeared as a heaven-sent deliverer.

The Egyptiac Society. This very notable society emerged in the lower valley of the Nile during the fourth millennium B.C. and became extinct in the fifth century of the Christian Era, after existing, from first to last, at least three times as long as our Western Society has existed so far. It was without 'parents' and without offspring; no living society can claim it as an ancestor. All the more triumphant is the immortality that it has sought and found in stone. It seems probable that the Pyramids, which have already borne inanimate witness to the existence of their creators for nearly five thousand years, will survive for hundreds of thousands of years to come. It is not inconceivable that they may outlast man himself and that, in a world where there are no longer human minds to read their message, they will continue to testify: 'Before Abraham was, I am.'

These vast pyramidal tombs, however, typify the history of the Egyptiac Society in more ways than one. We spoke of this society as existing for some four thousand years, but for half that period the Egyptiac Society was not so much a living organism as an organism dead but unburied. More than half of Egyptiac history is a gigantic epilogue.

If we trace that history we find that a little more than a quarter of its span was a period of growth. The impetus which manifested itself first in the mastery of a peculiarly formidable physical environment—in the clearing, draining and cultivation of the jungle-swamp that originally occupied the lower valley and delta of the Nile to the exclusion of man—and which then displayed its increasing momentum in the precocious political unification of the Egyptiac World at the end of the so-called Pre-Dynastic Age, reached its climax in the stupendous material performances of the fourth dynasty. This dynasty marks the zenith in the characteristic achievement of the Egyptiac Society: the co-ordination of human labour in great engineering enterprises, ranging from the reclamation of the swamps to the construction of the Pyramids. It was also the zenith in political administration and in art. Even in the sphere of religion, where wisdom is proverbially born of suffering, the so-called 'pyramid texts' testify that this age likewise saw the creation, the collision and the first stage in the interaction of the two religious movements—the worship of the Sun and the worship of Osiris—which came to their maturity after the Egyptiac Society had gone into its decline.

The zenith was passed and the decline set in at the transition from the fifth dynasty to the sixth, *circa* 2424 B.C., and at this point we begin to recognize the familiar symptoms of decline in the order in which they have presented themselves to us in the histories of other societies. The break-up of the Egyptiac united kingdom into a number of small states constantly at war with one another bears the unmistakable stamp of a time of troubles. The Egyptiac time of troubles was followed in about 2070 B.C. by a universal state, founded by the local dynasty of Thebes and consolidated by the twelfth dynasty, *circa* 2000–1788 B.C. After the twelfth dynasty the universal state broke down, and the consequent interregnum brought its Völkerwanderung in the invasion of the Hyksos.

Here, then, might seem to be the end of this society. If we had followed our usual procedure of exploration and had worked backwards from the fifth century of the Christian Era, we should probably have paused at this point and said: 'We have now traced Egyptiac history back, from its last fading foot-prints in the fifth century after Christ, for twenty-one centuries, and have struck on a Völkerwanderung following a universal state. We have traced the Egyptiac Society to its source and discern beyond its beginnings the latter end of an earlier society, which we will call "Nilotic".'

We shall refuse to adopt this course, because, if we now resume our exploration in the forward direction, we shall not find a new society but something quite different. The barbarian 'successor state' is overthrown; the Hyksos are expelled; and the universal state with its capital at Thebes is restored, consciously and deliberately.

This restoration was, from our present standpoint, the sole significant event in Egyptiac history (except the abortive revolution of Ikhnaton) between the sixteenth century B.C. and the fifth century after Christ. The duration of this universal state, repeatedly overthrown and re-established, fills the whole of these two millennia. There is no new society. If we study the religious history of the Egyptiac Society we find that here, too, after the interregnum, a religion prevailed that had been taken over from the dominant minority of the preceding age of decline. Yet it did not prevail without a struggle, and it first secured its position by coming to terms with a universal church which had been created in the preceding age of decline by the Egyptiac internal proletariat out of the religion of Osiris.

The religion of Osiris came from the Delta, not from Upper Egypt, where the political history of the Egyptiac Society was made. The main thread of Egyptiac religious history is the rivalry between this god of terrestrial and subterranean nature—the spirit of vegetation that alternately appears above ground and disappears beneath it—and the sun god of Heaven, and this theological conflict was bound up with, and was indeed a theological expression of, the political and social conflict between the two sections of society in which the two worships arose. The worship of the sun god, Re, was controlled by the priesthood of Heliopolis, and Re was conceived in the image of the Pharaoh, whereas the worship of Osiris was a popular religion. It was a conflict between an established state-church and a popular religion with an appeal to the individual believer.

The crucial difference between the two religions in their original forms was the difference in the prospects that they offered to their devotees after death. Osiris ruled the multitudes of the dead in a shadow world underground. Re—for a consideration—redeemed his devotees from death and raised them alive to the sky. But this apotheosis was reserved for those who could pay the price, a price which was constantly rising until solar immortality became virtually the monopoly of the Pharaoh and those members of his court to whose immortalization-equipment he chose to contribute. The Great Pyramids are the monuments of this endeavour to secure personal immortality by architectural extravagance.

Meanwhile the religion of Osiris gained ground. The immortality that it offered might be a poor thing compared with residence in Re's sky-heaven, but it was the one consolation to which the masses could look forward under the grinding oppression to which they were subjected in this life in order to secure eternal bliss for their masters. The Egyptiac Society was splitting into a dominant minority and an internal proletariat. Confronted with this danger, the priesthood of Heliopolis sought to render Osiris innocuous by taking him into partnership, but in this transaction Osiris succeeded in taking far more than he gave. When he entered into the Pharaoh's solar cult he captured the solar ritual of apotheosis for the mass of mankind. The monument of this religious syncretism is the so-called Book of the Dead—'an Everyman's guide to Immortality' which dominated the religious life of the Egyptiac Society throughout the two millennia of its 'epilogue'. The idea that Re demanded righteousness rather than pyramids prevailed, and Osiris appears as a judge in the underworld, consigning the dead to the destinies that their lives on Earth have deserved.

Here, under the Egyptiac universal state, we discern the lineaments of a universal church created by an internal proletariat. What would have been the future of this Osirian church if the Egyptiac universal state had not been restored? Would it have become the chrysalis of a new society? First of all, we should have expected to see it captivate the Hyksos, as the Christian Church captivated the Barbarians. But it did not; hatred of the Hyksos led it to combine in an unnatural union with the dead religion of the dominant minority, and in this process the Osirian religion was perverted and degraded. Immortality was once again up for sale, though the price was no longer a pyramid but only a few texts on a roll of papyrus. We may conjecture that in this business as in others the mass production of a cheap article for a small margin of profit brought the manufacturer the best return. Thus the 'restoration' in the sixteenth century B.C. was something more than a rehabilitation of the universal state; it was an amalgamation of the living tissues of the Osirian Church with the dead tissues of the moribund Egyptiac Society in a single mass—a kind of social concrete that took two millennia to weather away.

The best proof that the restored Egyptiac Society was void of life was the complete failure of the one attempt to raise it from the dead. This time one man, the Pharaoh Ikhnaton, sought to repeat by an instantaneous gesture the act of religious creation that had been performed in vain by the Osirian Church of the internal proletariat during the centuries of the long-past time of troubles. By sheer genius Ikhnaton created a new conception of God and man, life and nature, and expressed it in a new art and poetry; but dead societies cannot thus be brought to life. His failure is the proof that we are justified in regarding the social phenomena of Egyptiac history from the sixteenth century B.C. onwards as an epilogue rather than as the history from cradle to grave of a new society.

The Andean, Yucatec, Mexic and Mayan Societies. America before the coming of the Spanish conquistadores yields the four societies here named. The Andean Society in Peru had already reached the condition of a universal state, the Inca Empire, when it was destroyed by Pizarro in 1530. The Mexic Society was approaching a similar condition, the predestined universal state being the Aztec Empire. At the time of Cortez's expedition the city state of Tlaxcala was the only remaining independent Power of any importance, and the Tlaxcalans in consequence supported Cortez. The Yucatec Society in the peninsula of Yucatan had been absorbed by the Mexic Society some four hundred years earlier. Both the Mexic and the Yucatec societies were affiliated to an earlier society, the Mayan, which seems to have achieved a higher and more humane civilization than its successors. It came to a rapid and mysterious end in the seventh century after Christ, leaving as the record of its existence the ruins of its great cities in the rain-soaked forests of Yucatan. This society excelled in astronomy, turned to practical account in a system of chronology which was remarkably exact in its calculations. The horrible religious rites discovered by Cortez in Mexico appear to be a grossly barbarized version of the old religion of the Mayas.

Our researches have thus yielded us nineteen societies, most of them related as parent or offspring to one or more of the others: namely the Western, the Orthodox, the Iranic, the Arabic (these last two being now united in the Islamic), the Hindu, the Far Eastern, the Hellenic, the Syriac, the Indic, the Sinic, the Minoan, the Sumeric, the Hittite, the Babylonic, the Egyptiac, the Andean, the Mexic, the Yucatec and the Mayan. We have expressed doubt as to the separate existence of the Babylonic apart from the Sumeric, and some of the other pairs might perhaps be regarded as single societies with an 'epilogue' on the Egyptiac analogy. But we will respect their individualities until we find good reason for doing otherwise. Indeed it is probably desirable to divide the Orthodox Christian Society into an Orthodox-Byzantine and an Orthodox-Russian Society, and the Far Eastern into a Chinese and a Korean-Japanese Society. This would raise our numbers to twenty-one. Further explanation and defence of our proceedings must be reserved for the next chapter.

III. THE COMPARABILITY OF SOCIETIES

(1) CIVILIZATIONS AND PRIMITIVE SOCIETIES

BEFORE we proceed with the systematic comparison of our twenty-one societies, which is the purpose of this book, we must meet certain possible objections *a limine*. The first and simplest argument against the procedure we propose may be stated thus: 'These societies have no common characteristic beyond the fact that all of them are "intelligible fields of study", and this characteristic is so vague and general that it can be turned to no practical account.'

The answer is that societies which are 'intelligible fields of study' are a genus within which our twenty-one representatives constitute one particular species. Societies of this species are commonly called civilizations, to distinguish them from primitive societies which are also 'intelligible fields of study' and which form another, in fact *the* other, species within this genus. Our twenty-one societies must, therefore, have one specific feature in common in the fact that they alone are in process of civilization.

Another difference between the two species at once suggests itself. The number of known civilizations is small. The number of known primitive societies is vastly greater. In 1915 three Western anthropologists, setting out to make a comparative study of primitive societies and confining themselves to those about which adequate information was available, registered about 650, most of them alive to-day. It is impossible to form any conception of the number of primitive societies which must have come into and passed out of existence since man first became human, perhaps 300,000 years ago, but it is evident that the numerical preponderance of primitive societies over civilizations is overwhelming.

Almost equally overwhelming is the preponderance of civilizations over primitive societies in their individual dimensions. The primitive societies, in their legions, are relatively short-lived, are restricted to relatively narrow geographical areas and embrace relatively small numbers of human beings. It is probable that if we could take a census of the membership of the five living civilizations up to date, during the small number of centuries through which they have yet lived, we should find that each of our Leviathans, singly, has embraced more human beings than could be mustered by all the primitive societies taken together since the emergence of the human race. However, we are studying not individuals but societies, and the significant fact for our purpose

is that the number of societies in process of civilization known to
have existed has been comparatively small.

(2) THE MISCONCEPTION OF 'THE UNITY OF CIVILIZATION'

The second argument against the comparability of our twenty-
one civilizations is the contrary of the first. It is that there are
not twenty-one distinct representatives of such a species of society
but only one civilization—our own.

This thesis of the unity of civilization is a misconception into
which modern Western historians have been led by the influence
of their social environment. The misleading feature is the fact
that, in modern times, our own Western Civilization has cast the
net of its economic system all round the World, and this economic
unification on a Western basis has been followed by a political
unification on the same basis which has gone almost as far; for
though the conquests of Western armies and governments have
been neither as extensive nor as thorough as the conquests of
Western manufacturers and technicians, it is nevertheless a fact
that all the states of the contemporary world form part of a single
political system of Western origin.

These are striking facts, but to regard them as evidence of the
unity of civilization is a superficial view. While the economic and
poli' cal maps have now been Westernized, the cultural map
remains substantially what it was before our Western Society
started on its career of economic and political conquest. On the
cultural plane, for those who have eyes to see, the lineaments of
the four living non-Western civilizations are still clear. But many
have not such eyes; and their outlook is illustrated in the use of the
English word 'natives' and of equivalent words in other Western
languages.

When we Westerners call people 'natives' we implicitly take
the cultural colour out of our perception of them. We see them
as wild animals infesting the country in which we happen to come
across them, as part of the local flora and fauna and not as men
of like passions with ourselves. So long as we think of them
as 'natives' we may exterminate them or, as is more likely
to-day, domesticate them and honestly (perhaps not altogether
mistakenly) believe that we are improving the breed, but we do
not begin to understand them.

But apart from illusions due to the world-wide success of the
Western Civilization in the material sphere, the misconception

of 'the unity of history'—involving the assumption that there is only one river of civilization, our own, and that all others are either tributary to it or else lost in the desert sands—may be traced to three roots: the egocentric illusion, the illusion of 'the unchanging East', and the illusion of progress as a movement that proceeds in a straight line.

As for the egocentric illusion, it is natural enough, and all that need be said is that we Westerners have not been its only victims. The Jews suffered from the illusion that they were not *a* but *the* 'chosen people'. What we call 'natives' they called 'gentiles', and the Greeks called 'barbarians'. But the finest flower of egocentricity is perhaps the missive presented in A.D. 1793 by the philosophic emperor of China, Ch'ien Lung, to a British envoy for delivery to his master, King George III:

'You, O King, live beyond the confines of many seas; nevertheless, impelled by your humble desire to partake of the benefits of our civilization, you have despatched a mission respectfully bearing your memorial. . . . I have perused your memorial; the earnest terms in which it is couched reveal a respectful humility on your part which is highly praiseworthy. . . .

'As to your entreaty to send one of your nationals to be accredited to my Celestial Court and to be in control of your country's trade with China, this request is contrary to all usage of my Dynasty and cannot possibly be entertained. . . . If you assert that your reverence for Our Celestial Dynasty fills you with a desire to acquire our civilization, our ceremonies and code of laws differ so completely from your own that, even if your envoy were able to acquire the rudiments of our civilization, you could not possibly transplant our manners and customs to your alien soil. Therefore, however adept the envoy might become, nothing would be gained thereby.

'Swaying the wide world, I have but one aim in view, namely, to maintain a perfect governance and to fulfil the duties of the state. Strange and costly objects do not interest me. If I have commanded that the tribute offerings sent by you, O King, are to be accepted, this was solely in consideration for the spirit which prompted you to despatch them from afar. Our Dynasty's majestic virtue has penetrated into every country under Heaven, and kings of all nations have offered their costly tribute by land and sea. As your ambassador can see for himself, we possess all things. I set no value on objects strange or ingenious, and have no use for your country's manufactures.'[1]

In the course of the century following the composition of this dispatch the pride of Ch'ien Lung's countrymen suffered a series of falls. It is the proverbial fate of pride.

The illusion of 'the unchanging East' is so obviously a popular

[1] Whyte, A. F.: *China and Foreign Powers*, p. 41.

illusion without foundation in serious study that a search for its causes has no great interest or importance. Perhaps it is due to the fact that 'the East', which in this context means anything from Egypt to China, was at one time far ahead of the West and now seems to be far behind; *ergo*, while we have been moving it must have stood still. More particularly we must remember that for the average Westerner the only familiar chapter of the ancient history of 'the East' used to be that contained in the narratives of the Old Testament. When modern Western travellers observed, with mingled astonishment and delight, that the life lived to-day on the Transjordanian border of the Arabian desert corresponded, point by point, with the description of the lives of the patriarchs in the Book of Genesis, the unchanging character of the East seemed proved. But what such travellers encountered was not 'the unchanging East' but the unchanging Arabian Steppe. On the Steppe the physical environment is so hard a taskmaster to human beings that their ability to adapt themselves is confined within very narrow limits. It imposes upon all human beings in all ages who have the hardihood to be its inhabitants a rigid and unvarying way of life. As proof of an 'unchanging East' such evidence is puerile. There are, for example, in the Western World Alpine valleys untouched by modern tourist invasion whose inhabitants live just as their predecessors must have lived in the days of Abraham. It would be as reasonable to deduce from these an argument for an 'unchanging West'.

The illusion of progress as something which proceeds in a straight line is an example of that tendency to over-simplification which the human mind displays in all its activities. In their 'periodizations' our historians dispose their periods in a single series end to end, like the sections of a bamboo stem between joint and joint or the sections of the patent extensible handle on the end of which an up-to-date modern chimney-sweep pokes his brush up the flue. On the brush-handle which our modern historians have inherited there were originally two joints only— 'ancient' and 'modern', roughly though not exactly corresponding to the Old Testament and the New Testament and to the dual back-to-back reckoning of dates B.C. and A.D. This dichotomy of historical time is a relic of the outlook of the internal proletariat of the Hellenic Society, which expressed its sense of alienation from the Hellenic dominant minority by making an absolute antithesis between the old Hellenic dispensation and that of the Christian Church, and thereby succumbed to the egocentric illusion (much more excusable in them, with their limited knowledge, than in us) of treating the transition from one of our twenty-one societies to another as the turning-point of all human history.[1]

As time has gone on, our historians have found it convenient to extend their telescopic brush-handle by adding a third section, which they have called 'medieval' because they have inserted it between the other two. But, while the division between 'ancient' and 'modern' stands for the break between Hellenic and Western history, the division between 'medieval' and 'modern' only stands for the transition between one chapter of Western history and another. The formula 'ancient + medieval + modern' is wrong; it should run 'Hellenic + Western (medieval + modern)'. Yet even this will not do, for, if we honour one chapter-division of Western history with a separate 'period', why refuse the same honour to the others? There is no warrant for laying greater stress on a division round about 1475 than for one round about 1075, and there is ample reason for supposing that we have recently passed into a new chapter whose beginnings may be placed round about 1875. So we have:

Western I ('Dark Ages'), 675–1075.
Western II ('Middle Ages'), 1075–1475.
Western III ('Modern'), 1475–1875.
Western IV ('Post-Modern'?), 1875–?

But we have strayed from the point, which is that an equation of Hellenic and Western history with History itself—'ancient and modern', if you like—is mere parochialism and impertinence. It is as though a geographer were to produce a book entitled 'World Geography' which proved on inspection to be all about the Mediterranean Basin and Europe.

There is another and very different concept of the unity of history which coincides with the popular and traditional illusions, so far discussed, in being at variance with the thesis of this book. Here we confront no idol of the market-place but a product of modern anthropological theorizing: we refer to the diffusion theory as set forth in G. Elliot Smith's *The Ancient Egyptians and the Origins of Civilization* and W. H. Perry's *The Children of the Sun: a Study in the Early History of Civilisation*. These writers believe in 'the unity of civilization' in a special sense: not as a fact of yesterday or to-morrow which has just been accomplished by the world-wide diffusion of the one and only Western Civilization,

---

[1] In the same way the founders of the French Revolutionary Republic, imagining that they were starting a new epoch of history and that all that lay behind them was a 'back number', started a new Year I on the 21st September, 1792; the common sense and conservatism of Napoleon dropped the scheme twelve years later, but for those twelve years it survives to incommode the student with its Fructidors and Thermidors.

but as a fact which was accomplished thousands of years ago by the diffusion of the Egyptiac Civilization—which happens to be one of the few dead civilizations to which we have attributed no 'offspring' whatsoever. They believe that the Egyptiac Society is the one and only instance in which such a thing as a civilization has ever been created independently, without assistance from outside. All other manifestations of civilization derive from Egypt, including those of the Americas, which Egyptiac influences must be supposed to have reached by way of Hawaii and Easter Island.

Now it is, of course, true that diffusion is a method by which many techniques, aptitudes, institutions and ideas, from the Alphabet to Singer's sewing machines, have been communicated by one society to another. Diffusion accounts for the present ubiquity of the Far Eastern beverage tea, the Arabic beverage coffee, the Central American beverage cocoa, the Amazonian material rubber, the Central American practice of smoking tobacco, the Sumerian practice of duodecimal reckoning as exemplified in our shilling, the so-called Arabic numerals which perhaps came originally from Hindustan—and so on. But the fact that the rifle attained its ubiquity through diffusion from a single centre where it was once, and once only, invented, is no proof that the bow and arrow attained its early ubiquity in the same manner. Nor does it follow that, because the power-loom spread all over the world from Manchester, the technique of metallurgy must be likewise traceable to a single point of origin. The evidence in this case is all the other way.

But in any case civilizations are not, in spite of the perverted notions of modern materialism, built of such bricks as these; they are not built of sewing-machines and tobacco and rifles, nor even of alphabets and numerals. It is the easiest thing in the world for commerce to export a new Western technique. It is infinitely harder for a Western poet or saint to kindle in a non-Western soul the spiritual flame that is alight in his own. While giving diffusion its due, it is necessary to emphasize the part that has been played in human history by original creation, and we may remind ourselves that the spark or germ of original creation may burst into flame or flower in any manifestation of life in virtue of the principle of the uniformity of nature. We may at least go so far as to place the *onus probandi* on the diffusionists' shoulders in cases where it is an open question whether or not diffusion is entitled to claim credit for any particular human achievement.

'There can be little doubt,' wrote Freeman in the year 1873, 'that many of the most essential inventions of civilized life have been invented over and over again, in distant times and countries, as different nations have reached those particular points of social advancement when those inventions were first needed. Thus, printing has been independently invented in China and in medieval Europe; and it is well known that a process essentially the same was in use for various purposes in Ancient Rome, though no one took the great step of applying to the reproduction of books the process which was familiarly used for various meaner purposes. What happened with printing we may believe also to have happened with writing, and we may take another illustration from an art of quite another kind. There can be no doubt, from comparing the remains of the earliest buildings in Egypt, Greece, Italy, the British Islands and the ruined cities of Central America, that the great inventions of the arch and the dome have been made more than once in the history of human art. . . . Nor need we doubt that many of the simplest and most essential arts of civilised life—the use of the mill, the use of the bow, the taming of the horse, the hollowing out of the canoe—have been found out over and over again in distant times and places. . . . So it is with political institutions also. The same institutions constantly appear very far from one another, simply because the circumstances which called for them have arisen in times and places very far from one another.'[1]

A modern anthropologist expresses the same idea:

'The resemblances in man's ideas and practices are chiefly traceable to the similarity in structure of the human brain everywhere, and in the consequent nature of his mind. As the physical organ is, at all known stages of man's history, substantially the same in constitution and nervous processes, so the mind has certain universal characteristics, powers and methods of action. . . . This similarity in the operation of the brain is seen in the nineteenth-century intellects of Darwin and Russell Wallace, which, working on the same data, arrived simultaneously at the theory of Evolution; and it accounts for numerous claims in the same age to priority with respect to the same invention or discovery. The similar operations of the common mind of the race—more fragmentary in their data, more rudimentary in their powers, and vaguer in their results—explain the appearance of such beliefs and institutions as Totemism, Exogamy, and the many purificatory rituals in most widely separated peoples and portions of the globe.'[2]

(3) THE CASE FOR THE COMPARABILITY OF CIVILIZATIONS

We have now dealt with two incompatible objections to our plan of comparative study: on the one hand that our twenty-one societies have no common characteristic save that of being 'intelligible fields of historical study'; on the other, that 'the unity of civilization' reduces the apparent plurality of civilizations to one.

[1] Freeman, E. A.: Comparative Politics, pp. 31–2.
[2] Murphy, J.: Primitive Man: His Essential Quest, pp. 8–9.

Yet our critics, even if they accept our answers to these objections, may make a stand at this point and deny that our twenty-one civilizations are comparable on the ground that they are not contemporary. Seven of them are still alive; fourteen are extinct, and of these at least three—the Egyptiac, the Sumeric and the Minoan—go back to 'the dawn of history'. These three, and perhaps others, are separated chronologically from the living civilizations by the whole span of 'historical time'.

The answer is that time is relative and that the spell of something less than six thousand years which bridges the interval between the emergence of the earliest known civilizations and our own day has to be measured for the purpose of our study on the relevant time-scale, that is in the terms of the time-spans of the civilizations themselves. Now, in surveying the relations of civilizations in time, the highest number of successive generations that we have met with in any case is three, and in each case these three, between them, more than cover our span of six thousand years, since the last term in each series is a civilization that is still alive.

The fact that, in our survey of civilizations, we have found in no case a higher number of successive generations than three means that this species is very young in terms of its own time-scale. Moreover, its absolute age up to date is very short compared with that of the sister species of the primitive societies, which is coeval with man himself and has therefore existed, to take an average estimate, for three hundred thousand years. It goes without saying that some civilizations go back to 'the dawn of history' because what we call history is the history of man in a 'civilized' society, but if by history we meant the whole period of man's life on Earth we should find that the period producing civilizations, far from being coeval with human history, covers only two per cent. of it, one-fiftieth part of the lifetime of mankind. Our civilizations may, then, be granted to be sufficiently contemporaneous with one another for our purpose.

Once again our critics, supposedly abandoning their argument on the time-span, might deny the comparability of civilizations on the ground of their differences in value. Are not most of what have been claimed as civilizations so nearly valueless, so 'uncivilized' in fact, that the establishment of parallels between their experiences and those of the 'real' civilizations (such as, of course, our own) is mere waste of intellectual energy? On this point the reader may be asked to suspend judgement until he has seen what comes of such intellectual exertions as we propose to demand of him. Meanwhile let him remember that value, like time, is a relative concept; that all our twenty-one societies, if measured against primitive societies, will be found to have achieved a good deal; and that all of them, if measured against any ideal standard, will be found to have fallen so far short that none of them is in a position to throw stones at the others.

In fact, we maintain that our twenty-one societies should be regarded, hypothetically, as philosophically contemporaneous and philosophically equivalent.

And lastly the critics, even if we suppose them to have gone along with us so far, may take the line that the histories of civilizations are nothing but strings of historical facts; that every historical fact is intrinsically unique; and that history does not repeat itself.

The answer is that, while every fact, like every individual, is unique and therefore incomparable in some respects, it may be also in other respects a member of its class and therefore comparable with other members of that class in so far as it is covered by the classification. No two living bodies, animal or vegetable, are exactly alike, but that does not invalidate the sciences of physiology, biology, botany, zoology and ethnology. Human minds are even more elusively diverse, but we admit psychology's right to exist and exert itself, however much we may differ as to the value of its achievements up to date. We equally admit a comparative study of primitive societies under the title of anthropology. What we propose is an attempt to do for the 'civilized' species of society something of what anthropology is doing for the primitive species.

But our position will be made clearer in a final section of this chapter.

(4) HISTORY, SCIENCE AND FICTION

There are three different methods of viewing and presenting the objects of our thought, and, among them, the phenomena of human life. The first is the ascertainment and recording of 'facts'; the second is the elucidation, through a comparative study of the facts ascertained, of general 'laws'; the third is the artistic re-creation of the facts in the form of 'fiction'. It is generally assumed that the ascertainment and recording of facts is the technique of history, and that the phenomena in the province of this technique are the social phenomena of civilizations; that the elucidation and formulation of general laws is the technique of science, and that, in the study of human life, the science is anthropology and the phenomena in the province of the scientific technique are the social phenomena of primitive societies; and, lastly, that fiction is the technique of the drama and the novel, and that the phenomena in the province of this technique are the personal relations of human beings. All this, in essentials, is to be found in the works of Aristotle.

The distribution of the three techniques between the three departments of study is, however, less watertight than might be supposed. History, for example, does not concern itself with the recording of all the facts of human life. It leaves alone the facts of social life in primitive societies, from which anthropology elucidates its 'laws'; and it hands over to biography the facts of individual lives—though nearly all individual lives that are of sufficient interest and importance to make them seem worth recording have been lived, not in primitive societies, but in one or other of those societies in process of civilization which are conventionally regarded as history's province. Thus history concerns itself with some but not all the facts of human life; and, on the other hand, besides recording facts, history also has recourse to fictions and makes use of laws.

History, like the drama and the novel, grew out of mythology, a primitive form of apprehension and expression in which—as in fairy tales listened to by children or in dreams dreamt by sophisticated adults—the line between fact and fiction is left undrawn. It has, for example, been said of the *Iliad* that anyone who starts reading it as history will find that it is full of fiction but, equally, anyone who starts reading it as fiction will find that it is full of history. All histories resemble the *Iliad* to this extent, that they cannot entirely dispense with the fictional element. The mere selection, arrangement and presentation of facts is a technique belonging to the field of fiction, and popular opinion is right in its insistence that no historian can be 'great' if he is not also a great artist; that the Gibbons and Macaulays are greater historians than the 'Dryasdusts' (a name coined by Sir Walter Scott—himself a greater historian in some of his novels than in any of his 'histories') who have avoided their more inspired confrères' factual inaccuracies. In any case, it is hardly possible to write two consecutive lines of historical narrative without introducing such fictitious personifications as 'England', 'France', 'the Conservative Party', 'the Church', 'the Press' or 'public opinion'. Thucydides[1] dramatized 'historical' personages by putting 'fictitious' speeches and dialogues into their mouths, but his *oratio*

---

[1] Thucydides is generally accounted the first and one of the greatest of severely factual historians, but F. M. Cornford has demonstrated in *Thucydides Mythistoricus* that his whole presentation of his subject is governed by the conventions of contemporary Greek tragedy.

recta, while more vivid, is really no more fictional than the laboured *oratio obliqua* in which the moderns present their composite photographs of public opinion.

On the other hand history has taken into her service a number of ancillary sciences which formulate general laws not about primitive societies but about civilizations: e.g. economics, political science and sociology.

Though it is not necessary to our argument, we might demonstrate that, just as history is not innocent of using the techniques associated with science and fiction, so science and fiction by no means confine themselves to what are supposed to be their own techniques. All sciences pass through a stage in which the ascertainment and recording of facts is the only activity open to them, and the science of anthropology is only just emerging from that phase. Lastly, the drama and the novel do not present fictions, complete fictions and nothing but fictions regarding personal relationships. If they did, the product, instead of deserving Aristotle's commendation that it was 'truer and more philosophical than history', would consist of nonsensical and intolerable fantasies. When we call a piece of literature a work of fiction we mean no more than that the characters could not be identified with any persons who have lived in the flesh, nor the incidents with any particular events that have actually taken place. In fact, we mean that the work has a fictitious personal foreground; and, if we do not mention that the background is composed of authentic social facts, that is simply because this seems so self-evident that we take it for granted. Indeed, we recognize that the highest praise we can give to a good work of fiction is to say that it is 'true to life', and that 'the author shows a profound understanding of human nature'. To be more particular: if the novel deals with a fictitious family of Yorkshire woollen-manufacturers, we might praise the author by saying that he evidently knows his West Riding mill-towns through and through.

None the less, the Aristotelian distinction between the techniques of history, science and fiction remains valid in a general way, and we shall perhaps see why this is so if we examine these techniques again, for we shall find that they differ from each other in their suitability for dealing with 'data' of different quantities. The ascertainment and record of particular facts is all that is possible in a field of study where the data happen to be few. The elucidation and formulation of laws is both possible and necessary where the data are too numerous to tabulate but not too numerous to survey. The form of artistic creation and expression called fiction is the only technique that can be employed or is worth employing where the data are innumerable. Here, as between the three techniques, we have an intrinsic difference of a quantitative order. The techniques differ in their utility for handling different quantities of data. Can we discern a corresponding difference in the quantities of the data that actually present themselves in the respective fields of our three studies?

To begin with the study of personal relations, which is the province of fiction, we can see at once that there are few individuals whose personal relations are of such interest and importance as to make them fit subjects for that record of particular personal facts which we call biography. With these rare exceptions students of human life in the field of personal relations are confronted with innumerable examples of universally familiar experiences. The very idea of an exhaustive recording of them is an absurdity. Any formulation of their 'laws' would be intolerably platitudinous or intolerably crude. In such circumstances the data cannot be significantly expressed except in some notation which gives an intuition of the infinite in finite terms; and such a notation is fiction.

Having now found, in quantitative terms, at least a partial explanation of the fact that, in the study of personal relations, the technique of fiction is normally employed, let us see if we can find similar explanations for the normal employment of the law-making technique in the study of primitive societies and the fact-finding technique in the study of civilizations.

The first point to observe is that both these other studies are concerned with human relations, but not with the relations of the familiar, personal kind which come within the direct experience of every man, woman and child. The social relations of human beings extend beyond the farthest possible range of personal contacts, and these impersonal relations are maintained through social mechanisms called institutions. Without institutions societies could not exist. Indeed, societies themselves are simply institutions of the highest kind. The study of societies and the study of institutional relations are one and the same thing.

We can see at once that the quantity of data confronting students of institutional relations between people is very much smaller than the quantity confronting students of people's personal relations. We can see further that the quantity of recorded institutional relations that are relevant to the study of primitive societies will be much greater than the quantity of those relevant to the study of 'civilized' societies, because the number of known primitive societies runs to over 650, whereas our survey of societies in process of civilization has enabled us to identify no more than, at the outside, twenty-one. Now 650 examples, while far from necessitating the employment of fiction, are just enough to enable the student to make a beginning with the formulation of laws. On the other hand, students of a phenomenon of which only a dozen or two dozen examples are known are discouraged from attempting more than a tabulation of facts; and this, as we have seen, is the stage in which 'history' has remained so far.

At first sight it may seem a paradox to assert that the quantity of data which students of civilizations have at their command is inconveniently small, when our modern historians are complaining that they are overwhelmed by the mass of their materials. But it remains true that the facts of the highest order, the 'intelligible fields of study', the *comparable units* of history, remain inconveniently few for the application of the scientific technique, the elucidation and formulation of laws. None the less, at our own peril, we intend to hazard the attempt, and the results of it are embodied in the remainder of this book.

II

THE GENESES OF CIVILIZATIONS

IV. THE PROBLEM AND HOW NOT TO SOLVE IT

(1) THE PROBLEM STATED

As soon as we approach the problem why and how societies in process of civilization have come into existence, we realize that our list of twenty-one societies of this kind falls, as far as this problem is concerned, into two groups. Fifteen of our societies are affiliated to predecessors of the same species. Of these a few are so closely affiliated that their separate individuality may be a matter for argument, while at the other end of the scale a few are so loosely affiliated that the metaphor implied in the term affiliation may seem to carry us too far. But let that pass. The fifteen more or less affiliated societies are in a different group from the six which, so far as we can discern, have emerged direct from primitive life. It is to the genesis of these six that we propose to direct our attention at present. They are the Egyptiac, the Sumeric, the Minoan, the Sinic, the Mayan and the Andean.

What is the essential difference between the primitive and the higher societies? It does not consist in the presence or absence of institutions, for institutions are the vehicles of the impersonal relations between individuals in which all societies have their existence, because even the smallest of primitive societies is built on a wider basis than the narrow circle of an individual's direct personal ties. Institutions are attributes of the whole genus 'societies' and therefore common properties of both its species. Primitive societies have their institutions—the religion of the annual agricultural cycle; totemism and exogamy; tabus, initiations and age-classes; segregations of the sexes, at certain stages of life, in separate communal establishments—and some of these institutions are certainly as elaborate and perhaps as subtle as those which are characteristic of civilizations.

Nor are civilizations distinguished from primitive societies by the division of labour, for we can discern at least the rudiments of the division of labour in the lives of primitive societies also. Kings, magicians, smiths and minstrels are all 'specialists'— though the fact that Hephaestus, the smith of Hellenic legend, is lame, and Homer, the poet of Hellenic legend, is blind, suggests that in primitive societies specialism is abnormal and apt to be confined to those who lack the capacity to be 'all-round men' or 'jacks of all trades'.

An essential difference between civilizations and primitive societies *as we know them* (the *caveat* will be found to be important) is the direction taken by mimesis or imitation. Mimesis is a generic feature of all social life. Its operation can be observed both in primitive societies and in civilizations, in every social activity from the imitation of the style of film-stars by their humbler sisters upwards. It operates, however, in different directions in the two species of society. In primitive societies, as we know them, mimesis is directed towards the older generation and towards dead ancestors who stand, unseen but not unfelt, at the back of the living elders, reinforcing their prestige. In a society where mimesis is thus directed backward towards the past, custom rules and society remains static. On the other hand, in societies in process of civilization, mimesis is directed towards creative personalities who command a following because they are pioneers. In such societies, 'the cake of custom', as Walter Bagehot called it in his *Physics and Politics*, is broken and society is in dynamic motion along a course of change and growth.

But if we ask ourselves whether this difference between primitive and higher societies is permanent and fundamental, we must answer in the negative; for, if we only know primitive societies in a static condition, that is because we know them from direct observation only in the last phases of their histories. Yet, though direct observation fails us, a train of reasoning informs us that there must have been earlier phases in the histories of primitive societies in which these were moving more dynamically than any 'civilized' society has moved yet. We have said that primitive societies are as old as the human race, but we should more properly have said that they are older. Social and institutional life of a kind is found among some of the higher mammals other than man, and it is clear that mankind could not have become human except in a social environment. This mutation of sub-man into man, which was accomplished, in circumstances of which we have no record, under the aegis of primitive societies, was a more profound change, a greater step in growth, than any progress which man has yet achieved under the aegis of civilization.

Primitive societies, as we know them by direct observation, may be likened to people lying torpid upon a ledge on a mountainside, with a precipice below and a precipice above; civilizations may be likened to companions of these sleepers who have just risen to their feet and have started to climb up the face of the cliff above; while we for our part may liken ourselves to observers whose field of vision is limited to the ledge and to the lower slopes of the upper precipice and who have come upon the scene at the moment when the different members of the party happen to be in these respective postures and positions. At first sight we may be inclined to draw an absolute distinction between the two groups, acclaiming the climbers as athletes and dismissing the recumbent figures as paralytics; but on second thoughts we shall find it more prudent to suspend judgement.

After all, the recumbent figures cannot be paralytics in reality; for they cannot have been born on the ledge, and no human muscles except their own can have hoisted them to this halting-place up the face of the precipice below. On the other hand, their companions who are climbing at the moment have only just left this same ledge and started to climb the precipice above; and, since the next ledge is out of sight, we do not know how high or how arduous the next pitch may be. We only know that it is impossible to halt and rest before the next ledge, wherever that may lie, is reached. Thus, even if we could estimate each present climber's strength and skill and nerve, we could not judge whether any of them have any prospect of gaining the ledge above, which is the goal of their present endeavours. We can, however, be sure that some of them will never attain it. And we can observe that, for every single one now strenuously climbing, twice that number (our extinct civilizations) have fallen back on to the ledge, defeated.

We have failed to find the immediate object of our search, a permanent and fundamental point of difference between primitive societies and civilizations, but incidentally we have obtained some light on the ultimate objective of our present inquiry: the nature of the geneses of civilizations. Starting with the mutation of primitive societies into civilizations we have found that this consists in a transition from a static condition to a dynamic activity; and we shall find that the same formula holds good for the emergence of civilizations through the secessions of internal proletariats from the dominant minorities of pre-existent civilizations which have lost their creative power. Such dominant minorities are static by definition; for to say that the creative minority of a civilization in growth has degenerated or atrophied into the dominant minority of a civilization in disintegration is only another way of saying that the society in question has lapsed from a dynamic activity into a static condition. Against this static condition the secession of a proletariat is a dynamic reaction; and in this light we can see that, in the secession of a proletariat from a dominant minority, a new civilization is generated through the transition of a society from a static condition to a dynamic activity, just as it is in the mutation which produces a civilization out of a primitive society. The geneses of all civilizations—the unrelated and the related class alike—could be described in the phrase of General Smuts: 'Mankind is once more on the move.'

This alternating rhythm of static and dynamic, of movement and pause and movement, has been regarded by many observers in many different ages as something fundamental in the nature of the Universe. In their pregnant imagery the sages of the Sinic Society described these alternations in terms of Yin and Yang— Yin the static and Yang the dynamic. The nucleus of the Sinic character which stands for Yin seems to represent dark coiling clouds overshadowing the Sun, while the nucleus of the character which stands for Yang seems to represent the unclouded sun-disk emitting its rays. In the Chinese formula Yin is always mentioned first, and, within our field of vision, we can see that our breed, having reached the 'ledge' of primitive human nature 300,000 years ago, has reposed there for ninety-eight per cent of that period before entering on the Yang-activity of civilization. We have now to seek for the positive factor, whatever it may be, which has set human life in motion again by its impetus. And first we will explore two avenues which will turn out to be blind alleys.

(2) RACE

It seems obvious that the positive factor which, within the last 6,000 years, has shaken part of mankind out of the Yin state of primitive societies 'on the ledge' into the Yang state of civilizations 'on the cliff' must be sought either in some special quality in the human beings who made the transition or in some special feature of the environment in which the transition has taken place or in some interaction between the two. We will first consider the possibility that one or other of these factors taken by itself will give us what we are looking for. Can we attribute the geneses of civilizations to the virtues of some particular race or races?

Race is a term used to denote the possession of some distinctive and inheritable quality in particular groups of human beings. The supposed attributes of race which concern us here are distinctive psychic or spiritual qualities supposedly innate in certain societies. Psychology, however, and particularly social psychology, is a study which is still in its infancy; and all discussions of race up to date, when race is put forward as a factor productive of civilization, depend on the assumption that there is a correlation between valuable psychic qualities and certain manifest physical characteristics.

The physical characteristic most commonly emphasized by Western advocates of racial theories is colour. It is, of course, just conceivable that spiritual and mental superiority is somehow linked up with, and therefore positively correlated with, comparative absence of skin pigmentation, though it seems biologically improbable. However, the most popular of the racial theories of civilization is that which sets upon a pedestal the xanthotrichous, glaucopian, dolichocephalic variety of *homo leucodermaticus*,[1] called by some the Nordic man and by Nietzsche 'the blond beast'; and it is worth while inquiring into the credentials of this idol of the Teutonic market-place.

Nordic man was first placed on his pedestal by a French aristocrat, the Comte de Gobineau, early in the nineteenth century, and his idolization of 'the blond beast' was an incident in the controversies that arose out of the French Revolution. When the French nobility were being dispossessed of their estates, exiled or guillotined, the pedants of the revolutionary party, who were never happy unless they could present the events of their day in a 'classical' guise, proclaimed that the Gauls, after fourteen centuries of subjection, were now driving their Frankish conquerors back into the outer darkness beyond the Rhine from which they had come during the Völkerwanderung, and were resuming possession of the Gallic soil which, despite the long barbarian usurpation, had never ceased to be their own.

To this nonsense Gobineau replied with some more telling nonsense of his own. 'I accept your identification', he replied in effect. 'Let us agree that the populace of France is descended from the Gauls and the aristocracy from the Franks; that both races have bred pure; and that there is a definite and permanent correlation between their physical and psychic characteristics. Do you really imagine that the Gauls stand for civilization and the Franks for barbarism? Whence came such civilization as you Gauls ever acquired? From Rome. And what made Rome great? Why, a primeval infusion of that same Nordic blood that flows in my Frankish veins. The first Romans—and likewise the first Greeks, the Achaeans of Homer—were fair-haired conquerors who had descended from the invigorating north and established their dominion over the feebler natives of the enervating Mediterranean. In the long run, however, their blood was diluted and their race enfeebled; their power and their glory declined. The

---

[1] 'Is't not possible to understand in another tongue?' asks Horatio. It is; to wit, 'yellow-haired, grey-eyed, long-headed variety of white-skinned man'.—EDITOR.

time had come for another rescue party of fair-haired conquerors to descend from the north and set the pulse of civilization beating again, and among these were the Franks.'

Such is Gobineau's amusing account of a series of facts which we have already handled in a very different manner in our sketches of the origins first of the Hellenic and afterwards of the Western Civilization. His political *jeu d'esprit* gained plausibility from a contemporary discovery of which Gobineau was quick to take advantage. It was discovered that almost all the living languages of Europe, as well as Greek and Latin, and the living languages of Persia and Northern India as well as classical Iranian and classical Sanskrit, were related to one another as members of one vast linguistic family. It was rightly inferred that there must have been an original and primeval 'Aryan' or 'Indo-European' language, from which all known members of the family derived their descent. It was wrongly inferred that the peoples among whom these kindred languages were current were physically related in the same degree as the languages themselves, and that they were all descended from a primitive 'Aryan' or 'Indo-European' race which had spread, conquering and to conquer, east and west and north and south from its original home: a race which had brought forth the religious genius of Zarathustra and the Buddha, the artistic genius of Greece, the political genius of Rome and— fitting climax—our noble selves! Why, this race was responsible for practically all the achievements of human civilization!

The hare which the vivacious Frenchman started was run by heavy-footed German philologists who improved the word Indo-European into Indo-Germanic and located the original home of this imaginary race in the dominions of the King of Prussia. Shortly before the outbreak of the war of 1914–18 Houston Stewart Chamberlain, an Englishman who had fallen in love with Germany, wrote a book called *The Foundations of the Nineteenth Century* in which he added Dante and Jesus Christ to the list of Indo-Germans.

Americans also had their uses for the 'Nordic man'. Alarmed by the overwhelming immigration of Southern Europeans during the quarter of a century before 1914, such writers as Madison Grant and Lothrop Stoddard demanded a restriction of immigration as the only way of preserving—not American social standards but the purity of the American branch of the Nordic race.

The British Israelite doctrine is a theory of the same type using different terminology and supporting imaginary history with quaint theology.

It is curious to notice that, whereas the racial propagandists of our own civilization insist on fair skins as the mark of spiritual superiority, exalting Europeans over other races and Nordics over other Europeans, the Japanese employ a different physical test. It so happens that the bodies of the Japanese are remarkably free from hair, and they have as their neighbours in their northern island a primitive community of quite a different type, a physical type not unlike that of the average European, called the Hairy Ainu. Very naturally, therefore, the Japanese associate hairlessness with spiritual superiority, and, though their claim may be as baseless as our plea for the superiority of fair skins, it is superficially more plausible, for the hairless man is certainly, *quâ* hairlessness, somewhat farther removed from his cousin, the ape.

Ethnologists, classifying White men in accordance with their physical types, long heads and round heads, fair skins and dark skins, and all the rest of it, have sorted out three main White 'races', which they call Nordic, Alpine and Mediterranean. For what it is worth, we will reckon up the number of civilizations to which each of these races has made a positive contribution. The Nordics have contributed to four, possibly five: the Indic, the Hellenic, the Western, the Russian Orthodox Christian and possibly the Hittite. The Alpines have contributed to seven, possibly nine: the Sumeric, the Hittite, the Hellenic, the Western, both the Russian offshoot and the main body of the Orthodox Christian, the Iranic and possibly the Egyptiac and the Minoan. The Mediterraneans have contributed to ten: the Egyptiac, the Sumeric, the Minoan, the Syriac, the Hellenic, the Western, the main body of the Orthodox Christian, the Iranic, the Arabic and the Babylonic. Of the other divisions of the human race, the Brown (meaning thereby the Dravidian peoples in India and the Malays in Indonesia) have contributed to two: the Indic and the Hindu. The Yellow race have contributed to three: the Sinic and both the Far Eastern civilizations, namely the main body in China and the Japanese offshoot. The Red race of America are, of course, the sole contributors to the four American civilizations. The Black races alone have not contributed positively to any civilization— as yet. The White races hold the lead, but it is to be remembered that there are many White peoples that are as innocent of having made any contribution to any civilization as the Blacks themselves. If anything positive emerges from this classification it is that half our civilizations are based on contributions from more than one race. The Western and the Hellenic have three contributors each and, if the Yellow, Brown and Red races were analysed into 'sub-races', like the Nordic, Alpine and Mediterranean divisions of the White race, we should probably be able to produce a plurality of contributors to all our civilizations. What the value of these sub-divisions may be and whether at any time they represented historically and socially distinct peoples is another matter; the whole subject is exceedingly obscure.

But enough has been said to justify us in dismissing the theory that a superior race has been the cause and author of the transition from Yin to Yang, from static to dynamic, in one part of the world after another since a date some six thousand years ago.

(3) ENVIRONMENT

Modern Western minds have been led to emphasize, and over-emphasize, the racial factor in history owing to the expansion of our Western Society over the world during the last four centuries. This expansion brought the peoples of the West into contact, and often unfriendly contact, with peoples differing from themselves not only in culture but in physique, and the notion of superior and inferior biological types was just what one might expect to result from such contacts, especially in the nineteenth century, when Western minds had been rendered biology-conscious by the work of Charles Darwin and other scientific investigators.

The Ancient Greeks also expanded, by way of trade and colonization, into the world around them, but it was a much smaller world containing a wide diversity of cultures but not a wide diversity of physical types. The Egyptian and the Scythian might be far apart from each other and from their Greek observer (Herodotus, for example) in their manner of life, but they were not physically different from him in the sensational way in which the Negro of West Africa and the Red Man of America differed from the European. It was natural, therefore, that the Greeks should find some factor other than biological inheritance of physical characteristics, i.e. race, to account for the differences of culture they observed around them. They found their explanation in differences of geographical habitat, soil and climate.[1]

There is a treatise entitled *Influences of Atmosphere, Water and Situation*, dating from the fifth century B.C. and preserved among the collected works of the Hippocratean School of Medicine, which illustrates Greek views on this subject. Here we read, for example, that

'Human physiognomies may be classified into the well-wooded and

---

[1] Mr. Bernard Shaw is here on the side of the Greeks. Readers of the Preface to *John Bull's Other Island* will remember that he dismisses with scorn the concept of a 'Celtic race' and attributes all the differences between the English and the Irish to the difference between the climates of their respective islands.

well-watered mountain type, the thin-soiled waterless type, the meadowy marshy type, the well-cleared and well-drained lowland type. . . . Inhabitants of mountainous, rocky, well-watered country at a high altitude, where the margin of seasonal climatic variation is wide, will tend to have large-built bodies constitutionally adapted for courage and endurance. . . . Inhabitants of sultry hollows covered with water-meadows, who are more commonly exposed to warm winds than to cold, and who drink tepid water, will, in contrast, not be large built or slim, but thickset, fleshy and dark-haired, with swarthy rather than fair complexions, and with less phlegm than bile in their constitutions. Courage and endurance will not be innate in their characters to the same degree, but will be capable of being produced in them by the co-efficient of institutions. . . . Inhabitants of rolling, wind-swept, well watered country at a high altitude will be large-built and un-individualized, with a vein of cowardice and tameness in their characters. . . . In the majority of cases, you will find that the human body and character vary in accordance with the nature of the country.'[1]

But the favourite Hellenic illustrations of the 'environment theory' were furnished by the contrast between the effect of life in the Lower Nile Valley on the physique, character and institutions of the Egyptians and the effect of life on the Eurasian Steppe on the physique, character and institutions of the Scythians.

Both the race theory and the environment theory try to account for the observed diversity in the psychical (intellectual and spiritual) behaviour and performance of different fractions of mankind by supposing that this psychical diversity is fixedly and permanently correlated, in the relation of effect to cause, with certain elements of observed diversity in the non-psychical domain of nature. The race theory finds the differentiating cause in the diversity of human physique, the environment theory in the diverse climatic and geographical conditions in which different societies live. The essence of both theories is the correlation between two sets of variables, in the one case character and physique, in the other case character and environment, and this correlation must be proved to be fixed and permanent if the theories founded on it are to be established. Under this test we have already seen the race theory break down, and we shall now see that the environment theory, though less preposterous, will fare no better. What we have to do is to test the Hellenic theory on its two favourite examples, the Eurasian Steppe and the Nile Valley. We must find other areas of the Earth's surface geographically and climatically similar to each of these two regions. If all of

---

[1] Hippocrates: *Influences of Atmosphere, Water and Situation*, chs. 13 and 24, translated by Toynbee, A. J.: *Greek Historical Thought from Homer to the Age of Heraclius*, pp. 167–8.

them can show populations resembling, in character and institutions, the Scythians in the one case and the Egyptians in the other, the environment theory will be vindicated; but if not, it will be refuted.

Let us take first the Eurasian Steppe, that vast area of which the Greeks knew only the south-western corner. We may set beside it the Afrasian Steppe which stretches from Arabia across Northern Africa. Is the similarity between the Eurasian and Afrasian steppes matched by any corresponding similarity between the respective human societies that have emerged in these two areas? The answer is in the affirmative. Both have produced the nomadic type of society, a nomadism which displays just those resemblances and differences—differences, for example, in the animals domesticated—that we should expect to find in view of the resemblances and differences between the two areas. But under further tests the correlation breaks down; for we find that other parts of the world which offer environments for nomad societies—the prairies of North America, the Llanos of Venezuela, the Pampas of Argentina and the Australian grasslands—have not produced nomadic societies of their own. Their potentialities are not open to question, for they have been realized by the enterprise of our Western Society in modern times; and the pioneering Western stockmen—North American cowboys, South American gauchos and Australian cattlemen—who have won and held these untenanted ranges for a few generations, in the van of the advancing plough and mill, have captivated the imagination of mankind as triumphantly as the Scythian, the Tatar and the Arab. The potentialities of the American and Australian steppes must have been powerful indeed if they could transform into nomads, if only for a generation, the pioneers of a society which had no nomadic traditions, having lived by agriculture and manufacture ever since it first emerged. It is all the more remarkable that the peoples whom the first Western explorers found in occupation had never been stimulated by their environment into nomadism but had found no better use for these nomads' paradises than to take them as hunting-grounds.

If we next test the theory by a survey of areas resembling the Lower Nile Valley, our experience will be the same.

The Lower Nile Valley is, so to speak, a 'sport' in the landscape of the Afrasian Steppe. Egypt has the same dry climate as the vast area surrounding it, but it has one exceptional asset—an unfailing supply of water and alluvium, provided by the great river which rises, beyond the limits of the Steppe, in an area of abundant rainfall. The creators of the Egyptiac Civilization used this asset to produce a society in sensational contrast with the nomadism on either side of them. Then is the special environment offered by the Nile in Egypt the positive feature to which the genesis of the Egyptiac Civilization is due? To establish this thesis we have to show that in every other separate area in which an environment of the Nilotic type is offered, a similar civilization has independently emerged.

The theory stands the test in a neighbouring area where the required conditions are fulfilled, namely the lower valley of the Euphrates and Tigris. Here we find both similar physical conditions and a similar society, the Sumeric. But it breaks down in the much smaller but similar Jordan Valley, which has never been the seat of a civilization. It probably also breaks down in the Indus Valley—that is, if we are right in surmising that the Indus Culture was brought there ready made by Sumerian colonists. The Lower Ganges Valley may be ruled out of the test as too moist and tropical and the Lower Yangtse and Lower Mississippi valleys as too moist and temperate, but the most captious critic cannot deny that the environmental conditions offered by Egypt and Mesopotamia are also offered by the valleys of the Rio Grande and the Colorado River in the United States. Under the hands of the modern European settler, equipped with resources which he has brought with him from the other side of the Atlantic, these rivers of America have performed the miracles which the Nile and Euphrates performed for Egyptiac and Sumeric engineers. But this magic has never been taught by the Colorado or the Rio Grande to people who were not adepts at it already through having learnt it elsewhere.

On the showing of this evidence the environmental factor cannot be the positive factor which brought the 'fluvial' civilizations into existence; and we shall be confirmed in this conclusion if we glance at some other environments which have produced civilizations in one area but not in another.

The Andean Civilization came into existence on a high plateau, and its achievement was in sharp contrast with the savagery ensconced in the Amazonian forests below. Was, then, the plateau the reason why the Andean Society forged ahead of its savage neighbours? Before we admit the idea we ought to glance at the same equatorial latitudes in Africa, where the East African highlands fringe the forests of the Congo Basin. We shall find that in Africa the plateau was no more productive of a 'civilized' society than the tropical forests of the great river valley.

Similarly, we observe that the Minoan Civilization emerged in a cluster of islands situated in an inland sea and blessed with the climate of the Mediterranean, but a similar environment failed to evoke another civilization of the archipelago type round the Inland Sea of Japan. Japan never gave birth to an independent civilization but was occupied by an offshoot of a continental civilization that had emerged in the interior of China.

The Sinic Civilization is sometimes represented as the offspring of the Yellow River because it happened to emerge in the Yellow River Valley, but the Danube Valley with much the same disposition of climate and soil and plain and mountain failed to produce a similar civilization.

The Mayan Civilization emerged amid the tropical rainfall and vegetation of Guatemala and British Honduras, but no such civilization ever arose out of savagery in the similar conditions on the Amazon and the Congo. These two river basins, it is true, lie actually astride of the equator, while the Mayan homeland is fifteen degrees north. If we follow the fifteenth parallel of latitude round to the other side of the world we stumble upon the tremendous ruins of Angkor Wat amid the tropical rainfall and vegetation of Cambodia. Surely these are comparable with the ruined Mayan cities of Copan and Ixkun? But archaeological evidence shows that the civilization represented by Angkor Wat was not native to Cambodia but was an offshoot of a Hindu Civilization that had emerged in India.

We might pursue the subject farther, but we have, perhaps, said enough to convince the reader that neither race nor environment, taken by itself, can be the positive factor which, within the last six thousand years, has shaken humanity out of its static repose on the level of primitive society and started it on the hazardous quest of civilization. In any case, neither race nor environment, as hitherto envisaged, has offered, or apparently can offer, any clue as to why this great transition in human history occurred not only in particular places but at particular dates.

V. CHALLENGE AND RESPONSE

(1) THE MYTHOLOGICAL CLUE

IN our search so far for the positive factor in the geneses of civilizations we have been employing the tactics of the classical school of modern physical science. We have been thinking in abstract terms and experimenting with the play of inanimate forces—race and environment. Now that these manœuvres have ended in our drawing blank, we may pause to consider whether our failures may not have been due to some mistake of method. Perhaps, under the insidious influence of the spirit of an outgoing age, we have fallen victims to what we will call the 'apathetic fallacy'. Ruskin warned his readers against the 'pathetic fallacy' of imaginatively endowing inanimate objects with life; but it is equally necessary for us to be on our guard against the converse error of applying to historical thought, which is a study of living creatures, a scientific method devised for the study of inanimate nature. In our final attempt to solve the riddle let us follow Plato's lead and try the alternative course. Let us shut our eyes, for the moment, to the formulae of science in order to open our ears to the language of mythology.

It is clear that if the geneses of civilizations are not the result of biological factors or of geographical environment acting separately, they must be the result of some kind of interaction between them. In other words, the factor which we are seeking to identify is something not simple but multiple, not an entity but a relation. We have the choice of conceiving this relation either as an interaction between two inhuman forces or as an encounter between two superhuman personalities. Let us yield our minds to the second of these two conceptions. Perhaps it will lead us towards the light.

An encounter between two superhuman personalities is the plot of some of the greatest dramas that the human imagination has conceived. An encounter between Yahweh and the Serpent is the plot of the story of the Fall of Man in the Book of Genesis; a second encounter between the same antagonists, transfigured by a progressive enlightenment of Syriac souls, is the plot of the New Testament which tells the story of the Redemption; an encounter between the Lord and Satan is the plot of the Book of Job; an encounter between the Lord and Mephistopheles is the plot of Goethe's *Faust*; an encounter between Gods and Demons is the plot of the Scandinavian *Voluspa*; an encounter between Artemis and Aphrodite is the plot of Euripides' *Hippolytus*.

We find another version of the same plot in that ubiquitous and ever-recurring myth—a 'primordial image' if ever there was one—of the encounter between the Virgin and the Father of her Child. The characters in this myth have played their allotted parts on a thousand different stages under an infinite variety of names: Danae and the Shower of Gold; Europa and the Bull; Semele the Stricken Earth and Zeus the Sky that launches the thunderbolt; Creusa and Apollo in Euripides' *Ion*; Psyche and Cupid; Gretchen and Faust. The theme recurs, transfigured, in the Annunciation. In our own day in the West this protean myth has re-expressed itself as the last word of our astronomers on the genesis of the planetary system, as witness the following *credo*:

'We believe ... that some two thousand million years ago ... a second star, wandering blindly through space, happened to come within hailing distance of the Sun. Just as the Sun and Moon raise tides on the Earth, this second star must have raised tides on the surface of the Sun. But they would be very different from the puny tides which the small mass of the Moon raises in our oceans; a huge tidal wave must have travelled over the surface of the Sun, ultimately forming a mountain of prodigious height, which would rise ever higher and higher as the cause of the disturbance came nearer and nearer. And, before the second star began to recede, its tidal pull had become so powerful that this mountain was torn to pieces and threw off small fragments of itself, much as the crest of a wave throws off spray. These small fragments have been circulating round their parent sun ever since. They are the planets, great and small, of which our Earth is one.'[1]

Thus out of the mouth of the mathematical astronomer, when all his complex calculations are done, there comes forth, once again, the myth of the encounter between the Sun Goddess and her ravisher that is so familiar a tale in the mouths of the untutored children of nature.

The presence and potency of this duality in the causation of the civilizations whose geneses we are studying is admitted by a Modern Western archaeologist whose studies begin with a concentration on environment and end with an intuition of the mystery of life:

'Environment ... is not the total causation in culture-shaping. ... It is, beyond doubt, the most conspicuous single factor. ... But there is still an indefinable factor which may best be designated quite frankly as *x*, the unknown quantity, apparently psychological in kind. ... If *x* be not the most conspicuous factor in the matter, it certainly is the most important, the most fate-laden.'[2]

In our present study of history this insistent theme of the super-

[1] Jeans, Sir James: *The Mysterious Universe*, pp. 1 and 2.
[2] Means, P. A.: *Ancient Civilizations of the Andes*, pp. 25–6.

human encounter has asserted itself already. At an early stage we observed that 'a society . . . is confronted in the course of its life by a succession of problems' and that 'the presentation of each problem is a challenge to undergo an ordeal'.

Let us try to analyse the plot of this story or drama which repeats itself in such different contexts and in such various forms. We may begin with two general features: the encounter is conceived of as a rare and sometimes as a unique event; and it has consequences which are vast in proportion to the vastness of the breach which it makes in the customary course of nature.

Even in the easy-going world of Hellenic mythology, where the gods saw the daughters of men that they were fair, and had their way with so many of them that their victims could be marshalled and paraded in poetic catalogues, such incidents never ceased to be sensational affairs and invariably resulted in the births of heroes. In the versions of the plot in which both parties to the encounter are superhuman, the rarity and momentousness of the event are thrown into stronger relief. In the Book of Job, 'the day when the Sons of God came to present themselves before the Lord, and Satan came also among them', is evidently conceived of as an unusual occasion; and so is the encounter between the Lord and Mephistopheles in the 'Prologue in Heaven' (suggested, of course, by the opening of the Book of Job) which starts the action of Goethe's *Faust*. In both these dramas the consequences on Earth of the encounter in Heaven are tremendous. The personal ordeals of Job and Faust represent, in the intuitive language of fiction, the infinitely multiple ordeal of mankind; and, in the language of theology, the same vast consequence is represented as following from the superhuman encounters that are portrayed in the Book of Genesis and in the New Testament. The expulsion of Adam and Eve from the Garden of Eden, which follows the encounter between Yahweh and the Serpent, is nothing less than the Fall of Man; the passion of Christ in the New Testament is nothing less than Man's Redemption. Even the birth of our planetary system from the encounter of two suns, as pictured by our modern astronomer, is declared by the same authority to be 'an event of almost unimaginable rarity'.

In every case the story opens with a perfect state of Yin. Faust is perfect in knowledge; Job is perfect in goodness and prosperity; Adam and Eve are perfect in innocence and ease; the Virgins—Gretchen, Danae and the rest—are perfect in purity and beauty. In the astronomer's universe the Sun, a perfect orb, travels on its course intact and whole. When Yin is thus complete, it is ready to pass over into Yang. But what is to make it pass? A change in a state which, by definition, is perfect after its kind can only be started by an impulse or motive which comes from outside. If we think of the state as one of physical equilibrium, we must bring in another star. If we think of it as one of psychic beatitude or *nirvana*, we must bring another actor on to the stage: a critic to set the mind thinking again by suggesting doubts; an adversary to set the heart feeling again by instilling distress or discontent or fear or antipathy. This is the role of the Serpent in Genesis, of Satan in the Book of Job, of Mephistopheles in *Faust*, of Loki in the Scandinavian mythology, of the Divine Lovers in the Virgin myths.

In the language of science we may say that the function of the intruding factor is to supply that on which it intrudes with a stimulus of the kind best calculated to evoke the most potently creative variations. In the language of mythology and theology, the impulse or motive which makes a perfect Yin-state pass over into new Yang-activity comes from an intrusion of the Devil into the universe of God. The event can best be described in these mythological images because they are not embarrassed by the contradiction that arises when the statement is translated into logical terms. In logic, if God's universe is perfect, there cannot be a Devil outside it, while, if the Devil exists, the perfection which he comes to spoil must have been incomplete already through the very fact of his existence. This logical contradiction, which cannot be logically resolved, is intuitively transcended in the imagery of the poet and prophet, who give glory to an omnipotent God yet take it for granted that He is subject to two crucial limitations.

The first limitation is that, in the perfection of what He has created already, He cannot find an opportunity for further creative activity. If God is conceived of as transcendent, the works of creation are as glorious as ever they were but they cannot 'be changed from glory into glory'. The second limitation on God's power is that when the opportunity for fresh creation is offered to Him from outside He cannot but take it. When the Devil challenges Him He cannot refuse to take the challenge up. God is bound to accept the predicament because He can refuse only at the price of denying His own nature and ceasing to be God.

If God is thus not omnipotent in logical terms, is He still mythologically invincible? If He is bound to take up the Devil's challenge, is He also bound to win the ensuing battle? In Euripides' *Hippolytus*, where God's part is played by Artemis and the Devil's by Aphrodite, Artemis is not only unable to decline the combat but is foredoomed to defeat. The relations between the Olympians are anarchic and Artemis in the epilogue can console herself only by making up her mind that one day she will play the Devil's role herself at Aphrodite's expense. The result is not creation but destruction. In the Scandinavian version destruction is likewise the outcome in Ragnarök—when 'Gods and Demons slay and are slain'—though the unique genius of the author of *Voluspa* makes his Sibyl's vision pierce the gloom to behold the light of a new dawn beyond it. On the other hand, in another version of the plot, the combat which follows the compulsory acceptance of the challenge takes the form, not of an exchange of fire in which the Devil has the first shot and cannot fail to kill his man, but of a wager which the Devil is apparently bound to lose. The classic works in which this wager *motif* is worked out are the Book of Job and Goethe's *Faust*.

It is in Goethe's drama that the point is most clearly made. After the Lord has accepted the wager with Mephistopheles in Heaven, the terms are agreed on Earth, between Mephistopheles and Faust, as follows:

> *Faust.* Comfort and quiet!—no, no! none of these
> For me—I ask them not—I seek them not.
> If ever I upon the bed of sloth
> Lie down and rest, then be the hour in which
> I so lie down and rest my last of life.
> Canst thou by falsehood or by flattery
> Delude me into self-complacent smiles,
> Cheat me into tranquillity? Come then,
> And welcome, life's last day—be this our wager.
> *Meph.* Done.
> *Faust.*   Done, say I: clench we at once the bargain.
> If ever time should flow so calmly on,
> Soothing my spirits in such oblivion
> That in the pleasant trance I would arrest
> And hail the happy moment in its course,
> Bidding it linger with me . . . .
> Then willingly do I consent to perish.[1]

The bearing of this mythical compact upon our problem of the geneses of civilizations can be brought out by identifying Faust, at the moment when he makes his bet, with one of those 'awakened sleepers' who have risen from the ledge on which they had been lying torpid and have started to climb on up the face of the cliff. In the language of our simile, Faust is saying: 'I have made up my mind to leave this ledge and climb this precipice in search of the next ledge above. In attempting this I am aware that I am

---

[1] Goethe's *Faust*, ll. 1692-1706 (John Anster's translation).

leaving safety behind me. Yet, for the sake of the possibility of achievement, I will take the risk of a fall and destruction.'

In the story as told by Goethe the intrepid climber, after an ordeal of mortal dangers and desperate reverses, succeeds in the end in scaling the cliff triumphantly. In the New Testament the same ending is given, through the revelation of a second encounter between the same pair of antagonists, to the combat between Yahweh and the Serpent which, in the original version in Genesis, had ended rather in the manner of the combat between Artemis and Aphrodite in the *Hippolytus*.

In Job, *Faust* and the New Testament alike it is suggested, or even declared outright, that the wager cannot be won by the Devil; that the Devil, in meddling with God's work, cannot frustrate but can only serve the purpose of God, who remains master of the situation all the time and gives the Devil rope for the Devil to hang himself. Then has the Devil been cheated? Did God accept a wager which He knew He could not lose? That would be a hard saying; for if it were true the whole transaction would have been a sham. An encounter which was no encounter could not produce the consequences of an encounter—the vast cosmic consequence of causing Yin to pass over into Yang. Perhaps the explanation is that the wager which the Devil offers and which God accepts covers, and thereby puts in real jeopardy, a part of God's creation but not the whole of it. The part really is at stake; and, though the whole is not, the chances and changes to which the part is exposed cannot conceivably leave the whole unaffected. In the language of mythology, when one of God's creatures is tempted by the Devil, God Himself is thereby given the opportunity to re-create the World. The Devil's intervention, whether it succeeds or fails on the particular issue—and either result is possible—has accomplished that transition from Yin to Yang for which God has been yearning.

As for the human protagonist's part, suffering is the keynote of it in every presentation of the drama, whether the player of the part is Jesus or Job or Faust or Adam and Eve. The picture of Adam and Eve in the Garden of Eden is a reminiscence of the Yin-state to which primitive man attained in the food-gathering phase of economy, after he had established his ascendancy over the rest of the flora and fauna of the Earth. The Fall, in response to the temptation to eat of the Tree of the Knowledge of Good and Evil, symbolizes the acceptance of a challenge to abandon this achieved integration and to venture upon a fresh differentiation out of which a fresh integration may—or may not—arise. The expulsion from the Garden into an unfriendly world in which the

Woman must bring forth children in sorrow and the Man must eat bread in the sweat of his face, is the ordeal which the acceptance of the Serpent's challenge has entailed. The sexual intercourse between Adam and Eve, which follows, is an act of social creation. It bears fruit in the birth of two sons who impersonate two nascent civilizations: Abel the keeper of sheep and Cain the tiller of the ground.

In our own generation, one of our most distinguished and original-minded students of the physical environment of human life tells the same story in his own way:

'Ages ago a band of naked, houseless, fireless savages started from their warm home in the torrid zone and pushed steadily northward from the beginning of spring to the end of summer. They never guessed that they had left the land of constant warmth until in September they began to feel an uncomfortable chill at night. Day by day it grew worse. Not knowing its cause, they travelled this way or that to escape. Some went southward, but only a handful returned to their former home. There they resumed the old life, and their descendants are untutored savages to this day. Of those who wandered in other directions, all perished except one small band. Finding that they could not escape the nipping air, the members of this band used the loftiest of human faculties, the power of conscious invention. Some tried to find shelter by digging in the ground, some gathered branches and leaves to make huts and warm beds, and some wrapped themselves in the skins of the beasts that they had slain. Soon these savages had taken some of the greatest steps towards civilization. The naked were clothed; the houseless sheltered; the improvident learnt to dry meat and store it, with nuts, for the winter; and at last the art of preparing fire was discovered as a means of keeping warm. Thus they subsisted where at first they thought that they were doomed. And in the process of adjusting themselves to a hard environment they advanced by enormous strides, leaving the tropical part of mankind far in the rear.'[1]

A classical scholar likewise translates the story into the scientific terminology of our age:

'It is . . . a paradox of advancement that, if Necessity be the mother of Invention, the other parent is Obstinacy, the determination that you will go on living under adverse conditions rather than cut your losses and go where life is easier. It was no accident, that is, that civilization, as we know it, began in that ebb and flow of climate, flora and fauna which characterizes the four-fold Ice Age. Those primates who just "got out" as arboreal conditions wilted retained their primacy among the servants of natural law, but they forewent the conquest of nature. Those others won through, and became men, who stood their ground when there were no more trees to sit in, who "made do" with meat when fruit did not ripen, who made fires and clothes rather than

[1] Huntington, Ellsworth: *Civilization and Climate*, pp. 405–6.

follow the sunshine; who fortified their lairs and trained their young and vindicated the reasonableness of a world that seemed so reasonless.'[1]

The first stage, then, of the human protagonist's ordeal is a transition from Yin to Yang through a dynamic act—performed by God's creature under temptation from the Adversary—which enables God Himself to resume His creative activity. But this progress has to be paid for; and it is not God but God's servant, the human sower, who pays the price. Finally, after many vicissitudes, the sufferer triumphant serves as the pioneer. The human protagonist in the divine drama not only serves God by enabling Him to renew His creation but also serves his fellow men by pointing the way for others to follow.

(2) THE MYTH APPLIED TO THE PROBLEM

The Unpredictable Factor

By the light of mythology we have gained some insight into the nature of challenges and responses. We have come to see that creation is the outcome of an encounter, that genesis is a product of interaction. Let us now return to our immediate quest: our search for the positive factor that has shaken part of mankind out of 'the integration of custom' into 'the differentiation of civilization' within the last six thousand years. Let us review the origins of our twenty-one civilizations in order to ascertain, by an empirical test, whether the conception of 'Challenge-and-Response' answers to the factor of which we are in search any better than the hypotheses of race and environment, which we have already weighed in the balance and found wanting.

In this fresh survey we shall still be concerned with race and environment, but we shall regard them in a new light. We shall no longer be on the look-out for some simple cause of the geneses of civilizations which can be demonstrated always and everywhere to produce an identical effect. We shall no longer be surprised if, in the production of civilizations, the same race or the same environment appears to be fruitful in one instance and sterile in another. In fact, we shall no longer make the scientific postulate of the Uniformity of Nature, which we rightly made so long as we were thinking of our problem in scientific terms as the function of a play of inanimate forces. We shall be prepared now to recognize that, even if we were exactly acquainted with all the racial, environmental, and other data that are capable of being formulated

[1] Myres, J. L.: Who were the Greeks?, pp. 277-8.

scientifically, we should not be able to predict the outcome of the interaction between the forces which these data represent, any more than a military expert can predict the outcome of a battle or campaign from an 'inside knowledge' of the dispositions and resources of both the opposing general staffs, or a bridge expert the outcome of a game from a similar knowledge of all the cards in every hand.

In both these analogies 'inside knowledge' is not sufficient to enable its possessor to predict results with any exactness or assurance because it is not the same thing as complete knowledge. There is one thing which must remain an unknown quantity to the best-informed onlooker because it is beyond the knowledge of the combatants, or players, themselves; and it is the most important term in the equation which the would-be calculator has to solve. This unknown quantity is the reaction of the actors to the ordeal when it actually comes. These psychological momenta, which are inherently impossible to weigh and measure and therefore to estimate scientifically in advance, are the very forces which actually decide the issue when the encounter takes place. And that is why the very greatest military geniuses have admitted an incalculable element in their successes. If religious, they have attributed their victories to God, like Cromwell; if merely superstitious, to the ascendancy of their 'star', like Napoleon.

The Genesis of the Egyptiac Civilization

When dealing with environment in the previous chapter we assumed, as the Hellenic authors of the environment theory naturally assumed, that environment is a static factor; more particularly, that within the limits of 'historic' time the physical conditions presented by the Afrasian Steppe and the Nile Valley have been always the same as they are to-day and as they were twenty-four centuries ago when the Greeks spun their theories round them. But in fact we know that this has not been so.

'While Northern Europe was covered in ice as far as the Harz, and the Alps and the Pyrenees were capped with glaciers, the Arctic high pressure deflected southwards the Atlantic rainstorms. The cyclones that to-day traverse Central Europe then passed over the Mediterranean Basin and the Northern Sahara and continued, undrained by Lebanon, across Mesopotamia and Arabia to Persia and India. The parched Sahara enjoyed a regular rainfall, and farther east the showers were not only more bountiful than to-day but were distributed over the whole year, instead of being restricted to the winter. . . .

'We should expect in North Africa, Arabia, Persia and the Indus Valley parklands and savannahs, such as flourish to-day north of the Mediterranean. . . . While the mammoth, the woolly rhinoceros and the reindeer were browsing in France and Southern England, North Africa was supporting a fauna that is found to-day on the Zambesi in Rhodesia. . . .

'The pleasant grasslands of North Africa and Southern Asia were naturally as thickly populated by man as the frozen steppes of Europe, and it is reasonable to suspect that in this favourable and indeed stimulating environment man would make greater progress than in the ice-bound north.'[1]

But after the close of the Ice Age our Afrasian area began to experience a profound physical change in the direction of desiccation; and simultaneously two or more civilizations arose in an area which had previously, like all the rest of the inhabited world, been occupied solely by primitive societies cf the palaeolithic order. Our archaeologists encourage us to look upon the desiccation of Afrasia as a challenge to which the geneses of these civilizations were the responses.

'Now we are on the brink of the great revolution, and soon we shall encounter men who are masters of their own food supply through possession of domesticated animals and the cultivation of cereals. It seems inevitable to connect that revolution with the crisis produced by the melting of the northern glaciers and consequent contraction of the Arctic high pressure over Europe and diversion of the Atlantic rainstorms from the South Mediterranean Zone to their present course across Central Europe.

'That event would certainly tax the ingenuity of the inhabitants of the former grassland zone to the utmost. . . .

'Faced with the gradual desiccation consequent upon the re-shift northward of the Atlantic cyclone belt as the European glaciers contracted, three alternatives were open to the hunting populations affected. They might move northward or southward with their prey, following the climatic belt to which they were accustomed; they might remain at home eking out a miserable existence on such game as could withstand the drought; or they might—still without leaving their homeland—emancipate themselves from dependence on the whims of their environment by domesticating animals and taking to agriculture.'[2]

In the event, those that changed neither their habitat nor their way of life paid the penalty of extinction for their failure to respond to the challenge of desiccation. Those that avoided changing their habitat by changing their way of life and transforming themselves from hunters into shepherds became the nomads of the Afrasian Steppe. Their achievement and fate will demand our attention in another part of this book. Of those that elected to change their habitat rather than change their way of life, the

[1] Childe, V. G.: *The Most Ancient East*, ch. ii.
[2] Ibid., ch. iii.

communities which avoided the drought by following the cyclone belt as it shifted northward exposed themselves, unintentionally, to a new challenge—the challenge of the northern seasonal cold—which evoked a new creative response in such as did not succumb to it; while the communities which avoided the drought by retreating southward into the monsoon belt came under the soporific influence emanating from the climatic monotony of the Tropics. Fifthly and finally there were communities that responded to the challenge of desiccation by changing their habitat and their way of life alike, and this rare double reaction was the dynamic act which created the Egyptiac and Sumeric civilizations out of some of the primitive societies of the vanishing Afrasian grasslands.

The change in these creative communities' way of life was the thoroughgoing transformation of food-gatherers and hunters into cultivators. The change in their habitat was small in point of distance but vast if measured by the difference in character between the grasslands which they abandoned and the new physical environment in which they now made their home. When the grasslands overlooking the lower valley of the Nile turned into the Libyan Desert and the grasslands overlooking the lower valley of the Euphrates and Tigris into the Rub' al-Khāli and the Dasht-i-Lūt, these heroic pioneers—inspired by audacity or by desperation—plunged into the jungle-swamps of the valley bottoms, never before penetrated by man, which their dynamic act was to turn into the Land of Egypt and the Land of Shinar. To their neighbours, who took the alternative courses described above, their venture must have seemed a forlorn hope; for in the outlived age when the area which was now beginning to turn into the Afrasian Steppe had been an earthly paradise the Nilotic and Mesopotamian jungle-swamp had been a forbidding and apparently impenetrable wilderness. As it turned out, the venture succeeded beyond the most sanguine hopes in which the pioneers can ever have indulged. The wantonness of nature was subdued by the works of man; the formless jungle-swamp made way for a pattern of ditches and embankments and fields; the lands of Egypt and Shinar were reclaimed from the wilderness and the Egyptiac and Sumeric societies started on their great adventures.

The Lower Nile Valley into which our pioneers descended was not only very different from the valley as we see it to-day, after sixty centuries of skilled labour have left their mark on it; it was almost equally different from what it would be to-day if man had left its re-fashioning to nature. Even as comparatively late as the times of the Old and the Middle Kingdom—that is to

say, several millennia after the days of the pioneers—the hippo-
potamus, the crocodile and a variety of wild fowl, none of which
are now found below the First Cataract, were common objects in
the lower valley, as is proved by the evidence of sculptures and
paintings which survive from that period. What is true of the birds
and animals is true also of the vegetation. Though desiccation
had set in, Egypt still had rainfall and the Delta was a waterlogged
marsh. It is probable that the Lower Nile above the Delta resembled in those days the Upper Nile country of the Bahr-al-
Jabal in the Equatorial Province of the Sudan and that the Delta
itself resembled the region round Lake No where the Bahr-al-
Jabal and the Bahr-al-Ghazal mingle their waters. What follows
is a present-day description of this dismal country:

'The scenery of the Bahr-al-Jabal throughout its course through
the Sudd [reed-pack] region is monotonous to a degree. There are
no banks at all, except at a few isolated spots, no semblance of any ridge
on the water's edge. Reedy swamps stretch for many kilometres upon
either side. Their expanse is only broken at intervals by lagoons of open
water. Their surface is only a few centimetres above that of the water-
level in the river when at its lowest, and a rise of half a metre floods
them to an immense distance. These marshes are covered with a dense
growth of water-weeds, extending in every direction to the horizon. . . .
'Throughout this whole region, more especially between Bor and
Lake No, it is extremely rare to see any sign of human life. . . . The
whole region has an aspect of desolation beyond the power of words to
describe. It must be seen to be understood.'[1]

It is uninhabited because the people who live on its outskirts
are not confronted, here and now, as the fathers of the Egyptiac
Civilization were confronted when they were squatting on the
borders of the Lower Nile Valley six thousand years ago, with the
hard choice of plunging into the forbidding Sudd or clinging to
an ancestral habitat in process of transformation from an earthly
paradise into an inhospitable desert. If our scholars are right in
their surmise, the forefathers of these people who now live on
the margin of the Sudanese Sudd were living, in what is now the
Libyan Desert, cheek by jowl with the founders of the Egyptiac
Civilization at the time when these responded to the challenge of
desiccation by making their momentous choice. At that time, it
would seem, the ancestors of the modern Dinka and Shilluk
parted with their heroic neighbours and followed the line of least
resistance by retreating southwards to a country where they
could continue to live, without changing their way of life, in

[1] Garstin, Sir William: *Report upon the Basin of the Upper Nile, 1904*, pp.
98–9.

physical surroundings partly identical with those to which they were accustomed. They settled in the Tropical Sudan, within the range of the equatorial rains, and here their descendants remain to this day living the self-same life as their remote ancestors. In their new home the sluggish and unambitious emigrants found what their souls desired.

'On the Upper Nile there dwell to-day people allied to the oldest Egyptians in appearance, stature, cranial proportions, language and dress. These are ruled by rain-maker magicians or by divine kings who were until recently ritually slain, and the tribes are organised in totemic clans. . . . It really looks as if among these tribes on the Upper Nile social development had been arrested at a stage that the Egyptians had traversed before their history began. There we have a living museum whose exhibits supplement and vivify the prehistoric cases in our collections.'[1]

The parallel between earlier conditions in one part of the Nile Basin and present-day conditions in another part invites certain speculations. Supposing that the challenge of desiccation had never been presented to the inhabitants of the Nile Basin in those parts of it which, under present conditions, are beyond the range of the equatorial rains: in that event would the delta and lower valley of the Nile have been left in the original state of nature? Would the Egyptiac Civilization never have arisen? Would these people be squatting still on the edge of an untamed Lower Nile Valley as the Shilluk and Dinka are now squatting on the edge of the Bahr-al-Jabal? And there is another line of speculation which concerns not the past but the future. We may remind ourselves that on the time-scale of the universe, or of our planet, or of life, or even of the *genus homo*, a span of six thousand years is a negligible lapse of time. Supposing that another challenge, as formidable as that which presented itself to the inhabitants of the Lower Nile Valley yesterday, at the end of the Ice Age, were to present itself to the inhabitants of the Upper Nile Basin to-morrow: is there any reason to believe that they are incapable of responding by some equally dynamic act which might have equally creative effects?

We need not require that this hypothetical challenge to the Shilluk and Dinka shall be of the same kind as that presented to the fathers of the Egyptiac Civilization. Let us imagine that the challenge comes not from the physical but from the human environment, not from a change of climate but from the intrusion of an alien civilization. Is not this very challenge being actually presented under our eyes to the primitive inhabitants of Tropical

[1] Childe, V. G.: *The Most Ancient East*, pp. 10–11.

Africa by the impact of our Western Civilization—a human agency which, in our generation, is playing the mythical role of Mephistopheles towards every other extant civilization and towards every extant primitive society on the face of the Earth? The challenge is still so recent that we cannot yet forecast the ultimate response that any of the challenged societies will make to it. We can only say that the failure of the fathers to respond to one challenge would not condemn the children to fail in face of another challenge when their hour came.

The Genesis of the Sumeric Civilization

We can deal with this problem briefly, for here we have a challenge identical with that which confronted the fathers of the Egyptiac Civilization and a response which was of the same kind. The desiccation of Afrasia likewise impelled the fathers of the Sumeric Civilization to come to grips with the jungle-swamp of the lower valley of the Tigris and Euphrates and to transform it into the Land of Shinar. The material aspects of these two geneses almost coincide. The spiritual characteristics of the two resultant civilizations, their religion, their art, and even their social life, display much less similarity—another indication that, in the field of our studies, identic causes cannot be presumed, *a priori*, to produce identic effects.

The ordeal through which the fathers of the Sumeric Civilization passed is commemorated in Sumeric legend. The slaying of the dragon Tiamat by the god Marduk and the creation of the World out of her mortal remains signifies the subjugation of the primeval wilderness and the creation of the Land of Shinar by the canalization of the waters and the draining of the soil. The story of the Flood records nature's revolt against the shackles which man's audacity had placed on her. In the Biblical version, a literary heritage of the Jews from their exile by the waters of Babylon, 'the Flood' has become a household word of our Western Society. It has remained for modern archaeologists to discover the original version of the legend and also to find direct evidence of a particular flood of abnormal severity in a thick layer of flood-laid clay which intervenes between the earliest and the later strata deposited by human habitation on the sites of certain historic seats of the Sumeric culture.

The basin of the Tigris and Euphrates, like the basin of the Nile, displays for our observation a 'museum' in which we can study the normal aspect of inanimate nature in the wilderness which man has transformed, together with the life that was lived in this wilderness by the first Sumeric pioneers. In Mesopotamia, however, this museum is not to be found, as in the Nile Basin, by travelling up-stream. It lies in the new delta at the head of the Persian Gulf which has been laid down by the confluence of the sister streams in times posterior not only to the genesis of the Sumeric Civilization but to its extinction and also to the extinction of its Babylonic successor. These marshes, which have gradually come into existence during the last two or three thousand years, have remained in their virgin state down to this day only because no human society with the will to master them has appeared on the scene. The marshmen by whom they are haunted have learnt to adapt themselves to this environment in a passive way, as is indicated by their nickname, 'the web-feet', which they received from British soldiers who encountered them in the war of 1914–18, but they have never yet girded themselves for the task, which the fathers of the Sumeric Civilization accomplished in similar country near by some five or six thousand years ago, of transforming the marshes into a network of canals and fields.

The Genesis of the Sinic Civilization

If we consider next the genesis of the Sinic Civilization in the lower valley of the Yellow River we shall find a human response to a challenge from physical nature which was perhaps even more severe than the challenge of the Two Rivers and of the Nile. In the wilderness which man once transformed into the cradle of the Sinic Civilization, the ordeal of marsh and bush and flood was capped by the ordeal of a temperature which varied seasonally between extremes of summer heat and winter cold. The fathers of the Sinic Civilization do not seem to have differed in race from the peoples occupying the vast region to the south and south-west which extends from the Yellow River to the Brahmaputra and from the Tibetan Plateau to the China Sea. If certain members of that wide-spread race created a civilization while the rest remained culturally sterile, the explanation may be that a creative faculty, latent in all alike, was evoked in those particular members, and in those only, by the presentation of a challenge to which the rest did not happen to be exposed. The precise nature of that challenge is impossible to determine in the present state of our knowledge. What we can say with certainty is that the fathers of the Sinic Civilization in their home by the Yellow River did not enjoy the fancied but delusive advantage of an easier environment than their neighbours. Indeed, none of the related peoples farther south, in the valley of the Yangtse, for example, where this civilization did *not* originate, can have had so hard a fight for life.

The Geneses of the Mayan and Andean Civilizations

The challenge to which the Mayan Civilization was a response was the luxuriance of the tropical forest.

'The Mayan culture was made possible by the agricultural conquest of the rich lowlands where the exuberance of nature can only be held in check by organized effort. On the highlands the preparation of the land is comparatively easy, owing to scanty natural vegetation and a control vested in irrigation. On the lowlands, however, great trees have to be felled and fast-growing bushes kept down by untiring energy. But when nature is truly tamed she returns recompense many-fold to the daring farmer. Moreover, there is reason to believe that the removal of the forest cover over large areas affects favourably the conditions of life which under a canopy of leaves are hard indeed.'[1]

This challenge, which called the Mayan Civilization into existence to the north of the Isthmus of Panama, found no response on the other side of the Isthmus. The civilizations which arose in South America responded to two quite different challenges, from the Andean Plateau and from the adjoining Pacific Coast. On the plateau the fathers of the Andean Civilization were challenged by a bleak climate and a grudging soil; on the coast they were challenged by the heat and drought of an almost rainless equatorial desert at sea-level, which could only be made to blossom as the rose by the works of man. The pioneers of the civilization on the coast conjured their oases out of the desert by husbanding the scanty waters that descended from the western scarp of the plateau and giving life to the plains by irrigation. The pioneers on the plateau transformed their mountain-sides into fields by husbanding the scanty soil on terraces preserved by a ubiquitous system of laboriously constructed retaining walls.

The Genesis of the Minoan Civilization

We have now explained in terms of responses to challenges from the physical environment the geneses of five out of our six un-related civilizations. The sixth was a response to a physical challenge that we have not yet encountered in this survey, the challenge of the sea.

Whence came these pioneers of 'the thalassocracy of Minos'? From Europe, Asia or Africa? A glance at the map would suggest that they would have come from Europe or Asia, for the islands are very much nearer to these mainlands than to North Africa— being, in fact, the peaks of submerged mountain ranges which, but for a collapse in prehistoric times and the inflow of the waters,

[1] Spinden, H. J.: *Ancient Civilizations of Mexico and Central America*, p. 65.

would run continuously from Anatolia to Greece. But we are faced with the disconcerting, yet indubitable, testimony of archaeologists that the oldest remains of human habitation are found in Crete, an island comparatively distant from both Greece and Anatolia, though it is nevertheless nearer to both of them than it is to Africa. Ethnology supports the suggestion that archaeology throws out; for it appears to be established that among the earliest known inhabitants of the continents facing the Aegean there were certain clearly marked distinctions of physical type. The earliest known inhabitants of Anatolia and Greece were 'broad-heads'; the earliest known inhabitants of the Afrasian grasslands were 'long-heads'; and an analysis of the oldest relics of human physique in Crete seems to indicate that the island was first occupied wholly or mainly by 'long-heads', while the 'broad-heads', though they eventually became predominant, were originally either not represented in the population of Crete at all or only in a small minority. This ethnological evidence points to the conclusion that the first human beings to secure a footing in any part of the Aegean Archipelago were immigrants from the desiccation of the Afrasian grasslands.

We have, then, to add a sixth to the five responses to this desiccation that we have already noted. To those who stayed where they were and perished; to those who stayed where they were and became nomads; to those who went south and retained their old way of life, like the Dinka and Shilluk; to those who went north and became neolithic agriculturists on the European Continent; to those who plunged into the jungle-swamps and made the Egyptiac and Sumeric civilizations, we must add those who, going north and striking, not the comparatively easy passages offered by then surviving isthmuses or still existing straits, but the intimidating void of the open Mediterranean, accepted this further challenge, crossed the broad sea, and made the Minoan Civilization.

If this analysis is correct, it offers a fresh illustration of the truth that, in the geneses of civilizations, the interplay between challenges and responses is the factor which counts above all others—in this case above proximity. If proximity had been the determining factor in the occupation of the Archipelago, then the inhabitants of the nearest continents, Europe and Asia, would have been the first occupants of the Aegean islands. Many of the islands are 'within a stone's throw' of these mainlands, whereas Crete is two hundred miles from the nearest point in Africa. Yet the islands nearest to Europe and Asia, which apparently were not occupied until a much later date than Crete, appear to have been occupied concurrently by 'long-heads' and 'broad-heads'; which suggests that, after the Afrasians had laid the foundations of the Minoan Civilization, others entered into their labours, either from mere imitation of the pioneers or because some pressure or challenge which we cannot precisely identify forced them too, in their time, to make the same response as the original Afrasian occupants of Crete had already made under still more formidable conditions.

The Geneses of the Affiliated Civilizations

When we pass from the 'unrelated' civilizations, which arose out of the Yin-state of primitive society, to those later civilizations that were in varying ways and degrees related to 'civilized' predecessors, it is obvious that in their case, though there may have been some degree of physical challenge to stimulate them too, the principal and essential challenge was a human challenge arising out of their relationship to the society to which they were affiliated. This challenge is implicit in the relation itself, which begins with a differentiation and culminates in a secession. The differentiation takes place within the body of the antecedent civilization, when that civilization begins to lose the creative power through which, in its period of growth, it had at one time inspired a voluntary allegiance in the hearts of the people below its surface or beyond its borders. When this happens, the ailing civilization pays the penalty for its failing vitality by being disintegrated into a dominant minority, which rules with increasing oppressiveness but no longer leads, and a proletariat (internal and external) which responds to this challenge by becoming conscious that it has a soul of its own and by making up its mind to save its soul alive. The dominant minority's will to repress evokes in the proletariat a will to secede; and a conflict between these two wills continues while the declining civilization verges towards its fall, until, when it is *in articulo mortis*, the proletariat at length breaks free from what was once its spiritual home but has now become a prison-house and finally a City of Destruction. In this conflict between a proletariat and a dominant minority, as it works itself out from beginning to end, we can discern one of those dramatic spiritual encounters which renew the work of creation by carrying the life of the Universe out of the stagnation of autumn through the pains of winter into the ferment of spring. The secession of the proletariat is the dynamic act, in response to the challenge, through which the change from Yin to Yang is brought about; and in this dynamic separation the 'affiliated' civilization is born.

Can we discern a physical challenge also at the geneses of our affiliated civilizations? We saw, in our second chapter, that the affiliated civilizations were related in differing degrees to their predecessors in the matter of their geographical location. At one end of the scale, the Babylonic Civilization developed wholly within the homeland of its antecedent Sumeric Society. Here a physical challenge can hardly have entered into the genesis of the new civilization at all, except in so far as, during the interregnum between the two civilizations, their common cradle may have relapsed to some extent into its primitive state of nature and to that extent have challenged the fathers of the later civilization to repeat the initial achievement of their predecessors.

When, however, the affiliated civilization has broken new ground and established its home partly or wholly outside the area of the antecedent civilization, there will have been a challenge from the new and unmastered physical environment. Thus, our Western Civilization was exposed at its genesis to a challenge from the forests and the rains and the frosts of Transalpine Europe which had not confronted the antecedent Hellenic Civilization. The Indic Civilization was exposed at its genesis to a challenge from the moist tropical forests of the Ganges Valley which had not confronted its predecessor, the Sumeric Civilization's outlying province or counterpart in the Indus Valley.[1] The Hittite Civilization was exposed at its genesis to a challenge from the Anatolian Plateau which had not confronted the antecedent Sumeric Civilization. The challenge to which the Hellenic Civilization was exposed at its genesis—the challenge of the sea—was precisely the same as that which had confronted the antecedent Minoan Civilization. This challenge, however, was entirely new to the external proletariat beyond the European land-frontier of 'the thalassocracy of Minos'; and these continental barbarians, Achaeans and the like, when they took to the sea in the post-Minoan Völkerwanderung, were facing and surmounting as great an ordeal as the pioneers of the Minoan Civilization had themselves faced and surmounted in their day.

In America the Yucatec Civilization was exposed at its genesis to the challenge of the waterless, treeless and almost soil-less limestone shelf of the Yucatan Peninsula, and the Mexic Civilization to the challenge of the Mexican Plateau, neither of which challenges had been encountered by the antecedent Mayan Civilization.

There remain the Hindu, the Far Eastern, the Orthodox

---

[1] We have omitted Mr. Toynbee's discussion, earlier in the book, of the question whether this Indus Valley Culture was a separate civilization or a province of the Sumeric. He leaves the point undetermined, but in Chapter II treats 'the Indus Valley Culture' as part of the Sumeric Society.—EDITOR.

Christian, the Arabic and the Iranic civilizations. These do not seem to have been exposed to any obvious physical challenge; for their homelands, though not, like that of the Babylonic Civilization, identical with the homelands of their antecedent civilizations, had already been subdued by these or by other civilizations. We saw reason, however, to subdivide the Orthodox Christian and the Far Eastern civilizations. The offshoot of the Orthodox Christian Civilization in Russia was exposed to a challenge from forests and rains and frosts still more severe than that with which our Western Civilization had to contend; and the offshoot of the Far Eastern Civilization in Korea and Japan was exposed to a challenge from the sea entirely different from any challenge which had confronted the pioneers of the Sinic Civilization.

We have now shown that our affiliated civilizations, while in all cases necessarily exposed to a human challenge inherent in the disintegration of the antecedent civilizations from which they sprang, were also in some cases, though not in others, exposed to a challenge from the physical environment, resembling the challenges encountered by the unrelated civilizations. To complete this stage of our inquiry, we ought to ask whether the unrelated societies, in addition to their physical challenges, were exposed to human challenges arising out of their differentiation from primitive societies. On this point we can only say that historical evidence is entirely lacking—as one might expect. It may well be that our six unrelated civilizations did encounter, in that 'prehistoric' past in which their geneses are shrouded, human challenges comparable in kind to the challenges offered to the affiliated societies by the tyranny of the dominant minorities of their predecessors. But to enlarge on this subject would be to speculate in a void.

VI. THE VIRTUES OF ADVERSITY[1]

A Stricter Test

WE have been led to reject the popular assumption that civilizations emerge when environments offer unusually easy conditions of life and to advance an argument in favour of exactly the opposite view. The popular view arises from the fact that a modern observer of such a civilization as the Egyptiac—and in this context the Ancient Greeks were 'moderns' like ourselves—takes for granted the land as man has made it, and assumes that it was like that when the pioneers first took it in hand. We have tried to show what the Lower Nile Valley was really like when the pioneers first took it in hand by giving a picture of certain parts of the Upper Nile Valley as they are to-day. But this difference in the geographical site may have prevented our illustration from being entirely convincing, and in the present chapter we propose to drive our point home by citing cases in which a civilization has first succeeded and subsequently failed on the same site, and the country, unlike Egypt, has reverted to its pristine condition.

Central America

One remarkable instance is the present state of the birthplace of the Mayan Civilization. Here we find the ruins of immense and magnificently decorated public buildings which now stand, far away from any present human habitations, in the depth of the tropical forest. The forest, like some sylvan boa-constrictor, has literally swallowed them up and is now devouring them at its leisure, prising the fine-hewn close-laid stones apart with its writhing roots and tendrils. The contrast between the present aspect of the country and the aspect which it must have worn when the Mayan Civilization was in being is so great that it is almost beyond imagination. There must have been a time when these immense public buildings stood in the heart of large and populous cities, and when those cities lay in the midst of wide expanses of cultivated land. The transitoriness of human achievement and the vanity of human wishes are poignantly exposed by the return of the forest, engulfing first the fields and then the houses and finally the palaces and temples themselves. Yet that is not the most significant lesson to be learnt from the present state of Copan or Tikal or Palenque. The ruins speak still more

[1] Mr. Toynbee entitles this chapter Χαλεπὰ τὰ Καλά, which means 'The beautiful is difficult' or 'High quality involves hard work'.—EDITOR.

eloquently of the intensity of the struggle with the physical environment which the creators of the Mayan Civilization must have waged in their day. In her very revenge, which reveals her in all her gruesome power, Tropical Nature testifies to the courage and vigour of the men who once, if only for a season, succeeded in putting her to flight and keeping her at bay.

Ceylon

The equally arduous feat of conquering the parched plains of Ceylon for agriculture is commemorated in the breached dams and overgrown floors of the tanks which were once constructed on the wet side of the hill country, on a colossal scale, by the Sinhalese converts to the Indic philosophy of the Hīnayāna.

'To realize how such tanks came into being one must know something of the history of Lanka. The idea underlying the system was simple but very great. It was intended by the tank-building kings that none of the rain which fell in such abundance in the mountains should reach the sea without paying tribute to man on the way.

'In the middle of the southern half of Ceylon is a wide mountain zone, but to the east and north dry plains cover thousands of square miles, and at present are very sparsely populated. In the height of the monsoon, when armies of storm-swept clouds rush on day after day to match their strength against the hills, there is a line drawn by nature that the rains are unable to pass. . . . There are points where the line of demarcation of the two zones, the wet and the dry, is so narrow that within a mile one seems to pass into a new country. . . . The line curves from sea to sea and appears to be stable and unaffected by the operations of man, such as felling forests.'[1]

Yet the missionaries of the Indic Civilization in Ceylon once achieved the *tour de force* of compelling the monsoon-smitten highlands to give water and life and wealth to the plains which nature had condemned to lie parched and desolate.

'Hill streams were tapped and their water guided into the giant storage-tanks below, some of them four thousand acres in extent; and, from those, channels ran on to other larger tanks farther from the hills and from them to others still more remote. And below each great tank and each great channel were hundreds of little tanks, each the nucleus of a village, all, in the long run, fed from the wet mountain zone. So gradually the ancient Sinhalese conquered all, or nearly all, of the plains that are now so empty of men.'[2]

The arduousness of the labour involved in holding for a man-made civilization these naturally barren plains is demonstrated by two outstanding features in the landscape of Ceylon to-day:

[1] Still, John: *The Jungle Tide*, pp. 74–5.
[2] Ibid., pp. 76–7.

the relapse of that once irrigated and populated tract into its primeval barrenness, and the concentration of the modern tea, coffee and rubber planters in the other half of the island, where the rain falls.

The North Arabian Desert

A celebrated and indeed almost hackneyed illustration of our theme is the present state of Petra and Palmyra—a spectacle which has inspired a whole series of essays in the philosophy of history from Volney's *Les Ruines* (1791) onwards. To-day these former homes of the Syriac Civilization are in the same state as the former homes of the Mayan Civilization, though the hostile environment which has taken its revenge on them is the Afrasian Steppe instead of the tropical forest. The ruins tell us that these elaborate temples and porticoes and tombs must, when they stood intact, have been the ornaments of great cities; and here the evidence of archaeology, which is our sole means of composing a picture of the Mayan Civilization, is reinforced by the written testimony of historical records. We know that the pioneers of the Syriac Civilization who conjured these cities up out of the desert were masters of the magic which Syriac legend ascribes to Moses.

These magicians knew how to bring water out of the dry rock and how to find their way across the untrodden wilderness. In their prime, Petra and Palmyra stood in the midst of irrigated gardens such as still surround Damascus. But Petra and Palmyra did not live then, any more than Damascus lives to-day, exclusively or even principally on the fruits of their narrow-verged oases. Their rich men were not market-gardeners but merchants, who kept oasis in communion with oasis, and continent with continent, by a busy caravan-traffic from point to point across the intervening tracts of steppe and desert. Their present state reveals not only the final victory of the desert over man but the dimensions of the previous victory of man over the desert.

Easter Island

In a different scene we may draw a similar conclusion concerning the origins of the Polynesian Civilization[1] from the present state of Easter Island. At the time of its modern discovery this outlying island in the South-East Pacific was inhabited by two races: a race of flesh and blood, and a race of stone; an apparently primitive population of Polynesian physique and a highly accomplished population of statues. The living inhabitants in that

[1] This is one of the 'arrested civilizations' discussed later. See pp. 164 *seqq.*

generation possessed neither the art of carving statues such as these nor the science of navigating the thousand miles of open sea that separate Easter Island from the nearest sister island of the Polynesian Archipelago. Before its discovery by European seamen the island had been isolated from the rest of the world for an unknown length of time. Yet its dual population of flesh and stone testifies just as clearly as the ruins of Palmyra or Copan to a vanished past which must have been utterly different from the present.

Those human beings must have been begotten, and those statues carved, by Polynesian navigators who once found their way across the Pacific in flimsy open canoes, without chart or compass. And this voyage can hardly have been an isolated adventure which brought one boat-load of pioneers to Easter Island by a stroke of luck that was not repeated. The statue population is so numerous that it must have taken many generations to produce it. Everything points to a state of affairs in which the navigation across those thousand miles of open sea was carried on regularly over a long period of time. Eventually, for some reason unknown to us, the sea, once traversed victoriously by man, closed round Easter Island, as the desert closed round Palmyra and the forest round Copan. The men of stone, like the statue in Housman's poem, quitted themselves like stone, but the men of flesh and blood begot in each generation ruder and more incompetent offspring.

The evidence of Easter Island is, of course, in flat contradiction to the popular Western view of the South Sea Islands as an earthly paradise and their inhabitants as children of nature in the state of Adam and Eve before the Fall. The mistaken idea arises from the assumption that one portion of the Polynesian environment constitutes the whole of it. The physical environment consists, in fact, of water as well as land, water which presents a formidable challenge to any human beings who try to cross it without possessing any better means than such as were at the disposal of the Polynesians. It was by responding boldly and successfully to the challenge of the 'salt, estranging sea', by achieving the *tour de force* of a regular maritime traffic between island and island, that the pioneers won their footing on the specks of dry land which are scattered through the watery wilderness of the Pacific almost as sparsely as the stars are scattered through space.

New England

Before closing this review of reversions to a state of nature, the writer may permit himself to cite two instances—one somewhat out of the way and the other exceedingly obvious—which happen to have come within his own personal observation.

I[1] was once travelling in a rural part of the State of Connecticut in New England when I came across a deserted village—a not uncommon spectacle in those parts, as I was told, yet a spectacle which is nevertheless surprising and disconcerting to a European. For some two centuries, perhaps, Town Hill—such was its name—had stood with its plank-built Georgian church in the middle of the village green, its cottages, its orchards and its cornfields. The church still stood, preserved as an ancient monument; but the houses had vanished, the fruit-trees had gone wild and the corn-fields had faded away.

Within the last hundred years those New Englanders had played a part disproportionate to their numbers in wresting from wild nature the whole breadth of the American Continent from the Atlantic to the Pacific, yet at the same time they had allowed nature to recapture from them this village in the heart of their homeland, where their forefathers had lived for perhaps two hundred years. The rapidity, the thoroughness, the *abandon* with which nature had re-asserted her domain over Town Hill as soon as man had relaxed his grip, surely gave the measure of the exertions which man had formerly made to tame that barren soil. Only an energy as intense as the energy which the breaking-in of Town Hill had called into play could have been sufficient for 'the Winning of the West'. The deserted site explained the miracle of the mushroom cities of Ohio and Illinois and Colorado and California.

The Roman Campagna

The effect produced on me by Town Hill was produced on Livy by the Roman Campagna, when he marvelled that an in-numerable company of yeoman warriors should formerly have subsisted in a region which in his day, as in ours,[2] was a wilder-ness of barren grey fell and feverish green swamp. This latter-day wilderness has reproduced the pristine state of the forbidding landscape which was once transformed by Latin and Volscian pioneers into a cultivated and populous countryside; and the energy generated in the process of breaking-in this narrow plot of dour Italian soil was the energy which afterwards conquered the World from Egypt to Britain.

[1] i.e. Mr. Toynbee, to whom (and not the Editor) the pronoun refers where-ever it occurs in this volume.
[2] No longer quite so, for the government of Mussolini left behind it one honourable and enduring monument in the result of its strenuous and successful efforts to reclaim this district for man.

Perfida Capua

Having studied the character of certain environments which have actually been the scenes of the geneses of civilizations or of other signal human achievements, and having found that the conditions they offered to man were not easy but rather the opposite, let us pass on to a complementary study. Let us examine certain other environments in which the conditions offered have been easy and study the effect on human life which these environments have produced. In attempting this study we must distinguish between two different situations. The first is one in which people are introduced to an easy environment after having lived in a difficult one. The second is that of people in an easy environment who have never, so far as one knows, been exposed to any other environment since their pre-human ancestors became men. In other words we have to distinguish between the effect of an easy environment on man in process of civilization and on primitive man.

In classical Italy Rome found her antithesis in Capua. The Capuan Campagna was as kindly to man as the Roman Campagna was dour; and, while the Romans went forth from their forbidding country to conquer one neighbour after another, the Capuans stayed at home and allowed one neighbour after another to conquer them. From her last conquerors, the Samnites, Capua was delivered, at her own request, by the intervention of Rome herself; and then, at the most critical moment of the most critical war of Roman history, on the morrow of the battle of Cannae, Capua repaid Rome by opening her gates to Hannibal. Both Rome and Hannibal were of one mind in regarding Capua's change of sides as the most important result of the battle and perhaps the decisive event of the war. Hannibal repaired to Capua and there took up his winter quarters—whereupon something happened which falsified everybody's expectations. A winter spent in Capua so demoralized Hannibal's army that it was never the same instrument of victory again.

The Advice of Artembares

Herodotus has a story which is very much to the point in this context. A certain Artembares and his friends came to Cyrus with the following suggestion:

' "Now that Zeus has put down Astyages from his seat and has given the dominion to the Persians as a nation and to you, Sire, as an individual, why should we not emigrate from the confined and rocky territory which we at present possess, and occupy a better? There are many near at hand and many more at a distance, of which we have only to take our choice in order to make a greater impression on the world than we make as it is. This is a natural policy for an imperial people, and we shall never have a finer opportunity of realizing it than now, when our empire is established over vast populations and over the entire continent of Asia."

'Cyrus, who had listened and had not been impressed, told his petitioners to do as they wished, but he qualified his advice by telling them in the same breath to prepare their minds for exchanging positions with their present subjects. Soft countries, he informed them, invariably breed soft men.'[1]

The Odyssey and the Exodus

If we turn to documents of ancient literature even more cele- brated than the History of Herodotus, we find that Odysseus was never in greater danger from the Cyclops and other aggressive antagonists than from the charmers who called him to a life of ease—Circe with her hospitality which ended in the pig-sty; the Lotus-eaters, in whose land, according to a later authority, 'it was always afternoon'; the Sirens, against whose enchanting voices he stopped his sailors' ears with wax, after which he bade them strap him to the mast; and Calypso, divinely fairer than Penelope and inhumanly inferior as a helpmeet for a mortal man.

As for the Israelites of the Exodus, the austere writers of the Pentateuch provided no Sirens or Circes to lead them astray, but we read that they were continually hankering after 'the flesh pots of Egypt'. If they had had their way we may be sure that they would never have produced the Old Testament. Fortunately Moses was of the same school of thought as Cyrus.

The Doasyoulikes

A critic might contend that the examples we have just produced are not very convincing. Of course, he will say, a people trans- ferred from a hard to an easy condition of life will be 'spoilt', like a starving man who stuffs himself with a full meal; but those who have enjoyed easy conditions all the time might well be expected to make a good job of it. We must turn, then, to the second of the two situations which we distinguished above—the situation of people in an easy environment who have never, so far as is known, been in any other. In this case the disturbing factor of transition is eliminated, and we are able to study the effect of easy conditions in the absolute. Here is an authentic picture of it from Nyasaland, as seen by a Western observer half a century ago:

[1] Herodotus, Bk. IX, ch. 122.

'Hidden away in these endless forests, like birds' nests in a wood, in terror of one another and of their common foe, the slaver, are small native villages; and here in his virgin simplicity dwells Primeval Man, without clothes, without civilization, without learning, without religion—the genuine child of nature, thoughtless, careless and contented. This man is apparently quite happy; he has practically no wants. . . . The African is often blamed for being lazy, but it is a misuse of words. He does not need to work; with so bountiful a nature round him it would be gratuitous to work. His indolence, therefore, as it is called, is just as much a part of himself as his flat nose, and as little blameworthy as slowness in a tortoise.'[1]

Charles Kingsley, that Victorian exponent of the strenuous life who preferred the north-east wind to the south-west one, wrote a little story called 'The History of the Great and Famous Nation of the Doasyoulikes, who came away from the country of Hardwork because they wanted to play on the Jews' Harp all day long'. They paid the penalty by degenerating into gorillas.

It is amusing to observe the differing attitudes towards 'Lotus-eaters' displayed by the Hellenic poet and the modern Western moralist. For the Hellenic poet the Lotus-eaters and their Lotus-land are most formidably attractive, a snare of the devil in the path of the civilizing Greek. Kingsley, on the other hand, displays the modern British attitude in regarding his Doasyoulikes with such contemptuous disapproval that he is immune from their attractions; he feels it a positive duty to annex them to the British Empire, not for our good, of course, but for theirs, and to provide them with trousers and Bibles.

Our concern, however, is neither to approve nor to disapprove but to understand. The moral is found in the early chapters of the Book of Genesis; it was only *after* Adam and Eve had been expelled from their Eden Lotus-land that their descendants set about inventing agriculture, metallurgy and musical instruments.

[1] Drummond, H.: *Tropical Africa*, pp. 55–6.

VII. THE CHALLENGE OF THE ENVIRONMENT
(1) THE STIMULUS OF HARD COUNTRIES
Lines of Inquiry

WE have now, perhaps, established the truth that ease is inimical to civilization. Can we next proceed one step farther? Can we say that the stimulus towards civilization grows positively stronger in proportion as the environment grows more difficult? Let us review the evidence in favour of this proposition and then the evidence against it, and see what inference emerges. Evidence indicating that the difficulty and the stimulus of an environment are apt to increase *pari passu* is not hard to lay hands upon. Rather, we are likely to be embarrassed by the wealth of illustrations that leap to the mind. Most of these illustrations present themselves in the form of comparisons. Let us begin by sorting out our illustrations into two groups in which the points of comparison relate to the physical environment and the human environment respectively; and let us first consider the physical group. It subdivides itself into two categories: comparisons between the respective stimulating effects of physical environments which present different degrees of difficulty; and comparisons between the respective stimulating effects of old ground and new ground, apart from the intrinsic nature of the terrain.

The Yellow River and the Yangtse

Let us, as a first example, consider the different degrees of difficulty presented by the lower valleys of the two great rivers of China. It seems that when man first took in hand the watery chaos of the lower valley of the Yellow River (Hwang Ho), the river was not navigable at any season; in the winter it was either frozen or choked with floating ice, and the melting of this ice every spring produced devastating floods which repeatedly changed the river's course by carving out new channels, while the old channels turned into jungle-covered swamps. Even to-day, when some three or four thousand years of human effort have drained the swamps and confined the river within embankments, the devastating action of the floods has not been eliminated. As recently as 1852 the channel of the Lower Hwang Ho was entirely changed and its outflow into the sea shifted from the southern to the northern side of the Shantung Peninsula, a distance of over a hundred miles. The Yangtse, on the other hand, must always have been navigable, and its floods, though they occasionally assume devastating proportions, are less frequent than those of the Yellow River. In the Yangtse Valley, moreover, the winters are less severe. Nevertheless, it was on the Yellow River and not on the Yangtse that the Sinic Civilization came to birth.

Attica and Boeotia

Any traveller who enters or leaves Greece, not by sea but through the northern continental hinterland, cannot fail to be struck by the fact that the home of the Hellenic Civilization is more rocky and 'bony' and 'difficult' than the lands to the north which never produced a civilization of their own. Similar contrasts, however, may be observed within the Aegean area itself.

For instance, if one travels by train from Athens along the railway which eventually leads, through Salonika, to Central Europe, one passes, on the first stage of the journey, through a stretch of country which gives the Western or Central European traveller an anticipatory glimpse of the scenery with which he is familiar. After the train has been climbing slowly for hours round the eastern slopes of Mount Parnes through a typical Aegean landscape of stunted pines and jagged limestone crags, the traveller is astonished to find himself being rattled down into a lowland country of gently undulating deep-soiled ploughlands. Of course this landscape is nothing but a 'sport'; he will not see the like again until he has put Nish behind him and is descending the Morava to the Middle Danube. What was this exceptional piece of country called during the lifetime of the Hellenic Civilization? It was called Boeotia; and in Hellenic minds the word 'Boeotian' had a quite distinctive connotation. It stood for an ethos which was rustic, stolid, unimaginative, brutal—an ethos out of harmony with the prevailing genius of the Hellenic culture. This discord was accentuated by the fact that, just behind the range of Cithaeron and just round the corner of Parnes where the railway winds its way nowadays, lay Attica, 'the Hellas of Hellas': the country whose ethos was the quintessence of Hellenism lying cheek by jowl with the country whose ethos affected normal Hellenic sensibilities like a jarring note. The contrast was summed up in the piquant phrases: 'Boeotian swine' and 'Attic salt'.

The point of interest for our present study is that this cultural contrast which impressed itself so vividly on the Hellenic consciousness was geographically coincident with an equally striking contrast in physical environment. For Attica is 'the Hellas of Hellas' not only in her soul but in her physique. She stands to the other countries of the Aegean as they stand to the regions beyond. If you approach Greece from the west and enter through the avenue of the Corinthian Gulf you may flatter yourself that your eye has grown accustomed to the Greek landscape—beautiful but forbidding—before the view is shut out by the cliff-like banks of the deep-cut Corinth Canal. But when your steamer emerges into the Saronic Gulf you will be shocked afresh by an austerity of landscape for which the scenery on the other side of the Isthmus had not fully prepared you; and this austerity attains its climax when you round the corner of Salamis and see Attica spread out before your eyes. In Attica, with her abnormally light and stony soil, the process called denudation, washing the flesh off the mountain bones and burying it in the sea, which Boeotia has escaped down to this day, was already complete in Plato's time, as is attested by his graphic description of it in the *Critias*.

What did the Athenians do with their poor country? We know that they did the things which made Athens 'the education of Hellas'. When the pastures of Attica dried up and her plough-lands wasted away, her people turned from stock-breeding and grain-growing—the staple pursuits of Greece in that age—to devices which were peculiarly their own: olive-cultivation and the exploitation of the subsoil. The gracious tree of Athena not only keeps alive but flourishes on the bare rock. Yet man cannot live by olive oil alone. To make a living from his olive groves the Athenian must exchange his Attic oil for Scythian grain. To place his oil on the Scythian market he must pack it in jars and ship it overseas—activities which called into existence the Attic potteries and the Attic merchant marine, and also, since trade requires currency, the Attic silver-mines.

But these riches were merely the economic foundation for the political and artistic and intellectual culture which made Athens 'the education of Hellas' and 'Attic salt' the antithesis of Boeotian animality. On the political plane the result was the Athenian Empire. On the artistic plane, the prosperity of the potteries gave the Attic vase-painter his opportunity for creating a new form of beauty which, two thousand years later, enraptured the English poet Keats; while the extinction of the Attic forests compelled Athenian architects to translate their work from the medium of timber into that of stone and so led to the creation of the Parthenon.

Byzantium and Calchedon

The enlargement of the area of the Hellenic World, the cause of which we mentioned in our first chapter (see p. 4), offers another Hellenic illustration of our theme: the contrast between the two Greek colonies, Calchedon and Byzantium, which were planted, the former on the Asiatic, the latter on the European, side of the entrance to the Bosphorus from the Sea of Marmara.

Herodotus tells us that, a century or so after the foundation of the two cities, the Persian governor Megabazus

'made a *mot* which won him immortal celebrity among the Hellespontine Greeks. At Byzantium he heard that the Calchedonians had planted their city seventeen years earlier than the Byzantines had planted theirs; and he had no sooner heard it than he remarked: "Then the Calchedonians must have been blind men all that time." He meant that they must have been blind to choose the worse site when the better was at their disposal.'[1]

But it is easy to be wise after the event, and in Megabazus's day (at the time of the Persian invasions of Greece) the respective destinies of the two cities had already declared themselves. Calchedon still was what she had always meant to be, an ordinary agricultural colony, and from the agricultural point of view her site was, and is, immensely superior to that of Byzantium. The Byzantines came later, and took the leavings. As an agricultural community they failed, perhaps chiefly because of the continual raiding of the Thracian barbarians. But in their harbour, the Golden Horn, they had accidentally stumbled on the possession of a gold-mine; for the current which comes down the Bosphorus is in favour of any vessel trying to make the Golden Horn from either direction. Polybius, writing in the second century B.C., about five hundred years after the foundation of the Greek colony and nearly five hundred years before its promotion, as Constantinople, to the rank of an oecumenical capital, says:

'The Byzantines occupy a site which, from the twin standpoints of security and prosperity, is the most favourable of all sites in the Hellenic World to seaward and the most unprepossessing of all to landward. To seaward Byzantium commands the mouth of the Black Sea so absolutely that it is impossible for any merchantman to pass either in or out against the Byzantines' will.'[2]

Yet perhaps Megabazus secured by his *mot* a reputation for discernment which he hardly deserved. There can be no reasonable doubt that, if the colonists who took Byzantium had arrived twenty years earlier, they would have chosen the then vacant site of Calchedon; and it is also probable that, if their agricultural efforts had been less hampered by the Thracian raiders, they would have been less disposed to develop the commercial possibilities of their site.

[1] Herodotus, Bk. IV, ch. 144.
[2] Polybius, Bk. IV, ch. 38.

Israelites, Phoenicians and Philistines

If we turn now from Hellenic history to Syriac, we shall find that the various elements of population that entered Syria, or held their own there, at the time of the post-Minoan Völker-wanderung, distinguished themselves relatively thereafter in close proportion to the relative difficulty of the physical environment in the different districts in which they happened to have made themselves at home. It was not the Aramaeans of 'Abana and Pharpar, rivers of Damascus', who took the lead in the development of the Syriac Civilization; nor was it those other Aramaeans who settled on the Orontes where long afterwards the Greek Seleucid dynasty made a capital city at Antioch; nor was it those tribes of Israel who halted east of the Jordan to fatten their 'bulls of Bashan' on the fine pastures of Gilead. Most remarkable of all, the primacy of the Syriac World was not retained by those refugees from the Aegean who came to Syria not as barbarians but as heirs of the Minoan Civilization and took possession of the ports and lowlands south of Carmel—the Philistines. This people's name has acquired a connotation as contemptuous as that of the Boeotians among the Greeks; and, even if we admit that Boeotians and Philistines may neither of them have been as black as they were painted, and that we owe our knowledge of them both almost entirely to their rivals, what is that but to say that their rivals have outstripped them and won, at their expense, the respectful attention of posterity?

The Syriac Civilization has three great feats to its credit. It invented the Alphabet; it discovered the Atlantic; and it arrived at a particular conception of God which is common to Judaism, Zoroastrianism, Christianity and Islam but alien alike from the Egyptiac, Sumeric, Indic and Hellenic veins of religious thought. Which were the Syriac communities by whom these achievements were contributed?

As regards the Alphabet we really do not know. Though its invention is traditionally attributed to the Phoenicians, it *may* have been transmitted in an elementary form by the Philistines from the Minoan World; so in the present state of our knowledge the credit for the Alphabet must be left unallocated. Let us pass to the other two.

Who were those Syriac seafarers who ventured to sail the whole length of the Mediterranean to the Pillars of Hercules and out beyond? Not the Philistines, in spite of their Minoan blood; these turned their backs upon the sea and fought a losing battle for the fertile plains of Esdraelon and the Shephelah against tougher fighters than themselves, the Israelites of the hill country of Ephraim and Judah. The discoverers of the Atlantic were the Phoenicians of Tyre and Sidon.

These Phoenicians were a remnant of the Canaanites, the peoples in occupation before the incoming of Philistines and Hebrews—a fact expressed genealogically in an early chapter of Genesis where we read that Canaan (son of Ham, son of Noah) 'begat Sidon, his firstborn'. They survived because their homes, along the middle section of the Syrian coast, were not sufficiently inviting to attract invaders. Phoenicia, which the Philistines left alone, presents a remarkable contrast to the Shephelah in which the Philistines settled. On this section of the coast there is no fertile plain; the Lebanon Range rises sheer from the sea—so sheer that there is hardly room for road or railway. The Phoenician cities could not communicate easily, even with one another, except by sea, and Tyre, the most famous of them, is perched, like a seagull's nest, on a rocky island. Thus, while the Philistines were browsing like sheep in clover, the Phoenicians, whose maritime horizon had hitherto been restricted to the short range of the coastwise traffic between Byblus and Egypt, now launched out Minoan-fashion into the open sea and founded a second home for their own version of the Syriac Civilization along the African and Spanish shores of the Western Mediterranean. Carthage, the imperial city of this Phoenician overseas world, outstripped the Philistines even in their chosen field of land warfare. The most famous military champion of the Philistines is Goliath of Gath; he cuts a poor figure beside the Phoenician Hannibal.

But the physical discovery of the Atlantic is surpassed, as a feat of human prowess, by the spiritual discovery of monotheism; and that was the feat of a Syriac community stranded by the Völkerwanderung in a physical environment even less inviting than the Phoenician coast: the hill-country of Ephraim and Judah. Apparently this patch of thin-soiled forest-covered hill country had remained unoccupied until it was populated by the vanguard of the Hebrew nomads who had drifted into the fringes of Syria out of the North Arabian Steppe, in and after the fourteenth century B.C., during the interregnum following the decay of 'the New Empire' in Egypt. Here they transformed themselves from nomadic stock-breeders into sedentary tillers of a stony ground, and here in obscurity they lived until the Syriac Civilization had passed its zenith. As late as the fifth century B.C., at a date when all the great prophets had already said their say, the very name of Israel was unknown to Herodotus and the Land of Israel was still masked by the Land of the Philistines in the Herodotean panorama

of the Syriac World. He writes of 'the Land of the Philistines'[1]—
and Filastin or Palestine it remains to this day.

A Syriac fable tells how the God of the Israelites once tested a
king of Israel with the most searching test that a god can apply
to a mortal.

'The Lord appeared to Solomon in a dream by night; and God said:
"Ask what I shall give thee." And Solomon said, ". . . Give . . . thy
servant an understanding heart." . . . And the speech pleased the Lord,
that Solomon had asked this thing. And God said unto him: "Because
thou hast asked this thing, and hast not asked for thyself long life;
neither hast asked riches for thyself, nor hast asked the life of thine
enemies; but hast asked for thyself understanding to discern judgment;
behold, I have done according to thy words: lo, I have given thee a wise
and an understanding heart, so that there was none like thee before
thee, neither after thee shall any arise like unto thee. And I have also
given thee that which thou hast not asked, both riches and honour, so
that there shall not be any among the kings like unto thee all thy days." '[2]

The fable of Solomon's Choice is a parable of the history of
the Chosen People. In the power of their spiritual understanding
the Israelites surpassed the military prowess of the Philistines
and the maritime prowess of the Phoenicians. They had not
sought after those things which the Gentiles seek, but had sought
first the Kingdom of God; and all those things were added to
them. As for the life of their enemies, the Philistines were
delivered into Israel's hands. As for riches, Jewry entered into
the inheritance of Tyre and Carthage, to conduct transactions on
a scale beyond Phoenician dreams in continents beyond Phoenician knowledge. As for long life, the Jews live on—the same
peculiar people—to-day, long ages after the Phoenicians and
Philistines have lost their identity. Their ancient Syriac neighbours have gone into the melting-pot and been re-minted, with
new images and superscriptions, while Israel has proved impervious to this alchemy—performed by History in the crucibles of
universal states and universal churches and wanderings of the
nations—to which we Gentiles all in turn succumb.

Brandenburg and the Rhineland

From Attica and Israel to Brandenburg might seem a far cry
and a steep descent, yet on its own level it offers an illustration of
the same law. As you travel through the unprepossessing country
which formed the original domain of Frederick the Great—
Brandenburg, Pomerania and East Prussia—with its starveling

[1] Herodotus, Bk. II, ch. 104, and Bk. VII, ch. 89.
[2] 1 Kings iii. 5–13.

pine plantations and sandy fields, you might fancy you were traversing some outlying portion of the Eurasian Steppe. In whichever direction you travel out of it, to the pastures and beech-woods of Denmark, the black earth of Lithuania or the vineyards of the Rhineland, you pass into easier and pleasanter country. Yet the descendants of the medieval colonists who occupied these 'bad lands' have played an exceptional part in the history of our Western Society. It is not only that in the nineteenth century they mastered Germany and in the twentieth led the Germans in a strenuous attempt to provide our society with its universal state. The Prussian also taught his neighbours how to make sand produce cereals by enriching it with artificial manures; how to raise a whole population to a standard of unprecedented social efficiency by a system of compulsory education and of unprecedented social security by a system of compulsory health and unemployment insurance. We may not like him but we cannot deny that we have learnt from him lessons of importance and value.

Scotland and England

There is no need to argue the point that Scotland is a 'harder' land than England, nor to elaborate the notorious difference of tempera-ment between the traditional Scotsman—solemn, parsimonious, precise, persistent, cautious, conscientious and well educated—and the traditional Englishman—frivolous, extravagant, vague, spas-modic, careless, free and easy and ill grounded in book-learning. The English may regard this traditional comparison as rather a joke; they regard most things as rather a joke; but the Scots do not. Johnson used to chaff Boswell with his apparently oft re-peated *mot* that the finest prospect a Scotsman ever sees is the road to England; and before Johnson was born a wit of Queen Anne's day said that, if Cain had been a Scotsman, his punish-ment would have been reversed and, instead of being condemned to be a wanderer on the face of the Earth, he would have been sentenced to stay at home. The popular impression that the Scots have played a part disproportionate to their numbers in the making of the British Empire and in the occupancy of the high places of church and state is undoubtedly well founded. The classic parlia-mentary conflict of Victorian England was between a pure-bred Scot and a pure-bred Jew, and, of Gladstone's successors in the premiership of the United Kingdom down to this day, nearly half have been Scots.[1]

[1] Rosebery, Balfour, Campbell-Bannerman and MacDonald; and one can add Bonar Law—of Scots-Irish family and born in Canada, but his mother was pure Scots and he made his home in Glasgow. That makes five. There have been seven non-Scots.—EDITOR.

The Struggle for North America

The classic illustration of our present theme in our own Western history is the outcome of the competition between half a dozen different groups of colonists for the mastery of North America. The victors in this contest were the New Englanders, and in the preceding chapter we have already taken note of the unusual difficulty of the local environment which first fell to the lot of the ultimate masters of the Continent. Let us now compare this New England environment, of which the site of Town Hill is a fair specimen, with the earliest American environments of the New Englanders' unsuccessful competitors: the Dutch, the French, the Spaniards and the other English colonists who settled along the southern section of the Atlantic seaboard, in and around Virginia.

In the middle of the seventeenth century, when all these groups had found their first footing on the fringes of the American mainland, it would have been easy to predict the coming conflict between them for the possession of the interior, but the most far-sighted observer then alive would not have been likely to hit the mark if he had been asked, in 1650, to pick the winner. He might have had the acumen to rule out the Spaniards in spite of their two obvious assets: their ownership of Mexico, the only North American region that had been broken in by a previous civilization, and the reputation then still enjoyed, but no longer deserved, by Spain among European Powers. He might have discounted Mexico in view of its outlying position, and discounted Spanish prestige in consideration of Spain's failures in the European war (the Thirty Years' War) just concluded. 'France', he might have said, 'will succeed to the military primacy of Spain in Europe, Holland and England to her naval and commercial primacy at sea. The competition for North America lies between Holland, France and England. On a short view Holland's chances might appear to be the most promising. She is superior to both England and France at sea, and in America she holds a splendid water-gate to the interior, the valley of the Hudson. But on a longer view France seems likely to be the winner. She holds a still finer water-gate, the St. Lawrence, and she has it in her power to exhaust and immobilize the Dutch by using against their homeland her overwhelming military superiority. But both the English groups', he might have added, 'I can confidently rule out. Possibly the southern English colonists, with their relatively genial soil and climate, will survive as an enclave, cut off from the interior by the French or the Dutch—whichever of them wins the Mississippi Valley. One thing is certain, however: the little group of settlements in bleak and barren New England is bound to disappear, cut off, as they are, from their kinsfolk by the Dutch on the Hudson, while the French press in upon them from the St. Lawrence.'

Let us suppose that our imaginary observer lives to see the turn of the century. By 1701 he will be congratulating himself on having rated French prospects higher than Dutch; for these latter had tamely surrendered the Hudson to their English rivals in 1664. Meanwhile the French had pushed up the St. Lawrence on to the Great Lakes and over the portage to the Mississippi Basin. La Salle had followed the river down to its mouth; a new French settlement, Louisiana, had been established there; and its port, New Orleans, clearly had a great future before it. As between France and England, our observer would see no reason to alter his forecast. The New Englanders had perhaps been saved from extinction by the acquisition of New York, but only to enjoy the same modest future prospects as their southern kinsfolk. The future of the Continent seemed virtually decided; the winners would be the French.

Shall we endow our observer with superhuman length of life, in order that he may review the situation once more in the year 1803? If we preserve him alive till then, he will be forced to confess that his wits have not been worthy of his longevity. By the end of 1803 the French flag has disappeared off the political map of North America altogether. For forty years past Canada has been a possession of the British Crown, while Louisiana, after being ceded by France to Spain and retroceded again, has just been sold by Napoleon to the United States—the new Great Power that has emerged out of the thirteen British colonies.

In this year 1803 the United States have the Continent in their pockets and the scope of prophecy is reduced. It only remains to forecast which section of the United States is going to pocket the larger share of this vast estate. And surely this time there can be no mistake. The Southern States are the manifest masters of the Union. Look how they are leading in the final round of the competition in an inter-American race for the Winning of the West. It is the backwoodsmen of Virginia who have founded Kentucky—the first new State to be established west of those mountain ranges which have so long conspired with the French to keep the English settlers from penetrating the interior. Kentucky lies along the Ohio and the Ohio leads to the Mississippi. Meanwhile the new cotton-mills of Lancashire are offering these Southerners an ever-expanding market for the cotton crop which their soil and climate enable them to raise.

'Our Yankee cousin', the Southerner observes in 1807, 'has just invented a steam-boat which will navigate our Mississippi up-stream, and a machine for carding and cleaning our cotton-bolls. Their "Yankee notions" are more profitable to us than they are to the ingenious inventors.'

If our aged and unlucky prophet takes the Southerners' pros-pects at what was undoubtedly then and for some time later the Southerners' own valuation, he must indeed be in his dotage. For in this last round of the competition the Southerner is destined to meet as swift and crushing a defeat as has already overtaken the Dutch and the French.

In the year 1865 the situation is already transformed, out of all recognition, from what it was in 1807. In the Winning of the West the Southern planter has been outstripped and outflanked by his Northern rival. After almost winning his way to the Great Lakes through Indiana and getting the best of the bargain over Missouri (1821), he has been decisively defeated in Kansas (1854–60) and he has never reached the Pacific. The New Englanders are now masters of the Pacific coast all the way from Seattle to Los Angeles. The Southerner had counted on his Mississippi steam-boats to draw the whole of the West into a Southern system of economic and political relations. But 'Yankee notions' have not ceased. The railway locomotive has succeeded the steam-boat, and has taken away from the Southerner more than the steam-boat ever gave him; for the potential value of the Hudson Valley and New York, as the main gateway from the Atlantic to the West, has been actualized at last in the Railway Age. Railway traffic from Chicago to New York is surpassing river traffic from St. Louis to New Orleans. The lines of communication within the Continent have been switched from the vertical direction to the horizontal. The North-West has been detached from the South and welded on to the North-East in interest and in sentiment.

Indeed the Easterner, who once presented the South with the river-steamer and the cotton-gin, has now won the heart of the North-Westerner with a double gift; he has come to him with a locomotive in one hand and a reaper-and-binder in the other, and so provided him with solutions for both his problems: transport and labour. By these two 'Yankee notions' the allegiance of the North-West has been decided and the Civil War lost by the South before it has been fought. In taking up arms in the hope of redressing her economic reverses by a military counter-stroke, the South has merely consummated a *débâcle* that was already inevitable.

It may be said that all the different groups of colonists in North America had severe challenges to meet from their environments.

In Canada the French had to encounter almost Arctic winters and in Louisiana the vagaries of a river almost as treacherous and devastating as the Yellow River of China, of which we took note in the first of the comparisons in this series. Still, taking all in all—soil, climate, transport facilities and the rest—it is impossible to deny that the original colonial home of the New Englanders was the hardest country of all. Thus North American history tells in favour of the proposition: the greater the difficulty, the greater the stimulus.

(2) THE STIMULUS OF NEW GROUND

So much for comparisons between the respective stimulating effects of physical environments which present different degrees of difficulty. Let us now approach the same question from a different angle by comparing the respective stimulating effects of old ground and new ground, apart from the intrinsic nature of the terrain.

Does the effect of breaking new ground act as a stimulus in itself? The question is answered in the affirmative in the myth of the Expulsion from Eden and in the myth of the Exodus from Egypt. In their removal out of the magic garden into the work-a-day world Adam and Eve transcend the food-gathering economy of primitive man and give birth to the founders of an agricultural and a pastoral civilization. In their exodus from Egypt the Children of Israel give birth to a generation which helps to lay the foundations of the Syriac Civilization. When we turn from myths to the history of religions we find these intuitions confirmed. We find, for example, that—to the consternation of those who ask 'Can any good thing come out of Nazareth?'—the Messiah of Jewry does come out of that obscure village in 'Galilee of the Gentiles', an outlying piece of new ground which had been conquered for Jewry by the Maccabees rather less than a century before the date of Jesus's birth. And when the indomitable growth of this Galilaean grain of mustard-seed turns the consternation of Jewry into active hostility, and this not only in Judaea itself but among the Jewish *diaspora*, the propagators of the new faith deliberately 'turn to the Gentiles' and proceed to conquer new worlds for Christianity on ground far beyond the farthest limits of the Macca-baean kingdom. In the history of Buddhism it is the same story, for the decisive victories of this Indic faith are not won on the old ground of the Indic World. The Hīnayāna first finds an open road in Ceylon, which was a colonial annex of the Indic Civiliza-tion. And the Mahāyāna starts its long and roundabout journey towards its future domain in the Far East by capturing the

Syriacized and Hellenized Indic province of the Panjab. It is on the new ground of these alien worlds that the highest expressions of both the Syriac and the Indic religious genius eventually bear their fruit—in witness to the truth that 'a prophet is not without honour save in his own country and in his own house'.

A convenient empirical test of this social law is offered by those civilizations of the 'related' class which have arisen partly on ground already occupied by the respective antecedent civilization and partly on ground which the related civilization has taken over on its own account. We can test the respective stimulating effects of old and new ground by surveying the career of any one of these 'related' civilizations, marking the point or points within its domain at which its achievements in any line have been most distinguished, and then observing whether the ground on which such points are located is old ground or new.

Taking first the Hindu Civilization, let us mark the local sources of the new creative elements in Hindu life—particularly in religion, which has always been the central and supreme activity of the Hindu Society. We find these sources in the South. It was here that all the distinctive features of Hinduism took shape: the cult of gods represented by material objects or images and housed in temples; the emotional personal relation between the worshipper and the particular god to whose worship he has vowed himself; the metaphysical sublimation of image-worship and emotionalism in an intellectually sophisticated theology (Šankara, the founder of Hindu theology, was born about A.D. 788 in Malabar). And was Southern India old ground or new? It was new ground, which had not been incorporated into the domain of the preceding Indic Society until the last stage of that society's existence, in the time of the Mauryan Empire, which was its 'universal state' (circa 323–185 B.C.).

The Syriac Society gave birth to two affiliated societies, the Arabic and the Iranic, of which the latter, as we have seen, proved the more successful, eventually absorbing its 'sister'. In what areas did the Iranic Civilization most conspicuously flourish? Almost all its great achievements in war, politics, architecture and literature were accomplished at one or other of the two extremities of the Iranic World, either in Hindustan or in Anatolia, culminating respectively in the Mughal and in the Ottoman Empire. The site of both these achievements was new ground, beyond the range of the antecedent Syriac Civilization, ground wrested in the one case from the Hindu and in the other from the Orthodox Christian Society. By comparison with these achievements the history of the Iranic Civilization in its central regions, in

Iran itself for example, the old ground taken over from the Syriac Civilization, was quite undistinguished.

In what regions has the greatest vigour been displayed by the Orthodox Christian Civilization? A glance at its history shows that its social centre of gravity has lain in different regions at different times. In the first age after its emergence from the post-Hellenic interregnum the life of Orthodox Christendom was most vigorous in the central and north-eastern parts of the Anatolian Plateau. Thereafter, from the middle of the ninth century onwards, the centre of gravity shifted from the Asiatic to the European side of the Straits and, as far as the original stem of the Orthodox Christian Society is concerned, it has remained in the Balkan Peninsula ever since. In modern times, however, the original stem of Orthodox Christendom has been far outstripped in historical importance by its mighty offshoot in Russia.

Are these three areas to be regarded as old ground or new? In the case of Russia the question hardly needs answering. As for Central and North-Eastern Anatolia, it was certainly new ground so far as the Orthodox Christian Society was concerned, though two thousand years earlier it had been the home of the Hittite Civilization. The Hellenization of this area was retarded and always imperfect, and its first, and perhaps its only, contribution to the Hellenic culture was made in the last phase of the life-span of the Hellenic Society by the Cappadocian Fathers of the Church in the fourth century of the Christian Era.

The remaining centre of gravity of the Orthodox Christian Society, the interior of the Balkan Peninsula, was also new ground, for the veneer of Hellenic Civilization in a Latin medium with which this region had been thinly overlaid in the lifetime of the Roman Empire had been destroyed without leaving a trace during the interregnum which followed that empire's dissolution. The destruction here was more thoroughgoing than in any western province of the Empire except Britain. The Christian Roman provincials were not simply conquered but were practically exterminated by the pagan barbarian invaders, and these barbarians eradicated all elements of local culture so effectively that when their descendants repented of the evil their fathers had done they had to obtain fresh seed from outside in order to start cultivation again, three centuries later. Thus the soil had lain fallow here for twice as long as the soil of Britain had lain fallow at the date of Augustine's mission. So the region in which the Orthodox Christian Civilization established its second centre of gravity was ground which had very recently been reclaimed *de novo* from the wilderness.

Thus all the three regions in which the Orthodox Christian Society specially distinguished itself were new ground, and it is still more remarkable to observe that Greece itself, the radiant focus of the preceding civilization, played an altogether insignificant part in the history of the Orthodox Christian Society until, in the eighteenth century of the Christian Era, it became the water-gate through which Western influence forced an entry into the Orthodox Christian World.

Turning now to Hellenic history, let us ask the same question regarding the two regions which successively held primacy in the early history of the Hellenic Society : the Asiatic coast of the Aegean and the European peninsula of Greece. Were these flowerings on new or on old ground, from the standpoint of the preceding Minoan Civilization ? The ground was new ground, here again. On the European Greek peninsula the Minoan Civilization, even at its widest extension, had held no more than a chain of fortified positions on its southern and eastern coastline, and on the Anatolian coast the failure of our modern archaeologists to find traces of the presence, or even of the influence, of the Minoan Civilization has been so signal that it can hardly be attributed to chance, but seems to indicate that, for some reason, this coast did not come within the Minoans' range. Conversely, the Cyclades Islands, which had been one of the centres of the Minoan culture, played a subordinate role in Hellenic history as humble servants of the successive masters of the sea. The part played in Hellenic history by Crete itself, the earliest and always the most important centre of the Minoan culture, is even more surprising.

Crete might have been expected to retain importance not only for historical reasons, as the place in which the Minoan culture had attained its culmination, but for geographical reasons as well. Crete was by far the largest island of the Aegean Archipelago and it lay athwart two of the most important sea routes in the Hellenic World. Every ship that sailed from the Peiraeus for Sicily had to pass between the western end of Crete and Laconia; every ship that sailed from the Peiraeus for Egypt had to pass between the eastern end of Crete and Rhodes. Yet, whereas Laconia and Rhodes each played a leading part in Hellenic history, Crete remained aloof, obscure and benighted from first to last. While Hellas all round was giving birth to statesmen and artists and philosophers, Crete produced nothing more reputable than medicine-men, mercenaries and pirates, and the latter-day Cretan became a Hellenic by-word, like the Boeotian. Indeed he has passed judgement on himself in a hexameter which has been embedded in the canon of Christian Scripture. 'One of themselves, even a prophet of their own, said: "The Cretans are always liars, evil beasts, slow bellies." '[1]

Finally, let us apply the same test to the Far Eastern Society, which is affiliated to the Sinic Society. At what points in its domain has this Far Eastern Society shown the greatest vigour? The Japanese and the Cantonese stand out unmistakably as its most vigorous representatives to-day, and both these peoples have sprung from soil which is new ground from the standpoint of Far Eastern history. The south-eastern seaboard of China was not incorporated into the domain of the 'apparented' Sinic Society until a late phase of Sinic history, and even then only on the superficial plane of politics as a frontier province of the Han Empire. Its inhabitants remained barbarians. As for the Japanese Archipelago, the off-shoot of the Far Eastern Civilization which was transplanted thither by way of Korea in the sixth and seventh centuries of the Christian Era was propagated there on ground that showed no trace of any previous culture. The strong growth of this offshoot of the Far Eastern Civilization on the virgin soil of Japan is comparable to the growth of the offshoot of the Orthodox Christian Civilization which was transplanted from the Anatolian Plateau to the virgin soil of Russia.

If it is true, as our evidence suggests, that new ground provides a greater stimulus to activity than old ground, one would expect to find such stimulus specially marked in cases where the new ground is separated from the old by a sea voyage. This special stimulus of transmarine colonization appears very clearly in the history of the Mediterranean during the first half of the last millennium (1000–500) B.C., when its western basin was being colonized competitively by maritime pioneers from three different civilizations in the Levant. It appears, for instance, in the degree to which the two greatest of these colonial foundations, Syriac Carthage and Hellenic Syracuse, outstripped their parent cities, Tyre and Corinth. The Achaean colonies in Magna Graecia (southern Italy and Sicily) became busy seats of commerce and brilliant centres of thought, while the parent Achaean communities along the northern coast of the Peloponnese remained in a backwater until after the Hellenic Civilization had passed its zenith. Similarly the Epizephyrian Locrians in Italy far surpassed the Locrians who remained in Greece.

The most striking case of all is that of the Etruscans, the third party competing with Phoenicians and Greeks in the colonization

---

[1] Κρῆτες ἀεὶ ψεῦσται, κακὰ θηρία, γαστέρες ἀργοί: the Epistle to Titus, i. 12. The author of the line is said to be Epimenides.

of the Western Mediterranean. The Etruscans who went west, unlike the Greeks and Phoenicians, were not content to remain within sight of the sea across which they had come. They pushed inland from the west coast of Italy across the Appennines and the Po to the foot of the Alps. The Etruscans who stayed at home, however, attained the very nadir of obscurity, for they are unknown to history and no record of the precise location of their homeland survives, though Egyptian records indicate that the original Etruscans took part with the Achaeans in the post-Minoan Völkerwanderung and had their base of operations somewhere on the Asiatic coast of the Levant.

The stimulating effect of a sea-crossing is perhaps greatest of all in a transmarine migration occurring in the course of a Völkerwanderung. Such occurrences seem to be uncommon. The only instances which the writer of this Study can call to mind are the migration, during the post-Minoan Völkerwanderung, of Teucrians, Aeolians, Ionians and Dorians across the Aegean to the west coast of Anatolia, and of Teucrians and Philistines to the coast of Syria; the migration of the Angles and Jutes to Britain during the post-Hellenic Völkerwanderung; the consequent migration of Britons across the Channel to what then came to be called Brittany; the contemporary migration of the Irish Scots to Argyll; and the migration of the Scandinavian Vikings in the Völkerwanderung which followed the abortive evocation of the ghost of the Roman Empire by the Carolingians: six instances in all. Of these, the Philistine migration proved comparatively unproductive, in circumstances already described (see pp. 92–4), and the subsequent history of the Bretons was undistinguished, but the other four overseas migrations present certain striking phenomena which are not to be observed in the far more numerous instances of migration overland.

These overseas migrations have in common one and the same simple fact: in transmarine migration the social apparatus of the migrants has to be packed on board ship before it can leave the shores of the old country, and then be unpacked again at the end of the voyage. All kinds of apparatus—persons and property, techniques and institutions and ideas—are subject to this law. Anything that cannot stand the sea voyage at all has to be left behind, and many things—not only material objects—which the migrants do take with them, have to be taken to pieces, never perhaps to be reassembled in their original form. When unpacked, they are found to have suffered 'a sea change into something rich and strange'. When such a transmarine migration occurs in the course of a Völkerwanderung, the challenge is the more formidable and the stimulus the more intense because the society that is making the response is not one that is already socially progressive (like the Greek and Phoenician colonizers discussed above), but one that is still in that static condition which is the last state of primitive man. The transition, in a Völkerwanderung, from this passivity to a sudden paroxysm of storm and stress produces a dynamic effect on the life of any community, but this effect is naturally more intense when the migrants take ship than when they trek over solid ground, carrying with them much of the social apparatus which has to be discarded by the seafarer.

'This change of outlook [after the voyage overseas] gave birth to a new conception of gods and men. The local deities whose power was co-extensive with the territory of their worshippers were replaced by a corporate body of gods ruling the World. The holy-place with its blot-house which had formed the centre of Middlegarth was raised on high and turned into a divine mansion. Time-honoured myths setting forth the doings of mutually independent deities were worked up into a poetical mythology, a divine saga, on the same lines that had been followed by an earlier race of Vikings, the Homeric Greeks. This religion brought a new god to birth: Odin, the leader of men, the lord of the battlefield.'[1]

In somewhat similar fashion the overseas migration of the Scots from Ireland to North Britain prepared the way for the entry of a new religion. It is no accident that the transmarine Dalriada became the headquarters of St. Columba's missionary movement with its focal point in Iona.

One distinctive phenomenon of transmarine migration is the intermingling of diverse racial strains, for the first piece of social apparatus that has to be abandoned is the primitive kin-group. No ship will hold more than one ship's company, and a number of ships sailing together for safety and combining in their new home-land may well be drawn from different localities—in contrast with the usual process of migration overland, in which a whole kin-group is apt to pack its women and children and household stuff into ox-carts and move off *en masse* at a snail's pace over *terra firma*.

Another distinctive phenomenon of transmarine migration is the atrophy of a primitive institution which is perhaps the supreme expression of undifferentiated social life before this is refracted, by a clarifying social consciousness, on the separate planes of economics and politics and religion and art: the institution of the ἐνιαυτὸς δαίμων and his cycle. If we wish to see this ritual in its

---

[1] Grönbech, V.: *The Culture of the Teutons*, Pt. II, pp. 306–7.

glory in the Scandinavian World, we must study its development among the Scandinavians who stayed at home. By contrast 'in Iceland the May Day game, the ritual wedding and the wooing scene seem hardly to have survived the settlement, partly, no doubt, because the settlers were mainly of a travelled and enlightened class, and partly because these rural observances are connected with agriculture, which could not be an important branch of activity in Iceland'.[1]

Since even in Iceland there was an agriculture of some sort, we must regard the former of the two suggested reasons as the more important.

The thesis of the work we have just quoted is that the Scandinavian poems committed to writing in the Icelandic compilation called *The Elder Edda* are derived from the spoken words of the primitive Scandinavian fertility-drama—the only element in the ritual which the emigrants were able to cut away from its deeply embedded local roots and to take on board ship with them. According to this theory the development of the primitive ritual into drama was arrested among those Scandinavians who migrated overseas; and the theory is supported by an analogy from Hellenic history. For it is a well-established fact that, although the Hellenic Civilization first came to flower in transmarine Ionia, the Hellenic drama, based on primitive rituals, sprang from the continental soil of the Greek Peninsula. The counterpart, in Hellas, of the sanctuary at Upsala was the theatre of Dionysus in Athens. On the other hand it was in Ionia, in Iceland and in Britain that the transmarine migrants—Hellenic, Scandinavian and Anglo-Saxon—produced the epic poetry of 'Homer', *The Edda* and *Beowulf*.

The Saga and the Epic arise in response to a new mental need, a new awareness of strong individual personalities and of momentous public events. 'That lay is praised of men the most which ringeth newest in their ears', Homer declares. Yet there is one thing in an epic lay more highly prized than its novelty, and that is the intrinsic human interest of the story. The interest in the present predominates just so long as the storm and stress of the Heroic Age continues; but the social paroxysm is transitory and, as the storm abates, the lovers of Epic and Saga come to feel that life in their time has grown relatively tame. Therewith they cease to prefer new lays to old, and the latter-day minstrel, responding to his hearers' change of mood, repeats and embellishes the tales of the older generation. It was in this later age that the art of Epic and Saga attained its literary zenith; none the less, these mighty works would never have come into existence but for the stimulus originally exerted by the ordeal of oversea migration.

[1] Phillpotts, B. S.: *The Elder Edda and Ancient Scandinavian Drama*, p. 204.

We arrive at the formula: 'Drama . . . develops in the home country, Epic among migrating peoples.'[1]

The other positive creation that emerges from the ordeal of transmarine migration in the course of a Völkerwanderung is not literary but political. This new kind of polity is based not on kinship but on contract.

The most famous examples, perhaps, are the city states founded by the sea-faring Greek migrants on the coast of Anatolia in the districts subsequently known as Aeolis, Ionia and Doris, for the scanty records of Hellenic constitutional history seem to show that the principle of organization by law and locality instead of by custom and kinship asserted itself first in these Greek settlements overseas and was afterwards imitated in European Greece. In the oversea city states thus founded, the 'cells' of the new political organization would be, not kindreds, but ships' companies. Having co-operated at sea as men do co-operate when they are 'all in the same boat' amid the perils of the deep, they would continue to feel and act in the same way ashore when they had to hold a hardly won strip of coast against the menace of a hostile hinterland. On shore, as at sea, comradeship would count for more than kin, and the orders of a chosen and trusted leader would override the promptings of custom. In fact a collection of ships' companies joining forces to conquer a new home for themselves overseas would turn spontaneously into a city state articulated into local 'tribes' and governed by an elective magistracy.

When we turn to the Scandinavian Völkerwanderung, we can discern the rudiments of a similar political development. If the abortive Scandinavian Civilization had come to birth instead of being swallowed up by that of Western Europe, the part once played by the city states of Aeolis and Ionia might have been played by the five city states of the Ostmen on the Irish coast or by the five boroughs (Lincoln, Stamford, Leicester, Derby and Nottingham) which were organized by the Danes to guard the landward frontier of their conquests in Mercia. But the finest flowering of an oversea Scandinavian polity was the republic of Iceland, founded on the apparently unpromising soil of an Arctic island five hundred miles away from the nearest Scandinavian *point d'appui* in the Faroe Islands.

As for the political consequences of the transmarine migrations of the Angles and Jutes to Britain, it is perhaps something more than a coincidence that an island which was occupied at the dawn of Western history by immigrants who had shaken off the shackles of the primitive kin-group in crossing the sea should afterwards

---

[1] Phillpotts, B. S.: *The Elder Edda*, p. 207.

have been the country in which our Western Society achieved
some of its most important steps in political progress. The Danish
and Norman invaders who followed on the heels of the Angles,
and who share the credit for subsequent English political achievements, enjoyed the same liberating experience. Such a combination of peoples offered an unusually favourable soil for political
cultivation. It is not surprising that our Western Society should
have succeeded, in England, in creating first 'the King's Peace'
and thereafter parliamentary government, while on the Continent
our Western political development was retarded by the survival
of the kin-group among the Franks and Lombards, who had not
been relieved of that social incubus at the outset by the liberating
transit of the sea.

(3) THE STIMULUS OF BLOWS

Having now examined the stimulus of physical environments,
we may complete this part of our study by surveying the field of
human environments in the same way. We may distinguish, first,
between those human environments which are geographically
external to the societies upon which they act and those which are
geographically intermingled with them. The former category will
cover the action of societies or states upon their neighbours when
both parties start by being in exclusive occupation of particular
areas. From the standpoint of the organizations which play the
passive role in such social intercourse, the human environment
with which they are confronted is 'external' or 'foreign'. The
second of our two categories will cover the action of one social
'class' upon another, where the two classes are in joint occupation
of the same area—using the term 'class' in its widest meaning.
The relationship in this case is 'internal' or 'domestic'. Leaving
this internal human environment for later examination, we may
begin by making a further subdivision between the external impact when it takes the form of a sudden blow and its incidence in the
form of a continuous pressure. We have here, therefore, three
subjects of inquiry: external *blows*, external *pressures* and internal
penalizations.

What is the effect of sudden blows? Does our proposition 'the
greater the challenge the greater the stimulus' hold good here?
The first test cases that naturally occur to the mind are cases where
a military power has first been stimulated by successive contests
with its neighbours and has then suddenly been prostrated by an
adversary against whom it has never measured its strength before.
What usually happens when incipient empire-builders are thus

dramatically overthrown in mid-career? Do they usually remain lying, like Sisera, where they have fallen, or do they rise again from their mother earth, like the giant Antaeus of Hellenic mythology, with their strength redoubled? The historic examples indicate that the latter alternative is the normal one.

What, for example, was the effect of the *Clades Alliensis* upon the fortunes of Rome? The catastrophe overtook her only five years after her victory in her long duel with Etruscan Veii had placed her at last in a posture to assert her hegemony over Latium. The overthrow of the Roman army at the Allia and the occupation of Rome herself by barbarians from the back of beyond might have been expected to wipe out at one stroke the power and prestige which Rome had just won. Instead, Rome recovered from the Gallic disaster so rapidly that, less than half a century later, she was able to engage with ultimate success in longer and more arduous encounters with her Italian neighbours, which extended her authority over all Italy.

Again, what was the effect on the fortunes of the 'Osmanlis when Timur Lenk (Tamerlane) took Bāyezīd Yilderim · (the Sultan Bajazet) captive on the field of Angora? This catastrophe overtook the 'Osmanlis just when they were on the point of completing their conquest of the main body of Orthodox Christendom in the Balkan Peninsula. It was at this critical moment that they were prostrated, on the Asiatic side of the Straits, by a thunderbolt from Transoxania. A general collapse of their uncompleted edifice of empire is what might have been expected. But it was not what happened in fact; and, half a century later, Mehmed the Conqueror was able to place the coping-stone on Bāyezīd's building by taking possession of Constantinople.

The histories of Rome's unsuccessful rivals show how a crushing defeat nerves a community to more purposeful activity even though further defeat, after a more stubborn resistance than before, frustrates the purpose. The defeat of Carthage in the First Punic War stimulated Hamilcar Barca to conquer for his country an empire in Spain which surpassed the empire she had just lost in Sicily. Even after the defeat of Hannibal in the Second Punic War the Carthaginians twice astonished the world in the half-century that elapsed before their final destruction, first by the rapidity with which they paid off their war indemnity and recovered their commercial prosperity, and secondly by the heroism with which their whole population, men, women and children, fought and died in the final struggle. Again, it was only after his crushing defeat at Cynoscephalae that Philip V of Macedon, hitherto a somewhat futile monarch, set himself to transform his country

into so formidable a power that his son Perseus was able to challenge Rome single-handed and come near to defeating her before
his stubborn resistance was finally broken at Pydna.

Another example of the same kind, though with a different outcome, is furnished by the five interventions of Austria in the
Revolutionary and Napoleonic Wars. Her first three interventions
brought her not only defeats but discredit. After Austerlitz,
however, she began to gird up her loins. If Austerlitz was her
Cynoscephalae, Wagram was her Pydna; but, more fortunate than
Macedon, she was able to intervene once again with victorious
effect in 1813.

Still more striking is the performance of Prussia in the same
cycle of wars. During the fourteen years that culminated in the
catastrophe of Jena and the surrenders that immediately followed,
she had pursued a policy at once futile and ignominious. There
followed, however, the heroic winter campaign of Eylau, and the
severity of the terms dictated at Tilsit only added to the stimulus
which the shock of Jena had first administered. The energy
evoked in Prussia by this stimulus was extraordinary. It regene-
rated not only the Prussian army but also the Prussian administrative and educational systems. In fact it transformed the
Prussian state into a chosen vessel for holding the new wine of
German nationalism. It led through Stein and Hardenberg and
Humboldt to Bismarck.

This cycle has repeated itself in our own day in a manner too
painfully familiar to call for comment. The German defeat in the
war of 1914–18 and the exacerbation of that defeat by the French
occupation of the Ruhr Basin in 1923–4 have issued in the
demonic, though abortive, Nazi *revanche*.[1]

But the classic example of the stimulating effect of a blow is the
reaction of Hellas in general, and Athens in particular, to the
onslaught of the Persian Empire—the Syriac universal state—in
480–479 B.C. The pre-eminence of the Athenian rebound was
proportionate to the severity of Athenian sufferings, for while the
fertile fields of Boeotia were saved by the treachery of their owners
to the Hellenic cause and the fertile fields of Lacedaemon by the
prowess of the Athenian fleet, the poor land of Attica was devastated systematically in two successive seasons, Athens herself was

---

[1] Mr. Toynbee wrote this part of his book in the summer of 1931, when Dr.
Brüning was still Chancellor, but after the Nazi movement had already secured
those sensational and ominous gains in the Reichstag elections of September
1930 which raised the party's representation from 12 out of 491 seats to 107
out of 577. He wrote: 'It is already evident that the blows which have been
rained on Germany since the armistice of 1918 are having the same stimulating
effect as the blows inflicted on Prussia a century before in 1806–7.'—EDITOR.

occupied and her temples were destroyed. The whole population of Attica had to evacuate the country and cross the sea to the Peloponnese as refugees; and it was in this situation that the Athenian fleet fought and won the battle of Salamis. It is no wonder that the blow which aroused this indomitable spirit in the Athenian people should have been the prelude to achievements unique in the history of mankind for their brilliance and multitude and variety. In the rebuilding of her temples, which was for Athenians the most intimate symbol of their country's resurrection, Periclean Athens displayed a vitality far superior to that of post-1918 France. When the French recovered the battered shell of Reims cathedral they performed a pious restoration of each shattered stone and splintered statue. When the Athenians found the Hekatompedon burnt down to its foundations, they let the foundations lie and proceeded, on a new site, to build the Parthenon.[1]

The stimulus of blows finds its most obvious illustrations in reactions from military disasters, but examples can be sought and found elsewhere. Let us confine ourselves to a single supreme case, that presented in the field of religion by the Acts of the Apostles. These dynamic acts, which were eventually to win the whole Hellenic World for Christianity, were conceived at the moment when the Apostles were spiritually prostrated by the abrupt withdrawal of their Master's personal presence so soon after it had appeared to be miraculously restored. This second loss might have been more desolating than the Crucifixion itself. Yet the very heaviness of the blow evoked in their souls a proportionately powerful psychological reaction which is projected mythologically in the appearance of two men in white apparel and in the descent of the Pentecostal tongues of fire. In the power of the Holy Ghost they preached the divinity of the crucified and vanished Jesus not only to the Jewish populace but to the Sanhedrin, and within three centuries the Roman Government itself capitulated to a Church which the Apostles had founded at the hour when their spirits were at their lowest ebb.

(4) THE STIMULUS OF PRESSURES

We have now to examine cases in which the impact takes the different form of a continuous external pressure. In terms of political geography the peoples, states or cities which are exposed to such pressure fall, for the most part, within the general category

[1] London after the Great Fire of A.D. 1666 likewise had the courage of its contemporary architectural convictions and built Wren's St. Paul's instead of attempting a Gothic restoration. What would our own generation of Londoners have done to-day if Westminster Abbey or Wren's St. Paul's had been destroyed by German bombs?—EDITOR.

of 'marches' or frontier provinces, and the best way to study this particular kind of pressure empirically is to make some survey of the part played by exposed marches, in the histories of the communities to which they belong, in comparison with the part played by more sheltered territories in the interior of the domains of the same communities.

In the Egyptiac World

On no less than three momentous occasions in the history of the Egyptiac Civilization the course of events was directed by Powers originating in the south of Upper Egypt; the foundation of the United Kingdom *circa* 3200 B.C., the foundation of the universal state *circa* 2070 B.C., and its restoration *circa* 1580 B.C., were all carried out from this narrowly circumscribed district; and this seed-bed of Egyptiac empires was in fact the southern march of the Egyptiac World which was exposed to pressure from the tribes of Nubia. During the latter course of Egyptiac history, however—the sixteen centuries of twilight between the decline of the New Empire and the ultimate extinction of the Egyptiac Society in the fifth century after Christ—political power reverted to the Delta, which was the march confronting both Northern Africa and South-Western Asia, as persistently as it had been apt to revert to the southern march during the preceding two thousand years. Thus the political history of the Egyptiac World, from beginning to end, may be read as a tension between two poles of political power which in every age were located respectively in the southern and in the northern march. There are no examples of great political events originating at points in the interior.

Can we offer any reason why the influence of the southern march predominated in the first half of the time-span of Egyptiac history and the influence of the northern march in the second half? The reason would seem to be that, after the military conquest of the Nubians and their cultural assimilation under Thothmes I (*circa* 1557–1505 B.C.), the pressure on the southern march declined or vanished, whereas about the same time or soon afterwards the pressure on the Delta from the barbarians of Libya and the kingdoms of South-Western Asia very markedly increased. Thus not only does the influence of frontier provinces predominate in Egyptiac political history over the influence of central provinces, but the most threatened march at any given time enjoys the predominant influence.

In the Iranic World

The same result in quite different circumstances is revealed by the contrasted histories of two Turkish peoples, the 'Osmanlis and the Qaramanlis, who each occupied a part of Anatolia, the western advanced bastion of the Iranic World, in the fourteenth century of the Christian Era.

These two Turkish communities were both of them 'successor states' of the Anatolian Saljuq sultanate, a Muslim Turkish Power which had been established in Anatolia in the eleventh century, just before the beginning of the Crusades, by Saljuq Turkish adventurers who made provision for themselves in this world and the next by thus enlarging the borders of Dar-al-Islam at Orthodox Christendom's expense. When this sultanate broke up in the thirteenth century of the Christian Era, the Qaramanlis seemed to have the finest, and the 'Osmanlis the poorest, prospects of all the Saljuqs' heirs. The Qaramanlis inherited the kernel of the former Saljuq domain with its capital, Qōniyah (Konieh, Iconium), while the 'Osmanlis found themselves in possession of a piece of the husk.

In fact the 'Osmanlis had received the leavings of the Saljuq estate because they were the latest comers and had arrived in humble circumstances. Their eponym, 'Osmān, was the son of one Ertoghrul, the leader of a nameless band of refugees, an insignificant fragment of the human wreckage which had been hurled to the farthest extremities of Dar-al-Islam by the tremendous impact of the Mongol wave when it broke upon the north-eastern marches of the Iranic Society from the heart of the Eurasian Steppe. The last of the Anatolian Saljuqs had assigned to these refugee fathers of the 'Osmanlis a strip of territory on the north-western edge of the Anatolian Plateau, where the Saljuq territories marched with those still held by the Byzantine Empire along the Asiatic shores of the Sea of Marmara: an exposed position appropriately called *Sultan Önü*, the Sultan's battle-front. These 'Osmanlis may well have envied the good fortune of the Qaramanlis, but beggars cannot be choosers. 'Osmān accepted his lot and set himself to enlarge his borders at his Orthodox Christian neighbours' expense, taking as his first objective the Byzantine city of Brusa. The capture of Brusa took him nine years (A.D. 1317–26), but the 'Osmanlis have justly called themselves by his name, for 'Osmān was the true founder of the Ottoman Empire.

Within thirty years of the fall of Brusa the 'Osmanlis had gained a footing on the European shore of the Dardanelles, and it was in Europe that they made their fortune. Yet before the end of this same century they had conquered the Qaramanlis and other Turkish communities of Anatolia with their left hand at the same time as they were subduing Serbs and Greeks and Bulgars with their right.

Such was the stimulus of a political frontier, for an examination of the preceding epoch of history shows that there were no special hero-breeding qualities in the geographical environment of the 'Osmanlis' original base of operations in Anatolia, as contrasted with that of the unadventurous and deservedly forgotten Qaramanlis, such as would bring Sultan Önü within the field of the first section of this chapter. If we turn back to the time before the irruption of the Saljuq Turks in the third quarter of the eleventh century of the Christian Era, when Anatolia was still within the frontiers of the East Roman Empire, we find that the territory afterwards occupied by the Qaramanlis was almost coincident with the former district of the Anatolic Army Corps, which in the earliest age of Orthodox Christian history had held the primacy among the corps of the East Roman Army. In other words, the East Roman predecessors of the Qaramanlis in the district of Qōniyah held that pre-eminence in Anatolia which was held in the later age by the 'Osmanli occupants of Sultan Önü; and the reason is plain. At that earlier date the Qōniyah district had been a frontier province of the East Roman Empire *vis-à-vis* the Arab Caliphate, while the territory afterwards occupied by the 'Osmanlis was in that age enjoying the comfortable obscurity of the interior position.

In Russian Orthodox Christendom

We find here, as elsewhere, that the vitality of the society has tended to concentrate itself, successively, in one march after another as the relative strengths of the various external pressures on the several marches have varied in intensity. The Russian region in which the Orthodox Christian Civilization first took root at the time of its original transplantation across the Black Sea and across the Eurasian Steppe from Constantinople was the upper basin of the Dniepr. From there it was transferred in the twelfth century to the upper basin of the Volga by the frontiersmen who were enlarging their borders in this direction at the expense of the primitive pagan Finns of the north-eastern forests. Soon afterwards, however, the seat of vitality withdrew to the Lower Dniepr to meet a crushing pressure from the nomads of the Eurasian Steppe. This pressure, suddenly imposed upon the Russians as a result of the Mongol Bātū Khan's campaign of A.D. 1237, was extreme and prolonged; and it is interesting to observe that, in this instance as in others, a challenge of unusual severity evoked a response which was remarkably original and creative.

This response was nothing less than the evolution of a new manner of life and a new social organization which enabled a sedentary society, for the first time in history, not merely to hold its own against the Eurasian nomads, not merely to chastise them by transitory punitive expeditions, but actually to make an enduring conquest of nomad ground and to change the face of the landscape by transforming the nomads' cattle-ranges into peasants' fields and replacing their mobile camps by permanent villages. The Cossacks, who performed this unprecedented feat, were frontiersmen of Russian Orthodox Christendom who were tempered in the furnace and fashioned on the anvil of border warfare against Eurasian nomads (Bātū Khan's 'Golden Horde') in the two following centuries. They owe the name they have made legendary—Cossacks—to their enemies; it is simply the Turkish word *qazaq*, meaning an outlaw who refuses to acknowledge the authority of his 'legitimate' nomad overlord.[1] The far-flung Cossack communities which—at the moment of their annihilation in the Russian Communist Revolution of 1917—were écheloned right across Asia from the Don to the Ussuri, were all derived from a single mother-community, the Cossacks of the Dniepr.

These original Cossacks were a semi-monastic military brotherhood with points of resemblance to the Hellenic brotherhood of the Spartans and to the Crusading Orders of Knighthood. In their methods of conducting their truceless warfare against the nomads they realized that, if a civilization is to wage war with success against barbarians, it must fight them with other weapons and resources than their own. Just as modern Western empire-builders have overwhelmed their primitive opponents by bringing to bear against them the superior resources of industrialism, so the Cossacks overwhelmed the nomads by availing themselves of the superior resources of agriculture. And as modern Western generalship has reduced the nomads to military impotence on their own ground by outmatching their mobility with such instruments as railways, motor cars and aeroplanes, so the Cossacks reduced the nomads to military impotence in their own way by seizing upon the rivers, the one natural feature of the Steppe which was not under the nomads' control and which told against them instead of in their favour. To nomad horsemen the rivers were formidable as obstacles and useless for transport, whereas the

[1] In fact the Turkish meaning of 'Cossack' seems to be much the same as the Irish meaning of 'Tory'. But in its literal sense *qazaq* appears to mean 'digger', i.e. a tributary tiller of the soil on the fringe of the Steppe, who would naturally be recalcitrant to the nomad's overlordship. In other words, the *qazaq* is the Cain of the story of Cain and Abel—a story that is told from the nomad's point of view (see pp. 168–9).

Russian peasant and lumberman was expert in river navigation. Accordingly the Cossacks, while learning to vie with their nomad adversaries in the art of horsemanship, did not forget to be watermen, and it was by boat and not on horseback that they eventually won their way to the dominion of Eurasia. They passed from the Dniepr to the Don and from the Don to the Volga. Thence in 1586 they crossed the watershed between the Volga and the Ob and by 1638 their exploration of Siberian waterways had brought them to the shores of the Pacific on the Sea of Okhotsk.

In the same century in which the Cossacks thus signalized their victorious reaction to the nomad pressure on the south-east, another frontier became the principal recipient of external pressure and the principal focus of Russian vitality. In the seventeenth century of the Christian Era, Russia experienced for the first time in her history a formidable pressure from the Western World. A Polish army occupied Moscow for two years (1610–12), and soon afterwards the Sweden of Gustavus Adolphus barred out Russia from the Baltic by making herself mistress of the whole eastern coastline of that sea from Finland to the northern frontier of Poland, which at that time ran to within a few miles of Riga. But the century had barely closed when Peter the Great retorted to this Western pressure by founding Petersburg in A.D. 1703, on territory reconquered from the Swedes, and displaying the flag of a Russian navy, in Western style, on Baltic waters.

In the Western World over against the Continental Barbarians

When we pass to the history of our own Western Civilization we find that at first, not unnaturally, the heaviest external pressure was felt on its eastward, or landward, frontier over against the barbarians of Central Europe. This frontier was not only victoriously defended but was continuously pushed back until the barbarians had disappeared from the scene. Thereafter our Western Civilization found itself in contact on its eastern frontiers no longer with barbarians but with rival civilizations. At present we are concerned to draw examples of the stimulating effects of frontier pressure only from the first part of this span of history.

In the first phase of Western history the stimulating effect of the pressure of the Continental barbarians declared itself in the emergence of a new social structure, the still half-barbarian principality of the Franks. The Merovingian régime, in which the Frankish principality was first embodied, had its face turned towards the Roman past, but the succeeding Carolingian régime looked to the future; for, though it incidentally evoked a ghost of

the Roman Empire, that ghost was only evoked—in the spirit of
the cry 'Debout les morts!'—in order to assist the living in carrying out their task. And in what part of the Frankish domain was
this substitution of the vital and positive Carolings for the decadent and *fainéant* Merovings accomplished? Not in the interior
but on the frontier; not in Neustria (roughly equivalent to Northern
France), on soil fertilized by ancient Roman culture and sheltered
from barbarian inroads, but in Austrasia (the Rhineland), in a
territory which bestrode the Roman frontier and was exposed to
constant assaults from the Saxons of the North European forest
and from the Avars of the Eurasian Steppe. The measure of the
stimulus from this external pressure is given by the achievements
of Charlemagne, his eighteen Saxon campaigns, his extirpation of
the Avars and the 'Carolingian Renaissance', which was one of
the first manifestations of cultural and intellectual energy in our
Western World.

This Austrasian reaction to the stimulus of pressure was followed
by a relapse. Accordingly we find it succeeded by a Saxon reaction which came to a head, rather less than two centuries later,
in the career of Otto I. The enduring achievement of Charlemagne's career had been the incorporation of the domain of the
Saxon barbarians into Western Christendom; but by this very
success he had prepared the way for the transfer of the frontier,
and with it the stimulus, from his own victorious Austrasia to
conquered Saxony. In Otto's day the same stimulus evoked in
Saxony the same reaction that had been evoked by it, in Charlemagne's day, in Austrasia. Otto smote the Wends as Charlemagne had smitten the Saxons, and thereafter the frontiers of
Western Christendom were pushed back steadily farther eastwards.

In the thirteenth and fourteenth centuries the task of Westernizing the last remaining Continental barbarians was carried on no
longer under the leadership of hereditary monarchs who, like
Charlemagne and Otto, had assumed the Roman Imperial title,
but through the instrumentality of two new institutions: the city
state and the militant monastic order. The Hansa towns and the
Teutonic Knights, between them, advanced the bounds cf Western
Christendom from the Oder to the Dvina. That was the last round
in this secular conflict; for before the close of the fourteenth
century the Continental barbarians, who had been pressing on the
frontiers of three successive civilizations, the Minoan, the Hellenic
and the Western, for three thousand years, had been wiped off the
face of the earth. By A.D. 1400 Western Christendom and Orthodox
Christendom, which had once been entirely isolated from one
another on the Continent by intervening bands of barbarians, had

come to march with one another along a line extending across the whole breadth of the Continent from the Adriatic to the Arctic.

It is interesting to observe how, on this moving frontier between an advancing civilization and a retreating barbarism, the reversal of the direction of pressure, which became constant from the time when Otto I took up Charlemagne's work, was followed by a progressive transference of stimulus as the Western counter-offensive proceeded. For example, the Duchy of Saxony suffered the same eclipse after Otto's victories over the Wends that Austrasia had suffered, two centuries earlier, after Charlemagne's victories over the Saxons. Saxony lost her hegemony in A.D. 1024 and broke into fragments sixty years later. But the Imperial dynasty which followed the Saxon dynasty did not originate farther east on the advancing frontier, as the Saxon dynasty had originated eastward of the Carolingian. Instead, the Franconian dynasty and all subsequent dynasties bearing the Imperial title—Hohenstaufen, Luxemburg, and Hapsburg—originated on one or other of the confluents of the Rhine. The now distant frontier did not impart its stimulus to these Imperial successor dynasties, and we shall not be surprised to find that, in spite of the eminence of certain individual emperors, such as Frederick Barbarossa, the Imperial power steadily declined from the latter part of the eleventh century onwards.

Yet the empire resuscitated by Charlemagne survived, a ghost of a ghost no doubt, 'neither Holy nor Roman nor an Empire', to play a vital part once again in the political life of the Western Society. It owed its recovery of vitality to the fact that, at the latter end of the Middle Ages, a series of dynastic arrangements and accidents installed the Rhenish House of Hapsburg in Austria, where it eventually shouldered altogether new frontier responsibilities and responded to a new stimulus that these brought with them. To this subject we must now pass on.

In the Western World over against the Ottoman Empire

The impact of the Ottoman Turks on the Western World began in earnest with the hundred years' war between the 'Osmanlis and Hungary which culminated in the extinction of the medieval kingdom of Hungary in the battle of Mohacz (A.D. 1526). Hungary, standing at bay under the leadership of John Hunyadi and his son Matthias Corvinus, was the most stubborn opponent the 'Osmanlis had as yet encountered. The disparity, however, between the respective forces of the two combatants, in spite of the reinforcement of Hungary by its union with Bohemia from 1490 onwards, was so great that the effort proved to be beyond

Hungary's strength. The upshot was the battle of Mohacz; and it was only a disaster of this magnitude that could produce a sufficient psychological effect to bring the remnant of Hungary together with Bohemia and Austria into a close and enduring union under the Hapsburg dynasty which had been ruling Austria since A.D. 1440. This union endured nearly four hundred years—only to dissolve in the same year, 1918, that saw the final break-up of the Ottoman Power which had delivered the dynamic blow at Mohacz four centuries back.

Indeed, from the moment of the Danubian Hapsburg Monarchy's foundation its fortunes followed those of the hostile Power whose pressure had called it into existence. The heroic age of the Danubian Monarchy coincided chronologically with the period during which the Ottoman pressure was felt by the Western World most severely. This heroic age may be taken as beginning with the first abortive Ottoman siege of Vienna in 1529 and ending with the second in 1682–3. In these two supreme ordeals the Austrian capital played the same role in the desperate resistance of the Western World to the Ottoman assault as Verdun played in the French resistance to the German assault in the war of 1914–18. Both sieges of Vienna were turning-points in Ottoman military history. The failure of the first brought to a standstill the tide of Ottoman conquest which had been flooding up the Danube Valley for a century past—and the map shows, what many will find hard to believe without verification, that Vienna is more than half-way from Constantinople to the Straits of Dover. The failure of the second siege was followed by an ebb which continued thereafter, in spite of all pauses and fluctuations, until the Turkish frontier had been pushed back from the south-eastern outskirts of Vienna, where it had stood from 1529 to 1683, to the north-western outskirts of Adrianople.

The Ottoman Empire's loss, however, has not proved the Danubian Hapsburg Monarchy's gain, for the heroic age of the Danubian Monarchy did not survive the Ottoman Empire's decline. The collapse of the Ottoman Power, which threw open a field in South-Eastern Europe for other forces to occupy, simultaneously released the Danubian Monarchy from the pressure which had stimulated it hitherto. The Danubian Monarchy followed into decline the Power whose blows had originally called it into existence, and eventually shared the Ottoman Empire's fate.

If we take a glance at the Austrian Empire in the nineteenth century, when the once-menacing 'Osmanli had become 'the sick man of Europe', we find that it was now suffering under a double disability. Not only was it in this age no longer a frontier state; its

supernational organization which had proved an effective response
to the Ottoman challenge of the sixteenth and seventeenth centuries had become a stumbling-block to the newfangled nationalist
ideals of the nineteenth. The Hapsburg Monarchy spent the last
century of its existence in attempts—all doomed to failure—at
hindering the inevitable revision of the map on nationalist lines.
At the price of renouncing the hegemony over Germany and the
possession of territory in Italy, the Monarchy contrived to go on
living side by side with the new German Empire and the new
Italian Kingdom. By accepting the Austro-Hungarian *Ausgleich*
of 1867 and its Austro-Polish corollary in Galicia, it succeeded
in identifying its own interests with the national interests of the
Magyar and Polish as well as the German elements in its dominions.
But it would not or could not come to terms with its Roumanians
and Czechoslovaks and Jugoslavs, and the pistol-shots of Sarajevo
proved the signal for its obliteration from the map.

Finally, let us glance at the contrasting attitudes of 'inter-war'
Austria and 'inter-war' Turkey. From the war of 1914–18 they
both emerged as republics and both of them shorn of the empires
which had once made them neighbours and adversaries. But there
the resemblance ended. The Austrians were at once the hardest
hit and the most submissive of the five peoples that had found
themselves on the losing side. They accepted the new order
passively, with supreme resignation as well as with supreme regret.
By contrast, the Turks were the only one of the five peoples who
took up arms again, less than a year after the armistice, against the
victorious Powers and successfully insisted upon a drastic revision
of the peace treaty which the victors had intended to impose upon
them. In so doing the Turks renewed their youth and changed
their destiny. They were now no longer fighting, under a decadent
Ottoman dynasty, to preserve this or that province of a derelict
empire. Deserted by their dynasty, they were once again waging
a frontier war and following a leader chosen on his merits like
their first Sultan 'Osmān, and this not to extend their homelands
but to preserve them. The battlefield of In Önü, on which the
decisive action of the Graeco-Turkish war of 1919–22 was fought,
lies in that original patrimony which the last of the Saljuqs had
assigned to the first of the 'Osmanlis six hundred years before. The
wheel had come full circle.

In the Western World on its Western Frontiers

In its early days our Western Society experienced pressure not
only along its Continental eastern frontier but also on three fronts
in the west: the pressure of the so-called 'Celtic Fringe' in the

British Isles and Brittany; the pressure of the Scandinavian Vikings in the British Isles and along the Atlantic coast of Continental Europe; and the pressure of the Syriac Civilization represented by the early Muslim conquerors in the Iberian Peninsula. We will deal first with the pressure of 'the Celtic Fringe'.

How is it that the struggle for existence between the primitive and ephemeral barbarian principalities of the so-called Heptarchy has resulted in the emergence of two progressive and enduring states of our Western body politic? If we glance at the process by which the Kingdoms of England and Scotland have replaced 'the Heptarchy', we shall find that the determining factor at every stage has been a response to some challenge presented by external pressure. The genesis of the Kingdom of Scotland can be traced back to a challenge which was presented to the Anglo-Saxon principality of Northumbria by the Picts and Scots. The present capital of Scotland was founded by Edwin of Northumbria (whose name it still bears) as the frontier fortress of Northumbria over against the Picts beyond the Firth of Forth and the Britons of Strathclyde. The challenge was presented when the Picts and Scots conquered Edinburgh in A.D. 954 and thereafter compelled Northumbria to cede to them the whole of Lothian. This cession raised the following issue: Was this lost march of Western Christendom to retain its Western Christian culture in spite of the change of political régime, or was it to succumb to the alien 'Far Western' culture of its Celtic conquerors? Far from succumbing, Lothian responded to the challenge by taking its conquerors captive, as conquered Greece had once captivated Rome.

The culture of the conquered territory exercised such an attraction upon the Scottish kings that they made Edinburgh their capital and came to feel and behave as though Lothian were their homeland and the Highlands an outlying and alien part of their dominions. In consequence the eastern seaboard of Scotland up to the Moray Firth was colonized, and the 'Highland Line' pushed back, by settlers of English origin from Lothian under the auspices of Celtic rulers and at the expense of a Celtic population who were the Scottish kings' original kinsfolk. By a consequent and not less paradoxical transfer of names, 'the Scottish language' came to mean the English dialect spoken in Lothian instead of meaning the Gaelic dialect spoken by the original Scots. The ultimate consequence of the conquest of Lothian by the Scots and Picts was not to set back the north-western boundary of Western Christendom from the Forth to the Tweed but to push it forward till it embraced the whole island of Great Britain.

Thus a conquered fragment of one of the principalities of the

English 'Heptarchy' actually became the nucleus of the present Kingdom of Scotland, and it is to be observed that the fragment of Northumbria which performed this feat was the march between Tweed and Forth and not the interior between Tweed and Humber. If some enlightened traveller had visited Northumbria in the tenth century, on the eve of the cession of Lothian to the Scots and Picts, he would surely have said that Edinburgh had no great future and that if any Northumbrian town was going to become the permanent capital of a 'civilized' state, that town would be York. Situated in the midst of the largest arable plain of Northern Britain, York had already been the military centre of a Roman province and a metropolitan see of the Church, and had quite recently become the capital of the ephemeral Scandinavian realm of the 'Danelaw'. But the Danelaw had submitted in A.D. 920 to the King of Wessex; thereafter York sank to the level of an English provincial town; and to-day nothing but the unusual size of Yorkshire among English counties recalls the fact that a greater destiny once seemed to be in store for her.

Of the Heptarchic principalities south of the Humber, which one was to take the lead and form the nucleus of the future Kingdom of England? We notice that by the eighth century of the Christian Era the leading competitors were not the principalities nearest to the Continent but Mercia and Wessex, both of which had been exposed to a frontier stimulus from the unsubdued Celts of Wales and Cornwall. We also notice that, in the first round of this contest, Mercia had drawn ahead. King Offa of Mercia commanded greater power than any of the kings of Wessex in his day, for the pressure of Wales on Mercia was stronger than the pressure of Cornwall on Wessex. Though the resistance of the 'West Welsh' in Cornwall has left an undying echo in the legend of Arthur, this resistance seems nevertheless to have been overcome by the West Saxons with comparative ease. The severity of the pressure on Mercia, on the other hand, is attested philologically by the name Mercia itself ('the March' *par excellence*) and archaeologically by the remains of the great earthwork, stretching from the estuary of the Dee to the estuary of the Severn, which bears the name of Offa's Dyke. At that stage it looked as though the future lay, not with Wessex, but with Mercia. In the ninth century, however, when the challenge from 'the Celtic fringe' was outclassed by a new and far more formidable challenge from Scandinavia, these prospects were falsified. This time Mercia failed to respond, while Wessex under the leadership of Alfred responded triumphantly and thereby became the nucleus of the historic Kingdom of England.

The Scandinavian pressure on the oceanic seaboards of Western Christendom resulted not only in the coalescence of the Kingdom of England under the House of Cerdic out of the Heptarchy but also in the articulation of the Kingdom of France under the House of Capet out of the derelict fragments of the western part of Charlemagne's empire. In face of this pressure England found her capital, not in Winchester, the previous capital of Wessex, within range of the West Welsh but comparatively remote from the Scandinavian danger, but in London, which had borne the heat and burden of the day and which had perhaps given the long battle its decisive turn in A.D. 895 by repelling the attempt of a Danish armada to ascend the Thames. Similarly, France found its capital not in Laon, which had been the seat of the last Carolingians, but in Paris, which had stood in the breach under the father of the first of the Capetian kings and had brought the Vikings to a halt in their ascent of the Seine.

Thus the response of Western Christendom to the maritime challenge from Scandinavia gave birth to the new kingdoms of England and France. Further, in the process of gaining the upper hand over these adversaries, the French and English peoples forged the potent military and social instrument of the Feudal System, while the English also gave artistic expression to the emotional experience of their ordeal in a new outburst of epic poetry of which a fragment survives in *The Lay of the Battle of Maldon*.

We must also observe that France repeated in Normandy the achievement of the English in Lothian by winning the Scandinavian conquerors of Normandy as recruits for the civilization of the conquered. Little more than a century after Rollo and his companions had made with the Carolingian Charles the Simple the pact which secured them a permanent settlement on the Atlantic seaboard of France (A.D. 912), their descendants were extending the bounds of Western Christendom in the Mediterranean at the expense of Orthodox Christendom and Islam, and were spreading the full light of the Western Civilization, as it now shone in France, into the insular kingdoms of England and Scotland which till then had still lain in the penumbra. Physiologically the Norman Conquest of England might be regarded as the final achievement of the previously frustrated ambitions of the Viking barbarians, but culturally such an interpretation is mere nonsense. The Normans repudiated their Scandinavian pagan past by coming not to destroy the law of Western Christendom in England but to fulfil it. On the field of Hastings, when the Norman warrior-minstrel Taillefer rode singing into battle in the van of the Norman knights, the language on his lips was not Norse but French and the matter of which he was inditing was not the saga of Sigurd but the Chanson de Roland. When the Western Christian Civilization had thus captivated the Scandinavian invaders of its own domain, it is no wonder that it was able to set the seal upon its victory by supplanting the abortive Scandinavian Civilization in Scandinavia itself. We shall return to this subject later when we collect for comparative treatment a list of 'abortive' civilizations.

We have left till last the frontier pressure which came first in point of time, exceeded all others in intensity, and seemed overwhelming in its potency when measured against the apparently puny force of our civilization in its cradle; indeed, in the judgement of Gibbon, it came near to relegating our Western Society to a place on the list of abortive civilizations.[1] The Arab onslaught upon the infant civilization of the West was an incident in the final Syriac reaction against the long Hellenic intrusion upon the Syriac domain; for when the Arabs took up the task in the strength of Islam they did not rest until they had recovered for the Syriac Society the whole of its former domain at its widest extension. Not content with reconstituting as an Arab empire the Syriac universal state which had originally been embodied in the Persian empire of the Achaemenidae, they went on to reconquer the ancient Phoenician domain of Carthage in Africa and Spain. In the latter direction they crossed, in A.D. 713, in the footsteps of Hamilcar and Hannibal, not only the Straits of Gibraltar but also the Pyrenees; and thereafter, though they did not emulate Hannibal's passage of the Rhone and the Alps, they broke ground which Hannibal never trod when they carried their arms to the Loire.

The discomfiture of the Arabs by the Franks under Charlemagne's grandfather at the Battle of Tours in A.D. 732 has assuredly been one of the decisive events of history; for the Western reaction to Syriac pressure which there declared itself continued in force and increased in momentum on this front until, some seven or eight centuries later, its impetus was carrying the Portuguese vanguard of Western Christendom right out of the Iberian Peninsula and onwards overseas round Africa to Goa, Malacca and Macao, and the Castilian vanguard across the

---

[1] 'A victorious line of march had been prolonged above a thousand miles from the rock of Gibraltar to the banks of the Loire; the repetition of an equal space would have carried the Saracens to the confines of Poland and the Highlands of Scotland. . . . Perhaps the interpretation of the Koran would now be taught in the schools of Oxford, and her pulpits might demonstrate to a circumcised people the sanctity and truth of the revelation of Mahomet.'—Gibbon, E.: *The History of the Decline and Fall of the Roman Empire*, ch. lii.

Atlantic to Mexico and on across the Pacific to Manila. These Iberian pioneers performed an unparalleled service for Western Christendom. They expanded the horizon, and thereby potentially the domain, of the society they represented until it came to embrace all the habitable lands and navigable seas of the globe. It is owing in the first instance to this Iberian energy that Western Christendom has grown, like the grain of mustard seed in the parable, until it has become 'the Great Society': a tree in whose branches all the nations of the Earth have come and lodged.

The evocation of Iberian Christian energy by the stimulus of pressure from the Moors is attested by the fact that this energy gave out as soon as the Moorish pressure ceased to be exerted. In the seventeenth century the Portuguese and Castilians were supplanted in the new world that they had called into existence by interlopers—Dutch, English and French—from the Transpyrenaean parts of Western Christendom, and this discomfiture overseas coincided in date with the removal of the historic stimulus at home through the extirpation, by massacre, expulsion or forcible conversion, of the remaining 'Moriscos' of the Peninsula.

It seems, then, that the relation of the Iberian marches to the Moors resembles the relation of the Danubian Hapsburg Monarchy to the 'Osmanlis. Each was vigorous so long as the pressure was formidable; and then, as soon as the pressure slackened, each of them, Spain, Portugal and Austria, began to relax and lose the lead among the competing Powers of its own Western World.

(5) THE STIMULUS OF PENALIZATIONS

Lame Smiths and Blind Poets

When a living organism is penalized, by comparison with other members of its species, through losing the use of a particular organ or faculty, it is apt to respond to this challenge by specializing in the use of some other organ or faculty until it has secured an advantage over its fellows in this second field of activity to offset its handicap in the first. The blind, for example, are apt to develop a more delicate sense of touch than is usually possessed by people who enjoy the use of their eyes. Somewhat similarly we find that, in a body social, a group or class which is socially penalized—either by accident or by its own act or by the act of other members of the society in which it lives—is apt to respond to the challenge of being handicapped in, or altogether excluded from, certain fields of activity by concentrating its energies on other fields and excelling in these.

It may be convenient to start from the simplest case: a situation in which certain physical handicaps inhibit certain individuals from following the ordinary avocations of the society of which they are members. Let us remind ourselves, for example, of the predicament in which a blind man or a lame man finds himself in a barbarian society where the ordinary male member is, when needed, a warrior. How does the lame barbarian react? Though his feet cannot carry him into battle, his hands can still forge weapons and armour for his fellows to wield and wear, and he acquires a skill in handicraft which makes them as dependent on him as he is on them. He becomes the workaday prototype of lame Hephaestus (Vulcan) or lame Weland (Wayland Smith) in the world of mythology. And how does the blind barbarian react? His predicament is worse, for he cannot use his hands in the smithy; yet he can still use them to strike a harp in harmony with his voice and he can use his mind to make poetry out of the deeds he cannot perform, though he learns of them at second hand from the artless soldier's tales of his fellows. He becomes the means to that immortality of renown which the barbarian warrior desires.

> A race of heroes brave and strong
> Before Atrides fought and died:
> No Homer lived; no sacred song
>   Their great deeds sanctified:
> Obscure, unwept, unknown they lie,
> Opprest with clouds of endless night;
> No poet lived to glorify
>   Their names with light.[1]

Slavery

Of the penalizations imposed not by accident of nature but by the hand of man, the most obvious, the most universal and the most severe has been enslavement. Take, for example, the record of the vast concourse of immigrants who were brought to Italy as slaves from all the countries round the Mediterranean during those two terrible centuries between the Hannibalic War and the establishment of the Augustan Peace. The handicap under which these slave immigrants began their new life is almost beyond imagination. Some of them were heirs to the cultural heritage of the Hellenic Civilization, and these had seen their whole spiritual and material universe tumble about their ears when their cities had been sacked and they and their fellow citizens haled to the slave-market. Others, coming from the Oriental 'internal proletariat' of the Hellenic Society, had lost their social heritage already, but not their capacity for the grievous personal suffering that slavery

[1] Horace: *Odes*, IV, ix (*Vixere fortes*, &c.), De Vere's translation.

inflicts. There was an ancient Greek saying that 'the day of enslavement deprives man of half of his manhood', and this saying was terribly fulfilled in the debasement of the slave-descended urban proletariat of Rome, which lived not by bread alone but by 'bread and shows' (*panem et circenses*) from the second century B.C. to the sixth of the Christian Era, till the flesh-pots failed and the people perished off the face of the Earth. This long-drawn-out life-in-death was the penalty of failure to respond to the challenge of enslavement, and no doubt that broad path of destruction was trodden by the majority of those human beings of many different origins and antecedents who were enslaved *en masse* in the most evil age of Hellenic history. Yet some there were who did respond to the challenge and did succeed in 'making good', in one fashion or another.

Some rose in their masters' service until they became the responsible administrators of great estates; and Caesar's estate itself, when it had grown into the universal state of the Hellenic World, continued to be administered by Caesar's freedmen. Others, whom their masters established in petty business, purchased their freedom from the savings that their masters had allowed them to retain and eventually rose to affluence and eminence in the Roman business world. Others remained slaves in This World to become philosopher-kings or fathers of churches in another, and the true-born Roman who might justly despise the illegitimate authority of a Narcissus or the *nouveau-riche* ostentation of a Trimalchio would delight to honour the serene wisdom of the lame slave Epictetus, while he could not but marvel at the enthusiasm of the nameless multitude of slaves and freedmen whose faith was moving mountains. During the five centuries between the Hannibalic War and the conversion of Constantine the Roman authorities saw this miracle of servile faith being performed under their eyes and repeated—in defiance of their efforts to arrest it by physical force—until eventually they themselves succumbed to it. For the slave immigrants who had lost their homes and families and property still kept their religion. The Greeks brought the Bacchanalia, the Anatolians the worship of Cybele ('Diana of the Ephesians', a Hittite goddess who had long outlived the society in which she had been conceived), the Egyptians brought the worship of Isis, the Babylonians the worship of the stars, the Iranians the worship of Mithra, the Syrians Christianity. 'The Syrian Orontes has poured its waters into the Tiber', wrote Juvenal in the second century of the Christian Era; and the confluence of these waters raised an issue which revealed the limitations on the slave's subjection to his master.

The issue was whether an immigrant religion of the internal proletariat was to swamp the indigenous religions of the dominant minority of the Hellenic Society. When once the waters had met it was impossible that they should not mingle; and, when once they had mingled, there was little doubt as to which current would prevail if nature were not counteracted by art or force. For the tutelary gods of the Hellenic World had already withdrawn from the intimate life-giving communion in which they had once lived with their worshippers, whereas the gods of the proletariat had proved themselves to be their worshippers' 'refuge and strength, a very present help in time of trouble'. In face of these prospects the Roman authorities halted for five centuries between two opinions. Should they take the offensive against the foreign religions or should they take them to their hearts? Every one of the new gods appealed to some section of the Roman governing class: Mithra to the soldiers, Isis to the women, the heavenly bodies to the intellectuals, Dionysus to the Philhellenes and Cybele to the fetish-worshippers. In the year 205 B.C., in the crisis of the Hannibalic War, the Roman Senate anticipated Constantine's reception of Christianity more than five centuries later by receiving, with official honours, the magic stone or meteorite, fallen from heaven and charged with the divinity of Cybele, which they had imported as a talisman from Anatolian Pessinus. Twenty years later they anticipated Diocletian's persecution of the Christians by suppressing the Hellenic Bacchanalia. The long-drawn-out Battle of the Gods was the counterpart of an earthly contest between the slave immigrants and their Roman masters; and in this dual contest the slaves and the slaves' gods won.

The stimulus of penalization is also illustrated by racial discrimination as exemplified in the caste system of the Hindu Society. Here we see races or castes, excluded from one trade or profession, making good in another. The Negro slave immigrant of modern North America has, however, been subject to the twofold penalization of racial discrimination and legal servitude, and to-day, eighty years after the second of these handicaps has been removed, the first weighs as heavily as ever on the coloured freedman. There is no need to enlarge here upon the appalling injuries inflicted by the slave-traders and slave-owners of our Western World, European and American, upon the Negro race; what we are concerned to observe—and after our examination of the Hellenic parallel we observe this without surprise—is that the American Negro, finding the scales thus, to all seeming, permanently and overwhelmingly weighted against him in This World, has turned to another world for consolation.

The Negro appears to be answering our tremendous challenge with a religious response which may prove in the event, when it can be seen in retrospect, to bear comparison with the ancient Oriental's response to the challenge from his Roman masters. The Negro has not, indeed, brought any ancestral religion of his own from Africa to captivate the hearts of his White fellow-citizens in America. His primitive social heritage was of so frail a texture that, save for a few shreds, it was scattered to the winds on the impact of our Western Civilization. Thus he came to America spiritually as well as physically naked; and he has met the emergency by covering his nakedness with his enslaver's cast-off clothes. The Negro has adapted himself to his new social environment by rediscovering in Christianity certain original meanings and values which Western Christendom has long ignored. Opening a simple and impressionable mind to the Gospels, he has discovered that Jesus was a prophet who came into the world not to confirm the mighty in their seats but to exalt the humble and meek. The Syrian slave immigrants who once brought Christianity into Roman Italy performed the miracle of establishing a new religion which was alive in the place of an old religion which was already dead. It is possible that the Negro slave immigrants who have found Christianity in America may perform the greater miracle of raising the dead to life. With their childlike spiritual intuition and their genius for giving spontaneous aesthetic expression to emotional religious experience, they may perhaps be capable of kindling the cold grey ashes of Christianity which have been transmitted to them by us until, in their hearts, the divine fire glows again. It is thus perhaps, if at all, that Christianity may conceivably become the living faith of a dying civilization for the second time. If this miracle were indeed to be performed by an American Negro Church, that would be the most dynamic response to the challenge of social penalization that had yet been made by man.

Phanariots, Qāzānlis and Levantines

The social penalization of religious minorities within a single and otherwise homogeneous community is so familiar a fact that it hardly needs illustration. Everyone is aware of the vigorous response to such a challenge that was made by the English Puritans of the seventeenth century; how those who stayed at home, by the instrumentality first of the House of Commons and afterwards of Cromwell's Ironsides, turned the English Constitution inside out and assured the ultimate success of our experiment of parliamentary government, and how those who crossed the seas laid the foundations of the United States. It is of greater interest to study some less familiar examples in which the privileged and the penalized denominations belonged to different civilizations, though included within the same body politic through *force majeure* exerted by the dominant party.

In the Ottoman Empire the main body of Orthodox Christendom had been endowed, by intruders of alien faith and culture, with a universal state which the Orthodox Christian Society could not do without yet had proved unable to establish for itself; and the Orthodox Christians had to pay for their social incompetence by ceasing to be masters in their own house. The Muslim conquerors who established and maintained the *Pax Ottomanica* in the Orthodox Christian World exacted payment, in the form of religious discrimination, for the political service they were rendering to their Christian subjects; and here, as elsewhere, the adherents of the penalized denomination responded by becoming experts in those pursuits to which their activities were now forcibly confined.

In the old Ottoman Empire none who were not 'Osmanlis might govern or bear arms, and in large tracts of the Empire even the ownership and cultivation of land passed from the subject Christians into the hands of their Muslim masters. In these circumstances the several Orthodox Christian peoples came—for the first and last time in their histories—to an unavowed and perhaps not even consciously designed but none the less effective mutual understanding. They could now no longer indulge in their favourite pastime of fratricidal war nor enter the liberal professions, so they tacitly parcelled out among themselves the humbler trades, and as traders gradually regained a footing within the walls of the imperial capital from which they had been deliberately evicted wholesale by Mehmed the Conqueror. The Vlachs from the Rumelian highlands established themselves in towns as grocers; the Greek-speaking Greeks of the Archipelago and the Turkish-speaking Greeks of landlocked Anatolian Qaraman set up business on a more ambitious scale; the Albanians became masons; the Montenegrins hall-porters and commissionaires; even the bucolic Bulgars found a living in the suburbs as grooms and market-gardeners.

Among the Orthodox Christian reoccupants of Constantinople there was one Greek group, the so-called Phanariots, who were stimulated by the challenge of penalization to such a degree that they actually rose to be virtual partners and potential supplanters of the 'Osmanlis themselves in the administration and control of the Empire. The Phanar, from which this clique of aspiring Greek families derived their name, was the north-western corner of

Stamboul, which the Ottoman Government had abandoned to its Orthodox Christian subjects resident in the capital as the equivalent of a ghetto. Thither came the Oecumenical Patriarch after the church of Santa Sophia had been converted into a mosque, and in this apparently unpromising retreat the Patriarchate became the rallying-point and instrument of the Greek Orthodox Christians who had prospered in trade. These Phanariots developed two special accomplishments. As merchants on a grand scale they entered into commercial relations with the Western World and acquired a knowledge of Western manners, customs and languages. As managers of the affairs of the Patriarchate they acquired a wide practice and a close understanding of Ottoman administration, since, under the old Ottoman system, the Patriarch was the official political intermediary between the Ottoman Government and all its Orthodox Christian subjects of every tongue in every province. These two accomplishments made the fortunes of the Phanariots when, in the secular conflict between the Ottoman Empire and the Western World, the tide definitely turned against the 'Osmanlis after the second unsuccessful siege of Vienna in A.D. 1682–3.

This change of military fortunes introduced certain formidable complications into Ottoman affairs of state. Before the reverse of 1683 the 'Osmanlis had always been able to count upon settling their relations with the Western Powers by the simple application of force. Their military decline confronted them with two new problems. They had now to negotiate at the conference table with Western Powers whom they could not defeat in the field, and they had to consider the feelings of their Christian subjects whom they could no longer be sure of holding down. In other words they could no longer dispense with skilled diplomatists and skilled administrators; and the necessary fund of experience, which the 'Osmanlis themselves lacked, was possessed by the Phanariots alone among their subjects. In consequence the 'Osmanlis were constrained to disregard the precedents and tamper with the principles of their own régime by conferring upon the opportunely competent Phanariots the monopoly of four high offices of state which were key-positions in the new political situation of the Ottoman Empire. Thus in the course of the eighteenth century of the Christian Era the political power of the Phanariots was steadily enhanced, and it looked as though the result of Western pressure might be to endow the Empire with a new governing class drawn from among the victims of centuries of racial and religious penalization.

In the end the Phanariots failed to achieve their 'manifest

destiny' because, towards the end of the eighteenth century, the Western pressure on the Ottoman body social attained a degree of intensity at which its nature underwent a sudden transformation. The Greeks, having been the first of the subjects of the Ottoman Empire to enter into intimate relations with the West, were also the first to become infected with the new Western virus of nationalism—an after-effect of the shock of the French Revolution. Between the outbreak of the French Revolution and the Greek War of Independence the Greeks were under the spell of two incompatible aspirations. They had not given up the Phanariot ambition of entering into the whole heritage of the 'Osmanlis and keeping the Ottoman Empire intact as a 'going concern' under Greek management; and at the same time they had conceived the ambition of establishing a sovereign independent national state of their own—a Greece which should be Greek as France was French. The incompatibility of these two aspirations was demonstrated conclusively in 1821 when the Greeks attempted to realize them both simultaneously.

When the Phanariot Prince Hypsilanti crossed the Pruth from his base in Russia in order to make himself master of the Ottoman Empire and the Maniot chief Petro Bey Mavromikhalis descended from his mountain fastness in the Morea in order to establish an independent Greece, the outcome was a foregone conclusion. The resort to arms spelt the ruin of Phanariot aspirations. The reed on which the 'Osmanlis had been leaning for more than a century pierced their hand, and their fury at this betrayal nerved them to break the treacherous staff in pieces and to stand at all costs on their own feet. The 'Osmanlis retorted to Prince Hypsilanti's act of war by destroying at one blow the fabric of power which the Phanariots had been peacefully building up for themselves since 1683; and this was the first step in eradicating all non-Turkish elements from the remnant of the Ottoman heritage—a process which reached its climax in the eviction of the Orthodox Christian minority from Anatolia in 1922. In fact, the first explosion of Greek nationalism kindled the first spark of its Turkish counterpart.

Thus, after all, the Phanariots just failed to secure that 'senior partnership' in the Ottoman Empire for which they seemed to be destined. Yet the fact that they came within an ace of success is evidence of the vigour with which they had responded to the challenge of penalization. Indeed the history of their relation with the 'Osmanlis is an excellent illustration of the social 'law' of challenge-and-response; and the antithesis between Greek and Turk, which has attracted so much interest and excited so much animus, is explicable only in these terms and not in the racial and religious terms which have been in fashion on both sides in the popular polemics. Turcophils and Graecophils agree in attributing the historical differences in ethos between Greek Christians and Turkish Muslims to some ineradicable quality of race or some indelible imprint of religion. They disagree only in inverting the social values which they assign to these unknown quantities in the two cases. The Graecophil postulates an inherent virtue in Greek blood and in Orthodox Christianity and an inherent vice in Turkish blood and in Islam. The Turcophil simply transposes the vice and the virtue. Actually the common assumption underlying both these views is contradicted by unquestionable matters of fact.

It is unquestionable, for instance, in the matter of physical race, that the blood of Ertoghrul's Central Asian Turkish followers which flows in the veins of the modern Turk is no more than an infinitesimal tincture. The Ottoman Turkish people has grown into a nation by assimilating the Orthodox Christian population in whose midst the 'Osmanlis have been living for the last six centuries. Racially there can by now be very little to choose between the two peoples.

If this sufficiently refutes the *a priori* racial explanation of the Graeco-Turkish antithesis, we may refute the *a priori* religious explanation by a glance at another Turkish Muslim people which is living, and has long been living, in circumstances resembling, not those of the Ottoman Turks but those of the 'Osmanlis' former Orthodox Greek subjects. On the Volga there exists a Turkish Muslim community called the Qāzānlis, who have been subject for some centuries to the Orthodox Christian government of Russia, and suffered much the same racial and religious penalizations under that alien régime as the 'Osmanlis imposed on Orthodox Christians. And what sort of people are these Qāzānlis? We read that they are

'distinguished by their sobriety, honesty, thrift and industry. . . . The chief occupation of the Qāzān Turk is trade. . . . His chief industries are soap-boiling, spinning and weaving. . . . He makes a good shoemaker and coachman. . . . Till the end of the sixteenth century no mosques were tolerated in Qāzān and the Tatars were compelled to live in a separate quarter, but the predominance of the Muslims gradually prevailed.'[1]

In essentials this description of Turks penalized by Russians in the days of the Czars might be a description of Orthodox Christians penalized by Turks in the heyday of the Ottoman Empire. The

[1] The British Admiralty: *Manual on the Turanians and Pan-Turanianism*, pp. 181–4.

common experience of being penalized on account of religion has been the governing factor in the development of both communities; and in the course of centuries their identic reaction to this common experience has bred in them a 'family likeness' to each other which has quite effaced the diversity between the original imprints of Orthodox Christianity and Islam.

This 'family likeness' is shared by adherents of certain other religious denominations who have been penalized on account of their religious allegiance and who have responded in the same way, for example the Roman Catholic 'Levantines' within the old Ottoman Empire. The Levantines, like the Phanariots, could escape from their penalization by abandoning their religion and adopting that of their masters. Few, however, cared to take this course; instead, like the Phanariots, they set themselves to exploit the limited opportunities left open by their arbitrarily imposed disabilities, and in doing so they displayed that curious and un-attractive combination of toughness of character and obsequious-ness of manner which seems to be characteristic of all social groups placed in this particular situation. It made no difference that the Levantine might be descended physically from one of the most warlike and imperious and high-spirited among the peoples of Western Christendom: medieval Venetians and Genoese or modern French, Dutch and English. In the stifling atmosphere of their Ottoman ghetto they must either make the same response to the challenge of religious penalization as their fellow victims of diverse origins or else succumb.

In the earlier centuries of their dominance the 'Osmanlis, knowing the peoples of Western Christendom—the Franks, as they called them—only through their Levantine representatives, assumed that Western Europe was wholly inhabited by such 'lesser breeds without the law'. A wider experience led them to revise their opinion, and the 'Osmanlis came to draw a sharp distinction between the 'fresh-water Franks' and their 'salt-water' namesakes. The 'fresh-water Franks' were those who had been born and bred in Turkey in the Levantine atmosphere and had responded by developing the Levantine character. The 'salt-water Franks' were those who had been born and bred at home in Frankland and had come out to Turkey as adults with their characters already formed. The Turks were puzzled to find that the great psychological gulf which divided them from the 'fresh-water Franks' who had always lived in their midst did not inter-vene when they had to deal with the Franks from beyond the seas. The Franks who were geographically their neighbours and compatriots were psychologically aliens, whereas the Franks who came from a far country turned out to be men of like passions with themselves. But the explanation was really very simple. The Turk and the salt-water Frank could understand one another because there was a broad similarity between their respective social backgrounds. Each had grown up in an environment in which he was the master of his own house. On the other hand they both found difficulty in understanding or respecting the fresh-water Frank because the fresh-water Frank had a social background which was equally foreign to both of them. He was not a son of the house but a child of the ghetto; and this penalized existence had developed in him an ethos from which the Frank brought up in Frankland and the Turk brought up in Turkey had both remained free.

The Jews

We have now noticed, without discussing at any length, the results of religious discrimination in the case where the victims of penalization belong to the same society as the perpetrators of it, the English Puritans being one of several familiar examples; and we have discussed at greater length examples from the history of the Ottoman Empire of the case where the victims of religious discrimination belong to a different civilization from their persecutors. There remains the case where the victims of religious discrimination represent an extinct society which only survives as a fossil. A list of such fossils was given on an early page (see p. 8), and every one of them would furnish illustrations of the results of such penalizations; but by far the most notable is one of the fossil remnants of the Syriac Society, the Jews. Before passing to a consideration of this long-drawn-out tragedy, the end of which is not yet,[1] we may notice that another Syriac remnant, the Parsees, have played the same role within the Hindu Society as the Jews have played elsewhere, developing much the same expertness in trade and finance; and yet another Syriac remnant, the Armenian Gregorian Monophysites, have played much the same part in the World of Islam.

The characteristic qualities of the Jews under penalization are well known. What we are concerned here to find out is whether these qualities are due, as is commonly assumed, to the 'Jewishness' of the Jews, regarded either as a race or as a religious sect, or whether they are simply produced by the impact of penalization. The conclusions already drawn from other examples may

[1] Mr. Toynbee wrote this part of his book before the Nazi persecution of the Jews opened a new and more terrible chapter of the story; that chapter, therefore, finds no place in what follows.—EDITOR.

prejudice us in favour of the latter view, but we will approach the evidence with an open mind. The evidence can be tested in two ways. We can compare the ethos displayed by the Jews when they are being penalized on account of their religion with the ethos when the penalization has been relaxed or wholly remitted. We can also compare the ethos of Jews who are or have been penalized with the ethos of other Jewish communities to whom the stimulus of penalization has never been administered.

At the present time the Jews who display most conspicuously the well-known characteristics commonly called Jewish and popularly assumed in Gentile minds to be the hall-mark of Judaism always and everywhere are the Ashkenazi Jews of Eastern Europe, who, in Rumania and in adjoining territories which used to be included in the so-called 'Jewish Pale' of the Russian Empire, have been kept morally, if not juridically, in the ghetto by the backward Christian nations among whom their lot is cast. The Jewish ethos is already less conspicuous among the emancipated Jews of Holland, Great Britain, France and the United States; and, when we consider how short a time has passed since the legal emancipation of the Jews in these latter countries took place, and how far from being complete their moral emancipation still is, even in the relatively enlightened countries of the West, we shall not underrate the significance of the change of ethos which is already apparent here.[1]

We may also observe that, among the emancipated Jews of the West, those of Ashkenazi origin who have come from the Jewish Pale still appear distinctly more 'Jewish' in ethos than the rarer Sephardim in our midst who have come originally from Dar-al-Islam; and we can account for this difference by reminding ourselves of the diversity in the history of those two Jewish communities.

The Ashkenazim are descended from Jews who took advantage of the opening up of Europe by the Romans and made a perquisite of the retail trade of the semi-barbarous Transalpine provinces. Since the conversion and break-up of the Roman Empire these Ashkenazim have had to suffer doubly from the fanaticism of the Christian Church and from the resentment of the barbarians. A barbarian cannot bear to see a resident alien living a life apart and making a profit by transacting business which the barbarian lacks

---

[1] As a public-school master I (the editor) may remark that I have several times observed that Jewish boys at a public school who happen to be good athletes, and thus find open to them the readiest road to the esteem of their schoolfellows, display far less of the 'Jewish ethos' than other less fortunate Jewish boys. The average Gentile boy simply does not reckon them as Jews at all, whatever their physiognomy and their surnames may be.—EDITOR.

the skill to transact himself. Acting on these feelings, the Western Christians have penalized the Jew as long as he has remained indispensable to them and have expelled him as soon as they have felt themselves capable of doing without him. Accordingly the rise and expansion of Western Christendom have been accompanied by an eastward drift of the Ashkenazim from the ancient marches of the Roman Empire in the Rhineland to the modern marches of Western Christendom in the Pale. In the expanding interior of Western Christendom the Jews have been evicted from one country after another as successive Western peoples have attained a certain level of economic efficiency—as, for example, they were evicted from England by Edward I (A.D. 1272–1307)— while, in the advancing Continental fringe, these Jewish exiles from the interior have been admitted and even invited to one country after another, in the initial stages of Westernization, as commercial pioneers, only to be penalized and eventually evicted once again as soon as they have once again ceased to be indispensable to the economic life of their transitory asylum.

In the Pale this long trek of the Ashkenazi Jews from west to east was brought to a halt and their martyrdom reached its climax; for here, at the meeting-point of Western and Russian Orthodox Christendom, the Jews have been caught and ground between the upper and the nether millstone. At this stage, when they sought to repeat their performance of trekking eastward, 'Holy Russia' barred the way. It was fortunate, however, for the Ashkenazim that by this time the leading nations of the West, which had been the first to evict the Jews in the Middle Ages, had risen to a level of economic efficiency at which they were no longer afraid of exposing themselves to Jewish economic competition—as for example the English by the time of the Commonwealth, when the Jews were readmitted to England by Cromwell (A.D. 1653–58). The emancipation of the Jews in the West came just in time to give the Ashkenazim of the Pale a new western outlet when their old eastward drift was brought up against the blank wall of 'Holy Russia's' western border. During the past century the tide of Ashkenazi migration has been ebbing back from east to west: from the Pale into England and the United States. It is not to be wondered at that, with these antecedents, the Ashkenazim whom this ebb-tide has deposited among us should display the so-called Jewish ethos more conspicuously than their Sephardi co-religionists whose lines have fallen in more pleasant places.

The less sharply accentuated 'Jewishness' which we observe among the Sephardi immigrants from Spain and Portugal is explained by the antecedents of the Sephardim in Dar-al-Islam.

The representatives of the Jewish Dispersion in Persia and in the provinces of the Roman Empire which ultimately fell to the Arabs found themselves in a comparatively happy position. Their status under the 'Abbasid Caliphate was certainly not less favourable than that of Jews in those Western countries where Jews have been emancipated to-day. The historic calamity of the Sephardim was the gradual transfer of the Iberian Peninsula from the Moors to the Western Christians which was completed at the end of the fifteenth century. They were presented by their Christian conquerors with a choice between the three alternatives of annihilation, expulsion or conversion. Let us glance at the latter state of those Peninsular Sephardim who saved their lives in one of the two alternative ways and whose posterity is therefore alive to-day. Those who preferred to go into exile found asylum among the enemies of Catholic Spain and Portugal: in Holland, in Turkey or in Tuscany.[1] Those who went to Turkey were encouraged by their 'Osmanli protectors to settle in Constantinople, Salonica and the lesser urban centres of Rumili in order to fill a vacuum left by the eviction or ruin of the previous Greek urban middle class. In these favourable circumstances the Sephardi refugees in the Ottoman Empire were able to specialize and prosper in trade without paying the price of developing an Ashkenazi ethos.

As for the Marranos, the Iberian Jews who, four or five centuries ago, agreed to conform to the Christian religion, their distinctive Jewish characteristics have been attenuated to vanishing-point. There is every reason to believe that in Spain and Portugal to-day there is a strong tincture of the blood of these Jewish converts in Iberian veins, especially in the upper and middle classes. Yet the most acute psychoanalyst would find it difficult, if samples of living upper- and middle-class Spanish and Portuguese were presented to him, to detect those who had Jewish ancestors.

In modern times a party among the emancipated Jews of the West has sought to complete the emancipation of their community by endowing it with a national state of the modern Western kind. The ultimate aim of the Zionists is to liberate the Jewish people from the peculiar psychological complex induced by centuries of penalization; and in this ultimate aim the Zionists are at one with the rival school of emancipated Jewish thought. The Zionists agree with the Assimilationists in wishing to cure the Jews of being a 'peculiar people'. They part company with them, however, in their estimate of the Assimilationists' prescription, which they regard as inadequate.

[1] Disraeli regarded himself—and probably rightly, though his account of his family history was highly imaginative—as descended from some of these last.

The ideal of the Assimilationists is that the Jew in Holland, England or America should become simply a Dutchman, Englishman or American 'of Jewish religion'. They argue that there is no reason why a Jewish citizen in any enlightened country should fail to be a completely satisfied and assimilated citizen of that country simply because he happens to go to synagogue on Saturday instead of to church on Sunday. To this the Zionists have two replies. In the first place they point out that, even if the Assimilationist prescription were capable of producing the result that its advocates claim for it, it is only applicable in those enlightened countries whose fortunate Jewish citizens are a mere fraction of World Jewry. In the second place they contend that, even under the most favourable conditions, the Jewish problem cannot be solved in this way because to be a Jew is something more than to be a person 'of Jewish religion'. In the eyes of the Zionists, a Jew who tries to turn himself into a Dutchman, an Englishman or an American is simply mutilating his Jewish personality without having any prospect at all of acquiring the full personality of a Dutchman or whatever the Gentile nationality of his choice may be. If the Jews are to succeed in becoming 'like all the other nations' the process of assimilation, so the Zionists contend, must be carried out on a national and not on an individual basis. Instead of individual Jews making the vain attempt to assimilate themselves to individual Englishmen or Dutchmen, the Jewish people must assimilate itself to the English people or the Dutch by acquiring— or reacquiring—a national home where the Jew, like the Englishman in England, will be master in his own house.

Though the Zionist movement as a practical undertaking is only half a century old, its social philosophy has already been justified by results. In the Jewish agricultural settlements in Palestine the children of the ghetto have been transformed out of all recognition into a pioneering peasantry which displays many of the characteristics of the Gentile colonial type. The tragic misfortune of the experiment is its failure to conciliate the pre-existent Arab population of the country.

It remains to record the existence of some little-known groups of Jews who have escaped penalization throughout their history by withdrawal into remote 'fastnesses' where they display all the characteristics of sturdy peasants or even of wild highlanders. Such are the Jews of the Yaman in the south-west corner of Arabia, the Falasha in Abyssinia, the Jewish highlanders of the Caucasus and the Turkish-speaking Jewish Krimchaks of the Crimea.

VIII. THE GOLDEN MEAN

(1) ENOUGH AND TOO MUCH

WE have now reached a point at which we can bring our present argument to a head. We have ascertained that civilizations come to birth in environments that are unusually difficult and not unusually easy, and this has led us on to inquire whether or not this is an instance of some social law which may be expressed in the formula: 'the greater the challenge, the greater the stimulus'. We have made a survey of the responses evoked by five types of stimulus—hard countries, new ground, blows, pressures and penalizations—and in all five fields the result of our survey suggests the validity of the law. We have still, however, to determine whether its validity is absolute. If we increase the severity of the challenge *ad infinitum*, do we thereby ensure an infinite intensification of the stimulus and an infinite increase in the response when the challenge is successfully met? Or do we reach a point beyond which increasing severity produces diminishing returns? And, if we go beyond this point, do we reach a further point at which the challenge becomes so severe that the possibility of responding to it successfully disappears? In that case the law would be that 'the most stimulating challenge is to be found in a mean between a deficiency of severity and an excess of it'.

Is there such a thing as an excessive challenge? We have not yet encountered an example of such, and there are several extreme cases of the operation of challenge-and-response which we have not yet mentioned. We have not yet cited the case of Venice—a city, built on piles driven into the mud banks of a salt lagoon, which has surpassed in wealth and power and glory all the cities built on *terra firma* in the fertile plain of the Po; nor Holland—a country which has been actually salvaged from the sea, but yet has distinguished herself in history far above any other parcel of ground of equal area in the North European plain; nor Switzerland, saddled with her portentous load of mountains. It might seem that the three hardest pieces of ground in Western Europe have stimulated their inhabitants to attain, along different lines, the highest level of social achievement that has as yet been attained by any peoples of Western Christendom.

But there are other considerations. Extreme in degree though these three challenges are, they are limited in range to only one of the two realms which constitute the environment of any society. They are challenges of difficult ground, no doubt, but on the

human side—blows, pressures and penalizations—the severity
of this physical situation has been not a challenge but a relief; it
has shielded them from human ordeals to which their neighbours
were exposed. Venice on her mud banks, insulated from the
Continent by her lagoons, was exempt from foreign military
occupation for almost a thousand years (A.D. 810–1797). Holland,
too, has more than once saved her vital centres by temporarily
reversing the mechanism which keeps her in existence and 'opening the dikes'. What a contrast to the histories of neighbouring
Lombardy and neighbouring Flanders, the two habitual battle-
fields of Europe.

It is, of course, easy enough to cite examples of communities
that have failed to respond to particular challenges. That proves
nothing, for almost every challenge that has eventually evoked a
victorious response turns out, on inquiry, to have baffled or
broken one respondent after another before the moment when,
at the hundredth or the thousandth summons, the victor has
entered the lists at last. Such is the notorious 'prodigality of
nature', of which a host of examples spring to the mind.

For instance, the physical challenge of the North European
forest effectually baffled primitive man. Unequipped with implements for felling the forest trees and ignorant of how to turn the
rich underlying soil to account by cultivation, even if he had been
capable of clearing it of trees, primitive man in Northern Europe
simply avoided the forest and squatted on the sand-dunes and
chalk downs where his remains in the shape of dolmens, flint-
mines and the like are now found—seeking out lands which his
successors scorned as 'bad lands' when the forest was falling to
their axes. For primitive man the challenge of the temperate
forest was actually more formidable than that of the frozen tundras;
and in North America his line of least resistance eventually led
him Pole-ward beyond the forests' northern fringe to find his
destiny in creating the Eskimo culture in response to the challenge
of the Arctic Circle. Yet primitive man's experience does not
prove that the challenge of the North European forest was excessive
in the sense of being beyond human power of effective response;
for the barbarians who followed on his heels were able to make
some impression with the aid of tools and techniques acquired,
perhaps, from civilizations with which they were in touch, until,
in the fullness of time, the pioneers of the Western and the Russian
Orthodox Civilization 'came and saw and conquered'.

In the second century B.C. the southern vanguard of the North
European forest in the Po valley had been subdued by Roman
pioneers after having from time immemorial baffled the Romans'

precursors. The Greek historian Polybius, who visited the country immediately after it had been opened up, draws a striking contrast between the inefficient and poverty-stricken life of Rome's Gallic predecessors, whose last survivors were then still living this life in the backwoods at the foot of the Alps, and the cheapness and plenty which prevailed in adjoining districts which Rome had taken in hand. A similar picture was often drawn in the early nineteenth century contrasting the squalid failure of the Redskins with the bustling vitality of the Anglo-American pioneers in the primeval forest of Kentucky or Ohio.

When we turn from the physical to the human environment, we find the same. A challenge which has defeated one respondent is afterwards proved by the victorious response of some later competitor to be not insuperable.

Let us consider, for example, the relation between the Hellenic Society and the North European barbarians. The pressure here was reciprocal, of each on the other, but let us confine our attention to the pressure of the Hellenic Society on the barbarians. As this civilization radiated deeper and deeper into the interior of the Continent one layer of barbarians after another was confronted with a question of life or death. Was it going to succumb to the impact of this potent alien force and suffer a disintegration of its own social fabric in order to become food for assimilation into the tissues of the Hellenic body social? Or was it going to resist assimilation and be enrolled, in virtue of its resistance, in the recalcitrant external proletariat of the Hellenic Society, which would in due course be 'in at the death' of that society and gorge itself on its corpse? In short, would it be the carcass or the vulture? This challenge was presented successively to the Celts and the Teutons. The Celts after a long struggle broke down; after which the Teutons responded with success.

The breakdown of the Celts was impressive, because they had had a good start and had taken spectacular advantage of it to begin with. They were given their opportunity by an error of tactics on the part of the Etruscans. These Hittite converts to the culture of their Hellenic competitors in the opening up of the Western Mediterranean were not content with securing their foothold on the west coast of Italy; their pioneers rashly pushed inland across the Appennines and scattered far and wide over the basin of the Po. In this they overtaxed their strength, while stimulating the Celts to destroy them. The result was a *furor Celticus* that was sustained for about two centuries and carried Celtic avalanches not only over the Appennines into Rome (in the *Clades Alliensis* of 390 B.C.), but also into Macedonia (279–6 B.C.)

and Greece and eastwards into Anatolia, where they left their mark and their name as 'Galatians'. Hannibal used the Celtic conquerors of the Po Basin as allies, but they failed, and the *furor Celticus* stimulated the response of Roman imperialism. In their western *Lebensraum* from Rimini to Rhine and Tyne as well as in their eastern outposts on Danube and Halys the Celts were disintegrated, swallowed and eventually digested by the Roman Empire.

This disintegration of the Celtic layer of European barbarism exposed the Teutonic layer, which lay next behind it, to the same challenge. How must the prospects of the Teutons have appeared to a historian of the Augustan Age, who recalled the complete destruction of an abortive *furor Teutonicus* by Marius and had watched Caesar throw Teutonic Ariovistus neck and crop out of Gaul? He would have foretold that the Teutons would go the way of the Celts, and would probably give much less trouble in the process; but he would have been wrong. The Roman frontier reached the Elbe for a moment only, to withdraw immediately to the Rhine–Danube line and to remain there; and, when a frontier between civilization and barbarism stands still, time always works in the barbarians' favour. The Teutons, unlike the Celts, were proof against assaults of the Hellenic culture, whether delivered by soldiers, traders or missionaries. By the fifth century of the Christian Era, when the Goths and Vandals were harrying the Peloponnese and holding Rome to ransom and occupying Gaul and Spain and Africa, it was abundantly plain that the Teutons had succeeded where the Celts had failed; and this was proof that, after all, the pressure of the Hellenic Civilization was not so severe that a successful response to it was impossible.

Again, the intrusion of Hellenism upon the Syriac World in the train of Alexander the Great presented a standing challenge to the Syriac Society. Was it, or was it not, to rise up against the intrusive civilization and cast it out? Confronted with this challenge, the Syriac Society made a number of attempts to respond, and these attempts all had one common feature. In every instance the anti-Hellenic reaction took a religious movement for its vehicle. Nevertheless there was a fundamental difference between the first four of these reactions and the last one. The Zoroastrian, the Jewish, the Nestorian and the Monophysite reactions were failures; the Islamic reaction was a success.

The Zoroastrian and Jewish reactions were attempts to combat the ascendancy of Hellenism with the aid of religions already rife in the Syriac World before the Hellenic intrusion. In the strength of Zoroastrianism the Iranians in the eastern domain of the Syriac Civilization rose up against Hellenism and expelled it,

within two centuries of Alexander's death, from all the region
east of the Euphrates. At that point, however, the Zoroastrian
reaction reached its limit and the remnant of Alexander's conquests was salvaged for Hellenism by Rome. Nor did the Jewish
reaction under the Maccabees succeed in its more audacious
attempt to liberate the western homeland of the Syriac Civilization, within sight of the Mediterranean, by an uprising from within.
The momentary triumph over the Seleucids was avenged by
Rome. In the great Romano-Jewish war of A.D. 66–70, the Jewish
community in Palestine was ground to powder, and the Abomination of Desolation, which the Maccabees had once cast out from
the Holy of Holies, came back to stay when Hadrian planted on
the site of Jerusalem the Roman colony of Aelia Capitolina.

As for the Nestorian and Monophysite reactions, they were
alternative attempts at turning against Hellenism a weapon which
the intruding civilization had forged for itself from a blend of
Hellenic and Syriac metal. In the syncretistic religion of primitive
Christianity the essence of the Syriac religious spirit had been
Hellenized to a degree which rendered it congenial to Hellenic
and uncongenial to Syriac souls. The Nestorian and Mono-
physite 'heresies' were both of them attempts to de-Hellenize
Christianity, and both of them failed as reactions against the
Hellenic intrusion. Nestorianism was ignominiously driven out
eastward beyond the Euphrates. Monophysitism held its ground
in Syria and Egypt and Armenia by winning the hearts of a never
Hellenized peasantry; but it was never able to wean away from
Orthodoxy and Hellenism a dominant minority inside the city walls.

A Greek contemporary of the Emperor Heraclius who had
witnessed the victory of the East Roman Empire in its last trial
of strength with the Persian Sasanids and the victory of the
Orthodox Christian hierarchy in its last trial of strength with
Nestorian and Monophysite heretics, might have been betrayed,
about the year 630 of the Christian Era, into giving thanks to God
for having made the earthly trinity of Rome, Catholicism and
Hellenism invincible. Yet at this very moment the fifth Syriac
reaction against Hellenism was impending. The Emperor
Heraclius himself was condemned not to taste of death until he
had seen 'Umar the Successor of Muhammad the Prophet coming
into his kingdom to undo, utterly and for ever, the work of all
the Hellenizers of Syriac domains from Alexander onwards. For
Islam succeeded where its predecessors had failed. It completed
the eviction of Hellenism from the Syriac World. It reintegrated,
in the Arab Caliphate, the Syriac universal state which Alexander
had ruthlessly cut short, before its mission had been fulfilled,

when he overthrew the Persian Achaemenidae. Finally, Islam
endowed the Syriac Society, at last, with an indigenous universal
church and thereby enabled it, after centuries of suspended
animation, to give up the ghost in the assurance that it would not
now pass away without leaving offspring; for the Islamic Church
became the chrysalis out of which the new Arabic and Iranic
civilizations were in due course to emerge.

The foregoing examples indicate that we have not yet hit upon
the right method for dealing with the problem now before us,
which is to find an unequivocal instance in which a challenge has
been proved to be excessive. We must approach the problem on
other lines.

(2) COMPARISONS IN THREE TERMS

A New Approach to the Problem

Can we find some alternative method of search that promises
better results? Let us try the effect of starting our inquiry from
the opposite end. Hitherto we have started with a challenge that
has defeated a respondent. Let us now start from instances in
which a challenge has administered an effective stimulus and provoked a successful response. In the various sections of the previous chapter we have examined many instances of this kind and
have compared the example of successful response with parallel
cases in which the same party, or a comparable party, responded
with less success to the same, or a comparable, challenge when the
challenge was less severe. Let us now reconsider some of these
comparisons between two terms and see whether we can increase
our two terms to three.

Let us look in each case for some third historical situation in
which the challenge has been not less severe but more severe than
in the situation from which we have started. If we succeed in
finding a third term of this kind, then the situation from which
we have started—that of the successful response—becomes a
middle term between two extremes. At these two extremes the
severity of the challenge is respectively less and greater than at
the mean. What about the success of the response? In the situation where the challenge was less we have already found that the
response was less. But what about the third situation, which we
are now introducing for the first time? Here, where the severity of
the challenge is at its highest, shall we find that the success of the
response is at its highest also? Suppose that we find, on the contrary, that an increase in the severity of the challenge beyond the
mean degree is not accompanied by any increase in the success

of the response but that, on the contrary, the response declines. If this proves to be so, we shall have found that the interaction of challenge and response is subject to a 'law of diminishing returns'; we shall conclude that there is a mean range of severity at which the stimulus is at its highest, and we will call this degree the optimum, as contrasted with the maximum.

Norway—Iceland—Greenland

We have already found that it was in Iceland, and not in Norway, Sweden or Denmark, that the abortive Scandinavian Civilization achieved its greatest triumphs both in literature and in politics. The achievement was a response to a twofold stimulus, the stimulus of overseas migration and the stimulus of a bleaker and barrener country than that which these Scandinavian seafarers had left behind. Now suppose the same challenge had been repeated with redoubled severity; suppose the Norsemen had travelled five hundred miles on and settled in a country as much bleaker than Iceland as Iceland is bleaker than Norway. Would this Thule beyond Thule have bred a Scandinavian community twice as brilliant in literature and politics as that of Iceland? The question is not hypothetical, for the conditions which we have postulated were actually fulfilled when the Scandinavian seafarers pushed on to Greenland. And the answer to the question is not in doubt. The Greenland settlement proved a failure; over a span of little less than half a millennium the Greenlanders were being slowly worsted in a tragic losing battle against a physical environment which was too severe even for them.

Dixie—Massachusetts—Maine

We have already compared the severity of the physical challenge presented by the harsh climate and stony soil of New England with the less severe challenge presented by Virginia and the Carolinas to the British-American colonists, and have shown how, in the struggle for the control of the Continent, it was the New Englanders who outdistanced all their rivals. Evidently the Mason and Dixon Line roughly corresponds with the southern limit of an area of optimum challenge. We have now to ask ourselves whether this area of highest climatic stimulus has another limit on the northern side, and as soon as we have framed the question we are aware that the answer is obviously affirmative.

The northern limit of the optimum climatic area actually partitions New England; for, when we speak of New England and the part it has played in American history, we are really thinking of only three of its five little States—of Massachusetts, Connecticut and Rhode Island, and not of New Hampshire and Maine. Massachusetts has always been one of the leading English-speaking communities of the North American Continent. In the eighteenth century she took a leading part in resistance to the British colonial régime and, in spite of the immense development of the United States since that time, Massachusetts has maintained her position in the intellectual sphere and to some extent in the industrial and commercial spheres as well. Maine, on the other hand, though actually a part of Massachusetts until her establishment as a separate state in 1820, has always been unimportant, and survives to-day as a kind of museum piece—a relic of seventeenth-century New England inhabited by woodmen and watermen and hunters. These children of a hard country now eke out their scanty livelihood by serving as 'guides' for pleasure-seekers who come from the North American cities to spend their holidays in this Arcadian state, just because Maine is still what she was when many of these cities had not yet begun to arise out of the wilderness. Maine to-day is at once one of the longest-settled regions of the American Union and one of the least urbanized and sophisticated.

How is this contrast between Maine and Massachusetts to be explained? It would appear that the hardness of the New England environment, which stands at its optimum in Massachusetts, is accentuated in Maine to a degree at which it brings in diminishing returns of human response. And, if we carry our survey still farther north, we are confirmed in this surmise. New Brunswick, Nova Scotia and Prince Edward Island are the least prosperous and progressive provinces of the Dominion of Canada. Farther north again, Newfoundland has in recent years been compelled to abandon an unequal struggle to stand on her own feet and has accepted a thinly veiled form of crown colony government in return for assistance from Great Britain. Farther north again, in Labrador, we reach conditions such as confronted the Norse settlers in Greenland—a maximum challenge which, far from being optimum, might more truly be described as 'pessimum'.

Brazil—La Plata—Patagonia

The Atlantic seaboard of South America obviously presents parallel phenomena. In Brazil, for example, the greater part of the national wealth, equipment, population and energy is concentrated in the small fraction of this vast territory which lies south of the twentieth degree of southern latitude. Moreover, Southern Brazil itself is inferior in civilization to regions farther south, on either side of the La Plata estuary, the Republic of Uruguay and the Argentinian State of Buenos Aires. It is evident that, along the South American Atlantic seaboard, the equatorial sector is not stimulating but positively relaxing; but there is also evidence that the more stimulating temperate climate of the Rio de la Plata estuary is an optimum; for if we follow the coast farther south again we shall find an increase of 'pressure', no doubt, but a decline of response as we traverse the bleak plateau of Patagonia. If we choose to go still farther we shall fare still worse, for we shall find ourselves among the numbed and starved savages who just manage to keep alive among the frosts and snows of Tierra del Fuego.

Galloway—Ulster—Appalachia

Let us next consider an instance in which the challenge has been not exclusively physical but partly physical and partly human.

At the present day there is a notorious contrast between Ulster and the rest of Ireland. While Southern Ireland is a rather old-fashioned agricultural country, Ulster is one of the busiest work-shops in the modern Western World. Belfast ranks with Glasgow, Newcastle, Hamburg or Detroit, and the modern Ulsterman has as great a reputation for being efficient as he has for being unaccommodating.

In response to what challenge has the Ulsterman made himself what he now is? He has responded to the dual challenge of migrating across the sea from Scotland and of contending, after his arrival in Ulster, with the native Irish inhabitants whom he found in possession and proceeded to dispossess. This twofold ordeal has had a stimulating effect which may be measured by comparing the power and wealth of Ulster at the present day with the relatively modest circumstances of those districts on the Scottish side of the border between Scotland and England and along the Lowland fringe of the 'Highland Line' from which the original Scottish settlers in Ulster were recruited at the beginning of the seventeenth century.[1]

The modern Ulstermen, however, are not the only surviving overseas representatives of this stock; for the Scottish pioneers who migrated to Ulster begot 'Scotch-Irish' descendants who re-emigrated in the eighteenth century from Ulster to North America, and these survive to-day in the fastnesses of the Appalachian Mountains, a highland zone which runs through half a dozen states of the American Union from Pennsylvania to Georgia. What has been the effect of this second transplantation? In the seventeenth century the subjects of King James crossed St.

[1] It will be seen that the term 'Galloway', which we have employed in the paragraph heading, is not an entirely adequate description of the homeland area from which the Ulster colonists were drawn.—EDITOR.

George's Channel and took to fighting the Wild Irish instead of the Wild Highlanders. In the eighteenth century their great-grandchildren crossed the Atlantic to become 'Indian fighters' in the American backwoods. Obviously this American challenge has been more formidable than the Irish challenge in both its aspects, physical and human. Has the increased challenge evoked an increased response? If we compare the Ulsterman and the Appalachian of to-day, two centuries after they parted company, we shall find that the answer is once again in the negative. The modern Appalachian has not only not improved on the Ulsterman; he has failed to hold his ground and has gone downhill in a most disconcerting fashion. In fact, the Appalachian 'mountain people' to-day are no better than barbarians. They have relapsed into illiteracy and witchcraft. They suffer from poverty, squalor and ill-health. They are the American counterparts of the latter-day White barbarians of the Old World—Rifis, Albanians, Kurds, Pathans and Hairy Ainus; but, whereas these latter are belated survivals of an ancient barbarism, the Appalachians present the melancholy spectacle of a people who have acquired civilization and then lost it.

Reactions to the Ravages of War

In the Ulster-Appalachia case the challenge was both physical and human, but the operation of the 'law of diminishing returns' appears quite as clearly in other instances in which the challenge is presented in the human sphere exclusively. Consider, for example, the effects of the challenge presented by devastation in war. We have already recorded two cases in which severe challenges of this kind met with triumphant responses: Athens responded to the devastation of the Persian invasion by becoming 'the education of Hellas', and Prussia responded to the devastation of the Napoleonic invasion by becoming the Germany of Bismarck. Can we find a challenge of this kind which proved too severe, a devastation whose wounds festered and in the long run proved mortal? We can.

The devastation of Italy by Hannibal did not, like those other less searing visitations, turn out to have been a blessing in disguise. The devastated arable lands of Southern Italy were transformed partly into pasture-lands and partly into vineyards and olive orchards, and the new rural economy, planting and stock-breeding alike, was worked by slave labour in place of the free peasantry which had once tilled the soil before Hannibal's soldiers burnt the peasant's cottage and before weeds and briars invaded his deserted fields. This revolutionary change from subsistence farming to cash-crop farming and from husbandry to the application of servile man-power undoubtedly increased for a time the monetary value of the produce of the land; but this was more than offset by the social evils it entailed—the depopulation of the countryside and the congregation of a pauper proletariat of ex-peasants in the towns. The attempt to arrest these evils by legislation, made by the Gracchi in the third generation after Hannibal's evacuation of Italy, only aggravated the distemper of the Roman Commonwealth by precipitating a political revolution without bringing the economic revolution to a halt. Political strife became inflamed into civil war, and, a hundred years after the tribunate of Tiberius Gracchus, the Romans acquiesced in the establishment of the permanent dictatorship of Augustus as a drastic remedy for a desperate state of affairs. Thus the devastation of Italy by Hannibal, so far from stimulating the Roman people as Xerxes' devastation of Attica had once stimulated the Athenians, actually gave them a shock from which they never recovered. The chastisement of devastation, which had proved stimulating when administered with Persian vigour, became deadly when inflicted with Punic intensity.

Chinese Reactions to the Challenge of Emigration

We have compared already the effects of varying degrees of physical challenge on different groups of British emigrants. Let us now consider the reaction of Chinese emigrants to varying degrees of human challenge. When the Chinese coolie emigrates to British Malaya or the Dutch East Indies he is apt to reap a reward for his enterprise. By facing the social ordeal of leaving his familiar home and entering an alien social environment, he exchanges an economic environment in which he is enervated by age-long social traditions for one in which he is stimulated to better himself, and not infrequently he makes his fortune. Suppose, however, that we intensify the social ordeal which is the price of economic opportunity. Suppose that, instead of sending him to Malaya or Indonesia, we send him to Australia or California. In these 'White Man's countries' our enterprising coolie, if he gains admission at all, will undergo an ordeal of vastly greater severity. Instead of merely finding himself a stranger in a strange land, he will have to endure deliberate penalization in which the law itself will discriminate against him instead of coming to his aid as it does in Malaya, where an official 'Protector of Chinese' is appointed by a benevolent colonial administration. Does this severer social ordeal evoke an economic response of proportionately greater vigour? It does not, as we can see if we compare the levels of prosperity which are in fact attained by the Chinese in Malaya and Indonesia with the levels attained by immigrants of the same gifted race in Australia and California.

Slavs—Achaeans—Teutons—Celts

Let us next reconsider the challenge which a civilization presents to a barbarism: a challenge that has been presented in Europe to successive layers of barbarians in successive ages by the radiation of various civilizations into the interior of this once dark continent.

When we study this drama our attention is caught by one instance in which the challenge has evoked a response of extraordinary brilliance. The Hellenic Civilization is perhaps the finest flower of the species that has ever yet come to bloom, and it was generated, in response to a challenge from the Minoan Civilization, by European barbarians. When the maritime Minoan Civilization established a footing on the Greek Peninsula, the Achaean barbarians of the hinterland were neither exterminated nor subjected nor assimilated. Instead, they managed to retain their identity as an external proletariat of the Minoan thalassocracy without failing to learn the arts of the civilization which they were holding at bay. In due course they took to the sea, overwhelmed the thalassocrats on their own element and became thereafter the true fathers of the Hellenic Civilization. The Achaean claim to the paternity of Hellenism is vindicated, as we have seen already, by a religious test, for the gods of the Olympian Pantheon manifestly display in their lineaments their derivation from Achaean barbarism, while any vestiges of a Hellenic church derived from the Minoan World are only to be found, if at all, in the side-chapels and crypts of the temple of Hellenic religion—in certain local cults, subterranean mysteries and esoteric creeds.

The measure of the stimulus in this instance is given by the brilliance of Hellenism; but we can measure it in another way by comparing the fortunes of this Achaean layer of barbarians with the fortunes of another layer which happened to be so remote and sheltered that it remained virtually immune from the radiation of any civilization whatever for two thousand years after the Achaeans had received the Minoan challenge and made their brilliant response. These were the Slavs, who had ensconced themselves in the Pripet Marshes when these dregs of the Continent had been yielded up to man by the retreating ice-cap. Here they went on living the primitive life of European barbarism century after century, and, when the Teutonic Völkerwanderung ended the long Hellenic drama which the Achaean Völkerwanderung had begun, there these Slavs still were.

At this late hour of the European barbarians' day the Slavs were at last routed out of their fastness by the nomad Avars, who had been tempted to stray beyond the limits of their native Eurasian Steppe in order to take a hand in the Teutons' game of pillaging and wrecking the Roman Empire. In the strange environment of an agricultural world these lost children of the Steppe sought to adapt their old manner of life to their new circumstances. On the Steppe the Avars had made their living as herdsmen of cattle; in the cultivated lands on which they had now trespassed these herdsmen found that the appropriate local livestock was a human peasantry, and they therefore set themselves, rationally enough, to become herdsmen of human beings. Just as they would have raided their nomadic neighbours' cattle in order to stock some newly conquered pastureland, so they now looked round for a human breed of cattle to re-stock the depopulated provinces of the Roman Empire that had fallen into their hands. They found what they wanted in the Slavs, herded them into droves, and stationed them in a vast circle round the Hungarian Plain on which they pitched their own camp. This, it appears, was the process by which the western vanguard of the Slav host—the forefathers of the present Czechs, Slovaks and Jugoslavs—made their belated and humiliating début in history.

This contrast between the Achaeans and the Slavs shows that, for a primitive society, complete immunity from the challenge of encounters with civilizations is a very serious handicap. It shows, in fact, that this challenge has a stimulating effect when its severity is of a certain degree. But suppose that we accentuate the challenge; suppose that we raise the degree of energy which the Minoan Society radiated to higher potencies. Shall we thereby elicit a response even more brilliant than that of the Achaean fathers of Hellenism, or will the 'law of diminishing returns' again come into play? On this point we need not speculate in a void, for between the Achaeans and the Slavs there have lain several other layers of barbarians who have been exposed to the radiation of various civilizations in various degrees. What became of them?

One instance in which European barbarians have succumbed to a radiation of destructive intensity has come to our notice already. We have seen how the Celts were eventually exterminated or subjected or assimilated after a transitory outburst of energy in response to a stimulus which the Celts had received through the medium of the Etruscans. We have contrasted the ultimate failure of the Celts with the relative success of the Teutons in holding their own against the Hellenic impact. We have noted that the Teutonic layer of European barbarians, unlike the Celtic layer,

resisted the disintegrating action of Hellenism to such effect that
the Teutons were able to take their place in the external proletariat of the Hellenic World and to dispatch the Hellenic Society
in its death agonies with the *coup de grâce*. By comparison with
the Celtic *débâcle* this Teutonic reaction was a success; but as
soon as we compare the Teutonic achievement with the Achaean
we are reminded that the Teutons won nothing better than a
Pyrrhic victory. They came in at the death of the Hellenic Society
only to receive their own death-blow, on the spot, from the rival
proletarian heirs of the defunct society. The victor on this field
was not the Teutonic war-band but the Roman Catholic Church
into which the internal proletariat of the Hellenic Society had
incorporated itself. Before the close of the seventh century of
the Christian Era every one of those Arian or heathen Teutonic
war-bands that had ventured to trespass on Roman ground had
been either converted to Catholicism or wiped out of existence.
The new civilization, affiliated to the Hellenic, was related to its
predecessor through the internal and not through the external
proletariat. Western Christendom was essentially the creation of
the Catholic Church—in contrast to Hellenism, which was
essentially the creation of the Achaean barbarians.

Let us now arrange our present series of challenges in the order
of an ascending scale of severity. The Slavs were long immune
from the challenge altogether and were patently the worse for
being without the stimulus. The Achaeans received what, to
judge from their response, must be regarded as the optimum
challenge. The Teutons held their own against the challenge of
the Hellenic Civilization but were subsequently worsted by the
challenge of Catholicism. The Celts, encountering the Hellenic
Society in its prime—in contrast to the Teutons, who encountered
it in its decline—were overwhelmed by it. The Slavs and the
Celts experienced the extremes—an insipid immunity on the one
hand and an overwhelming bombardment on the other. The
Achaeans and the Teutons occupy the position of 'middle terms'
in a comparison which, this time, contains four terms instead of
three; but the mean in the sense of the optimum experience was
that of the Achaeans.

(3) TWO ABORTIVE CIVILIZATIONS

The 'Rearguard' of the Teutonic Völkerwanderung

Is it possible to define more closely the point at which the law
of diminishing returns is brought into play in the series of challenges between radiating civilizations and European barbarians?

It is; for there are two examples which we have not yet taken into account. These are the conflict between the Roman Church, as parent of our Western Society, and the abortive Far Western Christendom of 'the Celtic Fringe', and the conflict between our Western Society in its early stages and the Far Northern or Scandinavian Society of the Vikings. In both these conflicts the antagonist was a barbarian 'rearguard' which had always remained beyond the range of Roman rule and had held itself in reserve at the time when the Teutonic vanguard was plunging its sword into the dying body of the Hellenic Society—to destroy and, as it turned out, to be destroyed. Moreover both these rearguards achieved a degree of success which, while falling short of that of the Achaeans, greatly surpassed that of the Teutons who come next below the Achaeans in our four-term comparison as at present stated. The Achaeans succeeded in producing a great civilization supplanting the Minoan Civilization which they attacked. The Teutonic vanguard enjoyed a transitory 'good time' in the congenial orgy of destruction, but achieved nothing, or almost nothing, of positive value. The Far Western Christians and the Far Northern Vikings, on the other hand, each got as far as begetting a civilization, but in each case the embyro succumbed to a challenge which proved too strong for it. We have already referred by implication more than once to the existence of abortive civilizations—civilizations which we did not include in our original list because the essence of a civilization is to be found in its achievement of maturity, whereas these are victims of 'infant mortality'. The course of our argument now presents an opportunity for examining two of them.[1]

The Abortive Far Western Christian Civilization

The Celtic Fringe reacted to Christianity in a way that was all its own. Unlike the Gothic converts to Arianism or the Anglo-Saxon converts to Catholicism these Celts did not take the alien religion as they happened to find it. Instead of allowing it to break up their native tradition they moulded it to fit their own barbarian social heritage. 'No other race', says Renan, 'showed such originality in its way of taking Christianity.' Perhaps we can discern this even in the reactions of the Christianized Celts of Britain under Roman rule. We know very little about them, but we know that they produced, in Pelagius, a heresiarch who made a

[1] In the following chapter we shall come across yet another and different group: the 'arrested civilizations'. These will be found to be victims, not of 'infant mortality', but of 'infantile paralysis'. They are civilizations which came to birth, but failed, like certain children of fairyland (Peter Pan, for example), to grow up.

stir throughout the Christian World of his day. More important in
the long run than Pelagianism, however, was the work of Pelagius's
fellow countryman and contemporary Patrick, who carried Christianity beyond the frontier of the Roman World to Ireland.

The English transmarine Völkerwanderung (the Anglo-Saxon
invasion of Britain), which dealt the British Celts a crushing blow,
made the Irish Celts' fortune. Its effect was to segregate Ireland,
in the period immediately after the seeds of Christianity had been
sown there, from those former Roman provinces in Western
Europe in which a new Christian civilization, oriented towards
Rome, was developing. It was this segregation, at the most forma-
tive stage of early growth, that made it possible for the embryo
of a separate and distinctive 'Far Western Christian Society', with
its nucleus in Ireland, to emerge simultaneously with the emergence of the nascent Continental Western Christendom. The
originality of this Far Western Christendom is manifest alike in
its ecclesiastical organization, in its ritual and hagiography, and in
its literature and art.

Within a hundred years of St. Patrick's mission (which may be
dated A.D. 432–61) the Irish Church had not only developed its distinctive features but had in many respects shot ahead of Continental Catholicism. This is proved by the warmth of the welcome
which, when the period of segregation was over, Irish missionaries
and scholars received in Britain and on the Continent and by the
eagerness with which British and Continental students sought out
the Irish schools. The period of Irish cultural superiority extends
from the date of the foundation of the monastic university at Clon-
macnois in Ireland in A.D. 548 to the foundation of the Irish
monastery of St. James at Ratisbon in 1090. But this transmission
of culture was not the only social consequence of the renewal of
contact between Insular and Continental Christendom. Another
consequence was a contest for power. The issue at stake was
whether the future civilization of Western Europe should derive
from an Irish or from a Roman embryo; and on this issue the Irish
were defeated long before they lost their cultural ascendancy.

The struggle was brought to a head in the seventh century by a
competition between the disciples of St. Augustine of Canterbury
and those of St. Columba of Iona for the conversion of the Angles
of Northumbria—the dramatic encounter of their representatives
at the Synod of Whitby (A.D. 664) and the Northumbrian king's
decision in favour of St. Wilfrid, the champion of Rome. The
Roman victory was clinched almost immediately when Theodore
of Tarsus came over from the Continent as Archbishop of Canterbury to organize the Church in England on the Roman diocesan

system with metropolitan sees at Canterbury and York. In the course of the next half-century all the communities of the Celtic Fringe—Picts, Irish, Welsh and Bretons, and lastly Iona itself— accepted the Roman tonsure and the Roman method of calculating the date of Easter, which had been the points formally in dispute at Whitby. But there were other differences which did not entirely disappear until the twelfth century.

From the time of the Synod of Whitby onwards the Far Western Civilization was isolated and doomed. It suffered severely from the Viking raids on Ireland in the ninth century of the Christian Era, when not a single Irish monastery escaped pillage. So far as is known, not a single work in Latin was written in Ireland in the ninth century, though at this very time the scholarship of the Irish refugees on the Continent stood at its zenith. The Scandinavian challenge, which was literally the making of England and France because it stimulated the English and French peoples to the optimum degree, presented itself to Ireland in her renewed isolation with such excessive severity that she could win no more than a Pyrrhic victory—the defeat of the invaders by Brian Boru at Clontarf. The final blow was the opening of the Anglo-Norman conquest of Ireland by the Angevin king Henry II, with a Papal blessing, in the middle of the twelfth century. Instead of founding a new civilization of their own it was the fate of the spiritual pioneers of the Celtic Fringe to be laid under contribution by the very competitors who were robbing them of their birthright of independent creation. Irish scholarship was made to minister to the progress of the Continental Western Civilization when Irish scholars, fleeing from Ireland as refugees from Scandinavian onslaughts, were enlisted in the service of the Carolingian Renaissance, in which Johannes Scotus Erigena, the Irish Hellenist, philosopher and theologian, was undoubtedly the greatest figure.

The Abortive Scandinavian Civilization

It will be seen that, in the contest between Rome and Ireland for the privilege of becoming the creator of the new Western Civilization, Rome only just succeeded in gaining the upper hand. And while the nascent Western Christendom was still in its infancy it had to engage, after the briefest breathing-space, in a second struggle for the same prize—this time in conflict with the Teutonic rearguard of the North European barbarians which had been holding itself in reserve in Scandinavia. This time the circumstances were more formidable. The trial was made on the military as well as on the cultural plane, and the two contending parties were severally stronger and also more alien from one another than the rival Irish and Roman embryos of a future Western Christendom had found themselves two centuries earlier.

The histories of the Scandinavians and of the Irish, before their respective contests with Western Christendom began, run parallel to this extent, that both had enjoyed a period of isolation from their future antagonist. The Irish Christians had been isolated by the irruption of Anglo-Saxon pagans into England. The Scandinavians were isolated from Roman Christendom before the end of the sixth century of the Christian Era by the interposition of the pagan Slavs who drifted overland along the southern shores of the Baltic from the line of the Niemen to the line of the Elbe, into the vacuum left by the emigration of the Teutonic barbarians who had evacuated this region because they had been involved in the post-Hellenic Völkerwanderung while the Scandinavians had stayed at home. Thus the Irish found themselves isolated from their fellow Christians and the Scandinavians from their fellow Teutons by wedges of more barbarous interlopers. There was, however, a fundamental difference. Whilst the previous radiation out of the Roman Empire had kindled among the Irish, before the Anglo-Saxon irruption, a spark of Christianity which burst into flame during the period of isolation, the Scandinavians remained pagans.

The Scandinavian Völkerwanderung, like other Völkerwanderungen, was the reaction of a barbarian society to the impact of a civilization, in this case embodied in Charlemagne's empire. This empire proved a fiasco because it was both grandiose and premature. It was an ambitious political superstructure piled up recklessly on rudimentary social and economic foundations; and the arch-instance of its unsoundness was the *tour de force* of Charlemagne's conquest of Saxony. When Charlemagne set out in A.D. 772 to bring Saxony within the fold of Roman Christendom by military conquest, he was making a disastrous breach with the policy of peaceful penetration, conducted by Irish and English missionaries for a century past, which had effectively extended the borders of Christendom by converting the Bavarians, Thuringians, Hessians and Frisians. The ordeal of the Franco-Saxon thirty years' war overstrained the weak tissues of the nascent Western Society and aroused in the souls of the Scandinavians the same *furor barbaricus* that had once been awakened in the souls of the Celts when the ambitious expansion of the Etruscans came to a halt at the foot of the Alps.

The Scandinavian expansion in the eighth to eleventh centuries after Christ surpassed the Celtic expansion of the fifth to third centuries B.C. both in extension and in intensity. The abortive envelopment of the Hellenic World by the Celts which had carried their right wing into the heart of Spain and their left wing into the heart of Asia Minor was dwarfed by the operations of the Vikings, who threatened Orthodox as well as Western Christendom by extending their left wing into Russia and their right into North America. Again, the two Christian civilizations were in greater jeopardy when the Vikings were attempting to force their way along the Thames, the Seine and the Bosphorus past London, Paris and Constantinople than was the Hellenic Civilization when the Celts were momentarily masters of Rome and Macedonia. Again, the abortive Scandinavian Civilization which began to unfold itself in Iceland before its chill beauty was melted into formlessness by the warm breath of Christianity, far surpassed in both achievement and promise the rudimentary Celtic culture, relics of which have been discovered by modern archaeologists.[1]

It is of the nature of the method pursued in this study that the same historical events should recur in different contexts. We have already described the challenge presented by the Scandinavian invasions to the peoples of England and France and shown that they rose victoriously to that challenge by achieving their own unity and, still more, by converting the Scandinavian settlers and incorporating them into their own civilization (see p. 123). Just as, after the doom of the Celtic Christian culture, its sons contributed to the enrichment of Roman Christendom, so the Normans became the spearhead of Latin aggression two centuries later. Indeed a historian has described the First Crusade, in a vivid oxymoron, as a Christianized Viking expedition. We have also described the significance of Iceland in the life of the abortive Scandinavian Civilization and speculated on the strange results that might have followed if the Scandinavian pagans had equalled the achievement of the Achaeans and, driving Christianity underground, had established throughout Western Europe their own pagan culture as the one and only successor of the Hellenic Civilization in that area. We have still to glance at the conquest and extinction of the Scandinavian Civilization in its own homelands.

This conquest was achieved by a reversion to the tactics which Charlemagne had discarded. The self-defence of Western Christendom had been conducted, perforce, on military lines, but, as soon as the militant Western defensive had brought the militant Scandinavian offensive to a halt, the Westerners resumed the tactics of peaceful penetration. After converting, and thus seducing from their original allegiance, the Scandinavian settlers in Western

---

[1] The 'La Tène culture', so named from the site at the outflow of the Lake of Neuchâtel where the first striking remains of it were discovered.

Christian lands, Western Christendom applied the same tactics to the Scandinavians who had remained at home. And at this point one of the outstanding virtues of the Scandinavians assisted in their undoing—their remarkable receptivity: a characteristic noticed by a contemporary Western Christian scholar and expressed by him in a couple of rather bad hexameters:[1] They take over the customs and language of those who join their standards, so that the result is a single race.'

It is curious, for example, to find that Scandinavian rulers, even before their conversion to Christianity, made a hero out of Charlemagne and showed an inclination to name their sons Karlus or Magnus. If in the same generation Muhammad and 'Umar had become favourite christian names among the rulers of Western Christendom, we should certainly have concluded that this new fashion boded ill for the prospects of Western Christendom in its struggle with Islam.

In the Scandinavian kingdoms of Russia, Denmark and Norway the formal outward act of conversion to Christianity was imposed upon the people wholesale by the arbitrary fiat of three Scandinavian princes who reigned contemporaneously near the end of the tenth century. In Norway there was at first a strenuous resistance, but in Denmark and Russia the change was accepted with apparent passivity. Thus the Scandinavian Society was not only conquered but was partitioned, for Orthodox Christendom, which had borne its share of the Viking onslaught, shared also in the religious and cultural counter-offensive which followed.

'The ambassadors or merchants of [the Scandinavian principality of] Russia compared the idolatry of the woods with the elegant superstition of Constantinople. They had gazed with admiration on the dome of St. Sophia: the lively pictures of saints and martyrs, the riches of the altar, the number and vestments of the priests, the pomp and order of the ceremonies; they were edified by the alternate succession of devout silence and harmonious song; nor was it difficult to persuade them that a choir of angels descended each day from Heaven to join in the devotion of the Christians.'[2]

The conversion of Iceland itself followed almost immediately in the year 1000, and it was the beginning of the end of the Icelandic culture. It is true that the subsequent Icelandic scholars who committed the Sagas to writing, collected the Eddic poems and made the classic digests of Scandinavian mythology, genealogy

[1] Moribus et lingua, quoscumque venire videbant,
Informant propria, gens efficiatur ut una.
William of Apulia, *De Gestis Normanorum*, in Muratori, *Scriptores Rerum Italicarum*.
[2] Gibbon, E.: *The History of the Decline and Fall of the Roman Empire*, ch. lv.

and law were all endowed with a Christian as well as a Northern cultural heritage; they did their work some hundred and fifty to two hundred and fifty years after the conversion. But this backward-looking scholarship was the last feat of the Icelandic genius. We may contrast the role of the Homeric poems in Hellenic history. These also were a work of 'backward-looking scholarship' in that they were not given literary form by 'Homer' until after the heroic age which had inspired them was over. But the Hellenic genius, having achieved the epics, passed on to further achievements of equal magnitude in other fields, whereas the Icelandic achievement petered out after reaching its 'Homeric' peak about A.D. 1150–1250.

(4) THE IMPACT OF ISLAM ON THE CHRISTENDOMS

To conclude this part of our inquiry let us see whether the impacts of Islam upon the Christendoms will furnish yet another of those 'comparisons in three terms' with which the reader is by this time familiar. We have already noticed in another connexion a challenge from Islam which evoked an optimum response. The challenge presented to the Franks in the eighth century of the Christian Era evoked a counter-offensive extending over many centuries which not only drove the adherents of Islam out of the Iberian Peninsula but also, travelling on beyond its original objective, carried the Spaniards and Portuguese overseas to all the continents of the world. In this case, too, we may notice a phenomenon which we have already observed in considering the defeat of the Far Western and Scandinavian civilizations. Before it was entirely rooted out and destroyed the Iberian Muslim culture was exploited for the benefit of its victorious antagonist. The scholars of Muslim Spain contributed unintentionally to the philosophical edifice erected by the medieval Western Christian schoolmen, and some of the works of the Hellenic philosopher Aristotle first reached the Western Christian World through Arabic translations. It is also true that many 'Oriental' influences on Western culture which have been attributed to infiltration through the Crusaders' principalities in Syria really came from Muslim Iberia.

The Muslim attack on Western Christendom through Iberia and over the Pyrenees was not really as formidable as it looked, owing to the length of the line of communications between this front and the fountain-heads of Islamic energy in South-Western Asia, and it is not difficult to find a quarter in which the lines of communication were shorter and the Muslim attack proved in consequence too severe. This region is Anatolia, at that time the citadel of the Orthodox Christian Civilization. In the first phase of their attack the Arab aggressors sought to put 'Rūm' (as they called it, i.e. 'Rome') out of action and to overwhelm Orthodox Christendom altogether by striking right across Anatolia at the Imperial City itself. Constantinople was unsuccessfully besieged by the Muslims in A.D. 673–7 and again in 717–18. Even after the failure of the second siege, when the frontier between the two Powers settled down along the line of the Taurus Mountains, what remained of the Anatolian domain of Orthodox Christendom was regularly raided by the Muslims twice a year.

The Orthodox Christians responded to this pressure by a political expedient; and this response was successful on a short view, inasmuch as it availed to keep the Arabs at bay. On a long view, on the other hand, it was unfortunate on account of its pernicious effects on the inward life and growth of the Orthodox Christian Society. The expedient was the evocation of a 'ghost' of the Roman Empire in the Orthodox Christian World by Leo the Syrian, about two generations before the same feat was attempted unsuccessfully (and therefore more or less innocuously) by Charlemagne in the West. The most disastrous effect of Leo the Syrian's achievement was the aggrandizement of the Byzantine State, at the expense of the Orthodox Church, and the consequent internecine hundred years' war between the Eastern Roman Empire and Patriarchate on the one side and the Bulgarian Empire and Patriarchate on the other. This self-inflicted wound was the death of the Orthodox Christian Society in its original form and its original home. These facts suffice to show that the challenge presented by the Islamic impact to Orthodox Christendom, unlike its challenge to Western Christendom, was excessive.

Can we find a case in which the Islamic impact failed to stimulate through being insufficiently severe? We can; for the results are to be seen to this day in Abyssinia. The Monophysite Christian community which has survived in this African fastness has become one of the social curiosities of the world: first, on account of its sheer survival, in almost complete isolation from other Christian communities, ever since the Muslim Arabs conquered Egypt thirteen centuries ago, and secondly on account of its extraordinarily low cultural level. Though Christian Abyssinia was admitted, with some hesitation, to membership in the League of Nations, she was a byword for disorder and barbarism: the disorder of feudal and tribal anarchy and the barbarism of the slave-trade. In fact, the spectacle presented by the one African state, apart from Liberia, that had retained its complete independence was perhaps the best justification that could be found for the partitioning of the rest of Africa among the European Powers.

Consideration shows that the peculiarities of Abyssinia—the survival of her independence and the stagnation of her culture—both derive from the same cause: the virtual impregnability of the highland fastness in which this fossil is ensconced. The wave of Islam and the mightier wave of our modern Western Civilization have washed round the foot of the escarpment and momentarily broken over its crest without ever permanently submerging the summit.

The occasions on which these hostile waves have swept up on to the highlands have been few and brief. Abyssinia was in danger of Muslim conquest in the first half of the sixteenth century, when the Muslim inhabitants of the lowlands on the Red Sea coast forestalled the Abyssinians in the acquisition of fire-arms; but the newfangled weapons which the Somalis had acquired from the 'Osmanlis reached the Abyssinians from the Portuguese just in time to save them from destruction. Thereafter, when the Portuguese had served their turn and begun to make themselves a nuisance by trying to convert the Abyssinians from Monophysitism to Catholicism, the Western version of Christianity was suppressed and all Western visitors were expelled from the country in the sixteen-thirties—at the same time as a similar policy was being carried out by Japan.

The British Abyssinian expedition of 1868 proved a complete success but was without ulterior consequences—unlike the 'opening of Japan' by the American navy fifteen years earlier. However, at the time of the 'scramble for Africa' in the last years of the nineteenth century, some European Power was bound to tackle Abyssinia, and the Italians made the attempt. This time the part played by the Portuguese two-and-a-half centuries before was played by the French, who supplied the Emperor Menelik with breech-loading rifles which enabled him to inflict a resounding defeat on the Italian invader at Adowa in 1896. When the Italians —malignantly fortified by the deliberate cultivation of a neo-barbarism in themselves—returned to the charge with greater resolution in 1935, it looked for the moment as though they had succeeded in putting an end to the ancient impregnability of Abyssinia as well as to the new-born promise of collective security for a tormented Western World. But within four years of the proclamation of an Italian Empire of Ethiopia Mussolini's intervention in the general war of 1939–45 had impelled the British— who had refrained from coming to Abyssinia's assistance in 1935-6 for the sake of saving the League of Nations—to save their own skins in 1941–2 by performing for Abyssinia, after all, the same obliging service that the French and the Portuguese had performed for her in previous emergencies.

These four foreign attacks are all that Abyssinia has had to face during the sixteen centuries since her adoption of Christianity, and the first three, at any rate, were repelled too quickly to be stimulating. Otherwise her experience has been a blank, and might serve as a refutation of the saying that the nation is happy which has no history. Her record contains little but monotonous and meaningless violence against a background of apathy, a word which, in the original Greek,[1] means invulnerability to the pains of experience or, in other words, imperviousness to its stimulus. In 1946, notwithstanding the valiant efforts at reform that were then being made by the Emperor Haile Selassie and his band of liberal-minded lieutenants, it remained to be seen whether the fourth foreign attack on Abyssinia would have any more stimulating effect than its predecessors.

[1] For the philosophic ideals of invulnerability and imperturbability, see p. 438 below.

III

THE GROWTHS OF CIVILIZATIONS

IX. THE ARRESTED CIVILIZATIONS

(1) POLYNESIANS, ESKIMOS AND NOMADS

IN the preceding part of this Study we have been wrestling with the admittedly difficult question of how civilizations come into existence, but the problem now before us might be thought to be too easy to deserve consideration as a problem at all. Once a civilization is born, and provided that it is not nipped in the bud, as has been the fate of what we have called abortive civilizations, may not its growth be expected as a matter of course? The best way to find an answer to this question is to ask another one: Do we find, as a matter of historical fact, that civilizations which have surmounted the successive perils of birth and of infancy do in fact invariably grow to 'manhood'—in other words, do they invariably proceed in due course to achieve a control over their environment and way of life which justifies us in including them in the list compiled in the second chapter of this book? The answer is that some do not. In addition to the two classes already noticed, developed civilizations and abortive civilizations, there is a third, which we must call arrested civilizations. It is the existence of civilizations which have kept alive but failed to grow that compels us to study the problem of growth; and our first step will be to collect and study the available specimens of civilizations of this category.

We can readily lay hands on half-a-dozen specimens. Among the civilizations that have come to birth in response to physical challenges there are the Polynesians, the Eskimos and the Nomads, and among civilizations that have arisen in response to human challenges there are certain peculiar communities, like the 'Osmanlis in the Orthodox Christian World and the Spartans in the Hellenic World, which have been called into existence by local accentuations of the prevalent human challenges when these have been keyed up, through peculiar circumstances, to pitches of unusual severity. These are all examples of arrested civilizations, and we can see at once that they all present a picture of the same general predicament.

All these arrested civilizations have been immobilized in consequence of having achieved a *tour de force*. They are responses to challenges of an order of severity on the very borderline between the degree that affords stimulus to further development and the degree that entails defeat. In the imagery of our fable of the climbers' pitch (see pp. 49–50) they are like climbers who have been brought up short and can go neither backward nor forward. Their posture is one of perilous immobility at high tension; and we may add that four out of the five we have mentioned were in the end compelled to accept defeat. Only one of them, the Eskimo culture, is still maintaining itself.

The Polynesians, for instance, ventured upon the *tour de force* of audacious oceanic voyaging. Their skill was to perform these stupendous voyages in frail open canoes. Their penalty was to remain, for an unknown but undoubtedly lengthy period of time, in exact equilibrium with the Pacific—just able to cross its vast empty spaces, but never able to cross them with any margin of security or ease—until the intolerable tension found its own relief by going slack, with the result that these former peers of the Minoans and the Vikings had degenerated into incarnations of the Lotus-eaters and Doasyoulikes, losing their grip upon the ocean and resigning themselves to being marooned, each in his own insular paradise, until the Western mariner descended upon them. We need not dwell here upon the Polynesians' latter end, since we have touched upon it already apropos of Easter Island (see p. 83).

As for the Eskimos, their culture was a development of the North American Indian way of life specially adapted to the conditions of life round the shores of the Arctic Ocean. The Eskimos' *tour de force* was to stay at or on the ice in the winter and hunt seals. Whatever the historical incentive may have been, it is evident that, at some point in their history, the forefathers of the Eskimos grappled audaciously with the Arctic environment and adapted their life to its exigencies with consummate skill. To prove this assertion it is only necessary to recite the catalogue of the material appliances which the Eskimos have elaborated or invented: 'kayak, umiak (women's boat), harpoon and bird-dart with throwing-board, the three-pronged salmon-spear, the compound bow, strengthened by a backing of sinews, the dog sledge, the snow-shoe, the winter house and the snow house with the lamps for burning blubber oil, and the platform, the summer tent and lastly the skin garments'.[1]

These are the outward and visible signs of an amazing feat of wit and will; and yet

'in certain directions, for instance as regards social organization, the

[1] Steensby, H. P.: *An Anthropological Study of the Origin of the Eskimo Culture*, p. 43.

Eskimo display somewhat inferior development. But it is a question whether this inferior social differentiation is due to primitiveness, or whether it is not rather a result of the natural conditions under which the Eskimo have lived from time immemorial. No deep knowledge of the Eskimo culture is needed to see that it is a culture which has been obliged to employ an immensely large part of its force simply to develop the means wherewith to gain a livelihood.'[1]

The penalty which the Eskimos have had to pay for their audacity in grappling with the Arctic environment has been the rigid conformation of their lives to the annual cycle of the Arctic climate. All the bread-winners of the tribe are obliged to carry on different occupations at the different seasons of the year, and the tyranny of Arctic Nature imposes almost as exacting a time-table on the Arctic hunter as is imposed on any factory worker by the human tyranny of 'scientific management'. Indeed, we may be inclined to ask ourselves whether the Eskimos are the masters of Arctic Nature or her slaves. We shall meet with an equivalent question, and we shall find it equally difficult to answer, when we come to examine the lives of the Spartans and the 'Osmanlis. But we must first consider the fate of another arrested civilization which has been evoked, like that of the Eskimos, by a physical challenge.

While the Eskimos grappled with the ice and the Polynesians with the ocean, the Nomad, who has taken up the challenge of the Steppe, has had the audacity to grapple with an equally intractable element; and indeed, in its relationship to man, the Steppe, with its surface of grass and gravel, actually bears a greater resemblance to 'the unharvested sea' (as Homer so often calls it) than it bears to *terra firma* that is amenable to hoe and plough. Steppe-surface and water-surface have this in common, that they are both accessible to man only as a pilgrim and a sojourner. Neither offers him anywhere on its broad surface, apart from islands and oases, a place where he can settle down to a sedentary existence. Both provide strikingly greater facilities for travel and transport than those parts of the Earth's surface on which human communities are accustomed to make their permanent homes, but both exact, as a penalty for trespassing on them, the necessity of constantly moving on, or else moving off their surface altogether on to the coasts of *terra firma* which surround them. Thus there is a real similarity between the Nomadic horde which annually follows the same orbit of summer and winter pasture-ranges and the fishing fleet which cruises from bank to bank according to the season; between the convoys of merchantmen which exchange

---

[1] Steensby, op. cit., p. 42.

the products of opposite shores of the sea and the camel caravans by which opposite shores of the Steppe are linked with one another; between the water-pirate and the desert-raider; and between those explosive movements of population which impel Minoans or Norsemen to take ship and break like tidal waves on the coasts of Europe or the Levant and those other movements which impel Nomad Arabs or Scyths or Turks or Mongols to swing out of their annual orbits and break with equal violence and suddenness upon the settled lands of Egypt or 'Iraq or Russia or India or China.

It will be seen that the Nomads', like the Polynesians' and the Eskimos', response to the challenge of physical nature is a *tour de force*, and in this case, unlike the other cases, the historical incentive is not altogether a matter of conjecture. We are entitled to infer that Nomadism was evoked by the same challenge that evoked the Egyptiac and Sumeric and Minoan Civilizations and that drove the forefathers of the Dinka and Shilluk into Equatoria —namely, desiccation. The clearest light that we have as yet on the origins of Nomadism has been thrown by the researches of the Pumpelly Expedition in the Transcaspian oasis of Anau.

Here we find the challenge of desiccation, in its first incidence, stimulating certain communities which had previously lived by hunting to eke out their livelihood in less favourable conditions by taking to a rudimentary form of agriculture. The evidence shows that this agricultural stage definitely preceded Nomadism.

Agriculture also had another—indirect but not less important— effect upon the social history of these *ci-devant* hunters; it gave them an opportunity of entering into an altogether new relation towards wild animals. For the art of domesticating wild animals, which the hunter, by the very nature of his occupation, is unable to develop beyond very narrow limits, has vastly greater possibilities for the agriculturist. The hunter may conceivably domesticate the wolf or the jackal with whom he disputes or shares his prey by turning the wild beast into a partner, but it is almost inconceivable that he should domesticate the game which is his quarry. It is not the hunter with his hound but the agriculturist with his watch-dog who has it in his power to accomplish the further transformation which produces the shepherd and his sheep-dog. It is the agriculturist who possesses food-supplies which are attractive to ruminants like the ox or the sheep, that would not, like dogs, be attracted by the huntsman's meat.

Archaeological evidence at Anau indicates that this further step in social evolution had been accomplished in Transcaspia by the time when Nature gave her screw of desiccation its second turn. By achieving the domestication of ruminants, Eurasian man had potentially recovered the mobility which he had forfeited in his previous metamorphosis from hunter into cultivator, and in response to the further incidence of the old challenge he made use of his new-found mobility in two quite different ways. Some of the Transcaspian oasis-cultivators simply used their mobility in order to emigrate progressively—moving ever farther on as the climatic trend towards desiccation increased in severity—so as always to keep abreast of the physical environment in which they could continue to practise their existing way of life. They changed their habitat in order not to change their habits. But others parted company with them in order to respond to the same challenge in a more audacious fashion. These other Eurasians likewise abandoned the now untenable oases and launched themselves and their families and flocks and herds upon the inhospitable surface of the Steppe. These others, however, did not embark as fugitives seeking a farther shore. They abandoned their former staple of agriculture as their ancestors had abandoned their former staple of hunting, and staked their existence on their latest acquired art, that of the stock-breeder. They flung themselves upon the Steppe, not to escape beyond its bounds but to make themselves at home on it. They became Nomads.

When we compare the civilization of the Nomad who has abandoned agriculture and held his ground on the Steppe with the civilizations of his brethren who have preserved their agricultural heritage by changing their habitat, we shall observe that Nomadism displays a superiority in several ways. In the first place the domestication of animals is obviously a higher art than the domestication of plants, inasmuch as it is a triumph of human wit and will over a less tractable material. The shepherd is a greater virtuoso than the husbandman, and this truth has been expressed in a famous passage of Syriac mythology.

'Adam knew Eve his wife; and she conceived, and bare Cain. . . . And she again bare his brother Abel. And Abel was a keeper of sheep, but Cain was a tiller of the ground. And in process of time it came to pass that Cain brought of the fruit of the ground an offering unto the Lord. And Abel, he also brought of the firstlings of his flock and of the fat thereof. And the Lord had respect unto Abel and to his offering; but unto Cain and to his offering he had not respect.'[1]

The Nomad's life is, indeed, a triumph of human skill. He manages to live off coarse grasses that he cannot eat himself by transforming them into the milk and flesh of his tame animals, and in order to find subsistence for his cattle, in season and out of season, from the natural vegetation of the bare and parsimonious

---

[1] Genesis iv. 1–5.

Steppe he has to adapt his life and movements with meticulous accuracy to a seasonal time-table. In fact the *tour de force* of Nomadism demands a rigorously high standard of character and behaviour, and the penalty that the Nomad has had to pay is essentially the same as the Eskimo's. The formidable environment which he has succeeded in conquering has insidiously enslaved him. The Nomads, like the Eskimos, have become the prisoners of an annual climatic and vegetational cycle; in acquiring the initiative on the Steppe they have forfeited the initiative in the world at large. They have not, indeed, passed across the stage of the histories of civilizations without having left their mark. From time to time they have broken out of their own domain into the domains of neighbouring sedentary civilizations, and on some of these occasions they have momentarily carried all before them; but these outbreaks have never been spontaneous. When the Nomad has issued from the Steppe and trespassed on the cultivator's garden, he has not been moved by a deliberate intention to depart from his customary cycle. He has responded mechanically to forces beyond his control.

There are two such external forces to which he is subject: one force which pushes and another force which pulls. He is sometimes pushed off the Steppe by an increase of desiccation which puts his former habitat beyond even his powers of endurance; and again he is occasionally pulled out of the Steppe by the suction of a social vacuum which has arisen in the domain of some adjacent sedentary society through the operation of historic processes such as the breakdown of a sedentary civilization and the consequent Völkerwanderung—causes which are quite extraneous to the Nomad's own experiences. A survey of the great historic interventions of the Nomads in the histories of the sedentary societies seems to show that all these interventions can be traced to one or other of these causes.[1]

Thus, in spite of these occasional incursions into the field of historical events, Nomadism is essentially a society without a history. Once launched on its annual orbit, the Nomadic horde revolves in it thereafter and might go on revolving for ever if an external force against which Nomadism is defenceless did not eventually bring the horde's movements to a standstill and its life to an end. This force is the pressure of the sedentary civilizations round about; for, though the Lord may have respect for Abel and his offering and not for Cain and his, no power can save Abel from being slain by Cain.

[1] Mr. Toynbee makes an exhaustive survey on these lines in a long appendix to this chapter which cannot be reproduced here.—EDITOR.

'Recent meteorological research indicates that there is a rhythmic alternation, possibly of world-wide incidence, between periods of relative desiccation and humidity, which causes alternate intrusions of Peasants and Nomads into one another's spheres. When desiccation reaches a degree at which the Steppe can no longer provide pasture for the quantity of cattle with which the Nomads have stocked it, the herdsmen swerve from their beaten track of annual migration and invade the surrounding cultivated countries in search of food for their animals and themselves. On the other hand, when the climatic pendulum swings back and the next phase of humidity attains a point at which the Steppe becomes capable of bearing cultivated roots and cereals, the Peasant makes his counter-offensive upon the pastures of the Nomad. Their respective methods of aggression are very dissimilar. The Nomad's outbreak is as sudden as a cavalry charge. The Peasant's is an infantry advance. At each step he digs himself in with mattock or steam plough, and secures his communications by building roads or railways. The most striking recorded examples of Nomad explosion are the intrusions of the Turks and Mongols, which occurred in what was probably the last dry period but one. An imposing instance of Peasant encroachment is the subsequent eastward expansion of Russia. Both types of movement are abnormal, and each is extremely unpleasant for the party at whose expense it is made. But they are alike in being due to a single uncontrollable physical cause.

'The relentless pressure of the cultivator is probably more painful in the long run, if one happens to be the victim of it, than the Nomad's savage onslaught. The Mongol raids were over in two or three generations; but the Russian colonization which has been the reprisal for them has been going on for over four hundred years—first behind the Cossack lines, which encircled and narrowed down the pasturelands from the north, and then along the Transcaspian Railway, which stretched its tentacles round their southern border. From the Nomad's point of view, a Peasant Power like Russia resembles those rolling and crushing machines with which Western industrialism shapes hot steel according to its pleasure. In its grip the Nomad is either crushed out of existence or racked into the sedentary mould, and the process of penetration is not always peaceful. The path was cleared for the Transcaspian Railway by the slaughter of Türkmens at Göktepé. But the Nomad's death-cry is seldom heard. During the European War, while people in England were raking up the Ottoman Turks' Nomadic ancestry in order to account for their murder of 600,000 Armenians, 500,000 Turkish-speaking Central Asian Nomads of the Kirghiz Qāzāq Confederacy were being exterminated—also under superior orders—by that "justest of mankind", the Russian muzhik.'[1]

Nomadism was doomed in Eurasia from that moment in the seventeenth century when two sedentary empires, the Muscovite and the Manchu, stretched their tentacles round the Eurasian

---

[1] Toynbee, A. J.: *The Western Question in Greece and Turkey*, pp. 339–42.

Steppe from opposite quarters. To-day our Western Civilization, which has now spread its tentacles over the entire surface of the globe, is completing the extirpation of Nomadism in all its other ancient domains. In Kenya the pasture-lands of the Masai have been cut up and cut down to make way for European farmers. In the Sahara the Imoshagh are seeing their hitherto impenetrable desert fastness invaded by aeroplanes and by the eight-wheeled automobile. Even in Arabia, the classic home of Afrasian Nomadism, the Badu are being forcibly converted into fallāhīn, and this by no alien power but by the deliberate policy of an Arab of the Arabs, ʿAbd-al-Aziz Āl-Saʿūd, the king of the Najd and the Hijāz, and the temporal head of the Wahhābī community of puritanical Muslim zealots. When a Wahhābī potentate in the heart of Arabia is fortifying his authority with armoured cars and solving his economic problems with petrol pumps and artesian wells and concessions to American oil interests, it is evident that the last hour of Nomadism has struck.

Thus Abel has been slain by Cain, and we are left to inquire whether the curse of Cain is duly descending upon his slayer.

'And now art thou cursed from the Earth, which hath opened her mouth to receive thy brother's blood from thy hand; when thou tillest the ground, it shall not henceforth yield unto thee her strength; a fugitive and a vagabond shalt thou be upon the Earth'.[1]

The first clause of Cain's curse has manifestly proved ineffective; for though the oasis-cultivator has certainly found himself unable to raise crops from the desiccated steppe-land, his migrations have carried him into regions whose climatic conditions have favoured him; and thence he has returned, with the driving force of industrialism behind him, to claim Abel's grasslands as his own also. Whether Cain will prove to be the master or the victim of the industrialism that he has created, remains to be seen. In the year 1933, when the new economic world order was threatened with breakdown and dissolution, it seemed not impossible that Abel might be avenged after all; and that *Homo Nomas*, *in articulo mortis*, might yet linger on to see his slayer, *Homo Faber*, go down, distraught, to Sheol.[2]

(2) THE ʿOSMANLIS

So much for the civilizations that have suffered arrest as the penalty for a *tour de force* in response to some physical challenge.

[1] Genesis iv. 11–12.
[2] If Mr. Toynbee had been writing in 1945, as his present editor was, he would have needed to make only superficial alterations in this passage.—EDITOR.

We now pass on to cases in which the superlative challenge has been not physical but human.

The superlative challenge to which the Ottoman system was a response was the geographical transference of a Nomadic community from its native environment on the Steppe to a new environment in which it was confronted with the novel problem of exercising dominion over alien communities of human beings. We have already seen[1] how the Avar Nomads, when they found themselves expatriated from their cattle ranges on the Steppe and stranded *in partibus agricolarum*, tried to deal with the sedentary population which they had conquered as though it were a human flock and sought to transform themselves from shepherds of sheep into shepherds of men. Instead of living off the wild herbage of the Steppe through the transforming medium of tame animals, the Avars (like many other Nomad hordes who have done the same) proposed to live off the cultivated crops of the ploughland through the transforming medium not of animal digestion but of human labour. The analogy is tempting to apply, and it works out in practice up to a point; but the empirical test discovers in it one almost fatal flaw.

On the Steppe the composite society constituted by the Nomads and their non-human flocks is the most suitable instrument that can be devised for dealing with that kind of physical environment; and the Nomad is not, strictly speaking, a parasite on his non-human partners. There is a reasonable exchange of benefits: if the flocks have to yield not only their milk but their meat to the Nomads, the Nomads have in the first instance secured for the flocks their means of livelihood. Neither could exist in any considerable numbers on the Steppe without the aid of the other. On the other hand, in an environment of fields and cities, a composite society of expatriated Nomads and indigenous 'human cattle' is economically unsound, since the 'shepherds of men' are always economically—though not always politically—superfluous and therefore parasitic. From the economic standpoint they have ceased to be shepherds keeping watch over their flocks and have turned into drones exploiting the worker-bees. They have become a non-productive ruling class maintained by the labour of a productive population which would be better off economically if they were not there.

For this reason the empires established by Nomad conquerors have generally suffered rapid decadence and premature extinction. The great Magribī historian Ibn Khaldūn (A.D. 1332–1406) was thinking in terms of Nomad empires when he assessed the average

[1] On p. 152 above.

duration of empires at not more than three generations or a hundred and twenty years. Once the conquest is achieved the Nomad conqueror degenerates because he has passed out of his own element and become economically superfluous, while his human cattle recuperate because they have remained on their own ground and not ceased to be economically productive. The 'human cattle' reassert their manhood by expelling or assimilating their shepherd masters. The dominion of the Avars over the Slavs probably lasted less than fifty years, and proved the making of the Slavs and the undoing of the Avars. The empire of the Western Huns lasted no longer than the life-span of a single individual, Attila. The empire of the Mongol Il-Khans in Iran and 'Iraq lasted less than eighty years, and the empire of the Great Khans in Southern China no longer. The Hyksos' (Shepherd Kings') empire in Egypt lasted a bare century. The span of more than two centuries during which the Mongols and their immediate local predecessors, the Kin, ruled continuously over Northern China (*circa* A.D. 1142–1368) and the longer span of over three centuries and a half during which the Parthians were masters of Iran and 'Iraq (*circa* 140 B.C.–A.D. 226/232) were distinctly exceptional.

By these standards of comparison the duration of the Ottoman Empire over the Orthodox Christian World was unique. If we date its establishment from the conquest of Macedonia in A.D. 1372 and the beginning of its end from the Russo-Turkish treaty of Küchük Qaynarjy in A.D. 1774, we shall be assigning it a period of four centuries without reckoning the time it took, before that, to rise and, after that, to fall. What is the explanation of its relative durability? A partial explanation can, no doubt, be found in the fact that the 'Osmanlis, though economically an incubus, served a positive political purpose by providing the Orthodox Christian World with the universal state which it was unable to achieve for itself. But we can carry our explanation much farther than that.

We have seen that the Avars and their like, when they have trespassed from the Desert on to the Sown, have attempted—and failed—to deal with their new situation as 'shepherds of men'. Their failure seems less surprising when we consider that these unsuccessful Nomad empire-builders *in partibus agricolarum* have not attempted to find any sedentary human equivalent for one of the essential partners in the composite society of the Steppe. For this Steppe society does not consist simply of the human shepherd and his flock. In addition to the animals which he keeps in order to live on their products, the Nomad keeps other animals—the dog, the camel, the horse—whose function is to help him in his work. These auxiliary animals are the *chef-d'œuvre* of the Nomadic

Civilization and the key to its success. The sheep and the cow have merely to be tamed, though that is difficult enough, in order to be of service to man. The dog and camel and horse cannot perform their more sophisticated services until they have been not only tamed but trained into the bargain. The training of his non-human auxiliaries is the Nomad's crowning achievement; and it is the adaptation of this higher Nomad art to sedentary conditions that distinguishes the Ottoman Empire from the Avar Empire and accounts for its vastly greater durability. The Ottoman Pādishāhs maintained their empire by training slaves as human auxiliaries to assist them in keeping order among their 'human cattle'.

This remarkable institution of making soldiers and administrators out of slaves—an idea which is so congenial to the Nomad genius and so alien from ours—was not an Ottoman invention. We find it in other Nomad empires over sedentary peoples—and this precisely in those that have had the longest duration.

We catch glimpses of military slavery in the Parthian Empire, for one of the armies that frustrated Mark Antony's ambition to emulate Alexander the Great was reported to have borne only 400 free men on its strength out of 50,000 effectives. In the same way and on the same ground a thousand ears later the 'Abbāsid Caliphs maintained their authority by pur asing Turkish slaves from the Steppe and training them to be soldiers and administrators. The Umayyad Caliphs of Cordova maintained a slave bodyguard recruited for them by their Frankish neighbours. The Franks supplied the Cordovan slave-market by making slave-raids across the opposite frontier of the Frankish dominions. The barbarians thus captured happened to be Slavs; and this is the origin of the word 'slave' in the English language.

A more celebrated example of the same phenomenon, however, was the Mamlūk régime in Egypt. The word mamlūk means in Arabic something possessed or owned, and the Mamlūks were originally the slave warriors of the dynasty founded by Saladin, the Ayyūbids. In A.D. 1250, however, these slaves got rid of their masters and took over the Ayyūbid slave-system on their own account, recruiting their corps not by procreation but by the purchase of relays of slaves from abroad. Behind the façade of a puppet Caliphate this self-owned slave-household ruled Egypt and Syria, and held the redoubtable Mongols in check at the line of the Euphrates, from A.D. 1250 to A.D. 1517, when they met more than their match in the slave-household of the 'Osmanlis. Even that was not the end of them, for under the Ottoman régime in Egypt they were permitted to perpetuate themselves as before, by the same method of training and from the same sources of recruitment. As the Ottoman Power declined the Mamlūk Power reasserted itself, and in the eighteenth century the Ottoman Pasha of Egypt came to be virtually a state-prisoner of the Mamlūks, as the Cairene 'Abbāsid Caliphs had been before the Turkish conquest. At the turn of the eighteenth and nineteenth centuries of the Christian Era it seemed an open question whether the Ottoman heritage in Egypt would revert to the Mamlūks or fall to some European Power—Napoleonic France or England. Actually both these alternatives were ruled out by the genius of the Albanian Muslim adventurer, Mehmed 'Ali, but he found more difficulty in settling with the Mamlūks than in keeping the British and French at bay. It needed all his ability and ruthlessness to exterminate this self-perpetuating slave-corps after it had kept itself alive on the alien soil of Egypt, by constant drafts of Eurasian and Caucasian man-power, for over five hundred years.

In discipline and organization, however, the Mamlūk slave-household was far surpassed by the somewhat younger slave-household created by the Ottoman dynasty for the establishment and maintenance of its dominion over the Orthodox Christian World. To exercise dominion over the entire body social of an alien civilization is evidently the hardest task that a Nomad conqueror could set himself, and this audacious enterprise called out, in 'Osmān and his successors down to Suleymān the Magnificent (A.D. 1520–66), a supreme display of the Nomad's social capacities.

The general character of the Ottoman slave-household is conveyed in the following passage from a brilliant study by an American scholar.[1]

'The Ottoman ruling institution included the Sultan and his family, the officers of his household, the executive officers of the Government, the standing army of cavalry and infantry and a large body of young men who were being educated for service in the standing army, the Court and the Government. These men wielded the sword, the pen and the sceptre. They conducted the whole of the government except the mere rendering of justice in matters that were controlled by the Sacred Law, and those limited functions that were left in the hands of subject and foreign groups of non-Muslims. The most vital and characteristic features of this institution were, first, that its personnel consisted, with few exceptions, of men born of Christian parents or the sons of such; and, second, that almost every member of the Institution came into it as the Sultan's slave, and remained the Sultan's slave throughout life—no matter to what height of wealth, power and greatness he might attain. . . .

[1] Lybyer, A. H.: *The Government of the Ottoman Empire in the Time of Suleiman the Magnificent*, pp. 36, 45–6, 57–8.

'The royal family . . . may rightly be included in the slave-family [because] the mothers of the Sultan's children were slaves: the Sultan himself was the son of a slave. . . . Long before Suleymān's time, the Sultans had practically ceased either to obtain brides of royal rank or to give the title of wife to the mothers of their children. . . . The Ottoman system deliberately took slaves and made them ministers of state. It took boys from the sheep-run and the plough-tail and made them courtiers and the husbands of princesses; it took young men whose ancestors had borne the Christian name for centuries, and made them rulers in the greatest of Muhammadan states, and soldiers and generals in invincible armies whose chief joy was to beat down the Cross and elevate the Crescent. . . . Grandly disregarding the fabric of fundamental customs which is called "human nature", and those religious and social prejudices which are thought to be almost as deep as life itself, the Ottoman system took children for ever from parents, discouraged family cares among its members through their most active years, allowed them no certain hold upon property, gave them no definite promise that their sons and daughters would profit by their success and sacrifice, raised and lowered them with no regard for ancestry or previous distinction, taught them a strange law, ethics and religion, and ever kept them conscious of a sword raised above their heads which might put an end at any moment to a brilliant career along a matchless path of human glory.'

The exclusion of the free-born Ottoman aristocracy from the government, which seems to us the strangest part of the system, was justified by results; for when the free Muslims did at last force an entry into the household, in the later years of Suleymān's reign, the system began to break down and the Ottoman Empire entered on its decline.

So long as the system stood intact, recruits were obtained from various Infidel sources of supply: from beyond the frontiers by capture in war, by purchase in the slave-market or by voluntary enlistment; from within the Empire by a periodical levy of children by conscription. The recruits were then put through an elaborate education, with selection and specialization at every stage. Discipline was severe and punishment savage, while on the other hand there was a deliberate and unceasing appeal to ambition. Every boy who entered the Ottoman Pādishāh's slave-household was aware that he was a potential Grand Vizier and that his prospects depended on his prowess as shown in his training.

We have a vivid and detailed description of this educational system in its heyday from a first-hand observer, the Flemish scholar and diplomat Ogier Ghiselin de Busbecq, who was the ambassador of the Hapsburg Court to Suleymān the Magnificent, and his conclusions are as flattering to the 'Osmanlis as they are the reverse towards the methods of contemporary Western Christendom.

'I have', he says, 'envied the Turks this system of theirs. It is always the way of the Turks, whenever they come into possession of a man of uncommonly good parts, to rejoice and be exceeding glad, as though they had found a pearl of great price. And, in bringing out all that there is in him, they leave nothing undone that labour and thought can do—especially where they recognize military aptitude. Our Western way is different indeed! In the West, if we come into possession of a good dog or hawk or horse, we are delighted, and we spare nothing in our efforts to bring the creature to the highest perfection of which its kind is capable. In the case of a man, however—supposing that we happen to come upon a man of signal endowments—we do not take anything like the same pains, and we do not consider that his education is particularly our business. So we Westerners obtain many sorts of pleasure and service from a well-broken-in horse, dog and hawk, while the Turks obtain from a man whose character has been cultivated by education the vastly greater return that is afforded by the vast superiority and pre-eminence of human nature over the rest of the animal kingdom.'[1]

In the end the system perished because everybody pressed in to share its privileges. Towards the end of the sixteenth century of the Christian Era, admission to the Janissary Corps was made open to all free Muslims except Negroes. Numbers were increased; discipline and efficiency declined. By the middle of the seventeenth century these human watch-dogs had 'returned to nature' by reverting into wolves who harried the Pādishāh's human cattle instead of watching over them and keeping them in order. The Orthodox Christian subject population was now cheated of the *Pax Ottomanica* which had originally reconciled it to bearing the Ottoman yoke. In the great war of A.D. 1682–99 between the Ottoman Empire and the Powers of Western Christendom, a war which ended with the first of a series of losses of Ottoman territory which continued thereafter till A.D. 1922, the superiority in discipline and efficiency passed definitively from the Ottoman to the Western camp.

The sequel to this decay of the Ottoman slave-household has brought to light the insuperable rigidity which was its fatal defect. Once thrown out of gear, it could be neither repaired nor remodelled. The system had become an incubus, and the Turkish rulers of later days were reduced to imitating the methods of their Western enemies, a policy long pursued half-heartedly and inefficiently but at last carried through with drastic completeness by

[1] Busbecq, O. G.: *Exclamatio, sive de Re Militari contra Turcam instituenda Consilium* (Leyden, 1633), p. 439.

Mustafā Kemāl in our own day. This metamorphosis is as wonderful a *tour de force* in its way as the creation of the slave-household by the early Ottoman statesmen. Yet a comparison of the results of these two performances brings out the relative triviality of the second. The makers of the Ottoman slave-household forged an instrument which enabled a tiny band of Nomads, who had been ejected from their native Steppe, not merely to hold their own in an unfamiliar world but to impose peace and order upon a great Christian society which had gone into disintegration and to threaten the life of a yet greater Christian society which has since cast its shadow over all mankind. Our latter-day Turkish statesmen have simply filled part of the vacuum which has been left in the Near East by the disappearance of the incomparable structure of the old Ottoman Empire by erecting on the desolate site a ready-made go-down of a standard Western pattern in the shape of a Turkish national state. In this commonplace villa-residence the Turkish legatees of the arrested Ottoman Civilization are to-day content—like the Zionist legatees of the fossilized Syriac Civilization next door and the Irish legatees of the abortive Far Western Civilization in the next street—to live henceforth in comfortable banality as a welcome escape from the no longer tolerable status of being 'a peculiar people'.

As for the slave-household itself, it had been ruthlessly 'put down'—the proper fate of a watch-dog who has gone wrong and taken to worrying the sheep—by Mahmūd II in A.D. 1826, in the middle of the Graeco-Turkish war, fifteen years after the analogous institution of the Mamlūks had been destroyed by Mahmūd's nominal subject—sometimes ally and sometimes rival—Mehmed 'Ali of Egypt.

(3) THE SPARTANS

The Ottoman institution came perhaps as near as anything in real life could to realizing the ideal of Plato's Republic, but it is certain that Plato himself, when he conceived his Utopia, had the actual institutions of Sparta in mind; and in spite of the difference in scale between Ottoman and Spartan operations there is a close resemblance between the 'peculiar institutions' with which each of these peoples equipped itself for the accomplishment of its *tour de force*.

As we noticed in the very first example cited in this Study (see p. 4), the Spartans made a peculiar response to the common challenge which was presented to all Hellenic states in the eighth century B.C. when the population of Hellas was outgrowing its means of subsistence. The normal solution which was found for this common problem was colonization: the extension of the area in Hellenic hands by the discovery of new lands overseas and their conquest and settlement at the expense of the local 'barbarians'. This proved a fairly simple matter on account of the inefficiency of the barbarian resistance. The Spartans, however, who, almost alone among Greek communities of any importance, did not live in sight of the sea, chose instead to conquer their Greek neighbours, the Messenians. This act confronted them with a challenge of unusual severity. The first Sparto-Messenian war (*circa* 736–720 B.C.) was child's-play compared with the second (*circa* 650–620 B.C.), in which the subject Messenians, tempered by adversity, rose in arms against their masters. Though they failed to achieve their own freedom, the Messenians succeeded in deflecting the whole course of Spartan development. The Messenian revolt was so terrible an experience that it left Spartan society 'fast bound in misery and iron'. Thenceforth the Spartans were never able to relax, never able to extricate themselves from their post-war reaction. Their conquest took the conquerors captive, much as the Eskimos have been enslaved by their conquest of an Arctic environment. As the Eskimos are fettered to the rigours of their annual cycle of livelihood, so the Spartans were fettered to the task of holding down their Messenian Helots.

The Spartans equipped themselves for performing their *tour de force* by the same method as the 'Osmanlis, adapting existing institutions to fulfil new needs. But whereas the 'Osmanlis could draw upon the rich social heritage of Nomadism, the Spartans' institutions were an adaptation of the very primitive social system of the Dorian barbarians who had invaded Greece in the post-Minoan Völkerwanderung. Hellenic tradition attributed this achievement to Lycurgus. But Lycurgus was not a man—only a god; and its real authors were probably a series of statesmen living as late as the sixth century B.C.

In the Spartan system as in the Ottoman, the outstanding feature, which accounts both for its efficiency and for its fatal rigidity and ultimate breakdown, was its grand disregard for human nature. The Spartan *agôgê* did not go so far as the Ottoman slave-household in disregarding the claims of birth and heredity; and the free citizen landholders of Sparta were in exactly the opposite situation from the free Muslim landed gentry of the Ottoman Empire. Virtually the whole duty of maintaining the Spartan dominion over Messenia was imposed upon them. At the same time, within the Spartiate citizen-body itself, the principle of equality was rigidly enforced. Every Spartiate held from the state an allotment of land of equal size, or equal productivity, and each of these allotments, cultivated by Messenian serfs (Helots), was sufficient to provide maintenance for the Spartiate and his family and thus enable him to devote the whole of his own energies to the art of war. Every Spartiate child, unless 'reprieved' as a weakling and put out to die by exposure, was condemned from the age of seven onwards to the Spartan curriculum of military education. There were no exemptions, and the girls were trained in athletics as well as the boys. Girls, like boys, competed naked before a male audience, and the Spartans seem in such matters to have achieved a sexual self-control or indifference similar to that of the modern Japanese. The production of Spartiate children was controlled on drastically eugenic lines, and a weakling husband was encouraged to secure a better male than himself to sire the children of his family. According to Plutarch, the Spartans

'saw nothing but vulgarity and vanity in the sexual conventions of the rest of mankind, who take care to serve their bitches and their mares with the best sires that they can manage to borrow or hire, yet lock their women up and keep them under watch and ward in order to make sure that they shall bear children exclusively to their husbands—as though this were a husband's sacred right even if he happens to be feeble-minded or senile or diseased'.[1]

The reader will notice the curious parallel between Plutarch's remarks on the Spartan system and the comments, already quoted, of Busbecq on the slave-household of the 'Osmanlis.

The leading features in the Spartan system were the same as in the Ottoman—supervision, selection, specialization and the competitive spirit—and in both cases these features were not confined to the educational stage. The Spartiate served fifty-three years with the colours. In some respects the claims made on him were more exacting than those made on the Janissaries. The Janissaries were discouraged from marrying, but if they married were allowed to live in married quarters; the Spartiate, though compelled to marry, was forbidden to lead a home-life. Even after marriage he continued to eat and sleep in his barracks. The result was the almost incredible and certainly crushing public spirit, a spirit which the English find difficult and repulsive even under the pressure of war and quite intolerable at other times, which has made the word 'Spartan' a by-word ever since. One aspect of that spirit is illustrated by the story of the Three Hundred at Thermopylae, or the story of the boy and the fox. On the other side, we have to remember that the last two years of the Spartiate

[1] Plutarch: *Lycurgus*, ch. xv.

boy's education were generally spent in the Secret Service, which was simply an official murder-gang, patrolling the countryside by night for the purpose of destroying any Helots who showed signs of insubordination, or indeed of inconvenient character and initiative in any shape or form.

The 'single-track' genius of the Spartan system leaps to the eye of any visitor to the present-day Sparta Museum; for this museum is totally unlike any other collection of Hellenic works of art. In such collections the visitor's eye seeks out and finds and dwells on the masterpieces of the Classical Age, which approximately coincides with the fifth and fourth centuries B.C. In the Sparta Museum, however, the Classical art is conspicuous by its absence. The pre-Classical exhibits are remarkable for their promise, but when one looks for their sequel one looks in vain. There is a complete gap in the sequence, and all that follows is a crop of standardized and uninspired work of the Hellenistic and Roman periods. The date at which the early Spartan art breaks off is approximately that of the overseership of Chilon in the middle of the sixth century B.C., and for that reason this statesman is often assumed to have been one of the authors of the system. The almost equally abrupt resumption of artistic production in the age of decadence is posterior to 189–188 B.C., when the system was forcibly abolished by a foreign conqueror. It is a curious illustration of the rigidity of the system that it lasted for two centuries after its *raison d'être* had disappeared—after Messenia had been irrevocably lost. Before this date the epitaph on Sparta had been written by Aristotle in the form of a general proposition.

'Peoples ought not to train themselves in the art of war with an eye to subjugating neighbours who do not deserve to be subjugated [i.e. fellow-Greeks, not 'lesser breeds without the law', whom Greeks called barbarians]. . . . The paramount aim of any social system should be to frame military institutions, like all its other institutions, with an eye to the circumstances of peace-time, when the soldier is off duty.'[1]

(4) GENERAL CHARACTERISTICS

Two characteristics, common to all these arrested societies, stand out conspicuously—caste and specialization; and both these phenomena can be embraced in a single formula: the individual living creatures which each of these societies embraces are not all of a single type but are distributed among two or three markedly different categories. In the Eskimo Society there are two castes: the human hunters and their canine auxiliaries. In the Nomadic Society there are three: the human shepherds, their

[1] Aristotle: *Politics*, 1333 B–1334 A.

animal auxiliaries and their cattle. In the Ottoman Society we find the equivalents of the three castes of the Nomadic Society with the substitution of human beings for animals. Whereas the polymorphic body social of Nomadism is constituted by the assemblage in a single society of human beings and animals who could none of them survive on the Steppe without their partners, the polymorphic Ottoman body social is constituted by the opposite process of differentiating a naturally homogeneous humanity into human castes which are treated as though they were different species of animals; but for our present purpose this difference can be ignored. The Eskimo's dog and the Nomad's horse and camel are half humanized by their partnership with man, whereas the Ottoman subject population, the Ra'iyeh (which means 'flock'), and the Laconian Helots are half dehumanized through being treated as cattle. Other human partners in these associations are specialized into 'monsters'. The perfect Spartiate is a Martian, the perfect Janissary a monk, the perfect Nomad a Centaur, the perfect Eskimo a Merman. The whole point of the contrast which Pericles draws, in the Funeral Oration, between Athens and her enemy is that the Athenian is a man, made in the image of God, whereas the Spartan is a war-robot. As for the Eskimos and the Nomads, the descriptions given by observers all agree in asserting that these specialists have carried their skill to such a point that the man-boat in the one case and the man-horse in the other manœuvre as organic units.

Thus Eskimos, Nomads, 'Osmanlis and Spartiates achieve what they achieve by discarding as far as possible the infinite variety of human nature and assuming an inflexible animal nature instead. Thereby they have set their feet on the path of retrogression. Biologists tell us that animal species which have adapted themselves too nicely to highly specialized environments are at a dead end and have no future in the evolutionary process. That is exactly the fate of the arrested civilizations.

Parallels with such a fate are furnished both by the imaginary human societies called Utopias and by the actual societies achieved by the social insects. If we enter into the comparison we shall find in the ant-heap and in the bee-hive, as well as in Plato's *Republic* or in Mr. Aldous Huxley's *Brave New World*, the same outstanding features as we have learnt to recognize in all the arrested civilizations—caste and specialization.

The social insects rose to their present social heights, and came to a permanent standstill at those altitudes, many millions of years before *Homo Sapiens* began to emerge above the mean level of the rank and file of the vertebrate order. As for the Utopias, they are static *ex hypothesi*. For these works are always programmes of action masquerading in the disguise of imaginary descriptive sociology; and the action which they are intended to evoke is nearly always the 'pegging', at a certain level, of an actual society which has entered on a decline that must end in a fall unless the downward movement can be artificially arrested. To arrest a downward movement is the utmost to which most Utopias aspire, since Utopias seldom begin to be written in any society until after its members have lost the expectation of further progress. Hence in almost all Utopias—with the noteworthy exception of that work of English genius which has given this whole genre of literature its name—an invincibly stable equilibrium is the aim to which all other social ends are subordinated and, if need be, sacrificed.

This is true of the Hellenic Utopias which were conceived at Athens in the schools of philosophy that arose in the age immediately following the catastrophe of the Peloponnesian War. The negative inspiration of these works is a profound hostility to Athenian democracy. For, after the death of Pericles, the democracy had dissolved its brilliant partnership with Athenian culture; it had developed a crazy militarism that had brought devastation upon the world in which Athenian culture had flourished; and it had capped its failure to win the war with the judicial murder of Socrates.

The first concern of the Athenian post-war philosophers was to repudiate everything that for two centuries past had made Athens politically great. Hellas, they held, could only be saved by an alliance between Athenian philosophy and the Spartan social system. In adapting the Spartan system to their own ideas they sought to improve upon it in two ways: first by working it out to its logical extremes and secondly by the imposition of a sovereign intellectual caste (Plato's 'Guardians'), in the likeness of the Athenian philosophers themselves, upon the Spartiate military caste, which is to be taught to play second fiddle in the Utopian orchestra.

In their condonation of caste, in their *penchant* towards specialization and in their passion for establishing an equilibrium at any price, the Athenian philosophers of the fourth century B.C. show themselves docile pupils of the Spartan statesmen of the sixth. In the matter of caste the thought of Plato and Aristotle is tainted with that racialism which has been one of the besetting sins of our own Western Society in recent times. Plato's conceit of 'the Noble Lie' is a delicate device for suggesting that between one human being and another there may be such profound differences as to constitute a distinction like that between one animal species and another. Aristotle's defence of slavery is along the same lines. He holds that some men are meant 'by nature' to be slaves, though he admits that in actual fact many are enslaved who ought to be free and many free who ought to be slaves.

In Plato's Utopias and Aristotle's alike (Plato's *Republic* and *Laws* and the last two Books of Aristotle's *Politics*) the aim is not the happiness of the individual but the stability of the community. Plato proclaims a ban on poets which might have issued from the mouth of a Spartan overseer; and he advocates a general censorship over 'dangerous thought' which has its latter-day parallels in the regulations of Communist Russia, National-Socialist Germany, Fascist Italy and Shintoist Japan.

The Utopian programme proved a forlorn hope for the salvation of Hellas, and its barrenness was demonstrated experimentally, before Hellenic history had run its course, by the mass-production of artificially manufactured commonwealths in which the main Utopian precepts were duly translated into practice. The single commonwealth laid out on a patch of waste land in Crete, which is postulated in Plato's *Laws*, was actually multiplied a thousandfold in the city states founded by Alexander and the Seleucidae *in partibus Orientalium* and by the Romans *in partibus Barbarorum* during the next four centuries. In these 'Utopias in real life' the little bands of Greeks or Italians who were fortunate enough to be enrolled as colonists were liberated for their cultural task of making the light of Hellenism shine upon the outer darkness by having assigned to them an ample labour-force of 'Natives' to do their dirty work. A Roman colony in Gaul might be endowed with the entire territory and population of a barbarian tribe.

In the second century after Christ, when the Hellenic World was enjoying an Indian Summer which contemporaries, and even posterity, long mistook for a Golden Age, it looked as though Plato's most audacious hopes had been fulfilled and transcended. From A.D. 96 to 180 a series of philosopher-kings sat upon a throne which dominated the entire Hellenic World, and a thousand city states were living side by side in peace and concord under this philosophic-imperial aegis. Yet the cessation of evils was only a pause, for all was not well beneath the surface. An impalpable censorship, inspired by the atmosphere of the social environment more effectively than it could ever have been imposed by imperial fiat, was eliminating intellectual and artistic vitality with a vengeance which would have disconcerted Plato if he could have returned to see his whimsical precepts so literally realized. And the uninspired respectable prosperity of the second century was followed by the chaotic passionate misery of the third, when the fallāhīn turned and rent their masters. By the fourth century the tables had been completely turned; for the once privileged ruling class of the Roman municipalities, in so far as it survived at all, was now everywhere in chains. Chained to their kennels and with their tails between their legs, the conscript aldermen of the municipalities of the Roman Empire *in extremis* could hardly be recognized as the ideological descendants of Plato's magnificent 'human watch-dogs'.

If we glance, in conclusion, at a few of the numerous modern Utopias we shall find the same Platonic characteristics. Mr. Aldous Huxley's *Brave New World*, written in a satirical vein, to repel rather than to attract, starts from the assumption that modern industrialism can be made tolerable only by a rigid segregation of 'natural' castes. This is achieved by sensational developments of biological science, supplemented by psychological techniques. The result is a stratified society of alphas, betas, gammas, deltas and epsilons which is simply Plato's invention or the 'Osmanlis' achievement carried to extremes, with the difference that Mr. Huxley's alphabetical castes are conditioned into really becoming so many different species of 'animals', like the human, the canine and the graminivorous species that co-operate in the Nomadic Society. The epsilons, who do the dirty work, really like it and want nothing else. They have been made that way in the procreational laboratory. Mr. Wells' *The First Men in the Moon* portrays a society in which 'every citizen knows his place. He is born to that place, and the elaborate discipline of training and education and surgery he undergoes fits him at last so completely to it that he has neither ideas nor organs for any purpose beyond it.'

Typical and interesting again from a slightly different standpoint is Samuel Butler's *Erewhon*. Four hundred years before the narrator's visit, the Erewhonians had realized that they were being enslaved by their mechanical inventions. The man-machine combination was becoming a sub-human entity like the man-boat of the Eskimos and the man-horse of the Nomads. So they scrapped their machines and pegged their society at the level it had reached before the opening of the Industrial Age.

NOTE. *Sea and Steppe as Language-conductors*

At the beginning of our account of Nomadism we noted that the Steppe, like 'the unharvested sea', while it provides no resting-place for sedentary mankind, affords greater facilities for travel and transport than cultivated lands. This resemblance between sea and Steppe is illustrated by their function as language-conductors. It is well known that a seafaring people is apt to spread its own language round the coasts of any sea or ocean on which it has made itself at home. Ancient Greek mariners once put the Greek language into currency all round the Mediterranean. The prowess of Malayan seamanship has propagated the Malay family of languages as far as Madagascar on the one side and the Philippines on the other. In the Pacific the Polynesian language is still spoken with extraordinary uniformity from Fiji to Easter Island and from New Zealand to Hawaii, though many generations have passed since the vast spaces which separate these islands were regularly traversed by Polynesian canoes. Again, it is because 'Britannia rules the waves' that English has lately become a language with a world-wide currency.

A corresponding dissemination of languages round the cultivated coasts of the Steppe, through the traffic of the Nomad steppe-mariners, is attested by the geographical distribution of four living languages or groups of languages: Berber, Arabic, Turkish and Indo-European.

The Berber languages are spoken to-day by the Nomads of the Sahara and also by the sedentary peoples of the Sahara's northern and southern coasts. It is natural to assume that the northern and southern branches of this family of languages were propagated into their present domains by Berber-speaking Nomads who trespassed, in times past, out of the Desert into the Sown in both directions.

Arabic is similarly spoken to-day, not only on the northern coasts of the Arabian Steppe, in Syria and 'Irāq, but on its southern coasts, in the Hadramaut and the Yaman and on its western coasts in the Nile Valley. It has also been carried farther westward again from the Nile Valley into the Berber domain, where it is now spoken as far afield as the North African coast of the Atlantic and the northern shore of Lake Chad.

Turkish has been disseminated to various coasts of the Eurasian Steppe and is spoken to-day, in one dialect or another, throughout a solid block of Central Asian territory extending from the east coast of the Caspian to the Lob Nor and from the northern escarpment of the Iranian Plateau to the western face of the Altai Mountains.

This present distribution of the Turkish family of languages gives the key to the present distribution of the Indo-European family, which (as its name implies) is now so strangely sundered into two isolated geographical groups, one domiciled in Europe and the other in Iran and India. The present Indo-European linguistic map becomes intelligible if we assume that the languages of this family were originally propagated by Nomads who were tenants of the Eurasian Steppe before the propagators of the Turkish languages made themselves at home there. Europe and Iran both have 'seaboards' on the Eurasian Steppe, and this great waterless ocean is the natural medium of communication between them. The only difference between this case and the three cases previously cited is that in this case the language group has lost its hold on the intervening Steppe region across which it was once disseminated.

X. THE NATURE OF THE GROWTHS OF CIVILIZATIONS

(1) TWO FALSE TRAILS

WE have found by observation that the most stimulating challenge is one of mean degree between an excess of severity and a deficiency of it, since a deficient challenge may fail to stimulate the challenged party at all, while an excessive challenge may break his spirit. But what about the challenge with which he is just capable of coping? On a short view this is the most stimulating challenge imaginable; and, in the concrete instances of the Polynesians and the Eskimos and the Nomads and the 'Osmanlis and the Spartans, we have observed that such challenges are apt to evoke *tours de force*. We have also observed, however, that in the next chapter of the story these *tours de force* exact, from those who have performed them, a fatal penalty in the shape of an arrest in their development. Therefore, on the longer view, we must pronounce that the evocation of the greatest immediate response is not the ultimate test of whether any given challenge is the optimum from the standpoint of evoking the greatest response on the whole and in the end. The real optimum challenge is one which not only stimulates the challenged party to achieve a single successful response but also stimulates him to acquire momentum that carries him a step farther: from achievement to a fresh struggle, from the solution of one problem to the presentation of another, from Yin to Yang again. The single finite movement from a disturbance to a restoration of equilibrium is not enough if genesis is to be followed by growth. And, to convert the movement into a repetitive, recurrent rhythm, there must be an *élan vital* (to use Bergson's term) which carries the challenged party through equilibrium into an overbalance which exposes him to a fresh challenge and thereby inspires him to make a fresh response in the form of a further equilibrium ending in a further overbalance, and so on in a progression which is potentially infinite.

This *élan*, working through a series of overbalances, can be detected in the course of the Hellenic Civilization from its genesis up to its zenith in the fifth century B.C.

The first challenge presented to the new-born Hellenic Civilization was the challenge of chaos and ancient night. The disintegration of the apparented Minoan Society had left a welter of social debris—marooned Minoans and stranded Achaeans and Dorians. Would the sediment of an old civilization be buried under the shingle which the new torrent of barbarism had brought down in spate? Would the rare patches of lowland in the Achaean landscape be dominated by the wilderness of highlands that ringed them round? Would the peaceful cultivators of the plains be at the mercy of the shepherds and brigands of the mountains?

This first challenge was victoriously met; it was decided that Hellas should be a world of cities and not of villages, of agriculture and not of pasturage, of order and not of anarchy. Yet the very success of their response to this first challenge exposed the victors to a second. For the victory which ensured the peaceful pursuit of agriculture in the lowlands gave a momentum to the growth of population, and this momentum did not come to a standstill when the population reached the maximum density which agriculture in the Hellenic homeland could support. Thus the very success of the response to the first challenge exposed the infant Hellenic Society to a second, and it responded to this Malthusian challenge as successfully as to the challenge of chaos.

The Hellenic response to the challenge of over-population took the form of a series of alternative experiments. The easiest and most obvious expedient was adopted first and was applied until it began to bring in diminishing returns. Thereupon a more difficult and less obvious expedient was adopted and applied, in place of the first, until this time a solution of the problem was achieved.

The first method was to employ the techniques and institutions which the lowlanders of Hellas had created in the process of imposing their wills upon their highland neighbours at home in order to conquer new domains for Hellenism overseas. With the military instrument of the hoplite phalanx and the political instrument of the city state, a swarm of Hellenic pioneers established a Magna Graecia in the toe of Italy at the expense of barbarian Itali and Chônes, a new Peloponnese in Sicily at the expense of barbarian Sikels, a new Hellenic pentapolis in Cyrenaica at the expense of barbarian Libyans, and a Chalcidicê on the north coast of the Aegean at the expense of barbarian Thracians. Yet, once again, the very success of the response brought down a new challenge upon the victors. For what they had done was in itself a challenge to the other Mediterranean peoples; and eventually the non-Hellenic peoples were stimulated to bring the expansion of Hellas to a standstill: partly by resisting Hellenic aggression with borrowed Hellenic arts and arms, and partly by co-ordinating their own forces on a greater scale than the Hellenes themselves were able to achieve. Thus the Hellenic expansion, which had begun in the eighth century B.C., was brought to a standstill in the course of the sixth. Yet the Hellenic Society was still confronted by the challenge of over-population.

In this new crisis in Hellenic history the required discovery was made by Athens, who became 'the education of Hellas' through learning, and teaching, how to transmute the expansion of the Hellenic Society from an extensive into an intensive process—a significant transmutation of which we shall have more to say later in this chapter. This Athenian response has already been described (see p. 4) and the description need not be repeated here.

This rhythm of growth was apprehended by Walt Whitman when he wrote: 'It is provided in the essence of things that from any fruition of success, no matter what, shall come forth something to make a greater struggle necessary', and in a more pessimistic vein by his Victorian contemporary William Morris when he wrote: 'I pondered . . . how men fight and lose the battle, and the thing that they fought for comes about in spite of their defeat, and when it comes turns out to be not what they meant, and other men have to fight for what they meant under another name.'

Civilizations, it would seem, grow through an *élan* which carries them from challenge through response to further challenge, and this growth has both outward and inward aspects. In the Macrocosm growth reveals itself as a progressive mastery over the external environment; in the Microcosm as a progressive self-determination or self-articulation. In either of these manifestations we have a possible criterion of the progress of the *élan* itself. Let us examine each manifestation in turn from this standpoint.

In considering first the progressive conquest of the external environment, we shall find it convenient to subdivide the external environment into the human environment, which for any society consists of the other human societies with which it finds itself in contact, and the physical environment constituted by non-human nature. Progressive conquest of the human environment will normally express itself in the form of a geographical extension of the society in question, whereas progressive conquest of the non-human environment will normally express itself in the form of improvements in technique. Let us begin with the former, namely geographical expansion, and see how far this deserves to be considered an adequate criterion of the real growth of a civilization.

Our readers would be unlikely to quarrel with us if we asserted, without more ado and without troubling to marshal any of the voluminous and overwhelming evidence, that geographical expansion, or 'painting the map red', is no criterion whatever of the real growth of a civilization. Sometimes we find that a period of geographical expansion coincides in date with, and is a partial manifestation of, qualitative progress—as in the case of the early Hellenic expansion just cited in another connexion. More often geographical expansion is a concomitant of real decline and coincides with a 'time of troubles' or a universal state—both of them stages of decline and disintegration. The reason is not far to seek. Times of trouble produce militarism, which is a perversion of the human spirit into channels of mutual destruction, and the most successful militarist becomes, as a rule, the founder of a universal state. Geographical expansion is a by-product of this militarism, in interludes when the mighty men of valour turn aside from their assaults upon their rivals within their own society to deliver assaults upon neighbouring societies.

Militarism, as we shall see at a later point in this Study, has been by far the commonest cause of the breakdowns of civilizations during the last four or five millennia which have witnessed the score or so of breakdowns that are on record up to the present date. Militarism breaks a civilization down by causing the local states into which the society is articulated to collide with one another in destructive fratricidal conflicts. In this suicidal process the entire social fabric becomes fuel to feed the devouring flame in the brazen bosom of Moloch. This single art of war makes progress at the expense of the divers arts of peace; and, before this deadly ritual has completed the destruction of all its votaries, they may have become so expert in the use of their implements of slaughter that, if they happen for a moment to pause from their orgy of mutual destruction and to turn their weapons for a season against the breasts of strangers, they are apt to carry all before them.

Indeed a study of Hellenic history might suggest a conclusion exactly the converse of that which we have rejected. We have noticed already that, at one stage in its history, the Hellenic Society met the challenge of over-population by geographical expansion: and that after some two centuries (*circa* 750–550 B.C.) this expansion was brought to a halt by surrounding non-Hellenic Powers. Thereafter the Hellenic Society was on the defensive, assaulted by the Persians from the east in its homelands and by the Carthaginians from the west in its more recently acquired domains. During this period, as Thucydides saw it, 'Hellas was repressed from all sides over a long period of time', and, as Herodotus saw it, 'was overwhelmed by more troubles than in the twenty preceding generations'.[1] The modern reader finds it difficult to realize that in these melancholy sentences the two greatest Greek historians are describing the age which, in the sight of posterity, stands out in retrospect as the acme of the Hellenic Civilization:

[1] Thucydides, Bk. I, ch. 17; Herodotus, Bk. VI, ch. 98.

the age in which the Hellenic genius performed those great acts of creation, in every field of social life, which have made Hellenism immortal. Herodotus and Thucydides felt as they did about this creative age because it was an age in which, in contrast to its predecessor, the geographical expansion of Hellas was held in check. Yet there can be no disputing that, during this century, the *élan* of the growth of the Hellenic Civilization was greater than ever before or after. And, if these historians could have been endowed with superhuman longevity to enable them to watch the sequel, they would have been amazed to observe that the breakdown marked by the Atheno-Peloponnesian War was followed by a fresh outburst of geographical expansion—the expansion of Hellenism overland, inaugurated by Alexander—far surpassing in material scale the earlier maritime expansion of Hellas. During the two centuries that followed Alexander's passage of the Hellespont, Hellenism expanded in Asia and the Nile Valley at the expense of all the other civilizations that it encountered—the Syriac, the Egyptiac, the Babylonic and the Indic. And for some two centuries after that it continued to expand, under the Roman aegis, in the barbarian hinterlands in Europe and North-West Africa. Yet these were the centuries during which the Hellenic Civilization was palpably in process of disintegration.

The history of almost every civilization furnishes examples of geographical expansion coinciding with deterioration in quality. We will select only two.

The Minoan culture attained its widest range of radiation in the phase which our modern archaeologists have labelled 'Late Minoan III', and this phase did not begin until after the sack of Cnossos *circa* 1425 B.C.: that is to say, not until after the catastrophe in which the Minoan universal state, the 'Thalassocracy of Minos', had broken up and given place to the interregnum in which the Minoan Society went into liquidation. The hall-mark of decadence is stamped upon all the material products of the Minoan culture dating from this third phase of the Late Minoan period, as conspicuously as these products outrange all previous Minoan products in geographical distribution. It looks almost as if a deterioration in quality of craftsmanship was the price which had to be paid for an expansion of output.

In the history of the Sinic Society, the predecessor of the present Far Eastern Society, it is much the same again. During the age of growth the domain of the Sinic Civilization does not extend beyond the basin of the Yellow River. It is during the Sinic time of troubles—'the Period of Contending States', as the Chinese call it—that the Sinic World incorporates into itself the Yangtse Basin on the south and the plains beyond the Peiho on the opposite side. Ts'in She Hwangti, the founder of the Sinic universal state, carries his political frontiers up to the line still delimited by the Great Wall; the Han dynasty, which enters into the Ts'in emperor's labours, pushes still farther afield to the south. Thus, in Sinic history, the periods of geographical expansion and social disintegration are contemporaneous.

Finally, if we turn to the unfinished history of our own Western Civilization and consider its early expansions at the expense of the abortive Far Western and Scandinavian civilizations, its expansion from the Rhine to the Vistula at the expense of North-European barbarism and from the Alps to the Carpathians at the expense of the Hungarian advance-guard of Eurasian Nomadism, and its subsequent maritime expansion into every corner of the Mediterranean basin from the Straits of Gibraltar to the mouths of the Nile and the Don in the widespread but ephemeral movement of conquest and commerce for which the most convenient short title is 'the Crusades', we may agree that all these, like the early maritime expansion of Hellas, are examples of geographical enlargement neither accompanied nor followed by any arrest in the expanding civilization's true growth. But when we survey the resumed and this time world-wide expansion of recent centuries we can only pause and wonder. The question here, which so closely concerns us, is one to which, in our generation, a prudent man will offer no confident answer.

We will now pass on to the next division of our subject and consider whether the progressive conquest of the physical environment by improvements in technique will provide us with an adequate criterion of the true growth of a civilization. Is there evidence of a positive correlation between an improvement in technique and a progress in social growth?

This correlation is taken for granted in the classification invented by modern archaeologists, in which a supposed series of stages in the improvement of material technique is taken as indicative of a corresponding succession of chapters in the progress of civilization. In this scheme of thought, human progress is represented as a series of 'Ages' distinguished by technological labels: the Palaeolithic Age, the Neolithic Age, the Chalcolithic Age, the Copper Age, the Bronze Age, the Iron Age, to which may be added the Machine Age in which we ourselves are privileged to live. In spite of the wide currency which this classification enjoys, it will be well to examine critically its claim to represent stages in the progress of civilization; for, without prejudice to the empirical test, we can point out several grounds on which it is suspect even *a priori*.

It is suspect, in the first place, by reason of its very popularity, for it appeals to the preconceptions of a society which has been fascinated by its own recent technical triumphs. Its popularity is an illustration of the indubitable fact—taken as the starting-point of the first chapter of this Study—that each generation is apt to design its history of the past in accordance with its own ephemeral scheme of thought.

A second reason for regarding the technological classification of social progress with suspicion is because it is a manifest example of the tendency of a student to become the slave of the particular materials for study which chance has placed in his hands. From the scientific standpoint it is a mere accident that the material tools which 'pre-historic' man has made for himself should have survived while his psychic artifacts, his institutions and ideas, have perished. Actually, while this mental apparatus is in use, it plays a vastly more important part than any material apparatus can ever play in human lives; yet, because a discarded material apparatus leaves, and a discarded psychic apparatus does not leave, a tangible detritus, and because it is the business of the archaeologist to deal with human detritus in the hope of extracting from it a knowledge of human history, the archaeological mind tends to picture *Homo Sapiens* only in his subordinate role of *Homo Faber*. When we turn to the evidence we shall find cases of technique improving while civilizations remain static or go into decline, as well as examples of the converse situation in which technique remains static while civilizations are in movement—either forward or backward as the case may be.

For instance, a high technique has been developed by every one of the arrested civilizations. The Polynesians have excelled as navigators, the Eskimos as fishermen, the Spartans as soldiers, the Nomads as tamers of horses, the 'Osmanlis as tamers of men. These are all cases in which civilizations have remained static while technique has improved.

An example of technique improving while a civilization declines is afforded by the contrast between the Upper Palaeolithic Age in Europe and the Lower Neolithic, which is its immediate successor in the technological series. The Upper Palaeolithic Society remained content with implements of rough workmanship, but it developed a fine aesthetic sense and did not neglect to discover certain simple means of giving it pictorial expression. The deft and vivid charcoal sketches of animals, which survive on the walls of Palaeolithic Man's cave-dwellings, excite our admiration. The

Lower Neolithic Society took infinite pains to equip itself with finely ground tools, and possibly turned these tools to account in a struggle for existence with Palaeolithic Man, in which *Homo Pictor* went down and left *Homo Faber* master of the field. In any case the change, which inaugurates a striking progress in terms of technique, is distinctly a set-back in terms of civilization; for the art of Upper Palaeolithic Man died with him.

Again, the Mayan Civilization never progressed technologically beyond the Stone Age, whereas the affiliated Mexic and Yucatec Civilizations made remarkable progress in the working of various metals during the five hundred years before the Spanish conquest. Yet it cannot be doubted that the Mayan Society achieved a much finer civilization than the two very second-rate societies that were affiliated to it.

Procopius of Caesarea, the last of the great Hellenic historians, prefaces his history of the wars of the Emperor Justinian—wars which actually sounded the death-knell of the Hellenic Society—with a claim that his subject was superior in interest to those chosen by his predecessors because his own contemporaries' military technique was superior to that employed in any previous wars. In truth, if we were to isolate the history of the technique of war from the other strands of Hellenic history, we should find a continuous progress from first to last, through the period of the growth of that civilization and onward through its decline as well; and we should also find that each step in the progress of this technique had been stimulated by events that were disastrous for civilization.

To begin with, the invention of the Spartan phalanx, the first signal Hellenic military improvement on record, was an outcome of the Second Sparto-Messenian War, which brought the Hellenic Civilization in Sparta to a premature halt. The next signal improvement was the differentiation of the Hellenic infantryman into two extreme types: the Macedonian phalangite and the Athenian peltast. The Macedonian phalanx, armed with long two-handed pikes in place of short one-handed stabbing-spears, was more formidable in its impact than its Spartan predecessor, but it was also more unwieldy and more vulnerable if it once lost formation. It could not safely go into action unless its flanks were guarded by peltasts, a new type of light infantry who were taken out of the ranks and trained as skirmishers. This second improvement was the outcome of a century of deadly war, from the outbreak of the Atheno-Peloponnesian War to the Macedonian victory over Thebans and Athenians at Chaeronea (431–338 B.C.), which saw the first breakdown of the Hellenic Civilization. The next signal improvement was made by the Romans when they succeeded in combining the advantages and avoiding the defects of both peltast and phalangite in the tactics and equipment of the legionary. The legionary was armed with a couple of throwing-spears and a stabbing-sword, and went into action in open order in two waves, with a third wave, armed and ordered in the old phalanx style, in reserve. This third improvement was the outcome of a fresh bout of deadly warfare, from the outbreak of the Hannibalic War in 220 B.C. to the end of the Third Romano-Macedonian War in 168 B.C. The fourth and last improvement was the perfection of the legion, a process, begun by Marius and completed by Caesar, which was the outcome of a century of Roman revolutions and civil wars ending in the establishment of the Roman Empire as the Hellenic universal state. Justinian's cataphract—the armoured rider on an armoured mount whom Procopius presents to his readers as the *chef-d'œuvre* of Hellenic military technique—does not represent a further stage in this native Hellenic line of development. The cataphract was an adaptation, by the last decadent generations of the Hellenic Society, of the military instrument of their Iranian contemporaries, neighbours and antagonists, who had first made Rome aware of their prowess when they defeated Crassus at Carrhae in 55 B.C.

Nor is the art of war the only kind of technique that is apt to make its progress in inverse ratio to the general progress of the body social. Let us now take a technique which stands at the farthest remove from the art of war: the technique of agriculture, which is generally regarded as *par excellence* the sovereign art of peace. If we revert to Hellenic history we shall find that an improvement in the technique of this art has been the accompaniment of a decline in a civilization.

At the outset we seem to be entering on a different story. Whereas the first improvement in the Hellenic art of war was purchased at the price of an arrest in the growth of the particular community that invented it, the first comparable improvement in Hellenic agriculture had a happier sequel. When Attica, on Solon's initiative, led the way from a régime of mixed farming to a régime of specialized agriculture for export, this technical advance was followed by an outburst of energy and growth in every sphere of Attic life. The next chapter of the story, however, takes a different and a sinister turn. The next stage of technical advance was an increase in the scale of operations through the organization of mass-production based on slave labour. This step appears to have been taken in the colonial Hellenic communities in Sicily, and perhaps first in Agrigentum; for the Sicilian Greeks found an expanding market for their wine and oil among the neighbouring barbarians. Here the technical advance was offset by a grave social lapse, for the new plantation slavery was a far more serious social evil than the old domestic slavery. It was worse both morally and statistically. It was impersonal and inhuman, and it was on a grand scale. It eventually spread from the Greek communities in Sicily to the great area of Southern Italy which had been left derelict and devastated by the Hannibalic War. Wherever it established itself it notably increased the productivity of the land and the profits of the capitalist, but it reduced the land to social sterility; for wherever slave-plantations spread they displaced and pauperized the peasant yeoman as inexorably as bad money drives out good. The social consequence was the depopulation of the countryside and the creation of a parasitic urban proletariat in the cities, and more particularly in Rome itself. Not all the efforts of successive generations of Roman reformers, from the Gracchi onwards, could avail to rid the Roman World of this social blight which the last advance in agricultural technique had brought upon it. The plantation-slave system persisted until it collapsed spontaneously in consequence of the breakdown of the money economy on which it was dependent for its profits. This financial breakdown was part of the general social *débâcle* of the third century after Christ; and the *débâcle* was doubtless the outcome, in part, of the agrarian malady which had been eating away the tissues of the Roman body social during the previous four centuries. Thus this social cancer eventually extinguished itself by causing the death of the society upon which it had fastened.

The development of plantation slavery in the cotton states of the American Union, in consequence of improvements in the technique of the manufacture of cotton goods in England, is another and very familiar example of the same order. The American Civil War cut out the cancer so far as the mere fact of slavery was concerned, but it by no means eradicated the social evils involved in the existence of a race of freedmen of negro stock in the midst of an American society that was otherwise of European origin.

The lack of correlation between progress in technique and progress in civilization is apparent in all these cases in which techniques have improved while civilizations have remained stationary or suffered set-backs. The same thing is apparent in the cases, which we have next to consider, in which techniques have remained stationary while civilizations have been moving either forward or backward.

For example, an immense step forward in human progress was

made in Europe between the Lower and the Upper Palaeolithic Age.

'The Upper Palaeolithic culture is associated with the end of the fourth glacial epoch. In place of the remains of Neanderthal Man we find the remains of several types, none of which show any affinity to Neanderthal Man. On the contrary, they all approximate more or less closely to Modern Man. At one bound we seem, when looking at the fossil remains of this epoch in Europe, to have passed into the modern period as far as human bodily form is concerned.'[1]

This transfiguration of the human type in the middle of the Palaeolithic Age is possibly the most epoch-making event that has ever yet occurred in the course of human history; for at that moment Sub-Man succeeded in turning himself into Man, while Man, in all the time that has elapsed since Sub-Man's achievement made Man human, has never yet succeeded in attaining a super-human level. This comparison gives us the measure of the psychic advance which was achieved when *Homo Neanderthalensis* was transcended and *Homo Sapiens* emerged. Yet this immense psychic revolution was not accompanied by any corresponding revolution in technique; so that, on the technological classification, the sensitive artists who drew the pictures we still admire in the Upper Palaeolithic cave-dwellings have to be confounded with 'the Missing Link', while in reality—as measured by wisdom and stature alike and by every trait that is distinctive of humanity—this *Homo Palaeolithicus Superior* is divided from *Homo Palaeolithicus Inferior* by just as great a gulf as is our latter-day *Homo Mechanicus*.

This instance in which a technique has remained stationary while a society has advanced finds its converse in cases in which techniques have remained stationary while societies have declined. For example, the technique of iron-working, which had been originally introduced into the Aegean World at the moment of the great social relapse when the Minoan Society was going into dissolution, remained stationary—neither improving nor declining —at the time of the next great social relapse when the Hellenic Civilization went the way of its Minoan predecessor. Our Western World inherited the technique of iron-working from the Roman World unimpaired, and also the techniques of the Latin Alphabet and of Greek mathematics. Socially there had been a cataclysm. The Hellenic Civilization had gone to pieces and an interregnum had ensued out of which the new Western Civilization eventually emerged. But there was no corresponding break in the continuity of these three techniques.

[1] Carr-Saunders, A. M.: *The Population Problem*, pp. 116–17.

(2) PROGRESS TOWARDS SELF-DETERMINATION

The history of the development of technique, like the history of geographical expansion, has failed to provide us with a criterion of the growth of civilizations, but it does reveal a principle by which technical progress is governed, which may be described as a law of progressive simplification. The ponderous and bulky steam-engine with its elaborate 'permanent way' is replaced by the neat and handy internal-combustion engine which can take to the roads with the speed of a railway train and almost all the freedom of action of a pedestrian. Telegraphy with wires is replaced by telegraphy without wires. The incredibly complicated scripts of the Sinic and Egyptiac societies are replaced by the neat and handy Latin Alphabet. Language itself shows the same tendency to simplify itself by abandoning inflexions in favour of auxiliary words, as may be illustrated by a comparative view of the histories of the languages of the Indo-European family. Sanskrit, the earliest surviving example of this family, displays an amazing wealth of inflexions side by side with a surprising poverty of particles. Modern English, at the other end of the scale, has got rid of nearly all its inflexions but has recouped itself by the development of prepositions and auxiliary verbs. Classical Greek represents a middle term between these two extremes. In the Modern Western World dress has been simplified from the barbaric complexity of Elizabethan costume to the plain modes of to-day. The Copernican astronomy, which has replaced the Ptolemaic system, presents, in far simpler geometrical terms, an equally coherent explanation of a vastly wider range of movement of the heavenly bodies.

Perhaps simplification is not quite an accurate, or at least not altogether an adequate, term for describing these changes. Simplification is a negative word and connotes omission and elimination, whereas what has happened in each of these cases is not a diminution but an enhancement of practical efficiency or of aesthetic satisfaction or of intellectual grasp. The result is not a loss but a gain; and this gain is the outcome of a process of simplification because the process liberates forces that have been imprisoned in a more material medium and thereby sets them free to work in a more etherial medium with a greater potency. It involves not merely a simplification of apparatus but a consequent transfer of energy, or shift of emphasis, from some lower sphere of being or of action to a higher. Perhaps we shall be describing the process in a more illuminating way if we call it, not simplification but etherialization.

In the sphere of human control over physical nature this development has been described with a finely imaginative touch by a modern anthropologist:

'We are leaving the ground, we are getting out of touch, our tracks grow fainter. Flint lasts for ever, copper for a civilization, iron for generations, steel for a lifetime. Who will be able to map the route of the London–Peking air express when the Age of Movement is over, or to-day to say what is the path through the aether of the messages which are radiated and received? But the frontiers of the petty vanished kingdom of the Iceni still sweep defensively across the southern frontier of East Anglia, from drained marsh to obliterated forest.'[1]

Our illustrations suggest that the criterion of growth, for which we are in search, and which we failed to discover in the conquest of the external environment, either human or physical, lies rather in a progressive change of emphasis and shifting of the scene of action out of this field into another field, in which the action of challenge-and-response may find an alternative arena. In this other field challenges do not impinge from outside but arise from within, and victorious responses do not take the form of surmounting external obstacles or of overcoming an external adversary, but manifest themselves in an inward self-articulation or self-determination. When we watch an individual human being or an individual society making successive responses to a succession of challenges, and when we ask ourselves whether this particular series is to be regarded as a manifestation of growth, we shall arrive at an answer to our question by observing whether, as the series proceeds, the action does or does not tend to shift from the first to the second of the two fields aforesaid.

This truth comes out very clearly in those presentations of history in which the attempt is made to describe processes of growth exclusively in terms of the external field from start to finish. Let us take as examples two outstanding presentations in these terms, which are each the work of a man of genius: M. Edmond Demolins' *Comment la Route crée le Type Social* and Mr. H. G. Wells' book *The Outline of History*.

The environment thesis is set out by M. Demolins in his preface with uncompromising terseness:

'There exists on the surface of the globe an infinite variety of populations; what is the cause which has created this variety? . . . The first and decisive cause of the diversity of races is the route which the peoples have followed. It is the route which creates both the race and the social type.'

When this provocative manifesto fulfils its purpose by stimu-

[1] Heard, Gerald: *The Ascent of Humanity*, pp. 277–8.

lating us to read the book in which the author's thesis is worked out, we find that he manages quite well so long as he is drawing his illustrations from the life of primitive societies. In such cases the character of the society can be explained with approximate completeness in terms of responses to challenges from the external environment only; but this, of course, is not an explanation of growth, since these societies are now static. M. Demolins is equally successful in explaining the state of the arrested societies. But when the author applies his formula to patriarchal village communities, the reader begins to be uneasy. In the chapters on Carthage and Venice, one feels sure that he has left something out, without being quite able to say what the omission is. When he seeks to explain the Pythagorean philosophy in terms of a portage-trade across the toe of Italy, one resists a temptation to smile. But the chapter entitled 'La Route des Plateaux—Les Types Albanais et Hellènes' pulls one up short. Albanian barbarism and Hellenic civilization to be bracketed together, just because their respective exponents happen to have arrived once upon a time at their respective geographical destinations by way of the same terrain! And the great human adventure that we know as Hellenism to be reduced to a kind of epiphenomenal by-product of the Balkan plateaux! In this unlucky chapter the argument of the book confutes itself by a *reductio ad absurdum*. When a civilization goes as far as the Hellenic Civilization went, an attempt to describe its growth exclusively in terms of responses to challenges from the external environment becomes positively ridiculous.

Mr. Wells also seems to lose his sureness of touch when he handles something mature instead of something primitive. He is in his element when he is exercising his imaginative powers in order to reconstruct some dramatic episode in some remote aeon of geological time. His story of how 'these little theriomorphs, these ancestral mammals' survived when the overgrown reptiles went under is almost worthy to rank with the Biblical Saga of David and Goliath. When the little theriomorphs turn into Palaeolithic hunters or Eurasian Nomads Mr. Wells, like M. Demolins, still comes up to our expectations. But he comes to grief in the annals of our own Western Society when he has to size up that singularly etherialized theriomorph William Ewart Gladstone. He fails here simply because he has failed to transfer his spiritual treasure, as his narrative proceeds, from the Macrocosm to the Microcosm; and this failure reveals the limitations of the magnificent intellectual achievement which *The Outline of History* represents.

Mr. Wells' failure may be measured by Shakespeare's success in solving the same problem. If we arrange the outstanding characters of the great Shakespearian gallery in an ascending order of etherialization, and if we bear in mind that the play-wright's technique is to reveal characters by displaying personalities in action, we shall observe that, as Shakespeare moves upward from the lower to the higher levels in our character-scale, he constantly shifts the field of action in which he makes the hero of each drama play his part, giving the Microcosm an ever larger share of the stage and pushing the Macrocosm ever farther into the background. We can verify this fact if we follow the series from Henry V through Macbeth to Hamlet. The relatively primitive character of Henry V is revealed almost entirely in his responses to challenges from the human environment around him: in his relations with his boon companions and with his father and in his communication of his own high courage to his comrades-in-arms on the morning of Agincourt and in his impetuous wooing of Princess Kate. When we pass to Macbeth, we find the scene of action shifting; for Macbeth's relations with Malcolm or Macduff, or even with Lady Macbeth, are equalled in importance by the hero's relations with himself. Finally, when we come to Hamlet, we see him allowing the Macrocosm almost to fade away, until the hero's relations with his father's murderers, with his spent flame Ophelia and with his outgrown mentor Horatio become absorbed into the internal conflict which is working itself out in the hero's own soul. In Hamlet the field of action has been transferred from the Macrocosm to the Microcosm almost completely; and in this masterpiece of Shakespeare's art, as in Aeschylus's *Prometheus* or in Browning's dramatic monologues, a single actor virtually monopolizes the stage in order to leave the greater scope for action to the surging spiritual forces which this one personality holds within itself.

This transference of the field of action, which we discern in Shakespeare's presentation of his heroes when we arrange them in an ascending order of spiritual growth, can also be discerned in the histories of civilizations. Here too, when a series of responses to challenges accumulates into a growth, we shall find, as this growth proceeds, that the field of action is shifting all the time from the external environment into the interior of the society's own body social.

For example, we have already noticed that, when our Western forefathers succeeded in repelling the Scandinavian onslaught, one of the means by which they achieved this victory over their human environment was by forging the potent military and social instrument of the feudal system. But in the next stage of Western history the social and economic and political differentiation of classes which feudalism entailed set up certain stresses and strains which in their turn produced the next challenge with which the growing society was confronted. Western Christendom had hardly rested from its labours in beating back the Vikings before it found its next task in the problem of replacing the feudal system of relations between classes by a new system of relations between sovereign states and their individual citizens. In this example of two successive challenges, the shift of the scene of action from the exterior to the interior field is plainly apparent.

We can observe the same tendency in other passages of history which we have already examined in different contexts. In Hellenic history, for example, we have seen that the earlier challenges all emanated from the external environment: the challenge of highland barbarism in Hellas itself and the Malthusian challenge, which was met by expansion overseas and involved as its consequence challenges from indigenous barbarians and rival civilizations, the challenges of these latter culminating in the simultaneous counter-attacks of Carthage and Persia in the first quarter of the fifth century B.C. Thereafter, however, this formidable challenge from the human environment was triumphantly surmounted in the four centuries beginning with Alexander's passage of the Hellespont and continuing with the victories of Rome. Thanks to these triumphs, the Hellenic Society now enjoyed a respite of some five or six centuries during which no serious challenge from the external environment was presented to it. But this did not mean that during those centuries the Hellenic Society was exempt from challenges altogether. On the contrary, as we have already noted, these centuries were a period of decline; that is to say, a period in which Hellenism was confronted by challenges to which it was failing to respond with success. We have seen what these challenges were and, if we now look into them again, we shall see that they were all of them internal challenges resulting from the victorious response to the previous external challenge, as the challenge presented by feudalism to our Western Society resulted from the previous development of feudalism as a means of response to the external pressure of the Vikings.

For example, the military pressure from the Persians and the Carthaginians stimulated the Hellenic Society to forge in self-defence two potent social and military instruments, the Athenian navy and the Syracusan tyrannis. These produced, in the next generation, internal strains and stresses in the Hellenic body social; these resulted in the Atheno-Peloponnesian War and in the reaction against Syracuse of her barbarian subjects and of her Greek allies; and these convulsions produced the first breakdown of the Hellenic Society.

In the following chapters of Hellenic history the arms turned outwards in the conquests of Alexander and the Scipios were soon turned inwards in the civil wars of rival Macedonian diadochi and rival Roman dictators. Similarly the economic rivalry between the Hellenic and Syriac societies for the mastery of the Western Mediterranean reappeared within the bosom of the Hellenic Society, after the Syriac competitor had succumbed, in the still more devastating struggle between the Oriental plantation-slaves and their Siceliot or Roman masters. The cultural conflict between Hellenism and the Oriental civilizations—Syriac and Egyptiac and Babylonic and Indic—likewise reappeared within the bosom of the Hellenic Society as an internal crisis in Hellenic, or Hellenized, souls: the crisis that declared itself in the emergence of Isis-worship and Astrology and Mithraism and Christianity and a host of other syncretistic religions.

> They cease not fighting, East and West,
> On the marches of my breast.[1]

In our own Western history, so far as it has gone up to date, we can detect a corresponding trend. In earlier ages the most conspicuous of the challenges that it encountered were presented by the human environment, beginning with the challenges of the Arabs in Spain and the Scandinavians, and ending with the challenge of the 'Osmanlis. Since then our modern Western expansion has been literally world-wide; and for the time being, at any rate, this expansion has relieved us completely from our old preoccupation with challenges from alien human societies.[2]

The only semblance of an effective external challenge to our society since the 'Osmanlis' second failure to take Vienna has been the challenge of Bolshevism which has confronted the Western World since Lenin and his associates made themselves masters of the Russian Empire in A.D. 1917. Yet Bolshevism has not yet threatened the ascendancy of our Western Civilization very far beyond the borders of the U.S.S.R.; and, even if one day the Communist dispensation were to fulfil the Russian Communists' hopes by spreading all over the face of the planet, a world-wide triumph of Communism over Capitalism would not mean the triumph of an alien culture, since Communism, unlike Islam, is

---

[1] Housman, A. E.: *A Shropshire Lad*, xxviii.
[2] Perhaps if Mr. Toynbee had been writing a few years later he would, at this point, have made an exception for the challenge of Japan.—EDITOR.

itself derived from a Western source, being a reaction from and a criticism of the Western Capitalism that it combats. The adoption of this exotic Western doctrine as the revolutionary creed of twentieth-century Russia, so far from signifying that Western culture is in jeopardy, really shows how potent its ascendancy has come to be.

There is a profound ambiguity in the nature of Bolshevism which is manifested in Lenin's career. Did he come to fulfil or to destroy the work of Peter the Great? In re-transferring the capital of Russia from Peter's eccentric stronghold to a central position in the interior, Lenin seems to be proclaiming himself the successor of the Arch-Priest Avvakum and the Old Believers and the Slavophils. Here, we might feel, is a prophet of Holy Russia, embodying the reaction of the Russian soul against the Western Civilization. Yet, when Lenin casts about for a creed, he borrows from a Westernized German Jew, Karl Marx. It is true that the Marxian creed comes nearer to a total repudiation of the Western order of society than any other creed of Western origin which a twentieth-century Russian prophet could have adopted. It was the negative and not the positive elements in the Marxian creed that made it congenial to a Russian revolutionary mind; and this explains why, in 1917, the still exotic apparatus of Western Capitalism in Russia was overthrown by an equally exotic Western anti-capitalist doctrine. This explanation is borne out by the metamorphosis which this Marxian philosophy appears to be undergoing in the Russian atmosphere, where we see Marxism being converted into an emotional and intellectual substitute for Orthodox Christianity, with Marx for its Moses and Lenin for its Messiah and their collected works for the scriptures of this new atheistic church militant. But the phenomena take on a different aspect when we turn our attention from faith to works and examine what Lenin and his successors have actually been doing to the Russian people.

When we ask ourselves what is the significance of Stalin's Five Year Plan, we can only answer that it was an effort to mechanize agriculture as well as industry and transport, to change a nation of peasants into a nation of mechanics, to transform the old Russia into a new America. In other words, it was a latter-day attempt at Westernization so ambitious and radical and ruthless that it puts Peter the Great's work into the shade. The present rulers of Russia are working with demonic energy to ensure the triumph in Russia of the very civilization that they are denouncing in the world at large. No doubt they dream of creating a new society which will be American in equipment but Russian in soul—though this is a strange dream to be dreamed by statesmen for whom a materialist

interpretation of history is an article of faith! On Marxian principles we must expect that, if a Russian peasant is taught to live
the life of an American mechanic, he will learn to think as the
mechanic thinks, to feel as he feels and to desire what he desires.
In this tug of war which we are witnessing in Russia between the
ideals of Lenin and the methods of Ford we may look forward to
seeing the ascendancy of the Western over the Russian Civilization
paradoxically confirmed.

The same ambiguity is revealed in the career of Gandhi, whose
involuntary furtherance of the same ubiquitous process of Westernization is still more ironical. The Hindu prophet sets out to sever
the threads of cotton which have entangled India in the meshes of
the Western World. 'Spin and weave our Indian cotton with your
Indian hands', he preaches. 'Do not clothe yourselves with the
products of Western power-looms; and do not, I conjure you,
seek to drive out these alien products by setting up on Indian soil
new Indian power-looms on the Western pattern.' This message,
which is Gandhi's real message, is not accepted by his countrymen.
They revere him as a saint, but they only follow his guidance in so
far as he resigns himself to leading them along the path of Westernization. And thus we see Gandhi to-day promoting a political
movement with a Western programme—the transformation of
India into a sovereign independent parliamentary state—with all
the Western political apparatus of conferences, votes, platforms,
newspapers and publicity. In this campaign the prophet's most
effective—though not his most obtrusive—supporters are those
very Indian industrialists who have done most to defeat the prophet's real mission, the men who have acclimatized the technique
of industrialism in India itself.[1]

Corresponding transmutations of external into internal challenges have followed the triumph of the Western Civilization over
its material environment. The triumphs of the so-called Industrial
Revolution in the technical sphere notoriously created a host of
problems in the economic and social spheres, a subject at once so
complicated and so familiar that we need not enlarge upon it here.
Let us call to our minds the now fast-fading picture of the pre-
mechanical road. This antique road is thronged with all kinds
of primitive wheeled vehicles: wheel-barrows and rickshaws and
ox-carts and dog-carts, with a stage-coach as the *chef-d'œuvre* of
muscular traction and a foot-propelled bicycle here and there as
a portent of things to come. Since the road is already rather

---

[1] Mr. Churchill called attention to this fact in his statement on India in the
House of Commons on the 10th September, 1942. His remarks were bitterly
attacked in the Indian nationalist press.—EDITOR.

crowded, there are a certain number of collisions; but nobody minds, because few are hurt and the traffic is scarcely interrupted. For the fact is, these collisions are not serious. They cannot be serious because the traffic is so slow and the force impelling it so feeble. The 'traffic problem' on this road is not the problem of avoiding collisions but the problem of getting the journey accomplished at all, roads being what they were in the old days. Accordingly, there is no sort of traffic regulation: no policeman on point-duty or signal lights.

And now let us turn our eyes to the road of to-day on which a mechanical traffic hums and roars. On this road the problems of speed and haulage have been solved, as is testified by the motor-lorry with its train of trucks that comes lumbering along with more than the momentum of a charging elephant and by the sports-car that goes whizzing past with the swiftness of a bee or a bullet. But, by the same token, the problem of collisions has become the traffic problem *par excellence*. Hence on this latter-day road the problem is no longer technological but psychological. The old challenge of physical distance has been transmuted into a new challenge of human relations between drivers who, having learned how to annihilate space, have thereby put themselves in constant danger of annihilating one another.

This change in the nature of the traffic problem has, of course, a symbolic as well as a literal significance. It typifies the general change that has occurred over the whole range of our modern Western social life since the emergence of the two dominant social forces of the age: Industrialism and Democracy. Owing to the extraordinary progress which our latter-day inventors have made in harnessing the energies of physical nature and in organizing the concerted actions of millions of human beings, everything that is now done in our society is done, for good or evil, with tremendous 'drive'; and this has made the material consequences of actions and the moral responsibility of agents far heavier than ever before. It may be that in every age of every society some moral issue is always the challenge that is fateful for the society's future; but, however that may be, there is no doubt that it is a moral challenge rather than a physical challenge that confronts our own society to-day.

'In the present-day thinker's attitude towards what is called mechanical progress, we are conscious of a changed spirit. Admiration is tempered by criticism; complacency has given way to doubt; doubt is passing into alarm. There is a sense of perplexity and frustration, as in one who has gone a long way and finds he has taken the wrong turning. To go back is impossible; how shall he proceed? Where will he find himself if he follows this path or that? An old exponent of applied mechanics may be forgiven if he expresses something of the disillusion with which, now standing aside, he watches the sweeping pageant of discovery and invention in which he used to take unbounded delight. It is impossible not to ask: Whither does this tremendous procession tend? What, after all, is its goal? What is its probable influence upon the future of the human race?'

These moving words propound a question which has been struggling to find expression in all our hearts; and they are words spoken with authority, for they were uttered by the President of the British Association for the Advancement of Science in his opening address at the hundred-and-first annual meeting of that historic body.[1] Is the new social driving power of Industrialism and Democracy to be employed in the great constructive task of organizing a Westernized World into an oecumenical society, or are we going to turn our new power to our own destruction?

In a perhaps rather simpler form the same dilemma once presented itself to the rulers of Ancient Egypt. When the Egyptiac pioneers had victoriously responded to their first physical challenge, when the water and soil and vegetation of the Lower Nile Valley had been subjected to the wills of human beings, the question arose how the lord and master of Egypt and the Egyptians would use the marvellous human organization ready to his hand and responsive to his will. It was a moral challenge. Would he employ the material power and the man-power at his command to improve the lot of his subjects? Would he lead them upward and onward to the level of well-being that had been attained already by the king himself and a handful of his peers? Would he play the generous part of Prometheus in Aeschylus's drama or the tyrannous part of Zeus? We know the answer. He built the Pyramids; and the Pyramids have immortalized these autocrats, not as ever-living gods but as grinders of the faces of the poor. Their evil reputations were handed down in Egyptiac folk-lore till they found their way into the immortal pages of Herodotus. As a nemesis for their misguided choice death laid his icy hand on the life of this growing civilization at the moment when the challenge which was the stimulus of its growth was transferred from the external to the internal field. In the somewhat similar situation of our own world to-day, when the challenge of Industrialism is being transferred from the sphere of technique to the sphere of morals, the outcome is still unknown, since our reaction to the new situation is still undecided.

However, we have reached the terminus of the argument of the

[1] Sir Alfred Ewing, as reported in *The Times*, 1st September, 1932.

present chapter. We conclude that a given series of successful responses to successive challenges is to be interpreted as a manifestation of growth if, as the series proceeds, the action tends to shift from the field of an external environment, physical or human, to the *for intérieur* of the growing personality or civilization. In so far as this grows and continues to grow, it has to reckon less and less with challenges delivered by external forces and demanding responses on an outer battlefield, and more and more with challenges that are presented by itself to itself in an inner arena. Growth means that the growing personality or civilization tends to become its own environment and its own challenger and its own field of action. In other words, the criterion of growth is progress towards self-determination; and progress towards self-determination is a prosaic formula for describing the miracle by which Life enters into its Kingdom.

XI. AN ANALYSIS OF GROWTH

(1) SOCIETY AND THE INDIVIDUAL

IF, as we have been led to think, self-determination is the criterion of growth, and if self-determination means self-articulation, we shall be analysing the process by which growing civilizations actually grow if we investigate the way in which they progressively articulate themselves. In a general way it is evident that a society in process of civilization articulates itself through the individuals who 'belong' to it, or to whom it 'belongs'. We can express the relation between the society and the individual indifferently by either of these formulae, contradictory though they are; and this ambiguity seems to show that both formulae are inadequate and that, before setting out on our new inquiry, we shall have to consider what is the relation in which societies and individuals stand to each other.

This is, of course, one of the stock questions of sociology, and there are two stock answers to it. One is that the individual is a reality which is capable of existing and of being apprehended by itself and that a society is nothing but an aggregate of atomic individuals. The other is that the reality is the society; that a society is a perfect and intelligible whole, while the individual is simply a part of this whole which cannot exist or be conceived as existing in any other capacity or setting. We shall find that neither of these views will bear examination.

The classic picture of an imaginary atomic individual is the Homeric description of the Cyclops, quoted by Plato for the same purpose as ours in quoting it now:

> Mootless are they and lawless. On the peaks
> Of mountains high they dwell, in hollow caves,
> Where each his own law deals to wife and child
> In sovereign disregard of all his peers.[1]

It is significant that this atomic way of life is ascribed to no ordinary human beings, and in fact no human beings have ever lived Cyclops-fashion, for man is essentially a social animal inasmuch as social life is a condition which the evolution of man out of sub-man pre-supposes and without which that evolution could not conceivably have taken shape. What, then, of the alternative answer which treats man as simply a part of a social whole?

'There are communities, such as those of bees and ants, where,

[1] *Odyssey*, Bk. IX, ll. 112–15, quoted by Plato: *Laws*, Bk. II, 640 B.

though no continuity of substance exists between the members, yet all work for the whole and not for themselves and each is doomed to death if separated from the society of the rest.

'There are colonies such as those of corals or of hydroid polyps where a number of animals, each of which by itself would unhesitatingly be called an individual, are found to be organically connected so that the living substance of one is continuous with that of all the rest. . . . Which is the individual now?

'Histology then takes up the tale and shows that the majority of animals, including man, our primal type of individuality, are built up of a number of units, the so-called cells. Some of these have considerable independence; and it is soon forced upon us that they stand in much the same general relation to the whole mass as do the individuals of a colony of coral polyps, or better of siphonophora, to the whole colony. This conclusion becomes strengthened when we find that there exist a great number of free-living animals, the protozoa, including all the simplest forms known, which correspond in all essentials, save their separate and independent existence, with the units building up the body of man. . . .

'In a sense . . . the whole organic world constitutes a single great individual, vague and badly co-ordinated, it is true, but none the less a continuing whole with interdependent parts: if some accident were to remove all the green plants, or all the bacteria, the rest of Life would be unable to exist.'[1]

Do these observations of organic nature hold good for mankind? Is the individual human being so far from possessing a Cyclopean independence that he is actually no more than a cell in the body social, or, on a wider view, a cellule in the vaster body of 'a single great individual' which is constituted by 'the whole organic world'? The well-known original frontispiece to Hobbes's *Leviathan* pictures the human body social as an organism built up out of a host of Anaxagorean *homoeomeriae* which are individual human beings —as though the social contract could have the magical effect of degrading a Cyclops into a cell. Herbert Spencer in the nineteenth century and Oswald Spengler in the twentieth have written of human societies as social organisms in sober earnest. To quote only from the latter:

'A civilization (*Kultur*) is born at the moment when, out of the primitive psychic conditions of a perpetually infantile [raw] humanity, a mighty soul awakes and extricates itself: a form out of the formless, a bounded and transitory existence out of the boundless and persistent. This soul comes to flower on the soil of a country with precise boundaries, to which it remains attached like a plant. Conversely a civilization dies if once this soul has realized the complete sum of its possibilities in the shape of peoples, languages, creeds, arts, states

[1] Huxley, J. S.: *The Individual in the Animal Kingdom*, pp. 36–8 and 125.

and sciences, and thereupon goes back into the primitive psyche from which it originally emerged.'[1]

An effective criticism of the thesis of this passage may be found in the work of an English writer which happened to appear in the same year as Spengler's book.

'Again and again social theorists, instead of finding and steadily employing a method and a terminology proper to their subject, have attempted to express the facts and values of society in terms of some other theory or science. On the analogy of the physical sciences they have striven to analyse and explain society as *mechanism*, on the analogy of biology they have insisted on regarding it as an *organism*, on the analogy of mental science or philosophy they have persisted in treating it as a *person*, sometimes on the religious analogy they have come near to confusing it with a God.'[2]

The biological and psychological analogies are perhaps least harmful and misleading when they are applied to primitive societies or to arrested civilizations, but they are manifestly unsuited to express the relation in which growing civilizations stand to their individual members. The inclination to introduce such analogies is merely an example of that myth-making or fictional infirmity of historical minds to which we have already referred: the tendency to personify and label groups or institutions—'Britain', 'France', 'the Church', 'the Press', 'the Turf' and so on—and to treat these abstractions as persons. It is sufficiently evident that the representation of a society as a personality or organism offers us no adequate expression of the society's relation to its individual members.

What then is the right way of describing the relation between human societies and individuals? The truth seems to be that a human society is, in itself, a system of relationships between human beings who are not only individuals but are also social animals in the sense that they could not exist at all without being in this relationship to one another. A society, we may say, is a product of the relations between individuals, and these relations of theirs arise from the coincidence of their individual fields of action. This coincidence combines the individual fields into a common ground, and this common ground is what we call a society.

If this definition is accepted, an important though obvious corollary emerges from it. Society is a 'field of action' but the *source* of all action is in the individuals composing it. This truth is forcibly stated by Bergson:

'We do not believe in the "unconscious" [factor] in history: "the

[1] Spengler, O.: *Der Untergang des Abendlandes*, vol. i, 15th–22nd ed., p. 153.
[2] Cole, G. D. H.: *Social Theory*, p. 13.

great subterranean currents of thought", of which there has been so
much talk, only flow in consequence of the fact that masses of men
have been carried away by one or more of their own number. . . . It
is useless to maintain that [social progress] takes place of itself, bit by
bit, in virtue of the spiritual condition of the society at a certain period
of its history. It is really a leap forward which is only taken when the
society has made up its mind to try an experiment; this means that the
society must have allowed itself to be convinced, or at any rate allowed
itself to be shaken; and the shake is always given by *somebody*.'[1]

These individuals who set going the process of growth in the
societies to which they 'belong' are more than mere men. They
can work what to men seem miracles because they themselves are
superhuman in a literal and no mere metaphorical sense.

'In giving to man the moral conformation which he required to be
a social animal, nature has probably done all that she was able to do for
the human species. But, just as men of genius have been found to push
back the bounds of the human intelligence, . . . so there have arisen
privileged souls who have felt themselves related to all souls and who,
instead of remaining within the limits of their group and keeping to
the [restricted] solidarity which has been established by nature, have
addressed themselves to humanity in general in an *élan* of love. The
apparition of each of these souls has been like the creation of a new
species composed of one unique individual.'[2]

The new specific character of these rare and superhuman souls
that break the vicious circle of primitive human social life and
resume the work of creation may be described as personality.
It is through the inward development of personality that individual
human beings are able to perform those creative acts, in the outward field of action, that cause the growths of human societies.
For Bergson it is the mystics who are the superhuman creators
par excellence, and he finds the essence of the creative act in the
supreme moment of the mystical experience. To pursue his analysis
in his own words:

'The soul of the great mystic does not come to a halt at the [mystical]
ecstasy as though that were the goal of a journey. The ecstasy may
indeed be called a state of repose, but it is the repose of a locomotive
standing in a station under steam pressure, with its movement continuing as a stationary throbbing while it waits for the moment to make
a new leap forward. . . . The great mystic has felt the truth flow into
him from its source like a force in action. . . . His desire is with God's
help to complete the creation of the human species. . . . The mystic's
direction is the very direction of the *élan* of life. It is that *élan* itself,
communicated in its entirety to privileged human beings whose desire

¹ Bergson, H.: *Les Deux Sources de la Morale et de la Religion*, pp. 333 and 373.
² Op. cit., p. 96.

it is thereafter to set the imprint of it upon the whole of mankind and—by a contradiction of which they are aware—to convert a species, which is essentially a created thing, into creative effort; to make a movement out of something which, by definition, is a halt.'[1]

This contradiction is the crux of the dynamic social relation which arises between human beings upon the emergence of mystically inspired personalities. The creative personality is impelled to transfigure his fellow men into fellow creators by re-creating them in his own image. The creative mutation which has taken place in the microcosm of the mystic requires an adaptative modification in the macrocosm before it can become either complete or secure; but *ex hypothesi* the macrocosm of the transfigured personality is also the macrocosm of his untransfigured fellow men, and his effort to transform the macrocosm in consonance with the change in himself will be resisted by their inertia, which will tend to keep the macrocosm in harmony with their unaltered selves by keeping it just as it is.

This social situation presents a dilemma. If the creative genius fails to bring about in his milieu the mutation which he has achieved in himself, his creativeness will be fatal to him. He will have put himself out of gear with his field of action; and in losing the power of action he will lose the will to live—even if his former fellows do not harry him to death, as abnormal members of the swarm or hive or herd or pack are harried to death by the rank and file in the static social life of gregarious animals or insects. On the other hand, if our genius does succeed in overcoming the inertia or active hostility of his former fellows and does triumphantly transform his social milieu into a new order in harmony with his transfigured self, he thereby makes life intolerable for men and women of common clay unless they can succeed in adapting their own selves, in turn, to the new social milieu that has been imposed on them by the triumphant genius's masterfully creative will.

This is the meaning of a saying attributed to Jesus in the Gospels:

'Think not that I am come to send peace on Earth: I came not to send peace but a sword.

'For I am come to set a man at variance against his father, and the daughter against her mother, and the daughter in law against her mother in law.

'And a man's foes shall be they of his own household.'[2]

---

[1] Op. cit., pp. 246–51. The reader will have noticed how close Bergson's philosophy of history comes to that of Carlyle.—EDITOR.

[2] Matthew x. 34–6; cf. Luke xii. 51–3.

How is it possible for social equilibrium to be restored when once the disturbing thrust of genius has made itself felt?

The simplest solution would be that uniform thrusts—uniform alike in vigour and in direction—should be made by each and every member of society independently. In such a case there would be growth without a trace of strain or tension. But, it need hardly be said, such hundred-per-cent responses to the call for creative genius do not in fact occur. History is, no doubt, full of examples of the fact that, when an idea—religious or scientific—is, as we say, 'in the air', it will take form in the minds of several inspired persons independently and almost simultaneously. But even in the most striking of such cases the plurality of independently and simultaneously inspired minds is to be counted in single figures as against the thousands or millions unresponsive to the call. The truth seems to be that the intrinsic uniqueness and individuality of any act of creation is never counteracted to more than a trifling extent by the tendency towards uniformity which arises from the fact that every individual is a potential creator and that all these individuals are living in the same atmosphere; so that the creator, when he arises, always finds himself overwhelmingly outnumbered by the inert uncreative mass, even when he has the good fortune to enjoy the companionship of a few kindred spirits. All acts of social creation are the work either of individual creators or, at most, of creative minorities; and at each successive advance the great majority of the members of the society are left behind. If we glance at the great religious organizations extant in the world to-day, Christian, Islamic and Hindu, we shall find that the great bulk of their nominal adherents, however exalted the creeds to which they profess lip-service, still live in a mental atmosphere which, so far as religion is concerned, is not far removed from a simple paganism. It is the same with the recent achievements of our material civilization. Our Western scientific knowledge and our technique for turning it to account is perilously esoteric. The great new social forces of Democracy and Industrialism have been evoked by a tiny creative minority, and the great mass of humanity still remains substantially on the same intellectual and moral level on which it lay before the titanic new social forces began to emerge. In fact the main reason why this would-be Western Salt of the Earth is in danger, to-day, of losing its savour is because the great mass of the Western body social has remained unsalted.

The very fact that the growths of civilizations are the work of creative individuals or creative minorities carries the implication that the uncreative majority will be left behind unless the pioneers can contrive some means of carrying this sluggish rear-guard along with them in their eager advance. And this consideration requires us to qualify the definition of the difference between civilizations and primitive societies on which we have hitherto worked. In an earlier part of this Study we found that primitive societies, as we know them, are in a static condition whereas the civilizations—other than the arrested civilizations—are in dynamic movement. We should now rather say that growing civilizations differ from static primitive societies in virtue of the dynamic movement, in their bodies social, of creative individual personalities; and we should add that these creative personalities, at their greatest numerical strength, never amount to more than a small minority. In every growing civilization the great majority of the participant individuals are in the same stagnant quiescent condition as the members of a static primitive society. More than that, the great majority of the participants in a growing civilization are, apart from a superimposed veneer of education, men of like passions with primitive mankind. Here we find the element of truth in the saying that human nature never changes. The superior personalities, geniuses, mystics or supermen—call them what you will—are no more than a leaven in the lump of ordinary humanity.

We have now to consider how those dynamic personalities who do succeed in breaking what Bagehot called 'the cake of custom' in their own *for intérieur* are actually able to consolidate their individual victory, and save it from being converted into a social defeat, by going on to break 'the cake of custom' in their social milieu. In order to solve this problem,

'a double effort is demanded: an effort on the part of some people to make a new invention and an effort on the part of all the rest to adopt it and adapt themselves to it. A society can be called a civilization as soon as these acts of initiative and this attitude of docility are both found in it together. As a matter of fact, the second condition is more difficult to secure than the first. The indispensable factor which has not been at the command of the uncivilized societies is in all probability not the superior personality (there seems no reason why nature should not have had a certain number of these felicitous vagaries at all times and places). The missing factor is more likely to have been the opportunity for individuals of this stamp to display their superiority and the disposition in other individuals to follow their lead.'[1]

The problem of securing that the uncreative majority shall in fact follow the creative minority's lead appears to have two solutions, the one practical and the other ideal.

'The one is by way of drill (*dressage*) ... the other is by mysticism ....

[1] Bergson, op. cit., p. 181.

The first method inculcates a morality consisting of impersonal habits; the second induces imitation of another personality, and even a spiritual union, a more or less complete identification with it.'[1]

The direct kindling of creative energy from soul to soul is no doubt the ideal way, but to rely upon it exclusively is a counsel of perfection. The problem of bringing the uncreative rank and file into line with the creative pioneers cannot be solved in practice, on the social scale, without bringing into play the faculty of sheer mimesis—one of the less exalted faculties of human nature, which has more in it of drill than of inspiration.

To bring mimesis into play is indispensable for the purpose in hand because mimesis, at any rate, is one of the ordinary faculties of primitive man. We have already noticed[2] that mimesis is a generic feature of social life, both in primitive societies and in civilizations, but that it operates in different ways in these two species of society. In static primitive societies mimesis is directed towards the older generation of the living members and towards the dead, in whom 'the cake of custom' is incarnated, whereas in societies in process of civilization the same faculty is directed towards the creative personalities who have broken new ground. The faculty is the same but it is turned in the opposite direction.

Can this revised version of a primitive social drill, this perfunctory and almost automatic 'right or left incline', really serve as an effective substitute for the 'strenuous intellectual communion and intimate personal intercourse' which Plato affirmed to be the only means of transmitting a philosophy from one individual to another? It can only be replied that the inertia of mankind in the mass has never in fact been overcome by the exclusive use of the Platonic method; and that, in order to draw the inert majority along in the active minority's train, the ideal method of direct individual inspiration has always had to be reinforced by the practical method of wholesale social drill—a habitual exercise of primitive mankind, which can be made to serve the cause of social progress when new leaders take command and issue new marching orders.

Mimesis may lead to the acquisition of social 'assets'—aptitudes or emotions or ideas—which the acquisitors had not originated and which they would never have possessed if they had not encountered and imitated those who possessed them. It is, in fact, a short cut; and at a later point in this Study we shall find that this short cut, though it may be an inevitable path towards a necessary goal, is also a dubious expedient which no less inevitably exposes a growing civilization to the peril of breakdown. It would be premature, however, to discuss that peril here.

[1] Op. cit., pp. 98–9.   [2] See p. 49.

(2) WITHDRAWAL AND RETURN: INDIVIDUALS

In the last section we have studied the course which is followed by creative personalities when they are taking the mystic path which is their highest spiritual level. We have seen that they pass first out of action into ecstasy and then out of ecstasy into action on a new and higher plane. In using such language we describe the creative movement in terms of the personality's psychic experience. In terms of his external relations with the society to which he belongs we shall be describing the same duality of movement if we call it withdrawal and return. The withdrawal makes it possible for the personality to realize powers within himself which might have remained dormant if he had not been released for the time being from his social toils and trammels. Such a withdrawal may be a voluntary action on his part or it may be forced upon him by circumstances beyond his control; in either case the withdrawal is an opportunity, and perhaps a necessary condition, for the anchorite's transfiguration; 'anchorite', in the original Greek, means literally 'one who goes apart'; but a transfiguration in solitude can have no purpose, and perhaps even no meaning, except as a prelude to the return of the transfigured personality into the social milieu out of which he had originally come: a native environment from which the human social animal cannot permanently estrange himself without repudiating his humanity and becoming, in Aristotle's phrase, 'either a beast or a god'. The return is the essence of the whole movement as well as its final cause.

This is apparent in the Syriac myth of Moses' solitary ascent of Mount Sinai. Moses ascends the mountain in order to commune with Yahweh at Yahweh's call; and the call is to Moses alone, while the rest of the Children of Israel are charged to keep their distance. Yet Yahweh's whole purpose in calling Moses up is to send him down again as the bearer of a new law which Moses is to communicate to the rest of the people because they are incapable of coming up and receiving the communication themselves.

'And Moses went up unto God; and the Lord called unto him out of the mountain, saying: "Thus shalt thou say to the house of Jacob and tell the Children of Israel." . . . And he gave unto Moses, when he had made an end of communing with him upon Mount Sinai, two tables of testimony . . . written with the finger of God.'[1]

The emphasis upon the return is equally strong in the account of the prophetic experience and the prophetic mission given by

---

[1] Exodus xix. 3 and xxxi. 18. See ch. xix, *passim*.

the Arabic philosopher Ibn Khaldūn in the fourteenth century of the Christian Era:

'The human soul has an innate disposition to divest itself of its human nature in order to clothe itself in the nature of the angels and to become an angel in reality for a single instant of time—a moment which comes and goes as swiftly as the flicker of an eyelid. Thereupon the soul resumes its human nature, after having received, in the world of angels, a message which it has to carry to its own human kind.'[1]

In this philosophic interpretation of the Islamic doctrine of prophecy we seem to catch an echo of a famous passage of Hellenic philosophy: Plato's simile of the Cave. In this passage Plato likens the ordinary run of mankind to prisoners in a cave, standing with their backs to the light and gazing at shadows cast upon a screen by the realities which are moving about behind them. The prisoners take it for granted that the shadows which they see on the back wall of the cave are the ultimate realities, since these are the only things that they have ever been able to see. Plato then imagines a single prisoner being suddenly released and compelled to turn round and face the light and walk out into the open. The first result of this re-orientation of vision is that the liberated prisoner is dazzled and confused. But not for long; for the faculty of vision is already in him and his eyes gradually inform him of the nature of the real world. He is then sent back to his cave again; and he is just as much dazzled and confused by the twilight now as he was by the sunlight before. As he formerly regretted his translation into the sunlight, so he now regrets his re-translation into the twilight, and with better reason; for in returning to his old companions in the cave who have never seen the sunlight he will be exposed to the risk of a hostile reception.

'There will assuredly be laughter at his expense, and it will be said of him that the only result of his escapade up there is that he has come back with his eyesight ruined. Moral: it is a fool's game even to make the attempt to go up aloft; "and as for the busybody who goes in for all this liberating and translating to higher spheres, if ever we have a chance to catch him and kill him, we will certainly take it".'

Readers of Robert Browning's poetry may be reminded at this point of his fantasy of Lazarus. He imagines that Lazarus, who was raised from the dead four days after his death, must have returned to 'the cave' a very different man from what he was before he left it, and he embodies a description of this same Lazarus of Bethany, in old age, forty years after his unique experience, in *An Epistle* of one Karshish, a travelling Arabian

[1] Ibn Khaldūn: *Muqaddamāt*, French translation by Baron M. de Slane, vol. ii, p. 437.

physician who writes periodical reports for the information of the head of his firm. According to Karshish the villagers of Bethany can make nothing of poor Lazarus; he has come to be regarded as a quite harmless variety of the village idiot. But Karshish has heard Lazarus's story, and is not so sure.

Browning's Lazarus failed to make his 'return' in any effective shape; he became neither a prophet nor a martyr, but suffered the returning Platonic philosopher's less exacting alternative fate of being tolerated but ignored. Plato himself has painted the ordeal of the return in such unattractive colours that it is almost surprising to find him imposing it remorselessly on his elect philosophers. But if it is essential to the Platonic system that the elect should acquire philosophy, it is equally essential that they should not remain philosophers only. The purpose and meaning of their enlightenment is that they should become philosopher-kings. The path which Plato lays down for them is unmistakably identical with the path that has been trodden by the Christian mystics.

Yet, while the path is identical, the spirit in which it is traversed by the Hellenic and by the Christian soul is not the same. Plato takes it for granted that the personal interest, as well as the personal desire, of the liberated and enlightened philosopher must be in opposition to the interest of the mass of his fellow men who still 'sit in darkness and in the shadow of death . . . fast bound in misery and iron'.[1] Whatever may be the interests of the prisoners, the philosopher, on Plato's showing, cannot minister to the needs of mankind without sacrificing his own happiness and his own perfection. For, when once he has attained enlightenment, the best thing for the philosopher himself is to remain in the light outside the cave and live there happy ever after. It was indeed a fundamental tenet of Hellenic philosophy that the best state of life is the state of contemplation—the Greek word for which has become our English word 'theory' which we habitually use as the opposite of 'practice'. The life of contemplation is placed by Pythagoras above the life of action, and this doctrine runs through the whole Hellenic philosophical tradition down to the Neo-platonists living in the latest age of the Hellenic Society in its dissolution. Plato affects to believe that his philosophers will consent to take a hand in the work of the world from a sheer sense of duty, but in fact they did not; and their refusal may be part of the explanation of the problem why the breakdown which the Hellenic Civilization had suffered in the generation before Plato was never retrieved. The reason why 'the great refusal' was made by the Hellenic philosophers is also clear. Their moral limitation was

[1] Psalm cvii. 10.

the consequence of an error in belief. Believing that the ecstasy and not the return was the be-all and end-all of the spiritual Odyssey on which they had embarked, they saw nothing but a sacrifice on the altar of duty in the painful passage from ecstasy to return which was really the purpose and culmination of the movement in which they were engaged. Their mystical experience lacked the cardinal Christian virtue of love which inspires the Christian mystic to pass direct from the heights of communion to the slums, moral and material, of the unredeemed workaday world.

This movement of Withdrawal-and-Return is not a peculiarity of human life which is only to be observed in the relations of human beings with their fellows. It is something that is characteristic of life in general, and becomes manifest to man in the life of the plants as soon as he has made this plant life his concern by taking up agriculture—a phenomenon which has led the human imagination to express human hopes and fears in agricultural terms. The annual withdrawal and return of the corn has been translated into anthropomorphic terms in ritual and mythology, as witness the rape and restoration of a Korê or Persephonê, or the death and resurrection of a Dionysus, Adonis, Osiris or whatever may be the local name for the universal corn-spirit or year-god, whose ritual and myth, with the same stock characters playing the same tragic drama under diverse names, is as widespread as the practice of agriculture itself.

Similarly, the human imagination has found an allegory of human life in the phenomena of withdrawal and return apparent in the life of plants, and in terms of this allegory it has wrestled with the problem of death, a problem which begins to torment human minds from the moment when, in growing civilizations, the higher personalities begin to disengage themselves from the mass of mankind.

'Some men will say: "How are the dead raised up? and with what body do they come?"

'Thou fool, that which thou sowest is not quickened except it die;

'And that which thou sowest, thou sowest not that body that shall be, but bare grain, it may chance of wheat or of some other grain;

'But God giveth it a body as it hath pleased him, and to every seed his own body. . . .

'So also is the resurrection of the dead. It is sown in corruption, it is raised in incorruption;

'It is sown in dishonour, it is raised in glory; it is sown in weakness, it is raised in power;

'It is sown a natural body, it is raised a spiritual body. . . .

'And so it is written: "The first man Adam was made a living soul; the last Adam was made a quickening spirit." . . .

'The first man is of the earth, earthy; the second man is the Lord from Heaven.'[1]

In this passage of the First Epistle of Paul to the Corinthians four ideas are presented in a succession which is also a crescendo. The first idea is that we are witnessing a resurrection when we behold the return of the corn in the spring after its withdrawal in the autumn. The second idea is that the resurrection of the corn is an earnest of the resurrection of dead human beings: a reaffirmation of a doctrine taught long before in the Hellenic Mysteries. The third idea is that the resurrection of human beings is possible and conceivable in virtue of some kind of transfiguration which their natures undergo through the act of God during the time of waiting that has to intervene between their death and their return to life. The earnest of this transfiguration of dead human beings is the manifest transfiguration of seeds into flowers and fruits. This change in human nature is to be a change in the direction of greater endurance, beauty, power and spirituality. The fourth idea in the passage is the last and most sublime. In the concept of the First and Second Man the problem of death is forgotten and the concern for the resurrection of the individual human being is momentarily transcended. In the advent of 'the Second Man who is the Lord from Heaven' Paul hails the creation of a new species composed of one unique individual, the *Adjutor Dei* whose mission it is to raise the rest of mankind to a super-human level by inspiring his fellow men with his own inspiration from God.

Thus the same *motif* of withdrawal and transfiguration leading up to a return in glory and power can be discerned in the spiritual experience of mysticism and in the physical life of the vegetable world and in human speculations on death and immortality and in the creation of a higher out of a lower species. This is evidently a theme of cosmic range; and it has furnished one of the primordial images of mythology, which is an intuitive form of apprehending and expressing universal truths.

One mythical variant of the *motif* is the story of the foundling. A babe born to a royal heritage is cast away in infancy—sometimes (as in the stories of Oedipus and Perseus) by his own father or grandfather, who is warned by a dream or an oracle that the child is destined to supplant him; sometimes (as in the story of Romulus) by a usurper, who has supplanted the babe's father and fears lest the babe should grow up to avenge him; and sometimes (as in the stories of Jason, Orestes, Zeus, Horus, Moses and Cyrus) by friendly hands that are concerned to save the babe from the

[1] 1 Corinthians xv. 35-8, 42-5, 47.

villain's murderous designs. In the next stage of the story the infant castaway is miraculously saved alive, and in the third and last chapter the child of destiny, now grown to manhood and wrought to a heroic temper by the hardships through which he has passed, returns in power and glory to enter into his kingdom.

In the story of Jesus the Withdrawal-and-Return *motif* perpetually recurs. Jesus is the babe born to a royal heritage—a scion of David or a son of God Himself—who is cast away in infancy. He comes down from Heaven to be born on Earth; He is born in David's own city of Bethlehem, yet finds no room in the inn and has to be laid in a manger, like Moses in his ark or Perseus in his chest. In the stable He is watched over by friendly animals, as Romulus is watched over by a wolf and Cyrus by a hound; He also receives the ministrations of shepherds, and is reared by a foster-father of humble birth, like Romulus and Cyrus and Oedipus. Thereafter He is saved from Herod's murderous design by being taken away privily to Egypt, as Moses is saved from Pharaoh's murderous design by being hidden in the bulrushes, and as Jason is placed beyond the reach of King Pelias by being hidden in the fastnesses of Mount Pelion. And then at the end of the story Jesus returns, as the other heroes return, to enter into His Kingdom. He enters into the Kingdom of Judah when, riding into Jerusalem, He is hailed by the multitudes as the Son of David. He enters into the Kingdom of Heaven in the Ascension.

In all this the story of Jesus conforms to the common pattern of the tale of the foundling babe, but in the Gospels the underlying *motif* of Withdrawal-and-Return presents itself in other shapes as well. It is present in each one of the successive spiritual experiences in which the divinity of Jesus is progressively revealed. When Jesus becomes conscious of His mission, upon His baptism by John, He withdraws into the wilderness for forty days and returns from His Temptation there in the power of the spirit. Thereafter, when Jesus realizes that His mission is to lead to His death, He withdraws again into the 'high mountain apart' which is the scene of His Transfiguration, and returns from this experience resigned and resolved to die. Thereafter, again, when He duly suffers the death of mortal man in the Crucifixion, He descends into the tomb in order to rise immortal in the Resurrection. And last of all, in the Ascension, He withdraws from Earth to Heaven in order to 'come again with glory to judge both the quick and the dead: whose Kingdom shall have no end'.

These crucial recurrences of the Withdrawal-and-Return *motif* in the story of Jesus likewise have their parallels. The withdrawal into the wilderness reproduces Moses' flight into Midian; the

Transfiguration on a 'high mountain apart' reproduces Moses' transfiguration on Mount Sinai; the death and resurrection of a divine being is anticipated in the Hellenic Mysteries; the tremendous figure which is to appear and dominate the scene, at the catastrophe which is to bring to an end the present mundane order, is anticipated in the Zoroastrian mythology in the figure of the Saviour and in the Jewish mythology in the figures of the Messiah and 'the Son of Man'. There is, however, one feature of the Christian mythology which seems to have no precedent; and that is the interpretation of the future coming of the Saviour or Messiah as the future return to Earth of an historical figure who had already lived on Earth as a human being. In this flash of intuition the timeless past of the foundling myth and the timeless present of the agrarian ritual are translated into the historical striving of mankind to reach the goal of human endeavour. In the concept of the Second Coming the *motif* of Withdrawal-and-Return attains its deepest spiritual meaning.

The flash of intuition in which the Christian concept of the Second Coming was conceived must evidently have been the response to a particular challenge of the time and place, and the critic who makes the mistake of supposing that things have nothing more in them than is to be found in their origins will depreciate this Christian doctrine on the ground that it originated in a disappointment: the disappointment of the primitive Christian community when they realized that their Master had actually come and gone without the looked-for result. He had been put to death, and, as far as could be seen, His death had left His followers without prospects. If they were to find heart to carry on their Master's mission, they must draw the sting of failure from their Master's career by projecting this career from the past into the future; they must preach that He was to come again in power and glory.

It is, indeed, true that this doctrine of a Second Coming has since been adopted by other communities that have been in the same disappointed or frustrated state of mind. In the myth of the Second Coming of Arthur, for example, the vanquished Britons consoled themselves for the failure of the historic Arthur to avert the ultimate victory of the English barbarian invaders. In the myth of the Second Coming of the Emperor Frederick Barbarossa (A.D. 1152–90) the Germans of the later Middle Ages consoled themselves for their failure to maintain their hegemony over Western Christendom.

'To the south-west of the green plain that girdles in the rock of Salzburg, the gigantic mass of the Untersberg frowns over the road which winds up a long defile to the glen and lake of Berchtesgaden. There, far up among its limestone crags, in a spot scarcely accessible to human foot, the peasants of the valley point out to the traveller the black mouth of a cavern and tell him that, within, Barbarossa lies amid his knights in an enchanted sleep, waiting the hour when the ravens shall cease to hover round the peak and the pear-tree blossom in the valley, to descend with his Crusaders and bring back to Germany the golden age of peace and strength and unity.'[1]

Similarly the Shi'ite community in the Muslim World, when they had lost their battle and become a persecuted sect, conceived the idea that the Twelfth Imām (twelfth lineal descendant of 'Alī, the son-in-law of the Prophet) had not died but had disappeared into a cave from which he continued to provide spiritual and temporal guidance for his people, and that one day he would reappear as the promised Mahdi and bring the long reign of tyranny to an end.

But if we turn our attention again to the doctrine of the Second Coming in its classic Christian exposition, we shall see that it is really a mythological projection into the future, in physical imagery, of the spiritual return in which the Apostles' vanquished Master reasserted His presence in the Apostles' hearts, when the Apostles took heart of grace to execute, in spite of the Master's physical departure, that audacious mission which the Master had once laid upon them. This creative revival of the Apostles' courage and faith, after a moment of disillusionment and despair, is described in the Acts—again in mythological language—in the image of the descent of the Holy Ghost on the Day of Pentecost.

After this attempt to grasp what Withdrawal-and-Return really means, we are in a better position to take an empirical survey of its working in human history through the interaction of creative personalities and creative minorities with their fellow human beings. There are famous historical examples of the movement in many different walks of life. We shall encounter it in the lives of mystics and saints and statesmen and soldiers and historians and philosophers and poets, as well as in the histories of nations and states and churches. Walter Bagehot expressed the truth we are seeking to establish when he wrote: 'All the great nations have been prepared in privacy and in secret. They have been composed far away from all distraction.'[2]

We will now pass rapidly in review a diversity of examples, beginning with creative individuals.

[1] Bryce, James: *The Holy Roman Empire*, ch. xi, *ad fin.*
[2] Bagehot, W.: *Physics and Politics*, 10th ed., p. 214.

Saint Paul

Paul of Tarsus was born into Jewry in a generation when the impact of Hellenism upon the Syriac Society was presenting a challenge which could not be evaded. In the first phase of his career he persecuted the Jewish followers of Jesus who were guilty, in Jewish Zealot eyes, of making a breach in the Jewish community's ranks. In the latter part of his career he turned his energies in an entirely different direction, preaching a new dispensation 'where there is neither Greek nor Jew, circumcision nor uncircumcision, Barbarian, Scythian, bond nor free',[1] and preaching this reconciliation in the name of the sect which he had formerly persecuted. This last chapter was the creative chapter of Paul's career; the first chapter was a false start; and between the two chapters a great gulf was fixed. After his sudden enlightenment on the road to Damascus, Paul 'conferred not with flesh and blood' but went into the desert of Arabia. Not until three years later did he visit Jerusalem and meet the original Apostles with a view to resuming practical activity.[2]

Saint Benedict

The life of Benedict of Nursia (*circa* A.D. 480–543) was contemporary with the death-throes of the Hellenic Society. Sent as a child from his Umbrian home to Rome in order to receive the traditional upper-class education in the humanities, he revolted from the life of the capital and withdrew into the wilderness at this early age. For three years he lived in utter solitude; but the turning-point of his career was his return to social life upon reaching manhood, when he consented to become the head of a monastic community: first in the valley of Subiaco and afterwards on Monte Cassino. In this last creative chapter of his career the saint improvised a new education to take the place of the obsolete system that he himself had rejected as a child, and the Benedictine community on Monte Cassino became the mother of monasteries which increased and multiplied until they had spread the Benedictine Rule to the uttermost parts of the West. Indeed this rule was one of the main foundations of the new social structure which was eventually raised in Western Christendom on the ruins of the ancient Hellenic order.

One of the most important features in Benedict's rule was the prescription of manual labour; for this meant, first and foremost, agricultural labour in the fields. The Benedictine movement was, on the economic plane, an agricultural revival: the first successful

[1] Colossians iii. 22.   [2] Galatians i. 15–18.

revival of agriculture in Italy since the destruction of the Italian peasant economy in the Hannibalic War. The Benedictine Rule achieved what had never been achieved by the Gracchan agrarian laws or the Imperial *alimenta*, because it worked, not, as state action works, from above downwards, but from below upwards, by evoking the individual's initiative through enlisting his religious enthusiasm. By virtue of this spiritual *élan* the Benedictine Order not only turned the tide of economic life in Italy; it also performed in medieval Transalpine Europe that strenuous pioneer work of clearing forests, draining marshes and creating fields and pastures which was performed in North America by the French and British backwoodsmen.

Saint Gregory the Great

Some thirty years after the death of Benedict, Gregory, holding the office of *Praefectus Urbi* in Rome, found himself faced with an impossible task. The city of Rome in A.D. 573 was in much the same predicament as the city of Vienna in A.D. 1920. A great city, which had become what it was in virtue of having been for centuries the capital of a great empire, now suddenly found itself cut off from its former provinces, deprived of its historic functions and thrown back on its own resources. In the year of Gregory's prefecture, the *Ager Romanus* was restricted approximately to the area which it had occupied some nine centuries back, before the Romans had embarked on their struggle with the Samnites for the mastery of Italy, but the territory which had then to support a little market-town had now to support a vast parasitic capital. The impotence of the old order to deal with the new state of affairs must have been borne in upon the mind of a Roman magnate who held the *Praefectura Urbis* at this time, and this painful experience would fully account for Gregory's complete withdrawal from the secular world two years later.

His withdrawal, like Paul's, was of three years' duration, and at the end of that period he was planning to undertake in person the mission that he afterwards undertook by proxy, for the conversion of the heathen English, when he was recalled to Rome by the Pope. Here, in various ecclesiastical offices and finally on the Papal throne itself (A.D. 590–604), he accomplished three great tasks. He reorganized the administration of the estates of the Roman Church in Italy and overseas; he negotiated a settlement between the Imperial authorities in Italy and the Lombard invaders; and he laid the foundations of a new empire for Rome in the place of her old empire which now lay in ruins—a new Roman Empire, established by missionary zeal and not by military force, which was eventually to conquer new worlds whose soil the legions had never trodden and whose very existence had never been suspected by the Scipios and Caesars.

The Buddha

Siddhārtha Gautama the Buddha was born into the Indic World in its time of troubles. He lived to see his native city state Kapilavastu sacked and his Sakyan kinsmen massacred. The small aristocratic republics of the early Indic World, of which the Sakyan community was one, appear to have been succumbing in Gautama's generation to rising autocratic monarchies built on a larger scale. Gautama was born a Sakya aristocrat at a moment when the aristocratic order was being challenged by new social forces. Gautama's personal retort to this challenge was to renounce a world which was becoming inhospitable to aristocrats of his ancestral kind. For seven years he sought enlightenment through ever-increasing asceticism. It was not until he had taken the first step towards returning to the world by breaking his fast that the light broke in upon him. And then, after he had attained the light for himself, he spent the rest of his life in imparting it to his fellow human beings. In order to impart it effectively, he allowed a company of disciples to gather round him and thus became the centre and head of a fraternity.

Muhammad

Muhammad was born into the Arabian external proletariat of the Roman Empire in an age when the relations between the Empire and Arabia were coming to a crisis. At the turn of the sixth and seventh centuries of the Christian Era the saturation-point had been reached in the impregnation of Arabia with cultural influences from the Empire. Some reaction from Arabia, in the form of a counter-discharge of energy, was bound to ensue; it was the career of Muhammad (whose lifetime was *circa* A.D. 570–632) that decided the form that this reaction was to take; and a movement of Withdrawal-and-Return was the prelude to each of the two crucial new departures upon which Muhammad's life-history hinges.

There were two features in the social life of the Roman Empire in Muhammad's day that would make a particularly deep impression on the mind of an Arabian observer because, in Arabia, they were both conspicuous by their absence. The first of these features was monotheism in religion. The second was law and order in government. Muhammad's life-work consisted in translating each of these elements in the social fabric of 'Rūm' into an

Arabian vernacular version and incorporating both his Arabianized monotheism and his Arabianized imperium into a single master-institution—the all-embracing institution of Islam—to which he succeeded in imparting such titanic driving-force that the new dispensation, which had been designed by its author to meet the needs of the barbarians of Arabia, burst the bounds of the peninsula and captivated the entire Syriac World from the shores of the Atlantic to the coasts of the Eurasian Steppe.

This life-work, upon which Muhammad appears to have embarked in about his fortieth year (*circa* A.D. 609), was achieved in two stages. In the first of these stages Muhammad was concerned exclusively with his religious mission; in the second stage the religious mission was overlaid, and almost overwhelmed, by the political enterprise. Muhammad's original entry upon a purely religious mission was a sequel to his return to the parochial life of Arabia after a partial withdrawal of some fifteen years' duration into the life of a caravan-trader between the Arabian oases and the Syrian desert-ports of the Roman Empire along the fringes of the North Arabian Steppe. The second, or politico-religious, stage in Muhammad's career was inaugurated by the Prophet's withdrawal or Hegira (*Hijrah*) from his native oasis of Mecca to the rival oasis of Yathrib, thenceforth known *par excellence* as Medina: 'the City' (of the Prophet). In the *Hijrah*, which has been recognized by Muslims as such a crucial event that it has been adopted as the inaugural date of the Islamic Era, Muhammad left Mecca as a hunted fugitive. After a seven years' absence (A.D. 622–9) he returned to Mecca, not as an amnestied exile, but as lord and master of half Arabia.

Machiavelli

Machiavelli (A.D. 1469–1527) was a citizen of Florence who was twenty-five years old when Charles VIII of France crossed the Alps and overran Italy with a French army in 1494. He thus belonged to a generation which was just old enough to have known Italy as she had been during her age of immunity from 'barbarian invasions'; and he lived long enough to see the peninsula become the international arena for trials of strength between sundry Transalpine or Transmarine Powers which found the prize and the symbol of their alternating victories in snatching from one another's grasp an oppressive hegemony over the once independent Italian city-states. This impact upon Italy of non-Italian Powers was the challenge which the generation of Machiavelli had to encounter and the experience through which they had to live; and the experience was the more difficult for the

Italians of this generation to meet inasmuch as it was one which
had not been tasted, either by them or by their forefathers, for
the best part of two-and-a-half centuries.

Machiavelli was endowed by nature with consummate political
ability; he had an insatiable zest for exercising his talents. Fortune
had made him a citizen of Florence, one of the leading city-states
of the peninsula, and merit won him, at the age of twenty-nine,
the post of Secretary to the Government. Appointed to this
important office in 1498, four years after the first French invasion,
he acquired a first-hand knowledge of the new 'barbarian' Powers
in the course of his official duties. After fourteen years of this
experience he had become perhaps better qualified than any other
living Italian for taking a hand in the urgent task of helping Italy
to work out her political salvation, when a turn in the wheel of
Florentine domestic politics suddenly expelled him from his field
of practical activity. In 1512 he was deprived of his Secretaryship
of State and in the following year he suffered imprisonment and
torture; and, although he was lucky enough to emerge again alive,
the price which he had to pay for his release from prison was a
perpetual rustication on his farm in the Florentine countryside.
The break in his career was complete; yet, in putting him to the
proof of this tremendous personal challenge, Fortune did not find
Machiavelli wanting in the power to make an effective response.

In a letter written very shortly after his rustication to a friend
and former colleague he describes in detail and with an almost
humorous detachment the manner of life which he has now
mapped out for himself. Rising with the sun, he devotes himself
during the hours of daylight to the humdrum social and sporting
activities suitable to the manner of life now forced upon him.
But that is not the end of his day.

'When the evening comes I return to the house and go into my study;
and at the door I take off my country clothes, all caked with mud and
slime, and put on court dress; and when I am thus decently re-clad I
enter into the ancient mansions of the men of ancient days. And there
I am received by my hosts with all lovingkindness, and I feast myself
on that food which alone is my true nourishment, and which I was
born for.'

In these hours of scholarly research and meditation was conceived and written *The Prince*; and the concluding chapter of the
famous treatise, which is an 'Exhortation to liberate Italy from the
Barbarians', reveals the intention that Machiavelli had in mind
when he took up his pen to write. He was addressing himself
once more to the one vital problem of contemporary Italian
statesmanship in the hope that perhaps, even now, he might help

to bring that problem to solution by transmuting into creative thought the energies which had been deprived of their practical outlet.

In fact, of course, the political hope that animates *The Prince* was utterly disappointed. The book failed to achieve its author's immediate aim; but this is not to say that *The Prince* was a failure, for the pursuit of practical politics by literary means was not the essence of the business which Machiavelli was going about when, evening after evening in his remote farm-house, he entered into the mansions of the men of ancient days. Through his writings Machiavelli was able to return to the world on a more etherial plane, on which his effect on the world has been vastly greater than the highest possible achievement of a Florentine Secretary of State immersed in the details of practical politics. In those magic hours of *catharsis* when he rose above his vexation of spirit Machiavelli succeeded in transmuting his practical energies into a series of mighty intellectual works—*The Prince, The Discourses on Livy, The Art of War* and *The History of Florence*—which have been the seeds of our modern Western political philosophy.

Dante

Two hundred years earlier the history of the same city furnished a curiously parallel example. For Dante did not accomplish his life-work till he had been driven to withdraw from his native city. In Florence, Dante fell in love with Beatrice, only to see her die before him, still the wife of another man. In Florence he went into politics only to be sentenced to exile, an exile from which he never returned. Yet, in losing his birthright in Florence, Dante was to win the citizenship of the world; for in exile the genius which had been crossed in politics after being crossed in love found its life-work in creating the *Divina Commedia*.

(3) WITHDRAWAL-AND-RETURN: CREATIVE MINORITIES

Athens in the Second Chapter of the Growth of the Hellenic Society

A conspicuous example of Withdrawal-and-Return, which has come to our notice in other connexions, is the behaviour of the Athenians in the crisis into which the Hellenic Society was thrown by the presentation of the Malthusian challenge in the eighth century B.C.

We have noticed that the first reaction of Athens to this problem of over-population was ostensibly negative. She did not, like so many of her neighbours, react to it by establishing colonies overseas, and she did not, like the Spartans, react to it by seizing the territory of adjoining Greek city-states and converting their inhabitants into serfs. In this age, so long as her neighbours were content to leave her alone, Athens continued to play an apparently passive role. The first glimpse of her demonic latent energy was to be seen in her violent reaction against the attempt of the Spartan king Cleomenes I to bring her under the Lacedaemonian hegemony. By her vigorous reaction against Lacedaemon, following her abstention from the colonizing movement, Athens had more or less deliberately segregated herself from the rest of the Hellenic World for upwards of two centuries. Yet these two centuries had not been for Athens a period of inactivity. On the contrary, she had taken advantage of this long seclusion to concentrate her energies upon solving the general Hellenic problem by an original solution of her own—an Athenian solution which proved its superiority by continuing to work when the colonizing solution and the Spartan solution were bringing in diminishing returns. It was only in her own good time, when she had remodelled her traditional institutions to suit her new way of life, that Athens at last returned to the arena. But, when she returned, it was with an impetus unprecedented in Hellenic history.

Athens proclaimed her return by the sensational gesture of throwing down the gauntlet to the Persian Empire. It was Athens who responded—when Sparta hung back—to the appeal of the Asiatic Greek insurgents in 499 B.C., and from that day onwards Athens stood out as the protagonist in the Fifty Years' War between Hellas and the Syriac universal state. For upwards of two centuries from the beginning of the fifth century B.C. onwards the role of Athens in Hellenic history was the absolute antithesis of the role that she had been playing for an equal period of time before. During this second period she was always in the thick of the mêlée of Hellenic inter-state politics, and it was not until she found herself hopelessly outclassed by the new Titans born of Alexander's Oriental adventure that she reluctantly renounced the status and the burdens of a Hellenic Great Power. Nor was her withdrawal after her final overthrow by Macedon in 262 B.C. the end of her active participation in Hellenic history. For, long before she fell behind in the military and political race, she had made herself 'the education of Hellas' in every other field. She had given the Hellenic culture a permanent Attic impress which it still retains in the eyes of posterity.

Italy in the Second Chapter of the Growth of the Western Society

We have already noticed, in touching upon Machiavelli, that Italy secured for herself during a period of over two centuries—

from the destruction of the Hohenstaufen in the middle of the thirteenth century to the French invasion at the end of the fifteenth century—a withdrawal from the tumultuous feudal semi-barbarism of Transalpine Europe. The greatest achievements of the Italian genius during those two-and-a-half centuries of immunity had not been extensive but intensive, not material but spiritual. In architecture, in sculpture, in painting, in literature and in almost every other province in the realm of aesthetic and general culture, the Italians had been performing works of creation which bear comparison with the achievements of the Greeks during an equal period in the fifth and fourth centuries B.C. Indeed the Italians sought inspiration from this Ancient Greek genius by evoking the ghost of the extinct Hellenic culture, looking back to the Greek achievement as something absolute, standard and classic, to be imitated but not surpassed; and we, following in their footsteps, established a system of 'classical' education which has only recently been giving way before the claims of latter-day technology. In fine, the Italians had used their hard-won immunity from alien domination to create, within their precariously sheltered peninsula, an Italian World in which the level of Western Civilization had been raised precociously to such a pitch that the difference in degree became tantamount to a difference in kind. By the close of the fifteenth century they felt themselves to be so far superior to other Westerners that—half in conceit and half in earnest—they revived the term 'barbarians' to describe the peoples beyond the Alps and across the Tyrrhene Sea. And then these latter-day 'barbarians' began to act in character by showing themselves politically and militarily wiser than the Italian children of light.

As the new Italian culture radiated out of the peninsula in all directions it quickened the cultural growth of the peoples round about, and quickened it first in the grosser elements of culture—such as political organization and military technique—in which the effect of radiation is always most prompt to make itself felt; and when the 'barbarians' had mastered these Italian arts they were able to apply them on a vastly larger scale than the scale of the Italian city-states.

The explanation of the 'barbarians'' success in achieving a scale of organization which the Italians had found to be beyond their powers lies in the fact that the 'barbarians' were applying the lessons learnt from the Italians in far easier circumstances than those that were the Italians' lot. Italian statesmanship was handicapped and 'barbarian' statesmanship facilitated by the operation of one of the regular laws of 'the Balance of Power'.

The Balance of Power is a system of political dynamics that comes into play whenever a society articulates itself into a number of mutually independent local states; and the Italian Society that had differentiated itself from the rest of Western Christendom had at the same time articulated itself in this very way. The movement to extricate Italy from the Holy Roman Empire had been carried through by a host of city-states which were striving, each for itself, to assert a right of local self-determination; thus the creation of an Italian World apart and the articulation of this world into a multiplicity of states were coeval events. In such a world the Balance of Power operates in a general way to keep the average calibre of states low in terms of every criterion for the measurement of political power: in territory, population and wealth. For any state which threatens to increase its calibre above the prevailing average becomes subject, almost automatically, to pressure from all the other states within reach; and it is one of the laws of the Balance of Power that this pressure is greatest at the centre of the group of states concerned and weakest at the periphery.

At the centre any move that any one state makes with a view to its own aggrandizement is jealously watched and adroitly countered by all its neighbours, and the sovereignty over a few square miles becomes a subject for the stubbornest contention. On the periphery, by contrast, competition is relaxed and small efforts will secure great results. The United States can expand unobtrusively from the Atlantic to the Pacific, and Russia can expand from the Baltic to the Pacific, while all the efforts of France or Germany will not suffice to obtain unchallenged possession of Alsace or of Posen.

What Russia and the United States are to the old and cramped nation-states of Western Europe to-day, those communities themselves four hundred years ago—a France politically Italianized by Louis XI, a Spain politically Italianized by Ferdinand of Aragon and an England politically Italianized by the early Tudors—were to such contemporary Italian city-states as Florence, Venice and Milan.

On a comparative view we can see that the Athenian withdrawal in the eighth, seventh and sixth centuries B.C. and the Italian withdrawal in the thirteenth, fourteenth and fifteenth centuries of the Christian Era display a strong resemblance to one another. In both cases the withdrawal, on the political plane, was complete and persistent. In both cases the self-segregating minority devoted its energies to the task of finding some solution for a problem that confronted the whole society. And in both cases the creative minority returned in the fullness of time, when its work of creation was accomplished, to the society which it had temporarily abandoned, and set its impress upon the whole body social. Moreover, the actual problems which Athens and Italy solved during their withdrawal were much the same. Like Attica in Hellas, Lombardy and Tuscany in Western Christendom served as a segregated social laboratory in which the experiment of transforming a locally self-sufficient agricultural society into an internationally interdependent industrial and commercial society was successfully carried out. And in the Italian as in the Athenian case there was a radical remodelling of traditional institutions in order to bring them into conformity with the new way of life. A commercialized and industrialized Athens changed over, on the political plane, from an aristocratic constitution based on birth to a bourgeois constitution based on property. A commercialized and industrialized Milan or Bologna or Florence or Siena changed over from the prevalent feudalism of Western Christendom to a new system of direct relations between the individual citizens and the locally sovereign governments whose sovereignty resided in the citizens themselves. These concrete economic and political inventions, as well as the impalpable and imponderable creations of the Italian genius, were communicated by Italy to Transalpine Europe from the close of the fifteenth century onwards.

At this stage, however, the respective courses of Western and Hellenic history diverge, on account of one essential point of dissimilarity between the position of the Italian city-states in Western Christendom and the position of Athens in Hellas. Athens was a city-state returning to a world of city-states; but the city-state pattern, on which the Italian world-within-a-world had likewise come to be organized in the course of the Middle Ages, was not the original basis of social articulation in Western Christendom. Its original basis was feudalism, and the greater part of Western Christendom was still organized on a feudal basis at the close of the fifteenth century, when the Italian city-states were re-absorbed into the main body of the Western Society.

This situation presented a problem which could, theoretically, be solved in either of two ways. In order to place itself in a position to adopt the new social inventions which Italy had to offer, Transalpine Europe might either break with its feudal past and rearticulate itself throughout on a city-state basis; or it might modify the Italian inventions in such a way as to make them workable on the feudal basis and the corresponding kingdom-state scale. In spite of the fact that city-state systems had achieved a considerable measure of success in Switzerland, Swabia, Franconia, the Netherlands and on the North German plain, where the key-points controlling inland and maritime waterways were the cities of the Hanseatic League, it was the non-city-state solution of the problem that was generally adopted beyond the Alps. And this brings us to another chapter of Western history and to another equally remarkable and fruitful withdrawal-and-return.

England in the Third Chapter of the Growth of the Western Society

The problem now confronting the Western Society was how to change over from an agricultural aristocratic to an industrial democratic way of life without adopting the city-state system. This challenge was taken up in Switzerland, in Holland and in England, and it eventually received an English solution. All these three countries were furnished with some degree of assistance from the geographical environment in their withdrawals from the general life of Europe: Switzerland by her mountains, Holland by her dykes and England by the Channel. The Swiss had successfully surmounted the crisis of the late medieval city-state cosmos by establishing a form of federation, and had maintained their independence, first against the Hapsburg and then against the Burgundian Power. The Dutch had established their independence against Spain and had federated as seven United Provinces. The English had been cured of their ambition to conquer Continental dependencies by their ultimate failure in the Hundred Years' War and, like the Dutch, they had repelled under Elizabeth the aggression of Catholic Spain. From that time onwards until the war of 1914–18 the avoidance of Continental entanglements was accepted, without further question, as one of the fundamental and perpetual aims of British foreign policy.

But these three local minorities were not all equally well placed for putting their common policy of withdrawal into effect. The Swiss mountains and the Dutch dykes were less effective barriers than the English Channel. The Dutch never entirely recovered from their wars with Louis XIV, and both Dutch and Swiss were for a time swallowed up in Napoleon's empire. Moreover the Swiss and the Dutch were handicapped in another way as aspirants for finding the solution of the problem that we have already described. They were neither of them fully centralized nation-states but were only loosely federated combinations of cantons and cities. Thus it fell to England, and, after the union of 1707, to the Anglo-Scottish United Kingdom of Great Britain, to play in the third chapter of the history of Western Christendom the part that Italy had played in the second.

It is to be noticed that Italy herself had begun to feel her way towards transcending the limits of the city-state unit, for, by the end of her period of withdrawal, some seventy or eighty independent city-states had been reduced through acts of conquest to some eight or ten larger combinations. But the result was inadequate in two respects. For one thing, these new Italian political units, though large by comparison with what had gone before, were still too small to hold their own against the 'barbarians' when the period of the invasions began. For another, the form of government evolved in these new larger units was always a tyranny, and the political virtue of the city-state system was lost in the process. It was this latter-day Italian despotic system which, crossing the Alps, was readily adapted to the larger Transalpine political units —by Hapsburgs in Spain, by Valois and Bourbons in France, by Hapsburgs again in Austria, and eventually by Hohenzollerns in Prussia. But this apparent line of advance proved a blind alley; for without the achievement of some kind of political democracy it was difficult for the Transalpine countries to emulate the prior Italian economic accomplishment—achieved in Italy under the city-state dispensation—of advancing from agriculture to commerce and industry.

In England, unlike France and Spain, the growth of autocratic monarchy was a challenge which evoked an effective response, and the English response was to breathe new life and import new functions into the traditional constitution of the Transalpine body politic, which was an English as well as a French and a Spanish heritage from the common past of Western Christendom. One of the traditional Transalpine institutions was the periodical holding of a parliament or conference between the Crown and the Estates of the Realm for the double purpose of ventilating grievances and obtaining a vote of supply for the Crown from the Estates as a *quid pro quo* for an honourable undertaking that well-founded grievances should be redressed. In the gradual evolution of this institution the Transalpine kingdoms had discovered how to overcome their regional problem of material scale—the problem of unmanageable numbers and impracticable distances—by inventing or rediscovering the legal fiction of 'representation'. The duty or right of every person concerned in the business done by parliament to take a personal part in the proceedings—a duty or right self-evident in a city-state—was attenuated in these unwieldy feudal kingdoms into a right to be represented by proxy and a duty on the proxy's part to shoulder the burden of travelling to the place where the parliament was to be held.

This feudal institution of a periodical representative and consultative assembly was well fitted for its original purpose of serving as a liaison between the Crown and its subjects. On the other hand it was originally not at all well fitted for the task to which it was successfully adapted in seventeenth-century England —the task of taking over the functions of the Crown itself and gradually superseding it as the mainspring of political authority.

Why was it that the English took up, and met successfully, a challenge with which no other contemporary Transalpine kingdom proved able to cope? The answer to this question will be found in the fact that England, being smaller than the Continental feudal kingdoms and possessed of better-defined frontiers, achieved far earlier than her neighbours a really national as distinct from a feudal existence. It is no mere paradox to say that the strength of English monarchy in the second, or medieval, chapter of the history of Western Christendom made possible its supersession by parliamentary government in the third chapter. No other country in the second chapter experienced such authoritative and disciplinary control as that exercised by William the Conqueror, the first and second Henrys, and the first and third Edwards. Under these strong rulers England was welded into a national unity long before anything like it was achieved in France or Spain or Germany. Another factor making for the same result was the predominance of London. In no other Western Transalpine kingdom did one single city so entirely dwarf all others. At the end of the seventeenth century, when the population of England was still insignificant in comparison with that of France or Germany and less than that of Spain or Italy, London was already in all probability the largest city in Europe. In fact, one may assert that England succeeded in solving the problem of adapting the Italian city-state system to public life on a national scale because, more than any of the other Transalpine nations, she had already achieved—through her small size, her firm frontiers, her strong kings and the predominance of her one great city—something of the compactness and self-consciousness of a city-state writ large.

Yet, even when full allowance is made for these favourable conditions, the English achievement of pouring the new wine of Renaissance Italian administrative efficiency into the old bottles of medieval Transalpine parliamentarism, without allowing these old bottles to burst, is a constitutional triumph that can only be regarded as an astonishing *tour de force*. And this English constitutional *tour de force* of carrying parliament across the gulf that divides the criticism of government from its conduct was performed for the Western Society by the English creative minority during the first phase of its withdrawal from Continental entanglements, a period covering the Elizabethan Age and the greater part of the seventeenth century. When, in response to the challenge from Louis XIV, the English made a partial and temporary return to the Continental arena, under the brilliant leadership of Marlborough, the Continental peoples began to take notice of what the islanders had been doing. The age of *Anglomanie*, as the French sometimes called it, set in. Montesquieu praised—and misunderstood—the English achievement. *Anglomanie*, in the form of a cult of constitutional monarchy, was one of the powder trains that fired the French Revolution, and it is a matter of common knowledge that, as the nineteenth century passed into the twentieth, all the peoples of the Earth became possessed of an ambition to clothe their political nakedness with parliamentary fig-leaves. This widespread worship of English political institutions at the latter end of the third chapter of Western history clearly corresponds with the worship of Italian culture at the latter end of the second phase, at the turn of the fifteenth and sixteenth centuries, an Italy-worship of which the most obvious illustration for Englishmen is the fact that more than three-quarters of Shakespeare's fictional plays are based on Italian tales. Indeed Shakespeare, in *Richard II*, alludes to, and mocks at, the *Italomanie* which his own choice of stories illustrates. The worthy old Duke of York is made to say that the foolish young king is led astray by—

> Report of fashions in proud Italy,
> Whose manners still our tardy apish nation
> Limps after in base imitation.[1]

The dramatist, in his usual anachronistic manner, is attributing to the age of Chaucer what was more characteristic of his own age—though, for that matter, Chaucer and his age saw the beginnings of it.

The English political invention of Parliamentary Government provided a propitious social setting for the subsequent English invention of Industrialism. 'Democracy' in the sense of a system of government in which the executive is responsible to a parliament which is representative of the people, and 'Industrialism' in the sense of a system of machine-production by 'hands' concentrated in factories, are the two master-institutions of our age. They have come to prevail because they offer the best solutions which our Western Society has been able to find for the problem of transposing the political and economic achievement of the Italian city-state culture from the city-state to the kingdom scale;

---

[1] Shakespeare: *Richard the Second*, Act i, sc. ii, ll. 21–3.

and both these solutions have been worked out in England in the age of what one of her latter-day statesmen has called her 'splendid isolation'.

What is to be Russia's Role in our Western History?

In the contemporary history of the Great Society into which our Western Christendom has expanded, can we again discern symptoms of that tendency of one age to overbalance into the next, and of one section of a whole society to solve in isolation the problem of the future while the rest are still working out the implications of the past, which signifies that the process of growth is still continuing? Now that the problems set to us by Italian solutions of earlier problems have themselves received their English solutions, are these English solutions giving rise to new problems in their turn? We are already alive, in our generation, to two new challenges to which we have been exposed by the triumph of Democracy and Industrialism. In particular, the economic system of Industrialism, which means local specialization in skilled and costly production for a world-wide market, demands the establishment of some kind of world order as its framework. And, in general, both Industrialism and Democracy demand from human nature a greater individual self-control and mutual tolerance and public-spirited co-operation than the human social animal has been apt to practise, because these new institutions have put an unprecedentedly powerful drive into all human social actions. It is generally agreed, for example, that, in the social and technological circumstances in which we now find ourselves, the continued existence of our civilization depends on the elimination of war as a method of settling our differences. Here we are only concerned to observe whether these challenges have evoked any fresh examples of a withdrawal, to be followed by a return.

It is too early to make any certain pronouncements upon a chapter of history that is clearly at present in its opening stages, but we may venture to speculate whether we have not here an explanation of the present posture of Russian Orthodox Christendom. In the Russian Communist movement we have already detected, under a Western masquerade, a 'Zealot' attempt to break away from the Westernization which had been imposed upon Russia two centuries before, by Peter the Great; and at the same time we have seen this masquerade passing over, willy-nilly, into earnest. We have concluded that a Western revolutionary movement, which has been taken up by an unwillingly Westernized Russia as an anti-Western gesture, has turned out to be a more potent agency of Westernization in Russia than any conventional application of the Western social creed; and we have tried to express this latest outcome of the social intercourse between Russia and the West in the formula that a relation which was once an external contact between two separate societies has been transformed into an internal experience of the Great Society into which Russia has now been incorporated. Can we go farther and say that Russia, being now incorporated into the Great Society, has at the same time been making a withdrawal from its common life in order to play the part of a creative minority which will strive to work out some solution for the Great Society's current problems? It is at least conceivable, and is believed by many admirers of the present Russian experiment, that Russia will make her return to the Great Society in this creative role.

XII. DIFFERENTIATION THROUGH GROWTH

WE have now completed our investigation of the process through which civilizations grow and, in the several instances which we have examined, the process seems to be one and the same. Growth is achieved when an individual or a minority or a whole society replies to a challenge by a response which not only answers that challenge but also exposes the respondent to a fresh challenge which demands a further response on his part. But although the process of growth may be uniform the experience of the various parties that undergo the challenge is not the same. The variety of experience in confronting a single series of common challenges is manifest when we compare the experiences of the several different communities into which any single society is articulated. Some succumb, while others strike out a successful response through a creative movement of Withdrawal-and-Return, while others neither succumb nor succeed but manage to survive until the member which has succeeded shows them the new pathway, along which they follow tamely in the footsteps of the pioneers. Each successive challenge thus produces differentiation within the society, and the longer the series of challenges the more sharply pronounced will this differentiation become. Moreover, if the process of growth thus gives rise to differentiation within a single growing society where the challenges are the same for all, then, *a fortiori*, the same process must differentiate one growing society from another where the challenges themselves differ in character.

A conspicuous illustration presents itself in the domain of art, for it is generally recognized that every civilization creates an artistic style of its own; and if we are attempting to ascertain the limits of any particular civilization in space or time we find that the aesthetic test is the surest as well as the subtlest. For example, a survey of the artistic styles that have prevailed in Egypt brings out the fact that the art of the Pre-Dynastic Age is not yet characteristically Egyptiac, whereas the Coptic art has discarded the characteristically Egyptiac traits; and on this evidence we can establish the time-span of the Egyptiac Civilization. By the same test we can establish the dates at which the Hellenic Civilization emerged from beneath the crust of the Minoan Society, and at which it disintegrated to make way for the Orthodox Christian Society. Again, the style of the Minoan artefacts enables us to delimit the extension in space of the Minoan Civilization in the various stages of its history.

If, then, it is accepted that every civilization has a style of its own in the domain of art, we have to inquire whether the qualitative uniqueness which is the essence of style can appear in this one domain without pervading all the parts and organs and institutions and activities of each separate civilization. Without entering on any ambitious inquiries in this direction we can assert this well-recognized fact that different civilizations lay differing degrees of emphasis on particular lines of activity. The Hellenic Civilization, for example, displays a manifest tendency towards a predominantly aesthetic outlook on life as a whole, illustrated by the fact that the Greek adjective καλός, which properly denotes what is aesthetically beautiful, is employed indiscriminately to stand, in addition, for what is morally good. On the other hand, the Indic Civilization, as well as the affiliated Hindu Civilization, displays an equally manifest tendency towards an outlook that is predominantly religious.

When we come to our own Western Civilization we find no difficulty in detecting our own bent or bias. It is, of course, a penchant towards machinery: a concentration of interest and effort and ability upon applying the discoveries of natural science to material purposes through the ingenious construction of material and social clockwork—material engines such as motor-cars, wrist-watches and bombs, and social engines such as parliamentary constitutions, state systems of insurance and military mobilization time-tables. And this has been our penchant longer than we commonly suppose. Western man was regarded as disgustingly materialistic by the cultivated élite of other civilizations long before the so-called 'Machine Age'. Anna Comnena, the Byzantine princess turned historian, sees our eleventh-century forebears in just this light, as appears in the mixture of horror with contempt which is her reaction to the mechanical ingenuity of the Crusaders' cross-bow, a Western novelty of her day which—with the characteristic precocity of lethal inventions—preceded by several centuries the invention of clockwork, which was medieval Western man's *chef-d'œuvre* in the application of his mechanical bent to the less fascinating arts of peace.

Some recent Western writers, more particularly Spengler, have pursued this subject of the 'characters' of the different civilizations to a point at which sober diagnosis passes over into arbitrary fantasy. We have perhaps said enough to establish the fact that differentiation of some kind does take place, and we should be in danger of losing our sense of proportion if we lost sight of the equally certain and more significant fact that the variety manifested in human life and institutions is a superficial phenomenon which masks an underlying unity without impairing it.

We have compared our civilizations to rock-climbers, and on the showing of this simile the several climbers, though they are certainly separate individuals, are all engaged on an identical enterprise. They are all attempting to scale the face of the same cliff from the same starting-point on a ledge below towards the same goal on a ledge above. The underlying unity is apparent here; and it appears again if we vary our simile and think of the growths of civilizations in terms of the Parable of the Sower. The seeds sown are separate seeds, and each seed has its own destiny. Yet the seeds are all of one kind; and they are all sown by one Sower in the hope of obtaining one harvest.

IV
THE BREAKDOWNS OF CIVILIZATIONS
XIII. THE NATURE OF THE PROBLEM

THE problem of the breakdowns of civilizations is more obvious than the problem of their growths. Indeed it is almost as obvious as the problem of their geneses. The geneses of civilizations call for explanation in view of the mere fact that this species has come into existence and that we are able to enumerate twenty-six representatives of it—including in that number the five arrested civilizations and ignoring the abortive civilizations. We may now go on to observe that, of these twenty-six, no less than sixteen are now dead and buried. The ten survivors are our own Western Society, the main body of Orthodox Christendom in the Near East, its offshoot in Russia, the Islamic Society, the Hindu Society, the main body of the Far Eastern Society in China, its offshoot in Japan, and the three arrested civilizations of the Polynesians, the Eskimos and the Nomads. If we look more closely at these ten survivors we observe that the Polynesian and Nomad societies are now in their last agonies and that seven out of the eight others are all, in different degrees, under threat of either annihilation or assimilation by the eighth, namely our own civilization of the West. Moreover, no less than six out of these seven (the exception being the Eskimo civilization, whose growth was arrested in infancy) bear marks of having already broken down and gone into disintegration.

One of the most conspicuous marks of disintegration, as we have already noticed, is a phenomenon in the last stage but one of the decline and fall, when a disintegrating civilization purchases a reprieve by submitting to forcible political unification in a universal state. For a Western student the classic example is the Roman Empire into which the Hellenic Society was forcibly gathered up in the penultimate chapter of its history. If we now glance at each of the living civilizations, other than our own, we notice that the main body of Orthodox Christendom has already been through a universal state in the shape of the Ottoman Empire; that the offshoot of Orthodox Christendom in Russia entered into a universal state towards the end of the fifteenth century, after the political unification of Muscovy and Novgorod; and that the Hindu Civilization has had its universal state in the Mughal Empire and its successor, the British Raj; the main body of the

Far Eastern Civilization in the Mongol Empire and its resuscitation at the hands of the Manchus; and the Japanese offshoot of the
Far Eastern Civilization in the shape of the Tokugawa Shogunate.
As for the Islamic Society, we may perhaps discern an ideological
premonition of a universal state in the Pan-Islamic Movement.

If we accept this phenomenon of a universal state as a token
of decline, we shall conclude that all the six non-Western civilizations alive to-day had broken down internally before they were
broken in upon by the impact of the Western Civilization from
outside. At a later stage of this Study we shall find reason for
believing that a civilization which has become the victim of a
successful intrusion has already in fact broken down internally
and is no longer in a state of growth. For our present purpose it
is enough to observe that of the living civilizations every one has
already broken down and is in process of disintegration except
our own.

And what of our Western Civilization? It has manifestly not
yet reached the stage of a universal state. But we found, in an
earlier chapter, that the universal state is not the first stage in
disintegration any more than it is the last. It is followed by what
we have called an 'interregnum', and preceded by what we have
called a 'time of troubles', which seems usually to occupy several
centuries; and if we in our generation were to permit ourselves to
judge by the purely subjective criterion of our own feeling about
our own age, the best judges would probably declare that our
'time of troubles' had undoubtedly descended upon us. But let
us leave this question open for the present.

We have already defined the nature of these breakdowns of
civilizations. They are failures in an audacious attempt to ascend
from the level of a primitive humanity to the height of some
superhuman kind of living, and we have described the casualties
in this great enterprise by the use of various similes. We have,
for example, compared them to climbers who fall to their death,
or to an ignominious state of life-in-death, upon the ledge from
which they have last started, before completing the 'pitch' and
reaching a new resting-place on the ledge above. We have also
described the nature of these breakdowns in non-material terms
as a loss of creative power in the souls of creative individuals or
minorities, a loss which divests them of their magic power to
influence the souls of the uncreative masses. Where there is no
creation there is no mimesis. The piper who has lost his cunning
can no longer conjure the feet of the multitude into a dance; and
if, in rage and panic, he now attempts to convert himself into a
drill-sergeant or a slave-driver, and to coerce by physical force a

people that he can now no longer lead by his old magnetic charm, then all the more surely and swiftly he defeats his own intention; for the followers who had merely flagged and fallen out of step as the heavenly music died away will be stung by a touch of the whip into active rebellion.

We have seen, in fact, that when, in the history of any society, a creative minority degenerates into a dominant minority which attempts to retain by force a position that it has ceased to merit, this change in the character of the ruling element provokes, on the other side, the secession of a proletariat which no longer admires and imitates its rulers and revolts against its servitude. We have also seen that this proletariat, when it asserts itself, is divided from the outset into two distinct parts. There is an internal proletariat, prostrate and recalcitrant, and an external proletariat beyond the frontiers who now violently resist incorporation.

On this showing, the nature of the breakdowns of civilizations can be summed up in three points: a failure of creative power in the minority, an answering withdrawal of mimesis on the part of the majority and a consequent loss of social unity in the society as a whole. With this picture of the nature of these breakdowns in our mind, we may now proceed to inquire into their cause: an inquiry which will occupy all the rest of this part of our Study.

XIV. DETERMINISTIC SOLUTIONS

WHAT, then, causes the breakdowns of civilizations? Before applying our own method, which involves the marshalling of the relevant concrete facts of history, we had better pass in review certain solutions of the problem which soar higher in search of their evidence and rely for proof either on unprovable dogmas or else on things outside the sphere of human history.

One of the perennial infirmities of human beings is to ascribe their own failure to forces that are entirely beyond their control. This mental manœuvre is particularly attractive to sensitive minds in periods of decline and fall; and in the decline and fall of the Hellenic Civilization it was a commonplace of various schools of philosophers to explain the social decay which they deplored but could not arrest as the incidental and inevitable effect of an all-pervasive onset of 'cosmic senescence'. This was the philosophy of Lucretius (cf. *De Rerum Natura*, Bk. II, ll. 1144–74) in the last generation of the Hellenic time of troubles, and the same theme recurs in a work of controversy written by one of the Fathers of the Western Church, St. Cyprian, when the Hellenic universal state was beginning to break up three hundred years later. He writes:

'You ought to be aware that the age is now senile. It has not now the stamina that used to make it upstanding, nor the vigour and robustness that used to make it strong. . . . There is a diminution in the winter rains that give nourishment to the seeds in the earth, and in the summer heats that ripen the harvests. . . . This is the sentence that has been passed upon the World; this is the law of God; that what has been must die, and what has grown up must grow old.'

Modern physical science has knocked the bottom out of this theory, at any rate so far as any civilization now extant is concerned. It is true that modern physicists envisage, in an unimaginably distant future, a 'running down' of the 'clock' of the Universe as a consequence of the inevitable transformation of matter into radiation, but that future is, as we have said, unimaginably distant. Sir James Jeans writes:

'Taking a very gloomy view of the future of the human race, let us suppose that it can only expect to survive for two thousand million years longer, a period about equal to the past age of the Earth. Then, regarded as a being destined to live for three-score years and ten, Humanity, although it has been born in a house only seventy years old, is itself only three days old. . . . Utterly inexperienced beings, we are standing at the first flush of the dawn of civilization. . . . In time the glory of the morning must fade into the light of common day, and this, in some far distant age, will give place to evening twilight, presaging the final eternal night. But we children of the dawn need give but little thought to the far-off sunset.'[1]

However, our latter-day Western advocates of a predestinarian or deterministic explanation of the breakdowns of civilizations do not attempt to link up the destinies of these human institutions with the destiny of the Physical Universe as a whole. They appeal instead to a law of senescence and death with a shorter wave-length, for which they claim jurisdiction over the whole kingdom of life on this planet. Spengler, whose method is to set up a metaphor and then proceed to argue from it as if it were a law based on observed phenomena, declares that every civilization passes through the same succession of ages as a human being; but his eloquence on this theme nowhere amounts to proof, and we have already noticed that societies are not in any sense living organisms. In subjective terms, societies are the intelligible fields of historical study. In objective terms, they are the common ground between the respective fields of activity of a number of individual human beings, who are themselves living organisms but who cannot conjure up a giant in their own image out of the intersection of their own shadows and then breathe into this unsubstantial body the breath of their own life. The individual energies of all the human beings who constitute the so-called 'members' of a society are the vital forces whose operation works out the history of that society, including its time-span. To declare dogmatically that every society has a predestined time-span is as foolish as it would be to declare that every play is bound to contain just so many acts.

We may dismiss the theory that breakdowns occur when each civilization draws near the close of its biological life-span, because civilizations are entities of a kind that is not subject to the laws of biology; but there is another theory which suggests that, for some reason unexplained, the biological quality of the individuals whose mutual relations constitute a civilization mysteriously declines after a certain or uncertain number of generations; in fact, that the experience of civilization is in the long run essentially and irremediably dysgenic.

> Aetas parentum, peior avis, tulit
> Nos nequiores, mox daturos
> Progeniem vitiosiorem.[2]

---

[1] Jeans, Sir J.: *Eos: or the Wider Aspects of Cosmogony*, pp. 12–13, 83–4.
[2] Horace: *Odes*, Bk. III, Ode vi, last stanza. It has been neatly, though not very poetically, rendered:
> Degenerate sires' degenerate seed,
> We'll soon beget a fourth-rate breed.

This is to put the cart before the horse, and mistake an effect of social decline for the cause of it. For though, in times of social decline, the members of the declining society may seem to dwindle into pygmies, or to stiffen into cripples, by contrast with the kingly stature and magnificent activity of their forefathers in the age of social growth, to ascribe the malady to degeneration is a false diagnosis. The biological heritage of the epigoni is the same as that of the pioneers, and all the pioneers' endeavours and achievements are potentially within their descendants' reach. The malady which inhibits the children of the decadence is no paralysis of their natural faculties but a breakdown of their social inheritance, which debars them from finding scope for their unimpaired faculties in effective and creative social action.

This untenable hypothesis that a racial degeneration is the cause of a social breakdown is sometimes supported by the observation that, during the interregnum that intervenes between the final dissolution of a decadent society and the emergence of a new-born society related to it by affiliation, there is frequently a Völkerwanderung in which the population of the identical home of the two successive societies is treated to an infiltration of 'new blood'. On the logic of *post hoc propter hoc* it is assumed that the fresh access of creative power which the new-born civilization displays in the course of its growth is the gift of this 'new blood' from the 'pure source' of a 'primitive barbarian race'; and it is then inferred that, conversely, the loss of creative power in the life of the antecedent civilization must have been due to some kind of racial anaemia or pyaemia which nothing but a fresh infusion of healthy blood could cure.

In support of this view an alleged case in point is cited from the history of Italy. It is pointed out that the inhabitants of Italy exhibited pre-eminent creative power in the last four centuries B.C. and again during a period of some six centuries from the eleventh to the sixteenth century of the Christian Era, and that these two periods are separated from one another by a millennium of decadence, prostration and convalescence in which it seemed for a time as if virtue had gone out of the Italians altogether. These striking vicissitudes in Italian history would be inexplicable, say the racialists, if it were not for the infusion of the new blood of the invading Goths and Lombards into Italian veins during the interval between the two great ages of Italian achievement. This elixir of life produced in due course, and after centuries of incubation, the Italian rebirth or Renaissance. It was for lack of fresh blood that Italy languished and declined under the Roman Empire after the demonic output of energy in the days of the Roman

Republic. And this energy which burst into action with the rise of the Republic was doubtless itself the product of an earlier infusion of fresh barbarian blood during the Völkerwanderung which preceded the birth of the Hellenic Civilization.

This racial explanation of Italian history up to the sixteenth century of the Christian Era has a superficial plausibility as long as we are content to stop at that point in time. But if we allow our thoughts to travel on from the sixteenth century to the present day we shall find that, after a further period of decadence in the seventeenth and eighteenth centuries, Italy was the scene, in the nineteenth century, of another resurrection so dramatic that the name (Risorgimento) is now applied, without qualification, exclusively to this modern repetition of a medieval Italian experience. And what infusion of pure barbarian blood had preceded this last outburst of Italian energy? The answer is, of course, 'None'. The main immediate cause, historians seem to agree, of the nineteenth-century Italian Risorgimento was the general shake-up and challenge administered to Italy by the experience of being conquered and temporarily ruled by a Revolutionary and Napoleonic France.

It is not more difficult to find non-racial explanations for the previous rise of Italy at the beginning of the second millennium of the Christian Era, and for her still earlier decline which declared itself in the course of the last two centuries B.C. This last-mentioned decline was evidently the nemesis of a Roman militarism which brought upon Italy all the appalling train of social evils that followed in the wake of the Hannibalic War. The beginnings of social recovery in Italy, during the post-Hellenic interregnum, can be traced with equal certainty to the work of creative personalities of the old Italian race, more particularly to Saint Benedict and to Pope Gregory the Great, who are the fathers not only of the rejuvenated Italy of the Middle Ages but of the new Western Civilization in which the medieval Italians were participants. Conversely, when we survey the districts of Italy which were overrun by the 'pure-blooded' Lombards, we find that the list excludes Venice and the Romagna and other districts which played parts in the Italian Renaissance as distinguished as theirs and far more distinguished than those played by the cities known to have been centres of Lombard authority: Pavia, Benevento and Spoleto. If we wanted to furbish up a racial explanation of Italian history we could easily submit evidence that Lombard blood had proved a taint rather than an elixir.

We can drive the racialists out of their one remaining stronghold in Italian history by suggesting a non-racial explanation for the rise of the Roman Republic. It can be explained as a response to the challenge of Greek and Etruscan colonization. Were the native peoples of the Italian Peninsula to resign themselves to that choice between extermination, subjugation or assimilation which had been forced by the Greeks on their cousins in Sicily and by the Etruscans upon the natives of Umbria? or were they to hold their own against the intruders by adopting the Hellenic Civilization of their own accord and on their own terms (as Japan has been adopting that of Western Europe), and thereby raising themselves to the Greek and Etruscan level of efficiency? The Romans decided to make this latter response, and in taking this decision they became the authors of their own subsequent greatness.

We have now disposed of three deterministic explanations of the breakdowns of civilizations: the theory that they are due to the 'running down' of the 'clockwork' of the Universe or to the senescence of the Earth; the theory that a civilization, like a living organism, has a life-span determined by the biological laws of its nature; and the theory that the breakdowns are due to a deterioration in the quality of the individuals participating in a civilization, as a result of their pedigrees' accumulating too long a tale of 'civilized' ancestors. We have still to consider one further hypothesis, generally referred to as the cyclical theory of history.

The invention of this theory of cycles in the history of Mankind was a natural corollary to the sensational astronomical discovery, apparently made in the Babylonic Society at some date between the eighth and sixth centuries B.C., that the three conspicuous and familiar cycles—the day-and-night, the lunar month and the solar year—were not the only examples of periodic recurrence in the movements of the heavenly bodies; that there was also a larger co-ordination of stellar movements embracing all the planets as well as Earth, Moon and Sun; and that 'the music of the spheres', which was made by the harmony of this heavenly chorus, came round full circle, chord for chord, in a great cycle which dwarfed the solar year into insignificance. The inference was that the annual birth and death of vegetation, which was manifestly governed by the solar cycle, had its counterpart in a recurrent birth and death of all things on the time-scale of the cosmic cycle.

The interpretation of human history in these cyclic terms evidently fascinated Plato (*Timaeus*, 21 E–23 C, and *Politicus*, 269 C–273 E), and the same doctrine reappears in one of the most famous passages in Virgil, from the Fourth Eclogue:—

Ultima Cumaei venit iam carminis aetas;
Magnus ab integro saeclorum nascitur ordo.
Iam redit et virgo, redeunt Saturnia regna,
Iam nova progenies caelo demittitur alto. . . .
Alter erit tum Tiphys et altera quae vehat Argo
Delectos heroas; erunt etiam altera bella
Atque iterum ad Troiam magnus mittetur Achilles.[1]

Virgil uses the cyclic theory to adorn a paean of optimism inspired by the Augustan pacification of the Hellenic World. But is it a matter for congratulation that 'the old wars will be refought'? Many individuals who have had reasonably successful and happy lives have declared with conviction that they would not like to live them over again, and is history at large more worthy of an 'encore' than the average biography? This question, which Virgil does not face, is answered by Shelley in the last chorus of his *Hellas*, which begins as a Virgilian reminiscence and ends on a note which is altogether Shelley's own:

The World's great age begins anew,
    The golden years return,
The Earth doth like a snake renew
    Her winter weeds outworn:
Heaven smiles, and faiths and empires gleam
Like wrecks of a dissolving dream. . . .

A loftier Argo cleaves the main,
    Fraught with a later prize;
Another Orpheus sings again,
    And loves and weeps and dies;
A new Ulysses leaves once more
Calypso for his native shore.

Oh write no more the tale of Troy,
    If Earth Death's scroll must be—
Nor mix with Laian rage the joy
    Which dawns upon the free,
Although a subtler Sphinx renew
Riddles of death Thebes never knew. . . .

Oh cease! must hate and death return?
    Cease! must men kill and die?
Cease! drain not to its dregs the urn
    Of bitter prophecy!
The World is weary of the past,—
Oh might it die or rest at last!

[1] 'Already the last age foretold in the Cumaean prophecy has come; the great order of the ages comes to birth again afresh. Already the Virgin and the Golden Age are returning; already a new race is being sent down from High Heaven. . . . There will be another Tiphys and another Argo to carry a chosen band of heroes. The old wars will be refought and once again great Achilles will be sent to Troy.'

If the law of the Universe is really the sardonic *Plus ça change plus c'est la même chose,* no wonder that the poet cries, in Buddhist mood, for release from the wheel of existence, which may be a thing of beauty so long as it is merely guiding the stars in their courses, but which is an intolerable treadmill for our human feet.

Does reason constrain us to believe, quite apart from any alleged influence of the stars, in a cyclic movement of human history? Have we not, in the course of this Study, ourselves given encouragement to such a supposition? What of those movements of Yin and Yang, Challenge and Response, Withdrawal and Return, Apparentation and Affiliation, which we have elucidated? Are they not variations on the trite theme that 'History repeats itself'? Certainly, in the movement of all these forces that weave the web of human history, there is an obvious element of recurrence. Yet the shuttle which shoots backwards and forwards across the loom of Time in a perpetual to-and-fro is all this time bringing into existence a tapestry in which there is manifestly a developing design and not simply an endless repetition of the same pattern. This, too, we have seen again and again. The metaphor of the wheel in itself offers an illustration of recurrence being concurrent with progress. The movement of the wheel is admittedly repetitive in relation to the wheel's own axle, but the wheel has only been made and fitted to its axle in order to give mobility to a vehicle of which the wheel is merely a part, and the fact that the vehicle, which is the wheel's *raison d'être,* can only move in virtue of the wheel's circular movement round its axle does not compel the vehicle itself to travel like a merry-go-round in a circular track.

This harmony of two diverse movements—a major irreversible movement which is born on the wings of a minor repetitive movement—is perhaps the essence of what we mean by rhythm; and we can discern this play of forces not only in vehicular traction and in modern machinery but likewise in the organic rhythm of life. The annual procession of the seasons, which brings with it the annual withdrawal and return of vegetation, has made possible the secular evolution of the Vegetable Kingdom. The sombre cycle of birth, reproduction and death has made possible the evolution of all the higher animals up to Man. The alternation of a pair of legs enables a walker to 'cover the ground'; the pumping actions of the lungs and the heart enable an animal to live out its life; the bars of music and the metres and stanzas of poetry enable the composer and the poet to expound their themes. The planetary 'Great Year' itself, which is perhaps the origin of the whole cyclic philosophy, can no longer be mistaken for the ultimate and all-embracing movement of a stellar cosmos in which our local solar system has now dwindled to the diminutiveness of a speck of dust under the mighty magnifying lenses of our latter-day Western astronomy. The repetitive 'music of the spheres' dies down to a mere subsidiary accompaniment, a species of 'Alberti bass',[1] in an expanding universe of star-clusters which are apparently receding from one another with incredible velocity, while the relativity of the space-time framework gives to each successive position of the vast astral array the irrevocable historic uniqueness of a dramatic situation in some play in which the actors are living personalities.

Thus the detection of periodic repetitive movements in our analysis of the process of civilization does not imply that the process itself is of the same cyclic order as they are. On the contrary, if any inference can legitimately be drawn from the periodicity of these minor movements, we may rather infer that the major movement which they bear along is not recurrent but progressive. Humanity is not an Ixion bound for ever to his wheel nor a Sisyphus for ever rolling his stone to the summit of the same mountain and helplessly watching it roll down again.

This is a message of encouragement for us children of the Western Civilization as we drift to-day alone, with none but stricken civilizations around us. It may be that Death the Leveller will lay his icy hand on our civilization also. But we are not confronted with any *Saeva Necessitas*. The dead civilizations are not dead by fate, or 'in the course of nature', and therefore our living civilization is not doomed inexorably in advance to 'join the majority' of its species. Though sixteen civilizations may have perished already to our knowledge, and nine others may be now at the point of death, we—the twenty-sixth—are not compelled to submit the riddle of our fate to the blind arbitrament of statistics. The divine spark of creative power is still alive in us, and, if we have the grace to kindle it into flame, then the stars in their courses cannot defeat our efforts to attain the goal of human endeavour.

---

[1] A musical term for the 'diddle-diddle' accompaniments common in eighteenth-century keyboard music. For 'diddle-diddle' we have the authority of the late Sir Donald Tovey.—EDITOR.

XV. LOSS OF COMMAND OVER THE ENVIRONMENT

(1) THE PHYSICAL ENVIRONMENT

IF we have proved to our satisfaction that the breakdowns of civilizations are not brought about by the operation of cosmic forces outside human control, we have still to find the true cause of these catastrophes; and we will first consider the possibility that these breakdowns are due to some loss of command over the society's environment. In attempting to solve this problem we will employ the distinction that we have already made between two kinds of environment: the physical and the human.

Do civilizations break down owing to loss of command over their physical environments? The degree of command over its physical environment possessed by any society can be measured, as we have already pointed out, by its technique; and we have already ascertained, while studying the problem of 'growth', that, if we set ourselves to plot out two sets of curves—one set representing the vicissitudes of civilizations and the other the vicissitudes of techniques—the two sets of curves not only fail to correspond but display wide discrepancies. We have found cases of technique improving while civilizations remain static or decline and cases of technique remaining static while civilizations are in movement, either forward or backward as the case may be.[1] We have therefore already gone a long way towards proving that loss of command over physical environment is not the criterion of the breakdowns of civilizations. In order to complete our proof, however, we have to show that, in cases where the breakdown of a civilization has been coincident with a decline in technique, the latter has not been the cause of the former. We shall find, as a matter of fact, that the decline in technique has been, not a cause, but a consequence or symptom.

When a civilization is in decline it sometimes happens that a particular technique, that has been both feasible and profitable during the growth-stage, now begins to encounter social obstacles and to yield diminishing economic returns; if it becomes patently unremunerative it may be deliberately abandoned. In such a case it would obviously be a complete inversion of the true order of cause and effect to suggest that the abandonment of the technique in such circumstances was due to a technical inability to practise it and that this technical inability was a cause of the breakdown of the civilization.

[1] See pp. 187–98.

An obvious case in point is the abandonment of the Roman roads in Western Europe, which was obviously not a cause but a consequence of the breakdown of the Roman Empire. These roads became derelict, not through a failure of technical skill, but because the society which required them, and had made them for its military and commercial purposes, had gone to pieces. Nor can the decline and fall of the Hellenic Civilization be traced back to a decline in technique by simply extending our vision from the single technique of road-making to embrace the whole technical apparatus of economic life.

'The economic explanation of the decay of the Ancient World must be rejected completely. . . . The economic simplification of ancient life was not the cause of what we call the decline of the Ancient World but one of the aspects of the more general phenomenon.'[1]

This more general phenomenon was 'the failure of administration and the ruin of the middle class'.

The abandonment of the Roman roads had a more or less contemporary parallel in the partial abandonment of the far older irrigation system in the alluvial delta of the Tigris-Euphrates Basin. In the seventh century of the Christian Era the reconditioning of these hydro-engineering works was left in default in a large section of South-Western 'Irāq after the works had been put out of action by a flood which had probably done no more serious damage than many floods that had come and gone in the course of four thousand years. Thereafter, in the thirteenth century, the whole irrigation system of 'Irāq was allowed to go to ruin. Why, on these occasions, did the inhabitants of 'Irāq abandon the conservation of a system which their predecessors had successfully maintained for some thousands of years without a break—a system on which the agricultural productivity and the maintenance of the dense population of the country depended? This lapse in a matter of technique was in fact not the cause but the consequence of a decline in population and prosperity which was itself due to social causes. Both in the seventh century of the Christian Era and afterwards in the thirteenth the Syriac Civilization was at so low an ebb in 'Irāq, and the consequent general state of insecurity was so extreme, that nobody had either the means of investing capital or the motive for employing energy in river conservancy and irrigation work. In the seventh century the true causes of the technical failure were the great Romano-Persian war of A.D. 603–28 and the subsequent over-running of 'Irāq by the primitive

---

[1] Rostovtzeff, M.: *The Social and Economic History of the Roman Empire*, pp. 302–5 and 482–5.

Muslim Arabs; in the thirteenth century, the Mongol invasion of A.D. 1258 which dealt the Syriac Society its *coup de grâce*.

We reach a similar conclusion when we follow out a train of investigation which is suggested by a remarkable finding of empirical observation in Ceylon.[1] In Ceylon at the present day the area which contains the ruined monuments of the Indic Civilization is coincident, not only with the area permanently afflicted by drought, but also with the area that is nowadays infested with malaria. This latter-day perversity of a water-supply which suffices for the anopheles mosquito while it is wholly inadequate for raising crops is at first sight a strange setting for a bygone civilization, and it is extremely unlikely that the malaria should have been already prevalent at the time when the pioneers of the Indic Society in Ceylon constructed their amazing system of waterworks. As a matter of fact it can be demonstrated that the malaria is a consequence of the ruin of the irrigation system and therefore posterior to its construction. This part of Ceylon became malarious because the breakdown of the irrigation system transformed the artificial watercourses into chains of stagnant pools and destroyed the fish which had lived in the watercourses and kept them clear of mosquito-grubs.

But why was the Indic irrigation system abandoned? Those bunds were breached and those channels were choked in the course of an incessant and devastating warfare. The works were deliberately sabotaged by invaders as a short cut to their military objective; and a war-worn people had not the heart to go on repairing a damage that had been inflicted on them so many times and seemed certain to be inflicted again. Thus the technical factor dwindles, in this case again, into an incidental and subordinate link in a chain of social cause and effect which has still to be traced back to its social origins.

This chapter in the history of the Indic Civilization in Ceylon has a close parallel in the history of the Hellenic Civilization. Here too we find that some of the regions where this now vanished civilization lived its most brilliant life and put forth its most vital energies have since become malarial swamps that have been reclaimed within living memory. The Copaic Marshes, which have been drained by the enterprise of a British company since A.D. 1887, after having been a pestilential swamp for at least two thousand years, were once the fields that fed the citizens of Orchomenos the Wealthy; and the Pomptine Marshes, drained and re-populated under Mussolini's régime after as long a period of desolation, once harboured a swarm of Volscian cities and Latin colonies. It has

[1] For a previous discussion of this subject in another aspect see pp. 81-2.

indeed been suggested that the 'loss of nerve' (the phrase is Professor Gilbert Murray's) which was at the heart of the Hellenic breakdown was caused by the entry of malaria into the Hellenic homelands. But there is reason to believe that in each of these areas, as in Ceylon, the reign of malaria did not begin until the reigning civilization had·passed its zenith. A modern authority[1] who has made the subject his own concludes that in Greece malaria did not become endemic until after the Peloponnesian War; and in Latium the disease does not seem to have gained the upper hand until after the Hannibalic War. It would obviously be absurd to suggest that the Greeks of the Post-Alexandrine Age and the Romans of the Age of the Scipios and the Caesars were inhibited by some technical inefficiency from continuing to cope with the water problems of the Copaic and Pomptine marshes which had been solved by their technically less expert forefathers. The explanation of the contrast is to be found not on the technical but on the social plane. The Hannibalic War and the Roman predatory and civil wars which followed in its train during the next two centuries had a profoundly disintegrating effect upon Italian social life. The peasant culture and economy were first undermined and finally swept away by the cumulative effect of a number of inimical forces: the devastations of Hannibal; the perpetual mobilization of the peasantry for military service; the agrarian revolution which substituted large-scale farming with slave-labour for the small-scale farming of a self-subsistent peasantry; and a mass migration from the countryside to parasitic cities. This combination of social evils amply accounts for man's retreat and the mosquito's advance during the seven centuries between the generation of Hannibal and the generation of Saint Benedict in Italy.

As for Greece, a similar combination of evils, going back to the Peloponnesian War, had resulted by the time of Polybius (206–128 B.C.) in a degree of depopulation which was more extreme than the rather later depopulation of Italy. In a famous passage Polybius lays his finger on the practice of restricting the size of families, by abortion or infanticide, as the principal cause of the social and political downfall of Greece in his day. It is apparent, then, that no failure in engineering technique is needed to explain why the Copaic, like the Pomptine, plain was allowed to transform itself from a granary into a nest of mosquitoes.

We shall arrive at corresponding conclusions if we pass from the practical technique of engineering to the artistic techniques of architecture and sculpture and painting and calligraphy and litera-

[1] Jones, W. H. S.: *Malaria and Greek History.*

ture. Why, for example, did the Hellenic style of architecture
go out of use between the fourth and seventh centuries of the
Christian Era? Why did the Ottoman Turks abandon the Arabic
Alphabet in 1928? Why is almost every non-Western society in
the world now discarding its traditional style in dress and in the
arts? And, for a start, we may as well bring the problem home to
ourselves by asking why our own traditional manners of music
and dancing and painting and sculpture are being abandoned by
a large section of our rising generation.

In our own case, is the explanation a loss of artistic technique?
Have we forgotten the rules of rhythm and counterpoint and
perspective and proportion which were discovered by the Italian
and other creative minorities in the second and third chapters of
our history? Obviously we have not. The prevailing tendency
to abandon our artistic traditions is not the result of technical
incompetence; it is the deliberate abandonment of a style which
is losing its appeal to a rising generation because this generation
is ceasing to cultivate its aesthetic sensibilities on the traditional
Western lines. We have wilfully cast out of our souls the great
masters who have been the familiar spirits of our forefathers; and,
while we have been wrapped in self-complacent admiration of the
spiritual vacuum that we have created, a Tropical African spirit
in music and dancing and statuary has made an unholy alliance
with a pseudo-Byzantine spirit in painting and bas-relief, and
has entered in to dwell in a house which it found swept and gar-
nished. The decline is not technical in origin but spiritual. In
repudiating our own Western tradition of art and thereby reducing
our faculties to a state of inanition and sterility in which they seize
upon the exotic and primitive art of Dahomey and Benin as though
this were manna in the wilderness, we are confessing before all
men that we have forfeited our spiritual birthright. Our abandonment of our traditional artistic technique is manifestly the consequence of some kind of spiritual breakdown in our Western
Civilization; and the cause of this breakdown evidently cannot
be found in a phenomenon which is one of its results.

The recent abandonment of the Arabic Alphabet by the Turks
in favour of the Latin Alphabet is to be explained on the same lines.
Mustafā Kemāl Ataturk and his disciples have been thorough-
going Westernizers within their own Islamic World. They have
lost faith in the traditions of their own civilization, and have
consequently discarded the literary medium through which it has
been transmitted. A similar explanation would account for the
discarding of other traditional scripts by other moribund civilizations of an earlier day: for instance, the hieroglyphic script in

Egypt and the cuneiform in Babylonia. A movement in favour of abolishing the Sinic script is now discernible in China and Japan.

An interesting example of the substitution of one technique for another is the abandonment of the Hellenic style of architecture in favour of the newfangled Byzantine style. In this case the architects of a society in its death-throes were abandoning the comparatively simple scheme of architrave on column in order to experiment in the unusually difficult problem of crowning a cruciform building with a circular dome, so there can have been no failure of technical competence. Is it credible that the Ionian architects who triumphantly solved the constructional problems of the church of the Haghia Sophia for the Emperor Justinian could not have built a Classical Greek temple if that had been the autocrat's will—and theirs? Justinian and his architects adopted a new style because the old style had become distasteful to them through its associations with the remains of a dead and rotting past.

The upshot of our investigation seems to be that the abandonment of a traditional artistic style is an indication that the civilization associated with that style has long since broken down and is now disintegrating. Like the disuse of an established technique, it is the consequence of breakdown, not the cause.

(2) THE HUMAN ENVIRONMENT

When we previously considered this subject in connexion with the growths of civilizations, we found that the degree of command over the human environment possessed by any given society at any stage in its history could be roughly measured in terms of geographical expansion; and we also found, from a study of examples, that geographical expansion was frequently accompanied by social disintegration. If this be so, it seems extremely improbable that the cause of this self-same breakdown and disintegration is to be found in the precisely opposite tendency—a tendency, that is to say, towards a decrease in command over the human environment, as measured by a successful encroachment of alien human forces. Nevertheless, the view has been widely held that civilizations, like primitive societies, lose their lives as the result of successful assaults upon them on the part of external powers; and a classic exposition of this view is given by Edward Gibbon in *The History of the Decline and Fall of the Roman Empire*. The theme is declared in the single sentence in which Gibbon sums up his story in retrospect: 'I have described the triumph of Barbarism and Religion.' The Hellenic Society, embodied in a Roman Empire which was at its zenith in the Age of the Antonines, is represented as having been overthrown by a simultaneous assault from two alien enemies attacking on two different fronts: the North European barbarians issuing out of the no-man's-land beyond the Danube and the Rhine and the Christian Church emerging from the subjugated but never assimilated Oriental provinces.

It never occurred to Gibbon that the Age of the Antonines was not the summer but the 'Indian summer' of Hellenic history. The degree of his hallucination is betrayed by the very title of his great work. The decline and fall of the Roman Empire! The author of a history that bears that name and that starts in the second century of the Christian Era is surely beginning his narrative at a point that is very near the end of the actual story. For the 'intelligible field of historical study' with which Gibbon is concerned is not the Roman Empire but the Hellenic Civilization, of whose far-advanced disintegration the Roman Empire itself was a monumental symptom. When the whole story is taken into account, the rapid decline of the Empire after the Antonine Age is seen to be not at all surprising. On the contrary, it would have been surprising if the Roman Empire had endured; for this Empire was already doomed before it was established.[1] It was doomed because the establishment of this universal state was nothing but a rally which could delay, but not permanently arrest, the already irretrievable ruin of the Hellenic Society.

If Gibbon had set himself to tell this longer story from its beginning he would have found that 'the triumph of Barbarism and Religion' was not the plot of the piece, but only an epilogue to it—not the cause of the breakdown but only an inevitable accompaniment of a dissolution in which the long process of disintegration was bound to end. More than that, he would have found that the triumphant Church and Barbarians were, after all, not external powers, but were really children of the Hellenic household who had been morally alienated from the dominant minority in the course of a time of troubles which had intervened between the Periclean breakdown and the Augustan rally. In fact, if Gibbon had carried his inquest back to the true beginning of the tragedy, he would have had to return a different verdict. He would have had to report that the Hellenic Society was a suicide who had attempted, when his life was already past saving, to avert the fatal consequences of his assault upon himself, and who eventually received a *coup de grâce* from his own mishandled and alienated children at a time when the Augustan rally had already given place to a third-century relapse and the patient was

---

[1] The unique case of the Egyptiac Empire, which endured for centuries long after it ought, on all analogies, to have been dead has been discussed on pp. 31–3.

manifestly dying from the after-effects of his old self-inflicted wounds.

In these circumstances the historian-coroner would not concentrate his attention on the epilogue but would try to determine exactly when and how the suicide had first laid violent hands upon himself. In prospecting for a date he would probably lay his finger on the outbreak of the Peloponnesian War in 431 B.C.—a social catastrophe which Thucydides, speaking through the mouth of one of the characters of his tragic drama, denounced at the time as 'a beginning of great evils for Hellas'. In reporting upon how the members of the Hellenic Society had perpetrated their self-destructive crime, he would probably lay equal emphasis on the twin evils of war between states and war between classes. Following in Thucydides' footsteps, he would perhaps single out, as specially notorious examples of each of these evils, the appalling punishment inflicted by the Athenians on the conquered Melians and the equally appalling faction-fights at Corcyra. In any case he would declare that the mortal blow was delivered six hundred years earlier than Gibbon supposed, and that the hand that dealt it was the victim's own.

If we now extend our inquest from this case to the cases of some of the other civilizations that are now either undoubtedly dead or apparently moribund, we shall find that the same verdict has to be returned.

For example, in the decline and fall of the Sumeric Society, 'the Golden Age of Hammurabi' (as it is called in the *Cambridge Ancient History*) represents an even later phase of 'the Indian summer' than that which presents itself in the Age of the Antonines; for Hammurabi is the Diocletian rather than the Trajan of Sumeric history. Accordingly we shall not identify the slayers of the Sumeric Civilization with the trans-frontier barbarians who descended on 'the Kingdom of the Four Quarters' in the eighteenth century B.C. We shall detect the fatal strokes in events that had occurred some nine hundred years earlier: the class war between Urukagina of Lagash and the local priesthood and the militarism of Urukagina's destroyer Lugalzaggisi; for those long-past catastrophes were the authentic beginning of the Sumeric time of troubles.

In the decline and fall of the Sinic Society 'the triumph of Barbarism and Religion' is represented by the foundation of Eurasian Nomad successor-states of the Sinic universal state in the basin of the Yellow River round about A.D. 300, and by the simultaneous invasion of the Sinic World by the Mahayanian form of Buddhism, which was one of the religions of the Sinic internal proletariat in the north-western provinces. But these triumphs, like those of 'Barbarism and Religion' in the Roman Empire, were only victories of a moribund society's external and internal proletariats, and they constitute no more than the last chapter of the whole story. The Sinic universal state itself represented a social rally after a time of troubles in which the Sinic body social had been torn in pieces by fratricidal warfare between a number of parochial states into which the Sinic Society had previously articulated itself. The fatal date that, in the Sinic tradition, corresponds to the Hellenic 431 B.C. is 479 B.C., which is the conventional starting-point of what the tradition called 'the Period of Contending States'. Probably, however, this conventional date is some two hundred and fifty years later than the actual event, and has been taken as the beginning of the Sinic time of troubles simply because it is also the traditional date of the death of Confucius.

As for the Syriac Society, which enjoyed its 'Indian summer' under the 'Abbasid Caliphate of Baghdad and which saw 'the triumph of Barbarism and Religion' in the invasions of the Nomad Turks and their conversion to the indigenous religion of Islam, we have to remember a point that we established much earlier in this Study—that the Syriac process of decline and fall was suspended for a thousand years by an Hellenic intrusion, and that the 'Abbasid Caliphate merely picks up the thread of Syriac history where the Achaemenian Empire had been compelled to drop it in the fourth century B.C.[1] We have therefore to push our investigations back into the Syriac time of troubles preceding the *Pax Achaemenia* inaugurated by Cyrus.

What caused the breakdown of a civilization which, during its brief foregoing age of growth, had proved its genius and displayed its vitality in the three immense discoveries of monotheism and the Alphabet and the Atlantic? At first glance it may seem as though we have stumbled here, at last, upon an authentic example of a civilization being struck down by the impact of an external human force. Did not the Syriac Civilization break down under the hail of blows with which it was belaboured by Assyrian militarism during the ninth, eighth and seventh centuries B.C.? So it might seem; but closer inspection shows that, when 'the Assyrian came down like the wolf on the fold', the Syriac World was no longer one fold with one shepherd. The tenth-century attempt to unite politically, under an Israelite hegemony, the group of Hebrew, Phoenician, Aramaean and Hittite cantons which lay in the fairway between the Babylonic and Egyptiac worlds had failed, and it was the resulting outbreak of Syriac fratricidal warfare that

[1] See pp. 17–19.

gave the Assyrians their opportunity. The breakdown of the Syriac Civilization is to be dated, not from the first crossing of the Euphrates by Asshur-nazirpal in 876 B.C., but from the dissolution of Solomon's empire after the death of its founder in 937 B.C.

Again, it is often said that the Orthodox Christian Civilization in its 'Byzantine' political embodiment—that 'Eastern Roman Empire' whose long-drawn-out trials are the subject of Gibbon's enormous epilogue—was destroyed by the Ottoman Turks. It would usually be added that the Muslim Turks only gave the *coup de grâce* to a society that had already been fatally mauled by the Western Christian invasion, impiously masquerading under the name of a Fourth Crusade, which deprived Byzantium of the presence of a Byzantine Emperor for more than half a century (A.D. 1204–61). But this Latin assault, like its Turkish successor, came from a source that was alien to the society that was its victim; and, if we were content to leave our analysis here, we should have to return a verdict of genuine 'murder' in a list of deaths which we have so far invariably diagnosed as suicides. As we see it, however, the fatal turning-point in Orthodox Christian history was neither the Turkish assault in the fourteenth and fifteenth centuries nor the Latin assault in the thirteenth century nor even the conquest of the heart of Anatolia by an earlier wave of Turkish invaders (the Saljuqs) in the eleventh century, but a strictly domestic event which precedes them all: the great Romano-Bulgarian war of A.D. 977–1019. This fratricidal conflict between the two Great Powers of the Orthodox Christian World at this time did not come to an end until one of them had been deprived of its political existence and the other had suffered wounds from which there is good reason for saying that it never recovered.

When the Ottoman Pādishāh Mehmed II conquered Constantinople in A.D. 1453 the Orthodox Christian Civilization was not brought to an end. By a curious paradox the alien conqueror supplied the society he had conquered with its universal state. Though the Christian church of the Haghia Sophia became a Muslim mosque, the Orthodox Christian Civilization continued to live out its life-span, much as the Hindu Civilization survived under another universal state of Turkish origin founded by the Mughal Akbar a century later, and continues to survive under the not more alien British Raj. But in due course a stirring of dissolution and the beginnings of a Völkerwanderung made themselves felt within that part of the Ottoman Turkish Empire which coincided with the domain of the Orthodox Christian Society. Greeks, Serbs and Albanians were manifestly on the move before the end of the eighteenth century. Why was it that these movements did not result in a 'triumph of Barbarism and Religion' such as we have already found at the latter end of the Hellenic, the Sinic and other societies?

The answer is that the mighty march of an irresistibly expanding Western Civilization was treading hard upon the heels of these abortive barbarian heirs of the Orthodox Christian Society. The triumph of Westernization, and not the triumph of Barbarism and Religion, was the process to which the break-up of the Ottoman Empire actually ministered. Instead of taking their natural form of barbarian principalities in the style of a 'Heroic Age', the successor-states of the Ottoman Empire were moulded by Western pressure, as fast as they emerged, into imitations of the national states members of a comity of Western states which was in the act of re-organizing itself on a basis of nationalism just at this time. In some cases an incipient barbarian successor-state transformed itself directly into one of these newfangled national states on the Western model—Serbia, for example, and Greece. On the other hand the barbarians who were still so little affected by Western radiation that they were incapable of turning their activities into a Western nationalistic channel paid the penalty of 'missing the 'bus'. The Albanians forfeited in the nineteenth century to the Greeks, Serbs and Bulgars a heritage which, in the eighteenth century, had seemed more brilliant than theirs, and barely succeeded in entering the Western comity of nations in the twentieth century with an insignificant patrimony.

Thus in the history of the Orthodox Christian Society the last act has been, not 'the triumph of Barbarism and Religion', but the triumph of an alien civilization which has been swallowing the moribund society whole and has been incorporating its fabric into its own social tissues.

We have stumbled here upon an alternative way in which a civilization may lose its identity. 'The triumph of Barbarism and Religion' means that the moribund society has been thrown on to the scrap-heap by an iconoclastic revolt on the part of its own external and internal proletariats, in order that one or other of these insurgent forces may win a free field for bringing a new society to birth. In this event the older society passes away, yet in a sense it still lives on vicariously, in the younger civilization's life, through the relationship which we have learnt to call 'Apparentation and Affiliation'. In the alternative event, when the old civilization is not thrown on to the scrap-heap to make way for its offspring but is swallowed and assimilated by one of its own contemporaries, the loss of identity is manifestly more complete in one sense though less so in another. The communities into which the moribund society is articulated may be spared the extreme agonies of social dissolution; they may pass from their old body social into their new one without an absolute break of historic continuity, as the Modern Greek people, for example, has re-fashioned itself as one of the nations of a Westernized World after having lived for four centuries the life of an Ottoman *millet*. From another point of view, however, the loss of identity will be more complete and not less; for the society that passes away through incorporation into another society preserves some continuity in its material fabric at the price of forfeiting altogether the chance of creating an affiliated society which may represent it in the next generation, as our own society is, in a very real sense, the represen-tative of the Hellenic Society, the Hindu of the Indic or the Far Eastern of the Sinic.

The instance in which this process of extinction through assimi-lation has come to our notice is the incorporation of the main body of the Orthodox Christian Society into the body social of our own Western Civilization. But we can see at once that all the other extant civilizations are in course of travelling along the same road. This is the current history of the offshoot of Orthodox Christendom in Russia; of the Islamic and Hindu societies; and of both branches of the Far Eastern Society. It is also true of the three extant arrested societies—Eskimos, Nomads and Polynesians—which are all in process of being incorporated in so far as the social radiation of Western Civilization is not destroying them outright. We can see, too, that a number of the civilizations now extinct lost their identity in the same way. The process of Westernization, which began to overtake Orthodox Christendom at the end of the seventeenth century, was brought to bear on the Mexic and Andean societies of the New World nearly two centuries earlier, and in both these cases the process seems now to be virtually complete. The Babylonic Society was incorporated into the Syriac Society in the last century B.C., and the Egyptiac Society was absorbed into the same Syriac body social a few centuries later. This Syriac assimilation of the Egyptiac Society—the longest lived and most firmly compacted and unified civilization that has ever yet been seen—is perhaps the most extraordinary feat of social assimilation so far known.

If we now glance at the group of living civilizations that are in process of being assimilated by our own Western Civilization, we shall find that the process is proceeding at different paces on different planes.

On the economic plane every one of these societies has been

caught in the network of relations which our Modern Western Industrialism has spread all over the habitable world.

> Their wiseacres have seen
> The electric light i' the West, and come to worship.[1]

On the political plane, also, the children of all these apparently moribund civilizations have been seeking admission to membership of the Western comity of states through various doors. On the cultural plane, however, there is no uniform corresponding tendency. In the main body of Orthodox Christendom the former *ra'īyeh* (human flock) of the Ottoman Empire—Greeks, Serbs, Rumans, Bulgars—appear to have welcomed the prospect of cultural as well as political and economic Westernization with open arms; and the present leaders of their former lords and masters, the Turks, have followed their example. But these cases seem to be exceptional. Arabs, Persians, Hindus, Chinese and even Japanese are accepting our Western culture with conscious mental and moral reservations, in so far as they are accepting it at all. As for the Russians, the equivocal character of their response to the challenge from the West has been considered on an earlier page and in another connexion (see pp. 239-40).

On this showing, the present tendency towards a unification of the World within a Western framework on the economic, political and cultural planes alike may prove to be neither so far advanced nor so well assured of ultimate success as it would appear to be at first sight. On the other hand, the four cases of the Mexic, the Andean, the Babylonic and the Egyptiac societies are sufficient to show that the loss of identity through assimilation can be just as complete as through the alternative process of dissolution in which the Hellenic, Indic, Sinic, Sumeric and Minoan societies met their end. We have now therefore to recall our attention to what is, after all, the objective of the present chapter and to consider whether the fates which these societies suffered or are now suffering—namely incorporation and assimilation by a neighbouring society—were the real causes of their breakdowns, or whether—as we found to be the case with the other group which we have already examined—the breakdowns had actually occurred before the incorporation and assimilation process started. If we reach the latter conclusion, we shall have completed our present inquiry and shall be in a position to state that a loss of command over a society's environment, whether the physical environment or the human, is *not* the prime cause of breakdowns for which we are seeking.

[1] Bridges, R.: *The Testament of Beauty*, Book I, ll. 594-5.

We have seen, for example, that the main body of Orthodox Christendom did not lose its identity through absorption until its universal state had run out into an interregnum, and that the real breakdown began with a Romano-Bulgarian war that was fought eight hundred years before any signs of Westernization made their appearance. The interval between the breakdown and the absorption of the Egyptiac Society is very much longer, for we have found reason to place that breakdown as far back as the transition from the Fifth to the Sixth Dynasty, *circa* 2424 B.C., when the sins of the Pyramid Builders were visited on their successors and the top-heavy political structure of 'the Old Kingdom' collapsed. In the case of the Far Eastern Society the interval between the breakdown and the beginnings of the process of incorporation is not as long as in Egyptiac history but is rather longer than in the history of Orthodox Christendom, for the breakdown of the Far Eastern Society can be equated with the decay of the T'ang dynasty in the last quarter of the ninth century of the Christian Era and the consequent onset of a time of troubles followed by successive embodiments of a universal state in empires founded by barbarians. The first of these embodiments, the *Pax Mongolica* established by Qubilay Khan, was less fortunate in its issue than the comparable versions of a Nomad Peace provided for the Hindu Society by Akbar and for the Orthodox Christian Society by Mehmed the Conqueror. The Chinese, acting on the principle of *timeo Danaos et dona ferentes* ('I fear the Greeks even when they bring benefits'), expelled the Mongols as the Egyptians had expelled the Hyksos. The Manchus had still to come and go before the stage was set for the act of Westernization.

In Russia and in Japan the impact of the Western Civilization occurred at a much earlier stage in the decline of the civilizations represented by those two now Westernized Great Powers; but in both cases the decline had already set in, for the Romanov Tsardom and the Tokugawa Shogunate, which Peter the Great and the Japanese authors of 'the Meiji Restoration' set themselves, respectively, to transform into national states members of the Western comity of nations, were both of them universal states which had been in existence for over two hundred years in the Russian case and over three hundred in the Japanese. In these cases there will be little inclination to suggest that the performances of Peter the Great and his Japanese counterparts should be regarded as breakdowns. On the contrary, these achievements were to all appearance so successful that many observers may incline to regard them as evidence that the societies which deliberately put themselves through this radical metamorphosis and which came through it—at any rate for the time being—without mishap, must still have been in the full *élan* of growth. The Russian and Japanese response offers, at any rate, a sharp contrast to the ineffectiveness of the 'Osmanlis, Hindus, Chinese, Aztecs and Incas in dealing with an identical challenge. Instead of undergoing a compulsory process of Westernization at the hands of their Western neighbours—Poles, Swedes, Germans or Americans—the Russians and the Japanese carried through their social metamorphosis with their own hands, and were thus enabled to enter the Western comity of nations as the equals of the Great Powers and not as colonial dependencies or 'poor relations'.

It is worth observing that in the early years of the seventeenth century, nearly a hundred years before Peter the Great and two-and-a-half centuries before 'the Meiji Restoration', both Russia and Japan had experienced and repelled a Western attempt at absorption on the lines familiar elsewhere. In the Russian case the impact took the crude form of a regular military invasion and a temporary occupation of Moscow by the forces of Russia's western neighbour the United Kingdom of Poland-Lithuania, on the pretext of supporting a pretender to the Russian throne, 'the false Dmitri'. In the Japanese case, where the impact took the more etherial form of the conversion of several hundred thousand Japanese souls to Catholicism by Spanish and Portuguese missionaries, it was quite possible that in due course this enthusiastic Christian minority might have sought to make itself master of Japan with the support of Spanish armadas based on the Philippines. But the Russians drove out the Poles, while the Japanese exorcised 'the White Peril' by expelling all resident Western missionaries and merchants, by forbidding Westerners to set foot henceforth on Japanese soil—with the exception of a few Dutch merchants licensed under ignominious conditions—and by exterminating the Japanese Catholic community by ruthless persecution. Having thus rid themselves of their 'Western Question', both Russians and Japanese imagined that they had only to retire into their own shells and 'live happy ever after'. When the course of time showed that this was not to be, they went on to make original and positive responses which we have already described.

Yet there are unmistakable indications that, before the first Portuguese ship sailed into Nagasaki or the first English ship into Archangel (an earlier herald of the West than the Polish invader in Moscow), both the Far Eastern Civilization in Japan and the Orthodox Christian in Russia had already broken down.

In Russian history the true 'time of troubles', in the sense in which that term is used in this Study, is not the bout of anarchy in the early years of the seventeenth century for which the term was originally coined by the Russians themselves. That was merely an interlude between the first and second phases of the Russian universal state, corresponding to the third-century bout of anarchy in the Hellenic World between the Age of the Antonines and the accession of Diocletian. The chapter of Russian history which corresponds to the chapter of Hellenic history between the Peloponnesian war and the *Pax Augusta*, and which therefore represents the Russian time of troubles in our sense, is the period of adversity which preceded the foundation of the Russian universal state through the union of Muscovy and Novgorod in A.D. 1478. On the same showing, the time of troubles in Japanese history is represented by the Kamakura and Ashikaga periods of feudal anarchy which preceded the disciplinary unification and pacification carried out by Nobunaga, Hideyoshi and Ieyasu; and the combined span of these two periods extends, according to the conventional dates, from A.D. 1184 to A.D. 1597.

If these be the true Russian and Japanese times of troubles, we have in both cases to inquire whether they were precipitated by some suicidal act or by the action of an external adversary. In the Russian case, the common explanation of the recognized breakdown contemporaneous with the Western Middle Ages is that it was due to the assault of the Mongol Nomads from the Eurasian Steppe. But we have already encountered and rejected in other cases—in the case of the older branch of the Orthodox Christian Society, for example—the plea that the Eurasian Nomads were the villains of the various pieces in which they played their part. Is it not possible that in Russia, likewise, the Orthodox Christian Society may have already brought about its breakdown, by its own act, before ever the Mongols crossed the Volga in A.D. 1238? An affirmative answer to this question is suggested by the break-up of the primitive Russian Principality of Kiev into a host of warring successor-states in the twelfth century of the Christian Era.

In Japan the case is much clearer. Here breakdown cannot be convincingly attributed to the Mongol assault which the Japanese successfully repelled from their shores in A.D. 1281; and when we inquire into the cause of this Marathonic triumph we find that, while no doubt they owed it in part to their insular position, it was due still more to the military efficiency which they had developed in the faction fights of a time of troubles which by that date had already been exercising them for more than a hundred years.

In the histories of the Hindu, Babylonic and Andean societies the process of absorption by an alien society supervened, as in the cases of Russia and Japan, when the declining societies were in their universal states. In these other three cases, however, the process took a more catastrophic turn, and these declining societies suffered an alien military conquest. In Hindu history the British conquest was preceded by a Muslim Turkish conquest which dates back, far behind the era of the 'Great Moguls', to the invasions of A.D. 1191–1204, and this first alien conquest, like its successors, Mughal and British, was notoriously due to the fact that the Hindu Society was by then already in a condition of chronic anarchy.

The Babylonic Society was absorbed into the Syriac after the conquest of its universal state, the empire of Nebuchadnezzar, by Cyrus the Persian. From that time onwards the Babylonic culture gradually gave way before the Syriac, of which the Achaemenian Empire was the first universal state; but the cause of the Babylonic breakdown is to be found in the preceding excesses of Assyrian militarism.

As for the Andean Society, it is of course manifestly true that the Inca Empire was destroyed by the impact of the Spanish Conquistadores, and it is probable that, if the peoples of the Western World had never found their way across the Atlantic, the Inca Empire would have lasted several centuries longer. But the destruction of the Inca Empire is not the same thing as the breakdown of the Andean Civilization, and we now know enough about Andean history to perceive that the breakdown had taken place long before and that the military and political rise of the Incas, in the century preceding the Spanish conquest, far from being identical with the cultural rise of the Andean Civilization, was actually a late incident in its decline.

The Mexic Civilization fell before the Conquistadores at an earlier stage, when the Aztec Empire, though already manifestly destined to become the universal state of its society, had not yet completely rounded off its conquests. We can express the difference by saying that the Andean Society was conquered in its Antonine Age and the Mexic Society in its Age of the Scipios; but an 'Age of the Scipios' is a phase of a time of troubles and is thus, by definition, the sequel to an antecedent breakdown.

In the Islamic World, on the other hand, Westernization gained the upper hand before any Islamic universal state was in sight, and its various member states—Persia, 'Irāq, Saʿūdī Arabia, Egypt, Syria, the Lebanon and the rest—are making the best of a rather bad job as 'poor relations' in the Western comity of nations. The Pan-Islamic movement seems to be abortive.

Several other civilizations, including some which grew to maturity, as well as the arrested and even the abortive civilizations, might be passed in review. But of the matured civilizations some, such as the Minoan, the Hittite and the Mayan, have histories still so imperfectly deciphered by modern scholarship that it might be rash to draw conclusions from them; the arrested civilizations would yield no result for the present inquiry, because they are, by definition, civilizations which achieved genesis but no subsequent growth; and the abortive civilizations would be unilluminating *a fortiori*.

(3) A NEGATIVE VERDICT

We may fairly conclude from the foregoing inquiry that the cause of the breakdowns of civilizations is not to be found in loss of command over the human environment, as measured by the encroachment of alien human forces upon the life of any society whose breakdown we may be investigating. In all the cases reviewed the most that an alien enemy has achieved has been to give an expiring suicide his *coup de grâce*. Where encroachment takes the form of a violent attack, at any stage in the history of a civilization except the very last, when it is *in articulo mortis*, the normal effect upon the life of the assaulted party would appear to be not destructive but positively stimulating. The Hellenic Society was stimulated, by the Persian attack at the beginning of the fifth century B.C., to its highest manifestations of genius. The Western Society was stimulated by the Norse and Magyar attacks of the ninth century of the Christian Era into performing those feats of valour and statesmanship which resulted in the foundation of the kingdoms of England and France and the reconstruction of the Holy Roman Empire by the Saxons. The medieval city-states of Northern Italy were stimulated by the incursions of the Hohenstaufen; the modern English and Dutch by the assaults of Spain; and the infant Hindu Society by the primitive Muslim Arab onslaught in the eighth century of the Christian Era.

The foregoing examples are all cases in which the assaulted party was still in a state of growth; but we can cite at least as many cases in which an alien assault has given a temporary stimulus to a society after this society has already broken down through its mishandling of itself. The classic instance is the repeated reaction of the Egyptiac Society to this stimulus; for this Egyptiac reaction was evoked and re-evoked over a period of two thousand years; and this long epilogue to Egyptiac history was inaugurated when the Egyptiac Society had already passed out of its universal state and had entered upon an interregnum which might have been expected to prove the prelude to a speedy dissolution. At this late stage the Egyptiac Society was stimulated to expel the Hyksos invaders, and long afterwards to expel by successive explosions of energy the Sea-raiders, the Assyrians and the Achaemenidae and, last of all, to offer stubborn and successful resistance to the process of Helle-nization to which Egypt was subjected by the Ptolemies.

There has been a similar series of reactions to external blows and pressures in the history of the Far Eastern Civilization in China. The expulsion of the Mongols by the Ming dynasty is reminiscent of the expulsion of the Hyksos by the Theban founders of 'the New Empire', and the resistance of the Egyptiac Society to Hellenization finds its analogue in the Chinese anti-Western movement which flared up in the Boxer Rising of A.D. 1900 and attempted, in A.D. 1925–7, to fight out its losing battle to the bitter end by borrowing the weapons of Russian communism.

These illustrations, which could be abundantly supplemented, are perhaps sufficient to support our thesis that the normal effect of blows and pressures from outside is stimulating and not destruc-tive; and, if this thesis is accepted, it confirms our conclusion that a loss of command over the human environment is not the cause of the breakdowns of civilizations.

EDITOR'S NOTE. Some readers may be inclined to feel that, in the fore-going chapter, the author has more than once, for the sake of the argu-ment on which he has embarked, pushed back the date of his 'break-downs' to an unreasonably early stage in the history of some of his civilizations. This feeling, if it is felt, may be due to a misunderstanding produced by an ambiguity in the meaning of the term 'breakdown'. When we speak of a man suffering a breakdown in health the suggestion is that, unless the breakdown be overcome by subsequent recovery, his active life is over. In fact we use 'breakdown' in common parlance to mean very much what Mr. Toynbee means when he writes 'disintegra-tion'. But 'breakdown' in this Study does not mean quite that; it means the termination of the period of growth. Analogies from organic life are always dangerous in the discussion of societies, but the reader may be reminded that growth terminates comparatively early in the life of a living organism. The difference between a living organism and a society, as the author was at pains to show in the chapter preceding that now concluded, is that a living organism has its life-span deter-mined by its very nature—'the days of our years are three score years and ten'—whereas history indicates no limits to the possible life-span of a society. In other words, a society does not ever die 'from natural causes', but always dies from suicide or murder—and nearly always from the former, as this chapter has shown. Similarly the termination of the growth-period, which is a natural event in the history of a living organism, is an 'unnatural' event, due to crime or blunder, in a society; and to this crime or blunder Mr. Toynbee has applied the term 'breakdown' for the purposes of this Study. It will be seen that, when the term is used in this sense, some of the most fruitful, illuminating and celebrated achievements and productions in the history of a civilization may come after the breakdown and, indeed, in consequence of it.

XVI. FAILURE OF SELF-DETERMINATION

(1) THE MECHANICALNESS OF MIMESIS

OUR inquiry into the cause of the breakdowns of civilizations has led us, so far, to a succession of negative conclusions. We have found out that these breakdowns are not acts of God—at any rate in the sense that lawyers attach to that phrase; nor are they vain repetitions of senseless laws of Nature. We have also found that we cannot attribute them to a loss of command over the environment, physical or human; they are due neither to failures in industrial or artistic techniques nor to homicidal assaults from alien adversaries. In successively rejecting these untenable explanations we have not arrived at the object of our search; but the last of the fallacies we have just cited has incidentally given us a clue. In demonstrating that the broken-down civilizations have not met their death from an assassin's hand we have found no reason to dispute the allegation that they have been victims of violence, and in almost every instance we have been led, by the logical process of exhaustion, to return a verdict of suicide. Our best hope of making some positive progress in our inquiry is to follow up this clue; and there is one hopeful feature in our verdict which we can observe at once. There is nothing original about it.

The conclusion at which we have arrived at the end of a rather laborious search has been divined with sure intuition by a modern Western poet:

> In tragic life, God wot,
> No villain need be! Passions spin the plot:
> We are betrayed by what is false within.

This flash of insight (from Meredith's *Love's Grave*) was not a new discovery. We can find it in earlier and higher authorities. It reveals itself in the last lines of Shakespeare's *King John*:

> This England never did, nor never shall,
> Lie at the proud foot of a conqueror,
> But when it first did help to wound itself.
> . . . Nought shall makes us rue
> If England to itself do rest but true.

It likewise reveals itself in the words of Jesus (Matt. xv. 18–20):

'Whatsoever entereth in at the mouth goeth into the belly and is cast out into the draught. But those things which proceed out of the mouth come forth from the heart; and they defile the man. For out of the heart proceed evil thoughts, murders, adulteries, fornications, thefts, false witness, blasphemies. These are the things which defile a man.'

What is the weakness which exposes a growing civilization to the risk of stumbling and falling in mid-career and losing its Promethean *élan*? The weakness must be radical; for, although the catastrophe of a breakdown is a risk and not a certainty, the risk is evidently high. We are faced with the fact that, of the twenty-one civilizations that have been born alive and have proceeded to grow, thirteen are dead and buried; that seven of the remaining eight are apparently in decline; and that the eighth, which is our own, may also have passed its zenith for all that we as yet know. On an empirical test, the career of a growing civilization would appear to be fraught with danger; and, if we recall our analysis of growth, we shall see that the danger lies in the very nature of the course which a growing civilization is bound to take.

Growth is the work of creative personalities and creative minorities; they cannot go on moving forward themselves unless they can contrive to carry their fellows with them in their advance; and the uncreative rank and file of mankind, which is always the overwhelming majority, cannot be transfigured *en masse* and raised to the stature of their leaders in the twinkling of an eye. That would be in practice impossible; for the inward spiritual grace through which an unillumined soul is fired by communion with a saint is almost as rare as the miracle that has brought the saint himself into the world. The leader's task is to make his fellows his followers; and the only means by which mankind in the mass can be set in motion towards a goal beyond itself is by enlisting the primitive and universal faculty of mimesis. For this mimesis is a kind of social drill; and the dull ears that are deaf to the unearthly music of Orpheus' lyre are well attuned to the drill sergeant's word of command. When the Piper of Hamelin assumes King Frederick William's Prussian voice, the rank and file, who have stood stolid hitherto, mechanically break into movement, and the evolution which he causes them to execute brings them duly to heel; but they can only catch him up by taking a short cut, and they can only find room to march in formation by deploying on the broad way which leadeth to destruction. When the road to destruction has perforce to be trodden on the quest of life, it is perhaps no wonder that the quest should often end in disaster.

Moreover, there is a weakness in the actual exercise of mimesis, quite apart from the way in which the faculty may be exploited. For, just because mimesis is a kind of drill, it is a kind of mechanization of human life and movement.

When we speak of 'an ingenious mechanism' or 'a skilled mechanic', the words call up the idea of a triumph of life over matter, of human skill over physical obstacles. Concrete examples suggest the same idea, from the gramophone or the aeroplane back to the first wheel and the first dug-out canoe; for such inventions have extended man's power over his environment by so manipulating inanimate objects that they are made to carry out human purposes, as the drill sergeant's commands are executed by his mechanized human beings. In drilling his platoon the sergeant expands himself into a Briareus whose hundred arms and legs obey his will almost as promptly as if they had been organically his own. Similarly the telescope is an extension of the human eye, the trumpet of the human voice, the stilt of the human leg, the sword of the human arm.

Nature has implicitly complimented man on his ingenuity by anticipating him in his use of mechanical devices. She has made extensive use of them in her *chef-d'œuvre*, the human body. In the heart and the lungs she has constructed two self-regulating machines that are models of their kind. By adjusting these and other organs so that they work automatically, Nature has released the margin of our energies from the monotonously repetitive tasks these organs perform, and has set these energies free to walk and talk and, in a word, bring into existence twenty-one civilizations! She has arranged that, say, ninety per cent. of the functions of any given organism shall be performed automatically and therefore with the minimum expenditure of energy, in order that the maximum amount of energy may be concentrated on the remaining ten per cent., in which Nature is feeling her way towards a fresh advance. In fact, a natural organism is made up, like a human society, of a creative minority and an uncreative majority of 'members'; and in a growing and healthy organism, as in a growing and healthy society, the majority is drilled into following the minority's lead mechanically.

But, when we have lost ourselves in admiration of these natural and human mechanical triumphs, it is disconcerting to be reminded that there are other phrases—'machine-made goods', 'mechanical behaviour'—in which the connotation of the word 'machine' is exactly the reverse, suggesting not the triumph of life over matter but the triumph of matter over life. Though machinery be designed to be the slave of man, it is also possible for man to become the slave of his machines. A living organism which is ninety per cent. mechanism will have greater opportunity or capacity for creativity than an organism which is fifty per cent. mechanism, as Socrates will have more time and opportunity to discover the secret of the

Universe if he has not got to cook his own meals, but the organism that is a hundred per cent. mechanism is a robot.

Thus a risk of catastrophe is inherent in the use of the faculty of mimesis which is the vehicle of mechanization in the social relationships of human beings; and it is evident that this risk will be greater when mimesis is called into play in a society which is in dynamic movement than in a society which is in a state of rest. The weakness of mimesis lies in its being a mechanical response to a suggestion from outside, so that the action performed is one which would never have been performed by the performer on his own initiative. Thus mimesis-action is not self-determined, and the best safeguard for its performance is that the faculty should become crystallized in habit or custom—as it actually is in primitive societies in the Yin-state. But when 'the cake of custom' is broken, the faculty of mimesis, hitherto directed backward towards elders or ancestors as incarnations of an unchanging social tradition, is reoriented towards creative personalities bent upon leading their fellows with them towards a promised land. Henceforth the growing society is compelled to live dangerously. Moreover the danger is perpetually imminent, since the condition which is required for the maintenance of growth is a perpetual flexibility and spontaneity, whereas the condition required for effective mimesis, which is itself a prerequisite of growth, is a considerable degree of machine-like automatism. The second of these requirements was what Walter Bagehot had in mind when, in his whimsical way, he told his English readers that they owed their comparative successfulness as a nation in large part to their stupidity. Good leaders, yes: but the good leaders would not have had good followers if the majority of these followers had determined to think everything out for themselves. And yet, if all are 'stupid', where will be the leadership?

In fact, the creative personalities in the vanguard of a civilization who have recourse to the mechanism of mimesis are exposing themselves to the risk of failure in two degrees, one negative and the other positive.

The possible negative failure is that the leaders may infect themselves with the hypnotism which they have induced in their followers. In that event, the docility of the rank and file will have been purchased at the disastrous price of a loss of initiative in the officers. This is what happened in the arrested civilizations, and in all periods in the histories of other civilizations which are to be regarded as periods of stagnation. This negative failure, however, is not usually the end of the story. When the leaders cease to lead, their tenure of power becomes an abuse. The rank and file mutiny;

the officers seek to restore order by drastic action. Orpheus, who
has lost his lyre or forgotten how to play it, now lays about him
with Xerxes' whip; and the result is a hideous pandemonium, in
which the military formation breaks down into anarchy. This is
the positive failure; and we have already, again and again, used
another name for it. It is that 'disintegration' of a broken-down
civilization which declares itself in the 'secession of the proletariat'
from a band of leaders who have degenerated into a 'dominant
minority'.

This secession of the led from the leaders may be regarded as
a loss of harmony between the parts which make up the whole
ensemble of the society. In any whole consisting of parts a loss of
harmony between the parts is paid for by the whole in a corresponding loss of self-determination. This loss of self-determination
is the ultimate criterion of breakdown; and it is a conclusion which
should not surprise us, seeing that it is the inverse of the conclusion,
reached in an earlier part of this Study, that progress towards self-
determination is the criterion of growth. We have now to examine
some of the forms in which this loss of self-determination through
loss of harmony is manifested.

(2) NEW WINE IN OLD BOTTLES

Adjustments, Revolutions and Enormities

One source of disharmony between the institutions of which a
society is composed is the introduction of new social forces—
aptitudes or emotions or ideas—which the existing set of institutions was not originally designed to carry. The destructive effect
of this incongruous juxtaposition of things new and old is pointed
out in one of the most famous of the sayings attributed to Jesus:

'No man putteth a piece of new cloth into an old garment, for that
which is put in to fill it up taketh from the garment, and the rent is
made worse. Neither do men put new wine into old bottles—else the
bottles break and the wine runneth out and the bottles perish; but they
put new wine into new bottles, and both are preserved.'[1]

In the domestic economy from which this simile is taken the
precept can, of course, be carried out to the letter; but in the
economy of social life men's power to order their affairs at will on
a rational plan is narrowly restricted, since a society is not, like a
wineskin or a garment, the property of a single owner but is the
common ground of many men's fields of action; and for that reason
the precept, which is common sense in household economy and

[1] Matt. ix. 16–17.

practical wisdom in the life of the spirit, is a counsel of perfection in social affairs.

Ideally, no doubt, the introduction of new dynamic forces ought to be accompanied by a reconstruction of the whole existing set of institutions, and in any actually growing society a constant re-adjustment of the more flagrant anachronisms is continually going on. But *vis inertiae* tends at all times to keep most parts of the social structure as they are, in spite of their increasing incongruity with new social forces constantly coming into action. In this situation the new forces are apt to operate in two diametrically opposite ways simultaneously. On the one hand they perform their creative work either through new institutions that they have established for themselves or through old institutions that they have adapted to their purpose; and in pouring themselves into these harmonious channels they promote the welfare of society. At the same time they also enter, indiscriminately, into any institutions which happen to lie in their path—as some powerful head of steam which had forced its way into an engine-house might rush into the works of any old engine that happened to be installed there.

In such an event, one or other of two alternative disasters is apt to occur. Either the pressure of the new head of steam blows the old engine to pieces, or else the old engine somehow manages to hold together and proceeds to operate in a new manner that is likely to prove both alarming and destructive.

To translate these parables into terms of social life, the explosions of the old engines that cannot stand the new pressures—or the bursting of the old bottles which cannot stand the fermentation of the new wine—are the revolutions which sometimes overtake anachronistic institutions. On the other hand, the baneful performances of the old engines which have stood the strain of being keyed up to performances for which they were never intended are the social enormities which a 'die-hard' institutional anachronism sometimes engenders.

Revolutions may be defined as retarded, and proportionately violent, acts of mimesis. The mimetic element is of their essence; for every revolution has reference to something that has happened already elsewhere, and it is always manifest, when a revolution is studied in its historical setting, that its outbreak would never have occurred of itself if it had not been thus evoked by a previous play of external forces. An obvious example is the French Revolution of A.D. 1789, which drew its inspiration in part from the events which had recently occurred in British America—events in which the French Government of the *Ancien Régime* had most suicidally assisted—and in part from the century-old achievement of England which had been popularized and glorified in France by two generations of *philosophes* from Montesquieu onwards.

The element of retardation is likewise of the essence of revolutions, and accounts for the violence which is their most prominent feature. Revolutions are violent because they are the belated triumphs of powerful new social forces over tenacious old institutions which have been temporarily thwarting and cramping these new expressions of life. The longer the obstruction holds out the greater becomes the pressure of the force whose outlet is being obstructed; and, the greater the pressure, the more violent the explosion in which the imprisoned force ultimately breaks through.

As for the social enormities that are the alternative to revolutions, they may be defined as the penalties which a society has to pay when the act of mimesis, which ought to have brought an old institution into harmony with a new social force, is not simply retarded but is frustrated altogether.

It is evident, then, that, whenever the existing institutional structure of a society is challenged by a new social force, three alternative outcomes are possible: either a harmonious adjustment of structure to force, or a revolution (which is a delayed and discordant adjustment) or an enormity. It is also evident that each and all of these three alternatives may be realized in different sections of the same society—in different national states, for example, if that is the manner in which the particular society is articulated. If harmonious adjustments predominate, the society will continue to grow; if revolutions, its growth will become increasingly hazardous; if enormities, we may diagnose a breakdown. A series of examples will illustrate the formulae that we have just presented.

The Impact of Industrialism on Slavery

Within the last two centuries two new dynamic social forces were set in motion, Industrialism and Democracy, and one of the old institutions on which these forces impinged was slavery. This pernicious institution, which had contributed so largely to the decline and fall of the Hellenic Society, never secured a firm foothold in the homelands of our Western Society, but, from the sixteenth century onwards, when Western Christendom expanded overseas, it came to be established in some of its new overseas dominions. However, for a long time the scale of this recrudescence of plantation slavery was not very formidable. At the moment when, at the end of the eighteenth century, the new forces of Democracy and Industrialism began to radiate out from

Great Britain into the rest of the Western World, slavery was still practically confined to the colonial fringes, and even there its area was contracting. Statesmen who were themselves slave-owners, such as Washington and Jefferson, not only deplored the institution but took a fairly optimistic view of the prospects of its peaceful extinction in the coming century.

This possibility, however, was ruled out by the outbreak of the Industrial Revolution in Great Britain, which immensely stimulated the demand for raw materials which plantation slave-labour produced. The impact of Industrialism thus gave the languishing and anachronistic institution of slavery a new lease of life. The Western Society was now faced with a choice between taking active steps to put an end to slavery immediately or else seeing this ancient social evil converted, by the new driving force of Industrialism, into a mortal danger to the very life of the society.

In this situation an anti-slavery movement came into action in many different national states of the Western World and achieved a number of pacific successes; but there was one important region in which the anti-slavery movement failed to make peaceful headway, and this was 'the cotton belt' in the Southern States of the North American Union. Here the champions of slavery remained in power for one whole generation longer, and in this short interval of thirty years—between 1833 when slavery was abolished in the British Empire and 1863 when it was abolished in the United States—the 'peculiar institution' of the Southern States, with the driving force of Industrialism behind it, swelled into a monstrous growth. After that the monster was brought to bay and destroyed; but this belated eradication of slavery in the United States had to be paid for at the price of a shattering revolution, the devastating effects of which are still apparent to-day. Such has been the price of this particular retardation of mimesis.

Still, our Western Society may congratulate itself that, even at this price, the social evil of slavery has been eradicated from its last Western stronghold; and for this mercy we have to thank the new force of Democracy, which came into the Western World a little in advance of Industrialism—for it is no accidental coincidence that Lincoln, the principal author of the eradication of slavery from its last Western stronghold, should be very widely and rightly regarded as the greatest of democratic statesmen. Since Democracy is the political expression of humanitarianism, and since humanitarianism and slavery are obviously mortal foes, the new democratic spirit put drive into the anti-slavery movement at the very time when the new Industrialism was putting drive into slavery. It can safely be said that if, in the struggle over slavery, the drive of Industrialism had not been largely neutralized by the drive of Democracy, the Western World would not have rid itself of slavery so easily.

The Impact of Democracy and Industrialism on War

It is a commonplace to say that the impact of Industrialism has increased the horrors of war as markedly as it increased the horrors of slavery. War is another ancient and anachronistic institution which is condemned on moral grounds almost as widely as slavery has been. On strictly intellectual grounds there is also a wide-spread school of thought which holds that war, again like slavery, 'does not pay' even those who think they profit by it. Just as, on the eve of the American Civil War, a Southerner, H. R. Helper, wrote a book entitled *The Impending Crisis of the South* to prove that slavery did not pay the slave-owners and, by a curious but easily explained confusion of thought, was condemned by the class whom he sought to enlighten as to their real interests, so, on the eve of the General War of 1914–18, Norman Angell wrote a book entitled *Europe's Optical Illusion* to prove that war brought a dead loss to the victors as well as the vanquished, and was condemned by a large section of a public that was as anxious for the preserva-tion of peace as the heretical author himself. Why then has our society been so much less successful up to the present in getting rid of war than in getting rid of slavery? The answer is manifest. In this case, unlike the other, the two driving forces of Democracy and of Industrialism have made their simultaneous impacts in the same direction.

If we cast our minds back to the state of the Western World on the eve of the emergence of Industrialism and Democracy, we shall notice that at that time, in the middle of the eighteenth century, war was in much the same condition as slavery: it was manifestly on the wane, not so much because wars were less frequent—though even that fact could perhaps be statistically proved[1]—as because they were being conducted with more moderation. Our eighteenth-century rationalists looked back with distaste on a recent past in which war had been keyed up to a horrid intensity by the impact of the drive of religious fanaticism. In the latter part of the seventeenth century, however, this demon had been cast out, and the immediate effect was to reduce the evil

[1] Though P. A. Sorokin, in the statistical evidence marshalled by him, finds that the incidence of war on the Western World was lighter, on the whole, in the nineteenth century than in the eighteenth (*Social and Cultural Dynamics*, vol. iii (New York 1937, American Book Co.), pp. 342 and 345–6).

of war to a minimum never approached in any other chapter of
our Western history before or since. This age of relatively
'civilized warfare' came to an end at the close of the eighteenth
century when war began to be keyed up once again by the impact
of Democracy and Industrialism. If we ask ourselves which of
these two forces has played the greater part in the intensification
of warfare during the last hundred and fifty years, our first impulse
will probably be to attribute the more important role to Industrialism. But we should be wrong. The first of the modern wars
in this sense was the cycle of wars inaugurated by the French
Revolution, and on these wars the impact of Industrialism was
inconsiderable and the impact of Democracy, French Revolutionary Democracy, all-important. It was not so much the
military genius of Napoleon as the revolutionary fury of the new
French armies that cut through the old-fashioned eighteenth-
century defence of the unrevolutionized Continental Powers like
a knife through butter and carried French arms all over Europe.
If evidence for this assertion is required it can be found in the
fact that the raw French levies had accomplished feats too hard
for the professional army of Louis XIV before Napoleon appeared
on the scene. And we may remind ourselves also that Romans
and Assyrians and other keyed-up militarist Powers of bygone
ages have destroyed civilizations without the aid of any industrial
apparatus, in fact with weapons that would have seemed rudimentary to a sixteenth-century matchlockman.

The fundamental reason why war was less atrocious in the
eighteenth century than either before or since was that it had
ceased to be a weapon of religious fanaticism and had not yet
become an instrument of nationalist fanaticism. During this
interval it was merely a 'sport of kings'. Morally, the use of war
for this more frivolous purpose may be all the more shocking, but
the effect in mitigating the material horrors of war is undeniable.
The royal players knew quite well the degree of licence that their
subjects would allow them, and they kept their activities well
within these bounds. Their armies were not recruited by conscription; they did not live off the country they occupied like
the armies of the Wars of Religion, nor did they wipe the works of
peace out of existence like the armies of the twentieth century.
They observed the rules of their military game, set themselves
moderate objectives and did not impose crushing terms on their
defeated opponents. On the rare occasions when these conventions
were broken, as by Louis XIV in his devastations of the Palatinate
in A.D. 1674 and A.D. 1689, such atrocities were roundly condemned not only by the victims but by neutral public opinion.

The classic description of this state of affairs comes from the pen of Edward Gibbon:

'In war the European forces are exercised by temperate and undecisive contests. The Balance of Power will continue to fluctuate, and the prosperity of our own or the neighbouring kingdoms may be alternately exalted or depressed; but these partial events cannot essentially injure our general state of happiness, the system of arts and laws and manners which so advantageously distinguish, above the rest of mankind, the Europeans and their colonists.'[1]

The author of this excruciatingly complacent passage lived just long enough to be shaken to the core by the beginning of a new cycle of wars which was to render his verdict obsolete.

Just as the intensification of slavery through the impact of Industrialism led to the launching of the anti-slavery movement, so the intensification of war through the impact of Democracy, and subsequently of course through the impact of Industrialism as well, has led to an anti-war movement. Its first embodiment in the League of Nations after the end of the General War of 1914–18 failed to save the World from having to go through the General War of 1939–45. At the price of this further affliction, we have now bought a fresh opportunity to attempt the difficult enterprise of abolishing war through a co-operative system of world government, instead of letting the cycle of wars run its course until it ends—too badly and too late—in the forcible establishment of a universal state by some single surviving power. Whether we in our world will succeed in achieving what no other civilization has ever yet achieved is a question that lies on the knees of the Gods.

The Impact of Democracy and Industrialism on Parochial Sovereignty

Why is it that Democracy, which its admirers have often proclaimed to be a corollary of the Christian Religion, and which showed itself not altogether unworthy of this high claim in its attitude towards slavery, has had an aggravating influence on the equally manifest evil of war? The answer is to be found in the fact that, before colliding with the institution of war, Democracy collided with the institution of parochial (or local) sovereignty; and the importation of the new driving forces of Democracy and Industrialism into the old machine of the parochial state has generated the twin enormities of political and economic nationalism. It is in this gross derivative form, in which the etherial spirit of Democracy has emerged from its passage through an alien medium, that Democracy has put its drive into war instead of working against it.

[1] Gibbon, E.: *The History of the Decline and Fall of the Roman Empire*, ch. xxxviii, *ad finem*.

Here again, our Western Society was in a happier posture in the Pre-Nationalistic Age of the eighteenth century. With one or two notable exceptions the parochial sovereign states of the Western World were not then the instruments of the general wills of their citizens but were virtually the private estates of dynasties. Royal wars and royal marriages were the two procedures through which conveyances of such estates, or of parts of them, from one dynasty to another were brought about, and, of the two methods, the latter was obviously to be preferred. Hence the familiar line in praise of the foreign policy of the House of Hapsburg: *Bella gerant alii; tu, felix Austria, nube.* ('Let others wage wars; you, happy Austria, go marry.') The very names of the three chief wars of the first half of the eighteenth century, the Wars of the Spanish, Polish and Austrian Successions, suggest that wars only occurred when matrimonial arrangements had got into an inextricable tangle.

There was no doubt something rather petty and sordid about this matrimonial diplomacy. A dynastic compact by which provinces and their inhabitants are transferred from one owner to another like estates with their livestock is revolting to the susceptibilities of our democratic age. But the eighteenth-century system had its compensations. It took the shine out of patriotism; but, with the shine, it took the sting. A well-known passage in Sterne's *Sentimental Journey* relates how the author went to France quite forgetting that Great Britain and France were engaged in the Seven Years' War. After a little trouble with the French police, the services of a French nobleman, whom he had never met before, enabled him to resume his journey without any further unpleasantness. When, forty years later, on the rupture of the treaty of Amiens, Napoleon gave orders that all British civilians between the ages of eighteen and sixty who happened to be in France at the moment should be interned, his action was regarded as an example of Corsican savagery and as an illustration of Wellington's subsequent dictum that he was 'not a gentleman', and indeed Napoleon offered excuses for his procedure; yet it was only what even the most humane and liberal government to-day would do as a matter of course and of common sense. War has now become 'total war', and it has become so because parochial states have become nationalist democracies.

By total war we mean a war in which it is recognized that the combatants are not only the selected 'chessmen' called soldiers and sailors but the whole populations of the countries concerned. Where shall we find the beginnings of this new outlook? Perhaps in the treatment meted out at the end of the Revolutionary War by the victorious British-American colonists to those among themselves who had sided with the mother country. These United Empire Loyalists were expelled bag and baggage—men, women and children—from their homes after the war was over. The treatment they received is in marked contrast with that meted out, twenty years before, by Great Britain, to the conquered French Canadians, who not only retained their homes but were allowed to preserve their legal system and their religious institutions. This first example of 'totalitarianism' is significant, for the victorious American colonists were the first democratized nation of our Western Society.[1]

The economic nationalism which has grown into as great an evil as our political nationalism has been engendered by a corresponding perversion of Industrialism working within the same constricting bonds of the parochial state.

Economic ambitions and rivalries were, of course, not unknown in the international politics of the pre-Industrial Age; indeed, economic nationalism received its classic expression in the 'mercantilism' of the eighteenth century, and the prizes of eighteenth-century warfare included markets and monopolies, as is illustrated by the famous section of the treaty of Utrecht allotting to Great Britain a monopoly of the slave-trade of the Spanish-American colonies. But eighteenth-century economic conflicts affected only small classes and restricted interests. In a predominantly agricultural age, when not only each country but each village community produced nearly all the necessities of life, English wars for markets might be called 'the sport of merchants' as reasonably as Continental wars for provinces have been called 'the sport of kings'.

This general state of economic equilibrium at low tension on a minute scale was violently disturbed by the advent of Industrialism; for Industrialism, like Democracy, is intrinsically cosmopolitan in its operation. If the real essence of Democracy is, as the French Revolution delusively proclaimed, a spirit of fraternity, the essential requirement of Industrialism, if it is to achieve its full potentiality, is world-wide co-operation. The social dispensation which Industrialism demands was truly proclaimed by the eighteenth-century pioneers of the new technique in their famous watchword 'Laissez faire! Laissez passer!'—freedom to manufacture, freedom to exchange. Finding the World divided into small economic units, Industrialism set to work, a hundred and

---

[1] Actually there is an earlier example: the expulsion by the British authorities of the French Acadians from Nova Scotia at the opening of the Seven Years' War; but this was a small-scale affair, atrocious though it was by eighteenth-century standards, and there were, or were supposed to be, strategic reasons for it.

fifty years ago, to re-shape the economic structure of the World in two ways, both leading in the direction of world unity. It sought to make the economic units fewer and bigger, and also to lower the barriers between them.

If we glance at the history of these efforts we shall find that there was a turning-point in it round about the sixties and seventies of the last century. Down to that date Industrialism was assisted by Democracy in its efforts to diminish the number of economic units and to lower the barriers between them. After that date both Industrialism and Democracy reversed their policies and worked in the opposite direction.

If we consider first the size of the economic units, we find that, at the end of the eighteenth century, Great Britain was the largest free-trade area in the Western World, a fact which goes far to explain why it was in Great Britain and not elsewhere that the Industrial Revolution began. But in A.D. 1788 the ex-British colonies in North America, by adopting the Philadelphian Con-stitution, irrevocably abolished all commercial barriers between the States and created what was to become, by natural expansion, the largest free-trade area, and by direct consequence the mightiest industrialized community, in the world to-day. A few years later the French Revolution abolished all the provincial tariff-frontiers which had hitherto broken up the economic unity of France. In the second quarter of the nineteenth century the Germans achieved an economic *Zollverein* which proved the precursor of political union. In the third quarter the Italians, by achieving political unity, secured economic unity at the same time. If we take the other half of the programme, the lowering of tariffs and other parochial barriers in the way of international trade, we find that Pitt, who proclaimed himself a disciple of Adam Smith, set going a movement in favour of free imports which was carried to com-pletion by Peel, Cobden and Gladstone in the middle years of the nineteenth century; that the United States, after experi-menting with high tariffs, moved steadily in the free-trade direc-tion from 1832 to 1860 and that both the France of Louis Philippe and Napoleon III and pre-Bismarckian Germany steered the same course.

Then the tide turned. Democratic nationalism, which in Ger-many and in Italy had united many states into one, henceforth set itself to disintegrate the multi-national Hapsburg, Ottoman and Russian Empires. After the end of the General War of 1914–18 the old free-trade unit of the Danubian Monarchy was split up into a number of successor-states each striving desperately for economic autarky (self-sufficiency), while another constellation of new states, and by consequence new economic compartments, inserted itself between a close-shorn Germany and a close-shorn Russia. Meanwhile, about a generation earlier, the movement towards free trade had begun to be reversed first in one country and then in another until, at long last, in 1931, the returning tide of 'mercantilism' reached Great Britain herself.

The causes of this abandonment of free trade are easily discerned. Free trade had suited Great Britain when she was 'the Workshop of the World'; it had suited the cotton-exporting States which largely controlled the government of the United States between 1832 and 1860. It had seemed for various reasons to suit France and Germany during the same period. But, as the nations one by one became industrialized, it suited their parochial interests on a short view to pursue a cut-throat industrial competition with all their neighbours, and, under the prevailing system of parochial state sovereignty, who was to say them nay?

Cobden and his followers had made an immense miscalculation. They had looked forward to seeing the peoples and the states of the World drawn into a social unity by the new and unprecedently close-knit web of world-wide economic relations which was being woven blindly, from a British node, by the youthful energies of Industrialism. It would be an injustice to the Cobdenites to dismiss the Victorian British free-trade movement as simply a masterpiece of enlightened self-interest. The movement was also the expression of a moral idea and of a constructive international policy; its worthiest exponents aimed at something more than making Great Britain the mistress of the world market. They also hoped to promote the gradual evolution of a political world order in which the new economic world order could thrive; to create a political atmosphere in which a world-wide exchange of goods and services could be carried on in peace and security— ever increasing in security and bringing with it at each stage a rise in the standard of living for the whole of mankind.

Cobden's miscalculation lay in the fact that he failed to forecast the effect of the impact of Democracy and Industrialism on the rivalries of parochial states. He assumed that these giants would lie quiet in the nineteenth century as they had done in the eighteenth until the human spiders who were now spinning a world-wide industrial web had had time to enmesh them all in their gossamer bonds. He relied upon the unifying and pacifying effects which it was in the nature of Democracy and Industrialism to produce in their native and untrammelled manifestations, in which Democracy would stand for fraternity and Industrialism for co-operation. He did not reckon with the possibility that these same forces, by forcing their new 'heads of steam' into the old engines of the parochial states, would make for disruption and world anarchy. He did not recall that the gospel of fraternity preached by the spokesmen of the French Revolution had led to the first of the great modern wars of Nationalism; or rather he assumed that this would prove to have been not only the first but also the last war of its kind. He did not realize that, if the narrow mercantile oligarchies of the eighteenth century had been able to set in motion wars for the furtherance of the comparatively unimportant luxury trades which constituted the international commerce of their day, then, *a fortiori*, the democratized nations would fight one another *à outrance* for economic objects in an age when the Industrial Revolution had transformed international commerce from an exchange of luxuries into an exchange of the necessities of life.

In fine, the Manchester School misunderstood human nature. They did not understand that even an economic world order cannot be built on merely economic foundations. In spite of their genuine idealism, they did not realize that 'Man shall not live by bread alone'. This fatal mistake was not made by Gregory the Great and the other founders of Western Christendom, from whom the idealism of Victorian England was ultimately derived. These men, whole-heartedly dedicated to a supra-mundane cause, had not consciously attempted to found a world order. Their worldly aim had been limited to the more modest material ambition of keeping the survivors of a shipwrecked society alive. The economic edifice raised, as a burdensome and thankless necessity, by Gregory and his peers was avowedly a makeshift; yet, in raising it, they took care to build on a religious rock and not on economic sands; and, thanks to their labours, the structure of the Western Society rested on a solid religious foundation and grew, in less than fourteen centuries, from its modest beginnings in one out-of-the-way corner, into the ubiquitous Great Society of our own day. If a solid religious basis was required for Gregory's unpretentious economic building, it seems unlikely, on this showing, that the vaster structure of a world order, which it is our task to build to-day, can ever be securely based upon the rubble foundations of mere economic interests.

The Impact of Industrialism on Private Property

Private property is an institution which is apt to establish itself in societies in which the single family or household is the normal unit of economic activity, and in such a society it is probably the most satisfactory system for governing the distribution of material wealth. But the natural unit of economic activity is now no longer the single family, the single village or the single national state, but the entire living generation of mankind. Since the advent of Industrialism our modern Western economy has transcended the family unit *de facto* and has therefore logically transcended the family institution of private property. Yet in practice the old institution has remained in force; and in these circumstances Industrialism has put its formidable 'drive' into private property, enhancing the man of property's social power while diminishing his social responsibility, until an institution which may have been beneficent in the pre-Industrial Age has assumed many of the features of a social evil.

In these circumstances our society to-day is confronted with the task of adjusting the old institution of private property to a harmonious relationship with the new force of Industrialism. The method of pacific adjustment is to counteract the maldistribution of private property which Industrialism inevitably entails by arranging for a deliberate, rational and equitable control and redistribution of private property through the agency of the state. By controlling key industries the state can curb the excessive power over other people's lives which is conferred by the private ownership of such industries, and it can mitigate the ill effects of poverty by providing social services financed by high taxation of wealth. This method has the incidental social advantage that it tends to transform the state from a war-making machine—which has been its most conspicuous function in the past—into an agency for social welfare.

If this pacific policy should prove inadequate, we may be fairly sure that the revolutionary alternative will overtake us in the shape of some form of Communism which will reduce private property to vanishing-point. This seems to be the only practical alternative to an adjustment, because the maldistribution of private property through the impact of Industrialism would be an intolerable enormity if not effectively mitigated by social services and high taxation. Yet, as the Russian experiment indicates, the revolutionary remedy of Communism might prove little less deadly than the disease itself; for the institution of private property is so intimately bound up with all that is best in the pre-industrial social heritage that its sheer abolition could hardly fail to produce a disastrous break in the social tradition of our Western Society.

The Impact of Democracy on Education

One of the greatest social changes that has been brought about by the advent of Democracy has been the spread of education.

In the progressive countries a system of universal compulsory gratuitous instruction has made education the birthright of every child—in contrast to the role of education in the pre-Democratic Age, when it was the monopoly of a privileged minority. This new educational system has been one of the principal social ideals of every state that aspires to an honourable position in the modern world-comity of nations.

When universal education was first inaugurated it was greeted by the liberal opinion of the day as a triumph of justice and enlightenment which might be expected to usher in a new era of happiness and well-being for mankind. But these expectations can now be seen to have left out of account the presence of several stumbling-blocks on this broad road to the millennium, and in this matter, as so often happens, it has been the unforeseen factors that have proved the most important.

One stumbling-block has been the inevitable impoverishment in the results of education when the process is made available for 'the masses' at the cost of being divorced from its traditional cultural background. The good intentions of Democracy have no magic power to perform the miracle of the loaves and fishes. Our mass-produced intellectual pabulum lacks savour and vitamins. A second stumbling-block has been the utilitarian spirit in which the fruits of education are apt to be turned to account when they are brought within everybody's reach. Under a social régime in which education is confined to those who have either inherited a right to it as a social privilege or have proved a right to it by their exceptional gifts of industry and intelligence, education is either a pearl cast before swine or else a pearl of great price which the finder buys at the cost of all that he has. In neither case is it a means to an end: an instrument of worldly ambition or of frivolous amusement. The possibility of turning education to account as a means of amusement for the masses—and of profit for the enterprising persons by whom the amusement is purveyed— has only arisen since the introduction of universal elementary education; and this new possibility has conjured up a third stumbling-block which is the greatest of all. The bread of universal education is no sooner cast upon the waters than a shoal of sharks arises from the depths and devours the children's bread under the educator's very eyes. In the educational history of England the dates speak for themselves. The edifice of universal elementary education was, roughly speaking, completed by Forster's Act in 1870; and the Yellow Press was invented some twenty years later—as soon, that is, as the first generation of children from the national schools had acquired sufficient purchasing-power—by a stroke of irresponsible genius which had divined that the educational philanthropist's labour of love could be made to yield a royal profit to a press-lord.

These disconcerting reactions to the impact of Democracy upon education have attracted the attention of the rulers of modern would-be totalitarian national states. If press-lords could make millions by providing idle amusement for the half-educated, serious statesmen could draw, not money perhaps, but power from the same source. The modern dictators have deposed the press-lords and substituted for crude and debased private entertainment an equally crude and debased system of state propaganda. The elaborate and ingenious machinery for the mass-enslavement of semi-educated minds, invented for private profit under British and American régimes of *laisser faire*, has been simply taken over by the rulers of states who have employed these mental appliances, reinforced by the cinema and the radio, for their own sinister purposes. After Northcliffe, Hitler—though Hitler was not the first in his line.

Thus, in countries where democratic education has been introduced, the people are in danger of falling under an intellectual tyranny engineered either by private exploitation or by public authority. If the people's souls are to be saved, the only way is to raise the standard of mass-education to a degree at which its recipients will be rendered immune against at any rate the grosser forms of exploitation and propaganda; and it need hardly be said that this is no easy task. Happily, there are certain disinterested and effective educational agencies grappling with it in our Western World to-day—such agencies as the Workers' Educational Association and the British Broadcasting Corporation in Great Britain and the extra-mural activities of universities in many countries.

The Impact of Italian Efficiency on Transalpine Governments

All our examples hitherto have been drawn from the latest phase of our Western history. We need do no more than remind the reader of the problem set by the impact of a new force on an old institution in an earlier chapter of that same history, for we have already examined this example in another connexion. The problem here set was how to secure a harmonious adjustment of the Transalpine feudal monarchies to the impact of the political efficiency generated in the city-states of Renaissance Italy. The easier and inferior way of adjustment was through keying up the monarchies themselves into tyrannies or despotisms on the pattern of those despotisms to which so many of the Italian states had already succumbed. The harder but better method was the keying-up of the medieval assemblies of Estates in the Trans-alpine kingdoms into organs of representative government which would be as efficient as the latter-day Italian despotisms and would at the same time provide, on the national scale, for as liberal a measure of self-government as the self-governing institutions of the Italian city-states in what had been, politically at any rate, their best days.

It was in England, for reasons which we have recalled elsewhere, that these adjustments were most harmoniously achieved, and England accordingly became the pioneer, or creative minority, in the next chapter of Western history, as Italy had been in the pre-ceding one. Under the adroit and nationally minded Tudors the monarchy began to develop into a despotism, but under the ill-fated Stuarts Parliament drew level with the Crown and finally drew ahead. Even so, the adjustment was not made without two revolutions, which were, however, in comparison with most revolutions, conducted with sobriety and restraint. In France the despotic tendency lasted much longer and went much farther, and the result was a far more violent revolution which ushered in a period of political instability the end of which is not yet in sight. In Spain and Germany the drift towards despotism continued down to our own day and the democratic counter-movements, thus inordinately long delayed, have found themselves involved in all the complications which have been outlined in the previous sections of this chapter.

The Impact of the Solonian Revolution on the Hellenic City-States

The Italian political efficiency which made its impact upon the Transalpine countries of the Western World at the transition from the second to the third chapter of Western history had a counter-part in Hellenic history in the economic efficiency which was achieved in certain states of the Hellenic World in the seventh and sixth centuries B.C., under the pressure of the Malthusian problem. For this new economic efficiency did not confine itself to Athens and the other states that originated it, but, radiating outwards, made impacts on both the domestic and the inter-national politics of the whole Hellenic city-state cosmos.

We have already described this economic new departure, which may be called the Solonian revolution. Essentially it was a change-over from subsistence farming to cash-crop farming accompanied by a development of commerce and industry. This solution of an economic problem, the pressure of population on land-space, called two new political problems into existence. On the one hand, the economic revolution brought into existence new social classes, urban commercial and industrial workers, artisans and sailors, for whom a place had to be found in the political scheme. On the other hand, the old isolation of one city-state from another gave place to an interdependence on the economic plane, and, when once a number of city-states had become interdependent economically, it was thenceforth impossible that they should remain, without disaster, in their pristine state of isolation on the plane of politics. The former of these problems resembles that which Victorian England solved by a series of parliamentary reform bills; the latter that which she hoped to solve through the free-trade movement. We will take these problems separately and in the order previously observed.

In the domestic political life of the Hellenic city-states the enfranchisement of the new classes involved a radical change in the basis of political association. The traditional kinship basis had to be replaced by a new franchise based on property. In Athens this change-over was carried through effectively, and for the most part smoothly, in a series of constitutional developments between the Age of Solon and the Age of Pericles. The comparative smoothness and effectiveness of the transition is proved by the smallness of the part that the *tyrannis* played in Athenian history; for it was a general rule in the constitutional history of these city-states that, when the process of following in the footsteps of the pioneer communities was unduly retarded, a condition of *stasis* (revolutionary class-war) supervened, which could only be resolved by the emergence of a 'tyrant' or, in our modern jargon borrowed from Rome, a dictator. At Athens, as elsewhere, a dictatorship proved an indispensible stage in the process of adjustment, but here the tyranny of Peisistratus and his sons was no more than a brief interlude between the Solonian and the Cleisthenean reform.

Other Greek city-states managed their adjustments much less harmoniously. Corinth underwent a prolonged, and Syracuse a repeated, dictatorship. At Corcyra the atrocity of the *stasis* has been immortalized in the pages of Thucydides.

Finally, we may take the case of Rome, a non-Greek community which was drawn into the Hellenic World as a result of the geographical expansion of the Hellenic Civilization during the period 725–525 B.C. It was not till after this cultural conversion that Rome entered on the course of economic and political development which was the normal career of a Hellenic or Hellenized city-state, and consequently in this chapter Rome passed through every stage with a time-lag of some hundred and fifty years behind the corresponding date in the history of Athens. For this time-lag Rome paid the penalty in an extreme and bitter *stasis* between the patrician monopolists of power by right of birth and the plebeian claimants to power by right of wealth and numbers. This Roman *stasis*, which lasted from the fifth century B.C. to the third, went to such lengths that the Plebs, on several occasions, seceded from the Populus by an actual geographical withdrawal, while it permanently established a plebeian anti-state—complete with its own institutions, assemblies and officers—within the bosom of the legitimate commonwealth. It was only thanks to external pressure that Roman statesmanship succeeded, in 287 B.C., in coping with this constitutional enormity by bringing state and anti-state into a working political unity; and, after the century-and-a-half of victorious imperialism which followed, the makeshift character of the settlement of 287 B.C. was rapidly revealed. The unannealed amalgam of patrician and plebeian institutions which the Romans had accepted as their ramshackle constitution proved so inept a political instrument for achieving new social adjustments that the violent and abortive careers of the Gracchi opened a second bout of *stasis* (131–31 B.C.) worse than the first. This time, after a century of self-laceration, the Roman body politic submitted itself to a permanent dictatorship; and since, by this time, Roman arms had completed their conquest of the Hellenic World, the Roman *tyrannis* of Augustus and his successors incidentally provided the Hellenic Society with its universal state.

The persistent ineptitude of the Romans in fumbling with their domestic problems presents an extreme contrast to their unrivalled ability in making, retaining and organizing their foreign conquests; and it is to be noticed that the Athenians, who were unrivalled in the success with which they exorcized *stasis* from their domestic politics, signally failed in the fifth century B.C. to create the then already urgently needed international order which the Romans succeeded in establishing after a fashion four hundred years later.

This international task, in which Athens failed, was the second of the two problems of adjustment set by the Solonian revolution. The obstacle in the way of creating the international political security which Hellenic international trade required was the inherited political institution of city-state sovereignty. From the opening of the fifth century B.C. onwards the whole of the rest of Hellenic political history can be formulated in terms of an endeavour to transcend city-state sovereignty and of the resistance which this endeavour evoked. Before the fifth century closed, the obstinacy of the resistance to this endeavour had brought the Hellenic Civilization to its breakdown, and, though the problem was solved after a fashion by Rome, it was not solved in time to prevent the disintegration of the Hellenic Society from running its course to a final breakdown. The ideal solution of the problem was to be found in a permanent limitation of city-state sovereignty by voluntary agreement between the city-states themselves. Unfortunately the most conspicuous of such attempts, the Delian League, achieved by Athens and her Aegean allies in the course of their victorious counter-offensive against Persia, was vitiated by the intrusion of the older Hellenic tradition of *hegemony*, the exploitation of an enforced alliance by its leading member. The Delian League became an Athenian Empire and the Athenian Empire provoked the Peloponnesian War. Four centuries later Rome succeeded where Athens had failed; but the chastisement with whips which Athenian imperialism inflicted on its small world was as nothing to the chastisement with scorpions which Roman imperialism inflicted on a much enlarged Hellenic and Hellenized society during the two centuries which followed the Hannibalic War and preceded the establishment of the Augustan Peace.

The Impact of Parochialism on the Western Christian Church

While the Hellenic Society broke down through failure to transcend in time its traditional parochialism, our Western Society failed—with consequences still hidden in the future—to maintain a social solidarity which was perhaps the most precious part of its original endowment. In the time of transition from the medieval to the modern chapter of our Western history one of the most significant expressions of the current social change was the rise of parochialism. In our generation it is not altogether easy for us to regard this change dispassionately on account of the vast evils which it has brought upon us in our own day, when it has become an anachronistic survival. Yet we can see that there was much to be said in favour of the abandonment of our medieval oecumenicalism five centuries ago. For all its moral grandeur it was a ghost from the past, a legacy from the universal state of the Hellenic Society, and there was always an unseemly discrepancy between the theoretical supremacy of the oecumenical idea and the actual anarchy of medieval practice. The new parochialism at any rate succeeded in living up to its less ambitious claims. However that may be, the new force won the day. In politics it displayed itself in a plurality of sovereign states; in letters in the form of new vernacular literatures; and in the field of religion it collided with the medieval Western Church.

The violence of this last collision was due to the fact that the Church, elaborately organized under the Papal hierocracy, was the master institution of the medieval dispensation. The problem was probably open to adjustment along lines which the Papacy had already reconnoitred when it was at the height of its power. For instance, in encountering the local impulse to make use of vernacular languages for liturgical purposes instead of Latin, the Roman Church had conceded to the Croats permission to translate the liturgy into their own language, probably because in this frontier district Rome found herself faced with the competition of her Eastern Orthodox rival, who, so far from insisting on her non-Greek converts accepting Greek as their liturgical language, showed a politic generosity in translating her liturgy into many tongues. Again, in dealing with the medieval predecessors of modern sovereign governments, the Popes, engaged, as they were, in a life-and-death struggle against the oecumenical claims of the Holy Roman Emperors, had shown themselves much more accommodating to the parochial claims of the kings of England, France, Castile and other local states to exercise control over the ecclesiastical organization within their own respective frontiers.

Thus the Holy See was not altogether unschooled in rendering unto Caesar the things which are Caesar's by the time when the full-fledged parochial neo-Caesarism asserted itself, and in the century before the so-called Reformation the Papacy went to considerable lengths in negotiating with secular sovereigns concordats which divided between Rome and the parochial rulers the control over the ecclesiastical hierarchy. This system of concordats was the unintended outcome of the abortive oecumenical councils held in the first half of the fifteenth century at Constance (A.D. 1414–18) and at Basel (A.D. 1431–49).

The Conciliar Movement was a constructive effort to neutralize the irresponsible, and often notoriously misused, authority of the self-styled Vicar of Christ by the introduction on an oecumenical scale of a system of ecclesiastical parliamentarism such as on the parochial scale had already proved its usefulness in the Feudal Age as a means of controlling the activities of medieval kings. But the Popes who encountered the Conciliar Movement hardened their hearts; and Papal intransigence proved disastrously successful. It succeeded in bringing the Conciliar Movement to naught, and, by thus rejecting a last opportunity for adjustment, it condemned Western Christendom to be rent by a violent internal discord between its ancient oecumenical heritage and its new parochial proclivities.

The result was a melancholy crop of revolutions and enormities. Among the former we need only mention the violent break-up of the Church into a number of rival churches each denouncing the other as the gang of Antichrist and setting in motion a whole cycle of wars and persecutions. Among the latter may be placed the usurpation by secular sovereigns of the 'divine right' supposedly inherent in the Papacy, a 'divine right' which is still working havoc in the Western World in the grim shape of a pagan worship of sovereign national states. Patriotism, which Dr. Johnson rather oddly described as 'the last refuge of a scoundrel' and which Nurse Cavell more discerningly declared to be 'not enough', has very largely superseded Christianity as the religion of the Western World. In any case, it is difficult to conceive of a sharper contradiction of the essential teaching of Christianity—and of all the other historic higher religions as well—than is embodied in this monstrous product of the impact of parochialism on the Western Christian Church.

The Impact of the Sense of Unity on Religion

The 'higher religions' with a mission to all mankind are relatively recent arrivals on the scene of human history. Not only are they unknown in primitive societies; they have not arisen even among societies in process of civilization until after a certain number of civilizations have broken down and travelled far on the way to disintegration. It is in response to the challenge presented by the disintegrations of civilizations that these higher religions have made their appearance. The religious institutions of civilizations of the unaffiliated class, like those of primitive societies, are bound up with the secular institutions of those societies and do not look beyond them. From a higher spiritual standpoint such religions are clearly inadequate, but they have one important negative merit: they foster a spirit of 'live and let live' between one religion and another. Under such conditions a plurality of gods and of religions in the world is taken for granted as a natural concomitant of a plurality of states and of civilizations.

In this social condition human souls are blind to the ubiquity and omnipotence of God, but they are immune from the temptation of succumbing to the sin of intolerance in their relations with other human beings who worship God under different forms and titles. It is one of the ironies of human history that the illumination which has brought into religion a perception of the unity of God and the brotherhood of mankind should at the same time have promoted intolerance and persecution. The explanation is, of course, that the idea of unity in its application to religion impresses the spiritual pioneers who embrace it as being so transcendently important that they are apt to plunge into any short cut which promises to hasten the translation of their idea into reality. This enormity of intolerance and persecution has shown its hideous countenance, almost without fail, whenever and wherever a higher religion has been preached. This fanatical temper flared up in the abortive attempt of the Emperor Ikhnaton to impose his vision of monotheism on the Egyptiac World in the fourteenth century B.C. An equally ardent fanaticism casts its lurid light over the rise and development of Judaism. A savage denunciation of any participation in the worships of kindred Syriac communities is the reverse side of that etherialization of the local worship of Yahweh into a monotheistic religion which was the positive and sublime spiritual achievement of the Hebrew Prophets. In the history of Christianity, both in its internal schisms and in its encounters with alien faiths, we see the same spirit breaking out again and again.

On this showing the impact of a sense of unity on religion is apt to beget a spiritual enormity, and the moral adjustment which meets the case is the practice of the virtue of toleration. The right motive for toleration is the recognition that all religions are quests in search of a common spiritual goal and that, even though some of these quests may be more advanced and more on the right lines than others, the persecution of a 'wrong' religion by a *soi-disant* 'right' religion is of its very nature a contradiction in terms, since, by indulging in persecution, the 'right' religion puts itself in the wrong and denies its own credentials.

In at least one noteworthy case such tolerance was enjoined by a prophet upon his followers on this high ground. Muhammad prescribed the religious toleration of Jews and Christians who had made political submission to the secular arm of Islam, and he gave this ruling expressly on the ground that these two non-Muslim religious communities, like the Muslims themselves, were 'People of the Book'. It is significant of the tolerant spirit which animated Primitive Islam that, without express sanction from the Prophet himself, a similar toleration was afterwards extended in practice to the Zoroastrians who came under Muslim rule.

The period of religious toleration upon which Western Christendom entered in the second half of the seventeenth century had its origins in a much more cynical mood. It can be called 'religious toleration' only in the sense that it was a toleration of religions; if we look to its motives it should rather be styled irreligious toleration. In this half-century the Catholic and Protestant factions rather suddenly abandoned their struggles, not because they had become convinced of the sin of intolerance but because they had come to realize that neither party could any longer make much headway against the other. At the same time they seem to have become aware that they no longer cared sufficiently for the theological issues at stake to relish making any further sacrifices for

their sake. They repudiated the traditional virtue of 'enthusiasm'
(which by derivation means being filled with the spirit of God)
and henceforth regarded it as a vice. It was in this spirit that
an eighteenth-century English bishop described an eighteenth-
century English missionary as 'a miserable enthusiast'.

Nevertheless toleration, from whatever motive it may derive, is
a sovereign antidote to the fanaticism which the impact of a sense
of unity on religion is apt to breed. The nemesis of its absence
is a choice between the enormity of persecution or a revolutionary
revulsion against religion itself. Such a revulsion is expressed in
the most famous line of Lucretius: *Tantum religio potuit suadere
malorum* ('Such an enormity of evil has religion been able to
instigate'); in Voltaire's 'Écrasez l'infame'; and in Gambetta's
'Le cléricalisme, voilà l'ennemi'.

The Impact of Religion on Caste

The Lucretian and Voltairean view that religion is itself an
evil—and perhaps the fundamental evil in human life—might be
supported by citing, from the annals of Indic and Hindu history,
the sinister influence which religion has incontestably exercised,
in the lives of these civilizations, upon the institution of caste.

This institution, which consists in the social segregation of two
or more geographically intermingled groups of human beings,
is apt to establish itself wherever and whenever one community
makes itself master of another community without being able or
willing either to exterminate the subject community or to assimilate it into its own body social. For example, a caste division has
arisen in the United States between the dominant white majority
and the negro minority, and in South Africa between the dominant
white minority and the negro majority. In the sub-continent of
India the institution of caste seems to have arisen out of the irruption of the Eurasian Nomad Aryas into the former domain of the
so-called Indus culture in the course of the first half of the second
millennium B.C.

It will be seen that this institution of caste has no essential
connexion with religion. In the United States and in South
Africa, where the Negroes have abandoned their ancestral religions and adopted the Christianity of the dominant Europeans,
the divisions between churches cut right across the divisions between races, though the black and white members of each church
are segregated from one another in their religious worship as in
other social activities. In the Indian case, on the other hand, we
may conjecture that from the first the castes were distinguished
from one another by differences of religious practice. It is evident,

however, that this religious differentiation must have been accentuated when the Indic Civilization developed the strongly religious bent which it has bequeathed to its successor. It is further evident that this impact of religiosity on the institution of caste must have seriously aggravated the banefulness of the institution. Caste is always on the verge of being a social enormity, but, when it is keyed up by receiving a religious interpretation and a religious sanction, its enormity is bound to grow to monstrous proportions.

In the actual event the impact of religion on caste in India has begotten the unparalleled social abuse of 'untouchability', and there has never been any effective move to abolish or even to mitigate 'untouchability' on the part of the Brahmans, the hieratic caste which has become master of the ceremonies of the whole system. The enormity survives, except in so far as it has been assailed by revolution.

The earliest known revolts against caste are those of Mahavira, the founder of Jainism, and of the Buddha, both about 500 B.C. If either Buddhism or Jainism had succeeded in captivating the Indic World, caste might have been got rid of. As it turned out, however, the role of universal church in the last chapter of the Indic decline and fall was played by Hinduism, a parvenu archaistic syncretism of things new and old; and one of the old things to which Hinduism gave a new lease of life was caste. Not content with preserving this old abuse, it elaborated it, and the Hindu Civilization has been handicapped from its outset by a far heavier burden of caste than ever weighed upon its predecessor.

In the history of the Hindu Civilization revolts against caste have expressed themselves in secessions from Hinduism under the attraction of some alien religious system. Some of these secessions have been led by Hindu reformers who have founded new churches combining expurgated versions of Hinduism with alien elements. For example Nanak (A.D. 1469–1538), the founder of Sikhism, borrowed elements from Islam, and Ram Mohan Roy (A.D. 1772–1833) created the Brahmō Samāj out of a combination between Hinduism and Christianity. In both these systems caste is rejected. In other cases secessionists have shaken the dust of Hinduism off their feet altogether and have entered the Islamic or the Christian fold; and such conversions have taken place on the largest scale in districts containing a high proportion of members of low castes and depressed classes.

This is the revolutionary retort to the enormity of 'untouchability', which has been evoked by the impact of religion on caste; and, as the masses of India are progressively stirred by the economic and intellectual and moral ferment of Westernization, the trickle of conversions among outcastes seems likely to swell to a flood, unless a harmonious adjustment of their religious-social system is achieved, in the teeth of Brahman opposition, by those members of the Hindu Society who honour the religious as well as the political ideals of the Banya Maḥatma Gandhi.

The Impact of Civilization on the Division of Labour

We have already observed that the division of labour is not entirely unknown in primitive societies, and it is illustrated by the specialization of smiths, bards, priests, medicine-men and the like. But the impact of civilization on the division of labour tends in a general way to accentuate the division to a degree at which it threatens not merely to bring in diminishing social returns but to become actually anti-social in its working; and this effect is produced in the lives of the creative minority and the uncreative majority alike. The creators are pushed into esotericism and the rank and file into lopsidedness.

Esotericism is a symptom of failure in the careers of creative individuals, and it may be described as an accentuation of the preliminary movement in the rhythm of Withdrawal-and-Return, resulting in a failure to complete the process. The Greeks censured those who failed in this way by applying to them the word $\iota\delta\iota\dot{\omega}\tau\eta\varsigma$. The $\iota\delta\iota\dot{\omega}\tau\eta\varsigma$, in fifth-century Greek usage, was a superior personality who committed the social offence of living by and for himself instead of putting his gifts at the service of the common weal; and the light in which such behaviour was regarded in Periclean Athens is illustrated by the fact that, in our modern vernaculars, the derivative of this Greek word (idiot) has come to mean an imbecile. But the real $\iota\delta\iota\dot{\omega}\tau\alpha\iota$ of our modern Western Society are not to be found in asylums. One group of them, *homo sapiens* specialized and degraded into *homo economicus*, supplies the Gradgrinds and Bounderbys of Dickensian satire. Another group believes itself to be at the opposite pole and to be numbered among the children of light, but in fact it falls under the same condemnation; these are the intellectual and aesthetic snobs and high-brows who believe that their art is 'for art's sake', the Bunthornes of Gilbertian satire. Perhaps the difference of date between Dickens and Gilbert exemplifies the fact that the former group were the more conspicuous in Early Victorian England and the latter group in the Late Victorian Age. They are at opposite poles, but it has been remarked of the North and South Poles of our planet that, though they are far apart, they suffer from the same climatic defects.

It remains to consider what we have called lopsidedness, the effect of the impact of civilization on the division of labour in the life of the uncreative majority.

The social problem that awaits the creator when he returns from his withdrawal into a renewed communion with the mass of his fellows is the problem of raising the average level of a number of ordinary human souls to the higher level that has been attained by the creator himself; and as soon as he grapples with this task he is confronted with the fact that most of the rank and file are unable to live on this higher level with all their hearts and wills and souls and strength. In this situation he may be tempted to try a short cut and resort to the device of raising some single faculty to the higher level without bothering about the whole personality. This means, *ex hypothesi*, the forcing of a human being into a lop-sided development. Such results are most easily obtainable on the plane of a mechanical technique, since, of all the elements in a culture, its mechanical aptitudes are easiest to isolate and to communicate. It is not difficult to make an efficient mechanic out of a person whose soul remains in all other departments primitive and barbarous. But other faculties can be specialized and hyper-trophied in the same way. Matthew Arnold's criticism, in *Culture and Anarchy* (1869), of the devout middle-class Nonconformist English Philistine in his 'Hebraizing backwater' was that he had specialized in what he wrongly believed to be the Christian Religion while neglecting the other—the 'Hellenic'—virtues which go to the making of a well-balanced personality.

We have come across this lopsidedness already in our examina-tion of the response to the challenge of penalization made by penalized minorities. We have observed that the tyrannical exclu-sion of these minorities from full citizenship has stimulated them to prosper and excel in the activities left open to them; and we have marvelled at and admired a whole gallery of *tours de force* in which these minorities stand out as the very incarnation of the invinci-bility of human nature. At the same time we cannot ignore the fact that some of these minorities—Levantines and Phanariots and Armenians and Jews—have the reputation of being 'not as other men are' for worse as well as for better. In the unhappy relations between Jews and Gentiles, which is the classic case, the Gentile who is disgusted and ashamed at the behaviour of his anti-Semitic fellow Goyyim is also embarrassed at finding himself constrained to admit that there is some element of truth in the caricature which the Jew-baiter draws as a justification for his own bestiality. The heart of the tragedy lies in the fact that a penalization which stimu-lates a penalized minority to a heroic response is apt to warp its human nature as well. And what is true of these socially penalized minorities is evidently likewise true of those technologically specialized majorities with which we are now concerned. This is a point to be borne in mind when we observe the ever-increasing intrusion of technological studies upon what used to be a liberal, if too unpractical, curriculum of education.

The fifth-century Greeks had a word for this lopsidedness: βαναυσία. The βάναυσος was a person whose activity was specialized, through a concentration on some particular technique, at the expense of his all-round development as a social animal. The kind of technique which was usually in people's minds when they used the term was some manual or mechanical trade pursued for private profit. But the Hellenic contempt for βαναυσία went farther than this, and implanted in Hellenic minds a contempt for professionalism of all kinds. The Spartan concentration on military technique was, for example, βαναυσία incarnate. Even a great statesman and saviour of his country could not escape the reproach if he lacked an all-round appreciation of the art of life.

'In refined and cultivated society Themistocles used to be girded at by people of so-called liberal education [for his lack of accomplishments] and used to be driven into making the rather cheap defence that he certainly could do nothing with a musical instrument, but that, if you were to put into his hands a country that was small and obscure, he knew how to turn it into a great country and a famous one.'[1]

Against this, perhaps rather mild, example of βαναυσία we may set a picture of Vienna in the golden age of Haydn, Mozart and Beethoven, where it is recorded that a Hapsburg Emperor and his Chancellor were both accustomed, in their hours of relaxation, to take part in the performance of string quartets.

This Hellenic sensitiveness to the dangers of βαναυσία has also expressed itself in the institutions of other societies. For example, the social function of the Jewish Sabbath and the Christian Sunday is to ensure that, for one day out of seven, a creature who has been cramped and blinkered by the professional specialization through which he has been earning his living for six days shall on the seventh remember his Creator and live the life of an integral human soul. Again, it is no accident that, in England, organized games and other sports should have grown in popularity with the rise of Industrialism; for such sport is a conscious attempt to counterbalance the soul-destroying specialization which the division of labour under Industrialism entails.

Unfortunately, this attempt to adjust life to Industrialism through sport has been partially defeated because the spirit and

---

[1] Plutarch: *Life of Themistocles*, ch. ii.

rhythm of Industrialism have invaded and infected sport itself. In the Western World of to-day professional athletes, more narrowly specialized and more extravagantly paid than any industrial technicians, now provide horrifying examples of βαναυσία at its acme. The writer of this Study recalls two football grounds he visited on the campuses of two colleges in the United States. One of them was flood-lighted in order that football players might be manufactured by night as well as by day, in continuous shifts. The other was roofed over in order that practice might go on, whatever the weather. It was said to be the largest span of roof in the world, and its erection had cost a fabulous sum. Round the sides were ranged beds for the reception of exhausted or wounded warriors. On both these American grounds I found that the players were no more than an infinitesimal fraction of the total student body; and I was also told that these boys looked forward to the ordeal of playing in a match with much the same apprehension as their elder brothers had felt when they went into the trenches in 1918. In truth, this Anglo-Saxon football was not a game at all.

A corresponding development can be discerned in the history of the Hellenic World, where the aristocratic amateurs whose athletic victories are celebrated in Pindar's Odes were replaced by teams of professionals, while the shows that were purveyed, in the post-Alexandrine Age, from Parthia to Spain by the Διονύσου Τεχνῖται ('United Artists Ltd.') were as different from the performances in Dionysus's own theatre at Athens as a music-hall revue is different from a medieval mystery play.

It is no wonder that, when social enormities defy adjustment in this baffling fashion, philosophers should dream of revolutionary plans for sweeping the enormities away. Plato, writing in the first generation after the Hellenic breakdown, seeks to cut the root of βαναυσία by planting his Utopia in an inland region with no facilities for maritime trade and little inducement towards any economic activity except subsistence farming. Thomas Jefferson, the fountain-head of an American idealism that has gone sadly astray, dreams the same dream at the opening of the nineteenth century. 'Were I to indulge my own theory', he writes, 'I should wish the States to practise neither commerce nor navigation but to stand with regard to Europe precisely on the footing of China'[1] (who kept her ports closed to European trade until forced to open them by British arms in 1840). Again, Samuel Butler imagines his Erewhonians deliberately and systematically destroying their machines as the only alternative to being enslaved by them.

[1] Quoted by Woodward, W. E.: *A New American History*, p. 260.

The Impact of Civilization on Mimesis

A re-orientation of the faculty of mimesis away from the elders towards the pioneers is, as we have seen, the change in the direction of this faculty which accompanies the mutation of a primitive society into a civilization; and the aim in view is the raising of the uncreative mass to the new level reached by the pioneers. But, because this resort to mimesis is a short cut, a 'cheap substitute' for the real thing, the attainment of the goal is apt to be illusory. The mass is not really enabled to enter the 'communion of saints'. Too often the natural primitive man, *homo integer antiquae virtutis*, is transmogrified into a shoddy 'man in the street', *homo vulgaris Northcliffii* or *homo demoticus Cleonis*. The impact of civilization on mimesis, in that event, begets the enormity of a pseudo-sophisticated urban crowd, signally inferior in many respects to its primitive ancestors. Aristophanes fought Cleon with the weapon of ridicule on the Attic stage, but off the stage Cleon won. The Cleonian 'man in the street', whose entry upon the stage of Hellenic history before the end of the fifth century B.C. is one of the unmistakable symptoms of social decline, eventually redeemed his soul by repudiating outright a culture which had failed to satisfy his spiritual hunger because he had only succeeded in filling his belly with the husks. As a spiritually awakened child of a dissident proletariat, he worked out his own salvation at last through the discovery of a higher religion.

Perhaps these examples may suffice to illustrate the part played in the breakdown of civilizations by the intractability of old institutions to the touch of new social forces—or, in biblical language, by the inadequacy of old bottles as receptacles for new wine.

(3) THE NEMESIS OF CREATIVITY: IDOLIZATION OF AN EPHEMERAL SELF

The Reversal of Roles

We have now made some study of two aspects of that failure of self-determination to which the breakdowns of civilizations appear to be due. We have considered the mechanicalness of mimesis and the intractability of institutions. We may conclude this part of our inquiry with a consideration of the apparent nemesis of creativity.

It looks as though it were uncommon for the creative responses to two or more successive challenges in the history of a civilization to be achieved by one and the same minority. Indeed, the party that has distinguished itself in dealing with one challenge is apt to fail conspicuously in attempting to deal with the next. This disconcerting yet apparently normal inconstancy of human fortunes is one of the dominant *motifs* of Attic drama and is discussed by Aristotle in his *Poetics* under the name of περιπέτεια or 'the reversal of roles'. It is also one of the principal themes of the New Testament.

In the drama of the New Testament the Christ, whose epiphany on Earth is the true fulfilment of Jewry's Messianic hope, is nevertheless rejected by the school of the Scribes and Pharisees which, only a few generations back, had come to the front by taking the lead in the heroic Jewish revolt against the triumphal progress of Hellenization. The insight and the uprightness which had brought the Scribes and Pharisees to the fore in that previous crisis desert them now in a crisis of greater import, and the Jews who respond are 'the publicans and harlots'. The Messiah Himself comes from 'Galilee of the Gentiles', and the greatest of His executors is a Jew from Tarsus, a pagan Hellenized city beyond the traditional horizon of the Promised Land. If the drama is looked at from a slightly different angle and on a rather broader stage, the role of the Pharisees can be assigned, as in the Fourth Gospel, to Jewry as a whole, and the role of the publicans and harlots to the Gentiles who accept St. Paul's teaching when it is rejected by the Jews.

The same *motif* of 'the reversal of roles' is the theme of a number of the parables and subsidiary incidents in the Gospel story. It is the point of the parables of Dives and Lazarus, the Pharisee and the Publican, the Good Samaritan in contrast to the Priest and the Levite, and the Prodigal Son in contrast to his respectable elder brother; and the same theme appears in the encounters of Jesus with the Roman centurion and with the Syrophoenician woman. If we include the Old and New Testaments in a single conspectus, we find the Old Testament drama of Esau forfeiting his birthright to Jacob answered by a 'reversal of roles' in the New Testament when the descendants of Jacob forfeit their birthright in their turn by rejecting Christ. The *motif* constantly recurs in the sayings of Jesus: 'Whosoever shall exalt himself shall be abased'; 'The last shall be first and the first last'; 'Except ye be converted and become as little children, ye shall not enter into the Kingdom of Heaven'. And He applies the moral to His own mission by quoting a verse from the hundred and eighteenth Psalm: 'The stone which the builders rejected, the same is become the head of the corner.'

The same idea runs all through the great works of Hellenic literature, and is summarily expressed in the formula ὕβρις — ἄτη: 'Pride goes before a fall.' Herodotus underlines the lesson in the lives of Xerxes and Croesus and Polycrates. Indeed the whole subject of his History might be taken to be the pride and fall of the Achaemenian Empire; and Thucydides, writing a generation later and in an apparently more objective and 'scientific' spirit, portrays much more impressively, because he discards the frank tendentiousness of 'the Father of History', the pride and fall of Athens. It is scarcely necessary to cite the favourite themes of Attic tragedy exemplified in the Agamemnon of Aeschylus, the Oedipus and Ajax of Sophocles, or the Pentheus of Euripides. A poet of the Sinic decline and fall expresses the same idea:

He who stands on tip-toe does not stand firm;
He who takes the longest strides does not walk the fastest. . . .
He who boasts of what he will do succeeds in nothing;
He who is proud of his work achieves nothing that endures.[1]

Such is the nemesis of creativity; and if the plot of this tragedy is really of common occurrence—if it is true that the successful creator in one chapter finds his very success a severe handicap in endeavouring to resume the creative role in the next chapter, so that the chances are always actually against 'the favourite' and in favour of 'the dark horse'—then it is plain that we have here run to earth a very potent cause of the breakdowns of civilizations. We can see that this nemesis would bring on social breakdowns in two distinct ways. On the one hand, it would diminish the number of possible candidates for playing the creator's role in face of any possible challenge, since it would rule out those who had successfully responded to the last challenge. On the other hand, this disqualification of those who had played the creator's part in the former generation would range these same ex-creators in the forefront of the opposition to whoever may be making the successful response to the new challenge; and these ex-creators, by the very fact of their earlier creativity, will now be in occupation of the key positions of power and influence in the society to which they and the potential new creators alike belong. In these positions they will not be helping the society forward any longer; they will be 'resting on their oars'.

While the attitude of 'resting on one's oars' may be described as a passive way of succumbing to the nemesis of creativity, the negativeness of this mental posture does not certify an absence of moral fault. A fatuous passivity towards the present springs from an infatuation with the past, and this infatuation is the sin of idolatry. For idolatry may be defined as an intellectually and morally blind worship of the creature instead of the Creator. It

---

[1] The *Tao-te King*, ch. 24 (translation by Waley, A., in *The Way and its Power*).

may take the form of an idolization of the idolator's own personality or society in some ephemeral phase of the never-ceasing movement through challenge and response to further challenge which is the essence of being alive; or it may take the limited form of an idolization of some particular institution or technique which once stood the idolater in good stead. It will be convenient to examine these different forms of idolatry separately, and we will start with the idolization of the self, because that will offer the clearest illustrations of the sin that we are now setting out to study. If it is indeed the truth

> That men may rise on stepping-stones
> Of their dead selves to higher things,[1]

then the idolater who commits the error of treating one dead self not as a stepping-stone but as a pedestal will be alienating himself from life as conspicuously as the Stylite devotee who maroons himself on a lonely pillar from the life of his fellows.

We have now perhaps sufficiently prepared the ground for a few historical illustrations of our present theme.

Jewry

The most notorious historical example of this idolization of an ephemeral self is the error of the Jews which is exposed in the New Testament. In a period of their history which began in the infancy of the Syriac Civilization and which culminated in the Age of the Prophets, the people of Israel and Judah raised themselves head and shoulders above the Syriac peoples round about by rising to a monotheistic conception of religion. Keenly conscious and rightly proud of their spiritual treasure, they allowed themselves to be betrayed into an idolization of this notable but transitory stage in their spiritual growth. They had indeed been gifted with unparalleled spiritual insight; but, after having divined a truth which was absolute and eternal, they allowed themselves to be captivated by a relative and temporary half-truth. They persuaded themselves that Israel's discovery of the One True God had revealed Israel itself to be God's Chosen People; and this half-truth inveigled them into the fatal error of looking upon a momentary spiritual eminence, which they had attained by labour and travail, as a privilege conferred upon them by God in an everlasting covenant. Brooding on a talent which they had perversely sterilized by hiding it in the earth, they rejected the still greater treasure which God offered them in the coming of Jesus of Nazareth.

[1] Tennyson: *In Memoriam.*

Athens

If Israel succumbed to the nemesis of creativity by idolizing itself as 'the Chosen People', Athens succumbed to the same nemesis by idolizing herself as 'the Education of Hellas'. We have already seen how Athens earned a transitory right to this glorious title by her achievements between the Age of Solon and the Age of Pericles; but the imperfection of what Athens had achieved was, or should have been, made manifest by the very occasion on which this title was conferred upon her by her own brilliant son. Pericles coined the phrase in a funeral oration which, according to Thucydides, he delivered in praise of the Athenian dead in the first year of the war which was the outward and visible sign of an inward and spiritual breakdown in the life of the Hellenic Society in general and of Athens in particular. This fatal war had broken out because one of the problems set by the Solonian economic revolution—the problem of creating a Hellenic political world order—had proved to be beyond the compass of the fifth-century Athenians' moral stature. The military overthrow of Athens in 404 B.C., and the greater moral defeat which the restored Athenian democracy inflicted on itself five years later in the judicial murder of Socrates, provoked Plato in the next generation to repudiate Periclean Athens and nearly all her works. Yet Plato's partly petulant and partly affected gesture did not impress his fellow citizens; and the epigoni of the Athenian pioneers who had made their city 'the Education of Hellas' sought to vindicate their claim to a forfeited title by the perverse method of proving themselves unteachable—as they continued to prove themselves by their inconsistent and futile policies right through the age of the Macedonian ascendancy down to the bitter end of Athenian history, when Athens subsided into stagnant obscurity as a provincial town of the Roman Empire.

Thereafter, when a new culture dawned on what had once been the free city-states of the Hellenic World, it was not in Athens that the seed fell on good ground. The account given in the Acts of the Apostles of the encounter between the Athenians and Saint Paul suggests that the Apostle to the Gentiles was not insensitive to the 'academic' atmosphere of a city which in his day had become the Hellenic Oxford and that when he addressed 'the dons' on 'Mars' Hill' he did his best to approach the subject from an angle congenial to this peculiar audience. Yet the narrative makes it appear that his preaching in Athens proved a failure, and, though in the sequel he found occasion to address Epistles to a number of the churches that he had founded in Greek cities, he never, so far as we know, attempted to convert with the pen these Athenians whom he had found so impervious to the spoken word.

Italy

If the Athens of the fifth century B.C. could fairly claim to be 'the Education of Hellas', a corresponding title might with justice be awarded by the modern Western World to the city-states of Northern Italy on the strength of their achievement in the Renaissance. When we examine the history of our Western Society during the four hundred years from the latter part of the fifteenth century to the latter part of the nineteenth, we find that its modern economic and political efficiency, as well as its modern aesthetic and intellectual culture, is of a distinctively Italian origin. This modern movement in the concerto of Western history was set in motion by an Italian impetus, and this impetus was a radiation of the Italian culture of the preceding age. In fact this chapter of Western history might well be called its Italistic Age, on the analogy of the so-called Hellenistic Age of Hellenic history in which the culture of fifth-century Athens was propagated, along the track of Alexander's armies, from the coasts of the Mediterranean to the remote landward frontier of a submerged Achaemenian Empire.[1] Yet we find ourselves again confronted with the same paradox; for, just as Athens played a part of ever increasing futility in the Hellenistic Age, so the contributions of Italy to the general life of the Western Society in the Modern Age were conspicuously inferior to those of her Transalpine disciples.

The comparative sterility of Italy throughout this Modern Age was manifest in all the medieval hearths and homes of Italian culture—in Florence, in Venice, in Milan, in Siena, in Bologna, in Padua; and the sequel, at the end of this modern period, is perhaps even more remarkable. Towards the close of this chapter the Transalpine nations had become competent to repay the debt they owed to Medieval Italy. The turn of the eighteenth and nineteenth centuries saw the beginning of a new cultural radiation across the Alps, this time in the reverse direction; and this inflow of Transalpine influences into Italy was the first cause of the Italian *Risorgimento*.

---

[1] 'Atticistic' would be a more accurate label than the customary term 'Hellenistic' for the three centuries intervening between the overthrow of the Achaemenian Empire by Alexander the Great and the establishment of the *Pax Romana* by Augustus. As Edwyn Bevan has pointed out, the strictly proper application of the epithet 'Hellenistic' would be, not to any chapter in the history of the Hellenic Civilization itself, but to the whole character of the two civilizations that are affiliated to the Hellenic Society and that, in the terminology employed in this Study, are called the Western and the Orthodox Christian.

The first strong political stimulus received by Italy from the other side of the Alps was her temporary incorporation into the Napoleonic Empire. The first strong economic stimulus was the re-opening of the trade route through the Mediterranean to India, which preceded the cutting of the Suez Canal and arose indirectly out of Napoleon's expedition to Egypt. These Transalpine stimuli did not, of course, produce their full effect until they had communicated themselves to Italian agents; but the Italian creative forces by which the *Risorgimento* was brought to harvest did not arise on any Italian ground that had already borne the harvest of a medieval Italian culture.

In the economic field, for example, the first Italian port to win for itself a share in modern Western maritime trade was neither Venice nor Genoa nor Pisa, but Leghorn; and Leghorn was the post-Renaissance creation of a Tuscan Grand Duke, who had planted there a settlement of crypto-Jews from Spain and Portugal. Though Leghorn was planted within a few miles of Pisa, her fortunes were made by these indomitable refugees from the opposite shore of the Western Mediterranean and not by the supine descendants of the medieval Pisan seafarers.

In the political field the unification of Italy was the achievement of an originally Transalpine principality which, before the eleventh century, had had no foothold on the Italian side of the Alps beyond the French-speaking Val d'Aosta. The centre of gravity of the dominions of the House of Savoy did not finally come to rest on the Italian side of the Alps till the liberty of the Italian city-states and the genius of the Italian Renaissance had successively passed away, and no Italian city that had been of first-class importance in the great age came within the dominions of the King of Sardinia, as the ruler of the dominions of the House of Savoy was now styled, until the acquisition of Genoa after the conclusion of the Napoleonic Wars. The Savoyard ethos was at that time still so alien from the city-state tradition that the Genoese chafed under the rule of His Sardinian Majesty until 1848, when the dynasty won adherents in all parts of the Italian Peninsula by putting itself at the head of the nationalist movement.

In 1848 the Austrian régime in Lombardy and Venetia was threatened simultaneously by a Piedmontese invasion and by risings in Venice and Milan and other Italian cities within the Austrian provinces; and it is interesting to reflect upon the difference in the historical importance of these two anti-Austrian movements, which took place at the same time and which both figure officially as blows struck in the common cause of Italian liberation. The risings in Venice and Milan were strokes for liberty, no doubt; but the vision of liberty which inspired them was the recollection of a medieval past. These cities were, in spirit, resuming their medieval struggles against the Hohenstaufen. Compared with their failures, which were unquestionably heroic, the military performance of the Piedmontese in 1848-9 was far from creditable, and the irresponsible breach of a prudent armistice was punished by the shameful defeat at Novara. But this Piedmontese disgrace proved more fruitful for Italy than the glorious defence of Venice and of Milan; for the Piedmontese army survived to secure its revenge (with very substantial French assistance) at Magenta ten years later, and the newfangled English-fashioned parliamentary constitution granted by King Charles Albert in 1848 became the constitution of a united Italy in 1860. On the other hand, the glorious feats performed by Milan and Venice in 1848 were not repeated; thereafter, these ancient cities remained passive under the reimposed Austrian yoke, and allowed their final liberation to be secured by Piedmontese arms and diplomacy.

The explanation of these contrasts would seem to be that the Venetian and Milanese exploits of 1848 were foredoomed to failure because the spiritual driving force behind them was not modern nationalism but an idolization of their own dead selves as medieval city-states. The nineteenth-century Venetians who responded to Manin's call in 1848 were fighting for Venice alone; they were striving to restore an obsolete Venetian republic, not to contribute to the creation of a united Italy. The Piedmontese, on the other hand, were not tempted to idolize an obsolete ephemeral self, because their past provided no self which could be made an object of idolatry.

The difference is summed up in the contrast between Manin and Cavour. Manin was an unmistakable Venetian who would have found himself quite at home in the fourteenth century. Cavour, with his French mother-tongue and his Victorian outlook, would have been as utterly out of his element in a fourteenth-century Italian city-state as his Transalpine contemporaries, Peel and Thiers, while he could have turned his gift for parliamentary politics and diplomacy, and his interest in scientific agriculture and railway building, to equally good account if fate had chosen to make him a landowner in nineteenth-century England or France instead of in nineteenth-century Italy.

On this showing, the role, in the Italian *Risorgimento*, of the uprising of 1848-9 was essentially negative, and its failure was a precious and, indeed, indispensable preliminary to the successes of 1859-70. In 1848 the old idols of medieval Milan and medieval

Venice were so battered and defaced that now at last they lost their fatal hold on their worshippers' souls; and this belated effacement of the past cleared the ground for the constructive leadership of the one Italian state that was not handicapped by any medieval memories.

South Carolina

If we extend our survey from the Old World to the New, we shall find a parallel illustration of the nemesis of creativity in the history of the United States. If we make a comparative study of the post-war histories of the several States of 'the Old South' which were members of the Confederacy in the Civil War of 1861–5 and were involved in the Confederacy's defeat, we shall notice a marked difference between them in the extent to which they have since recovered from that common disaster; and we shall notice that this difference is the exact inverse of an equally well-marked difference which had distinguished the same States in the period before the Civil War.

A foreign observer who visited the Old South in the fifth decade of the twentieth century would assuredly pick out Virginia and South Carolina as the two States in which there was least sign or promise of recovery; and he would be astonished to find the effects of even so great a social catastrophe as theirs persisting so starkly over so long a period. In these States the memory of that catastrophe is as green in our generation as if the blow had fallen only yesterday; and 'the War' still means the Civil War on many Virginian and South Carolinian lips, though two fearful wars have since supervened. In fact, twentieth-century Virginia or South Carolina makes the painful impression of a country living under a spell, in which time has stood still. This impression will be heightened through contrast by a visit to the State which lies between them. In North Carolina the visitor will find up-to-date industries, mushroom universities and a breath of the hustling, 'boosting' spirit which he has learnt to associate with the 'Yankees' of the North. He will also find that North Carolina has produced some of the great men of the twentieth century, such as Woodrow Wilson and Walter Page.

What explains the springlike burgeoning of life in North Carolina while the life of her neighbours still droops in an apparently unending 'winter' of their 'discontent'? If we turn for enlightenment to the past, we shall find our perplexity momentarily increased when we observe that, right up to the Civil War, North Carolina had been socially barren while Virginia and South Carolina had enjoyed spells of exceptional vitality. During the first forty years of the history of the American Union Virginia had been beyond comparison the leading State, producing four of the first five Presidents and also John Marshall, who, more than any other single man, adapted the ambiguities of the 'scrap of paper', composed by the Philadelphia Convention, to the realities of American life. And if, after 1825, Virginia fell behind, South Carolina, under the leadership of Calhoun, steered the Southern States into the course on which they suffered shipwreck in the Civil War. During all this time North Carolina was seldom heard of. She had a poor soil and no ports. Her impoverished small farmers, mostly descended from squatter immigrants who had failed to make good in either Virginia or South Carolina, were not to be compared with the Virginian squires or the South Carolinian cotton-planters.

The earlier failure of North Carolina in comparison with her neighbours on either side is easily explained; but what of their subsequent failure and her subsequent success? The explanation is that North Carolina, like Piedmont, has not been inhibited by the idolization of a once glorious past; she lost comparatively little by defeat in the Civil War because she had comparatively little to lose; and, having had less far to fall, she had that much less difficulty in recovering from the shock.

New Light on Old Problems

These examples of the nemesis of creativity show up in a new light a phenomenon which caught our attention in an earlier part of this Study, and which we called 'the stimulus of new ground'; for this phenomenon has reappeared in the foregoing examples: Galilaeans and Gentiles compared with Judaeans, Piedmont compared with Milan and Venice, and North Carolina compared with her neighbours to north and south; while, if we had pursued the same inquiry in the case of Athens, we could have shown that it was in Achaia and not in Attica that the Greeks of the third and second century B.C. came nearest to a solution of their intractable problem of federating city-states, in an abortive attempt to maintain their independence against the gigantic parvenu Great Powers that had arisen on the fringes of an expanded Hellenic World. We can now see that the superior fertility of the new ground is not invariably or entirely to be accounted for by the stimulus of the ordeal of breaking virgin soil. There is a negative as well as a positive reason why new ground is apt to be fruitful, namely its freedom from the incubus of ineradicable and no longer profitable traditions and memories.

We can also see the reason for another social phenomenon—

the tendency of a creative minority to degenerate into a dominant minority—which we singled out, early in this Study, as a prominent symptom of social breakdown and disintegration. While the creative minority is certainly not predestined to undergo this change for the worse, the creator is decidedly predisposed in this direction *ex officio creativitatis*. The gift of creativity, which, when originally brought into play, produces a successful response to a challenge, becomes in its turn a new and uniquely formidable challenge to the recipient who has turned this talent to best account.

(4) THE NEMESIS OF CREATIVITY: IDOLIZATION OF AN EPHEMERAL INSTITUTION

The Hellenic City-State

In examining the part played in the breakdown and disintegration of the Hellenic Society by the idolization of this institution— so brilliantly successful within its proper limits but at the same time, like all human creations, ephemeral—we shall have to distinguish between two different situations in which the idol stood as a stumbling-block in the way of the solution of a social problem.

The earlier, and graver, of the two problems is one which we have examined already in another context and can now, therefore, briefly dismiss. What we have called the Solonian economic revolution required, as one of its corollaries, some kind of political federation of the Hellenic World. The Athenian attempt to achieve this failed, and resulted in what we have diagnosed as the breakdown of the Hellenic Society. It is obvious that the cause of this failure was an inability on the part of all concerned to get over the stumbling-block of city-state sovereignty. But while this inescapable and central problem was left unsolved a secondary problem, which was of the Hellenic dominant minority's own seeking, came treading upon its heels when Hellenic history passed over from its second to its third chapter at the turn of the fourth and third centuries B.C.

The chief outward sign of this transition was a sudden increase in the material scale of Hellenic life. A hitherto maritime world, confined to the coasts of the Mediterranean Basin, expanded overland from the Dardanelles to India and from Olympus and the Appennines to the Danube and the Rhine. In a society which had swollen to these dimensions without having solved the spiritual problem of creating law and order between the states into which it was articulated, the sovereign city-state was so utterly dwarfed that it was no longer a practicable unit of political life. This was in itself by no means a misfortune; indeed, the passing of this traditional Hellenic form of parochial sovereignty might have been taken as a heaven-sent opportunity for shaking off the incubus of parochial sovereignty altogether. If Alexander had lived to ally himself with Zeno and Epicurus, it is conceivable that the Hellenes might have succeeded in stepping straight out of the city-state into the *Cosmopolis*; and in that event the Hellenic Society might have taken on a new lease of creative life. But Alexander's premature death left the World at the mercy of his successors, and the evenly balanced rivalries of the contending Macedonian warlords kept alive the institution of parochial sovereignty in the new era which Alexander had inaugurated. But on the new material scale of Hellenic life parochial sovereignty could be salvaged only on one condition. The sovereign city-state must make way for new states of higher calibre.

These new states were successfully evolved, but, as the result of a series of knock-out blows which Rome delivered, between 220 and 168 B.C., to all her rivals, the number of these states was abruptly reduced from the plural to the singular. The Hellenic Society, which had missed its opportunity of voluntary federation, now found itself clamped together in the bonds of a universal state. But the point of interest for our present purpose is that both the Roman response to the challenge that had defeated Periclean Athens, and all the preliminary contributions from other hands towards the making of it, were the work of members of the Hellenic Society who were not completely infatuated with the idol of city-state sovereignty.

The structural principle of the Roman state was something quite incompatible with such idolization; for this structural principle was a 'dual citizenship' dividing the citizen's allegiance between the local city-state in which he was born and the wider polity which Rome had created. This creative compromise was psychologically possible only in communities in which city-state idolatry had not acquired a strangle-hold over the citizens' hearts and minds.

The analogy between the problem of parochial sovereignty in the Hellenic World and the corresponding problem in our own world to-day needs no emphasis here. But this much may be said. On the showing of Hellenic history we may expect that our present Western problem will receive its solution—in so far as it receives one at all—in some quarter or quarters where the institution of national sovereignty has not been erected into an object of idolatrous worship. We shall not expect to see salvation come from the historic national states of Western Europe, where every political thought and feeling is bound up with a parochial sovereignty which is the recognized symbol of a glorious past. It is not in this Epimethean psychological environment that our society can look forward to making the necessary discovery of some new form of international association which will bring parochial sovereignty under the discipline of a higher law and so forestall the otherwise inevitable calamity of its annihilation by a knock-out blow. If this discovery is ever made, the laboratory of political experimentation where we may expect to see it materialize will be some body politic like the British Commonwealth of Nations, which has mated the experience of one ancient European national state with the plasticity of a number of new countries overseas; or else it will be some polity like the Soviet Union, which is attempting to organize a number of non-Western peoples into an entirely new kind of community based on a Western revolutionary idea. In the Soviet Union we may find an analogy to the Seleucid Empire, and in the British Empire to the Roman Commonwealth. Will these or such-like bodies politic on the outskirts of our modern Western cosmos eventually produce some form of political structure which will enable us to give more substance, before it is too late, to our inchoate international organization, which we are now making a second attempt to build up in place of our first inter-war essay at a League of Nations? We cannot tell; but we can almost feel sure that, if these pioneers fail, the work will never be done by the petrified devotees of the idol of national sovereignty.

The East Roman Empire

A classic case of the idolization of an institution bringing a society to grief is the fatal infatuation of Orthodox Christendom with a ghost of the Roman Empire, an ancient institution which had fulfilled its historic function and completed its natural term of life in serving as the apparented Hellenic Society's universal state.

Superficially the East Roman Empire presents an appearance of unbroken continuity as one and the same institution from the foundation of Constantinople by Constantine until the conquest of the Imperial City by the Ottoman Turks in A.D. 1453, more than eleven centuries later—or at any rate until the temporary eviction of the East Roman Imperial Government by the Latin Crusaders who seized Constantinople in A.D. 1204. But it would be more in accordance with realities to distinguish two different institutions insulated from one another in the time-dimension by an intervening interregnum. The original Roman Empire which had served as the Hellenic universal state indisputably came to an end in the West during the Dark Ages: *de facto* at the turn of the fourth and fifth centuries and officially in A.D. 476, when the last puppet Emperor in Italy was deposed by a barbarian war-lord, who thenceforth exercised authority in the name of the Emperor at Constantinople. It is perhaps not so readily recognized that the same fate overtook the original Roman Empire in the East, as well, before the Dark Ages were over. Its dissolution may be equated with the end of the strenuous and disastrous reign of Justinian in A.D. 565. There followed in the East a century-and-a-half of interregnum, by which we do not mean that there were not in fact persons styled Roman Emperors ruling or trying to rule from Constantinople during that period, but that this was an age of dissolution-and-incubation, in which the remains of a dead society were swept away and the foundations of a successor were laid. After that, however, in the first half of the eighth century, a ghost of the dead Roman Empire was conjured up by the genius of Leo Syrus. On this reading of the first chapter of Orthodox Christian history Leo Syrus was a disastrously successful Charlemagne; or, conversely, Charlemagne was a providentially unsuccessful Leo Syrus. Charlemagne's failure gave scope for the Western Christian Church and for a galaxy of Western parochial states to develop during the Middle Ages along the lines familiar to us. Leo's success clamped the strait waistcoat of a resuscitated universal state upon the Orthodox Christian body social almost before that infant society had learnt the use of its limbs. But this contrast in the outcome does not reflect any difference of aim, for Charlemagne and Leo alike were Epimethean worshippers of the same ephemeral and obsolete institution.

How are we to account for the fatally precocious superiority of Orthodox Christendom over the West in political constructiveness? One important factor, no doubt, was the difference in the degree of the pressure that was exerted upon both these Christendoms simultaneously by the aggression of the Muslim Arabs. In their assault upon the distant West the Arabs shot their bolt in recapturing for the Syriac Society its lost colonial domain in North Africa and Spain. By the time they had crossed the Pyrenees and were striking at the heart of the infant Western Society, the force of their offensive was already spent; and, when their wild ride round the southern and western rim of the Mediterranean brought them up short at Tours against an Austrasian shield-wall, their thrust glanced harmlessly off the solid target. Yet even this passive victory over a tired assailant was enough to make the fortunes of the Austrasian dynasty. It was the prestige won at Tours in A.D. 732 that marked Austrasia out as the leader among the rudimentary Powers of Western Christendom. If this relatively feeble impact of the Arab steel was able to touch off the Carolingian flash in the pan, it is not surprising that the solid structure of the East Roman Empire should have been called into existence in Orthodox Christendom to withstand the far more violent and far longer sustained assault from the same assailant to which Orthodox Christendom was subjected.

For this reason and for others[1] Leo Syrus and his successors succeeded in attaining a goal which in the West was never approached by Charlemagne or Otto I or Henry III even with Papal acquiescence, and *a fortiori* not by the later emperors who encountered Papal opposition. The Eastern Emperors, in their own dominions, turned the Church into a department of state and the Oecumenical Patriarch into a kind of under-secretary of state for ecclesiastical affairs, thus restoring the relationship between church and state which had been established by Constantine and maintained by his successors down to Justinian. The effect of this achievement declared itself in two ways, one of them general and the other particular.

The general effect was to check and sterilize the tendencies towards variety and elasticity, experimentation and creativeness in Orthodox Christian life; and we can roughly measure the damage done by noting some of the conspicuous achievements of the sister civilization in the West which have no Orthodox Christian counterpart. In Orthodox Christian history we not only find nothing that corresponds to the Hildebrandine Papacy; we miss also the rise and spread of self-governing universities and of self-governing city-states.

The particular effect was an obstinate unwillingness on the part of the reincarnated Imperial Government to tolerate the existence of independent 'barbarian' states within the area over which the civilization which it represented had expanded. This political intolerance led to the Romano-Bulgarian wars of the tenth century in which the East Roman Empire, though superficially the victor, suffered irremediable injury; and, as we have already indicated elsewhere, these wars caused the breakdown of the Orthodox Christian Society.

Kings, Parliaments and Bureaucracies

States of one kind or another, city-states or empires, are not the only kind of political institution that has attracted idolatrous

---

[1] In Mr. Toynbee's original work the East Roman Empire is treated at greater length and with greater elaboration than any previous historical illustration. See vol. iv, pp. 320-408.—EDITOR.

worship. Similar honours have been paid, with similar consequences, to the sovereign power in a state—a 'divine' king or an 'omnipotent' parliament—or again to some caste or class or profession on whose skill or prowess the existence of some state has been deemed to depend.

A classical example of the idolization of a political sovereignty incarnated in a human being is offered by the Egyptiac Society in the time of 'the Old Kingdom'. In another connexion we have noticed already that the acceptance, or exaction, of divine honours by the sovereigns of the Egyptiac United Kingdom was one symptom of a 'great refusal' of a call to a higher mission, a fatal failure to respond to the second challenge in Egyptiac history, and that this failure brought the Egyptiac Civilization to the early breakdown which cut short its precocious youth. The crushing incubus which this series of human idols imposed upon Egyptiac life is perfectly symbolized in the Pyramids, which were erected by the forced labour of their subjects in order to render the Pyramid-Builders magically immortal. Skill, capital and labour which should have been devoted to extending control over the physical environment in the interests of the whole society were misdirected into this idolatrous channel.

This idolization of a political sovereignty incarnated in a human being is an aberration that can be illustrated elsewhere also. If we look for an analogue in our modern Western history we can easily discern a vulgar version of a royal Son of Re in the French *roi soleil*, Louis XIV. This Western Sun King's palace at Versailles weighed as heavily upon the land of France as the Pyramids of Gizeh weighed upon the land of Egypt. 'L'État, c'est moi' might have been spoken by Cheops and 'Après moi le déluge' by Pepi II. But perhaps the most interesting example that the modern Western World affords of the idolization of a sovereign power is one on which an historical judgement cannot yet be pronounced.

In the apotheosis of 'the Mother of Parliaments' at Westminster the object of idolization is not a man but a committee. The incurable drabness of committees has co-operated with the obstinate matter-of-factness of modern English social tradition to keep this idolization of Parliament within reasonable limits; and an Englishman who looked out upon the world in 1938 might claim that his temperate devotion to his own political divinity was being handsomely rewarded. Was not the country which had preserved its loyalty to 'the Mother of Parliaments' in a happier case than its neighbours who had gone a-whoring after other gods? Had the Lost Ten Tribes of the Continent found either tranquillity or prosperity in their feverish adulation of outlandish Duces and

Fuehrers and Kommissars? Yet at the same time he would have to admit that the recent Continental offspring of the ancient insular institution of parliamentary government had proved a sickly brood, incompetent to bring political salvation to the non-British majority of the living generation of mankind, and incapable of holding their own against a war-begotten plague of dictatorships.

Perhaps the truth is that the very features of the Parliament at Westminster which are the secret of its hold upon an Englishman's respect and affection are so many stumbling-blocks in the way of making this venerable English institution into a political panacea for the World. Perhaps, in accordance with a law which we have already noticed—that those who respond successfully to one challenge are unfavourably placed for successful response to the next—the unique success of the Parliament at Westminster in outlasting the Middle Ages, by adapting itself to the exigencies of the 'Modern' (or Once-Modern) Age now concluded, makes it less likely to achieve another creative metamorphosis to meet the challenge of the post-Modern Age which is now upon us.

If we look into the structure of Parliament, we shall find that it is essentially an assembly of representatives of local constituencies. This is just what we should expect from the date and place of its origin; for the kingdoms of the medieval Western World were each a congeries of village communities, interspersed with small towns. In such a polity the significant grouping for social and economic purposes was that of neighbourhood; and in a society so constituted the geographical group was also the natural unit of political organization. But these medieval foundations of parliamentary representation have been undermined by the impact of Industrialism. To-day the link of locality has lost its significance for political as well as for most other purposes; and the English voter of our own generation, if we ask him who is his neighbour, will probably reply 'My fellow-railwayman or my fellow-miner, wherever he may live from Land's End to John o' Groats'. The true constituency has ceased to be local and has become occupational. But an occupational basis of representation is a constitutional *terra incognita* which 'the Mother of Parliaments' in her comfortable old age feels no inclination to explore.

To all this, no doubt, the twentieth-century English admirer of Parliament may justly reply with a *solvitur ambulando*. In the abstract he may admit that a thirteenth-century system of representation is unsuitable to a twentieth-century community, but he will point out that the theoretical misfit seems to work well enough. 'We English', he will explain, 'are so thoroughly at home with the institutions we have built up that, in our own country and among ourselves, we can make them work under any conditions. These foreigners, of course . . .'—and he shrugs his shoulders.

It may be that his confidence in his own political heritage will continue to justify itself, to the amazement of 'the lesser breeds without the law' who once so eagerly swallowed what they believed to be his political panacea and then violently rejected it after suffering acute indigestion. But, by the same token, it seems probable that England will not cap her seventeenth-century feat by becoming for a second time the creator of those new political institutions which a new age requires. When a new thing has to be found, there are only two ways of finding it, namely creation or mimesis; and mimesis cannot come into play until somebody has performed a creative act for his fellows to imitate. In the fourth chapter of our Western history, which has opened in our time, who will the new political creator be? We can discern at present no evidence in favour of any particular candidate for this prize; but we can predict with some confidence that the new political creator will not be any worshipper of 'the Mother of Parliaments'.

We may conclude this survey of institutional idols by glancing at the idolatrous worship of castes and classes and professions; and here we already have something to go upon. In studying the arrested civilizations we have come across two societies of the kind—the Spartans and the 'Osmanlis—in which the keystone of the arch was a caste that was virtually a corporate idol or deified Leviathan. If the aberration of idolizing a caste is capable of arresting a civilization's growth, it will also be capable of causing its breakdown; and, if we re-examine the breakdown of the Egyptiac Society with this clue in our hand, we shall perceive that the 'divine' kingship was not the only idolized incubus that weighed on the backs of the Egyptian peasantry of 'the Old Kingdom'. They had also to bear the burden of a bureaucracy of litterati.

The truth is that a deified kingship presupposes an educated secretariat. Without such support it could hardly maintain its statuesque pose on its pedestal. Thus the Egyptiac litterati were the power behind the throne, and, indeed, in point of time they were also before it. They were indispensable and they knew it; and they took advantage of this knowledge to 'bind heavy burdens and grievous to be borne and lay them on men's shoulders' while the Egyptiac scribes themselves would not move these same burdens 'with one of their fingers'. The privileged exemption of the litteratus from the common lot of the sons of toil is the theme of the Egyptiac bureaucracy's glorification of its own order in every age of Egyptiac history. The note is struck blatantly in *The Instruction of Duauf*: a work, composed during the Egyptiac time of troubles, which has been preserved to us in copies made a thousand years later, as a writing exercise, by the schoolboys of 'the New Empire'. In this 'instruction which a man named Duauf, the son of Khety, composed for his son named Pepi, when he voyaged up to the Residence, in order to put him in the School of Books, among the children of the magistrates', the gist of the ambitious father's parting exhortation to his aspiring child is:

'I have seen him that is beaten, him that is beaten: thou art to set thine heart on books. I have beheld him that is set free from forced labour: behold, nothing surpasseth books. . . . Every artisan that wieldeth the chisel, he is wearier than him that delveth. . . . The stone-mason seeketh for work in all manner of hard stone. When he hath finished it his arms are destroyed, and he is weary. . . . The field-worker, his reckoning endureth for ever . . . ; he too is wearier than can be told. . . . The weaver in the workshop, he fareth more ill than any woman. His thighs are upon his belly and he breatheth no air. . . . Let me tell thee, further, how it fareth with the fisherman. Is not his work upon the river, where it is mixed with the crocodiles? . . . Behold, there is no calling that is without a director except [that of] the scribe, and he is the director. . . .'

In the Far Eastern World there is a familiar analogue of the Egyptiac 'litteratocracy' in the incubus of the mandarin, which the Far Eastern Society inherited from the latest age of its predecessor. The Confucian litteratus used to flaunt his heartless refusal to lift a finger to lighten the load of the toiling millions by allowing his finger-nails to grow to lengths which precluded every use of the hand except the manipulation of the scribal brush, and through all the changes and chances of Far Eastern history he has emulated his Egyptiac confrère's tenacity in keeping his oppressive seat. Even the impact of Western culture has not unseated him. Though the examinations in the Confucian classics are now no more, the litteratus imposes upon the peasant as effectively as ever by flourishing in his face a diploma of the University of Chicago or of the London School of Economics and Political Science.

In the course of Egyptiac history the alleviation which the long-suffering people obtained—albeit too late—through the gradual humanization of the sovereign power was offset by successive additions to the class incubus. As though the burden of carrying a bureaucracy had not been enough, they were saddled, under 'the New Empire', with a priesthood which was organized into a powerful Pan-Egyptiac corporation under the presidency of a Chief Priest of Amon-Re at Thebes by the Emperor Thothmes III (*circa* 1480–1450 B.C.). Thenceforth the Egyptiac mandarin had a fellow-rider in the shape of an Egyptiac Brahman; and after that the broken-backed Egyptiac circus-horse was compelled to stumble on upon his everlasting round until the pair of riders was increased to a trio by the mounting of a *miles gloriosus* on the pillion behind the scribe and the pharisee.

The Egyptiac Society, which had been as free from militarism throughout its natural term of existence as the Orthodox Christian Society was during its time of growth, had been goaded by its encounter with the Hyksos—as the East Roman Empire was goaded by its encounter with Bulgaria—into militaristic courses. Not content with driving the Hyksos beyond the pale of the Egyptiac World, the Emperors of the Eighteenth Dynasty yielded to the temptation of passing over from self-defence to aggression by carving out an Egyptian Empire in Asia. This wanton adventure was easier to embark upon than to withdraw from; and when the tide turned against them the Emperors of the Nineteenth Dynasty found themselves compelled to mobilize the fast-waning strength of the Egyptiac body social to preserve the integrity of Egypt herself. Under the Twentieth Dynasty the aged and tormented frame was smitten with a paralytic stroke as the price of its final *tour de force* in flinging back the combined hosts of European, African and Asiatic barbarians hurled against it by the impetus of the post-Minoan Völkerwanderung. When the fallen body at last lay prostrate on the ground, the native litteratus and priest, who still sat tight in the saddle with no bones broken by the fall, were joined by the grandson of the Libyan invader, who now strolled back as a soldier of fortune into the Egyptiac World from whose frontiers his grandfather had been hurled back by the final feat of native Egyptiac arms. The military caste, begotten of these eleventh-century Libyan mercenaries, which continued to bestride the Egyptiac Society for a thousand years after, may have been less formidable to its opponents in the field than the Janissaries or the Spartiates, but it was doubtless just as burdensome at home to the peasantry beneath its feet.

(5) THE NEMESIS OF CREATIVITY: IDOLIZATION OF AN EPHEMERAL TECHNIQUE

Fishes, Reptiles and Mammals

If we now turn to consider the idolization of techniques, we may begin by recalling examples which have already come under our notice in which the extreme penalty has been paid. In the Ottoman and Spartan social systems the key-technique of being shepherds of human cattle or hunters of human game was idolized side by side with the institutions through which these activities were carried on. And when we pass from the arrested civilizations evoked by human challenges to those evoked by the challenges of physical nature we find that the idolatrous worship of a technique comprises the whole of their tragedy. The Nomads and the Eskimos have fallen into arrest through an excessive concentration of all their faculties on their shepherding and hunting techniques. Their single-track lives have condemned them to a retrogression towards an animalism which is the negation of human versatility; and if we now peer back into the pre-human chapters of the history of life on this planet we shall find ourselves confronted by other examples of the same law.

This law is enunciated in the following terms by a modern Western scholar who has made a comparative study of its operation in the non-human and in the human domain:

'Life starts in the sea. There it attains to an extraordinary efficiency. The fishes give rise to types which are so successful (such, for instance, as the sharks) that they have lasted on unchanged until to-day. The path of ascending evolution did not, however, lie in this direction. In evolution Dr. Inge's aphorism is probably always right: "Nothing fails like success." A creature which has become perfectly adapted to its environment, an animal whose whole capacity and vital force is concentrated and expended in succeeding here and now, has nothing left over with which to respond to any radical change. Age by age it becomes more perfectly economical in the way its entire resources meet exactly its current and customary opportunities. In the end it can do all that is necessary to survive without any conscious striving or unadapted movement. It can therefore beat all competitors in the special field; but equally, on the other hand, should that field change, it must become extinct. It is this success of efficiency which seems to account for the extinction of an enormous number of species. Climatic conditions altered. They had used up all their resources of vital energy in adapting themselves to things as they were. Like unwise virgins, they had no oil left over for further adaptations. They were committed, could not readjust, and so they vanished.'[1]

The fatally complete technical success of the fishes in adapting themselves to the physical environment of life in the marine overture to its terrestrial history is enlarged upon by the same scholar in the same context:

'At the level when life was confined to the sea and the fishes were developing, they threw up forms which evolved a spine, and so represented the vertebrates in the highest form then evolved. From the spine there spread out on each side, to aid the head, that fan of feelers which

[1] Heard, Gerald: *The Source of Civilization*, pp. 66–7.

in them became the fore-fins. In the shark—and almost all the fish—these feelers were specialized so as to become, no longer feelers, but paddles: amazingly efficient flukes for bringing the creature head-fore-most on its prey. Rapid reaction was everything, patient negotiation nothing; and these flukes not only ceased to be testers, explorers, examiners; they became increasingly efficient for water-movement and for nothing else. It looks as though pre-piscan pre-vertebrate life must have lived in warm shallow pools and perhaps always have been in touch with the floor, as to-day the gurnet by its feelers keeps contact with the solid bed. Once, however, swift unpremeditated movement became everything, specialization drove the fishes out into water where they lost touch with the bottom and all solids. . . . Water . . . became their only element. This meant [that] their power of being stimulated by new circumstances was greatly limited. . . .

'That type of fish, then, which gave rise to the next advancing order of animals must have been a creature which did not adopt this extreme specialization of the fin. For, first, it must have been a creature which kept in touch with the floor, and so remained more variously stimulated than the fishes which lost touch with a solid environment. And, secondly, it must have been a creature which, for the same reason, kept in touch with the shallows and kept this touch by means of forelimbs which, because they could not therefore become wholly specialized as water-driving flukes, retained a more generalized "inefficient" explora-tory and tentative character. The skeleton of such a creature has been discovered—a creature whose forelimbs are, it might almost be said, rather clumsy hands than proper fins; and through these members it looks as though the transition from shallow pool to flooded shore was made, the deep sea was left behind, the land was invaded and the amphibian arrived.'[1]

In this triumph of the fumbling amphibians in their competition with the deft and decisive fishes, we are witnessing an early perfor-mance of a drama which has since been re-played many times over with as many different changes in the cast. In the next perfor-mance that invites our attention, we shall find the fishes' part being taken by the amphibians' formidable progeny of the reptile tribe, while the amphibians' own part in the preceding performance falls to the ancestors of those mammalian animals in which the Spirit of Man has recently become incarnate. The primitive mammals were weak and puny creatures who unexpectedly inherited the Earth because the heritage had been left derelict by the magni-ficent reptiles who were the previous lords of creation; and the Mesozoic reptiles—like the Eskimos and the Nomads—were con-querors who forfeited their conquests by straying into the blind alley of over-specialization.

'[The] apparently abrupt ending up of the reptiles is, beyond all

[1] Heard, Gerald: *The Source of Civilization*, pp. 67–9.

question, the most striking revolution in the whole history of the Earth before the coming of mankind. It is probably connected with the close of a vast period of equable warm conditions and the onset of a new austerer age in which the winters were bitterer and the summers brief but hot. The Mesozoic life, animal and vegetable alike, was adapted to warm conditions and capable of little resistance to cold. The new life, on the other hand, was, before all things, capable of resisting great changes of temperature. . . .

'As for the mammals competing with and ousting the less fit reptiles . . . there is not a scrap of evidence of any such direct competition. . . . In the later Mesozoic a number of small jawbones are found, entirely mammalian in character. But there is not a scrap, not a bone, to suggest that there lived any Mesozoic mammal which could look a dinosaur in the face. . . . [They] seem to have been all obscure little beasts of the size of mice and rats.'[1]

The propositions put forward by Mr. Wells down to this point appear to be generally accepted. The reptiles were supplanted by the mammals because these unwieldy monsters had lost the ability to adapt themselves to new conditions. But, in the ordeal to which the reptiles succumbed, what was it exactly which enabled the mammals to survive? On this supremely interesting question the two writers we have hitherto drawn upon are in disagreement. According to Mr. Wells, the rudimentary mammals survived because they had hair which protected them against the oncoming cold. If this be all that there is to be said, we learn no more than that fur is a more effective armour than scales in certain conditions. Mr. Heard, however, suggests that the armour which saved the mammals' lives was not physical but psychic, and that the strength of this psychic defence lay in a spiritual defencelessness; in fact, that we have here a pre-human example of that principle of growth which we have called etherialization.

'The giant reptiles were themselves hopelessly decadent before the rise of the mammals. . . . They had begun [as] small, mobile and lively creatures. They grew so vast that these land-ironclads could scarcely move. . . . Their brains remained practically non-existent. . . . Their heads were no more than periscopes, breathing-tubes and pincers.

'Meanwhile, as they slowly swelled and hardened up to their doom . . . there was already being fashioned that creature which was to leap the boundary and limits then set for life, and start a new stage of energy and consciousness. And nothing could illustrate more vividly the principle that life evolves by sensitiveness and awareness; by being exposed, not by being protected; by nakedness, not by strength; by smallness, not by size. The fore-runners of the mammals . . . are minute rat-like creatures. In a world dominated by monsters the future is given to a creature which has to spend its time taking notice of others

[1] Wells, H. G.: *The Outline of History*, pp. 22–4.

and giving way to others. It is undefended, given fur instead of scales. It is unspecialized, given again those sensitive feeling forelimbs and, no doubt, those antennae—the long hairs on the face and head—to give it irritating stimulation all the time. Ears and eyes are highly developed. It becomes warm-blooded, so [that] it may be constantly conscious throughout the cold, when the reptile falls into anaesthetic coma. . . . So its consciousness is blown upon and developed. The varied continuous stimulant is reacted to with varied answer, because the creature, being unprecedented, is capable not of one but of many replies, none of which can settle the question for it.'[1]

If this is a faithful likeness of our ancestor, we may agree both that we ought to be proud of him and that we do not always show ourselves worthy of him.

The Nemesis in Industry

A hundred years ago Great Britain not only claimed to be, but actually was, 'the Workshop of the World'. To-day she is one of several competing workshops of the World, and her share of the business has tended for a long time past to grow relatively smaller. The thesis 'Is Britain finished?' has exercised innumerable pens and received a variety of answers. Perhaps, when all the factors are taken into account, we have done on the whole rather better than might have been expected in the last seventy years, though the subject obviously offers plenty of scope for pessimistic and upbraiding prophets of the type described in one of the most brilliant of Samuel Butler's inverted quotations.[2] If, however, one were to single out the point in which we have been most at fault, one would put his finger on the conservatism of our captains of industry who have idolized the obsolescent techniques which had made the fortunes of their grandfathers.

Perhaps a more instructive, because less generalized, example can be found in the United States. There will be no denying that, in the middle years of the nineteenth century, the Americans surpassed all other peoples in the variety and ingenuity of their industrial inventions and in their enterprise in exploiting such inventions for practical purposes. The sewing machine, the typewriter, the application of machinery to the craft of boot-making and the McCormick reaping machine are among the first of these 'Yankee notions' that spring to the mind. But there was one invention in the exploitation of which the Americans showed themselves decidedly backward in comparison with the British, and their backwardness here is the more striking because this

[1] Heard, Gerald: *The Source of Civilization*, pp. 71–2.
[2] 'A country is not without honour save in its own prophets.'

neglected invention was an improvement in a machine which the Americans themselves had invented at the very beginning of the century: namely, the steamship. The American paddle-steamer had proved an immensely important addition to the transport facilities of the rapidly expanding republic, all along the thousands of miles of navigable inland waterways with which North America is so richly endowed. It was no doubt a direct result of this successfulness that the Americans were much slower than the British to avail themselves of the later and superior device of the screw propeller for purposes of oceanic navigation. In this matter they were more strongly tempted to idolize an ephemeral technique.

The Nemesis in Warfare

In military history the analogue of the biological competition between the tiny soft-furred mammal and the massive armoured reptile is the saga of the duel between David and Goliath.

Before the fatal day on which he challenges the armies of Israel, Goliath has won such triumphant victories with his spear whose staff is like a weaver's beam and whose head weighs six hundred shekels of iron, and he has found himself so completely proof against hostile weapons in his panoply of casque and corselet and target and greaves, that he can no longer conceive of any alternative armament; and he believes that in this armament he is invincible. He feels assured that any Israelite who has the hardihood to accept his challenge will likewise be a spearman armed *cap-à-pie*, and that any such competitor in his own panoply is bound to be his inferior. So hard set is Goliath's mind in these two ideas that, when he sees David running forward to meet him with no armour on his body and nothing in his hand that catches the eye except his staff, Goliath takes umbrage instead of alarm and exclaims: 'Am I a dog, that thou comest to me with staves?' Goliath does not suspect that this youth's impertinence is a carefully considered manœuvre; he does not know that David, having realized, quite as clearly as Goliath himself, that in Goliath's accoutrements he cannot hope to be his match, has therefore rejected the panoply that Saul has pressed upon him. Nor does Goliath notice the sling, nor wonder what mischief may be hidden in the shepherd's bag. And so this luckless Philistine triceratops stalks pompously forward to his doom.

But as a matter of historical fact the individual hoplite of the post-Minoan Völkerwanderung—Goliath of Gath or Hector of Troy—did not succumb to David's sling or Philoctetes' bow but to the Myrmidons' phalanx, a Leviathan in which a multitude of hoplites set shoulder to shoulder and shield to shield.[1] While each single phalangite was a replica of Hector or Goliath in his accoutrements, he was the antithesis of the Homeric hoplite in his spirit; for the essence of the phalanx lay in the military discipline which had transformed a rabble of individual warriors into a military formation whose orderly evolutions could accomplish ten times as much as the uncoordinated efforts of an equal number of equally well-armed individual champions.

This new military technique, of which we already catch some anticipatory glimpses in the *Iliad*, made its indubitable entry upon the stage of history in the shape of the Spartan phalanx which marched through the rhythm of Tyrtaeus's verses to its socially disastrous victory in the Second Spartano-Messenian War. But this triumph was not the end of the story. After driving all its opposite numbers off the field, the Spartan phalanx 'rested on its oars', and in the course of the fourth century B.C. it saw itself ignominiously worsted: first, by an Athenian swarm of peltasts—a host of Davids with which the phalanx of Spartan Goliaths found itself quite unable to cope—and then by the tactical innovation of the Theban column. The Athenian and Theban techniques in their turn, however, were outmoded and overmatched at one stroke, in 338 B.C., by a Macedonian formation in which a highly differentiated skirmisher and phalangite had been skilfully integrated with a heavy cavalryman in a single fighting force.

Alexander's conquest of the Achaemenian Empire is the proof of the pristine efficiency of the Macedonian order of battle, and the Macedonian version of the phalanx remained the last word in military technique for a hundred and seventy years—from the battle of Chaeronea, which terminated the ascendancy of the citizen militias of the city-states of Greece, to the battle of Pydna, when the Macedonian phalanx went down in its turn before the Roman legion. The cause of this sensational περιπέτεια in Macedonian military fortunes was the senile adulation of an ephemeral technique. While the Macedonians were resting on their oars as unchallenged masters of all but the western fringes of the Hellenic World, the Romans had been revolutionizing the art of war in the light of an experience gained through their sufferings in their tremendous struggle with Hannibal.

The Roman legion triumphed over the Macedonian phalanx because it carried the integration of the light infantryman with the phalangite a long stage farther. The Romans, in fact, invented a new type of formation and a new type of armament which made it

[1] *Iliad*, xvi, ll. 211–17.

possible for any soldier, and any unit, to play at will either the light infantryman's or the hoplite's part, and to change over from one kind of tactics to the other at a moment's notice in the face of the enemy.

This Roman efficiency was, at the time of the Battle of Pydna, no more than a generation old; for in this Italian penumbra of the Hellenic World a phalanx of the pre-Macedonian type had been seen in the field as recently as the Battle of Cannae (214 B.C.), when the heavy Roman infantry, reverting to a battle order in the antique Spartan phalanx formation, had been rounded up from the rear by Hannibal's Spanish and Gallic heavy cavalry and had then been slaughtered like cattle by his African heavy infantry on either flank. This disaster had overtaken a Roman high command which—under the shock of a previous catastrophe at Lake Trasimene—had made up its mind to eschew experiments and play (as it most mistakenly supposed) for safety. In the hard school of their crowning defeat at Cannae the Romans had at last whole-heartedly embraced an improvement in infantry technique which transformed the Roman army, at a stroke, into the most efficient fighting force in the Hellenic World. There followed the triumphs of Zama, Cynoscephalae and Pydna, and then a series of wars of Roman against barbarian and of Roman against Roman in which, under a series of great captains from Marius to Caesar, the legion attained the greatest efficiency possible for infantry before the invention of fire-arms. At this very moment, however, when the legionary had become perfect after his own kind, he received the first of a long series of defeats from a pair of mounted men-at-arms with utterly different techniques, who eventually were to drive the legionary off the field. The victory of the horse-archer over the legionary at Carrhae in 53 B.C. forestalled by five years the classic combat of legionary against legionary at Pharsalus, a battle in which Roman infantry technique was probably at its zenith. The omen of Carrhae was confirmed at Adrianople more than four centuries later, when, in A.D. 378, the cataphract—a mailed cavalryman, armed with a lance—gave the legionary his *coup de grâce*. In this battle a Roman contemporary historian who was also a military officer, Ammianus Marcellinus, vouches for the fact that the Roman casualties amounted to two-thirds of the troops engaged, and expresses the opinion that there had been no military disaster to Roman arms on such a scale since Cannae.

For at least the last four of the six centuries between these two battles the Romans had rested on their oars, and that in spite of the warning given at Carrhae and repeated in the defeats of Valerian in A.D. 260 and of Julian in A.D. 363 by the Persian prototypes of the Gothic cataphracts who were the death of Valens and his legionaries in A.D. 378.

After the catastrophe of Adrianople, the Emperor Theodosius rewarded the barbarian horsemen for having annihilated the Roman infantry by hiring them to fill the yawning gap which they themselves had made in the Roman ranks; and, even when the Imperial Government had paid the inevitable price for this short-sighted policy, and had seen these mercenary barbarian troopers partition its western provinces into barbarian 'successor-states', the new native army which, at the eleventh hour, saved the eastern provinces from going the same way, was armed and mounted on the barbarian pattern. The supremacy of this heavy-armed lancer lasted for more than a thousand years and his spatial distribution is even more remarkable. His identity is unmistakable, whether his portrait is presented to us in some fresco, dating from the first century of the Christian Era, in a Crimean tomb; or on a third, fourth, fifth or sixth-century bas-relief cut by a Sasanian king into a cliff in Fars; or in the clay figurines portraying those Far Eastern men-at-arms who were the fighting force of the T'ang dynasty (A.D. 618–907); or in the eleventh-century tapestry at Bayeux which depicts the defeat of the antiquated English foot-soldiers of the day by William the Conqueror's Norman knights.

If this longevity and ubiquity of the cataphract are astonishing, it is also noteworthy that he becomes ubiquitous only in a degenerate form. The story of his discomfiture is told by an eye-witness.

'I was in the army of the Under-Secretary when he went forth to meet the Tatars on the western side of the City of Peace [Baghdad] on the occasion of its supreme disaster in the year A.H. 656 [A.D. 1258]. We met at Nahr Bashīr, one of the dependencies of Dujayl; and there would ride forth from amongst us, to offer single combat, a knight fully accoutred and mounted on an Arab horse, so that it was as though he and his steed together were [solid as] some great mountain. Then there would come forth to meet him from the Mongols a horseman mounted on a horse like a donkey, and having in his hand a spear like a spindle, wearing neither robe nor armour, so that all who saw him were moved to laughter. Yet ere the day was done the victory was theirs, and they inflicted on us a great defeat, which was the Key of Evil, and thereafter there befell us what befell us.'[1]

Thus the legendary encounter between Goliath and David, at the dawn of Syriac history, repeats itself at nightfall, perhaps twenty-three centuries later; and, though on this occasion the

---

[1] Browne, E. G.: *A Literary History of Persia*, vol. ii, p. 462, quoting Falak-ad-Dīn Muhammad b. Aydīmir as quoted by Ibn-at-Tiqtaqā in *Kitāb-al-Fakhrī*.

giant and the pygmy are on horseback, the outcome is the same.

The invincible Tatar qāzāq who overcame the 'Irāqī cataphract and sacked Baghdad and starved the 'Abbasid Caliph to death was a light horse-archer of the persistent Nomadic type which had first made itself known and dreaded in South-Western Asia through the Cimmerian and Scyth irruption at the turn of the eighth and seventh centuries B.C. But if David-on-horseback duly discomfited Goliath-on-horseback at the outset of the Tatar irruption from the Eurasian Steppe, the sequel to their encounter in this repetition of the story was also faithful to the original. We have seen that the mailed champion on foot who was laid low by David's sling was superseded thereafter not by David himself but by a disciplined phalanx of Goliaths. Hulāgū Khan's Mongol light horse, who had overcome the 'Abbasid Caliph's knights under the walls of Baghdad, were subsequently defeated again and again by the Mamluk masters of Egypt. In their accoutrements the Mamluks were neither better nor worse equipped than their fellow Muslim knights who had been overthrown outside Baghdad, but in their tactics they obeyed a discipline which gave them the mastery over both Mongol sharp-shooters and Frankish Crusaders. The knights of Saint Louis met their defeat at Mansūrah ten years before the Mongols received their first lesson from the same master.

By the close of the thirteenth century the Mamluks, having established their superiority over both the French and the Mongols, stood in the same position of unchallenged military supremacy within their own horizon as the Roman legionaries after Pydna. In this eminent but enervating situation the Mamluk, like the legionary, rested on his oars; and it is a curious coincidence that he was allowed to rest on them for almost exactly the same length of time before he was taken unawares by an old adversary armed with a new technique. Pydna is separated from Adrianople by 546 years; 548 years separate the Mamluk victory over Saint Louis from the Mamluk defeat at the hands of his successor Napoleon. During these five-and-a-half centuries, infantry had come into its own again. Before the first of these centuries had run its course the English long-bow had enabled an army of Davids-on-foot to defeat an army of Goliaths-on-horseback at Crécy, and the result had been driven home and confirmed by the invention of fire-arms and by a disciplinary system borrowed from the Janissaries.

As for the latter end of the Mamluks, the survivors of the Napoleonic assault and of the final destruction of the corps by Mehmed 'Alī, thirteen years later, withdrew to the Upper Nile and bequeathed their armament and technique to those mailed horsemen in the service of the Khalifah of a Sudanese Mahdi who went down under the fire of British infantry at Omdurman in 1898.

The French army which overthrew the Mamluks was already something different from the earliest version of the Western imitation of the Janissaries. It was a recent product of the French *levée en masse* which had succeeded in superseding, by successfully diluting, the small but superlatively well-drilled new-model Western army which had been brought to perfection by Frederick the Great. But the overthrow of the old Prussian army by the new Napoleonic army at Jena was to stimulate a Prussian pleiad of military and political men of genius to outdo the French in a further *tour de force* of combining the new numbers with the old discipline. The result was foreshadowed in 1813 and revealed in 1870. But in the next round the Prussian war-machine involved Germany and her allies in defeat by evoking an unforeseen response in the shape of a siege on an unprecedented scale. In 1918 the methods of 1870 went down before the new methods of trench warfare and economic blockade; and by 1945 it had been demonstrated that the technique which had won the war of 1914–18 was not the last link in this ever-lengthening chain. Each link has been a cycle of invention, triumph, lethargy and disaster; and, on the precedents thus set by three thousand years of military history, from Goliath's encounter with David to the piercing of a Maginot Line and a West Wall by the thrust of mechanical cataphracts and the pinpoint marksmanship of archers on winged steeds, we may expect fresh illustrations of our theme to be provided with monotonous consistency as long as mankind is so perverse as to go on cultivating the art of war.

(6) THE SUICIDALNESS OF MILITARISM

Κόρος, ῞Υβρις, ῎Ατη

Having concluded our survey of 'resting on one's oars', which is the passive way of succumbing to the nemesis of creativity, we may now go on to examine the active aberration which is described in the three Greek words κόρος, ὕβρις, ἄτη. These words have a subjective as well as an objective connotation. Objectively κόρος means 'surfeit', ὕβρις 'outrageous behaviour', and ἄτη 'disaster'.[1]

---

[1] The causal relation between surfeit and outrageous behaviour is neatly expressed by a Hebrew poet in the line 'Jeshurun waxed fat, and kicked'. (Deut. xxxii. 15). He kicked (ὕβρις) because he had waxed fat (κόρος), and the subsequent verses indicate that ἄτη is in store for him. The Jeshurun of this passage is Israel, when, in the prosperous days of Jeroboam II, he forsook Yahweh. The Captivity that was to lead to the extinction of these 'Ten Tribes' was only half a century ahead at that time.

Subjectively κόρος means the psychological condition of being spoilt by success; ὕβρις means the consequent loss of mental and moral balance; and ἄτη means the blind headstrong ungovernable impulse which sweeps an unbalanced soul into attempting the impossible. This active psychological catastrophe in three acts was the commonest theme—if we may judge by the handful of extant masterpieces—in the fifth-century Athenian tragic drama. It is the story of Agamemnon in Aeschylus's play of that name, and of Xerxes in his *Persae*; the story of Ajax in Sophocles' play of that name, of Oedipus in his *Oedipus Tyrannus*, and of Creon in his *Antigone*; and it is the story of Pentheus in Euripides' *Bacchae*. In Platonic language,

'If one sins against the laws of proportion and gives something too big to something too small to carry it—too big sails to too small a ship, too big meals to too small a body, too big powers to too small a soul— the result is bound to be a complete upset. In an outburst of ὕβρις the over-fed body will rush into sickness, while the jack-in-office will rush into the unrighteousness which ὕβρις always breeds.'[1]

In order to bring out the difference between the passive and the active methods of courting destruction, let us begin our survey of κόρος—ὕβρις—ἄτη in the military field, with which we have just brought our survey of 'resting on one's oars' to a close.

Both modes happen to be exemplified in the behaviour of Goliath. On the one hand, we have seen how he incurs his doom by vegetating in the once invincible technique of the individual hoplite champion without foreseeing or forestalling the new and superior technique which David is bringing into action against him. At the same time we may observe that his destruction at David's hands might have been averted if only his unenterprising-ness in technique had been accompanied by a corresponding passivity of ethos. Unfortunately for Goliath, however, this *miles gloriosus's* technological conservatism was not offset by any such moderation of policy; instead, he went out of his way to ask for trouble by issuing a challenge; he symbolizes a militarism at once aggressive and inadequately prepared. Such a militarist is so confident of his own ability to look after himself in the social—or anti-social—system in which all disputes are settled by the sword that he throws his sword into the scales. Its weight duly tips the balance in his favour and he points to his triumph as a final proof that the sword is omnipotent. In the next chapter of the story, however, it turns out that he has failed to prove his thesis *ad hominem* in the particular case which exclusively interests him; for the next event is his own overthrow by a stronger militarist

[1] Plato, *Laws*: 691 c.

than himself. He has proved a thesis which had not occurred to him: 'They that take the sword shall perish with the sword.'

With this introduction we may pass from the legendary duel of Syriac saga to consider a few of the examples offered by history.

Assyria

The disaster in which the Assyrian military power met its end in 614–610 B.C. was one of the completest yet known to history. It involved not only the destruction of the Assyrian war-machine but also the extinction of the Assyrian state and the extermination of the Assyrian people. A community which had been in existence for over two thousand years and had been playing an ever more dominant part in South-Western Asia for a period of some two-and-a-half centuries, was blotted out almost completely. Two hundred and ten years later, when Cyrus the Younger's ten thousand Greek mercenaries were retreating up the Tigris Valley from the battle-field of Cunaxa to the Black Sea coast, they passed in succession the sites of Calah and Nineveh and were struck with astonishment, not so much at the massiveness of the fortifications and the extent of the area they embraced, as at the spectacle of such vast works of man lying uninhabited. The weirdness of these empty shells, which testified by their inanimate endurance to the vigour of a vanished life, is vividly conveyed by the literary art of a member of the Greek expeditionary force who has recounted its experiences. Yet what is still more astonishing to a modern reader of Xenophon's narrative—acquainted as he is with the fortunes of Assyria through the discoveries of modern archaeologists—is the fact that Xenophon was unable to learn even the most elementary facts about the authentic history of these derelict fortress-cities. Although the whole of South-Western Asia, from] Jerusalem to Ararat and from Elam to Lydia, had been dominated and terrorized by the masters of these cities little more than two centuries before Xenophon passed that way, the best account he is able to give of them has no relation to their real history, and the very name of Assyria is unknown to him.

At first sight the fate of Assyria seems difficult to comprehend; for her militarists cannot be convicted, like the Macedonians, the Romans and the Mamluks, of 'resting on their oars'. When these other war-machines met with their fatal accidents each was hopelessly obsolete and shockingly out of repair. The Assyrian war-machine, on the other hand, was continuously overhauled, renovated and reinforced right down to the day of its destruction. The fund of military genius which produced the embryo of the hoplite in the fourteenth century before Christ, on the eve of

Assyria's first bid for predominance in South-Western Asia, and the embryo of the cataphract horse-archer in the seventh century before Christ, on the eve of Assyria's own annihilation, was also productive throughout the seven intervening centuries. The energetic inventiveness and the restless zeal for improvements, which were the notes of the latter-day Assyrian ethos in its application to the art of war, are attested unimpeachably by the series of bas-reliefs, found *in situ* in the royal palaces, in which the successive phases of the Assyrian military equipment and technique during the last three centuries of Assyrian history are recorded pictorially with careful precision and in minute detail. Here we find recorded continuous experiment and improvement in body armour, in the design of chariots, in the engines of assault and in the differentiation of specialized troops for special purposes. What then was the cause of Assyria's destruction?

In the first place the policy of the unremitting offensive, and the possession of a potent instrument for putting this policy into effect, led the Assyrian war-lords in the fourth and last bout of their militarism to extend their enterprises and commitments far beyond the bounds which their predecessors had kept. Assyria was subject to a perpetual prior call upon her military resources for the fulfilment of her task as warden of the marches of the Babylonic World against the barbarian highlanders in the Zagros and the Taurus on the one side and against the Aramaean pioneers of the Syriac Civilization on the other. In her three earlier bouts of militarism she had been content to pass from the defensive to the offensive on these two fronts without pressing this offensive *à outrance* and without dissipating her forces in other directions. Even so, the third bout, which occupied the two middle quarters of the ninth century B.C., evoked in Syria a temporary coalition of Syrian states which checked the Assyrian advance at Qarqar in 853 B.C., and it was met in Armenia by the more formidable *riposte* of the foundation of the kingdom of Urartu. In spite of these warnings Tiglath-Pileser III (746–727 B.C.), when he inaugurated the last and greatest of the Assyrian offensives, allowed himself to harbour political ambitions and to aim at military objectives which brought Assyria into collision with three new adversaries—Babylon, Elam and Egypt—each of whom was potentially as great a military power as Assyria herself.

Tiglath-Pileser put a conflict with Egypt in store for his successors when he set himself to complete the subjugation of the petty states of Syria; for Egypt could not remain indifferent to an extension of the Assyrian Empire up to her own frontier, and she was in a position to frustrate or undo the Assyrian empire-builders' work unless they made up their minds to round it off by embarking on the more formidable enterprise of subjugating Egypt herself. Tiglath-Pileser's bold occupation of Philistia in 734 B.C. may have been a strategic masterstroke which was rewarded by the temporary submission of Samaria in 733 and the fall of Damascus in 732. But it led to Sargon's brush with the Egyptians in 720 and Sennacherib's in 700, and these inconclusive encounters led on in their turn to Esarhaddon's conquest and occupation of Egypt in the campaigns of 675, 674 and 671. Thereupon it became manifest that, while Assyrian armies were strong enough to rout Egyptian armies and occupy the land of Egypt, and to repeat the feat, they were not strong enough to hold Egypt down. Esarhaddon himself was once more on the march for Egypt when death overtook him in 669; and, though the Egyptian insurrection was quelled by Asshurbanipal in 667, he had to reconquer Egypt once again in 663. By this time the Assyrian Government must have realized that in Egypt it was engaged on Psyche's Task, and when Psammetichus unobtrusively expelled the Assyrian garrisons in 658–651 Asshurbanipal turned a blind eye to what was happening. In thus cutting his Egyptian losses the King of Assyria was undoubtedly wise; yet this wisdom after the event was an admission that the energies expended on five Egyptian campaigns had been wasted. Moreover, the loss of Egypt was a prelude to the loss of Syria in the next generation.

The ultimate consequences of Tiglath-Pileser's intervention in Babylonia were far graver than those of his forward policy in Syria, since they led, by a direct chain of cause and effect, to the catastrophe of 614–610 B.C.

In the earlier stages of the Assyrian military aggression against Babylonia there is evidence of a certain political moderation. The conquering Power preferred the establishment of protectorates under puppet princes of native origin to outright annexation. It was only after the great Chaldaean insurrection of 694–689 that Sennacherib formally put an end to the independence of Babylonia by installing his son and designated successor, Esarhaddon, as Assyrian viceroy. But this policy of moderation failed to conciliate the Chaldaeans and merely encouraged them to retort with increasing effect to the Assyrian military challenge. Under the hammer-blows of Assyrian militarism the Chaldaeans set the anarchy of their own house in order and secured an alliance with the neighbouring kingdom of Elam. And, in the next stage, the abandonment of the policy of political moderation and the sacking of Babylon in 689 taught a lesson which was the opposite of that intended. In the white heat of the hatred which this act of Assyrian frightfulness aroused among the ancient urban population as well as among the intrusive Chaldaean nomads, citizens and tribesmen forgot their mutual antipathy and became fused together in a new Babylonian nation which could neither forget nor forgive, and which could never rest until it had brought its oppressor to the ground.

Yet for the best part of a century the stroke of the inevitable ἄτη was postponed by the progressive efficiency of the Assyrian military machine. In 639, for example, Elam was dealt such an annihilating blow that her derelict territory passed under the dominion of Persian highlanders from her eastern border and became the jumping-off ground from which the Achaemenidae made themselves masters of all South-Western Asia a century later. Immediately after Asshurbanipal's death in 626, however, Babylonia revolted once again, under the leadership of Nabopolassar, who found in the new kingdom of Media a more potent ally than Elam; and within sixteen years Assyria was wiped off the face of the map.

When we gaze back over the century-and-a-half of ever more virulent warfare which begins with Tiglath-Pileser's accession in 745 B.C. and closes with the Babylonian Nebuchadnezzar's victory over Pharaoh Necho at Carchemish in 605, the historical landmarks which stand out at first sight are the successive knock-out blows by which Assyria destroyed entire communities—razing cities to the ground and carrying whole populations away captive: Damascus in 732, Samaria in 722, Musasir in 714, Babylon in 689, Sidon in 677, Memphis in 671, Thebes in 663, Susa *circa* 639. Of all the capital cities of all the states within reach of Assyria's arm, only Tyre and Jerusalem remained inviolate at the time of the sack of Nineveh herself in 612. The loss and misery which Assyria inflicted on her neighbours is beyond all calculation; yet the legendary remark of the canting schoolmaster to the boy whom he is whipping—'It hurts you less than it hurts me'—would be a more pertinent critique of Assyrian military activities than the unashamedly truculent and naïvely self-complacent narratives in which the Assyrian war-lords have presented their own accounts of their performances. All Assyria's victims enumerated in this paragraph struggled back to life, and some of them had great futures ahead of them. Nineveh alone fell dead and never rose again.

The reason for this contrast of destinies is not far to seek. Behind the façade of her military triumphs, Assyria had been engaged in committing slow suicide. All that we know of her internal history during the period under review gives conclusive evidence of political instability, economic ruin, declining culture and wide-spread depopulation. The clearly attested progress of the Aramaic language at the expense of the native Akkadian in the Assyrian homeland during the last century-and-a-half of Assyria's existence shows that the Assyrian people was being peacefully supplanted by the captives of the Assyrian bow and spear in an age when the Assyrian military power stood at its zenith. The indomitable warrior who stood at bay in the breach at Nineveh in 612 was 'a corpse in armour', whose frame was only held erect by the massiveness of the military accoutrements in which this *felo de se* had smothered himself to death. When the Median and Babylonian storming party reached the stiff and menacing figure and sent it clattering and crashing down the moraine of ruined brickwork into the fosse below, they did not suspect that their terrible adversary was no longer a living man at the moment when they struck their daring, and apparently decisive, blow.

The doom of Assyria is typical of its kind. The tableau of the 'corpse in armour' conjures up a vision of the Spartan phalanx on the battlefield of Leuctra in 371 B.C. and of the Janissaries in the trenches before Vienna in A.D. 1683. The ironic fate of the militarist who is so intemperate in waging wars of annihilation against his neighbours that he deals unintended destruction to himself recalls the self-inflicted doom of the Carolingians or the Timurids, who built up great empires out of the agony of their Saxon or Persian victims, only to provide spoils for Scandinavian or Usbeg adventurers who lived to see and take their chance when the empire-builders paid for their imperialism by sinking into impotence within the space of a single lifetime. Another form of suicide which the Assyrian example calls to mind is the self-destruction of those militarists, whether barbarians or peoples of higher culture, who break into and break up some universal state or other great empire which has been giving a spell of peace to the peoples and lands over which it has spread its aegis. The conquerors ruthlessly tear the imperial mantle to shreds and expose the millions whom it has sheltered to the terrors of darkness and the shadow of death, but the shadow descends inexorably on the criminals as well as on their victims. Demoralized by the vastness of their prize, these new masters of a ravished world are apt, like the Kilkenny cats, to perform 'the friendly office' for one another until not one brigand of the band is left to feast upon the plunder.

We may watch how the Macedonians, when they have overrun the Achaemenian Empire and pressed beyond its farthest frontiers into India, next turn their arms with equal ferocity upon one another during the forty-two years between the death of Alexander in 323 B.C. and the overthrow of Lysimachus at Corupedium in 281. The grim performance was repeated a thousand years later when the Primitive Muslim Arabs emulated—and thereby undid—the Macedonians' work by overrunning, in twelve years, the Roman and Sasanian dominions in South-Western Asia over almost as wide a sweep of territory as had once been conquered, in eleven years, by Alexander. In this Arab act of brigandage the twelve years of conquest were followed by twenty-four years of fratricidal strife. Once again the conquerors fell on one another's swords, and the glory and profit of rebuilding a Syriac universal state was left to the usurping Umayyads and to the interloping 'Abbāsids instead of falling to the companions and descendants of the Prophet whose lightning conquests had prepared the way. The same suicidal Assyrian vein of militarism was displayed by the barbarians who overran the derelict provinces of the decadent Roman Empire, as has been already shown on an early page of this Study.

There is yet another variety of militaristic aberration of which we shall also find the prototype in the Assyrian militarism when we envisage Assyria in her proper setting as an integral part of the larger body social which we have called the Babylonic Society. In this society Assyria was a march whose special function was to defend not only herself but the rest of the world of which she formed a part from the predatory highlanders on the north and the east and from the aggressive pioneers of the Syriac Society on the south and the west. In articulating a march of this kind out of a previously undifferentiated social fabric a society stands to benefit in all its members; for while the march is stimulated in so far as it responds successfully to its proper challenge of resisting external pressures, the interior is relieved of pressure and set free to face other challenges and accomplish other tasks. This division of labour breaks down if the frontiersmen turn the arms which they have learnt to use against the outsider into a means of fulfilling ambitions at the expense of the interior members of their own society. What follows is essentially a civil war, and this explains the momentousness of the consequences that ultimately followed from the action of Tiglath-Pileser III in 745 B.C. when he turned his Assyrian arms against Babylonia. The aberration of the march which turns against the interior is, of its very nature, disastrous for the society as a whole, but for the marchman himself it is suicidal. His action is like that of a sword-arm that plunges the blade it wields into the body of which it is a member; or like the woodman who saws off the branch on which he is sitting, and so comes crashing down with it to the ground while the mutilated tree-trunk remains still standing.

Charlemagne

It was perhaps an intuitive misgiving at the misdirection of energies discussed in the preceding paragraph that moved the Austrasian Franks to protest so vehemently in A.D. 754 against their war-lord Pepin's decision to respond to Pope Stephen's call to arms against their brethren the Lombards. The Papacy had turned its eyes towards this Transalpine Power, and had whetted Pepin's ambition in 749 by crowning him king and thereby legitimizing his *de facto* authority, because Austrasia had distinguished herself in Pepin's generation by her services as a march on two fronts: against the pagan Saxons beyond the Rhine and against the Muslim Arab conquerors of the Iberian Peninsula who were pressing across the Pyrenees. In 754 the Austrasians were invited to divert their energies from the fields in which they had just been finding their true mission in order to destroy the Lombards, who stood in the way of the political ambitions of the Papacy. The misgivings of the Austrasian rank and file with regard to this enterprise were proved in the event to have been better justified than their leader's appetite for it; for in overriding the objections of his henchmen Pepin forged the first link in a chain of military and political commitments which bound Austrasia ever more tightly to Italy. His Italian campaign of 755-6 led on to Charlemagne's of 773-4, a campaign which disastrously interrupted the conquest of Saxony on which he had then just embarked. Thereafter, in the course of the next thirty years, his laborious operations in Saxony were interrupted again no less than four times by the intrusion of Italian crises which demanded his presence on the spot for periods of varying duration. The burdens imposed upon Charlemagne's subjects by his mutually contradictory ambitions aggravated to breaking-point the load which weighed upon Austrasia's back.

Timur Lenk

Timur in like fashion broke the back of his own Transoxania by squandering on aimless expeditions into Iran and 'Iraq and India and Anatolia and Syria the slender reserves of Transoxanian strength which ought to have been concentrated upon Timur's proper mission of imposing his peace on the Eurasian Nomads. Transoxania was the march of the sedentary Iranic Society over against the Eurasian Nomad World, and during the first nineteen years of his reign (A.D. 1362-80) Timur had attended to his proper business as warden of the marches. He had first repulsed and afterwards taken the offensive against the Chagatay Nomads, and he had rounded off his own dominions by liberating the oases of Khwarizm on the Lower Oxus from the Nomads of Juji's appanage. Upon the completion of this great task in A.D. 1380 Timur had a greater prize within his reach—no less than the succession to the great Eurasian empire of Chingis Khan; for in Timur's generation the Nomads were in retreat on all sectors of the long frontier between the Desert and the Sown, and the next chapter in the history of Eurasia was to be a race between the resurgent sedentary peoples round about for the prize of Chingis Khan's heritage. In this competition the Moldavians and Lithuanians were too remote to be in the running; the Muscovites were wedded to their forests and the Chinese to their fields; the Cossacks and the Transoxanians were the only competitors who had succeeded in making themselves at home on the Steppe without uprooting the sedentary foundations of their own way of life, and of the two the Transoxanian competitor seemed to have the better chance. Besides being stronger in himself and nearer to the heart of the Steppe he was also the first in the field, while, as champion of the Sunnah, he had potential partisans among the sedentary Muslim communities who were the outposts of Islam on the Steppe's opposite coasts.

For an instant Timur appeared to appreciate his opportunity and to grasp it with determination, but after a few bold and brilliant preliminary moves he made a right-about turn, directed his arms towards the interior of the Iranic World and devoted almost the whole of the last twenty-four years of his life to a series of barren and destructive campaigns in this quarter. The range of his victories was as sensational as their results were suicidal.

Timur's self-stultification is a supreme example of the suicidalness of militarism. His empire not only did not survive him but was devoid of all after-effects of a positive kind. Its only traceable after-effect is wholly negative. In sweeping away everything that it found in its path, in order to rush headlong to its own destruction, Timur's imperialism simply created a political and social vacuum in South-Western Asia; and this vacuum eventually drew the 'Osmanlis and the Safawis into a collision which dealt the stricken Iranic Society its death-blow.

The Iranic Society's forfeiture of the heritage of the Nomad World declared itself first on the plane of religion. Throughout the four centuries ending in Timur's generation Islam had been progressively establishing its hold over the sedentary peoples round the coasts of the Eurasian Steppe and had been captivating the Nomads themselves whenever they trespassed out of the Desert into the Sown. By the fourteenth century it looked as though nothing could now prevent Islam from becoming the religion of all Eurasia. But after Timur's career had run its course the progress of Islam in Eurasia came to a dead stop, and two centuries later the Mongols and the Calmucks were converted to the Lamaistic form of Mahayanian Buddhism. This astonishing triumph of a fossilized relic of the religious life of the long extinct Indic Civilization gives some measure of the extent to which the prestige of Islam had fallen in the estimation of the Eurasian Nomads during the two centuries that had elapsed since Timur's day.

On the political plane the Iranic culture which Timur had first championed and then betrayed proved equally bankrupt. The sedentary societies which ultimately performed the feat of taming Eurasian Nomadism politically were the Russians and the Chinese. This final conclusion of the monotonously repeated drama of Nomad history became predictable when, in the middle of the seventeenth century of the Christian Era, the Cossack servants of Muscovy and the Manchu masters of China ran into each other as they were feeling their way in opposite directions round the northern edge of the Steppe and fought their first battle for dominion over Eurasia in the neighbourhood of Chingis Khan's ancestral pastures in the upper basin of the Amur. The partition of Eurasia between these rivals was completed a century later.

It is a curious reflection that, if Timur had not turned his back on Eurasia and his arms against Iran in A.D. 1381, the present relations between Transoxania and Russia might have been the inverse of what they actually are. In those hypothetical circumstances Russia to-day might have found herself included in an empire of much the same extent as the area of the present Soviet Union but with quite a different centre of gravity—an Iranic empire in which Samarqand would be ruling Moscow instead of Moscow ruling Samarqand. This imaginary picture may appear outlandish because the actual course of events for five-and-a-half centuries has been so different, but at least as strange a picture will unfold itself if we plot out an alternative course for Western history on the assumption that Charlemagne's less violent and fatal diversion of his military energies had proved as disastrous for the Western Civilization as Timur's proved for the Iranic. On this analogy we shall have to picture Austrasia being submerged by the Magyars and Neustria by the Vikings in the darkness of the tenth century, and the heart of the Carolingian Empire remaining thereafter under this barbarian domination until in the fourteenth century the 'Osmanlis step in to impose the lesser evil of an alien domination upon these derelict marches of Western Christendom.

But the greatest of all Timur's acts of destruction was committed against himself. He has made his name immortal at the price of erasing from the mind of posterity all memory of the deeds for which he might have been remembered for good. To how many people in Christendom or Dār-al-Islām does Timur's name call up the image of a champion of civilization against barbarism, who led the clergy and people of his country to a hard-won victory at the end of a nineteen-years-long struggle for independence? To the vast majority of those to whom the name of Timur Lenk or Tamerlane means anything at all, it commemorates a militarist who perpetrated as many horrors in the span of twenty-four years as the last five Assyrian kings perpetrated in a hundred and twenty. We think of the monster who razed Isfarā'in to the ground in A.D. 1381; built 2,000 prisoners into a living mound and then bricked them over at Sabzawār in 1383; piled 5,000 human heads into minarets at Zirih in the same year; cast his Lūrī prisoners alive over precipices in 1386; massacred 70,000 people and piled the heads of the slain into minarets at Isfahan in 1387; massacred 100,000 prisoners at Delhi in 1398; buried alive 4,000 Christian soldiers of the garrison of Sivas after their capitulation in 1400; and built twenty towers of skulls in Syria in 1400 and 1401. In minds which know him only by such deeds Timur has caused himself to be confounded with the ogres of the Steppe—a Chingis and an Attila and the like—against whom he had spent the first and better half of his life in waging a Holy War. The crack-brained megalomania of this homicidal madman whose one idea is to impress the imagination of mankind with a sense of his military power by a hideous abuse of it is brilliantly conveyed in the hyperboles which the English poet Marlowe has placed in the mouth of his Tamburlaine:

> The God of war resignes his roume to me,
> Meaning to make me Generall of the world;
> Jove, viewing me in armes, lookes pale and wan,
> Fearing my power should pull him from his throne.
> Where ere I come the fatall sisters sweat,
> And griesly death by running to and fro,
> To do their ceassles homag to my sword. . . .
> Millions of soules sit on the bankes of Styx,
> Waiting the back returne of Charon's boat,
> Hell and Elysian swarme with ghosts of men,
> That I have sent from sundry foughten fields,
> To spread my fame through hell and up to heaven.[1]

The Margrave turned Moss-trooper

In analysing the careers of Timur and Charlemagne and the later Assyrian kings we have observed the same phenomenon in all three cases. The military prowess which a society develops

[1] Marlowe, Christopher: *Tamburlaine the Great*, ll. 2232–8, 2245–9.

among its frontiersmen for its defence against external enemies undergoes a sinister transformation into the moral malady of militarism when it is diverted from its proper field in the No-man's-land beyond the pale and is turned against the frontiers-men's own brethren in the interior. A number of other examples of this social evil will readily occur to our minds.

We shall think of Mercia turning against the other English 'successor-states' of the Roman Empire in Britain the arms which she had sharpened in performance of her original function as the English march against Wales; of the Plantagenet kingdom of England attempting in the Hundred Years' War to conquer the sister kingdom of France instead of attending to her proper business of enlarging the bounds of their common mother, Latin Christendom, at the expense of the Celtic Fringe; and of the Norman king Roger of Sicily turning his military energies to the extension of his dominions in Italy instead of carrying on his forebears' work of enlarging the bounds of Western Christendom in the Mediterranean at the expense of Orthodox Christendom and Dār-al-Islām. In like fashion the Mycenaean outposts of the Minoan Civilization on the European mainland misused the prowess which they had acquired in holding their own against the conti-nental barbarians, in order to turn and rend their mother Crete.

In the Egyptiac World the classic Southern March in the section of the Nile Valley immediately below the First Cataract trained itself in arms, in the execution of its duty of damming back the Nubian barbarians up-river, only to turn right-about against the communities of the interior and establish by brute force the United Kingdom of the Two Crowns. This act of militarism has been depicted by its perpetrator, with all the frankness of self-complacency, in one of the earliest records of the Egyptiac Civilization as yet discovered. The palette of Narmer displays the triumphant return of the Upper-Egyptian war-lord from the conquest of Lower Egypt. Swollen to a superhuman stature, the royal conqueror marches behind a strutting file of standard-bearers towards a double row of decapitated enemy corpses, while below, in the image of a bull, he tramples upon a fallen adversary and batters down the walls of a fortified town. The accompanying script is believed to enumerate a booty of 120,000 human captives, 400,000 oxen and 1,422,000 sheep and goats.

In this gruesome work of archaic Egyptiac art we have the whole tragedy of militarism as it has been acted over and over again since Narmer's time. Perhaps the most poignant of all the performances of this tragedy is that of which Athens was guilty when she trans-formed herself from 'the liberator of Hellas' into a 'tyrant city'.

This Athenian aberration brought upon all Hellas, as well as upon Athens herself, the never-retrieved disaster of the Atheno-Peloponnesian War. The military field, which we have been surveying in this chapter, is illuminating for the study of the fatal chain of κόρος—ὕβρις—ἄτη because military skill and prowess are edged tools which are apt to inflict fatal injuries on those who misuse them. But what is palpably true of military action is also true of other human activities in less hazardous fields where the train of gunpowder which leads from κόρος through ὕβρις to ἄτη is not so explosive. Whatever the human faculty or the sphere of its exercise may be, the presumption that, because a faculty has proved equal to the accomplishment of a limited task within its proper field, it may therefore be counted on to produce some inordinate effect in a different set of circumstances, is never anything but an intellectual and moral aberration and never leads to anything but certain disaster. We have now to proceed to an illustration of the working of this same sequence of cause and effect in a non-military field.

(7) THE INTOXICATION OF VICTORY

THE HOLY SEE

One of the more general forms in which the tragedy of κόρος—ὕβρις—ἄτη presents itself is the intoxication of victory—whether the struggle in which the fatal prize is won be a war of arms or a conflict of spiritual forces. Both variants of this drama could be illustrated from the history of Rome: the intoxication of a military victory from the breakdown of the Republic in the second century B.C. and the intoxication of a spiritual victory from the breakdown of the Papacy in the thirteenth century of the Christian Era. But as we have already dealt with the breakdown of the Roman Republic in another connexion we will confine ourselves here to the latter theme. The chapter in the history of the Roman See, the greatest of all Western institutions, with which we are concerned is that which began on the 20th December, A.D. 1046, with the opening of the Synod of Sutri by the Emperor Henry III, and closed on the 20th September, A.D. 1870, with the occupation of Rome by the troops of King Victor Emmanuel.

The Papal *Respublica Christiana* is unique among human institutions. Attempts to establish its character by analogies with institutions evolved in other societies reveal differences so fundamental that the supposed analogies turn out to be unprofitable. It can best be described, in negative terms, as an exact inversion of the Caesaro-Papal régime, against which it was a social reaction and a spiritual protest; and this description gives, better than any other, the measure of Hildebrand's achievement.

When the Tuscan Hildebrand took up his abode in Rome in the second quarter of the eleventh century, he found himself in a derelict outpost of the East Roman Empire which was occupied by a degenerate offshoot of the Byzantine Society. These latter-day Romans were militarily contemptible, socially turbulent, financially and spiritually bankrupt. They were unable to cope with their Lombard neighbours; they had lost the whole of the Papal estates at home and overseas; and when it was a question of raising the level of monastic life they had to turn for guidance to Cluny, beyond the Alps. The first attempts to regenerate the Papacy took the form of passing over Romans and appointing Transalpines. In this despised and alien Rome Hildebrand and his successors succeeded in creating the master-institution of Western Christendom. They won for Papal Rome an empire which had a greater hold on the human heart than the Empire of the Antonines, and which on the mere material plane embraced vast tracts of Western Europe beyond the Rhine and the Danube where the legions of Augustus and Marcus Aurelius had never set foot.

These Papal conquests were partly due to the constitution of the Christian Republic whose frontiers the Popes were enlarging; for it was a constitution which inspired confidence instead of evoking hostility. It was based on a combination of ecclesiastical centralism and uniformity with political diversity and devolution; and, since the superiority of the spiritual over the temporal power was a cardinal point in its constitutional doctrine, this combination made the note of unity predominant without depriving the adolescent Western Society of those elements of liberty and elasticity which are the indispensable conditions of growth. Even in those Central Italian territories over which the Papacy claimed secular as well as ecclesiastical authority the twelfth-century Popes gave encouragement to the movement towards city-state autonomy. At the turn of the twelfth and thirteenth centuries, when this civic movement was in full flood in Italy and when the Papal authority stood at its zenith over Western Christendom, a Welsh poet was 'pointing out . . . how strange it was that the Pope's censure, which in Rome could not move trifles, was elsewhere making the sceptres of kings tremble'.[1] Giraldus Cambrensis felt that he was here exposing a paradox which was a theme for satire. But the very reason why in this age a majority of the

[1] Mann, the Right Rev. Monsignor H. K.: *The Lives of the Popes in the Middle Ages*, vol. xi, p. 72.

princes and city-states of Western Christendom accepted the Papal supremacy with so little demur was because the Pope was not then under suspicion of attempting to trespass on the domain of the secular power.

This statesmanlike aloofness from secular and territorial ambitions was combined, in the Papal hierocracy at its zenith, with an energetic and enterprising use of the administrative gift which was the Byzantine legacy to Papal Rome. While in Orthodox Christendom this gift had been fatally applied to the *tour de force* of putting substance into a resuscitated ghost of the Roman Empire and thereby crushing an adolescent Orthodox Christian Society under the incubus of an institution too heavy for it to bear, the Roman architects of the *Respublica Christiana* turned their administrative resources to better account by building a lighter structure, on a new plan, upon broader foundations. The gossamer filaments of the Papal spider's web, as it was originally woven, drew medieval Western Christendom together into an unconstrained unity which was equally beneficial to the parts and to the whole. It was only later, when the fabric coarsened and hardened in the stress of conflict, that the silken threads changed into iron bands and that these came to weigh so heavily on the local princes and peoples that at last they burst their bonds in a temper in which they hardly cared if, in liberating themselves, they were destroying the oecumenical unity which the Papacy had established and preserved.

In that Papal work of creation it was not, of course, either a capacity for administration or an avoidance of territorial ambitions that was the vital creative force; the Papacy was able to be creative because it threw itself without hesitations or reservations into the task of giving leadership and expression and organization to an adolescent society's awakening desires for a higher life and a larger growth. It gave these aspirations form and fame, and thereby transformed them from the day-dreams of scattered minorities or isolated individuals into common causes which carried conviction that they were supremely worth striving for, and which swept men off their feet when they heard these causes preached by Popes who were staking upon them the fortunes of the Holy See. The victory of the Christian Republic was won by the Papal campaigns for the purification of the clergy from the two moral plagues of sexual incontinence and financial corruption, for the liberation of the life of the Church from the interference of secular Powers and for the rescue of the Oriental Christians and the Holy Places from the clutches of the Turkish champions of Islam. But this was not the whole of the Hildebrandine Papacy's work; for even in times of the severest stress the great Popes under whose leadership these 'Holy Wars' were fought had a margin of thought and will to spare for works of peace in which the Church was displaying her finest self and exercising her most creative activity: the nascent universities, the new forms of monastic life and the mendicant orders.

The fall of the Hildebrandine Church is as extraordinary a spectacle as its rise; for all the virtues which had carried it to its zenith seemed to change, as it sank to its nadir, into their own exact antitheses. The divine institution which had been fighting and winning a battle for spiritual freedom against material force was now infected with the very evil which it had set itself to cast out. The Holy See which had led the struggle against simony now required the clergy to pay their dues to a Roman receipt of custom for those ecclesiastical preferments which Rome herself had forbidden them to purchase from any local secular power. The Roman Curia which had been the head and front of moral and intellectual progress now turned itself into a fastness of spiritual conservatism. The ecclesiastical sovereign power now suffered itself to be deprived by its local secular underlings—the princes of the rising parochial states—of the lion's share of the product of the financial and administrative instruments which the Papacy itself had devised in order to make its authority effective. Finally, as the local prince of a Papal principality, the Sovereign Pontiff had to content himself with the paltry consolation-prize of sovereignty over one of the least of the 'successor-states' of his own lost empire. Has any institution ever given so great occasion as this to the enemies of the Lord to blaspheme? This is surely the most extreme example of the nemesis of creativity that we have yet encountered in our Study. How did this happen, and why?

How it happened is foreshadowed in the first recorded transaction of Hildebrand's public career.

The creative spirits of the Roman Church who set themselves in the eleventh century to rescue our Western Society from a feudal anarchy by establishing a Christian Republic found themselves in the same dilemma as their spiritual heirs who are attempting in our own day to replace an international anarchy by a world order. The essence of their aim was to substitute spiritual authority for physical force, and the spiritual sword was the weapon with which their supreme victories were won. But there were occasions on which it seemed as though the established régime of physical force was in a position to defy the spiritual sword with impunity; and it was in such situations that the Roman Church Militant was challenged to give its answer to the

Riddle of the Sphinx. Was the soldier of God to deny himself the use of any but his own spiritual arms at the risk of seeing his advance brought to a standstill? Or was he to fight God's battle against the Devil with the adversary's own weapons? Hildebrand accepted the latter alternative when, on being appointed by Gregory VI to be the guardian of the Papal treasury and finding it constantly looted by brigands, he raised an armed force and routed the brigands *manu militari*.

At the moment when Hildebrand took this action the inward moral character of his act was difficult to divine. At his last hour, forty years later, the answer to the riddle was already less obscure; for in 1085, when he was dying as a Pope in exile at Salerno, Rome herself lay prostrate under the weight of an overwhelming calamity which her bishop's policy had brought upon her only the year before. In 1085 Rome had just been looted and burnt by the Normans, whom the Pope had called in to assist him in a military struggle which had spread from the steps of St. Peter's altar—the Papal treasury—until it had engulfed the whole of Western Christendom. The climax of the physical conflict between Hildebrand and the Emperor Henry IV gave a foretaste of the deadlier and more devastating struggle which was to be fought out *à outrance*, more than a century-and-a-half later, between Innocent IV and Frederick II; and, by the time we come to the pontificate of Innocent IV, a lawyer turned militarist, our doubts will be at an end. Hildebrand himself had set the Hildebrandine Church upon a course which was to end in the victory of his adversaries—the World, the Flesh and the Devil—over the City of God which he was seeking to bring down to Earth.

> No Politick admitteth nor did ever admit
> the teacher into confidence; nay ev'n the Church,
> with hierarchy in conclave compassing to install
> Saint Peter in Caesar's chair, and thereby win for men
> the promises for which they had loved and worship'd Christ,
> relax'd his heavenly code to stretch her temporal rule.[1]

If we have succeeded in explaining how the Papacy became possessed by the demon of physical violence which it was attempting to exorcize, we have found the explanation of the other changes of Papal virtues into their opposing vices; for the substitution of the material for the spiritual sword is the fundamental change of which all the rest are corollaries. How was it, for example, that a Holy See whose main concern with the finances of the clergy had been the eradication of simony in the eleventh

---

[1] Bridges, Robert: *The Testament of Beauty*, iv, ll. 259-64.

century should in the thirteenth century have become so deeply engaged in allocating for the benefit of its nominees, and by the fourteenth century in taxing for its own benefit, those ecclesiastical revenues which it had once redeemed from the scandal of prostitution to secular Powers for the purchase of ecclesiastical preferment? The answer is simply that the Papacy had turned militarist and war costs money.

The outcome of the great war between the thirteenth-century Popes and the Hohenstaufen was the usual outcome of all wars that are fought out to the bitter end. The nominal victor succeeded in dealing the death-blow to his victim at the cost of sustaining fatal injuries himself; and the real victors over both belligerents were the neutral *tertii gaudentes*. When, half-a-century after the death of Frederick II, Pope Boniface VIII hurled against the King of France the Pontifical thunderbolt which had blasted the Emperor, the sequel demonstrated that, as a result of the deadly struggle of 1227–68, the Papacy had sunk to the level of weakness to which it had reduced the Empire, while the Kingdom of France had become as strong as either the Papacy or the Empire had been before they had destroyed each other. King Philippe le Bel burnt the Bull before Notre-Dame with the general approval of his clergy as well as his people, arranged the kidnapping of the Pope, and, after his victim's death, secured the transference of the seat of Papal administration from Rome to Avignon. There followed the 'Captivity' (1305–78) and the Schism (1379–1415).

It was now certain that the local secular princes would inherit, sooner or later, within their respective territories, the whole of the administrative and financial organization and power which the Papacy had been gradually building up for itself. The process of transfer was only a matter of time. We may notice, as landmarks on the road, the English Statutes of Provisors (A.D. 1351) and Praemunire (1353); the concessions which the Curia was compelled to make, a century later, to the secular Powers in France and Germany as the price of their withdrawal of support from the Council of Basel; the Franco-Papal Concordat of 1516 and the English Act of Supremacy passed in 1534. The transfer of the Papacy's prerogatives to secular governments had begun two hundred years before the Reformation and it worked itself out in the states which remained Catholic as well as in those which became Protestant. The sixteenth century saw the process completed; and it is, of course, no accident that the same century also saw the laying of the foundations upon which the 'totalitarian' states of the modern Western World have been built. The most significant single factor in this process, of which we have indicated some of the external landmarks, was the transference of devotion to these parochial secular states from an oecumenical Church.

This hold upon human hearts is the most precious of all the spoils which these successor-states have taken from the greater and nobler institution which they have plundered, since it is by commanding loyalty much more than by raising revenues and armies that these successor-states have kept themselves alive. By the same token it is this spiritual heritage from the Hildebrandine Church that has turned the once harmless and useful institution of the parochial state into the menace to civilization which it clearly is to-day. For the spirit of devotion, which was a beneficent creative power when directed through the channels of a *Civitas Dei* to God Himself, has degenerated into a destructive force when diverted from its original object and offered to idols made by human hands. Parochial states, as our medieval forebears knew, are man-made institutions which, being useful and necessary, deserve from us that same conscientious but unenthusiastic performance of minor social duties which we render in our time to our municipalities and county councils. To idolize these pieces of social machinery is to court disaster.

We have now perhaps found some answer to the question how the Papacy came to suffer its extraordinary περιπέτεια; but in describing the process we have not explained the cause. Why was it that the medieval Papacy became the slave of its own tools and allowed itself to be betrayed, by its use of material means, into being diverted from the spiritual ends to which those means had been intended to minister? The explanation appears to lie in the untoward effects of an initial victory. The dangerous game of fighting force with force, which is justifiable within limits which may be divined by intuition but which are perhaps impossible to define, had fatal results because, in the first instance, it succeeded all too well. Intoxicated by the successes which their hazardous manœuvre obtained for them in the earlier stages of their struggle with the Holy Roman Empire, Gregory VII (Hildebrand) and his successors persisted in the use of force until victory on this non-spiritual plane became an end in itself. Thus, while Gregory VII fought the Empire with the object of removing an Imperial obstacle to a reform of the Church, Innocent IV fought the Empire in order to destroy the Empire's own secular authority.

Can we identify the particular point at which the Hildebrandine policy 'went off the rails' or, in the language of an older tradition, turned aside from the strait and narrow way? Let us try to make out where it was that this wrong turning was taken.

By the year 1075 the double crusade against the sexual and the financial corruption of the clergy had been successfully launched throughout the Western World, and a signal victory had been gained by the moral prowess of a Roman See whose profligacy had been the greatest of all the scandals of the Church only half a century earlier. This victory had been Hildebrand's personal work. He had fought for it beyond the Alps and behind the Papal throne until the fight had carried him at last into the office that he had raised from the dust; and he had fought with every weapon, spiritual and material, that had come to his hand. It was at the moment of triumph, in the third year of his reign as Pope Gregory VII, that Hildebrand took a step which his champions can plausibly represent as having been almost inevitable and his critics—no less plausibly—as having been almost inevitably disastrous. In that year Hildebrand extended the field of battle from the sure ground of concubinage and simony to the debatable ground of Investiture.

Logically, perhaps, the conflict over Investiture might be justified as an inevitable sequel to the conflicts over concubinage and simony if all three struggles were looked upon as one single struggle for the liberation of the Church. To a Hildebrand at this critical point in his career it might seem labour lost to have freed the Church from her servitude to Venus and Mammon if he were to leave her still fettered by her political subjection to the secular Power. So long as this third shackle lay heavy upon her, would she not be debarred from doing her divinely appointed work for the regeneration of mankind? But this argument begs a question which Hildebrand's critics are entitled to ask, even though they cannot, in the nature of things, answer it conclusively one way or the other. In 1075, were the circumstances such that any clear-sighted and strong-minded occupant of the Papal throne was bound to assume that there was no longer any possibility of sincere and fruitful co-operation between the reforming party in the Church, as represented by the Roman Curia, and the secular Power in the Christian Commonwealth as represented by the Holy Roman Empire? On this question the onus of proof lies with the Hildebrandines on at least two accounts.

In the first place neither Hildebrand himself nor his partisans ever sought—either before or after the decree of 1075 prohibiting Lay Investiture—to deny that the secular authorities had a legitimate part to play in the procedure for the election of the clerical officers of the Church from the Pope himself downwards. In the second place, within the thirty years ending in 1075 the Roman See had been working hand in hand with the Holy Roman Empire in the older conflict over the issues of concubinage and simony.

It must be admitted that the co-operation of the Empire in these tasks had faltered and fallen short after the death of Henry III and during his son's minority, and that after Henry IV came of age, in 1069, his conduct had been unsatisfactory. It was in these circumstances that the Papacy embarked on the policy of limiting or prohibiting the intervention of the lay authority in ecclesiastical appointments. This may have been justifiable, but it must be admitted that it was a step of an almost revolutionary character; and if, in spite of all provocations, Hildebrand had forborne to throw down the gauntlet in 1075 it is conceivable that good relations might have been restored. It is difficult to resist the impression that Hildebrand was betrayed into an act of that impatience which is one of the hallmarks of ὕβρις, and the further impression that his nobler motives were alloyed by a desire to exact vengeance from the Imperial Power for the humiliation that it had inflicted on a degenerate Papacy at the Synod of Sutri in 1046. This last impression is strengthened by the fact that Hildebrand, on assuming the Papal tiara, took the name of Gregory, which had previously been borne by the Pope deposed on that occasion.

To raise the new issue of Investiture with a militancy which was bound to set Empire and Papacy at variance was the more hazardous inasmuch as this third issue happened to be far less clear than those others on which the two authorities had, not so long since, seen eye to eye.

One source of ambiguity arose from the fact that, by Hildebrand's day, it had become established that the appointment of a clerical officer of episcopal rank required the concurrence of several different parties. It was one of the primeval rules of ecclesiastical discipline that a bishop must be elected by the clergy and people of his see and must be consecrated by a quorum of the bishops of his province. And the secular Power had never at any time—since the issue had been raised by the conversion of Constantine—attempted to usurp the ritual prerogatives of the bishops or to challenge, at any rate in theory, the electoral rights of the clergy and people. The role which the secular authority had played *de facto*—without prejudice to the question of what the situation might be *de jure*—was that of nominating candidates and of exercising a right of veto over elections. Hildebrand had himself explicitly recognized this right on more than one occasion.

Further, by the eleventh century the traditional case for the exercise of some degree of secular control over clerical appointments had been reinforced by considerations of a practical kind. For the clergy had long, and to an increasing degree, been performing secular as well as ecclesiastical duties. By the year 1075 a very large part of the civil administration of Western Christendom was in the hands of clerics who held this secular authority by feudal tenure, so that the exemption of the clergy from Lay Investiture would carry with it an abrogation of the secular Power's jurisdiction over large tracts of its own proper field and the transformation of the Church into a civil as well as an ecclesiastical *imperium in imperio*. It is idle to suggest that these civil duties could have been transferred to secular administrators. Both parties to the conflict were well aware that a secular personnel capable of taking over such duties did not exist.

The gravity of Hildebrand's action in 1075 is revealed by the dimensions of the catastrophe which was its sequel. On this issue of Investiture Hildebrand staked the whole of the moral prestige which he had won for the Papacy in the previous thirty years; and his hold upon the consciences of the *Plebs Christiana* in Henry IV's Transalpine dominions was strong enough, in conjunction with the strength of Saxon arms, to bring the Emperor to Canossa. Yet, although Canossa may have dealt the Imperial dignity a blow from which it never quite recovered, the sequel was not an end but a resumption of the struggle. Fifty years of conflict had produced a breach between the Papacy and the Empire too wide and too deep to be closed by any politic compromise on the particular issue over which the conflict had originated. The controversy over Investitures might moulder in its grave after the Concordat of 1122, but the hostility that it had engendered went marching on, finding ever fresh issues in the hardness of men's hearts and the perversity of their ambitions.

We have examined the decision of Hildebrand in 1075 at some length because we believe it to have been the crucial decision conditioning all that followed. In the intoxication of victory Hildebrand set the institution which he himself had raised from the depths of ignominy to the heights of grandeur on the wrong road, and none of his successors was able to recover the right one. We need not pursue the story farther in any detail. The pontificate of Innocent III (1198–1216) is the Antonine Age or Indian summer of the Hildebrandine Papacy, but that Pope owed his pre-eminent position to accidental circumstances, such as the long minority in the Hohenstaufen line, and his career merely illustrates the fact that a superb administrator may be a purblind statesman. There followed the Papacy's war *à outrance* against Frederick II and his offspring; the tragedy of Anagni, which was the secular arm's vulgar *riposte* to Canossa; the Captivity and the Schism; the abortive parliamentarism of the Conciliar Movement; the paganization of the Vatican during the Italian Renaissance; the disruption of the Catholic Church through the Reformation; the indecisive but ferocious struggle inaugurated by the Counter-Reformation; the spiritual nullity of the Papacy in the eighteenth century and its active anti-liberalism in the nineteenth.

But the unique institution has survived;[1] and at this hour of decision at which we now live it is meet and right that all men and women in the Western World who 'have been baptized into Christ' as 'heirs according to the promise', and with us all the Gentiles who have become 'partakers of' the 'promise' and 'fellow heirs of the same body' through the adoption of our Western way of life, should call upon the Vicar of Christ to vindicate his tremendous title. Did not Peter's Master say to Peter himself that 'unto whomsoever much is given, of him shall be much required, and to whom men have committed much, of him they will ask the more'? To the Apostle at Rome our forefathers committed the destiny of Western Christendom, which was the whole of their treasure; and when 'that servant which knew his Lord's will' 'prepared not himself nor did according to his will' and was beaten in just retribution 'with many stripes', those blows fell with equal weight upon the bodies of 'the menservants and maidens' whose souls had been entrusted to the keeping of the *Servus Servorum Dei*. The punishment for the ὕβρις of the servant has been visited upon us; and it is for him who brought us to this pass to deliver us from it, whosoever we may be: Catholics or Protestants, believers or unbelievers. If, at this crucial moment, a second Hildebrand did arise, would our deliverer this time be forearmed, by the wisdom that is born of suffering, against that fatal intoxication of victory which ruined the great work of Pope Gregory VII?

[1] A well-known Roman Catholic man of letters once remarked in private conversation (and his name can therefore not be given): 'I believe that the Catholic Church is divine, and the proof of its divinity I take to be this: that no merely human institution conducted with such knavish imbecility would have lasted a fortnight.'—EDITOR.

THE DISINTEGRATIONS OF CIVILIZATIONS

XVII. THE NATURE OF DISINTEGRATION

(1) A GENERAL SURVEY

IN passing from the breakdowns of civilizations to their disintegrations we have to face a question like that which confronted us when we passed from the geneses of civilizations to their growths. Is disintegration a new problem on its own account or can we take it for granted as a natural and inevitable sequel to breakdown? When we considered the earlier question, whether growth was a new problem, distinct from the problem of genesis, we were led to answer the question in the affirmative by discovering that there were, in fact, a number of 'arrested' civilizations which had solved the problem of genesis but had failed to solve the problem of growth. And now again, at this later stage in our Study, we can meet the analogous question with the same affirmative answer by pointing to the fact that certain civilizations, after breakdown, have suffered a similar arrest and entered on a long period of petrifaction.

The classic example of a petrified civilization is presented by a phase in the history of the Egyptiac Society which we have already had occasion to consider. After the Egyptiac Society had broken down under the intolerable burden that was imposed on it by the Pyramid-builders, and when thereafter it had passed through the first and the second into the third of the three phases of disintegration—a 'time of troubles', a universal state and an interregnum—this apparently moribund society then departed unexpectedly and abruptly, at a moment when it was apparently completing its life course, from what we may provisionally regard as the standard pattern if we take for our norm the Hellenic example in which these three phases first came under our notice. At this point the Egyptiac Society refused to pass away and proceeded to double its life-span. When we take the time-measure of the Egyptiac Society from the moment of its galvanic reaction against the Hyksos invaders in the first quarter of the sixteenth century before Christ down to the obliteration of the last traces of an Egyptiac culture in the fifth century of the Christian Era, we find that this span of two thousand years is as long as the combined span of the birth, growth, breakdown and almost complete disintegration of the Egyptiac Society, reckoning back from the date of its passionate reassertion of itself in the sixteenth century before Christ to its first emergence above the primitive level at some unknown date in the fourth millennium B.C. But the life of the Egyptiac Society during the second half of its existence was a kind of life-in-death. During those two supernumerary millennia, a civilization whose previous career had been so full of movement and of meaning lingered on inert and arrested. In fact it survived by becoming petrified.

Nor does this example stand alone. If we turn to the history of the main body of the Far Eastern Society in China, in which the moment of breakdown may be equated with the break-up of the T'ang Empire in the last quarter of the ninth century of the Christian Era, we can trace the subsequent process of disintegration following its normal course through a 'time of troubles' into a universal state, only to be pulled up in the course of this stage by a reaction of the same abrupt and passionate kind as the Egyptiac reaction to the Hyksos invaders. The Southern Chinese revolt, under the leadership of the founder of the Ming dynasty, Hung Wu, against a Far Eastern universal state which had been established by the barbarian Mongols, is strongly reminiscent of the Theban revolt, under the leadership of the founder of the Eighteenth Dynasty, Amosis, against the 'successor-state' which had been erected on part of the derelict domain of the defunct Egyptiac universal state (the so-called 'Middle Empire') by the barbarian Hyksos. And there has been a corresponding similarity in the sequel. For the Far Eastern Society has prolonged its existence in a petrified form instead of passing expeditiously through disintegration into dissolution by way of a universal state running out into an interregnum.

We may add to these two examples the various fossilized fragments of otherwise extinct civilizations which have come to our notice: the Jains in India, the Hinayanian Buddhists in Ceylon, Burma, Siam and Cambodia, and the Lamaistic Mahayanian Buddhists of Tibet and Mongolia, all of them fossilized fragments of the Indic Civilization; and the Jews, Parsees, Nestorians and Monophysites, who are fossilized fragments of the Syriac Civilization.

If we cannot extend our list farther we can at least notice that, in the judgement of Macaulay, the Hellenic Civilization came within measurable distance of a similar experience in the third and fourth centuries of the Christian Era.

'The spirit of the two most famous nations of Antiquity was remarkably exclusive. . . . The fact seems to be that the Greeks admired only themselves and that the Romans admired only themselves and the Greeks. . . . The effect was narrowness and sameness of thought. Their minds, if we may so express ourselves, bred in and in, and were accordingly cursed with barrenness and degeneracy. . . . The vast despotism of the Caesars, gradually effacing all national peculiarities and assimilating the remotest provinces of the Empire to each other, augmented the evil. At the close of the third century after Christ the prospects of mankind [*sic*] were fearfully dreary. . . . That great community was then in danger of experiencing a calamity far more terrible than any of the quick, inflammatory, destroying maladies to which nations are liable—a tottering, drivelling, paralytic longevity, the immortality of the Struldbrugs, a Chinese civilization. It would be easy to indicate many points of resemblance between the subjects of Diocletian and the people of that Celestial Empire where, during many centuries, nothing has been learned or unlearned; where government, where education, where the whole system of life, is a ceremony; where knowledge forgets to increase and multiply, and, like the talent buried in the earth or the pound wrapped up in the napkin, experiences neither waste nor augmentation. The torpor was broken by two great revolutions, the one moral, the other political, the one from within, the other from without.'[1]

This merciful release for which, on Macaulay's showing, the Hellenic Society in the Imperial Age was indebted to the Church and the barbarians, is a relatively happy ending which cannot be taken for granted. So long as life persists it is always possible that, instead of being cut off sharp by Clotho's beneficently ruthless shears, it may stiffen by imperceptible degrees into the paralysis of life-in-death; and the possibility that this may be the destiny of our Western Society has haunted the mind of at least one distinguished historian of the present generation.

'I do not think the danger before us is anarchy, but despotism, the loss of spiritual freedom, the totalitarian state, perhaps a universal world totalitarian state. As a consequence of strife between nations or classes there might be local and temporary anarchy, a passing phase. Anarchy is essentially weak, and in an anarchic world any firmly organized group with rational organization and scientific knowledge could spread its dominion over the rest. And, as an alternative to anarchy, the World would welcome the despotic state. Then the World might enter upon a period of spiritual "petrifaction", a terrible order which for the higher activities of the human spirit would be death. The petrifaction of the Roman Empire and the petrifaction of China would appear less rigid because [in our case] the ruling group would have much greater scientific means of power. (Do you know Macaulay's essay on "History"? He argues that the barbarian invasions were a blessing in the long run because they broke up the petrifaction. "It cost Europe a thou-

---

[1] Macaulay, Lord: Essay on 'History'.

sand years of barbarism to escape the fate of China." There would be no barbarian races to break up a future world totalitarian state.)

'It seems to me possible that in such a totalitarian state, while philosophy and poetry would languish, scientific research might go on with continuous fresh discoveries. Greek science did not find the Ptolemaic realm an uncongenial environment, and I think, generally speaking, natural science may flourish under a despotism. It is to the interest of the ruling group to encourage what may increase their means of power. That, not anarchy, is for me the nightmare ahead, if we do not find a way of ending our present fratricidal strife. But there *is* the Christian Church there, a factor to be reckoned with. It may have to undergo martyrdom in the future world-state, but, as it compelled the Roman world-state in the end to make at any rate formal submission to Christ, it might again, by the way of martyrdom, conquer the scientific rationalist world-state of the future.'[1]

These reflections show that the disintegrations of civilizations present a problem which demands our study.

In studying the growths of civilizations we found that they could be analysed into successions of performances of the drama of challenge-and-response and that the reason why one performance followed another was because each of the responses was not only successful in answering the particular challenge by which it had been evoked but was also instrumental in provoking a fresh challenge, which arose each time out of the new situation that the successful response had brought about. Thus the essence of the nature of the growths of civilizations proved to be an *élan* which carried the challenged party through the equilibrium of a successful response into an overbalance which declared itself in the presentation of a new challenge. This repetitiveness or recurrency of challenge is likewise implied in the concept of disintegration, but in this case the responses fail. In consequence, instead of a series of challenges each different in character from a predecessor which has been successfully met and relegated to past history, we have the same challenge presented again and again. For example, in the history of the international politics of the Hellenic World, from the time when the Solonian economic revolution first confronted the Hellenic Society with the task of establishing a political world order, we can see that the failure of the Athenian attempt to solve the problem by means of the Delian League led on to Philip of Macedon's attempt to solve it by means of the Corinthian League, and Philip's failure to Augustus's attempt to solve it by the *Pax Romana*, upheld by a Principate. This repetition of the same challenge is in the very nature of the situation. When the outcome of each successive encounter is not victory but defeat,

[1] Dr. Edwyn Bevan, in a letter to the writer.

the unanswered challenge can never be disposed of, and is bound to present itself again and again until it either receives some tardy and imperfect answer or else brings about the destruction of the society which has shown itself inveterately incapable of responding to it effectively.

Can we say, then, that the alternative to petrifaction is total and absolute extinction? Before answering in the affirmative we may remind ourselves of the process of apparentation-and-affiliation which we noticed at an early stage of this Study. The Solonian *Respice finem* and a suspension of judgement may be for the present our wisest course.

In our study of the process of the growths of civilizations we began by looking for a criterion of growth before we attempted to analyse the process, and we will follow the same plan in our study of disintegrations. One step in the argument, however, we may spare ourselves. Having decided that the criteria of growth were not to be found in an increasing command over the human or the physical environment, we may fairly assume that loss of such command is not among the causes of disintegration. Indeed, the evidence, so far as it goes, suggests that an increasing command over environments is a concomitant of disintegration rather than of growth. Militarism, a common feature of breakdown and disintegration, is frequently effective in increasing a society's command both over other living societies and over the inanimate forces of nature. In the downward course of a broken-down civilization's career there may be truth in the Ionian philosopher Heracleitus's saying that 'war is the father of all things', and, since the vulgar estimates of human prosperity are reckoned in terms of power and wealth, it thus often happens that the opening chapters of a society's tragic decline are popularly hailed as the culminating chapters of a magnificent growth. Sooner or later, however, disillusionment is bound to follow; for a society that has become incurably divided against itself is almost certain to 'put back into the business' of war the greater part of those additional resources, human and material, which the same business has incidentally brought into its hands. For instance, we see the money-power and man-power won through Alexander's conquests being poured into the civil wars of Alexander's successors, and the money-power and man-power won by the Roman conquests of the second century B.C. being poured into the civil wars of the last century B.C.

Our criterion for the process of disintegration has to be sought for elsewhere; and the clue is given to us in the spectacle of that division and discord within the bosom of a society to which an increase in its command over its environment can so often be traced back. This is only what we should expect; for we have found already that the ultimate criterion and the fundamental cause of the breakdowns which precede disintegrations is an outbreak of internal discords through which societies forfeit their faculty of self-determination.

The social schisms in which this discord partially reveals itself rend the broken-down society in two different dimensions simultaneously. There are vertical schisms between geographically segregated communities and horizontal schisms between geographically intermingled but socially segregated classes.

So far as the vertical type of schism is concerned, we have already seen how frequently a reckless indulgence in the crime of inter-state warfare has been the main line of suicidal activity. But this vertical schism is not the most characteristic manifestation of the discord by which the breakdowns of civilizations are brought about; for the articulation of a society into parochial communities is, after all, a feature which is common to the whole genus of human societies, civilized and uncivilized, and inter-state warfare is merely an abuse of a potential instrument of self-destruction which is within the reach of any society at any time. On the other hand, the horizontal schism of a society along lines of class is not only peculiar to civilizations but is also a phenomenon which appears at the moment of their breakdowns and which is a distinctive mark of the periods of breakdown and disintegration, by contrast with its absence during the phases of genesis and growth.

We have already come across this horizontal type of schism. We encountered it when we were exploring the extension of our own Western Society backwards in the time-dimension. We found ourselves led back to the Christian Church and a number of barbarian war-bands which had come into collision with the Church in Western Europe inside the northern frontiers of the Roman Empire; and we observed that each of these two institutions—the war-bands and the Church—had been created by a social group which was not, itself, an articulation of our own Western body social and which could only be described in terms of another society, antecedent to ours: the Hellenic Civilization. We described the creators of the Christian Church as the internal proletariat, and the creators of the barbarian war-bands as the external proletariat, of this Hellenic Society.

Pursuing our inquiries farther, we found that both these proletariats had arisen through acts of secession from the Hellenic Society during a 'time of troubles' in which the Hellenic Society itself was manifestly no longer creative but was already in decline;

and, pushing our inquiry yet another stage back, we further found that these secessions had been provoked by an antecedent change in the character of the ruling element in the Hellenic body social. A 'creative minority' which had once evoked a voluntary allegiance from the uncreative mass, in virtue of the gift of charm which is the privilege of creativity, had now given place to a 'dominant minority' destitute of charm because it was uncreative. This dominant minority had retained its privileged position by force, and the secessions which had ultimately resulted in the creation of the war-bands and the Christian Church had been reactions to this tyranny. Yet this defeat of its own intentions—through the disruption of a society which it was attempting, by perverse methods, to hold together—is not the only achievement of the dominant minority that came to our notice. It has also left a monument of itself in the shape of the Roman Empire; and the Empire not only took shape earlier than either the Church or the war-bands; its mighty presence in the world in which these proletarian institutions grew up was a factor in the growth of both of them which cannot be left out of account. This universal state in which the Hellenic dominant minority encased itself was like the carapace of a giant tortoise; and, while the Church was reared under its shadow, the barbarians trained their war-bands by sharpening their claws on the tortoise-shell's outer face.

Finally, at a later point in this Study, we tried to obtain a clearer view of the nexus of cause and effect between the loss of the leading minority's faculty for creation and the loss of the faculty for attracting the majority by charm rather than by force. And here we put our finger on the creative minority's expedient of social drill—as a short cut for bringing the uncreative mass into line—in which we had already found the weak spot in the relation between minority and majority in the growth stage. On this showing, the estrangement between minority and majority which eventually comes to a head in the secession of the proletariat is the consequence of the breaking of a link which, even in the growth phase, had only been maintained by playing upon the well-drilled faculty of mimesis; and it is not surprising to find that mimesis fails when the leaders' creativity gives out, considering that, even in the growth phase, this link of mimesis has always been precarious by reason of a treacherous duality—the revenge of an unwilling slave—which is part of the nature of any mechanical device.

These are the threads of inquiry into the horizontal type of schism that are already in our hands; and perhaps the most promising way of pursuing our inquiry farther will be to draw these threads together and then spin out our strand.

Our first step will be to take a closer and wider survey of the three fractions—dominant minority and internal and external proletariats—into which it appears from the Hellenic example, as also from other examples at which we have glanced at earlier points in this Study, that a broken-down society splits when a horizontal schism rends its fabric. After that we will turn, as we did in our study of growths, from the macrocosm to the microcosm, and there we shall discover a complementary aspect of disintegration in the increasing distraction of the soul. Both these lines of search will lead us to the, at first sight, paradoxical discovery that the process of disintegration works out, in part at least, to a result which is logically incompatible with its nature—works out, that is to say, to a 'recurrence of birth' or 'palingenesia'.

When we have completed our analysis we shall find that the qualitative change which disintegration brings with it is exactly opposite in character to that which is the outcome of growth. We have seen that, in the process of growth, the several growing civilizations become increasingly differentiated from one another. We shall now find that, conversely, the qualitative effect of disintegration is standardization.

This tendency towards standardization is the more remarkable when we consider the extent of the diversity which it has to overcome. The broken-down civilizations bring with them, when they enter on their disintegration, the extremely diverse dispositions— a bent towards art or towards machinery or whatever the bent may be—that they have severally acquired during their growth. And they are also further differentiated from one another by the fact that their breakdowns overtake them at widely different ages. The Syriac Civilization, for example, broke down after the death of Solomon, *circa* 937 B.C., at a date probably less than two hundred years removed from the original emergence of this civilization out of the post-Minoan interregnum. On the other hand the sister Hellenic Civilization, which emerged out of the same interregnum coevally, did not break down till five hundred years later, in the Atheno-Peloponnesian War. Again, the Orthodox Christian Civilization broke down at the outbreak of the great Romano-Bulgarian War in A.D. 977, while the sister civilization, which is our own, was unquestionably growing for several centuries longer and— for all we yet know—may not have broken down even yet. If sister civilizations can run to such different lengths of growth-span, it is manifest that the growths of civilizations are not predestined to any uniform duration; and indeed we have failed to find any reason *a priori* why a civilization should not go on growing indefinitely, once it has entered on this stage. These considerations make it plain that the differences between growing civilizations are extensive and profound. Nevertheless, we shall find that the process of disintegration tends to conform in all cases to a standard pattern—a horizontal schism splitting the society into the three fractions already mentioned, and the creation, by each of these three fractions, of a characteristic institution: universal state, universal church and barbarian war-bands.

We shall have to take note of these institutions, as well as of their respective creators, if our study of the disintegrations of civilizations is to be comprehensive. But we shall find it convenient, so far as it may prove possible, to study the institutions for their own sake in separate parts of the book;[1] for these three institutions are something more than products of the disintegration process. They may also play a part in the relations between one civilization and another; and when we examine the universal churches we shall find ourselves compelled to raise the question whether churches can really be comprehended in their entirety in the framework of the histories of the civilizations in which they make their historical appearances, or whether we have not to regard them as representatives of another species of society which is at least as distinct from the species 'civilizations' as these latter are distinct from primitive societies.

This may prove to be one of the most momentous questions that a study of history can suggest to us, but it lies near the farther end of the inquiry we have just been sketching out.

(2) SCHISM AND PALINGENESIA

The German Jew Karl Marx (1818–83) has painted, in colours borrowed from the apocalyptic visions of a repudiated religious tradition, a tremendous picture of the secession of a proletariat and the ensuing class war. The immense impression which the Marxian materialist apocalypse has made upon so many millions of minds is in part due to the political militancy of the Marxian diagram; for, while this 'blue-print' is the kernel of a general philosophy of history, it is also a revolutionary call to arms. Whether the invention and vogue of this Marxian formula of the class war are to be taken as signs that our Western Society has its feet already set upon the path of disintegration, is a question which will occupy us in a later part of this Study,[1] when we come to look into the prospects of this Western Civilization of ours. In this place we have cited Marx for other reasons: first, because he is the classic exponent of class war for our world in our age; and, second,

[1] In the volumes of Mr. Toynbee's work not yet published.—EDITOR.

because his formula conforms to the traditional Zoroastrian and Jewish and Christian apocalyptic pattern in unveiling, beyond a violent climax, the vision of a gentle finale.

According to the Communist prophet's intuition of the operations of his familiar spirit, Historical Materialism or Determinism, the class war is bound to issue in a victorious proletarian revolution; but this bloody culmination of the struggle will also be the end of it; for the victory of the proletariat will be decisive and definitive and the 'Dictatorship of the Proletariat', by which the fruits of the victory are to be harvested during the post-revolutionary period, is not to be a permanent institution. A time is to come when a new society which has been classless from birth will be old enough and strong enough to dispense with the dictatorship. Indeed, in its final and permanent acme of well-being the New Society of the Marxian Millennium will be able to cast away not only the Dictatorship of the Proletariat but also every other institutional crutch, including the state itself.

The interest of the Marxian eschatology for our present inquiry lies in the surprising fact that this lingering political shadow of a vanished religious belief does accurately plot out the actual course which the class war or horizontal schism in a broken-down society is apt to follow as a matter of historical fact. History duly reveals to us in the phenomena of disintegration a movement that runs through war to peace; through Yang to Yin; and through an apparently wanton and savage destruction of precious things to fresh works of creation that seem to owe their special quality to the devouring glow of the flame in which they have been forged.

The schism itself is the product of two negative movements, each of which is inspired by an evil passion. First, the dominant minority attempts to hold by force the privileged position which it has ceased to merit. Then the proletariat repays injustice with resentment, fear with hate, violence with violence. Yet the whole movement ends in positive acts of creation: the universal state, the universal church and the barbarian war-bands.

Thus the social schism is not just a schism and nothing more. When we grasp the movement as a whole we find that we have to describe it as schism-and-palingenesia. And, considering that secession is manifestly a particular manner of withdrawal, we may classify the double movement of schism-and-palingenesia as one instance of the phenomenon we have already studied in a more general aspect under the heading of 'withdrawal-and-return'.

There is one respect in which this new variety of withdrawal-and-return might seem at first sight to differ from the examples we have previously studied. Were not they the achievements of creative minorities or individuals, and is not the seceding proletariat a majority, as opposed to a dominant minority? A moment's thought, however, suggests—what is obviously the true picture—that, though the secession is the work of a majority, the creative act of establishing a universal church is the work of a minority of creative individuals or groups within the proletarian majority. The uncreative majority in such a case consists of the dominant minority and of the rest of the proletariat. We found, also, it will be remembered, that in the growth stage the creative achievements of what we called the creative minority were never the work of the whole minority *en masse* but always that of one group or another within it. The difference between the two cases is that whereas, during growth, the uncreative majority consists of an impressionable rank and file which follows, by mimesis, in the track of the leaders, during disintegration the uncreative majority consists in part of an impressionable rank and file (the rest of the proletariat) and in part of a dominant minority which, apart from the responses of aberrant individuals, stands stiffly and proudly aloof.

XVIII. SCHISM IN THE BODY SOCIAL

(1) DOMINANT MINORITIES

NOTWITHSTANDING the fact that a certain fixity and uniformity of ethos is its characteristic mark, there cannot but be an element of variety even within a dominant minority. Though it may perform prodigies of sterilization in converting to its own barren *esprit de corps* the recruits whom it is continually drafting into its repeatedly self-decimated ranks, it cannot prevent itself from putting forth the creative powers that are revealed in the creation not only of a universal state but also of a school of philosophy. Accordingly we find that it is apt to include a number of members who depart very strikingly from the characteristic types of the closed corporation to which they belong.

These characteristic types are the militarist and the more ignoble exploiter who follows in his train. It is hardly necessary to cite examples from Hellenic history. We see the militarist at his best in an Alexander and the exploiter at his worst in a Verres, whose misgovernment of Sicily is exposed in the voluminous orations, or pamphlets, of Cicero. But the Roman universal state owed its long duration to the fact that its militarists and exploiters were followed, after the Augustan settlement, by the innumerable and mostly anonymous soldiers and civil servants who partly atoned for the misdeeds of their predatory predecessors by making it possible for this moribund society to bask for many generations in the pale sunshine of an 'Indian summer'.

Moreover the Roman public servant is neither the only nor the earliest epiphany of the Hellenic dominant minority in an altruistic role. In the age of the Severi, when the reign of the Stoic Emperor Marcus Aurelius was an accomplished fact of Roman history, and when a school of Stoic jurists was translating the Stoic ethos into terms of Roman law, it was obvious that the miracle of transforming the Roman wolf into a Platonic watch-dog had been the work of Greek philosophy. If the Roman administrator was an altruistic agent of the Hellenic dominant minority's practical ability, the Greek philosopher was a still nobler exponent of its intellectual power; and the golden chain of creative Greek philosophers, which ends with Plotinus (*circa* A.D. 203–62) in the generation that lived to see the Roman public service collapse, had begun with Socrates (*circa* 470–399 B.C.) in a generation that was already grown up when the Hellenic Civilization broke down.

To retrieve, or at any rate to mitigate, the tragic consequence of that breakdown was the Greek philosopher's, as well as the Roman administrator's, life-work; and the philosopher's labours produced a more valuable and durable result than the administrator's, just because they were less closely woven into the material texture of the disintegrating society's life. While the Roman administrators built the Hellenic universal state the philosophers endowed posterity with a κτῆμα εἰς ἀεί in the Academy and the Peripatus, the Stoa and the Garden, the Cynic's freedom of the highways and hedges and the Neoplatonist's unearthly Land of Heart's Desire.

If we extend our survey to the histories of the other broken-down civilizations we shall find the same noble streaks of altruism running side by side with the grim and sordid trails of the militarists and the exploiters. For example, the Confucian litterati who administered the Sinic universal state under the Han dynasty (202 B.C.–A.D. 221) attained a standard of service and acquired an *esprit de corps* which place them on a moral level with the Roman civil servants who were their contemporaries on the other side of the world during the latter half of their period of activity. Even the chinovniks who administered the Orthodox Christian universal state in Russia for two centuries from the reign of Peter the Great onwards, and who became a byword, at home as well as in the West, for their incompetence and corruption, did not acquit themselves so discreditably as is often supposed in wrestling with their gigantic dual task of maintaining the Muscovite Empire as a going concern and at the same time transforming it into a new-fangled polity on the Western pattern. In the main body of Orthodox Christendom the slave-household of the Ottoman Pādishāh, which has likewise become a byword for its oppression of the raʿīyeh, will also perhaps come to be remembered as an institution which performed at least one signal service for the Orthodox Society in imposing upon it that *Pax Ottomanica* which gave a self-tormented world a spell of quiet between two weary ages of anarchy. In the Far Eastern Society in Japan the feudal daimyos and their henchmen the Samurai, who preyed upon society, in preying upon one another, during the four centuries preceding the establishment of the Tokugawa Shogunate, survived to redeem their own past by lending themselves to Ieyasu's constructive work of converting a feudal anarchy into a feudal order; and at the opening of the next chapter of Japanese history they rose to a height of self-abnegation which is almost sublime, when they voluntarily divested themselves of their privileges because they were convinced that this sacrifice was required of them in order to enable Japan to hold her own in the environment of a Westernized World from which she could no longer hold aloof.

This vein of nobility which reveals itself in the Japanese Samurai is the virtue attributed even by their enemies to two other ruling minorities, the Incas of the Andean universal state and the Persian grandees who governed a Syriac universal state as vice-gerents of an Achaemenid King of Kings. The Spanish Conquistadores vouch for the virtues of the Incas. In the Greek portrait of the Persians, Herodotus's famous summary of the Persian boys' education— 'they train them from the age of five to the age of twenty to do three things, and three things only: to ride and to shoot and to speak the truth'—is not discredited by the companion picture that is presented to us of these same Persians in their manhood. There is the Herodotean tale of Xerxes' suite in the storm at sea doing obeisance to their Imperial Master and then leaping overboard in order to lighten the vessel. But the most impressive Greek testimonial to Persian virtues is that of Alexander the Great, who showed by grave acts, and not just by easy words, how highly he thought of the Persians after he had made their acquaintance. He had no sooner come to know these Persians by the searching test of their reaction to an overwhelming disaster than he took a decision that was not only bound to offend his own Macedonians but was the surest way of outraging their feelings that he could have hit upon if it had been his deliberate aim. He decided to take the Persians into partnership in the government of the empire which the prowess of his Macedonians had just wrested from them; and he put this policy into execution with characteristic thoroughness. He took a Persian grandee's daughter to wife; he bribed or browbeat his Macedonian officers into following his example; and he drafted Persian recruits into his Macedonian regiments. A people who could evoke this extraordinary tribute from the leader of their hereditary enemies—and this on the morrow of their utter defeat—must have been transparently endowed with the classic virtues of 'a ruling race'.

We have now managed to marshal a considerable array of evidence for the capacity of dominant minorities to produce an admirable governing class, and the evidence is borne out by the number of the universal states that they have created. Out of twenty civilizations that have broken down, no less than fifteen have passed through this stage on their road to dissolution. We can identify a Hellenic universal state in the Roman Empire; an Andean in the Empire of the Incas; a Sinic in the Empire of the Ts'in and Han dynasties; a Minoan in 'the thalassocracy of Minos'; a Sumeric in the Empire of Sumer and Akkad; a Babylonic in the

Neo-Babylonian Empire of Nebuchadnezzar; a Mayan in the 'Old Empire' of the Mayas; an Egyptiac in the 'Middle Empire' of the eleventh and twelfth dynasties; a Syriac in the Achaemenian Empire; an Indic in the Empire of the Mauryas; a Hindu in the Empire of the Great Moguls; a Russian Orthodox in the Muscovite Empire; a universal state of the main body of Orthodox Christendom in the Ottoman Empire; and in the Far Eastern World the Mongol Empire in China and the Tokugawa Shogunate in Japan.

Nor is this political capacity the only kind of creative power that is a common attribute of dominant minorities. We have already seen that the Hellenic dominant minority produced not only Roman administration but also Greek philosophy, and we can find at least three other cases in which a philosophy has been thought out by a dominant minority.

In the history of the Babylonic Society, for example, the terrible eighth century B.C., which saw the beginning of the hundred years' war between Babylonia and Assyria, seems also to have seen a sudden great advance in astronomical knowledge. In this age Babylonic men of science discovered that the rhythm of cyclic recurrence, which had been patent from time immemorial in the alternations of day and night, in the waxing and waning of the Moon, and in the solar cycle of the year, was also discernible on a vaster scale in the motions of the planets. These stars, which were traditionally named 'the wanderers' in allusion to their apparently erratic courses, now proved to be bound by as strict a discipline as the Sun and the Moon and the 'fixed' stars of the firmament in the cosmic cycle of the *magnus annus*; and this exciting Babylonic discovery had much the same effect as our recent Western scientific discoveries have had upon the discoverers' conception of the Universe.

The never broken and never varying order that had thus been found to reign in all the known movements of the stellar cosmos was now assumed to govern the Universe as a whole: material and spiritual, inanimate and animate. If an eclipse of the Sun or a transit of Venus could be dated to some precise moment hundreds of years back in the past, or predicted with equal certainty as bound to occur at some precise moment in the equally remote future, then was it not reasonable to assume that human affairs were just as rigidly fixed and just as accurately calculable? And since the cosmic discipline implied that all these members of the Universe that moved in so perfect a unison were 'in sympathy'— *en rapport*—with each other, was it unreasonable to assume that the newly revealed pattern of the movements of the stars was a key to the riddle of human fortunes, so that the observer who held this astronomical clue in his hands would be able to forecast his neighbour's destinies if once he knew the date and moment of his birth? Reasonable or not, these assumptions were eagerly made; and thus a sensational scientific discovery gave birth to a fallacious philosophy of determinism which has captivated the imagination of one society after another and is not quite discredited yet after a run of nearly 2,700 years.

The seductiveness of astrology lies in its pretension to combine a theory which explains the whole *machina mundi* with a practice which will enable Tom, Dick and Harry to spot the Derby winner here and now. Thanks to this twofold attraction, the Babylonic philosophy was able to survive the extinction of the Babylonic Society in the last century before Christ; and the Chaldean *mathematicus* who imposed it upon a prostrate Hellenic Society was represented until yesterday by the Court Astrologer at Peking and the Munejjim Bāshȳ at Istanbol.

We have dwelt on this Babylonic philosophy of determinism because it has a greater affinity than any of the Hellenic philosophies have with the still perhaps rather callow philosophical speculations of our own Western World in its present Cartesian Age. On the other hand, there are counterparts of almost all the Hellenic schools of thought in the philosophies of the Indic and Sinic worlds. The dominant minority of the disintegrating Indic Civilization brought forth the Jainism of the followers of Mahavira, the Primitive Buddhism of the earlier followers of Siddhartha Gautama, the transfigured Buddhism of the Mahāyāna (which differs from its acknowledged original at least as profoundly as Neoplatonism differs from the philosophy of the Socratics of the fourth century B.C.) and the diverse Buddhistic philosophies that are part of the mental apparatus of a post-Buddhaic Hinduism. The dominant minority of a disintegrating Sinic Civilization brought forth the moralized ritualism and ritualized morality of Confucius and the paradoxical wisdom of the Tao which is ascribed to the legendary genius of Lao-tse.

(2) INTERNAL PROLETARIATS

A Hellenic Prototype

When we pass from dominant minorities to proletariats, a closer examination of the facts will confirm here too our first impression that within each of these fractions of a disintegrating society there is a diversity of type. We shall also find that, in the range of this spiritual diversity, the internal and the external proletariats are at opposite poles. While the external proletariats have a gamut

which is narrower than that of the dominant minorities, the gamut
of the internal proletariats is very much wider. Let us reconnoitre
the wider field first.

If we wish to follow the genesis of the Hellenic internal proletariat from the beginning of the embryo stage, we cannot do better
than quote a passage from Thucydides in which the historian of
the breakdown of the Hellenic Society describes the consequent
social schism in its earliest phase, as it showed itself first at Corcyra.

'Such was the savagery of the class-war (*stasis*) at Corcyra as it
developed, and it made the deeper impression through being the first
of its kind—though eventually the upheaval spread through almost the
whole of the Hellenic World. In every country there were struggles
between the leaders of the proletariat and the reactionaries in their
efforts to procure the intervention of the Athenians and the Lacedae-
monians respectively. In peace-time they would have had neither the
opportunity nor the desire to call in the foreigner; but now there was
the war; and it was easy for any revolutionary spirits in either camp to
procure an alliance entailing the discomfiture of their opponents and a
corresponding reinforcement of their own faction. This access of class-
war brought one calamity after another upon the countries of Hellas—
calamities that occur and will continue to occur so long as human
nature remains what it is, though they may be aggravated or mitigated
or modified by successive changes of circumstance. Under the favourable conditions of peace-time both countries and individuals display a
sweeter reasonableness, because their hands are not forced by the logic
of events; but war eats away the margins of ordinary life and, in most
characters, adjusts the temperament to the new environment by its
brutal training. So the countries of Hellas became infected with the
class-war, and the sensation made by each successive outbreak had a
cumulative effect upon the next.'[1]

The first social effect of this state of affairs was to produce a
large and ever larger floating population of 'stateless' exiles.
During the growth period of Hellenic history such a plight had
been uncommon and was regarded as a dreadful abnormality.
The evil was not overcome by Alexander's great-hearted effort
to induce the reigning faction of the moment in each city-state to
allow its ejected opponents to return to their homes in peace; and
the fire made fresh fuel for itself; for the one thing that the exiles
found for their hands to do was to enlist as mercenary soldiers;
and this glut of military man-power put fresh drive into the wars
by which new exiles—and thereby more mercenaries—were being
created.

The effect of these direct moral ravages of the war spirit in
Hellas in uprooting her children was powerfully reinforced by the

[1] Thucydides: Bk. III, ch. 82.

operation of disruptive economic forces which the wars let loose. For example, the wars of Alexander and his successors in South-Western Asia gave military employment to one swarm of homeless Greeks at the cost of uprooting another. For the mercenaries were paid by putting into circulation the bullion which had been accumulating for two centuries in the Achaemenian treasuries; and this sudden increase in the volume of currency worked havoc among the peasants and artisans. Prices soared, and the financial revolution reduced to pauperism an element in the body social which had hitherto enjoyed a relative security. The same effect of pauperization was produced again, a hundred years later, by the economic consequences of the Hannibalic War, when the peasantry were uprooted from the soil of Italy, first by the direct devastation wrought by Hannibal's soldiery and then by the ever longer terms of Roman military service. Under this tribulation the pauperized descendants of an Italian peasantry that had been uprooted against its will had no recourse left except to make a profession out of the military career that had been imposed on their ancestors as a *corvée*.

In this cruel process of 'deracination' we cannot doubt that we are watching the genesis of the Hellenic internal proletariat—and this notwithstanding the fact that, at any rate in the earlier generations, the victims of the process were *ci-devant* aristocrats as often as not. For proletarianism is a state of feeling rather than a matter of outward circumstance. When we first made use of the term 'proletariat' we defined it, for our purpose, as a social element or group which in some way is 'in' but not 'of' any given society at any given stage of that society's history; and this definition covers the exiled Spartiate Clearchus and the other aristocratic captains of Cyrus the Younger's Greek mercenary force, whose antecedents Xenophon has sketched for us, as well as the meanest unemployed labourers who enlisted as mercenaries under the standard of a Ptolemy or a Marius. The true hall-mark of the proletarian is neither poverty nor humble birth but a consciousness—and the resentment that this consciousness inspires—of being disinherited from his ancestral place in society.

Thus the Hellenic internal proletariat was recruited first of all from the free citizens, and even from the aristocrats, of the disintegrating Hellenic bodies politic; and these first recruits had been disinherited in the first instance by being robbed of a spiritual birthright; but of course their spiritual impoverishment was often accompanied, and was almost always followed, by pauperization on the material plane, and they were soon reinforced by recruits from other classes who were material as well as spiritual proletarians from the start. The numbers of the Hellenic internal proletariat were vastly swollen by the Macedonian wars of conquest which swept the whole of the Syriac, Egyptiac and Babylonic societies into the Hellenic dominant minority's net, while the later conquests of the Romans swept in half the barbarians of Europe and North Africa.

These involuntary alien reinforcements of the Hellenic internal proletariat were perhaps at first more fortunate than their fellow proletarians of native Hellenic origin in one respect. Though they were morally disinherited and materially despoiled, they were not yet physically uprooted. But the slave-trade followed in the wake of the conqueror, and the last two centuries B.C. saw all the populations within range of the Mediterranean coast—both Western barbarians and cultivated Orientals—being laid under contribution in order to supply the demands of an insatiable Italian slave-labour market.

We now see that the internal proletariat of the disintegrating Hellenic Society was composed of three distinct elements: disinherited and uprooted members of the society's own body social; partially disinherited members of alien civilizations and primitive societies that had been conquered and exploited without being torn up by the roots; and doubly disinherited conscripts from these subject populations who were not only uprooted but were also enslaved and deported in order to be worked to death on distant plantations. The sufferings of these three sets of victims were as various as their origins were diverse, but these differences were transcended by their overwhelming common experience of being robbed of their social inheritance and being turned into exploited outcastes.

When we come to examine how these victims of injustice reacted to their fate, we shall not be surprised to find that one of their reactions was an explosion of savagery which surpassed in violence the cold-blooded cruelty of their oppressors and exploiters. A uniform note of passion rings through a pandemonium of desperate proletarian outbreaks. We catch this note in a series of Egyptiac insurrections against the Ptolemaic régime of exploitation; in the series of Jewish insurrections against a Seleucid and a Roman policy of Hellenization, from the rising of Judas Maccabaeus in 166 B.C. down to the last forlorn hope under the leadership of Bar Kōkabā in A.D. 132–5; in the reckless fury which moved the semi-Hellenized and highly sophisticated natives of Western Asia Minor to expose themselves twice over to Roman vengeance—under the Attalid Aristonicus in 132 B.C. and under Mithradates, King of Pontus, in 88 B.C. There is also the series of slave insurrections in Sicily and Southern Italy, culminating in the desperate exploit of the runaway Thracian gladiator Spartacus, who ranged up and down the length of the Italian Peninsula, defying the Roman wolf in his very lair, from 73 to 71 B.C.

Nor were these outbursts of exasperation confined to the alien elements in the proletariat. The savagery with which the Roman citizen-proletariat turned and rent the Roman plutocracy in the civil wars, and particularly in the paroxysm of 91–82 B.C., was quite equal to the savagery of a Judas Maccabaeus or a Spartacus; and the most Satanic of all the dark figures that stand out in sinister silhouette against the glare of a world in flames are the Roman revolutionary leaders who had been flung headlong, by some unusually violent turn of Fortune's wheel, out of the *Ordo Senatorius* itself: a Sertorius, a Sextus Pompeius, a Marius and a Catiline.

But suicidal violence was not the only response made by the Hellenic internal proletariat. There was another order of response altogether which found its highest expression in the Christian religion. The gentle, or non-violent, response is as genuine an expression of the will to secede as the violent response; for the gentle martyrs who are commemorated in the Second Book of Maccabees—the old scribe Eleazer and the Seven Brethren and their Mother—are the spiritual progenitors of the Pharisees, and the Pharisees are 'they who separate themselves'—a self-conferred title which would translate itself into 'secessionists' in language of Roman derivation. In the history of the Oriental internal proletariat of the Hellenic World from the second century B.C. onwards we see violence and gentleness striving for the mastery of souls until violence annihilates itself and leaves gentleness alone in the field.

The issue was raised at the outset; for the gentle way which was taken by the protomartyrs of 167 B.C. was swiftly abandoned by the impetuous Judas; and the immediate material success of this proletarian 'strong man armed'—tawdry and ephemeral though it was—so dazzled posterity that Jesus's most intimate companions were scandalized at their Master's predictions of his own fate, and were prostrated when these predictions came true. Yet a few months after the Crucifixion Gamaliel was already taking note of the executed leader's miraculously rallied disciples as men who might prove to have God on their side; and a few years later Gamaliel's own disciple Paul was preaching a crucified Christ.

This conversion of the first generation of Christians from the way of violence to the way of gentleness had to be purchased at the price of a shattering blow to their material hopes; and what was

done for Jesus's followers by the Crucifixion was done for
Orthodox Jewry by the destruction of Jerusalem in A.D. 70. A
new school of Judaism arose which renounced 'the notion that the
Kingdom of God was an external state of things which was just
upon the point of being manifested'.[1] With the signal but solitary
exception of the Book of Daniel, the apocalyptic writings in which
the Jewish way of violence had found literary expression were now
ejected from the canon of the Law and the Prophets; and the
contrary principle of abstaining from all efforts to promote the
fulfilment of God's will in This World by the work of human hands
has become so fast ingrained in the Jewish tradition that the
strictly orthodox *Agudath Israel* at this day look askance at the
Zionist movement and hold rigidly aloof from any participation
in the work of building up a Jewish 'national home' in twentieth-
century Palestine.

If this change of heart in Orthodox Jewry has enabled Jewry to
survive as a fossil, the corresponding change of heart in the companions of Jesus has opened the way to greater triumphs for the
Christian Church. To the challenge of persecution the Christian
Church responded in the gentle way of Eleazer and the Seven
Brethren, and its reward was the conversion of the Hellenic
dominant minority and afterwards of the barbarian war-bands of
the external proletariat.

The direct opponent of Christianity in the first centuries of its
growth was the primitive tribal religion of the Hellenic Society
in its latest guise: the idolatrous worship of the Hellenic universal
state in the personality of a Divus Caesar. It was the Church's
gentle but intransigent refusal to allow its members to practise this
idolatry, even in a merely formal and perfunctory way, that drew
upon it a series of official persecutions and finally compelled the
Roman Imperial Government to capitulate to a spiritual power
which it had failed to coerce. But though this primitive state-
religion of the Empire was maintained and imposed with the whole
strength of the Government's right arm, it had little hold over
human hearts. The conventional respect for it which the Roman
magistrate commanded the Christian to show by the performance
of a ritual act was the beginning and end of this state-religion.
There was nothing more in it than this for those non-Christians
who performed as a matter of course what was demanded of them
and who could not understand why the Christian insisted on sacrificing his life rather than comply with a trivial custom. The rivals
of Christianity which were powerful in themselves—through a
native power of attraction which needed no backing of political

[1] Burkitt, F. C.: *Jewish and Christian Apocalypses*, p. 12.

coercion—were neither this state-worship nor any other form of primitive religion but a number of 'higher religions' which sprang, like Christianity itself, from the Hellenic internal proletariat.

We can conjure up these rival 'higher religions' by reminding ourselves of the various sources from which the Oriental contingent of the Hellenic internal proletariat was derived. The Christian religion came from a people of Syriac antecedents. The Iranian half of the Syriac World contributed Mithraism. The worship of Isis came from the submerged northern half of the Egyptiac World. The worship of the Anatolian Great Mother Cybele may perhaps be regarded as a contribution from a Hittite Society which by this time had long been extinct on every plane of social activity except the religious—though, if we set ourselves to trace the Great Mother back to her ultimate origins, we shall find her originally at home in the Sumeric World under the name of Ishtar, before ever she established herself as Cybele at Pessinus in Anatolia or as the Dea Syra at Hierapolis or as the Mother Earth of remote Teutonic-speaking worshippers at her grove on a Holy Island in the North Sea or the Baltic.

A Minoan Lacuna and some Hittite Vestiges

When we seek for the histories of internal proletariats in other disintegrating societies we have to confess that in some cases evidence is scanty or altogether fails us. We know, for example, nothing about the internal proletariat of the Mayan Society. In the case of the Minoan Society our attention has already been caught by the tantalizing glimmer of a possibility that the vestiges of something which might be called a Minoan universal church may be preserved among the heterogeneous constituents of the historic Orphic Church which makes its appearance in Hellenic history from the sixth century before Christ onwards. We cannot, however, be certain that any of the practices and beliefs of Orphism derive from a Minoan religion. We know next to nothing, again, about the internal proletariat of the Hittite Civilization, which perished at an unusually tender age. We can only say that the wreckage of the Hittite Society seems gradually to have been assimilated in part by the Hellenic and in part by the Syriac Society, so that we should have to search the histories of these two alien societies for any vestiges of the Hittite body social.

The Hittite Society is one of the many disintegrating societies that have been devoured by a neighbour before the process of disintegration has been completed. In such cases it is natural that an internal proletariat should regard with indifference or even with satisfaction the fate that is befalling its dominant minority.

A test case is the behaviour of the internal proletariat in the Andean universal state when the Spanish Conquistadores suddenly broke in. The *orejones* were perhaps the most benevolent dominant minority that any disintegrating society has ever produced, but their benevolence availed them nothing in their day of trial. Their carefully tended human flocks and herds accepted Spanish conquest with the same unresponsive docility as they had shown in accepting the *Pax Incaica*.

We can also point to cases where an internal proletariat has greeted the conqueror of its dominant minority with positive enthusiasm. There is the welcome expressed in the eloquent apostrophes of 'Deutero-Isaiah' to the Persian conqueror of the Neo-Babylonian Empire which had taken the Jews into captivity. Two hundred years later the Babylonians themselves welcomed the Hellenic Alexander as their deliverer from the Achaemenian yoke.

The Japanese Internal Proletariat

Some clear tokens of the secession of a Japanese internal proletariat can be discerned in the history of the Far Eastern Society in Japan, which had run through its time of troubles and entered into its universal state before the Western Society swallowed it up. If we are looking, for example, for the counterparts of those citizens of the Hellenic city-states who were uprooted by the series of wars and revolutions which began in 431 B.C. and who found a disastrous outlet as mercenary soldiers, we shall observe an exact parallel in the *ronin*, or masterless unemployed men-at-arms, who were thrown off during the Japanese time of troubles by the feudal anarchy. Again, the *eta* or pariahs who survive as outcastes in the Japanese Society of to-day may be accounted for as a still unassimilated remnant of the Ainu barbarians of the Main Island who were forcibly incorporated into the Japanese internal proletariat as the barbarians of Europe and North Africa were incorporated by Roman arms into the Hellenic internal proletariat. In the third place we can discern the Japanese equivalent of those 'higher religions' in which the Hellenic internal proletariat sought and found its most effective response to the tribulations that it had to endure.

These religions were the Jōdo, the Jōdo Shinshu, the Hokke and the Zen, all of them founded within the century following the year A.D. 1175. These religions resemble their Hellenic equivalents in being all of them of alien inspiration, for all four of them are variations on the theme of the Mahāyāna. Three out of the four resemble Christianity to this extent that they taught the spiritual equality of the sexes. In addressing themselves to an unsophisticated public the apostles of these religions discarded Classical Chinese and wrote, when they did write, in the Japanese vernacular with a comparatively simple script. Their chief weakness as founders of religions was that, in their desire to bring salvation to as large a public as possible, they pitched their demands altogether too low. Some prescribed mere recitals of ritual formulae and others made little or no moral demand on their disciples. But it is to be remembered that the cardinal Christian doctrine of the Forgiveness of Sins has in various times and places been so misused and misunderstood by *soi-disant* Christian leaders as to expose them to either one or both of these charges. Luther, for example, attacked the sale of indulgences as practised by the Roman Church in his day as being the substitution of a commercial transaction, disguised under ritual forms, for Christian repentance, while at the same time, with his own interpretation of the Pauline Justification by Faith and his *Pecca fortiter*, he laid himself open to the charge of treating morality as a matter of indifference.

Internal Proletariats under Alien Universal States

A curious spectacle is offered by one group of disintegrating civilizations in which, after the indigenous dominant minority has been annihilated or overthrown, the course of outward events has still proceeded on normal lines. Three societies—the Hindu, the Far Eastern in China and the Orthodox Christian in the Near East—which have all duly passed through a universal state on the road from breakdown to dissolution, have each received this universal state as a gift, or imposition, from alien hands instead of constructing it for themselves. Iranic hands have supplied one universal state to the main body of Orthodox Christendom in the shape of the Ottoman Empire and another to the Hindu World in the Timurid (Mughal) Empire. British hands have since reconstructed this jerry-built Mughal Raj from the foundations. In China it has been the Mongols that have played the Ottoman or Mughal part, while the work of reconstruction on a firmer basis, which the British have undertaken in India, has been played in China by the Manchus.

When a disintegrating society is thus compelled to admit some alien architect to furnish it with its universal state, it is confessing that its own indigenous dominant minority has become totally incompetent and sterile; and the inevitable penalty for this premature senility is a humiliating disfranchisement. The alien who comes to do a dominant minority's work very naturally arrogates to himself a dominant minority's prerogative; and in an alien-built universal state the whole of the indigenous dominant minority is thus degraded to the ranks of the internal proletariat. The Mongol or Manchu Khāqān and the Ottoman Pādishāh and the Mughal or British Qaysar-i-Hind may still find it convenient to employ the services of the Chinese litteratus or the Greek Phanariot or the Hindu Brahman as the case may be; but that does not disguise from these agents the fact that they have lost their souls as well as their status. It is evident that in a situation like this, where the *ci-devant* dominant minority has become confounded in a common abasement with an internal proletariat upon which it has once looked down with disdain, we are unlikely to find the process of disintegration working itself out on normal lines.

In the internal proletariat of the Hindu Society in our own generation we can discern the twofold proletarian reaction of violence and gentleness in a contrast between the murders committed by a militant school of Bengali revolutionaries and the non-violence preached by the Gujerati Mahatma Gandhi; and we can infer a longer past history of proletarian fermentation from the presence of a number of religious movements in which the same two contrary tendencies are likewise represented. In Sikhism we see a warlike proletarian syncretism of Hinduism and Islam; in the Brahmō-Samāj a non-violent syncretism of Hinduism and Liberal Protestant Christianity.

In the internal proletariat of the Far Eastern Society in China under the Manchu régime we can see in the T'aip'ing movement, which dominated the social stage in the middle of the nineteenth century of the Christian Era, a work of the internal proletariat which is analogous to the Brahmō-Samāj in its debt to Protestant Christianity but to Sikhism in its militancy.

In the internal proletariat of the main body of Orthodox Christendom the 'Zealot' revolution at Salonica in the fifth decade of the fourteenth century of the Christian Era gives us a glimpse of a violent proletarian reaction at the darkest hour of the Orthodox Christian time of troubles—in the last generation before the Orthodox Christian Society was dragooned into a universal state by the drastic discipline of an Ottoman conqueror. The corresponding gentle reaction did not advance very far, but if, at the turn of the eighteenth and nineteenth centuries, the process of Westernization had not followed so hard on the heels of the break-up of the Ottoman Empire, we may conjecture that by the present day the Bektāshī movement might have won for itself throughout the Near East the position which it has actually succeeded in attaining in Albania.

The Babylonic and Syriac Internal Proletariats

If we now pass to the Babylonic World, we shall find that the ferment of religious experience and discovery in the souls of a sorely tried internal proletariat was as active in South-Western Asia under the Assyrian terror of the eighth and seventh centuries before Christ as it was on the Hellenized shores of the Mediterranean under the Roman terror some six centuries later.

Through the agency of Assyrian arms the disintegrating Babylonic Society expanded geographically in two directions, as the disintegrating Hellenic Society expanded through the conquests made by the Macedonians and the Romans. Eastwards, beyond the Zagros, in Iran, the Assyrians anticipated the Roman exploits in Europe beyond the Appennines by subjugating a host of primitive societies; westwards, beyond the Euphrates, they anticipated the Macedonians' exploits on the Asiatic side of the Dardanelles by subjugating two alien civilizations; and these, the Syriac and the Egyptiac, were actually identical with two of the four which were afterwards incorporated into the Hellenic internal proletariat after Alexander's campaigns. Nor were these alien victims of Babylonic militarism conquered without being uprooted. The classic examples of the deportation of a conquered population are the transplantation of the Israelites—the 'Lost Ten Tribes'—by the Assyrian war-lord Sargon and the transplantation of the Jews by the Neo-Babylonian war-lord Nebuchadnezzar to the heart of the Babylonic World in Babylonia itself.

The compulsory exchange of populations was the sovereign device of Babylonic imperialism for breaking the spirit of conquered peoples, and the atrocity was by no means exclusively inflicted on aliens and barbarians. In their own fratricidal warfare the dominant powers of the Babylonic World did not scruple to mete out the same treatment to one another, and the Samaritan community—of which a few hundred representatives can be seen still living under the shadow of Mount Gerizim—is a monument of the transplantation to Syria, by Assyrian hands, of deportees from several cities of Babylonia, including Babylon itself.

It will be seen that the *furor Assyriacus* did not spend itself before it had brought into existence a Babylonic internal proletariat which bore a singularly close resemblance to the Hellenic internal proletariat in its origin and composition and experience; and the two trees brought forth similar fruits. While the later incorporation of the Syriac Society into the Hellenic internal proletariat was to bear fruit in the birth of Christianity out of Judaism, the earlier incorporation of the same Syriac Society into the Babylonic internal proletariat bore fruit in the birth of Judaism itself out of the primitive religion of one of the parochial communities into which the Syriac Society had come to be articulated.

It will be seen that while Judaism and Christianity appear to be 'philosophically contemporary and equivalent' in so far as they can be regarded simply as products of similar stages in the histories of two alien societies, there is another angle of vision from which they present themselves as successive stages in a single process of spiritual enlightenment. In this latter picture Christianity stands not side by side with Judaism but on its shoulders, while they both tower above the primitive religion of Israel. Nor is the enlightenment of the Prophets of Israel and Judah in and after the eighth century before Christ the only intervening stage of which we have a record or a hint in the chronological and spiritual interval between Christianity and the primitive worship of Yahweh. Before and below the Prophets the Biblical tradition presents the figure of Moses, and before his figure the figure of Abraham. Whatever view we may take of the historical authenticity of these dim figures, it is to be observed that tradition places both Abraham and Moses in the same historical setting as the Prophets and as Christ. For the appearance of Moses is synchronized with the decadence of the 'New Empire' in Egypt and the appearance of Abraham with the last days of the Sumeric universal state, after its short-lived reconstruction by Hammurabi. Thus all four stages, as represented by Abraham, Moses, the Prophets and Jesus, illustrate the relationship between disintegrations of civilizations and new initiatives in religion.

The genesis of the higher religion of Judaism has left an incomparably full and clear record of itself in the books of the pre-exilic Prophets of Israel and Judah; and in these living records of a tremendous spiritual travail we see at issue the burning question that we have encountered elsewhere: the choice between the violent and the gentle way of facing the ordeal. Moreover gentleness gradually prevailed over violence in this case also; for the time of troubles, as it reached and passed its climax, delivered a series of hammer-blows which taught even the Die-hards of Judah the futility of replying to violence in kind. The new 'higher religion' which was born in eighth-century Syria, in Syriac communities pounded on their native threshing-floor by an Assyrian flail, was brought to maturity in sixth-century and fifth-century Babylonia among the uprooted and deported descendants of one of these battered peoples.

Like the Oriental slave deportees in Roman Italy, the Jewish exiles in Nebuchadnezzar's Babylonia were proof against any facile adaptability to the ethos of their conquerors:

'If I forget thee, O Jerusalem, let my right hand forget her cunning.
'If I do not remember thee, let my tongue cleave to the roof of my-mouth.'[1]

Yet the memory of their home which these exiles cherished in a strange land was not just a negative imprint: it was a positive act of inspired imaginative creation. In the unearthly light of this vision seen through a mist of tears the fallen fastness became transfigured into a holy city built upon a rock against which the gates of Hell should not prevail. And the captives who refused to indulge their captors' whim by singing them one of the songs of Sion, and stubbornly hanged their harps upon the willows by Euphrates' stream, were at that very moment composing an inaudible new melody on the invisible instrument of their hearts:

'By the waters of Babylon we sat down and wept when we remembered thee, O Sion';[2]

and in that weeping the enlightenment of Jewry was accomplished.

It is evident that, in the successive religious reactions of the Syriac conscripts in the ranks of an alien internal proletariat, the parallel between Babylonic and Hellenic history is very close; but the response evoked by the Babylonic challenge came not only from those victims who were members of an alien civilization but from the barbarian victims as well. Whereas the European and North African barbarians who were conquered by Roman arms made no religious discoveries of their own but simply accepted the seed sown among them by their fellow proletarians of Oriental origin, the Iranian barbarians who were passed under the Assyrian harrow begot a native prophet in the person of Zarathustra, the founder of Zoroastrianism. The date of Zarathustra is a matter of dispute and we cannot say for certain whether his religious discovery was an independent response to the Assyrian challenge or whether his voice was a mere echo of the cry of forgotten Israelite prophets who had been marooned in 'the cities of the Medes'. It is evident, however, that, whatever the original relations between these two 'higher religions' may have been, Zoroastrianism and Judaism met on equal terms in their maturity.

At any rate, when the Babylonic time of troubles was brought to an end by the overthrow of Assyria, and the Babylonic World passed into a universal state in the shape of the Neo-Babylonian Empire, it looked as though Judaism and Zoroastrianism would compete for the privilege of establishing a universal church within

---

[1] Ps. cxxxvii. 5–6. [2] Ps. cxxxvii. 1.

this political framework, much as Christianity and Mithraism competed for the same privilege within the framework of the Roman Empire.

This, however, was not to be, for the very sufficient reason that the Neo-Babylonian universal state proved to be ephemeral compared with its Roman equivalent. Nebuchadnezzar, the Babylonian Augustus, was not followed, at intervals of centuries, by a Trajan, a Severus and a Constantine. His immediate successors, Nabonidus and Belshazzar, are comparable rather with a Julian and a Valens. Within less than a century the Neo-Babylonian Empire was 'given to the Medes and Persians' and this Achaemenian Empire was politically Iranian and culturally Syriac in character. Thus the roles of dominant minority and internal proletariat were reversed.

In these circumstances the triumph of Judaism and Zoroastrianism might have been expected to be more sure and swift; but two hundred years later Fortune again intervened to give another unexpected turn to the course of events. She now delivered the Kingdom of the Medes and Persians into the hands of a Macedonian conqueror. A violent intrusion of the Hellenic Society upon the Syriac World broke the Syriac universal state in pieces long before its role was played out; and therewith the two higher religions which (as our somewhat scanty evidence suggests) had been spreading peacefully under the Achaemenian aegis were driven into the disastrous aberration of exchanging their proper religious function for a political role. Each on its own ground, they became champions of the Syriac Civilization in its struggle against an intrusive Hellenism. Judaism, in its advanced western position within sight of the Mediterranean, was inevitably cast for the forlorn hope, and it duly broke itself against the material power of Rome in the Romano-Jewish wars of A.D. 66–70, 115–17 and 132–5. Zoroastrianism, in its fastness east of Zagros, took up the struggle in the third century of the Christian Era under less desperately unequal conditions. In the Sasanian Monarchy it found a more potent weapon for an anti-Hellenic crusade than Judaism had been able to forge out of the petty principality of the Maccabees, and the Sasanidae gradually wore down the strength of the Roman Empire in a four hundred years' struggle which culminated in the internecine Romano-Persian wars of A.D. 572–91 and 603–28. Even so the Sasanian Power proved unequal to completing the task of evicting Hellenism from Asia and Africa, while Zoroastrianism had in the end to pay as heavily as Jewry for having lent itself to a political enterprise. At the present day the Parsees, like the Jews, survive as a mere 'diaspora'; and the petrified religions which still so potently hold the scattered members of the two communities together have lost their message to mankind, and have hardened into fossils of the extinct Syriac Society.

The impact of an alien cultural force did not merely divert these 'higher religions' into political paths; it also split them into fragments. After the transformation of Judaism and Zoroastrianism into instruments of political opposition, the Syriac religious genius took refuge among those elements in the Syriac population which were reacting to the Hellenic challenge in a gentle and not in a violent way; and, in giving birth to Christianity and Mithraism as its contributions to the spiritual travail of a Hellenic internal proletariat, Syriac religion found new expressions for the spirit and outlook which Judaism and Zoroastrianism had repudiated. Christianity in its turn, after having captivated, through the power of gentleness, the Hellenic conquerors of the Syriac World, broke up into three communions—a Catholic church which contracted an alliance with Hellenism and the two antithetical heresies of Nestorianism and Monophysitism which took over the militant political roles of Zoroastrianism and Judaism without achieving any more conclusive success in driving Hellenism off the Syriac field.

Two successive failures, however, did not reduce the militant Syriac opponents of Hellenism to apathy and despair. A third attempt followed and was crowned with success; and this final political triumph of the Syriac Society over Hellenism was achieved through the instrumentality of yet another religion of Syriac origin. At long last Islam overthrew the Roman Empire in South-Western Asia and North Africa and provided a universal church for a reconstructed Syriac universal state, the 'Abbāsid Caliphate.

The Indic and Sinic Internal Proletariats

The Indic Society, like the Syriac, had the course of its disintegration violently interrupted by an Hellenic intrusion; and it is interesting to see how far, in this case, a similar challenge evoked a similar response.

At the time when the Indic and Hellenic societies made their first contact—as a result of Alexander's raid into the Indus Valley—the Indic Society was on the point of entering its universal state, and its dominant minority had long since reacted to the ordeal of disintegration by creating the two philosophical schools of Jainism and Buddhism; but there is no evidence that its internal proletariat had produced any 'higher religion'. The Buddhist philosopher-king Açoka, who occupied the throne of the Indic universal state from 273 to 232 B.C., sought without success to convert his Hellenic neighbours to his philosophy. It was only at a later date that Buddhism took by storm the outlying, yet extensive and important, province of the post-Alexandrine Hellenic World which was occupied by the Greek kingdom of Bactria.

But Buddhism did not make this triumphant spiritual counter-conquest until it had undergone an extraordinary metamorphosis through which the old philosophy of the earlier followers of Siddhārtha Gautama[1] became transformed into the new religion of the Mahāyāna.

'The Mahāyāna is a truly new religion, so radically different from Early Buddhism that it exhibits as many points of contact with later Brahmanical religions as with its own predecessor. . . . It never has been fully realized what a radical revolution had transformed the Buddhist Church when the new spirit—which, however, was for a long time lurking in it—arrived at full eclosion in the first centuries A.D. When we see an atheistic, soul-denying philosophic teaching of a path to personal final deliverance, consisting in an absolute extinction of life and a simple worship of the memory of its human founder—when we see it superseded by a magnificent High Church with a Supreme God, surrounded by a numerous pantheon and a host of saints: a religion highly devotional, highly ceremonious and clerical, with an ideal of universal salvation of all living creatures, a salvation by the divine grace of Buddhas and Bodhisattvas, a salvation not in annihilation but in eternal life—we are fully justified in maintaining that the history of religions has scarcely witnessed such a break between new and old within the pale of what nevertheless continues to claim common descent from the same religious founder.'[2]

This transformed Buddhism that came to flower in the northeast of an expanded Hellenic World was in fact an Indic 'higher religion' comparable to others that in the same age were invading the heart of the Hellenic Society. What was the origin of this personal religion which was both the distinctive trait of the Mahā-

---

[1] It is a controversial question, which perhaps can never be conclusively answered, whether the Buddhist philosophy—described in the following passage from the work of a Russian scholar—against which the Mahāyāna was in revolt, was a replica or a misrepresentation of the personal teaching of Siddhārtha Gautama himself. Some scholars hold that, so far as we can catch glimpses of the Buddha's own personal teaching beneath the overlay of a systematized philosophy that is presented to us in the Hinayanian scriptures, we can divine that the Buddha himself did not disbelieve in the reality and permanence of the soul, and that the Nirvana which was the objective of his spiritual exercises was a condition of absolute extinction, not of life itself, but of the dross of passion which, so long as it clings to life, prevents life from being lived to the full.—A. J. T.

[2] Stcherbatsky, Th.: *The Conception of Buddhist Nirvana*, p. 36.

yāna and the secret of its success? This new leaven, which changed the spirit of Buddhism so profoundly, was as alien from the native vein of the Indic as it was from that of the Hellenic philosophy. Was it the fruit of the experience of the Indic internal proletariat, or was it a spark caught from the Syriac flame which had already kindled Zoroastrianism and Judaism? Evidence could be adduced in favour of either view, but we really are not in a position to choose between them. Suffice it to say that, with the arrival of this Buddhaic 'higher religion' on the scene, the religious history of the Indic Society begins to take the same course as that of the Syriac Society which we have already surveyed.

As a 'higher religion' which went forth from the bosom of the society in which it had arisen in order to evangelize a Hellenized world, the Mahāyāna is manifestly an Indic counterpart of Christianity and Mithraism; and with this key in our hands we can easily identify the Indic counterpart of those other rays into which the light of Syriac religion was diffracted by the interposition of the Hellenic prism. If we look for the Indic equivalent of those 'fossils' of the pre-Hellenic state of the Syriac Society that have survived in the Jews and the Parsees, we shall find what we are looking for in the latter-day Hinayanian Buddhism of Ceylon and Burma and Siam and Cambodia, which is a relic of the pre-Mahayanian Buddhist philosophy; and, just as the Syriac Society had to wait for the emergence of Islam in order to lay its hand upon a religion which was capable of serving as an effective instrument for casting Hellenism out, so we find that the complete and final expulsion of the intrusive Hellenic spirit from the Indic body social was accomplished, not through the Mahāyāna, but through the purely Indic, and utterly un-Hellenic, religious movement of post-Buddhaic Hinduism.

The history of the Mahāyāna corresponds, so far as we have at present taken it, with that of Catholic Christianity in that both found their field of action in the Hellenic World instead of converting the non-Hellenic society from which each had sprung. But there is a further chapter in the history of the Mahāyāna to which the history of the Christian Church offers no parallel. For Christianity, having taken up its abode in the domain of the moribund Hellenic Society, remained there and ultimately survived to provide churches for the two new civilizations, our own and that of Orthodox Christendom, which have been affiliated to the Hellenic. The Mahāyāna, on the other hand, passed out through the ephemeral Hellenic Bactrian kingdom across the highlands of Central Asia into the moribund Sinic World, and, at a double remove from the land of its birth, became the universal church of the Sinic internal proletariat.

The Legacy of the Sumeric Internal Proletariat

Two societies, the Babylonic and the Hittite, have been affiliated to the Sumeric Society, but in this case we cannot discover any universal church produced within the bosom of the Sumeric internal proletariat and bequeathed to the affiliated civilizations. The Babylonic Society seems to have taken over the religion of the Sumeric dominant minority, and the Hittite religion seems to have been derived in part from the same source. But we know very little about the religious history of the Sumeric World. We can only say that, if the worship of Tammuz and Ishtar really is a monument of the experience of the Sumeric internal proletariat, this attempted act of creation was abortive in the Sumeric Society itself, and only came to fruition elsewhere.

These Sumeric deities, male and female, had, indeed, a long career and extensive travels ahead of them, and one interesting feature of this subsequent history of theirs is the variation in their relative importance. In the Hittite version of the worship of this pair of divinities the figure of the goddess has dwarfed and overshadowed that of the god who plays towards her the diverse and indeed contradictory roles of son and lover, protégé and victim. By the side of Cybele-Ishtar, Attis-Tammuz dwindles to insignificance; and, in her remote north-western island sanctuary, lapped round by Ocean Stream, Nerthus-Ishtar seems to stand in solitary grandeur without any male consort. But, in the course of the pair's south-westward journey to Syria and Egypt, Tammuz increases in importance and Ishtar diminishes. The Atargatis whose worship spread from Bambyce to Ascalon would appear from her name to have been an Ishtar whose claim to veneration was based upon her function of serving as Attis' mate. In Phoenicia an Adonis-Tammuz was 'the Lord' whose yearly death an Astarte-Ishtar mourned; and in the Egyptiac World an Osiris-Tammuz overshadowed his sister-wife Isis as decidedly as Isis, in her turn, overshadowed Osiris when she subsequently won an empire for herself in the hearts of the Hellenic internal proletariat. This version of the Sumeric faith in which the dying god and not the mourning goddess was the figure on which the worshipper's devotion was concentrated seems even to have spread to the remote barbarians of Scandinavia, where a Balder-Tammuz was called 'the Lord', while his colourless consort Nanna still retained the personal name of the Sumeric mother-goddess.

(3) THE INTERNAL PROLETARIAT OF THE WESTERN WORLD

To complete our survey of internal proletariats we have to examine the case that lies nearest home. Do the characteristic phenomena reappear in the history of the West? When we call for the evidence of the existence of a Western internal proletariat we may find ourselves overwhelmed by an *embarras de richesses*.

We have already noticed that one of the regular sources of recruitment for an internal proletariat has been drawn upon by our Western Society on a stupendous scale. The man-power of no less than ten disintegrating civilizations has been conscripted into the Western body social during the last four hundred years; and on the common level of membership in our Western internal proletariat, to which they have been thus reduced, a process of standardization has been at work which has already blurred—and in some cases quite effaced—the characteristic features by which these heterogeneous masses were once distinguished from one another. Nor has our society been content to prey upon its own 'civilized' kind. It has also rounded up almost all the surviving primitive societies; and while some of these, like the Tasmanians and most of the North American Indian tribes, have died of the shock, others, like the Negroes of Tropical Africa, have managed to survive and set the Niger flowing into the Hudson and the Congo into the Mississippi—just as other activities of the same Western monster have set the Yangtse flowing into the Straits of Malacca.[1] The Negro slaves shipped across to America and the Tamil or Chinese coolies shipped to the equatorial or antipodean coasts of the Indian Ocean are the counterparts of the slaves who, in the last two centuries before Christ, were consigned from all the coasts of the Mediterranean to the ranches and plantations of Roman Italy.

There is another contingent of conscripted aliens in our Western internal proletariat who have been uprooted and disoriented spiritually without having been physically evicted from their ancestral homes. In any community that is attempting to solve the problem of adapting its life to the rhythm of an alien civilization, there is need for a special social class to serve as the human counterpart of the 'transformer' which changes an electric current from one voltage to another; and the class which is called into existence—often quite abruptly and artificially—in response to

---

[1] Juvenal, describing the influx of semi-Hellenized Syrian Orientals into the Rome of his day (early in the second century after Christ), wrote *in Tiberim defluxit Orontes*: The Orontes has flowed into the Tiber.

this demand, has come to be known generically, from the special Russian name for it, as the intelligentsia. The intelligentsia is a class of liaison officers who have learnt the tricks of the intrusive civilization's trade so far as may be necessary to enable their own community, through their agency, just to hold its own in a social environment in which life is ceasing to be lived in accordance with the local tradition and is coming more and more to be lived in the style imposed by the intrusive civilization upon the aliens who fall under its dominion.

The first recruits to this intelligentsia are military and naval officers who learn as much of the domineering society's art of war as may be necessary to save the Russia of Peter the Great from being conquered by a Western Sweden, or the Turkey and Japan of a later age from being conquered by a Russia who has by this time become sufficiently Westernized to be able to launch out on a career of aggression on her own account. Then comes the diplomatist who learns how to conduct with Western governments the negotiations that are forced upon his community by its failure to hold its own in war. We have seen the 'Osmanlis enlisting their *ra'iyeh* for this diplomatic work, until a further turn of the screw compels the 'Osmanlis to master for themselves this distasteful trade. Next come the merchants: the Hong merchants at Canton and the Levantine, Greek and Armenian merchants in the dominions of the Ottoman Pādishāh. And finally, as the leaven or virus of Westernism works deeper into the social life of the society which is in process of being permeated and assimilated, the intelligentsia develops its most characteristic types: the schoolmaster who has learnt the trick of teaching Western subjects; the civil servant who has picked up the practice of conducting the public administration according to Western forms; the lawyer who has acquired the knack of applying a version of the *Code Napoléon* in accordance with French judicial procedure.

Wherever we find an intelligentsia we may infer, not only that two civilizations have been in contact, but that one of the two is in process of being absorbed into the other's internal proletariat. We can also observe another fact in the life of an intelligentsia which is written large upon its countenance for all to read: an intelligentsia is born to be unhappy.

This liaison-class suffers from the congenital unhappiness of the hybrid who is an outcaste from both the families that have combined to beget him. An intelligentsia is hated and despised by its own people because its very existence is a reproach to them. Through its presence in their midst it is a living reminder of the hateful but inescapable alien civilization which cannot be kept at

bay and therefore has to be humoured. The Pharisee is reminded
of this each time he meets the Publican, and the Zealot each time
he meets the Herodian. And, while the intelligentsia thus has no
love lost on it at home, it also has no honour paid to it in the
country whose manners and tricks it has so laboriously and in-
geniously mastered.[1] In the earlier days of the historic association
between India and England the Hindu intelligentsia which the
British Rāj had fostered for its own administrative convenience
was a common subject of English ridicule. The more facile the
'babu's' command of English, the more sardonically the 'sahib'
would laugh at the subtle incongruity of the errors that inevitably
crept in; and such laughter was wounding even when good-
natured. The intelligentsia thus complies in double measure with
our definition of a proletariat by being 'in' but not 'of' two societies
and not merely one; and, while it may console itself in the first
chapter of its history by feeling that it is an indispensable organ
of both these bodies social, it is robbed of even this consolation
as time goes on. For the adjustment of supply to demand is
almost beyond the wit of man where man-power itself is the commodity, and in due course an intelligentsia comes to suffer from
overproduction and unemployment.

A Peter the Great wants so many Russian chinovniks or an East
India Company so many clerks, or a Mehmed 'Ali so many Egyptian mill-hands and shipwrights. Incontinently these potters in
human clay set to work to produce them, but the process of manu-
facturing an intelligentsia is more difficult to stop than to start;
for the contempt in which the liaison class is held by those who
profit by its services is offset by its prestige in the eyes of those
eligible for enrolment in it. The candidates increase out of all
proportion to the opportunities for employing them, and the
original nucleus of the employed intelligentsia becomes swamped
by an intellectual proletariat which is idle and destitute as well
as outcaste. The handful of chinovniks is reinforced by a legion
of 'Nihilists', the handful of quill-driving babus by a legion of
'failed B.A.s'; and the bitterness of the intelligentsia is incomparably greater in the latter state than in the former. Indeed, we
might almost formulate a social 'law' to the effect that an intelligentsia's congenital unhappiness increases in geometrical ratio with
the arithmetical progress of time. The Russian intelligentsia,
which dates from the close of the seventeenth century of the
Christian Era, has already discharged its accumulated spite in the

---

[1] It will perhaps have occurred to the reader that the intelligentsia, in Mr.
Toynbee's use of the term, is the social equivalent of the political animal
described as a 'quisling' during the General War of 1939–45.—EDITOR.

shattering Bolshevik Revolution of 1917. The Bengali intelligentsia, which dates from the latter part of the eighteenth century, is displaying to-day a vein of revolutionary violence which is not yet to be seen in other parts of British India, where the local intelligentsia did not come into existence till fifty or a hundred years later.

Nor is the rank growth of this social weed confined to the soil in which it is a native plant. It has latterly made its appearance in the heart of the Western World as well as in its semi-Westernized fringes. A lower-middle class which has received a secondary and even a university education without being given any corresponding outlet for its trained abilities was the backbone of the twentieth-century Fascist Party in Italy and National-Socialist Party in Germany. The demoniac driving force which carried Mussolini and Hitler to power was generated out of this intellectual proletariat's exasperation at finding that its painful efforts at self-improvement were not sufficient in themselves to save it from being crushed between the upper and nether millstones of Organized Capital and Organized Labour.

As a matter of fact we do not have to wait till the present century to see our Western internal proletariat being recruited from the native tissues of the Western body social; for in the Western as well as in the Hellenic World it is not only subjugated alien populations that have been torn up by the roots. The sixteenth-century and seventeenth-century Wars of Religion brought with them the penalization or eviction of Catholics in every country where power fell into the hands of the Protestant faction and the penalization and eviction of Protestants in every country where power fell into the hands of the Catholic faction, so that the descendants of French Huguenots are scattered from Prussia to South Africa and the descendants of Irish Catholics from Austria to Chile. Nor was the plague stayed by the peace of lassitude and cynicism in which the Wars of Religion came to a close. From the French Revolution onwards, political *stasis* began to be inspired by the *odium hactenus theologicum*, and fresh hosts of exiles were uprooted: the French aristocratic *émigrés* of 1789, the European Liberal *émigrés* of 1848, the Russian 'White' *émigrés* of 1917, the Italian and German democratic *émigrés* of 1922 and 1933, the Austrian Catholic and Jewish *émigrés* of 1938 and the millions of victims of the war of 1939–45 and its aftermath.

We have seen, again, how in Sicily and Italy during the Hellenic time of troubles the free population was uprooted from the countryside and chevied into the towns by an economic revolution in the conduct of agriculture: the replacement of small-scale mixed farming for subsistence by the mass production of specialized agricultural commodities by means of plantation slavery. In our modern Western history we have an almost exact repetition of this social disaster in the rural economic revolution which substituted cotton plantations worked by Negro slaves for the mixed farming of White freemen in the 'cotton belt' of the American Union. The 'White trash' which was thus degraded to the ranks of the proletariat was of the quality of the dispossessed and pauperized 'free trash' of Roman Italy, and this rural economic revolution in North America, with its twin cancerous growths of Negro slavery and White pauperdom, was only an exceptionally rapid and ruthless application of a similar rural economic revolution which was spread over three centuries of English history. The English had not introduced slave-labour but they had imitated the Roman and anticipated the American planters and stockbreeders by uprooting a free peasantry for the economic profit of an oligarchy, by turning ploughland into pasture and common land into enclosures. This modern Western rural economic revolution has not, however, been the principal cause of the flow of population from the countryside to the towns of our world. The principal motive force behind it has been not the push of an agrarian revolution replacing peasant holdings by latifundia but the pull of an urban industrial revolution replacing handicraft by steam-driven machines.

When this Western industrial revolution broke out first on English ground about a hundred and fifty years ago, its profitableness seemed so immense that the change was welcomed and blessed by the enthusiasts for Progress. While deploring the long hours of labour to which the first generation of the factory workers, including women and children, were condemned, and the sordid conditions of their new life in both factory and home, the panegyrists of the Industrial Revolution were confident that these were transitory evils which could and would be removed. The ironical sequel has been that this rosy prophecy has very largely come true, but that the blessings of the earthly paradise so confidently predicted are being neutralized by a curse which was hidden from the eyes of optimists and pessimists alike a century ago.[1] On the one hand, child labour has been abolished, women's labour has been tempered to women's strength, hours of labour have been shortened, the conditions of life and work in home and factory have been improved out of all recognition. But a world gorged with the wealth ground out by the magic industrial machine is at the same time overshadowed by the spectre of unemployment.

---

[1] A classic exposition of the optimism and the pessimism alike will be found in Macaulay's Essay on Southey's *Colloquies* (1830).—EDITOR.

Every time the urban proletarian draws his 'dole' he is reminded that he is 'in' a society but not 'of' it.

Enough has been said to indicate some of the many sources from which an internal proletariat has been recruited in our modern Western Society. We have now to ask whether here, as elsewhere, we find the two veins of violence and gentleness reappearing in our Western internal proletariat's reaction to its ordeal; and, if both tempers are displayed, which of the two is in the ascendant.

Manifestations of the militant temper in our Western under-world are at once apparent. It is unnecessary to catalogue the blood-stained revolutions of the last hundred and fifty years; but when we turn to look for evidence of a counteracting and con-structive spirit of gentleness, the traces are, unhappily, far to seek. It is true that many of the sufferers from the wrongs recorded in the earlier paragraphs of this chapter—exiled victims of religious or political persecution, deported African slaves, transported con-victs, uprooted peasantry—have made good, in the second or third if not in the first generation, in the new conditions imposed upon them. This may illustrate the recuperative powers of our civiliza-tion, but it gives no reward to our search. These are solutions of the proletarian's problem which escape the necessity of choice between the violent and the gentle response by escaping from the proletarian condition of life itself. In our search for modern Western exponents of the gentle response our only finds will be the English 'Quakers' and the German Anabaptist refugees in Moravia and the Dutch Mennonites; and even these rare specimens will slip through our fingers, for we shall find that they have ceased to be members of the proletariat.

In the first generation of the life of the English Society of Friends a vein of violence, which found vent in naked prophesy-ings and in noisy disturbances of the decorum of church services, drew down upon its members a savage chastisement both in England and in Massachusetts. This violence, however, was quickly and permanently superseded by a gentleness which became the Quakers' characteristic rule of life; and the Society of Friends for a time looked as though it might play in the Western World the classic role of the Primitive Christian Church on whose spirit and practice, as set forth in The Acts of the Apostles, they devoutly modelled their lives. But, while the Friends have never fallen away from the rule of gentleness, they have long travelled right out of the proletarian path, and have been, in a sense, the victims of their own virtues. It might even be said that they achieved material prosperity in their own despite; for much of their success in business can be traced to formidable decisions which they have taken, not for profit, but at the bidding of conscience. The first step in their undesigned pilgrimage to the shrine of material prosperity was taken, all unwittingly, when they migrated from the country to the towns, not because they were tempted by the lure of urban profits, but because this seemed the most obvious way of reconciling a conscientious objection to the payment of tithes to the Episcopalian Church with an equally conscientious objection to resisting the tithe-collector by force. Thereafter, when Quaker brewers took to making cocoa because they disapproved of intoxicants and when Quaker retail shopkeepers took to marking their goods with fixed prices because they scrupled to vary their price in 'the haggling of the market', they were deliberately risking their fortunes for their faith. But in the event they merely illustrated the truth of the proverb that 'honesty is the best policy' and the beatitude that 'the meek shall inherit the Earth'; and by the same token they removed their faith from the list of proletarian religions. Unlike their exemplars the Apostles, they were never ardent missionaries. They remained a select body, and their rule that a Quaker ceased to be a member of the Society if he married outside its ranks kept their numbers as low as their quality remained high.

The histories of the two groups of Anabaptists, though very different in many respects from that of the Quakers, are the same on the one point with which we are concerned. When, after violent beginnings, they adopted the rule of gentleness, they soon ceased to be proletarian.

Having drawn a blank so far in our search for a new religion reflecting the experience of our Western internal proletariat, we may remind ourselves that the Sinic internal proletariat found a religion in the Mahāyāna which was a transformation, out of all recognition, of the preceding Buddhist philosophy. In Marxian Communism we have a notorious example in our midst of a modern Western philosophy which has changed, in a lifetime, quite out of recognition into a proletarian religion, taking the path of violence and carving out its New Jerusalem with the sword on the plains of Russia.

If Karl Marx had been challenged by some Victorian *censor morum* to give his spiritual name and address, he would have described himself as a disciple of the philosopher Hegel, applying the Hegelian dialectic to the economic and political phenomena of his day. But the elements that have made Communism an explosive force are not of Hegel's creation; they bear on their face their certificate of origin from the ancestral religious faith of the West—a Christianity which, three hundred years after the philosophic challenge from Descartes, was still being drunk in by every Western child with its mother's milk and inhaled by every Western man and woman with the air they breathed. And such elements as cannot be traced to Christianity can be traced to Judaism, the 'fossilized' parent of Christianity which had been preserved by a Jewish Diaspora and volatilized through the opening of the ghettos and the emancipation of Western Jewry in the generation of Marx's grandparents. Marx has taken the goddess 'Historical Necessity' in place of Yahweh for his deity, and the internal proletariat of the Western World in place of Jewry for his chosen people, and his Messianic Kingdom is conceived of as a Dictatorship of the Proletariat; but the salient features of the Jewish Apocalypse protrude through this threadbare disguise.

However, it looks as if the religious phase in the evolution of Communism may prove ephemeral. The conservative national Communism of Stalin seems to have decisively defeated the revolutionary oecumenical Communism of Trotsky in the Russian field. The Soviet Union is no longer an outlaw society, out of communion with all the rest of the world. She has reverted to being what the Russian Empire was under a Peter or a Nicholas: a Great Power choosing her allies and her enemies on national grounds and irrespective of ideological considerations. And if Russia has moved to 'the right' her neighbours have moved to 'the left'. Not only the flash-in-the-pan of German National-Socialism and Italian Fascism but the apparently irresistible encroachment of planning on the once unregimented economies of the democratic countries suggests that the social structure of all countries in the near future is likely to be both national and socialist. Not only do the Capitalist and Communist régimes seem likely to continue side by side; it may well be that Capitalism and Communism—like intervention and non-intervention according to the sardonic dictum of Talleyrand—are becoming different names for very much the same thing. If this be so, we must decide that Communism has forfeited its prospects as a revolutionary proletarian religion: first, by being degraded from being a revolutionary panacea for all mankind into being a mere local variety of nationalism, and secondly by seeing the particular state that has enslaved it assimilate itself to the other states of the contemporary world by approximating to the latest standard type.

The upshot of our present inquiry seems to be that, while the evidence for the recruitment of an internal proletariat is at least as abundant in the recent history of our Western World as it is in the history of any other civilization, there is singularly little evidence in our Western history so far for the laying of any founda-

tions of a proletarian universal church or even for the emergence
of any strong-winged proletarian-born 'higher religions'. How is
this fact to be interpreted?

We have drawn many parallels between our own society and the
Hellenic, but there is one fundamental difference. The Hellenic
Society took over no universal church from its Minoan predecessor.
The condition of parochial paganism in which it broke down in
the fifth century B.C. was the condition in which it was born. But
parochial paganism was certainly not the first state, even if it comes
near to being the present state, of our own civilization, which was
once entitled to describe itself as Western Christendom. Moreover, even if we have now at last succeeded in sloughing off our
Christian heritage, the process of apostasy has been slow and
laborious, and with the best will in the world we are unlikely to
have carried it through with the thoroughness that we might wish;
for, after all, it is not so easy to get rid of a tradition in which we
and our forebears have been born and bred since the time, now
more than twelve hundred years ago, when our Western Christendom was born—a feeble infant—from the Church's womb.
When Descartes and Voltaire and Marx and Machiavelli and
Hobbes and Mussolini and Hitler have done their best to de-
christianize our Western life, we may still suspect that their
scouring and fumigating has been only partially effective. The
Christian virus or elixir is in our Western blood—if, indeed, it
is not just another name for that indispensable fluid—and it is
difficult to suppose that the spiritual constitution of the Western
Society can ever be refined to a paganism of Hellenic purity.

Besides, the Christian element in our system is not only ubiquitous: it is Protean; and one of its favourite tricks is to escape
eradication by insinuating a strong tincture of its own essence
into the very disinfectants that are so vigorously applied to sterilize
it. We have already noticed the Christian ingredient in a Communism which purports to be an anti-Christian application of
modern Western philosophy. The modern anti-Western prophets
of gentleness, Tolstoy and Gandhi, have never pretended to conceal their Christian inspiration.

Among the many diverse contingents of disinherited men and
women who have been subjected to the ordeal of being enrolled
in the Western internal proletariat, the worst sufferers of all have
been the primitive African Negroes transported as slaves to
America. In them we have found the Western analogue of the
slave-immigrants who were swept into Roman Italy from all the
other Mediterranean coasts during the last two centuries before
Christ, and we have observed that the Americo-African, like the

Italo-Oriental, plantation slaves met their tremendous social challenge with a religious response. In comparing the two at an earlier stage in this Study we dwelt upon the resemblance, but there is a quite equally significant difference. The Egyptian, Syrian and Anatolian slave-immigrants found consolation in the religions that they had brought with them; the Africans turned for consolation to the hereditary religion of their masters.

How is this difference to be accounted for? In part, no doubt, by the difference in the social antecedents of the two sets of slaves. The plantation-slaves of Roman Italy were largely drawn from an ancient and deeply cultivated Oriental population whose children might be expected to cling to their cultural heritage, whereas the African Negro slaves' ancestral religion was no more fit than any other element in their culture to hold its own against the overwhelmingly superior civilization of their White masters. This is a partial explanation of the difference in the sequel; but, to explain it completely, the cultural difference between the two sets of masters has to be taken into account.

The Oriental slaves in Roman Italy had actually nowhere else to look, outside their own native religious heritage, for religious consolation, since their Roman masters were living in a spiritual vacuum. In their case the pearl of great price was to be found in the heritage of the slaves and not in that of their masters, while in our Western case the spiritual treasure, as well as all the worldly wealth and power, has lain in the hands of the slave-driving dominant minority.

It is one thing, however, to possess a spiritual treasure and quite another thing to impart it; and, the more we think over it, the more astonishing we shall find it to be that these Christian slave-owners' hands should have been able to transmit to their primitive pagan victims the spiritual bread which they had done their best to desecrate by the sacrilegious act of enslaving their fellow-men. How could the slave-driver evangelist ever touch the heart of the slave whom he had morally alienated by doing him so grievous a wrong? The Christian religion must indeed be animated by an invincible spiritual power if it can win converts under such conditions. And, since a religion has no dwelling-place on Earth except in human souls, it follows that there must still be Christian men and women abroad in our neo-pagan world. 'Peradventure there be fifty righteous within the city';[1] and a glance at the American slave-mission field will show us some of these persisting Christians at work, for the American Negro convert to Christianity does not, of course, really owe his conversion to the ministrations

[1] Abraham pleading with Yahweh for the sparing of Sodom: Genesis xviii. 24.

of a plantation-gang overseer with a Bible in one hand and a whip in the other. He owes it to the John G. Fees and the Peter Clavers.

In this miracle of the slaves' conversion to the religion of their masters we can see the familiar schism between the internal proletariat and the dominant minority being healed in our Western body social by a Christianity which our dominant minority has been trying to repudiate; and the conversion of the American Negro is only one among many triumphs of a latter-day Christian missionary activity. In our war-ridden generation, in which the lately brilliant prospects of a neo-pagan dominant minority have been rapidly growing dim, the sap of life is visibly flowing once again through all the branches of our Western Christendom; and this spectacle suggests that perhaps, after all, the next chapter of our Western history may not follow the lines of the final chapter of Hellenic history. Instead of seeing some new church spring from the ploughed-up soil of an internal proletariat in order to serve as the executor and residuary legatee of a civilization that has broken down and gone into disintegration, we may yet live to see a civilization that has tried and failed to stand alone being saved, in spite of itself, from a fatal fall by being caught up in the arms of an ancestral church which it has vainly striven to push away and keep at arm's length. In that event a tottering civilization which has shamefully succumbed to the intoxication of a showy victory over physical nature, and has applied the spoils to laying up treasure for itself without being rich towards God, may be reprieved from the sentence—which it has passed upon itself— of treading out the tragic path of κόρος—ὕβρις—ἄτη; or, to translate this Hellenic language into a Christian imagery, an apostate Western Christendom may be given grace to be born again as a *Respublica Christiana* which was its own earlier and better ideal of what it should strive to be.

Is such spiritual rebirth possible? If we put Nicodemus's question—'Can' a man 'enter the second time into his mother's womb and be born?'—we may take his instructor's answer: 'Verily, verily, I say unto thee, except a man be born of water and of the spirit, he cannot enter into the Kingdom of God.'[1]

(4) EXTERNAL PROLETARIATS

The external, like the internal, proletariat brings itself into existence by an act of secession from the dominant minority of a civilization that has broken down, and the schism in which the secession results is in this case palpable; for, whereas the internal

[1] John iii. 4-5.

proletariat continues to be geographically intermingled with the dominant minority from which it is divided by a moral gulf, the external proletariat is not only morally alienated but is also physically divided from the dominant minority by a frontier which can be traced on the map.

The crystallization of such a frontier is indeed the sure sign that such a secession has taken place; for, as long as a civilization is still in growth, it has no hard and fast boundaries except on fronts where it happens to have collided with another civilization of its own species. Such collisions between two or more civilizations give rise to phenomena which we shall have occasion to examine in a later part of this Study,[1] but at present we will leave this contingency out of account and confine our attention to the situation in which a civilization has for its neighbour not another civilization but societies of the primitive species. In these circumstances we shall find that, as long as a civilization is in growth, its frontiers are indeterminate. If we place ourselves at the focus of growth in a growing civilization and proceed to travel outwards until we find ourselves sooner or later in an environment which is unmistakably and completely primitive, we shall not be able, at any point on such a journey, to draw a line and say: 'Here civilization ends and we enter the Primitive World.'

In fact, when a creative minority successfully performs its role in the life of a growing civilization, and the spark which it has kindled 'gives light unto all that are in the house', the light, as it radiates outward, is not arrested by the walls of the house, for in fact there are no walls and the light is not hid from the neighbours outside. The light shines as far as, in the nature of things, it can carry until it reaches vanishing-point. The gradations are infinitesimal, and it is impossible to demarcate the line at which the last glimmer of twilight flickers out and leaves the heart of darkness in undivided possession. In fact, the carrying-power of the radiation of growing civilizations is so great that, although civilizations are relatively a very recent achievement of mankind, they have long ago succeeded in permeating, at least in some degree, the whole array of surviving primitive societies. It would be impossible anywhere to discover a primitive society which had entirely escaped the influence of some civilization or other. In 1935, for example, a society previously quite unknown was discovered in the interior of Papua,[2] and this society possessed a technique of intensive agriculture which must, at some unknown date, have been acquired from some unidentified civilization.

---

[1] In the volumes not yet published.
[2] *The Times*, 14th August 1936, and Hides, J. G.: *Papuan Wonderland*.

This all-pervasiveness of the influence of civilizations in what remains of the Primitive World strikes us forcibly when we regard the phenomenon from the point of view of the primitive societies. If, on the other hand, we look upon it from the standpoint of a civilization, we shall be no less forcibly struck by the fact that the strength of the influence radiated wanes as the range increases. As soon as we have recovered from our astonishment at detecting the influence of Hellenic art in a coin that was struck in Britain in the last century before Christ or on a sarcophagus carved in Afghanistan in the first century of the Christian Era, we observe that the British coin looks like a caricature of its Macedonian original and that the Afghan sarcophagus is a shoddy product of 'commercial art'. At this remove mimesis has passed into travesty.

Mimesis is evoked by charm; and we can now see that the charm which is exercised, during the growth of a civilization, by a succession of creative minorities preserves the house not only from being divided against itself but also from being attacked by its neighbours—in so far, at least, as these neighbours are primitive societies. Wherever a growing civilization is in contact with primitive societies, its creative minority attracts their mimesis as well as the mimesis of the uncreative majority in its midst. But, if this is the normal relation between a civilization and the primitive societies round about so long as the civilization is in growth, a profound change sets in if and when the civilization breaks down and goes into disintegration. The creative minorities which have won a voluntary allegiance by the charm which their creativity exerts are replaced by a dominant minority which, lacking charm, relies on force. The surrounding primitive peoples are no longer charmed but are repelled; these humble disciples of the growing civilization then renounce their discipleship and become what we have called an external proletariat. Though 'in' the now broken-down civilization they are no longer 'of' it.[1]

The radiation of any civilization may be analysed into three elements—economic, political and cultural—and, so long as a society is in a state of growth, all three elements seem to be radiated with equal power or, to speak in human rather than physical terms, to exercise an equal charm. But, as soon as the civilization has ceased to grow, the charm of its culture evaporates. Its powers of economic and political radiation may, and indeed probably will, continue to grow faster than ever, for a successful cultivation of the pseudo-religions of Mammon and Mars and Moloch is emi-

---

[1] When we say 'in it', we do not mean geographically within it—for that, being 'external', they obviously are not—but 'in it' inasmuch as they continue willy-nilly to be in a state of active relationship with it.

nently characteristic of broken-down civilizations. But, since the cultural element is the essence of a civilization and the economic and political elements are relatively trivial manifestations of the life that it has in it, it follows that the most spectacular triumphs of economic and political radiation are imperfect and precarious.

If we look at the change from the standpoint of the primitive peoples, we shall express the same truth by saying that their mimesis of the broken-down civilization's arts of peace comes to an end, but that they continue to imitate its improvements—its technical gadgets—in the arts of industry, war and politics, not in order that they may become one with it—which was their aspiration so long as it charmed them—but in order that they may the more effectively defend themselves against the violence which is by now its most conspicuous characteristic.

In our foregoing survey of the experiences and reactions of internal proletariats we have seen how the path of violence has allured them, and also how, in so far as they have yielded to this temptation, they have only brought disaster on themselves. The Theudases and Judases inevitably perish with the sword; it is only when it follows a prophet of gentleness that the internal prole- tariat has a chance of taking its conquerors captive. The external proletariat, if it chooses (as it almost certainly will) to react with violence, is at no such disadvantage. Whereas the whole of the internal proletariat lies, *ex hypothesi*, within the dominant mino- rity's reach, some part at any rate of the external proletariat is likely to be beyond the effective range of the dominant minority's military action. In the contest that now ensues the broken-down civilization radiates force instead of attracting mimesis. In these circumstances the nearer members of the external proletariat are likely to be conquered and added to the internal proletariat, but a point will be reached where the dominant minority's qualitative superiority in military power is counterbalanced by the length of its communications.

When this stage is reached it brings with it the completion of a change in the nature of the contact between the civilization in question and its barbarian neighbours. So long as a civilization is in growth, its home territory, where it prevails in full force, is screened, as we have seen, from the impact of unreclaimed savagery by a broad threshold or buffer zone across which civiliza- tion shades into savagery in a long series of fine gradations. On the other hand, when a civilization has broken down and fallen into schism and when the consequent hostilities between the dominant minority and the external proletariat have ceased to be a running fight and have settled down into trench warfare, we find that the buffer zone has disappeared. The geographical transition from civilization to barbarism is now no longer gradual but is abrupt. To use the appropriate Latin words, which bring out both the kinship and the contrast between the two types of contact, a *limen* or threshold, which was a zone, has been replaced by a *limes* or military frontier, which is a line that has length without breadth. Across this line a baffled dominant minority and an unconquered external proletariat now face one another under arms; and this military front is a bar to the passage of all social radiation except that of military technique—an article of social exchange which makes for war and not for peace between those who give and take it.

The social phenomena which follow when this warfare becomes stationary along a *limes* will occupy our attention later.[1] Here it is sufficient to mention the cardinal fact that this temporary and precarious balance of forces inevitably tilts, with the passage of time, in favour of the barbarians.

A Hellenic Instance

The growth-phase of Hellenic history is rich in illustrations of the *limen* or buffer zone with which the home territory of a healthily growing civilization tends to surround itself. Towards continental Europe the quintessence of Hellas shaded off, north of Thermopylae, into semi-Hellenic Thessaly and, west of Delphi, into semi-Hellenic Aetolia, and these in their turn were screened by the demi-semi-Hellenism of Macedonia and Epirus from the undiluted barbarism of Thrace and Illyria. Towards Asia Minor, again, zones of diminishing Hellenism in the hinterlands of the Greek cities of the Asiatic coast are represented by Caria, Lydia and Phrygia. On this Asiatic border we can see Hellenism taking its barbarian conquerors captive for the first time in the full light of history. The spell was so strong that, in the second quarter of the sixth century B.C., the conflict between Philhellenes and Hellenophobes came to the forefront in Lydian politics; and, even when a Philhellenic aspirant to the Lydian throne, Pantaleon, was worsted by his half-brother Croesus, the protagonist of the anti-Hellenic party proved so impotent to swim against the pro-Hellenic tide that he became famous for being as generous a patron of Hellenic shrines as he was a credulous consultant of Hellenic oracles.

Even in the hinterlands overseas peaceful relations and gradual transitions seem to have been the rule. Hellenism spread rapidly in the hinterland of the Italian Magna Graecia, and the earliest

[1] In the volumes not yet published.

mention of Rome in extant literature is a notice, in a surviving fragment of a lost work from the hand of Plato's pupil, Heracleides Ponticus, in which this Latin commonwealth is described as 'a Hellenic city' (πόλιν Ἑλληνίδα Ῥώμην).

Thus on all the fringes of the Hellenic World in its growth stage we seem to see the gracious figure of Orpheus casting his spell upon the barbarians round about and even inspiring them to rehearse his magic music, on their own ruder instruments, to the still more primitive peoples of a farther hinterland. This idyllic picture vanishes in a trice, however, upon the Hellenic Civilization's breakdown. As the harmony breaks into a discord, the spell-bound listeners seem to awaken with a start; and, relapsing into their natural ferocity, they now hurl themselves against the sinister man-at-arms who has emerged from behind the gentle prophet's cloak.

The militant reaction of the external proletariat to the breakdown of the Hellenic Civilization was most violent and effective in Magna Graecia, where the Bruttians and Lucanians began to press upon the Greek cities and to occupy them one after another. Within a hundred years of the opening in 431 B.C. of a war which was 'the beginning of great evils for Hellas', the few remaining survivors among the formerly prosperous communities of Magna Graecia were summoning condottieri from the motherland to save them from being driven into the sea. And these erratic reinforcements were of such little avail for stemming the Oscan tide that the inflowing barbarians had already crossed the Straits of Messina before the whole movement was brought to an abrupt end by the intervention of the Oscans' Hellenized Roman kinsmen. Roman statesmanship and arms saved not merely Magna Graecia but the whole Italian Peninsula for Hellenism by taking the Oscans in the rear and imposing a common Roman Peace on Italian barbarians and Italiot Greeks alike.

Thus the South Italian front between Hellenism and barbarism was wiped out, and thereafter successive feats of Roman arms extended the dominion of the Hellenic dominant minority almost as far afield in Continental Europe and North-West Africa as it had already been extended in Asia by Alexander of Macedon. But the effect of this military expansion was not to eliminate the anti-barbarian fronts but to add to their length and to their distance from the centre of power. For several centuries they were stabilized; but the disintegration of the society continued to run its course until at long last the barbarians broke through.

We must now proceed to ask whether we can discern, in the external proletariat's reaction to the pressure of the Hellenic dominant minority, any symptoms of a gentle as well as a violent response; and whether we can credit the external proletariat with any creative activities.

At first sight it might seem that, in the Hellenic case at any rate, the answer to both questions must be in the negative. We can observe our anti-Hellenic barbarian in various postures and positions. As Ariovistus he is driven from the field by Caesar; as Arminius he holds his own against Augustus; as Odovacer he takes his revenge against Romulus Augustulus. But in all warfare there are the three alternatives of defeat, drawn battle and victory, and, in each alternative alike, violence monotonously rules and creativity is at a discount. We may be encouraged, however, to look farther by recalling that the internal proletariat also is apt to display an equal violence and an equal barrenness in its earlier reactions, while the gentleness which eventually expresses itself in such mighty works of creation as a 'higher religion' and a universal church usually requires both time and travail in order to gain the ascendancy.

In the matter of gentleness, for example, we can at any rate perceive a certain difference in degree in the violence of the different barbarian war-bands. The sack of Rome by the demi-semi-Hellenized Visigoth Alaric in A.D. 410 was a less merciless affair than the subsequent sack of the same city by the Vandals and Berbers in 455 or the sack which Rome might have suffered from Radagaisus in 406. The relative gentleness of Alaric is dwelt upon by St. Augustine:

'The dreaded atrocity of the barbarians has shown itself so mild in the event that churches providing ample room for asylum were designated by the conqueror and orders were given that in these sanctuaries nobody should be smitten with the sword and nobody carried away captive. Indeed, many prisoners were brought to these churches by soft-hearted enemies to receive their liberty, while none were dragged out of them by merciless enemies in order to be enslaved.'[1]

And there is the curious evidence relating to Alaric's brother-in-law and successor Atawulf that is reported by Augustine's disciple Orosius on the authority of 'a gentleman from Narbonne who had had a distinguished military career under the Emperor Theodosius'.

'This gentleman told us that at Narbonne he had become extremely intimate with Atawulf, and that he had often been told by him—and this with all the earnestness of a witness giving evidence—the story of his own life, which was often on the lips of this barbarian of abounding spirit, vitality and genius. According to Atawulf's own story, he had

[1] St. Augustine: *De Civitate Dei*, Bk. I, ch. 7.

started life with an eager craving to wipe out all memory of the name of Rome, with the idea of turning the whole Roman domain into an empire that should be—and be known as—the Empire of the Goths. . . . In time, however, experience had convinced him that on the one hand the Goths were utterly disqualified by their uncontrolled barbarity for a life under the rule of law, while on the other hand it would be a crime to banish the rule of law from the life of the state, since the state ceases to be itself when law ceases to reign in it. When Atawulf had divined this truth, he had made up his mind that he would at any rate make a bid for the glory, that was within his reach, of using the vitality of the Goths for the restoration of the Roman name to all—and perhaps more than all—its ancient greatness.'[1]

This passage is the *locus classicus* for evidence of a change from violence to gentleness in the ethos of the Hellenic external proletariat, and in the light of it we can identify certain accompanying symptoms of spiritual creativity, or at any rate originality, in partially reclaimed barbarian souls.

Atawulf himself, for example, like his brother-in-law Alaric, was a Christian. But his Christianity was not the Christianity of St. Augustine and the Catholic Church. On the European front the barbarian invaders of that generation, in so far as they were not still pagans, were Arians, and, although their original conversion to Arianism rather than Catholicism had been the result of chance, their subsequent fidelity to Arianism, after that heresy had lost its temporary vogue within the Christianized Hellenic World, was the result of deliberate preference. Their Arianism was henceforth a badge, deliberately worn and sometimes insolently displayed, of the conquerors' social distinction from the conquered population. This Arianism of the majority of the Teutonic successor-states of the Roman Empire persisted throughout the greater part of the interregnum period, A.D. 375–675. Pope Gregory the Great (A.D. 590–604), who, perhaps more than any other single man, may be regarded as the founder of the new civilization of Western Christendom which arose out of the void, played a part in bringing this Arian chapter of barbarian history to an end by converting to Catholicism the Lombard queen, Theodelinda. The Franks were never Arians but, at the conversion of Clovis and his baptism at Reims (A.D. 496), passed straight from paganism to Catholicism, a choice which powerfully assisted them to survive the interregnum and to build a state which became the political foundation-stone of the new civilization.

While an Arianism which its barbarian converts had taken as they found it thus eventually became the distinctive badge of these particular bands of barbarians, there were other barbarians on

¹ Orosius, P.: *Adversum Paganos*, Bk. VII, ch. 43.

other frontiers of the Empire who showed in their religious life a certain originality, inspired by something more positive than pride of caste. On the frontiers of the British Isles the barbarians of 'the Celtic Fringe', who had been converted to a Catholic and not to an Arian Christianity, re-moulded this to fit their own barbarian heritage, and on the frontier facing the Arabian section of the Afrasian Steppe the trans-frontier barbarians showed originality in a still higher degree. In the creative soul of Muhammad the radiation of Judaism and Christianity was transmuted into a spiritual force which discharged itself in the new 'higher religion' of Islam.

If we carry our investigations a stage farther back, we shall find that these religious reactions that we have just recorded were not the first that had been evoked from these primitive peoples by the radiation of the Hellenic Civilization. All genuinely and completely primitive religion is, in one guise or another, a cult of fertility. A primitive community mainly worships its own procreative power as displayed in the begetting of children and in the production of food, and the worship of destructive powers is either absent or subordinate. But, since the religion of primitive man is always a faithful reflection of his social conditions, a revolution in his religion is bound to take place when his social life is violently deranged by being brought into contact with an alien body social that is both close and hostile; and this is what happens when a primitive community which has been gradually and peacefully absorbing the beneficent influences of a growing civilization tragically loses sight of the gracious figure of Orpheus with his enchanting lyre and finds itself brusquely confronted, instead, by the ugly and menacing countenance of the dominant minority of a civilization that has broken down.

In this event the primitive community is transformed into a fragment of an external proletariat, and in this situation there is a revolutionary inversion of the relative importance of the procreative and destructive activities in the barbarian community's life. War now becomes the community's all-absorbing occupation, and, when war thus becomes more lucrative, as well as more exciting, than the trivial round and common task of food-getting, how can Demeter or even Aphrodite hope to hold her own against Ares as the supreme expression of the divine? The god is refashioned as the leader of a divine war-band. We have come across divinities of this barbaric strain in the Olympian Pantheon which was worshipped by the Achaean external proletariat of the Minoan thalassocracy; and we have seen that these deified brigands of Olympus have their counterparts in the denizens of Asgard, who were worshipped by the Scandinavian external proletariat of the

Carolingian Empire. Another pantheon of the same kind was worshipped by the Teutonic barbarians beyond the European frontiers of the Roman Empire before their conversion to Arianism or Catholicism; and the evocation of these predatory divinities in their militarized worshippers' own image must be reckoned as a creative work that has to be placed to the credit of the Teutonic external proletariat of the Hellenic World.

Having gleaned these wisps of creative activity in the field of religion, can we add to our slender harvest by drawing upon analogy once again? The 'higher religions' which are the glorious discoveries of the internal proletariats are notoriously associated with a sheaf of creative activities in the field of art. Have the 'lower religions' of the external proletariat any corresponding works of art to show?

The answer is certainly in the affirmative; for, as soon as we try to visualize the Olympian gods, we see them as they are portrayed in the Homeric epic. This poetry is associated with that religion as inseparably as Gregorian plainsong and Gothic architecture are associated with medieval Western Catholic Christianity. And the Greek epic poetry of Ionia has its counterpart in the Teutonic epic poetry of England and in the Scandinavian saga of Iceland. The Scandinavian saga is bound up with Asgard, and the English epic—of which *Beowulf* is the principal surviving masterpiece—with Woden and his divine *comitatus* as the Homeric epic is bound up with Olympus. In fact, epic poetry is the most characteristic and distinguished product of the reactions of external proletariats, the only κτῆμα εἰς ἀεί which their ordeals have bequeathed to humanity. No poetry that is the offspring of civilization ever will or ever can equal 'the unwearying splendour and the ruthless poignancy'[1] of Homer.

We have mentioned three examples of epic poetry, and it would be easy to add to this list and to show each example to be the reaction of an external proletariat to the civilization with which it has come into conflict. For example, the *Chanson de Roland* is the creation of the European wing of the external proletariat of the Syriac universal state. The French semi-barbarian Crusaders who broke through the Pyrenaean front of the Andalusian Umayyad Caliphate in the eleventh century of the Christian Era have inspired a work of art which is the parent of all the poetry that has ever been written since that day in any of the vernacular languages of the Western World. The *Chanson de Roland* outstrips *Beowulf* in historic importance as signally as it surpasses it in literary merit.[2]

---

[1] Lewis, C. S.: *A Preface to Paradise Lost*, p. 22.

[2] In his Study Mr. Toynbee deals, so far as historical evidence enables him,

(5) EXTERNAL PROLETARIATS OF THE WESTERN WORLD

When we come to the history of the relations between our own Western World and the primitive societies which it has encountered, we can discern an early stage in which, like Hellenism in its growth-phase, Western Christendom won converts through the attraction of its charm. The most signal of these early converts were the members of the abortive Scandinavian Civilization, who eventually succumbed—in their native lairs in the far north and in their distant settlements in Iceland, as well as in their encampments on Christian ground in the Danelaw and in Normandy— to the spiritual prowess of the civilization they had been assailing by force of arms. The contemporary conversion of the Nomad Magyars and forest-dwelling Poles was equally spontaneous, yet this early age of Western expansion is also marked by violent aggressions far surpassing the occasional subjugations and evictions of primitive neighbours chargeable to the score of the early Hellenes. We have Charlemagne's crusades against the Saxons and, two centuries later, the crusades of the Saxons against the Slavs between the Elbe and the Oder; and these atrocities were capped, in the thirteenth and fourteenth centuries, by the extermination of the Prussians beyond the Vistula at the hands of the Teutonic Knights.

On the north-western frontier of Christendom the same story repeats itself. The first chapter is the peaceful conversion of the English by a band of Roman missionaries, but this is followed by the coercion of the Far Western Christians by a series of turns of the screw which began with the decision of the Synod of Whitby in A.D. 664 and culminated in the armed invasion of Ireland by Henry II of England, with Papal approval, in 1171. Nor is this the end of the story. Habits of 'frightfulness', acquired by the English in their prolonged aggression against the remnants of the Celtic Fringe in the Highlands of Scotland and the bogs of Ireland, were carried across the Atlantic and practised at the expense of the North American Indians.

In the expansion of our Western Civilization over the whole planet in recent centuries the impetus of the expanding body has been so strong, and the disparity of resources between it and its

with the external proletariats of all the civilizations. I have omitted all these others, and proceed straight to the concluding section on the external proletariats of our Western Society. I need not say, nor apologize for the fact, that I have elsewhere, though less drastically, followed a similar plan. For example, in his chapter on the internal proletariats, Mr. Toynbee examines them all. I have omitted about half of them, retaining the half which seemed to present most features of interest.—EDITOR.

primitive antagonists so extreme, that the movement has swept on unchecked until it has reached, not an unstable *limes* but a *terminus* in the form of a natural frontier. In this world-wide Western offensive against the rear-guard of the primitive societies, extermination or eviction or subjugation has been the rule and conversion the exception. Indeed, we can count on the fingers of one hand the primitive societies that our modern Western Society has taken into partnership with itself. There are the Scottish Highlanders, one of those rare enclaves of untamed barbarians bequeathed to the modern Western World by a medieval Western Christendom; there are the Maoris of New Zealand; and there are the Araucanians in the barbarian hinterland of the Chilean province of the Andean universal state, with whom the Spaniards have had to deal since the Spanish conquest of the Inca Empire.

The test case is the history of the incorporation of the Scottish Highlanders after the failure of these White barbarians' last kick against the pricks in the Jacobite rising of 1745; for the social gulf between a Dr. Johnson or a Horace Walpole and the war-bands which carried Prince Charlie to Derby was probably not much less difficult to bridge than the gulf between the European settlers in New Zealand or Chile and the Maoris or Araucanians. At the present day the great-great-grandchildren of Prince Charlie's shaggy warriors are undoubtedly of one standardized social substance with the descendants of those bewigged and powdered Lowlanders and Englishmen who were the victors in the last round of a struggle that reached its end barely two hundred years ago; so much so that the very nature of the struggle has been transformed out of all recognition by popular mythology. The Scots have nearly persuaded the English, if not themselves, that the Highland tartan—which the citizens of Edinburgh in A.D. 1700 regarded very much as the citizens of Boston at the same date regarded the feathered headgear of an Indian chief—is the national dress of Scotland; and Lowland confectioners now sell 'Edinburgh Rock' in tartan-covered cartons.

Such barbarian *limites* as are to be found in the Westernized World of our own day are legacies from non-Western civilizations not yet completely absorbed into the Western body social. Among these, the North-West Frontier of India is of outstanding interest and importance, at any rate to the citizens of the particular Western parochial state that has taken it upon itself to provide a universal state for the disintegrating Hindu Civilization.

During the Hindu time of troubles (*circa* A.D. 1175–1575) this frontier was broken through again and again by Turkish and Iranian leaders of predatory war-bands. It was sealed for a time by the establishment in the Hindu World of a universal state represented by the Mughal Rāj. When the *Pax Mogulica* prematurely dissolved at the beginning of the eighteenth century of the Christian Era, the barbarians who rushed in—to contend for the possession of the carcass with the Marāthā protagonists of a militant Hindu reaction against an alien universal state—were the East Iranian Rohillas and Afghans; and when Akbar's work was re-performed by other alien hands and the Hindu universal state was re-established in the shape of a British Rāj, the defence of the North-West Frontier proved to be by far the heaviest of all the frontier commitments that the British empire-builders in India had to take over. Various frontier policies have been tried, and none of them has proved entirely satisfactory.

The first alternative which the British empire-builders essayed was to conquer and annex outright the whole of the East Iranian threshold of the Hindu World right up to the line along which the Mughal Rāj, at its apogee, had marched with its own Uzbeg successor-states in the Oxus-Jaxartes Basin and with the Safawī Empire in Western Iran. The adventurous reconnaissances which were carried out, from 1831 onwards, by Alexander Burnes, were followed by the still more hazardous step of dispatching a British-Indian military force to Afghanistan in 1838; but this ambitious attempt at a 'totalitarian' solution of the North-West Frontier problem had a disastrous ending. For, in the first flush of their triumphantly successful conquest of all India, south-east of the Indus basin, between 1799 and 1818, the British empire-builders had over-estimated their own strength and under-estimated the vigour and effectiveness of the resistance that their aggression would provoke among the untamed barbarians whom they were now proposing to subdue. In fact the operation ended, in 1841–2, in a disaster of greater magnitude than the Italian disaster in the Abyssinian highlands in 1896.

Since this resounding failure the British ambition to make a permanent conquest of the highlands has never been more than tentatively revived, and the variations of frontier policy since the conquest of the Panjab in 1849 have been tactical rather than strategic. Here, in fact, we have a *limes* of the same political order as the Rhine–Danube frontier of the Roman Empire during the opening centuries of the Christian Era. If and when the British-Indian dominant minority yield to the persuasions of the Hindu internal proletariat and quit the scene of their increasingly thankless labours, it will be interesting to see what this emancipated internal proletariat, when it is master in its own house, finds itself able to make of the North-West Frontier problem.

If we now ask ourselves whether the external proletariats gene-rated by our Western Society at various stages of its history in different quarters of the world have been stimulated by their ordeals to any acts of creativity in the spheres of poetry and religion, we shall at once be reminded of the brilliant creative work of those barbarian rear-guards in the Celtic Fringe and in Scandinavia whose attempts to give birth to civilizations on their own account were rendered abortive by their defeat in their struggle with the nascent civilization of Western Christendom. These encounters have been discussed in this Study already in another connexion, and we may pass on at once to consider the external proletariats generated by an expanding Western World in the Modern Age. In reconnoitring this broad landscape, we will content ourselves with a single example of barbarian creativity in each of the two spheres in which we have learnt to look for it.

In the poetic field we may take note of the 'heroic' poetry which was cultivated in the sixteenth and seventeenth centuries of the Christian Era by the Bosniak barbarians beyond the south-eastern frontier of the Danubian Hapsburg Monarchy. This example is interesting because at first sight it seems an exception to the rule that the external proletariat of a disintegrating civilization is not apt to be stimulated to the creation of 'heroic' poetry until the civilization in question has passed through its universal state and fallen into an interregnum which gives opportunity for a barba-rian Völkerwanderung. But the Danubian Hapsburg Monarchy, which, from the standpoint of London or Paris, was no more than one among several parochial Powers in a politically divided Western World, had all the appearance and properties of a Western universal state in the eyes of its own subjects and also in those of its non-Western neighbours and adversaries, against whom it served as a 'carapace' or shield for the whole body of a Western Christian Society whose sheltered members remained un-appreciative beneficiaries of the Monarchy's oecumenical mission.

The Bosniaks were a rear-guard of the Continental European barbarians who had previously had to endure the unusual—and unusually painful—experience of being taken between the fires of two aggressive civilizations, those of Western and of Orthodox Christendom. The radiation of the Orthodox Christian Civiliza-tion, which had been the first to reach the Bosniaks, had been rejected by them in its orthodox form, and had only been able to insinuate itself in the schismatic guise of Bogomilism. This heresy had drawn upon them the hostile attentions of both Christian civilizations, and in these circumstances they had wel-comed the arrival of the Muslim 'Osmanlis, abandoned their

Bogomilism and 'turned Turk' so far as religion was concerned. Thereafter, under Ottoman protection, these Jugoslav converts to Islam took to playing, on the Ottoman side of the Ottoman–Hapsburg frontier, the same part as was played on the Hapsburg side by Jugoslav Christian refugees from the territories which had fallen under Ottoman rule. The two opposing sets of Jugoslavs found an identical occupation in raiding, on the one side the Ottoman Empire and on the other side the Hapsburg Monarchy; and on the same fertile soil of border warfare two independent schools of 'heroic' poetry, both using the Serbo-Croat language, grew up and flourished side by side, apparently without exercising any influence on one another.

Our example of external-proletarian creativity in the religious field comes from a very different quarter, namely the nineteenth-century frontier of the United States over against the Red Indians.

It is remarkable that the North American Indians should have been capable of making any creative religious response at all to the challenge of European aggression, seeing that they were almost continuously 'on the run' from the moment of the arrival of the first English settlers down to the crushing of the last Indian attempt at armed resistance in the Sioux War of 1890, two hundred and eighty years later, and it is still more remarkable that this Indian response should have been of a gentle character. We should rather have expected the Indian war-bands either to create a pagan religion in their own likeness—an Iroquois Olympus or Asgard—or else to adopt the most militant elements in the Calvinistic Protestantism of their assailants. However, a series of prophets, from the anonymous Delaware Prophet of A.D. 1762 to Wovoka who arose about A.D. 1885 in Nevada, preached a gospel of quite another kind. They preached peace and urged their disciples to renounce the use of all the technical material 'improvements' that they had acquired from their white enemies,[1] beginning with the use of fire-arms. They proclaimed that, if their teaching were followed, the Indians were destined to a life of bliss in an earthly paradise in which the living would be rejoined by the souls of their ancestors, and that this Red Indian Messianic Kingdom was not to be conquered with tomahawks, much less with bullets. What results would have followed the adoption of such teaching we cannot say; it proved too hard and too high for the barbarian warriors to whom it was addressed, but in these gleams of gentle light on a dark and grim horizon we catch an arresting glimpse of the *anima naturaliter Christiana* in the bosom of primitive man.

[1] There is an obvious parallel here with the *swadeshi* movement in India.— EDITOR.

At the present moment it looks as though, for the few antique barbarian communities that remain on the map, the only chance of survival lies in adopting the tactics of the Abotrites and Lithuanians who, in the medieval chapter of the history of our Western expansion, had the foresight to anticipate a forcible by a voluntary conversion to the culture of an aggressive civilization which was too strong for them to resist. In our latter-day remnant of an antique barbarian world there are still standing out two closely beleaguered fastnesses of barbarism in each of which an enterprising barbarian war-lord has been making a determined effort to save a perhaps not yet quite hopeless situation by launching a vigorous cultural offensive-defensive.

In North-Eastern Iran it seems possible that the North-West Frontier problem of India may finally be solved, not by any drastic action against the untamed barbarians on the Indian side of the Indo-Afghan frontier, but rather by the voluntary Westernization of Afghanistan itself. For if this Afghan endeavour were to achieve success, one of its effects would be to place the war-bands on the Indian side between two fires and thereby make their position ultimately untenable. The Westernizing movement in Afghanistan was launched by King Amānallāh (A.D. 1919–29) with a radical excess of zeal which cost the royal revolutionary his throne; but Amānallāh's personal fiasco is less significant than the fact that this check has not proved fatal to the movement. By 1929 the process of Westernization had gone too far for the people of Afghanistan to put up with the unmitigated barbarian reaction of the brigand-rebel Bacha-i-Sakkā; and under the régime of King Nādir and his successor the Westernizing processh as been unobtrusively resumed.

But the outstanding Westernizer of a beleaguered barbarian fastness is 'Abd-al-'Azīz Āl Sa'ūd, the King of the Najd and the Hijāz: a soldier and statesman who, since 1901, has raised himself out of the political exile into which he was born until he has made himself master of all Arabia west of the Rub'-al-Khāli and north of the Yamanī kingdom of San'ā. As a barbarian war-lord Ibn Sa'ūd may be compared in point of enlightenment with the Visigoth Atawulf. He has apprehended the potency of modern Western scientific technique and has shown a discerning eye for those applications of it—artesian wells and motor-cars and aeroplanes— that are particularly effective in the Central Arabian Steppe. But above all he has seen that the indispensable foundation for a Western way of life is law and order.

When the last obstinate enclave has been eliminated, in one way or another, from the cultural map of a Westernized World, shall we be able to congratulate ourselves on having seen the last of barbarism itself? A complete elimination of the barbarism of the external proletariat would warrant no more than a mild elation, since we have convinced ourselves (if there is any virtue in this Study) that the destruction which has overtaken a number of civilizations in the past has never been the work of any external agency, but has always been in the nature of an act of suicide.

'We are betrayed by what is false within.'[1] The familiar barbarians of the antique type may have been effectively wiped out of existence through the elimination of the last remaining no-man's-land beyond anti-barbarian frontiers which have now been carried up to the limits set by physical nature on every front in the world. But this unprecedented triumph will have profited us nothing if the barbarians, in the hour of their extinction beyond the frontiers, have stolen a march on us by re-emerging in our midst. And is it not here that we find our barbarians embattled to-day? 'Ancient civilizations were destroyed by imported barbarians; we breed our own.'[2] Have we not seen, in our generation, a host of neo-barbarian war-bands recruited under our very eyes in one country after another—and these in the heart, and not on the outskirts, of what has hitherto been a Christendom? What else but barbarians in spirit were the fighting-men in these *Fascii di Combattimento* and these *Sturmabteilungen*? Were they not taught that they were the stepchildren of the society out of whose bosom they came and that, as an aggrieved party with a score to pay off, they were morally entitled to conquer 'a place in the sun' for themselves by the ruthless use of force? And is not this precisely the doctrine that the war-lords of the external proletariat—the Generics and the Attilas—have always proclaimed to their warriors as they have led them to plunder some world which, through its own fault, has lost the power to defend itself? Black shirts and not black skins were assuredly the badges of barbarism in the Italo-Abyssinian war of 1935–6, and the black-shirted barbarian is a more appalling portent than the black-skin whom he has made his prey. The black-shirt was a portent because he was deliberately sinning against inherited lights, and he was a menace because, for the commission of his sin, he had at his disposal an inherited technique which he was free to divert from God's to the Devil's service. But in arriving at this conclusion we have not yet dug down to the root of the matter, for we have not yet asked ourselves what the source might be from which this Italian neo-barbarism was derived.

---

[1] Meredith, G.: *Love's Grave.*
[2] Inge, W. R.: *The Idea of Progress*, p. 13.

Mussolini once declared that he thought 'for Italy as the great Englishmen who have made the British Empire have thought for England, as the great French colonizers have thought for France'.[1] Before we dismiss with contempt this Italian caricature of the deeds of our own forebears, we should reflect that a caricature may be an illuminating portrait. In the repulsive countenance of the Italian neo-barbarian apostate from the path of civilization we may be compelled to confess a recognition of some of the features of much-admired English models—a Clive, a Drake and a Hawkins.

But must we not pursue our importunate question still farther? Ought we not to remind ourselves that, on the evidence presented in this chapter, the dominant minorities are found to be the original aggressors in the warfare between dominant minorities and external proletariats? We have to remember that the annals of this warfare between 'civilization' and 'barbarism' have been written almost exclusively by the scribes of the 'civilized' camp. The classic picture of the external proletarian carrying his barbarous fire and slaughter into the fair domain of some unoffending civilization is therefore likely to be no objective presentation of the truth but an expression of the 'civilized' party's resentment at being made the target of a counter-attack which he has himself provoked. The complaint against the barbarian, as drafted by his mortal enemy, amounts perhaps to little more than:

> Cet animal est très méchant:
> Quand on l'attaque, il se défend![2]

(6) ALIEN AND INDIGENOUS INSPIRATIONS

A Widening of Horizons

At the very beginning of this Study, after having argued, from the example of English history, that the history of a national state was not intelligible taken by itself and apart from the doings of the rest of its kind, we made the assumption that the groups of kindred communities which we called societies—and which we found to be societies of a particular species known as civilizations —would prove to be 'intelligible fields of study'. In other words, we assumed that the course of the life of a civilization was self-determined, so that it could be studied and understood in and by itself, without requiring constant allowance for the play of alien social forces. This assumption has been borne out by our study

[1] Mussolini in an interview given to the French publicist M. de Kerillis, quoted in *The Times*, 1st August, 1935.
[2] 'Théodore P. K.': *La Ménagerie.*

of the geneses of civilizations and of their growths, and so far it has not been refuted by our study of their breakdowns and disintegrations. For, although a disintegrating society may split into fragments, each of these fragments turns out to be a chip of the old block. Even the external proletariat is recruited from elements within the disintegrating society's field of radiation. At the same time, however, our survey of the several fractions of societies in disintegration—and this is true not only of external proletariats but of internal proletariats and dominant minorities as well—has frequently required us to take alien as well as indigenous agents into account.

It has, in fact, become clear that, while the definition of a society as 'an intelligible field of study' can be accepted almost without qualification so long as it is still in growth, this definition can only be maintained with reservations when we come to the disintegration stage. True though it be that the breakdowns of civilizations are due to an inward loss of self-determination and not to any external blows, it is not true that the process of disintegration through which a broken-down civilization has to pass on its way to dissolution is equally intelligible without reference to external agencies and activities. In the study of the life of a civilization in the disintegration stage the 'intelligible field' has proved to be distinctly wider than the ambit of the single society under observation. This means that, in the process of disintegrating, the substance of a body social tends not merely to split into the three components that we have just been studying but also to resume its liberty to enter into new combinations with elements derived from foreign bodies. Thus we are now finding that the ground on which we took our stand at the beginning of this Study, and which has stood firm so far, is slipping away from under our feet. At the beginning we chose civilizations for the objects of our Study just because they presented the appearance of being 'intelligible fields' which lent themselves singly to being studied in isolation. We now find ourselves already on the move from this standpoint towards a different one which we shall have to take up when we examine the contacts of civilizations with one another.[1]

Meanwhile, it will be convenient at this point to distinguish and compare the respective effects of the alien and indigenous inspirations that can be discerned in the activities of the several fractions into which the body social of a society in disintegration is divided. We shall find that, in the works of a dominant minority and an external proletariat, an alien inspiration is apt to result in

[1] In the volumes not yet published.

discord and destruction, whereas in the works of an internal proletariat it is apt to produce the exactly opposite effects of harmony and creation.

Dominant Minorities and External Proletariats

We have seen that universal states are usually provided by dominant minorities indigenous to the society for which they perform this high-handed service. These indigenous empire-builders may be frontiersmen from the outer edge of the world upon which they confer the blessing of peace through the imposition of political unity; but this origin does not in itself convict them of having any alien tinge in their culture. We have, however, also noted cases in which the moral débâcle of the dominant minority has been so rapid that, by the time when the disintegrating society has been ripe for entering a universal state, there has no longer been any remnant of the dominant minority still possessed of the empire-building virtues. In such cases the task of providing a universal state is not usually allowed to remain unperformed. Some alien empire-builder steps into the breach and performs for the ailing society the task that ought to have been performed by native hands.

All universal states, alien and indigenous alike, are apt to be accepted with thankfulness and resignation, if not with enthusiasm; they are at any rate an improvement, in a material sense, upon the time of troubles that has preceded them. But as time passes 'a new king' arises 'who knew not Joseph'; in plain language, the time of troubles and the memory of its horrors recedes into a forgotten past, and the present—in which the universal state extends over the entire social landscape—comes to be judged as a thing in itself irrespective of its historical context. At this stage the fortunes of indigenous and alien universal states diverge. The indigenous universal state, whatever its real merits, tends to become more and more acceptable to its subjects and is more and more regarded as the only possible social framework for their life. The alien universal state, on the other hand, becomes more and more unpopular. Its subjects are more and more offended by its alien qualities and shut their eyes more and more firmly to the useful service which it has performed and perhaps still is performing for them.

An obvious pair of universal states for the illustration of this contrast is the Roman Empire which provided an indigenous universal state for the Hellenic World and the British Rāj which has provided the second of two alien universal states for the Hindu Civilization. Many quotations could be collected to illustrate the love and veneration with which the latter-day subjects of the Roman Empire regarded that institution, even after it had ceased to perform its task with tolerable efficiency and when it was in manifest dissolution. Perhaps the most striking of these tributes is a passage in the poem *De Consulatu Stilichonis* written in Latin hexameters by Claudian of Alexandria in A.D. 400.

> She—prouder boast than other conquerors knew—
> Gently her captives to her bosom drew;
> Mother not mistress, made the thrall her kin
> And 'neath her wing called all the nations in.
> Who owns, and owes not to her parent sway,
> His civick rights in utmost lands to-day?[1]

It would be easy to prove that the British Rāj has been in many respects a more benevolent and also perhaps a more beneficent institution than the Roman Empire, but it would be hard to find a Claudian in any of the Alexandrias of Hindustan.

If we look at the history of other alien universal states, we shall observe the same mounting tide of hostile feeling among their subjects as we find in British India. The alien Syriac universal state imposed by Cyrus on the Babylonic Society was so bitterly hated by the time it had completed the second century of its existence that in 331 B.C. the Babylonian priests were prepared to give an effusive welcome to the equally alien conqueror Alexander of Macedon, as in our day certain extreme nationalists in India might have been prepared to welcome a Clive from Japan. In Orthodox Christendom the alien *Pax Ottomanica* which had been welcomed in the first quarter of the fourteenth century of the Christian Era by the Greek adherents of the founder of the Ottoman commonwealth on the Asiatic shores of the Sea of Marmara had become an object of loathing to the Greek nationalists of A.D. 1821. The passage of five centuries had produced among Greeks a change of sentiment which was the exact inverse of the change in Gaul from the Romano-phobia of a Vercingetorix to the Romano-philia of a Sidonius Apollinaris.

Another prominent example of the hatred aroused by empire-builders of an alien culture is the animosity of the Chinese towards the Mongol conquerors who provided a distracted Far Eastern World with a sorely needed universal state, and this animosity might appear to present a curious contrast to the tolerance with which the same society accepted two-and-a-half centuries of Manchu domination at a later period. The explanation is to be found in the fact that the Manchus were backwoodsmen of

---

[1] Translation by R. A. Knox, in *The Making of Western Europe*, by C. R. L. Fletcher, p. 3.

the Far Eastern World who were not contaminated by any alien culture, whereas the Mongols' barbarism was mitigated, however slightly, by a tincture of Syriac culture derived from Nestorian Christian pioneers and by an open-minded readiness to enlist the services of able and experienced men whatever their provenance. That this is the real explanation of the unpopularity of the Mongol régime in China is made plain by Marco Polo's account of explosive contacts between the Chinese subjects and the Orthodox Christian soldiers and Muslim administrators of the Mongol Khāqān.

It was perhaps a tincture of Sumeric culture that made the Hyksos intolerable to their Egyptiac subjects, whereas the subsequent intrusion of the completely barbarian Libyans was accepted without resentment. In fact, we can venture to formulate something like a general social law to the effect that barbarian invaders who present themselves free from any alien cultural taint are apt to make their fortunes, while those who, before their Völkerwanderung, have acquired either an alien or a heretical tinge must go out of their way to purge themselves of it if they are to escape the otherwise inevitable doom of being either ejected or exterminated.

To take undiluted barbarians first: the Aryas and the Hittites and the Achaeans, each of whom invented a barbarian pantheon of their own during their sojourn on the threshold of a civilization, and who persisted in this barbarian worship after they had broken through and made their conquests, each also succeeded, notwithstanding this 'invincible ignorance', in founding new civilizations: the Indic, the Hittite and the Hellenic. Again, the Frankish and English and Scandinavian and Polish and Magyar converts from a native paganism to Western Catholic Christianity secured the opportunity to play full, and even leading, parts in the building up of Western Christendom. On the other hand the Hyksos worshippers of Set were evicted from the Egyptiac World and the Mongols were evicted from China.

An exception to our rule would seem to be presented by the Primitive Muslim Arabs. Here was a group of barbarians, belonging to the external proletariat of the Hellenic Society, who achieved a high degree of success in the Völkerwanderung which accompanied the dissolution of that society in spite of the fact that they clung to their own barbarian travesty of Syriac religion instead of adopting the Monophysite Christianity of their subjects in the provinces that they wrested from the Roman Empire. But the historic role of the primitive Muslim Arabs was altogether exceptional. Through their incidental conquest of the whole Sasanian

Empire in the course of their victorious assault upon the Oriental provinces of the Roman Empire, the barbarian successor-state of the Roman Empire which the Arabs founded on Syrian soil transformed itself into a restoration of the Syriac universal state which had been prematurely destroyed, a thousand years before, when the Achaemenidae had been overthrown by Alexander; and the vast new political mission with which the Muslim Arabs were thus, almost accidentally, endowed opened up a new horizon for Islam itself.

It would seem, therefore, that the history of Islam is a special case which does not invalidate the general results of our inquiry. In general we are justified in concluding that, for external proletariats and dominant minorities alike, an alien inspiration is a handicap because it is a fruitful source of friction and frustration for them in their dealings with the other two of the fractions into which a disintegrating society splits up.

Internal Proletariats

In contrast with these findings about dominant minorities and external proletariats we shall find that for internal proletariats an alien inspiration is not a curse but a blessing which confers on those who receive it an apparently superhuman power of taking their conquerors captive and of attaining the end to which they have been born. This thesis can best be tested by an examination of those 'higher religions' and universal churches which are the internal proletariat's characteristic works. Our survey of these has shown that their potency depends on the presence, and varies in proportion to the strength, of an alien spark of vitality in their spirit.

For example the worship of Osiris, which was the 'higher religion' of the Egyptiac proletariat, can be traced back tentatively, as we have seen, to an alien origin in the Sumeric worship of Tammuz; and the manifold and competing 'higher religions' of the Hellenic internal proletariat can all be traced back to various alien origins with certainty. In the worship of Isis the alien spark is Egyptiac; in the worship of Cybele it is Hittite; in Christianity and Mithraism it is Syriac; in the Mahāyāna it is Indic. The first four of these 'higher religions' were created by Egyptiac, Hittite and Syriac populations which had been conscripted into the Hellenic internal proletariat through Alexander's conquests, and the fifth was created by an Indic population likewise conscripted, in the second century B.C., through the Euthydemic Bactrian Greek princes' conquests in the Indic World. Profoundly though they differ from one another in their inward spiritual essence, all five of them have in common at least this superficial feature of being alien in their origin.

Our conclusion will not be shaken by a consideration of certain cases in which an attempt to conquer a society has been made by a higher religion without success. There is, for example, the abortive attempt of the Shī'ah sect of Islam to become the universal church of Orthodox Christendom under the Ottoman régime, and the abortive attempt of Catholic Christianity to become the universal church of the Far Eastern Society—in China during the last century of the Ming and the first century of the Manchu dynasties and in Japan at the moment of transition from the time of troubles to the Tokugawa Shogunate. The Shī'ah in the Ottoman Empire and Catholicism in Japan were both cheated of their prospective spiritual conquests by being exploited—or at any rate suspected of being exploited—for illegitimate political ends. The failure of Catholicism in China was due to the refusal of the Papacy to allow the Jesuit missionaries to carry on their work of translating an alien Catholic religious idiom into the traditional language of Far Eastern philosophy and ritual.

We may conclude that an alien spark is a help and not a hindrance to a 'higher religion' in winning converts; and the reason for this is not far to seek. An internal proletariat, alienated from the broken-down society from which it is in process of secession, is seeking a new revelation, and this is what the alien spark supplies; it is its newness which makes it attractive. But, before it can become attractive, the new truth has to be made intelligible; and, until this necessary work of exposition has been performed, the new truth will be inhibited from making its potential appeal. The victory of the Christian Church in the Roman Empire could not have been won if the Fathers of the Church, from St. Paul onwards, had not exerted themselves, during the first four or five centuries of the Christian era, to translate the Christian doctrine into terms of Hellenic philosophy; to build up the Christian ecclesiastical hierarchy on the pattern of the Roman civil service; to mould the Christian ritual on the model of the Mysteries; and even to convert pagan into Christian festivals and replace pagan cults of heroes by Christian cults of saints. It was an undertaking of this kind which was nipped in the bud by the Vatican's instructions to the Jesuit missionaries in China; and the conversion of the Hellenic World would have been as fatally arrested after the first excursions of Christian missionaries on to Gentile ground, if the Judaizing Christian opponents of St. Paul had been victorious in the conferences and conflicts described in The Acts of the Apostles and in the earlier Pauline epistles.

Our muster of 'higher religions' which appear to have had an indigenous inspiration will include Judaism and Zoroastrianism and Islam—three religions which have found their field in the Syriac World and have drawn their inspiration from the same quarter—and also Hinduism, which is clearly Indic both in its inspiration and in its field of operations. Hinduism and Islam must be regarded as exceptions to our 'law', but Judaism and Zoroastrianism will turn out on examination to be, after all, illustrations of it. For the Syriac populations among which Judaism and Zoroastrianism came to birth, between the eighth and the sixth century before Christ, were broken peoples which had been forcibly conscripted into the internal proletariat of the Babylonic Society by the Assyrian armies of the Babylonic dominant minority. It was this Babylonic aggression that evoked the Jewish and Zoroastrian religious responses from the Syriac souls that were subjected to the ordeal. On this showing we clearly ought to classify Judaism and Zoroastrianism as religions which were introduced by Syriac conscripts into the internal proletariat of the Babylonic Society. Judaism actually took shape 'by the waters of Babylon', as the Christian Church took shape in the Pauline congregations in the Hellenic World.

If the disintegration of the Babylonic Civilization had been as long drawn out as that of the Hellenic Civilization and had passed through all the same stages, then the birth and growth of Judaism and Zoroastrianism would present themselves, in historical perspective, as events in a Babylonic story—as the birth and growth of Christianity and Mithraism do, in fact, present themselves as events in Hellenic history. Our perspective has been thrown out by the fact that Babylonic history came to a premature close. The Chaldaean attempt at a Babylonic universal state collapsed; and the Syriac conscripts in its internal proletariat were able not only to throw off their chains but to turn the tables on their Babylonic conquerors by taking them captive in body as well as in spirit. The Iranians became converts to the Syriac and not to the Babylonic culture, and the Achaemenian Empire founded by Cyrus came to play the part of a Syriac universal state. It is in this perspective that Judaism and Zoroastrianism take on their present appearance of being Syriac religions with an indigenous inspiration. We can now see that they were, in their origin, religions of a Babylonic internal proletariat to which their Syriac inspiration was alien.

If a 'higher religion' has an alien inspiration—and we have found that this is a rule with only two notable exceptions—then obviously the nature of that religion cannot be understood without taking into account the contact of at least two civilizations: the civilization in whose internal proletariat the new religion arises and the civilization (or civilizations) from which its alien inspiration (or inspirations) is derived. This fact requires us to make a radical new departure; for it requires us to relinquish the basis on which this Study has so far been built up. So far we have been dealing in terms of civilizations; and we have assumed that any single civilization will afford a practicable 'field of study' in virtue of being a social whole, intelligible in isolation from whatever social phenomena might present themselves outside the spatial and temporal limits of this particular society. But now we find ourselves entangled in the same net as that in which, in our opening pages, we so confidently entangled those historians who believed that they could 'make sense' of an isolated national history. Henceforth we shall have to transcend the limits within which we have hitherto found ourselves able to work.

XIX. SCHISM IN THE SOUL

(1) ALTERNATIVE WAYS OF BEHAVIOUR, FEELING AND LIFE

THE schism in the body social, which we have been hitherto examining, is a collective experience and therefore superficial. Its significance lies in its being the outward and visible sign of an inward and spiritual rift. A schism in the souls of human beings will be found to underlie any schism that reveals itself on the surface of the society which is the common ground of these human actors' respective fields of activity; and the several forms which this inward schism may take must now engage our attention.

Schism in the souls of members of a disintegrating society displays itself in a variety of shapes because it arises in every one of the various ways of behaviour, feeling and life which we have found to be characteristic of the action of human beings who play their part in the geneses and growths of civilizations. In the disintegration phase each of these single lines of action is apt to split into a pair of mutually antithetical and antipathetic variations or substitutes, in which the response to a challenge is polarized into two alternatives—one passive and the other active, but neither of them creative. A choice between the active and the passive option is the only freedom that is left to a soul which has lost the opportunity (though not, of course, the capacity) for creative action through being cast for a part in the tragedy of social disintegration. As the process of disintegration works itself out, the alternative choices tend to become more rigid in their limitations, more extreme in their divergence and more momentous in their consequences. That is to say, the spiritual experience of schism in the soul is a dynamic movement, not a static situation.

To begin with, there are two ways of personal behaviour which are alternative substitutes for the exercise of the creative faculty. Both of them are attempts at self-expression. The passive attempt consists in an *abandon* (ἀκράτεια) in which the soul 'lets itself go' in the belief that, by giving free rein to its own spontaneous appetites and aversions, it will be 'living according to nature' and will automatically receive back from that mysterious goddess the precious gift of creativity which it has been conscious of losing. The active alternative is an effort at self-control (ἐγκράτεια) in which the soul 'takes itself in hand' and seeks to discipline its 'natural passions' in the opposite belief that nature is the bane of creativity and not its source and that to 'gain the mastery over nature' is the only way of recovering the lost creative faculty.

Then there are two ways of social behaviour which are alternative substitutes for that mimesis of creative personalities which we have found to be the necessary, though perilous, short cut on the road to social growth. Both these substitutes for mimesis are attempts to step out of the ranks of a phalanx whose 'social drill' has failed to work. The passive attempt to break this social deadlock takes the form of truancy. The soldier realizes with dismay that the regiment has now lost the discipline that has hitherto fortified his *moral*, and in this situation he allows himself to believe that he is absolved from his military duty. In this unedifying frame of mind the truant steps out of the ranks backwards, in the futile hope of saving his own skin by leaving his comrades in the lurch. There is, however, an alternative way of facing the same ordeal, which may be called martyrdom. In essence, the martyr is a soldier who steps out of the ranks on his own initiative in a forward direction in order to go beyond the demands of duty. While in normal circumstances duty demands that the soldier should risk his life to the minimum extent that may be necessary for the execution of his superior officer's orders, the martyr courts death for the vindication of an ideal.

When we pass from the plane of behaviour to that of feeling, we may first take note of two ways of personal feeling which are the alternative reactions to a reversal of that movement of *élan* in which the nature of growth seems to reveal itself. Both these feelings reflect a painful consciousness of being 'on the run' from forces of evil which have taken the offensive and established their ascendancy. The passive expression of this consciousness of continual and progressive moral defeat is a sense of drift. The routed soul is prostrated by a perception of its failure to control its environment; it comes to believe that the Universe, including the soul itself, is at the mercy of a power that is as irrational as it is invincible: the ungodly goddess with a double face who is propitiated under the name of Chance ($\tau\acute{v}\chi\eta$) or is endured under the name of Necessity ($\dot{a}\nu\acute{a}\gamma\kappa\eta$)—a pair of deities which have been given a literary incarnation in the choruses of Thomas Hardy's *Dynasts*. Alternatively, the moral defeat which desolates the routed soul may be felt as a failure to master and control the soul's own self. In that case, instead of a sense of drift we have a sense of sin.

We have also to notice two ways of social feeling which are alternative substitutes for the sense of style—a sense that is the subjective counterpart of the objective process of the differentiation of civilizations through their growth. Both these feelings betray a loss of this same sensitiveness to form, though in their respective ways of responding to this challenge they are poles apart. The passive response is a sense of promiscuity in which the soul surrenders itself to the melting-pot. In the medium of language and literature and art this sense of promiscuity declares itself in the currency of a *lingua franca* (κοινή) and of a similarly standardized and composite style of literature, painting, sculpture and architecture; in the realm of philosophy and religion it produces syncretisms. The active response takes the loss of a style of living which has been local and ephemeral as an opportunity, and a call, to adopt another style which partakes of what is universal and eternal: *quod ubique, quod semper, quod ab omnibus*. This active response is an awakening to a sense of unity which broadens and deepens as the vision expands from the unity of mankind, through the unity of the cosmos, to embrace the unity of God.

If we pass on, in the third place, to the plane of life, we shall encounter here again two pairs of alternative reactions, but on this plane the picture departs from the previous pattern in three respects. For one thing, the alternatives which here replace the single movement that is characteristic of the stage of growth are variations on that movement rather than substitutes for it. Secondly, both pairs of alternatives are variations on the same single movement—a movement which we have described as transference of the field of action from the macrocosm to the microcosm. Thirdly, the two pairs are differentiated from one another by a difference sufficiently profound to account for the duplication. In one pair the temper of the reactions is violent; in the other pair, gentle. In the violent pair the passive reaction may be described as archaism and the active as futurism; in the gentle pair the passive may be described as detachment and the active as transfiguration.

Archaism and futurism are alternative attempts to substitute a mere transfer in the time-dimension for that transfer of the field of action from one spiritual plane to another which is the characteristic movement of growth. In both, the effort to live in the microcosm instead of the macrocosm is abandoned for the pursuit of a Utopia which would be reached—supposing it could actually be found 'in real life'—without any challenge to face the arduous change of spiritual clime. This external Utopia is intended to do duty as an 'Other World'; but it is an 'Other World' only in the shallow and unsatisfying sense of being a negation of the macrocosm in its present state of being, here and now. The soul proposes to perform what is required of it by making its move from the present disintegrating state of society to a goal which is simply the same society as it may once have been in the past or as it may sometime come to be in the future.

Archaism may, in fact, be defined as a reversion from the mimesis of contemporary creative personalities to a mimesis of the ancestors of the tribe: that is to say, as a lapse from the dynamic movement of civilization to the static condition in which primitive mankind is now to be seen. It may be defined, again, as one of those attempts at a forcible stoppage of change which result, in so far as they succeed, in the production of social 'enormities'. Thirdly, it may be taken as an example of that attempt to 'peg' a broken-down and disintegrating society which in another context we found to be the common aim of the authors of Utopias. In corresponding terms we may define futurism as a repudiation of the mimesis of anybody, and also as one of those attempts at a forcible accomplishment of change which result, in so far as they succeed at all, in producing social revolutions that defeat their own purpose by tumbling over into reaction.

For those who put their trust in either of these would-be substitutes for the transfer of the field of action from the macrocosm to the microcosm, there lies in wait an ironical common fate. In seeking their alternative 'easy' options these defeatists are actually condemning themselves to the violent denouement which is bound to overtake them, because they are attempting something which is contrary to the order of nature. The quest of the inner life, hard though it may be, is no impossibility; but it is intrinsically impossible for the soul, in so far as it is living in the outward life, to extricate itself from its present place in the 'ever rolling stream' by taking a flying leap either backwards up-stream into the past or down-stream into the future. The archaistic and the futuristic Utopias alike are Utopias in the literal sense of the word: they are 'Nowheres'. These two alluring *alibis* are unattainable *ex hypothesi*; and the sole and certain effect of striking out towards either of them is to produce a troubling of the waters with a violence that brings no healing.

In its tragic climax futurism expresses itself as Satanism.

'The essence of the belief is that the World Order is evil and a lie; goodness and truth are persecuted rebels. . . . The belief has been held by many Christian saints and martyrs, and notably by the author of the Apocalypse. But we should notice that it is diametrically opposed to the teaching of almost all the great moral philosophers. Plato, Aristotle 'and the Stoics, St. Augustine and St. Thomas Aquinas, Kant and J. S. Mill and Comte and T. H. Green, all argue or assume that there exists in some sense a Cosmos or Divine Order; that what is good is in harmony with this order and what is bad is in discord against it. I notice that one of the Gnostic schools, in Hippolytus the Church Father, actually defines Satan as "the Spirit who works against the Cosmic Powers": the rebel or protestant who counteracts the will of the whole and tries to thwart the community of which he is a member.'[1]

This inevitable outcome of the spirit of revolution is an accepted commonplace among all men and women who are not themselves revolutionaries, and it is not difficult to lay our finger on historic illustrations of the working out of this spiritual law.

For example, in the Syriac Society, the Messianic form of futurism made its first appearance as a positive attempt to follow the way of gentleness. Instead of persisting in a disastrous attempt to maintain his political independence, here and now, against the assaults of Assyrian militarism, the Israelite bowed his neck to a present political yoke and reconciled himself to this painful act of resignation by transferring all his political treasure to the hope of a saviour-king who was to arise and restore the fallen national kingdom at some unknown future date. When we trace out the history of this Messianic Hope in the Jewish community, we find that it worked in favour of gentleness for more than four hundred years—from 586 B.C., when the Jews were carried away into a Babylonish Captivity by Nebuchadnezzar, until 168 B.C., when they were subjected to the Hellenizing persecution of Antiochus Epiphanes. Yet the discord between a confidently expected mundane future and an excruciatingly painful mundane present resolved itself into violence in the end. The martyrdom of Eleazer and the Seven Brethren was followed within two years by the armed insurrection of Judas Maccabaeus, and the Maccabees inaugurated that long line of ever more fanatically militant Jewish Zealots—the innumerable Theudases and Judases of Galilee—whose violence reached its appalling climax in the Satanic Jewish revolts of A.D. 66–70 and 115–17 and 132–5.

The nemesis of futurism, illustrated by this classic Jewish case, is not unfamiliar; but it is perhaps more surprising to find archaism overtaken by the same nemesis at the end of its own apparently opposite path; for, so far from being a commonplace, it may seem something of a paradox to suggest that a pandemonium of violence is the inevitable outcome of this retrograde movement likewise. Nevertheless, the facts of history show that it is so.

In the history of the political disintegration of the Hellenic Society the first statesmen to take the archaistic road were King Agis IV at Sparta and the tribune Tiberius Gracchus at Rome. Both were men of unusual sensitiveness and gentleness, and both set themselves the task of righting a social wrong, and thereby averting a social catastrophe, through a return to what they

[1] Murray, Gilbert: 'Satanism and the World Order', in *Essays and Addresses*, p. 203.

believed to have been the ancestral constitutions of their states in
the already half legendary 'golden age' before the breakdown. Their
aim was the restoration of concord; yet, because their archaistic
policy was an attempt to reverse the current of social life, it inevitably led them into a course of violence; and their gentleness of
spirit, which moved them to sacrifice their lives rather than go to
extremes in combating the counter-violence which their reluctant
violence had provoked, did not avail to arrest the avalanche of
violence which they had unintentionally set in motion. Their
self-sacrifice merely inspired a successor to take up their work and
seek to carry it through to success by a ruthless use of the violence
in which the martyr had shown himself half-hearted. The gentle
King Agis IV was followed by the violent King Cleomenes III
and the gentle tribune Tiberius Gracchus by his violent brother
Gaius. Nor was this, in either case, the end of the story. The
two gentle archaists let loose a flood of violence which did not sub-
side until it had swept away the whole fabric of the commonwealths which they had sought to save.

But if we now pursue our Hellenic and our Syriac illustrations
into the next chapters of the histories to which they belong, we
shall find that the pandemonium of violence, let loose by archaism
in the one case and by futurism in the other, was eventually
allayed by an astonishing resurrection of that very spirit of gentleness which the surging tide of violence had overborne and submerged. In the history of the Hellenic dominant minority the
gangsters of the last two centuries B.C. were followed, as we have
observed, by a breed of public servants with the conscience and
the ability to organize and maintain a universal state; and at the
same time the successors of the violent-handed archaizing reformers turned into a school of aristocratic philosophers—Arria,
Caecina Paetus, Thrasea Paetus, Seneca, Helvidius Priscus—who
took no satisfaction in the exercise of their hereditary dominance
even in the public interest, and who carried this abnegation to
a point of obediently committing suicide at the command of a
tyrant emperor. Similarly, in the Syriac wing of the internal
proletariat of the Hellenic World, the fiasco of the Maccabaean
attempt to establish by force of arms a Messianic Kingdom of This
World was followed by the triumph of a King of the Jews whose
Kingdom was not of This World; while, in the next generation, on
a narrower range of spiritual vision, the savagely heroic forlorn
hope of the militant Jewish Zealots was retrieved, in the hour of
annihilation, by the sublimely heroic non-resistance of the Rabbi
Johanan ben Zakkai, who separated himself from the Jewish
Zealots in order that he might quietly continue his teaching out

of earshot of the battle. When the news of the inevitable catastrophe was brought to him, and the disciple who brought it
exclaimed in anguish 'Woe to us, because the place is destroyed
where they make propitiation for the sins of Israel', the master
answered: 'My son, let it not grieve thee; we have yet one propitiation equal to it, and what is that but the bestowal of kindnesses?
—even as it is written "I desired kindness and not sacrifice".'

How was it that in both these cases a tide of violence, which
seemed to have swept away every barrier in its path, was brought
thus to a standstill and reversed? In either case the miraculous
reversal can be traced to a change in ways of life. In the souls of
the Roman fraction of the Hellenic dominant minority the ideal
of archaism had been supplanted by the ideal of detachment; in
the souls of the Jewish fraction of the Hellenic internal proletariat the ideal of futurism had been replaced by the ideal of transfiguration.

Perhaps we can apprehend the qualities of these two gentle
ways of life in the same view as their historical geneses if we
approach each of them first through the personality and life-
history of a notable convert: for example, Cato Minor, the Roman
archaist who became a Stoic philosopher, and Simon Bar-Jonas,
the Jewish futurist who became Peter the disciple of Jesus. In
both of these great men there was a streak of spiritual blindness
which obscured their greatness by misdirecting their energies so
long as they were pursuing the respective Utopias to the service
of which they had first thought to dedicate themselves. And in
each of them the long-baffled and bewildered soul was enabled,
through its conversion to a new way of life, to realize at last its
highest potentialities.

As the Quixotic champion of a romantically conceived Roman
πάτριος πολιτεία which had never existed 'in real life' in any past
age, Cato was almost a figure of fun. In the politics of a generation
which he refused to take as he found it he was perpetually chasing
the shadow and missing the substance; and, when at last he stumbled into playing a leading part in a civil war for the outbreak of
which he bore a large share of unadmitted responsibility, his
political make-believe was doomed to suffer a shattering disillusionment whatever the event might be, for the régime which
would have resulted from a victory of his associates would have
been at least as repugnant to Cato's archaistic ideal as the eventually victorious Caesarean dictatorship. In this dilemma the
Quixotic politician was redeemed from ineptitude by the Stoic
philosopher. The man who had lived as an archaist in vain now
met his death as a Stoic to such good purpose that, after all, he

gave Caesar—and Caesar's successors after him for more than a century—more trouble than all the rest of the Republican party put together. The story of Cato's last hours made an impression upon his contemporaries which can be recaptured down to this day by any reader of Plutarch's narrative. With the instinct of genius Caesar apprehended the gravity of the blow which had been dealt to his cause by the Stoic death of an antagonist whom he had never found it necessary to take very seriously as a live politician; and, in the midst of the titanic labour of reconstructing a world while he was stamping out the embers of a civil war, the militarily triumphant dictator found time to reply to Cato's sword with Caesar's pen—the only weapon, as this versatile genius well knew, which might avail to ward off an attack that had been transferred from the military to the philosophic plane by Cato's disconcerting gesture of turning his sword against his own breast. Yet Caesar was unable to vanquish the adversary who had struck this parting stroke; for Cato's death gave birth to a school of philosophic opponents of Caesarism who were inspired by their founder's example to put the new tyranny out of countenance by removing themselves, with their own hand, from a situation which they would not accept and could not mend.

The change-over from archaism to detachment is also vividly illustrated in the story of Marcus Brutus, as told by Plutarch and retold by Shakespeare. Brutus was married to Cato's daughter, and was also a party to that outstanding act of futile archaistic violence, the assassination of Julius Caesar. Yet we are given to understand that, even before the assassination, he was doubtful whether he was on the right track, and that after he had seen its results he was more doubtful still. After the battle of Philippi, in the last words which Shakespeare puts into his mouth, he accepts the Catonian solution which he had formerly condemned. As he commits suicide he says:

> Caesar, now be still:
> I killed not thee with half so good a will.

As for Peter, his futurism at first seemed as incorrigible as Cato's archaism. The first of the disciples to hail Jesus as the Messiah, he was also the foremost in protesting against his acknowledged Master's consequent revelation that his Messianic Kingdom was not to be a Jewish version of the Iranian world-empire of Cyrus; and so, having earned a special blessing as the reward for his impulsive faith, he immediately drew down upon himself a crushing rebuke for his obtuse and aggressive insistence that his Master's vision of his own kingdom must conform to the disciple's *idée fixe*:

'Get thee behind me, Satan; thou art an offence unto me. For thou savourest not the things that be of God, but those that be of men.'

Even when Peter's error had been held up before his eyes by his Master's terrible reproof, the lesson had so little effect that he failed again under the next test. When he was chosen out to be one of the three witnesses of the Transfiguration, he immediately took the vision of Moses and Elias standing at his Master's side as a signal for the beginning of a *Befreiungskrieg*, and betrayed his prosaic misconception of what the vision meant by proposing to build on the spot the nucleus of a camp ('three tabernacles' or tents) of the kind that the Theudases and Judases of Galilee were wont to establish in the wilderness during the brief interval of grace before the Roman authorities received intelligence of their activities and sent out flying columns of troops to disperse them. At the sound of this jarring note the vision vanished in an echo of admonition to accept the Messiah's own revelation of the Messiah's path. Yet this second lesson was still not enough to open Peter's eyes. Even at the climax of his Master's career—when all that the Master himself had foretold was patently coming true—the incorrigible futurist drew his sword to fight in the garden of Gethsemane; and it may be that his 'betrayal' of his Master later in the same evening was the result of the confusion of mind of one who had lost his futuristic faith at last without as yet confidently grasping any alternative to it.

Even after this crowning experience of his life, when the Crucifixion and the Resurrection and the Ascension had taught him at last that Christ's Kingdom was not of This World, Peter was still fain to believe that even in this transfigured kingdom the franchise must be restricted to the Jews, just as it would have been in the futurist's Messianic Utopia—as though a society that embraced God in Heaven as its King could be bounded on God's Earth by a frontier excluding from it all but one of the tribes of God's human creatures and children. In one of the last scenes in which Peter is displayed to us in the Acts of the Apostles, we see him characteristically protesting against the clear command which accompanied the vision of the sheet let down from Heaven. Yet Peter does not give place to Paul as the protagonist in the story until the narrative has recorded his comprehension, at last, of a truth which Paul the Pharisee had apprehended in a trice through a single overwhelming spiritual experience. The long work of Peter's enlightenment was completed when the vision on the roof was followed by the arrival of Cornelius's messengers at the gate. And in his confession of faith at Cornelius's house, and his defence of his action there before the Jewish-Christian community upon his return to Jerusalem, Peter preached the Kingdom of God in words that would have drawn no reproof from the Christ.

What are these two ways of life which produced these vast spiritual effects when they were respectively adopted in place of archaism by Cato and in place of futurism by Peter? Let us begin by taking note of the common differences between detachment and transfiguration on the one hand and archaism and futurism on the other, and then go on to the differences between detachment and transfiguration.

Transfiguration and detachment alike differ from both futurism and archaism in substituting a genuine change in spiritual clime, and not a mere transfer in the time-dimension, for the particular form of transference of the field of action from the macrocosm to the microcosm which we have found to be the criterion of the growth of a civilization. The kingdoms that are their respective goals are both of them 'otherworldly' in the sense that neither of them is an imaginary past or future state of mundane existence. This common 'otherworldliness', however, is their only point of resemblance; in every other respect they present a contrast to each other.

The way of life that we have called 'detachment' has been given a variety of names by various schools of adepts. From a disintegrating Hellenic World the Stoics withdrew into an 'invulnerability' (ἀπάθεια) and the Epicureans into an 'imperturbability' (ἀταραξία)—as illustrated by the somewhat self-consciously Epicurean declaration of the poet Horace, when he tells us that 'Fragments of a ruined world strike me unperturbed' (*impavidum*). From a disintegrating Indic World the Buddhists withdrew into an 'unruffledness' (nirvāna). It is a way that leads out of This World; its goal is an asylum; and the fact that that asylum excludes This World is the feature that makes it attractive. The impulse that carries the philosophic traveller along is a push of aversion and not a pull of desire. He is shaking off from his feet the dust of the City of Destruction, but he has no vision of 'yonder Shining Light'. 'The worldling says: "O beloved City of Cecrops"; and shalt thou not say: "O beloved City of Zeus"?'[1]—but Marcus's 'City of Zeus' is not the same as Augustine's *Civitas Dei* which is 'the city of the Living God'; and the journey is a withdrawal according to plan rather than a pilgrimage inspired by faith. For the philosopher a successful escape from This World is an end in itself, and it really does not matter what the philosopher does with himself when once he has crossed the threshold of his city of refuge. The Hellenic philosophers pictured the state of the liberated sage as

[1] Marcus Aurelius Antoninus: *Meditations*, Bk. IV, ch. 23.

one of blissful contemplation (θεωρία), and the Buddha (if his doctrine is faithfully reflected in the scriptures of the Hīnayāna) frankly declares that, so long as all possibility of returning has been ruled out once for all, the nature of the alternative state in which the *tathāgata* has come to rest is a matter of no consequence.

This unknowable and neutral Nirvāna or 'City of Zeus', which is the goal of detachment, is the very antithesis of the Kingdom of Heaven which is entered by way of the religious experience of transfiguration. While the philosophic 'Other World' is in essence a world that is exclusive of ours on Earth, the divine 'Other World' transcends the earthly life of man without ceasing to include it.

'And when he was demanded of the Pharisees, when the Kingdom of God should come, he answered them and said: "The Kingdom of God cometh not with observation; neither shall they say, Lo here! or Lo there! for, behold, the Kingdom of God is within you." '[1]

It will be seen that the Kingdom of God is as positive in its nature as the 'City of Zeus' is negative, and that, whereas the way of detachment is a sheer movement of withdrawal, the way of transfiguration is a movement of what we have already had occasion to call 'withdrawal-and-return'.

We have now set out in brief six pairs of alternative ways of behaviour, feeling and life that present themselves to the souls of men whose lot is cast in disintegrating societies. Before we proceed to examine them, pair by pair, in greater detail, we may pause for a moment to take our bearings by observing the links between the history of the soul and the history of society.

Granting that every spiritual experience must be that of some individual human being, shall we find that certain experiences, among those which we have been reviewing, are peculiar to members of certain fractions of a disintegrating society? We shall find that all four personal ways of behaviour and feeling—passive *abandon* and active self-control, passive sense of drift and active sense of sin—can be detected in members of the dominant minority and the proletariat alike. On the other hand, when we come to the social ways of behaviour and feeling, we shall have to distinguish, for our present purpose, between the passive and the active pair. The two passive social phenomena—the lapse into truancy and the surrender to a sense of promiscuity—are apt to appear first in the ranks of the proletariat and to spread from there to the ranks of the dominant minority, which usually succumbs to the sickness of 'proletarianization'. Conversely the two active social phenomena—the quest of martyrdom and the awakening to a

[1] Luke xvii. 20-1.

sense of unity—are apt to appear first in the ranks of the dominant minority and to spread from there to the proletariat. Finally, when we consider our four alternative ways of life, we shall find, conversely, that the passive pair, archaism and detachment, are apt to be associated in the first instance with the dominant minority and the active pair, futurism and transfiguration, with the proletariat.

(2) 'ABANDON' AND SELF-CONTROL

The particular manifestations of *abandon* and self-control which are characteristic of societies in disintegration are perhaps rather difficult to identify, just because these two ways of personal behaviour are apt to be exhibited by human beings in every variety of social circumstance. Even in the life of primitive societies we can distinguish an orgiastic and an ascetic vein, and also the annual cyclic alternation of these moods, according to the season, in the tribe's ceremonial corporate expression of its members' emotions. But by *abandon* as an alternative to creativity in the lives of disintegrating civilizations we mean something more precise than this primitive flux of feeling. We mean a state of mind in which antinomianism is accepted—consciously or unconsciously, in theory or in practice—as a substitute for creation. Examples of *abandon* in this sense can be identified with least uncertainty if we try to take them in a single synoptic view side by side with examples of self-control, which is the alternative substitute for creativity.

In the Hellenic time of troubles, for instance, in the first generation after the breakdown, a pair of incarnations of *abandon* and self-control are presented in Plato's portraits of Alcibiades and Socrates in *The Symposium* and of Thrasymachus and Socrates in *The Republic*—Alcibiades, the slave of passion, standing for *abandon* in practice, and Thrasymachus, the advocate of 'Might is right', standing for the same mood in theory.

In the next chapter of the Hellenic story we find the exponents of each of these attempts at self-expression in lieu of creation seeking an authoritative sanction for their respective ways of behaviour by claiming that these are ways 'of living according to nature'. This merit was claimed for *abandon* by those vulgar hedonists who took in vain, and brought into disrepute, the name of Epicurus, and who for this offence were chidden by the austere Epicurean poet Lucretius. On the other side we see the sanction of 'naturalness' claimed for the ascetic life by the cynics, of whom Diogenes in his tub is the exemplar, and in less crude fashion by the Stoics.

If we pass from the Hellenic to the Syriac World in its time of troubles, we shall find the same unreconciled opposition between *abandon* and self-control appearing in the contrast between the sedately sceptical theory of the Book of Ecclesiastes and the piously ascetic practice of the monastic community of the Essenes.

There is another group of civilizations—the Indic, the Babylonic, the Hittite and the Mayan—which seem, as they disintegrate, to be reverting to the ethos of primitive man in their apparent insensibility to the yawning breadth of the gulf between the abandoned sexualism of their religion and the exaggerated asceticism of their philosophy. In the Indic case there is a contradiction which at first sight looks insoluble between lingam-worship and yoga; and we are similarly shocked by the corresponding contrasts between the temple prostitution and the astral philosophy of a disintegrating Babylonic Society, between the human sacrifices and the penitential self-mortifications of the Mayas and between the orgiastic and the ascetic aspects of the Hittite worship of Cybele and Attis. Perhaps it was the common vein of sadistic extravagance which entered into their practice of *abandon* and of self-control alike that maintained, in the souls of the members of these four disintegrating civilizations, an emotional harmony between practices which seem to defy reconciliation when they are observed with the coldly analytic eye of an alien spectator.

Are these two conflicting ways of behaviour now re-performing their parts upon the broader stage of our Western Society in the modern chapter of its history? There is no lack of evidence of *abandon*; in the domain of theory it has found its prophet in Jean-Jacques Rousseau with his alluring invitation to 'return to nature', while, for the practice of *abandon* to-day, *si monumentum requiris, circumspice*. On the other hand we may search in vain for a counter-resurgence of asceticism, and may perhaps tentatively draw from this fact the cynical conclusion that, if our Western Civilization has indeed broken down, its disintegration cannot yet be very far advanced.

(3) TRUANCY AND MARTYRDOM

Truancy and martyrdom, in the unspecialized sense of both terms, are simply products of the vice of cowardice and the virtue of courage and as such are common phenomena of human behaviour in all ages and all types of society. The truancy and martyrdom, however, which we are now considering are special forms inspired by a particular attitude to life. The truancy of mere cowardice and the martyrdom of pure courage are not our concern. The truant soul of which we are in search is a soul whose truancy is inspired by a genuine feeling that the cause which it serves is not really worth the service that this cause demands of it. Similarly the martyr soul of which we are in search is the soul which goes to martyrdom not merely or mainly to render practical service to the furtherance of that cause but rather to satisfy a craving of the soul itself for deliverance from

> the heavy and the weary weight
> Of all this unintelligible world.[1]

Such a martyr, noble as he may be, is psychologically more than half a suicide. He is, in modern jargon, an escapist, as is also of course our truant an escapist of a more ignoble variety. The Roman archaist converts to the philosophy of detachment were martyrs in this sense. By their supreme act they felt that they did not so much deprive themselves of life as free themselves from it; and, if one were to seek an example of truancy from the same class in the same period of history, one could cite Mark Antony, a truant from Rome and Roman ideals of *gravitas* in the arms of a semi-orientalized Cleopatra.

Two centuries later, in the gathering gloom of the outgoing decades of the second century of the Christian Era, we behold in the person of Marcus Aurelius a prince whose title to the martyr's crown is not invalidated, but is on the contrary confirmed, by Death's refusal to cut this martyr's ordeal short by any *coup de grâce*; while in Marcus's son and successor Commodus we are presented with the spectacle of an imperial truant who makes scarcely an effort to shoulder the burden of his heritage before he turns tail and is off, in headlong moral flight, along the sordid cinder track of proletarianization. Born to be an emperor, he prefers to amuse himself as an amateur gladiator.

The Christian Church was the principal target for the parting strokes of a Hellenic dominant minority which turned savage in its death-agony; for this dying pagan ruling class refused to face the heart-rending truth that it was itself the author of its own downfall and destruction. Even *in articulo mortis* it tried to salvage a last shred of self-respect by persuading itself that it was perishing as the victim of a dastardly assault on the part of the proletariat; and, since the external proletariat was now marshalled in formidable war-bands which were able to defy or elude the Imperial Government's attempts at retaliation for their galling raids, the brunt fell upon the Christian Church, which was the master institution of the internal proletariat. Under the test of this ordeal the sheep of the Christian fold were divided unequivocally from

[1] Wordsworth, W.: *Tintern Abbey.*

the goats by the challenge of being called upon to make the tremendous choice between renouncing their faith or sacrificing their lives. The renegades were legion—indeed their numbers were so great that the problem of how to deal with them became the burning question of ecclesiastical politics as soon as the persecutions came to an end—but the tiny band of martyrs was spiritually potent out of all proportion to its numerical strength. Thanks to the prowess of these heroes who at the critical moment stepped forward from the Christian ranks to bear their witness at the cost of life itself, the Church emerged victorious; and that small but noble army of men and women have received no more than their due meed of fame in being remembered in history as 'the martyrs' *par excellence*, in antithesis to 'the traitors' (*traditores*) who delivered up the holy scriptures or the sacred vessels of the Church at the demand of the pagan Imperial authorities.

It may be objected that here is mere cowardice on the one side and pure courage on the other, and that this illustration is of no use for our present purpose. So far as the truants are concerned we have no material for replying to this charge; their motives are buried in ignominious oblivion; but for the motives of the martyrs there is abundant evidence to prove that something more—or less, if the reader prefers—than sheer disinterested courage was the mainspring of their inspiration. Men and women enthusiastically sought martyrdom as a sacrament, a 'second baptism', a means of forgiveness of sins and a secure passage to Heaven. Ignatius of Antioch, one of the notable Christian martyrs of the second century, speaks of himself as 'the wheat of God' and longs for the day when he shall be 'ground by the teeth of wild beasts into the pure bread of Christ'.

In our own modern Western World can we discern any traces of these two antithetical ways of social behaviour? Assuredly we can put our finger on a portentous modern Western act of truancy in '*la trahison des clercs*'; and the roots of this treason spring from a depth to which the gifted Frenchman who coined the phrase might perhaps hesitate to trace them[1]—though he has virtually confessed how deep-rooted the mischief is by choosing the medieval ecclesiastical name to denote and indict our modern 'intellectuals'. Their treason did not begin with the pair of treasonable acts which they have perpetrated within living memory—a cynical loss of faith in the recently established principles, and a nerveless surrender of the recently won gains, of Liberalism. The truancy which has given this latest exhibition of itself was set on foot, centuries earlier, when the 'clerks' repudiated their clerical origin

[1] See the book with this title by Julien Benda.

by trying to shift the rising edifice of our Western Christian Civilization from a religious to a secular basis. This was the original act of ὕβρις which is being requited in our day by an ἄτη that has been accumulating for centuries at compound interest.

If we cast our eyes some four hundred years back and then focus them on the patch of Western Christendom which is known as England, we shall there see in Thomas Wolsey—the precociously modern-minded clerk who pleaded guilty, in the hour of his political disgrace, of having served his God less well than he had served his king—a truant whose truancy was shown up in all its blackness, less than five years after its ignominious end, by the martyrdom of his contemporaries, Saint John Fisher and Saint Thomas More.

(4) THE SENSE OF DRIFT AND THE SENSE OF SIN

The sense of drift, which is the passive way of feeling the loss of the *élan* of growth, is one of the most painful of the tribulations that afflict the souls of men and women who are called upon to live their lives in an age of social disintegration; and this pain is perhaps a punishment for the sin of idolatry committed through worshipping the creature instead of the Creator; for in this sin we have already found one of the causes of those breakdowns from which the disintegrations of civilizations follow.

Chance and Necessity are the alternative shapes of the Power which appears to rule the world in the eyes of those afflicted with a sense of drift; and, though at first sight the two notions may appear to contradict one another, they prove, when probed, to be merely different facets of one identical illusion.

The notion of Chance is expressed in the literature of the Egyptiac time of troubles through the simile of the giddy spinning of a potter's wheel, and in the literature of the Hellenic time of troubles through the simile of a ship that has been abandoned, without a steersman, to the mercy of the winds and waves.[1] The anthropomorphism of the Greeks converted Chance into a Goddess, 'Our Lady Automatism'. Timoleon, the liberator of Syracuse, built her a chapel in which he offered sacrifices, and Horace dedicated an Ode to her.[2]

When we look into our own hearts we find this Hellenic goddess similarly enthroned, as is witnessed by the profession of faith to be found in the Preface of H. A. L. Fisher's *History of Europe*:

'One intellectual excitement has . . . been denied me. Men wiser

[1] Cf. Plato: *Politicus*, 272 D 6–273 E 4.
[2] Horace: *Odes*, Bk. I, Ode 35. O diva gratum quae regis Antium . . . .

and more learned than I have discerned in History a plot, a rhythm, a predetermined pattern. These harmonies are concealed from me. I can see only one emergency following upon another as wave follows upon wave; only one great fact with respect to which, since it is unique, there can be no generalizations; only one safe rule for the historian: that he should recognize in the development of human destinies the play of the contingent and the unforeseen.'

This modern Western belief in the omnipotence of Chance gave birth in the nineteenth century, when things still seemed to be going well with Western man, to the policy of *laissez-faire*: a philosophy of practical life which was founded on a faith in the miraculous enlightenment of self-interest. In the light of a transitorily gratifying experience our nineteenth-century grandfathers claimed to 'know that all things work together for good for them that love' the Goddess Chance. And even in the twentieth century, when the goddess had begun to show her teeth, she was still the oracle of British foreign policy. The view that was prevalent among the people, as well as in the Cabinet, of the United Kingdom during the fateful years which opened in the autumn of 1931 was accurately expressed in the following sentence from a leading article in a great English Liberal newspaper:

'A few years of peace are always a few years gained, and a war that is due in a few years' time may never come off at all.'[1]

The doctrine of *laissez-faire* cannot be claimed as an original Western contribution to the stock of human wisdom, for it was current coin in the Sinic World some two thousand years ago. This Sinic worship of Chance, however, differs from ours in deriving from a less sordid origin. The eighteenth-century French bourgeois came to believe in *laissez-faire laissez-passer* because he had noticed and envied and analysed the prosperity of his English 'opposite number' and had come to the conclusion that the bourgeoisie might prosper in France as well as in England if only King Louis could be induced to follow the example of King George in allowing the bourgeois to manufacture what he chose, without restrictions, and to send his goods to any market, free of tolls. On the other hand the line of least resistance along which a weary Sinic World allowed itself to drift during the earlier decades of the second century before Christ was conceived of, not as a packhorse's beaten track from a humming mill to a busy market, but as a way which was the truth and the life: the *tao* which 'meant "the way the Universe works"—and ultimately something very like God, in the more abstract and philosophical sense of that term'.[2]

---

[1] *The Manchester Guardian*, 13th July, 1936.
[2] Waley, A.: *The Way and its Power*, p. 30.

> Great Tao is like a boat that drifts;
> It can go this way; it can go that.[1]

But the Goddess of *laissez-faire* has another face, under which she is worshipped, not as Chance but as Necessity. The two notions of Necessity and Chance are simply different ways of looking at the same thing. For example, the disorderly motion of the rudderless ship, which stands in Plato's eyes for the chaos of a Universe abandoned by God, can be recognized, by a mind endowed with the necessary knowledge of dynamics and physics, as a perfect illustration of the orderly behaviour of waves and currents in the media of wind and water. When the human soul adrift apprehends that the force baffling it is not simply a negation of the soul's own will but is a thing in itself, then the countenance of the invisible goddess changes from the subjective or negative aspect in which she is known as Chance to the objective or positive aspect in which she is known as Necessity—but this without any corresponding change in the essential nature of the goddess or in the predicament of her victims.

The dogma of the omnipotence of Necessity on the physical plane of existence seems to have been introduced into Hellenic thought by Democritus—a philosopher whose long life-span (*circa* 460–360 B.C.) gave him time to grow to manhood before becoming a spectator of the breakdown of the Hellenic Civilization, and thereafter to watch the process of disintegration for three-score years and ten; but he seems to have ignored the problems involved in an extension of the empire of determinism from the physical to the moral sphere. Physical determinism was also the basis of the astral philosophy of the dominant minority of the Babylonic World, and the Chaldaeans did not shrink from extending the same principle to the lives and fortunes of human beings. It is quite possible that it was from Babylonic sources rather than from Democritus that Zeno, the founder of the Stoic philosophy, derived the thorough-going fatalism with which he infected his School, and which is everywhere apparent in the 'Meditations' of the most famous of Zeno's disciples, the Emperor Marcus Aurelius.

The modern Western World seems to have broken virgin soil in extending the empire of Necessity into the economic field—which is, indeed, a sphere of social life that has been overlooked or ignored by almost all the minds that have directed the thoughts of other societies. The classic exposition of economic determinism is, of course, the philosophy—or religion—of Karl Marx; but in the Western World of to-day the number of souls who testify by

[1] *Tao Te King*, ch. 34 (Waley's translation).

their acts to a conscious or unconscious conviction of economic determinism is vastly greater than the number of professing Marxians, and would be found to include a phalanx of arch-capitalists.

The sovereignty of Necessity in the psychical sphere has also been proclaimed by one faction, at least, in our fledgeling school of modern Western psychologists, who have been tempted to deny the existence of the soul—in the sense of a personality or self-determining whole—in the excitement of an apparent initial success in an endeavour to analyse the soul's processes of psychic behaviour. And, young though the science of psycho-analysis is, the worship of Necessity in the medium of soul-stuff can claim as its convert, in the hour of his brief triumph, the most notorious politician of the age.

'I go my way with the assurance of a somnambulist, the way which Providence has sent me.'

These words are quoted from a speech delivered by Adolf Hitler at Munich on the 14th March, 1936; and they sent a cold shudder through the frames of millions of European men and women beyond the frontiers of the Third Reich (and perhaps inside them too) whose nerves had not yet had time to recover from the preceding shock of the German military re-occupation of the Rhineland seven days before.

There is another version of the creed of psychical determinism which breaks the bounds of the narrow time-span of a single human life on Earth and carries the chain of cause and effect both backwards and forwards in time—backwards to the first appearance of man on this terrestrial stage and forwards to his final exit from it. The doctrine appears in two variants which seem to have arisen quite independently of one another. One variant is the Christian conception of Original Sin; the other is the Indic conception of *Karma* which has entered into both the philosophy of Buddhism and the religion of Hinduism. These two renderings of one doctrine agree in the essential point of making the spiritual chain of cause and effect run on continuously from one earthly life to another. In both the Christian and the Indic view the character and conduct of a human being alive to-day are held to have been causally conditioned by actions performed in other lives—or in one other life—lived in the past. To this extent the Christian and the Indic conceptions coincide, but beyond this point they diverge from one another.

The Christian doctrine of Original Sin affirms that a particular personal sin of the progenitor of the human race has entailed upon all his offspring a heritage of spiritual infirmity which they would have been spared if Adam had not fallen from grace; and that every descendant of Adam is doomed to inherit this Adamic blemish— in spite of the psychic insulation and individuality of each single soul, which is an essential tenet of the Christian religion. According to this doctrine, the capacity for transmitting an acquired spiritual characteristic to his physical descendants was possessed by Adam but by him alone of the race of which he is the progenitor.

This last feature of the doctrine of Original Sin is not found in the conception of *Karma*. According to this Indic doctrine, the spiritual characteristics that any individual acquires through his own acts are all transmitted, from first to last, for good or for evil, without exception; and the bearer of this cumulative spiritual heritage is not a genealogical tree representing a procession of successive separate personalities but is a spiritual continuum which appears and reappears in the world of sense in a series of reincarnations. According to the Buddhist philosophy, the continuity of *Karma* is the cause of this 'transmigration of souls' or metempsychosis which is one of the axioms of Buddhist thought.

Finally we have to take notice of the theistic form of determinism—a form which is perhaps the most bizarre and perverse of all, since in this theistic determinism an idol is worshipped in the likeness of the True God. The addicts of this covert idolatry still theoretically ascribe to the object of their worship all the attributes of a divine personality, while at the same time they insist upon the single attribute of transcendence with an emphasis so disproportionate that their God becomes transformed into a being as unaccountable, implacable and impersonal as Saeva Necessitas herself. The 'higher religions' that have emanated from the internal proletariat of the Syriac Society are the spiritual fields in which this idolatrous perversion of a transcendental theism seems most apt to break out. The two classic examples of it are the Islamic notion of *Qismet* and the doctrine of predestination as formulated by Calvin, the founder and organizer of the militant Protestantism of Geneva.

The mention of Calvinism raises a problem which has proved a puzzle to many minds and for which we must try to find some solution. We have suggested that a deterministic creed is an expression of that sense of drift which is one of the psychological symptoms of social disintegration, but it is an undeniable fact that many people who have been avowed determinists have actually been distinguished, both individually and collectively, by an uncommon energy, activity and purposefulness, as well as by an uncommon assurance.

'The central paradox of religious ethics—that only those are nerved with the courage to turn the world upside down who are convinced that already, in a higher sense, it is disposed for the best by a power of which they are the humble instruments—finds in [Calvinism] a special exemplification.'[1]

Calvinism, however, is only one of several notorious examples of a fatalistic creed which is apparently in contradiction with the conduct of its votaries. The temper displayed by the Calvinists (Genevan, Huguenot, Dutch, Scottish, English and American) has likewise been displayed by other theistic predestinarians: for example, by the Jewish Zealots, the Primitive Muslim Arabs and by other Muslims of other ages and races—for instance, by the Janissaries of the Ottoman Empire and the Mahdists of the Sudan. And in the nineteenth-century Western Liberal votaries of Progress and the twentieth-century Russian Communist Marxians we see two predestinarian sects of an atheistic turn of mind whose ethos is manifestly akin to that of their theistic fellow-worshippers of the idol of Necessity. The parallel between the Communists and the Calvinists has been drawn by the brilliant pen of the English historian whom we have quoted above:

'It is not wholly fanciful to say that, on a narrower stage but with not less formidable weapons, Calvin did for the bourgeoisie of the sixteenth century what Marx did for the proletariat of the nineteenth, or that the doctrine of Predestination satisfied the same hunger for an assurance that the forces of the Universe are on the side of the Elect as was to be assuaged in a different age by the theory of Historical Materialism. He . . . taught them to feel that they were a Chosen People, made them conscious of their great destiny in the Providential plan and resolute to realize it.'[2]

The historical link between sixteenth-century Calvinism and twentieth-century Communism is nineteenth-century Liberalism.

'Determinism was much in vogue by this time: but why should determinism be a depressing creed? The law which we cannot escape is the blessed Law of Progress—"that kind of improvement that can be measured by statistics". We had only to thank our stars for placing us in such an environment, and to carry out energetically the course of development which Nature has prescribed for us, and to resist which would be at once impious and futile. Thus the superstition of Progress was firmly established. To become a popular religion, it is only necessary for a superstition to enslave a philosophy. The Superstition of Progress had the singular good fortune to enslave at least three philosophies—those of Hegel, of Comte and of Darwin. The

[1] Tawney, R. H.: *Religion and the Rise of Capitalism*, p. 129.
[2] Op. cit., p. 112.

strange thing is that none of these philosophies is really favourable to the belief which it was supposed to support.'[1]

Are we then to infer that the acceptance of a deterministic philosophy is in itself a spur to confident and successful action? We are not; for the addicts of predestinarian creeds on whom their faith has had this fortifying and stimulating effect seem all of them to have made the bold assumption that their own will was coincident with the will of God or with the law of Nature or with the decrees of Necessity, and was therefore bound, *a priori*, to prevail. The Calvinist's Jehovah is a God who vindicates His Elect; the Marxian's Historical Necessity is an impersonal force that brings about the Dictatorship of the Proletariat. Such an assumption gives a confidence in victory which, as the history of war teaches, is one of the springs of *moral* and is therefore apt to justify itself by achieving the result which it has taken for granted in advance. '*Possunt quia posse videntur*'[2] (they can because they believe they can) was the secret of the success of the ultimately victorious crew in the Virgilian boat-race. In short, Necessity can operate as a potent ally when she is assumed to be one; but the assumption is, of course, an act of ὕβρις—and a supreme one—which invites its eventual confutation by the inexorable logic of events. Confidence in victory at last proved Goliath's bane when the long series of his successful combats was broken and terminated by his encounter with David. The Marxians have now lived on their assumption for nearly a hundred years, and the Calvinists for some four centuries, without having yet had the bubble pricked; but the Muslims, who committed themselves to the same proud but unproven belief some thirteen centuries ago and, in the strength of it, performed no less mighty deeds in their earlier history, have had time enough to fall on evil days; and the feebleness of their reaction to their latter-day tribulations indicates that Determinism is just as apt to sap *moral* in adversity as it is to stimulate it so long as the challenges encountered are within the range of an effective response. The disillusioned predestinarian who has been taught by harsh experience that his God is not, after all, on his side is condemned to arrive at the devastating conclusion that he and his fellow-homunculi are

> But helpless pieces in the game He plays
> Upon this chequer-board of nights and days,
> Hither and thither moves and checks and slays,
> And one by one back in the closet lays.[3]

---

[1] Inge, W. R.: *The Idea of Progress*, pp. 8–9.
[2] Virgil: *Aeneid*, Bk. V, l. 231.
[3] Fitzgerald, E.: *Rubáiyat of Omar Khayyám* (fourth edition), lxix.

While the sense of drift is a passive feeling, it has its active counterpart and antithesis in the sense of sin, which is an alternative reaction to an identical consciousness of moral defeat. In essence and in spirit the sense of sin and the sense of drift present the sharpest contrast to one another; for, while the sense of drift has the effect of an opiate in instilling into the soul an insidious acquiescence in an evil which is assumed to reside in external circumstances beyond the victim's control, the sense of sin has the effect of a stimulus because it tells the sinner that the evil is not external after all but is within him and is therefore subject to his will—if only he wills to carry out God's purpose and to render himself accessible to God's grace. There is here the whole difference between the Slough of Despond in which Christian for a time wallowed and the original impetus which started him running towards 'yonder wicket gate'.

There is none the less a kind of 'no-man's-land' in which the two moods overlap, as is implicitly assumed in the Indic conception of *Karma*; for although, on the one hand, *Karma*, like 'Original Sin', is conceived of as a spiritual heritage with which the soul is saddled without the option of repudiating it, the accumulation of the burden of *Karma*, as it stands at any given moment, may be increased or diminished by the deliberate and voluntary action of the individual in whom the soul at any given moment is embodied. The same passage to a conquerable Sin from an unconquerable Fate can be made along the Christian way of life; for the Christian soul is offered the possibility of purifying itself from the taint of Original Sin, which is its heritage from Adam, by seeking and finding God's grace, which is won solely as a Divine response to human effort.

An awakening to the sense of sin can be detected in the development of the Egyptiac conception of the life after death in the course of the Egyptiac time of troubles, but the classical case is the spiritual experience of the Prophets of Israel and Judah in the Syriac time of troubles. When these Prophets were discovering their truths and delivering their message, the society out of whose bosom they had arisen, and to whose members they were addressing themselves, was lying in helpless misery in the grip of the Assyrian tiger. For the souls whose body social was in this fearful plight it was a heroic spiritual feat to reject the obvious explanation of their misery as the work of an irresistible external material force and to divine that, in spite of superficial appearances, it was their own sin which was the cause of their tribulations and that it therefore lay in their own hands to win their true release.

This saving truth, which had been discovered by the Syriac

Society in the ordeal of its own breakdown and disintegration, was inherited from the Prophets of Israel and propagated in Christian guise by the Syriac wing of the internal proletariat of the Hellenic World. Without this instruction from an alien source in a principle which had already been apprehended by Syriac souls with an altogether un-Hellenic outlook, the Hellenic Society might never have succeeded in learning a lesson so much at variance with its own ethos. At the same time the Hellenes might have found it still more difficult than they did find it to take this Syriac discovery to heart if they had not, of their own motion, been moving in the same direction themselves.

This native awakening to a sense of sin can be traced in the spiritual history of Hellenism many centuries before a Hellenic trickle mingled with a Syriac stream in the river of Christianity. If we have been right in our interpretation of the origin, nature and intention of Orphism, there is evidence that, even before the Hellenic Civilization broke down, at least a few Hellenic souls had become so painfully conscious of a spiritual void in their native cultural heritage that they had resorted to the *tour de force* of artificially inventing the 'higher religion' with which the apparented Minoan Civilization had failed to endow them. It is at any rate certain that, in the very first generation after the breakdown of 431 B.C., the apparatus of Orphism was being used—and abused—for the purpose of providing satisfaction for souls that were already convicted of sin and were groping, however blindly, for release from it. For this we have the testimony of a passage of Plato which might almost have flowed from the pen of Luther.

'There are the quacks and diviners who peddle their wares to the rich and make them believe that these cheapjacks possess powers, procured from the Gods by sacrifices and incantations, for healing with diversions and festivities any sin that has been committed either by oneself or by one's forebears.... They follow these books [of Musaeus and Orpheus] in their hocus-pocus; and they persuade even governments, as well as private people, that a release and purification from sin can be obtained by means of sacrifices and agreeable child's-play. They further maintain that these "rites" (as they call them in this connexion) are as efficacious for the dead as they are for the living. "Rites" liberate us from the torments of the world beyond the grave, while a dreadful fate awaits us if we neglect here and now to make sacrifices.'[1]

This first glimpse of a native sense of sin in the souls of the Hellenic dominant minority looks as unpromising as it is repulsive.

[1] Plato: *Republic*, 364 B–365 A.

Yet four centuries later we find a native Hellenic sense of sin which has been purified out of all recognition in the fires of suffering; for there is an almost Christian note in the voice of the Hellenic dominant minority of the Augustan Age as it makes itself heard in the poetry of Virgil. The well-known passage at the end of the First Georgic is a prayer for delivery from a torturing sense of drift, and it takes the form of a confession of sin. Moreover, though the sin from which the poet implores Heaven for release is nominally an 'original sin' inherited from a legendary Trojan ancestor, the whole force of the passage impels the reader to realize that this is allegory and that the sin which the Romans were really expiating in Virgil's own day was the sin which they themselves had been committing during the two-centuries-long rake's progress upon which they had entered when they plunged into the Hannibalic War.

Within a century of the year when Virgil's poem was written the spirit that breathes through these passages had become predominant in a stratum of the Hellenic Society which had hardly yet come within range of the radiation of Christianity. In retrospect it is clear that the generations of Seneca and Plutarch and Epictetus and Marcus Aurelius were unwittingly preparing their hearts for an approaching enlightenment from a proletarian source out of which these sophisticated Hellenic intellectuals would never have augured the coming of any good thing. Both the unwitting preparation of the heart and—in the particular case chosen—the sophisticated rejection of the offer of proletarian enlightenment are portrayed with remarkable insight and felicity in Robert Browning's character-study *Cleon*. Cleon, an imaginary philosopher of the Hellenic dominant minority in the first century of the Christian Era, has been brought by his study of history to a state of mind which he describes as 'profound discouragement'. None the less, when it is suggested to him that he should refer to 'one Paulus' the problems he had admitted that he could not solve himself, his *amour-propre* is merely irritated.

> Thou canst not think a mere barbarian Jew
> As Paulus proves to be, one circumcised,
> Hath knowledge of a secret hid from us.[1]

The Hellenic and Syriac societies are assuredly not the only civilizations in which there has been an awakening to the sense of sin through the shock of seeing an ancient social structure collapse

---

[1] The appropriateness of Browning's fictitious poet Cleon as an illustration of the argument of the foregoing paragraph is not invalidated by the fact that the theological problem submitted by King Protus to Cleon was concerned not with the sense of sin but with the immortality of the soul.

in ruins. Without attempting to compile a list of such societies, we may ask, in conclusion, whether our own society should be added to it.

The sense of sin is, no doubt, a feeling with which our modern Western homunculus is quite familiar. A familiarity with it is indeed almost forced upon him; for the sense of sin is a cardinal feature of the 'higher religion' which we have inherited. In this case, however, familiarity seems to have latterly been breeding— not so much contempt as positive aversion; and the contrast between this temper of the modern Western World and the contrary temper of the Hellenic World in the sixth century B.C. shows up a vein of perversity in human nature. The Hellenic Society, starting life with the jejune and unsatisfying religious heritage of a barbarian pantheon, seems to have become conscious of its spiritual poverty and exerted itself to fill the void by inventing, in Orphism, a 'higher religion' of the kind that some other civilizations have inherited from their predecessors; and the character of the Orphic ritual and doctrine makes it clear that the sense of sin was the pent-up religious feeling for which the Hellenes of the sixth century were eager, above all, to find a normal outlet. In contrast to the Hellenic Society our Western Society is one of those more generously endowed civilizations which have grown up under the aegis of a 'higher religion' and within the chrysalis of a universal church; and it is perhaps just because Western man has always been able to take his Christian birthright for granted that he has so often depreciated it and come near to repudiating it. Indeed the cult of Hellenism, which has been so potent, and in many ways so fruitful, an ingredient in our Western secular culture since the Italian Renaissance, has been partly fostered and kept alive by a conventional conception of Hellenism as a way of life which gloriously combines with all our modern Western virtues and attainments an innate and effortless freedom from that sense of sin which Western man is now industriously purging out of his Christian spiritual heritage. It is no accident that the more up-to-date varieties of Protestantism, while retaining the concept of Heaven, have quietly discarded the concept of Hell and have surrendered the concept of the Devil to our satirists and comedians.

To-day the cult of Hellenism is being pushed into a corner by the cult of physical science, but the prospects for a recovery of the sense of sin have not been improved thereby. Our social reformers and philanthropists are very ready to regard the sins of the poor as misfortunes due to external circumstances—'What can you expect from the man, seeing that he was born in a slum?' And our psychoanalysts are equally ready to regard the sins of their patients as misfortunes due to internal circumstances, complexes and neuroses: in fact, to explain sin, and explain it away, as disease. In this line of thought they were anticipated by the philosophers of Samuel Butler's *Erewhon*, where, as the reader may remember, poor Mr. Nosnibor had to send for the family 'straightener' (*sc.* doctor) because he was suffering from an attack of embezzlement.

Will modern Western man repent of, and recoil from, his ὕβρις before it finds its nemesis in ἄτη? The answer cannot yet be forecast, but we may anxiously scan the landscape of our contemporary spiritual life for any symptoms that may give us ground for hope that we are regaining the use of a spiritual faculty which we have been doing our utmost to sterilize.

(5) THE SENSE OF PROMISCUITY

(*a*) VULGARITY AND BARBARISM IN MANNERS

A sense of promiscuity is a passive substitute for that sense of style which develops *pari passu* with the growth of a civilization. This state of mind takes practical effect in an act of self-surrender to the melting-pot; and in the process of social disintegration an identical mood manifests itself in every province of social life: in religion and literature and language and art, as well as in the wider and vaguer sphere of 'manners and customs'. It will be convenient to begin operations in this latter field.

In our search for evidence on this point we shall perhaps be inclined to turn our eyes with the greatest expectancy towards the internal proletariat, for we have already observed that the common and characteristic affliction of internal proletariats is the torture of being torn up by the roots; and this terrible experience of social deracination might be expected, above all other experiences, to produce a sense of promiscuity in the souls of those compelled to undergo it. This *a priori* expectation is not, however, borne out by the facts; for, more often than not, the ordeal to which an internal proletariat is subjected seems to strike that optimum degree of severity at which it acts as a stimulus, and we see the uprooted, expatriated and enslaved people of whom an internal proletariat is composed not only keeping a firm hold on the remnants of their social heritage but actually imparting it to the dominant minority who, *a priori*, might have been expected to impose their own culture pattern upon the mob of waifs and strays whom they have caught in their net and forced under their yoke.

It is still more surprising to see—as, again, we do see—the

dominant minority showing itself similarly receptive to the cultural influence of the external proletariat, considering that these truculent war-bands are insulated from the dominant minority by a military frontier and that their barbarian social heritage might have been expected to be lacking in both the charm and the prestige that manifestly still cling even to the tatters of those mellow civilizations to which the internal proletariat is heir in the persons of some, at least, of its involuntary recruits.

Nevertheless we do find, as a matter of fact, that, of the three fractions into which a disintegrating society is apt to split, it is the dominant minority that succumbs most readily to the sense of promiscuity, and the ultimate result of this proletarianization of the dominant minority is a disappearance of that schism in the body social which is the index and penalty of social breakdown. The dominant minority in the end atones for its sins by closing a breach that has been its own handiwork and merging itself in its own proletariats.

Before attempting to follow the course of this process of proletarianization along its two parallel lines—vulgarization by contact with the internal proletariat and barbarization by contact with the external proletariat—it may be convenient to glance at some of the evidence for the receptivity of empire-builders, since this predisposition may partly explain the sequel.

The universal states of which these empire-builders are the architects are, for the most part, the product of military conquest and we may therefore look for examples of receptivity in the sphere of military technique. The Romans, for example, according to Polybius, discarded their native cavalry equipment and adopted that of the Greeks whom they were in process of conquering. The Theban founders of 'the New Empire' of Egypt borrowed the horse-and-chariot as a weapon of war from their defeated antagonists, the once Nomad Hyksos. The victorious 'Osmanlis borrowed the Western invention of fire-arms, and, when the tide turned in this particular struggle, the Western World borrowed from the 'Osmanlis their immensely potent weapon of a disciplined, drilled and uniformed professional infantry.

But such borrowings are not confined to the military art. Herodotus notes that the Persians, while proclaiming themselves superior to all their neighbours, borrowed their civilian dress from the Medes and a number of outlandish indulgences, including unnatural vice, from the Greeks; and 'the Old Oligarch', in the course of his pungent criticisms of fifth-century Athens, remarks that his fellow-countrymen had been exposed, through their command of the sea, to a more extensive debasement by foreign customs than was to be seen in the cities of less enterprising Greek communities. As for ourselves, our tobacco-smoking commemorates our extermination of the red-skinned aborigines of North America, our coffee-drinking and tea-drinking and polo-playing and pyjama-wearing and Turkish baths commemorate the enthrone-ment of the Frankish man-of-business in the seat of the Ottoman Qaysar-i-Rum and of the Mughal Qaysar-i-Hind, and our jazzing commemorates the enslavement of the African Negro and his transportation across the Atlantic to labour on American soil in plantations which had taken the place of the hunting-grounds of the vanished Red Indians.

After this prefatory recital of some of the more notorious evidence for the receptivity of the dominant minority in a dis-integrating society, we may now proceed to our survey, first of the vulgarization of the dominant minority through its pacific inter-course with an internal proletariat which lies physically at its mercy, and then of its barbarization through its warlike inter-course with an external proletariat which eludes its yoke

While the intercourse of the dominant minority with the internal proletariat is pacific in the sense that the proletarians have already been conquered, it often happens that the first contact between the two parties as rulers and subjects takes the form of an introduc-tion of proletarian recruits into the empire-builders' permanent garrisons and standing armies. The history of the standing army of the Roman Empire, for example, is the story of a progressive dilution which began almost on the morrow of the Roman army's transformation from an *ad hoc* and amateur conscript force to a permanent and professional volunteer force by the act of Augustus. In the course of a few centuries an army which originally had been drawn almost entirely from the dominant minority came to be drawn almost entirely from the internal proletariat and, in the final phase, very largely from the external proletariat as well. The history of the Roman army is reproduced, with differences of detail, in that of the army of the Far Eastern universal state as reconstructed by Manchu empire-builders in the seventeenth century of the Christian Era, and in the history of the Arab standing army of the Umayyad and 'Abbasid Caliphates.

If we try to estimate the importance of the part that has been played by comradeship-in-arms in the breaking-down of the barrier between the dominant minority and the internal proletariat, we shall find, as we might expect, that this factor has been of greatest account in those cases where the dominant minority has been represented by empire-builders who have been not merely frontiersmen but men from the wrong side of the frontier—

empire-builders, that is, of barbarian origin. For the barbarian conqueror is likely to be even more receptive than the marchman to amenities of life which he finds in use among the peoples he has subjected. Such, at any rate, was the sequel to the comradeship-in-arms between the Manchus and their Manchurian Chinese subjects. The Manchus became thoroughly assimilated to the Chinese, and the same tendency to abandon *de jure* segregation in favour of *de facto* symbiosis can be traced in the history of the Primitive Muslim Arab conquerors of South-Western Asia, who were unconsciously restoring a Syriac universal state which had first taken form in the prematurely overthrown empire of the Achaemenidae.

When we turn to the histories of dominant minorities which have arisen—as dominant minorities normally do arise—from within the disintegrating society's pale, we shall not be able to leave the military factor out of account, but we shall find that here the comradeship-in-arms is apt to be replaced by a partnership in business. 'The Old Oligarch' observed that in thalassocratic Athens the slaves of alien origin had come to be undistinguishable in the streets from the lower class of citizens. In the latter days of the Roman Republic the management of the Roman aristocrats' households, with their huge personnel and elaborate organization, had already become the perquisite of the ablest of the freedmen of the nominal master; and, when Caesar's household actually went into partnership with the Senate and the People in the management of the Roman universal state, Caesar's freedmen became cabinet ministers. The imperial freedmen of the early Roman Empire enjoyed a plenitude of power comparable to that of those members of the Ottoman Sultan's slave-household who attained to the equally powerful—and equally precarious—office of Grand Vizier.

In all cases of symbiosis between the dominant minority and the internal proletariat both parties are affected, and the effect on each of them is to set them in motion on a course which leads to an assimilation to the other class. On the superficial plane of 'manners' the internal proletariat moves towards enfranchisement and the dominant minority towards vulgarization. The two movements are complementary and both are taking place all the time; but, while it is the enfranchisement of the proletariat that is the more conspicuous in the earlier phases, in the later chapters it is the vulgarization of the dominant minority that forces itself on our attention. The classic example is the vulgarization, in 'the Silver Age', of the Roman governing class: a sordid tragedy which has been inimitably recorded—or caricatured—in a Latin literature which still preserved its genius in the satirical vein after it had lost its last breath of inspiration in every other *genre*. This Roman rake's progress can be followed in a series of Hogarthian pictures in each of which the central figure is not merely an aristocrat but an emperor: Caligula, Nero, Commodus and Caracalla.

Of the last named we read in Gibbon:

'The demeanour of Caracalla was haughty and full of pride; but with the troops he forgot even the proper dignity of his rank, encouraged their insolent familiarity and, neglecting the essential duties of a general, affected to imitate the dress and manners of a common soldier.'

Caracalla's way of going 'proletarian' was neither so sensational nor so pathological as that of Nero the music-hall *artiste* or that of Commodus the gladiator, but it is perhaps of greater significance as a sociological symptom. A Hellenic dominant minority which had reached the last stage in the repudiation of its social heritage was fitly represented by the figure of an emperor who took refuge in the proletarian freedom of the barrack-room from a freedom of the Academy and the Stoa which he found intolerable just because he knew it was his birthright. Indeed, by this date, on the eve of the next relapse of the Hellenic Society after the respite of the Augustan rally, the relative volumes and momenta and speeds of the two mutually contrary streams of influence that flowed respectively from the dominant minority and from the internal proletariat had changed, in the proletarian stream's favour, to a degree at which the latter-day observer may find himself wondering whether, after all, he has not been watching the movement of a single current which now, at a certain moment, has simply reversed its direction.

If we now turn our eyes to the Far Eastern World we shall see the first chapter of our story of the proletarianization of the Roman governing class in the act of reproducing itself at the present day. It is illustrated in the following record from the pen of a living Western scholar who shows us the struggle for enfranchisement giving way to the drift towards proletarianization within the compass of the single generation that separates a Manchuized Chinese father from his proletarianized son:

'It was . . . possible, in Manchuria, for a Chinese from China proper to become in his own lifetime an out-and-out "Manchu". An instance of this phenomenon came within my own experience when I formed an acquaintance with a Chinese military officer and his old father. The father, born in Honan, had gone to Manchuria as a young man, had travelled over the most remote parts of the three provinces, and had finally settled down in Tsitsihar. One day I said to the young man:

"Why is it that you, who were born in Tsitsihar, speak just like the generality of Manchurian Chinese, while your father, who was born in Honan, has not only the speech, but exactly the manner and even gestures, of the old-fashioned Manchus of Manchuria?" He laughed, and said: "When my father was a young man it was difficult for a *min-jen* [non-'banner' Chinese, 'a civilian, one of the people'] to get on in the world up in the northern regions. The Manchus dominated everything. . . . But when I was growing up it was no longer any use to be a 'bannerman', and therefore I became like all the other young men of my generation." This is a story which illustrates the processes of the present as well as of the past; for the young Manchus of Manchuria are becoming rapidly indistinguishable from Manchuria-born Chinese.'[1]

But in A.D. 1946 an Englishman had no need either to read Gibbon or to book a berth on the Trans-Siberian express in order to study the process of proletarianization; he could study it at home. In the cinema he would see people of all classes taking an equal pleasure in films designed to cater for the taste of the proletarian majority, while in the club he would find that the black ball did not exclude the Yellow Press. Indeed, if our latter-day Juvenal was a family man he could stay indoors and still find his copy. He had merely to open his ears (which was perhaps easier than to close them) to the jazz or 'variety' which his children were conjuring out of the wireless set. And then when, at the end of the holidays, he saw his boys off to their public school—an institution whose social exclusiveness was an abomination to democrats—let him not forget to ask them to point out to him 'the bloods' among their schoolfellows assembling on the platform. As, at this passing show, our quizzical paterfamilias discreetly took smart young Commodus's measure, he would notice the rakish proletarian angle of the trilby hat and would observe that the *apache* scarf, with its convincing air of negligence, had really been carefully arranged to conceal the obligatory white collar. Here was proof positive that the proletarian style was *à la mode*. And, since a straw does really show which way the wind is blowing, the satirist's trivialities may be grist for the more ponderous mill of the historian.

When we pass from the vulgarization of the dominant minority through their pacific intercourse with the internal proletariat to examine the parallel process of their barbarization through their warlike intercourse with the external proletariat beyond the pale, we find that the plot of both plays is the same in its general structure. In the second of the two the *mise-en-scène* is an artificial military frontier—the *limes* of a universal state—across which the dominant minority and the external proletariat are seen confront-

---

[1] Lattimore, O.: *Manchuria, Cradle of Conflict* (1932), pp. 62–3.

ing each other, when the curtain rises, in a posture which, on both sides, is one of aloofness and hostility. As the play proceeds, the aloofness turns into an intimacy which does not, however, bring peace; and, as the warfare goes on, time tells progressively in the barbarian's favour, until at last he succeeds in breaking through the *limes* and overrunning the domain which the dominant minority's garrison has hitherto protected.

In the first act the barbarian enters the world of the dominant minority in the successive roles of hostage and mercenary, and in both capacities he figures as a more or less docile apprentice. In the second act he comes as a raider, unbidden and unwanted, who ultimately settles down as a colonist or a conqueror. Thus, between the first act and the second, the military ascendancy has passed into the barbarian's hands, and this sensational transfer of the kingdom, the power and the glory from the dominant minority's to the barbarian's banners has a profound effect on the dominant minority's outlook. It now seeks to retrieve its rapidly deteriorating military and political position by taking one leaf after another out of the barbarian's book; and imitation is assuredly the sincerest form of flattery.

Having thus sketched out the plot of the play, we may now return to its opening and watch the barbarian make his first appearance on the stage as the dominant minority's apprentice; see the dominant minority begin to 'go native'; catch a glimpse of the two adversaries at the fleeting moment at which, in their rival masquerades in one another's borrowed plumage, they assume the grotesque generic resemblance of the griffin to the chimaera; and finally watch the *ci-devant* dominant minority lose the last traces of its original form by sinking to meet the triumphant barbarian at a common level of unmitigated barbarism.

Our list of barbarian war-lords who have made their début as hostages in the hands of a 'civilized' Power includes some famous names. Theodoric served his apprenticeship as a hostage at the Roman Court of Constantinople and Scanderbeg his at the Ottoman Court of Adrianople. Philip of Macedon learnt the arts of war and peace at the Thebes of Epaminondas, and the Moroccan chieftain 'Abd al-Karīm, who annihilated a Spanish expeditionary force at Anwal in 1921 and, four years later, shook the French power in Morocco to its foundations, served an eleven months' apprenticeship in a Spanish prison at Melilla.

The list of barbarians who have 'come' and 'seen' as mercenaries, before imposing themselves as conquerors, is a long one. The Teutonic and Arab barbarian conquerors of Roman provinces in the fifth and seventh centuries of the Christian Era were descendants of many generations of Teutons and Arabs who had done their military service in the Roman forces. The Turkish bodyguard of the 'Abbasid Caliphs in the ninth century of the Christian Era prepared the way for the Turkish buccaneers who carved up the Caliphate into its eleventh-century successor-states. Other examples could be cited, and our list would be longer still if the historical records of the last agonies of civilizations were not so fragmentary as they are apt to be. But we may at least conjecture that the sea-roving barbarians who hovered round the fringes of the Minoan thalassocracy and sacked Cnossos *circa* 1400 B.C. had served their apprenticeship as the hirelings of Minos before they aspired to supplant him, and tradition tells that Vortigern, the British King of Kent, employed Saxon mercenaries before he was overthrown by those unverifiable marauders, Hengist and Horsa.

We can also espy several instances in which the barbarian mercenary has missed his 'manifest destiny'. For example, the East Roman Empire might have fallen a prey to the Varangian Guard if it had not been ravished by the Normans and the Saljūqs, carved up by the French and the Venetians and finally swallowed whole by the 'Osmanlis. And the Ottoman Empire, in its turn, would assuredly have been partitioned among the Bosniak and Albanian mercenaries who were fast asserting their mastery over the provincial pashas and even over the Sublime Porte itself at the turn of the eighteenth and nineteenth centuries of the Christian Era if the Frankish man-of-business had not come treading on the heels of the Albanian man-at-arms to give the last chapter of Ottoman history an unexpected turn by flooding the Levant with Western political ideas as well as with Manchester goods. The Oscan mercenaries, again, who found a market for their services in the Greek city-states of Campania and Magna Graecia and Sicily made a practice of ejecting or exterminating their Greek employers whenever they saw an opportunity, and there is little doubt that they would have carried on this game until there was not a single Greek community left west of the Straits of Otranto if the Romans had not, at the critical moment, taken the Oscan homelands in the rear.

These examples may suggest to us a contemporary situation in which we cannot yet foresee whether mercenaries will turn marauders or whether, if they do, their enterprises will, like those of the Oscan and the Albanian, be nipped in the bud or, like those of the Teuton and the Turk, go on to fruition. A present-day Indian might well speculate on the future role, in India's destinies, of those barbarians—entrenched in a warlike independence in their fastnesses beyond the limits of the Government of India's administration—from among whom no less than one-seventh of the Indian regular army was recruited in 1930. Were the Gurkha mercenaries and the Pathan raiders of that day marked out to be remembered in history as the fathers and grandfathers of barbarian conquerors who were to carve out on the plains of Hindustan the successor-states of the British Rāj?

In this example we are unacquainted with the second act of the play. To watch the progress of the drama in this phase we must return to the story of the relations between the Hellenic universal state and the European barbarians beyond the northern *limes* of the Roman Empire. On this historic stage we can watch from beginning to end the parallel processes by which a dominant minority sinks into barbarism while the barbarians are making their fortune at its expense.

The play opens in a liberal atmosphere of enlightened self-interest.

'The Empire was not an object of hatred to the barbarians. Indeed, they were often eager to be taken into its service, and many of their chiefs, like Alaric or Ataulphus [Atawulf], had no higher ambition than to be appointed to high military command. On the other hand there was a corresponding readiness on the Roman side to employ barbarian forces in war.'[1]

It appears that, about the middle of the fourth century of the Christian Era, the Germans in the Roman service started the new practice of retaining their native names; and this change of etiquette, which seems to have been abrupt, points to a sudden access of self-confidence and self-assurance in the souls of the barbarian *personnel* which had previously been content to 'go Roman' without reservations. This new insistence on their cultural individuality did not evoke on the Romans' part any counter-demonstration of anti-barbarian exclusiveness. So far from that, the barbarians in the Roman service began, at this very time, to be appointed to the consulship, which was the highest honour that the Emperor had to bestow.

While the barbarians were thus setting their feet on the topmost rungs of the Roman social ladder, the Romans themselves were moving in the opposite direction. For example, the Emperor Gratian (A.D. 375–383) succumbed to a newfangled form of inverted snobbery, a mania, not for vulgarity, but for barbarism, which led him to assume barbarian styles of dress and devote himself to barbarian field-sports. A century later we find Romans

---

[1] Dill, S.: *Society in the Last Century of the Western Empire*, p. 291.

actually enlisting in the war-bands of independent barbarian chieftains. For example, at Vouillé in A.D. 507, when Visigoths and Franks were fighting for the possession of Gaul, one of the casualties on the Visigoths' side was a grandson of Sidonius Apollinaris, who in his generation had still managed to live the life of a cultured classical man-of-letters. There is no evidence that at the opening of the sixth century of the Christian Era the descendants of the Roman provincials showed any less alacrity in following a *Führer* on the war-path than was shown by the contemporary descendants of barbarians to whom for centuries past the war-game had been the breath of life. By this time the two parties had reached cultural parity in a common barbarism. We have already seen how, in the fourth century, the barbarian officers in Roman service began to retain their barbarian names. The following century saw, in Gaul, the earliest examples of an inverse move, on the part of true-born Romans, to assume German names, and before the end of the eighth century the practice had become universal. By Charlemagne's time every inhabitant of Gaul, whatever his ancestry, was sporting a German name.

If we lay alongside this history of the decline and fall of the Roman Empire the parallel story of the barbarization of the Sinic World, the outstanding dates of which fall, throughout, some two centuries earlier, we shall find a significant difference in regard to this last point. The founders of the barbarian successor-states of the Sinic universal state were meticulous in disguising their barbarian nakedness by the adoption of correctly formed Sinic names, and it is perhaps not altogether fanciful to see a connexion between this difference of practice on an apparently trivial point and the eventual resuscitation of the Sinic universal state in a much more effective form than the parallel evocation of a 'ghost' of the Roman Empire by Charlemagne.

Before closing our inquiry into the barbarization of dominant minorities, we may pause to ask ourselves whether any of the symptoms of this social phenomenon are discernible in our own modern Western World. On first thoughts we shall perhaps be inclined to think that our question has received a conclusive answer in the fact that our society has embraced the whole world in its tentacles and that there are no longer external prole-tariats of any considerable dimensions left to barbarize us. But we must recall the rather disconcerting fact that, in the heart of our Western Society's 'New World' of North America, there is to-day a large and widespread population of English and Lowland Scottish origin, with a Protestant Western Christian social heri-tage, which has been unmistakably and profoundly barbarized by being marooned in the Appalachian backwoods after serving a preliminary term of exile on 'the Celtic Fringe' of Europe.

The barbarizing effect of the American frontier has been described by an American historian who is a master of the subject.

'In the settlement of America we have to observe how European life entered the continent and how America modified and developed that life and reacted on Europe. Our early history is the study of European germs developing in an American environment. . . . The frontier is the line of most rapid and effective Americanization. The wilderness masters the colonist. It finds him a European in dress, industries, tools, modes of travel and thought. It takes him from the railroad car and puts him in the birch canoe. It strips off the garments of civilization and arrays him in the hunting shirt and the moccasin. It puts him in the log cabin of the Cherokee and Iroquois and runs an Indian palisade around him. Before long he has gone to planting Indian corn and plowing with a sharp stick; he shouts the war-cry and takes the scalp in orthodox Indian fashion. In short, at the frontier the environment is at first too strong for the man. . . . Little by little he transforms the wilderness; but the outcome is not the old Europe. . . . The fact is that here is a new product that is American.'[1]

If this thesis is correct, then we are bound to declare that, in North America at any rate, a social pull of tremendous force has been exerted upon one section of our dominant minority by one section of its external proletariat. In the light of this American portent it would be rash to assume that the spiritual malady of barbarization is a portent which our modern Western dominant minority can afford altogether to ignore. It appears that even conquered and annihilated external proletariats can take their revenge.

(b) VULGARITY AND BARBARISM IN ART

If we pass from the general field of manners and customs to the special field of art, we shall find the sense of promiscuity betraying itself, here again, in the alternative forms of vulgarity and barbarism. In one or other of these forms the art of a disintegrating civilization is apt to pay for an abnormally wide and rapid diffusion by forfeiting that distinctiveness of style which is the sign-manual of fine quality.

Two classic examples of vulgarity are the fashions in which a disintegrating Minoan and a disintegrating Syriac Civilization successively radiated their aesthetic influence round the shores of the Mediterranean. The interregnum (*circa* 1425–1125 B.C.) which followed the overthrow of the Minoan thalassocracy is marked by the vulgar fashion labelled 'Late Minoan III' which outranges in

---

[1] Turner, F. J.: *The Frontier in American History*, pp. 3–4.

its diffusion all the earlier and finer Minoan styles; and similarly the time of troubles (*circa* 925–525 B.C.) which followed the breakdown of the Syriac Civilization is marked in Phoenician art by an equally vulgar and equally widespread mechanical combination of *motifs*. In the history of Hellenic art a corresponding vulgarity found expression in the excessively rich decoration which came into vogue with the Corinthian order of architecture —an extravagance which is the very antithesis of the distinctive note of the Hellenic genius; and, when we look for outstanding examples of this fashion, which reached its climax under the Roman Empire, we shall find them, not at the heart of the Hellenic World, but in the remains of the temple of a non-Hellenic deity at Ba'lbak or in the sarcophagi that were manufactured by Hellenic monumental masons to harbour the mortal remains of Philhellene barbarian war-lords on the far-eastern rim of the Iranian Plateau.

If we turn from the archaeological to the literary record of the disintegration of the Hellenic Society, we find that the 'highbrows' of the first few generations after the breakdown of 431 B.C. bewailed the vulgarization of Hellenic music; and we have already noticed in another context the vulgarization of the Attic drama at the hands of Διονύσου Τεχνῖται ('United Artists, Ltd.'). In the modern Western World we may observe that it was the floridly decadent and not the severely classical style of Hellenic art that inspired our Western Hellenizing fashions of baroque and rococo; and in the so-called 'chocolate-box' style of our Victorian commercial art we can discern an analogue of 'Late Minoan III' that bids fair to conquer the whole face of the planet in the service of a peculiarly Western technique of visually advertising the tradesman's wares.

The fatuousness of the 'chocolate-box' style is so desolating that it has provoked our own generation into attempting desperate remedies. Our archaistic flight from vulgarity into pre-Raphaelite Byzantinism is discussed in a later chapter, but in this place we have to take note of the contemporary and alternative flight from vulgarity into barbarism. Self-respecting Western sculptors of to-day who have not found a congenial asylum in Byzantium have turned their eyes towards Benin; and it is not only in the glyptic branch of art that a Western World whose resources of creativeness have apparently run dry has been seeking fresh inspiration from the barbarians of West Africa. West African music and dancing, as well as West African sculpture, have been imported, via America, into the heart of Europe.

To the layman's eye the flight to Benin and the flight to Byzantium seem equally unlikely to lead the latter-day Western artist to the recovery of his lost soul. And yet, even if he cannot save himself, he may conceivably be a means of salvation to others. Bergson observes that

'A mediocre teacher, giving mechanical instruction in a science that has been created by men of genius, may awake in some one of his pupils the vocation which he has never felt in himself';

and if the 'commercial art' of a disintegrating Hellenic World performed the astonishing feat of evoking the supremely creative art of Mahayanian Buddhism through its encounter with the religious experience of another disintegrating world on Indic ground, we cannot pronounce *a priori* that the modern Western 'chocolate-box' style is incapable of working similar miracles as it is flaunted round the globe on the advertiser's hoardings and sky-signs.

(c) *LINGUE FRANCHE*

In the field of language the sense of promiscuity reveals itself in the change from a local distinctiveness to a general confusion of tongues.

Though the institution of language exists for the purpose of serving as a means of communication between human beings, its social effect in the history of mankind hitherto has actually been, on the whole, to divide the human race and not to unite it; for languages have taken such a number of diverse forms that even those enjoying the widest currency have never yet been common to more than a fraction of mankind, and unintelligibility of speech is the hall-mark of the 'foreigner'.

In disintegrating civilizations at an advanced stage of their decline we are apt to see languages—following the fortunes of the peoples that speak them as their mother-tongues—waging inter-necine wars with one another and conquering, when victorious, wide dominions at their discomfited rivals' expense; and, if there is any grain of historical fact in the legend of a confusion of tongues in the land of Shinar at the foot of an unfinished ziggurat in a recently built city of Babel, the story perhaps takes us to Babylon in an age in which the Sumeric universal state was breaking up; for in the catastrophic last chapter of Sumeric history the Sumerian language became a dead language after having played an historic role as the original linguistic vehicle of the Sumeric culture, while even the Akkadian language, which had recently attained an upstart parity with it, had now to contend with a host of external proletarian vernaculars brought into the derelict domain by barbarian war-bands. The legend of the confusion of tongues is true to life in fastening upon this state of mutual unintelligibility as being a sovereign impediment to concerted social action in face of a new and unprecedented social crisis; and this association of linguistic diversity with social paralysis can be illustrated by examples which stand out conspicuously in the full light of history.

In the Western World of our own generation this was one of the fatal weaknesses of the Danubian Hapsburg Monarchy which perished in the General War of 1914–18; and even in the inhumanly efficient slave-household of the Ottoman Pādishāh in its age of maturity, in A.D. 1651, we see the curse of Babel descending upon the *Ich-oghlans* within the precincts of the seraglio and reducing them to impotence at the critical moment of a palace revolution. In their excitement the boys forgot their artificially acquired 'Osmanli idiom, and the astonished ears of the spectators were smitten with the sound of 'a tumult . . . with different voices and languages—for some cried in Georgian, others Albanian, Bosnian, Mingrelian, Turkish and Italian'.[1] The circumstances of this trivial incident in Ottoman history are, however, inverted in the momentous event of the Coming of the Holy Spirit as recorded in the second chapter of The Acts of the Apostles. In that scene the tongues which are spoken are foreign to the lips of the speakers: unlettered Galilaeans who have hitherto never spoken and seldom heard any other language than their native Aramaic. Their sudden outbreak into other tongues is represented as being a miraculous gift from God.

This enigmatic passage has been variously interpreted, but there will be no dispute about the point in it which here concerns us. It is clear that, in the view of the writer of the Acts, the gift of tongues was the first enhancement of their natural faculties which was needed by Apostles who had been charged with the tremendous task of converting all mankind to a newly revealed 'higher religion'. Yet the society into which the Apostles were born was far less ill-supplied with *lingue franche* than our world is to-day. The Aramaic mother-tongue of the Galilaeans would carry any speaker of it northwards as far as the Amanus, eastwards as far as the Zagros, and westwards as far as the Nile, while the Greek in which The Acts themselves were written would carry the Christian missionary overseas as far as Rome and beyond.

If we now proceed to examine the causes and the consequences of the transformation of local mother-tongues into oecumenical *lingue franche*, we shall find that a language which wins this kind of victory over its rivals usually owes its success to the social

[1] Rycaut, P.: *The Present State of the Ottoman Empire* (1668), p. 18.

advantage of having served, in an age of social disintegration, as
the tool of some community that has been potent either in war or
in commerce. We shall also find that languages, like human beings,
are unable to win victories without paying a price; and the price
a language pays for becoming a *lingua franca* is the sacrifice of its
native subtleties; for it is only on the lips of those who have
learnt it in infancy that any language is ever spoken with that
perfection which is the dower of nature and the despair of art.
This judgement can be verified by a survey of the evidence.

In the history of the disintegration of the Hellenic Society we
see two languages one after the other—first Attic Greek and subsequently Latin—starting as the respective mother-tongues of
two tiny districts—Attica and Latium—and then spreading outwards until, on the eve of the Christian Era, we find Attic Greek
employed in a chancery on the bank of the Jhelum and Latin in
camps on the banks of the Rhine. The expansion of the domain of
Attic Greek began with the first establishment of an Athenian
thalassocracy in the fifth century B.C., and was afterwards enor-
mously extended as a result of Philip of Macedon's adoption of
the Attic dialect as the official language of his chancery. As for
Latin, it followed the flag of the victorious Roman legions. If,
however, after admiring the expansion of these languages, we
study their contemporary development from the standpoint of
the philologist and the literary connoisseur, we shall be equally
impressed by their vulgarization. The exquisite parochial Attic
of Sophocles and Plato degenerates into the vulgar κοινή of
the Septuagint and Polybius and the New Testament, while the
literary medium of Cicero and Virgil eventually becomes the
'Dog Latin' which did duty for all serious forms of international
intercourse in the affiliated Western Christian Society until the
beginning of the eighteenth century. Milton, for example, was the
'Latin Secretary' of Cromwell's government. In the Hungarian
Parliament, 'Dog Latin' continued to be the medium for the
transaction of business until 1840, and its abandonment was one
of the detonators of a fratricidal struggle of intermingled nationa-
lities which burst out in 1848.

In the disintegration of the Babylonic and Syriac civilizations
the ruins of the two simultaneously collapsing societies became
intermingled, ever more indistinguishably, the thicker they came
to be strewn over their common *Trümmerfeld*. Across the
broken surface of this promiscuous debris the Aramaic language
spread itself with the luxuriance of a weed, though, unlike both
Greek and Latin, Aramaic owed little or nothing to the patronage
of successful conquerors. Yet the currency of the Aramaic

language, remarkable in its day, seems short-lived and narrow-verged by comparison with that of the Aramaic Alphabet and script. One of the variants of this script reached India, where it was used by the Buddhist Emperor Açoka to convey his prākrit texts in two out of the fourteen inscriptions of his that are known to us. Another variant, the so-called Sogdian, gradually made its way north-eastwards from the Jaxartes to the Amur, and by A.D. 1599 it had provided an alphabet for the Manchus. A third variant of the Aramaic Alphabet became the vehicle of the Arabic language.

If we turn next to the abortive cosmos of city-states with its main focus in Northern Italy which arose in Western Christendom in the so-called 'medieval' age, we shall see the Tuscan dialect of Italian eclipsing its rivals as Attic eclipsed the rival dialects of Ancient Greek, and at the same time being propagated all round the shores of the Mediterranean by Venetian and Genoese traders and empire-builders; and this pan-Mediterranean currency of Tuscan Italian outlived the prosperity and even the independence of the Italian city-states. In the sixteenth century Italian was the service language of an Ottoman Navy that was driving the Italians out of Levantine waters; and in the nineteenth century, again, the same Italian was the service language of a Hapsburg Navy whose Imperial masters were successful, from 1814 to 1859, in thwarting Italian national aspirations. This Italian *lingua franca* of the Levant, with its Italian base almost buried under the load of its miscellaneous foreign accretions, is such an admirable example of the genus which it represents that its historic name has come to bear a generic meaning.

Latterly, however, this vulgarized Tuscan has been replaced, even in its congenial Levantine haunts, by a vulgarized French. The fortune of the French language has been made by the fact that, during the time of troubles of the broken-down cosmos of Italian and German and Flemish city-states—a phase in the history of this sub-society's disintegration which set in towards the close of the fourteenth century and lasted until the close of the eighteenth—France carried off the victory in the contest among the Great Powers round the periphery of this still expanding society for the control of its decaying centre. From the age of Louis XIV onwards French culture exerted an attraction which kept pace with French arms; and, when Napoleon at length achieved his Bourbon forerunners' ambition of piecing together a mosaic with a French design out of all the broken fragments of city-states which strewed the face of Europe at the French nation's doors from the Adriatic to the North Sea and the Baltic, the

Napoleonic Empire proved itself to be a cultural force as well as a military system.

It was, indeed, its cultural mission that was the Napoleonic Empire's undoing; for the ideas of which it was the carrier (in the clinical sense) were the expression of a modern Western culture which was still in growth. Napoleon's mission was to provide a 'sub-universal' state for the sub-society of the city-state cosmos at the heart of Western Christendom. But it is the function of a universal state to provide repose for a society long distracted by a time of troubles. A universal state inspired by dynamic and revolutionary ideas is a contradiction in terms, a lullaby performed on a trombone. The 'ideas of the French Revolution' were not calculated to act as a sedative which might reconcile the Italians and Flemings and Rhinelanders and Hanseatics to the yoke of the French empire-builders by whom these ideas were being introduced. So far from that, the revolutionary impact of Napoleonic France gave these stagnating peoples a stimulating shock which roused them from their torpor and inspired them to rise up and overthrow the French Empire as a first step towards taking their places as new-born nations in a modern Western World. Thus the Napoleonic Empire carried within itself the Promethean seeds of its own inevitable failure in its Epimethean role of serving as the universal state of a decadent world which once, in its long-past noonday, had created the splendours of Florence and Venice and Bruges and Lübeck.

The actual task which the Napoleonic Empire did perform, involuntarily, was to tow the stranded galleons of a derelict medieval armada back into the racing current of Western life, and at the same time to stimulate their listless crews into making their vessels seaworthy; and this actual French performance would have been a short and thankless business in the nature of the case even if Napoleon had not provoked the unconquerable hostility of nation states—Britain, Russia and Spain—beyond the limits of the city-state cosmos which, on our showing, was his proper sphere of action. Yet in the Great Society of to-day there is one substantial legacy of the two-hundred-years-long role, with its brief Napoleonic culmination, which was sustained by France in the last phase of the city-state cosmos. The French language has succeeded in establishing itself as the *lingua franca* of that central portion of our Western World, and it has even extended its dominion to the far extremities of the former domains of the Spanish and Ottoman Empires. A knowledge of French will still carry the traveller through Belgium and Switzerland and the Iberian Peninsula and Latin America and Rumania and Greece and Syria and Turkey and Egypt. Throughout the British occupation of Egypt French never ceased to be the language of official communication between the representatives of the Egyptian Government and their British advisers, and when the British High Commissioner, Lord Allenby, on the 23rd November, 1924, read to the Egyptian Prime Minister, in English, two communications conveying an ultimatum provoked by the assassination of the Sirdar, the unusual choice of language was doubtless intended to be taken as a mark of displeasure. Even so, written copies of these British communications were deposited in French at the same time. Viewed from this standpoint, Napoleon's Egyptian Expedition in the wake of medieval Italian seafarers, which is usually regarded as an irrelevant and futile divagation in the career of a European conqueror, wears the appearance of a fruitful endeavour to sow seeds of French culture on a soil that was as receptive as it was far afield.

If the French *lingua franca* is a monument of the decline and fall of a medieval sub-society within the Western body social, we may see in the English *lingua franca* a product of that gigantic process of *pammixia* that has expanded and diluted our modern Western World into a 'Great Society' of world-wide range. This triumph of the English language was a corollary of the triumph of Great Britain herself in a military, political and commercial struggle for the mastery of a new world overseas, both east and west. English has become the native language of North America and the dominant *lingua franca* of the Indian sub-continent. It has also a wide currency in China and Japan. We have already found Italian in use as the service language in the navies of the enemies of the Italian states, and similarly we find, in the China of 1923, the Russian Communist agent, Borodin, using English as his medium of communication with the Chinese representative of the Kuomintang Party in political operations designed to drive the British out of the treaty ports. English is also used as a medium of communication between educated Chinese coming from provinces where different Chinese dialects are spoken, and the vulgarization, on alien lips, of the classic Tuscan and classic Attic tongues has its counterpart in the babu English of India and the pidgin-English of China.

In Africa we can trace the progress of an Arabic *lingua franca* as it has pushed its way westwards from the west coast of the Indian Ocean towards the Lakes, and southwards from the south coast of the Sahara into the Sudan, in the train of successive bands of Arab or semi-Arabicized stock-breeders and slave-raiders and traders. And the linguistic consequences of this movement can still be studied to-day in the life; for, while the physical impact of Arab intruders has been brought to a standstill by European intervention, the linguistic impact of the Arabic language upon the native vernaculars has actually received fresh impetus from an 'opening-up' of Africa that has latterly been taken out of Arab hands. Under European flags which signify the imposition of a Western régime, the Arabic language enjoys better facilities for its advancement than ever before. Perhaps the greatest benefit of all conferred upon Arabic by the European colonial governments has been the official encouragement that they have given—for the sake of supplying an administrative need of their own—to the mixed languages that have arisen on the different cultural coasts on which the flowing tide of Arabic has been seeping in through native mangrove swamps. It is French imperialism on the Upper Niger and British imperialism on the Lower Niger and British and German imperialism in the East African hinterland of Zanzibar that have respectively made the fortunes of Fulani and Hausa and Swahili; and all these languages are linguistic alloys— with an African base and an Arabic infusion—that have been reduced to writing in the Arabic Alphabet.

(d) SYNCRETISM IN RELIGION

In the field of religion the syncretism or amalgamation of rites, cults and faiths is the outward manifestation of that inward sense of promiscuity which arises from the schism in the soul in an age of social disintegration. This phenomenon may be taken, with some assurance, as a symptom of social disintegration because the apparent examples of religious syncretism in the histories of civilizations in their growth-stage turn out to be illusory. For example, when we see the parochial mythologies of innumerable city-states being co-ordinated and harmonized into a single Pan-Hellenic system by the labours of Hesiod and other archaic poets, we are watching a mere juggling with names which is not accompanied by any corresponding fusion of different rites or blending of diverse religious emotions. Again, when we see Latin *numina* being identified with Olympian divinities—a Jupiter with a Zeus or a Juno with a Hera—what we are watching is, in effect, a replacement of primitive Latin animism by a Greek anthropomorphic pantheon.

There is a different class of identifications between names of gods in which these verbal equations do occur in an age of disintegration and also do bear witness to a sense of promiscuity, but which, nevertheless, will be found on examination to be no genuine religious phenomena but merely politics under a religious mask. Such are the identifications that are made between the names of different local gods in an age when a disintegrating society is being forcibly unified on the political plane by wars of conquest between the different parochial states into which the society had previously articulated itself during its growth-phase. For example, when, in the concluding chapters of Sumeric history, Enlil the Lord (Bel) of Nippur was merged into Marduk of Babylon, and when Marduk-Bel of Babylon in his turn went incognito for a time under the name of Kharbe, the *pammixia* thus commemorated was purely political. The first change records the rehabilitation of the Sumeric universal state through the prowess of a Babylonian dynasty, and the second the conquest of that universal state by Kassite war-lords.

Parochial gods who come to be identified with one another in a disintegrating society as a consequence of the unification of different parochial states or the transfer of political authority over such unified empires from one group of war-lords to another, are apt to have a certain antecedent affinity with one another in virtue of their being in most cases the ancestral gods of different sections of one and the same dominant minority. For this reason, the amalgamation of godheads demanded by *raison d'état* does not, as a rule, go seriously against the grain of religious habit and sentiment. To find examples of a religious syncretism that cuts deeper than *raison d'état* and touches the quick of religious practice and belief, we must turn our attention from the religion which the dominant minority inherits from a happier past to the philosophy which it strikes out for itself in response to the challenges from a time of troubles, and we must watch rival schools of philosophy colliding and blending not only with one another but also with the new higher religions produced by the internal proletariats. Since these higher religions, too, collide with one another besides colliding with the philosophies, it will be convenient to glance first at the relations between the higher religions *inter se* and the philosophies *inter se* in their originally separate social spheres before we go on to consider the more dynamic spiritual results that follow when the philosophies on the one side come into relation with the higher religions on the other.

In the disintegration of the Hellenic Society the generation of Posidonius (*circa* 135–51 B.C.) seems to mark the beginning of an epoch in which the several schools of philosophy, which had hitherto delighted in lively and acrimonious controversy, now tended with one accord, with the solitary exception of the Epicureans, to notice and emphasize the points which united them rather than those which divided them, until a time came, in the first and second centuries of the Roman Empire, when every non-Epicurean philosopher in the Hellenic World, whatever he might call himself, subscribed to much the same eclectic set of tenets. A similar tendency towards promiscuity in philosophy displays itself in the history of the disintegration of the Sinic Society at the corresponding stage. In the second century B.C., which was the first century of the Empire of the Han, eclecticism was equally the note of the Taoism which was at first in favour at the Imperial Court and of the Confucianism which supplanted it.

This syncretism between rival philosophies has its parallel in the relations between rival higher religions. For example, in the Syriac World from the generation of Solomon onwards we find a strong tendency towards *rapprochement* between the Israelitish worship of Yahweh and the worships of the local Baalim of neighbouring Syriac communities; and the date is significant, because we have seen reason to believe that the death of Solomon heralded the breakdown of the Syriac Society. No doubt the remarkable and momentous feature of the religious history of Israel in that age is the exceptional success of the Prophets in combating the sense of promiscuity and diverting the stream of Israelitish religious development out of the facile channel of syncretism into a new and arduous course which was peculiar to Israel itself. Yet when we look at the credit instead of the debit side of the Syriac account of reciprocal religious influences, we shall recall that the Syriac time of troubles may have seen the worship of Yahweh make an impact on the religious consciousness of the peoples of Western Iran in whose midst a 'diaspora' of Israelitish deportees had been planted by the Assyrian militarists; and it is at any rate certain that there was a powerful counter-impact of the Iranian upon the Jewish religious consciousness in the time of the Achaemenian Empire and afterwards. By the second century B.C. the mutual interpenetration of Judaism and Zoroastrianism had gone to such lengths that our modern Western scholars find the utmost difficulty in determining and disentangling the respective contributions that these two sources made to the stream which was fed by their united waters.

Similarly, in the development of the higher religions of the internal proletariat of the Indic World, we see a fusion, which goes much deeper than a mere equation of names, between the worship of Krishna and the worship of Vishnu.

Such breaches in the barriers between religion and religion or philosophy and philosophy in times of disintegration open the way for *rapprochements* between philosophies and religions; and in these philosophico-religious syncretisms we shall find that the attraction is mutual and that the move is made from both sides. Just as, astride the military frontiers of a universal state, we have watched the soldiers in the imperial garrisons and the warriors in the barbarian war-bands gradually approximating towards one another in their ways of life until at length the two social types cease to be distinguishable, so, in the interior of a universal state, we can watch a corresponding movement of convergence between the adherents of the philosophic schools and the devotees of the popular religions. And the parallel runs true; for, in this case as in that, we find that, though the representatives of the proletariat do come a certain distance to meet the representatives of the dominant minority, the latter go so much farther along their own path of proletarianization that the eventual fusion takes place almost entirely on proletarian ground. In studying the *rapprochement* from both sides it will therefore be convenient to survey the shorter spiritual journey of the proletarian party first before attempting to follow the longer spiritual journey of the dominant minority.

When higher religions of the internal proletariat find themselves face to face with the dominant minority, their advance along the path of adaptation may sometimes stop short at the preliminary step of commending themselves to the dominant minority's notice by assuming the outward fashions of the dominant minority's style of art. Thus, in the disintegration of the Hellenic World, the unsuccessful rivals of Christianity all sought to promote the success of their missionary enterprises on Hellenic ground by recasting the visual representations of their divinities in forms likely to prove agreeable to Hellenic eyes. But none of them made any appreciable move towards taking the further step of Hellenizing itself inwardly as well as outwardly. It was Christianity alone that went the length of expressing its creed in the language of Hellenic philosophy.

In the history of Christianity the intellectual Hellenization of a religion whose creative essence was of Syriac origin was foreshadowed in the employment of the Attic, instead of the Aramaic, κοινή as the linguistic vehicle of the New Testament; for the very vocabulary of this sophisticated tongue carried with it a host of philosophic implications.

'In the Synoptic Gospels Jesus is regarded as the Son of God, and this belief is carried on and deepened in the body of the Fourth Gospel. But also in the prologue to the Fourth Gospel the idea is thrown out that the Saviour of the World is the Creative Logos of God. Implicitly, then, though the statement is not made explicitly, the Son of God and the Logos of God are one and the same: the Son as the Logos is identified with the creative wisdom and purpose of Deity, the Logos as the Son is hypostatized into a person beside the person of the Father. At one bound the philosophy of the Logos has become a religion.'[1]

This device of preaching religion in the language of philosophy was one of the heirlooms which Christianity had inherited from Judaism. It was Philo the Jewish philosopher of Alexandria (*circa* 30 B.C.–A.D. 45) who sowed the seed from which Philo's Christian fellow-citizens, Clement and Origen, were to reap so rich a harvest two centuries later; and it was perhaps from the same quarter that the author of the Fourth Gospel gained his vision of the Divine Logos with which he identifies his Incarnate God. No doubt this Alexandrian Jewish forerunner of the Alexandrian Christian Fathers was led into the path of Hellenic philosophy through the gate of the Greek language; for it was assuredly no accident that Philo lived and philosophized in a city in which the Attic κοινή had become the vernacular language of a local Jewish community that had so utterly lost command of Hebrew, and even of Aramaic, that it had been driven to desecrate its Holy Scriptures by translating them into a Gentile language. Yet in the history of Judaism itself this Jewish father of a Christian philosophy is an isolated figure; and his ingenious effort to derive the Platonic philosophy from the Mosaic Law remained, for Judaism, a *tour de force* without consequences.

When we pass from Christianity to Mithraism, its rival in a competition for the spiritual conquest of the Hellenic World, we observe that, on its voyage westward from its Iranian homeland, Mithra's barque took on board a heavy cargo of the Babylonic astral philosophy. In a similar fashion the Indic higher religion of Hinduism despoiled a senile Buddhist philosophy in order to acquire for itself the weapons with which it drove its philosophical rival out of their common homeland in the Indic World. And it is the opinion of at least one eminent modern Egyptologist that the proletarian worship of Osiris only won its way into the citadel of the Egyptiac dominant minority's hereditary pantheon by usurping from Re the ethical role—originally quite foreign to the Osirian faith—of a divinity that reveals and vindicates righteousness. But this 'spoiling of the Egyptians' cost the proletarian religion dear; for the Osirian religion had to pay for its borrowed plumes by putting itself into the hands of the party that was constrained to lend them. The master-stroke of the old Egyptiac priesthood was to place itself at the disposal—and in so doing also place itself at the head—of a rising religious movement which it

[1] More, P. E.: *Christ the Word: The Greek Tradition from the Death of Socrates to the Council of Chalcedon*, vol. iv, p. 298.

found itself unable to suppress or hold at bay, and thereby to raise itself to a pinnacle of power which it had never attained before.

The capture of the Osirian religion by the priests of the old Egyptiac pantheon has its parallels in the capture of Hinduism by the Brahmans and the capture of Zoroastrianism by the Magi. But there is another and still more insidious way in which a proletarian religion is apt to fall into the hands of a dominant minority; for the priesthood which gains control of a proletarian church and then abuses this control in order to govern it in the dominant minority's spirit and interest need not be an ancient priesthood belonging to the dominant minority by descent; it may actually be recruited from the leading lights of the proletarian church itself.

In an early chapter of the political history of the Roman Republic the *stasis* between Plebeians and Patricians was brought to an end by a 'deal' in which the Patricians took the leaders of the Plebeians into partnership on the tacit understanding that these leaders of the unprivileged class would betray their trust and leave their rank and file in the lurch. In a similar fashion on the religious plane, the rank and file of Jewry had been betrayed and deserted, before the time of Christ, by their own former leaders, the Scribes and Pharisees. These Jewish 'separatists' had lived to deserve their self-chosen name in a sense which was the opposite of their intention at the time when they assumed it. The original Pharisees were Jewish puritans who separated themselves from the Hellenizing Jews when these renegades were joining the camp of an alien dominant minority, whereas the distinguishing mark of the Pharisees in the time of Christ was their separation from the rank and file of the loyal and devout members of the Jewish community to whom they still hypocritically professed to be setting a good example. This is the historical background of the scathing denunciation of the Pharisees which echoes through the pages of the Gospels. The Pharisees had become the Jewish ecclesiastical counterparts of Jewry's Roman political masters. In the tragedy of the Passion of Christ we see them actively ranging themselves at the side of the Roman authorities in order to compass the death of a prophet of their own race who had been putting them to shame.

If we pass now to our examination of the complementary movement in which the philosophies of the dominant minority make their approach towards the religions of the internal proletariat, we shall find that on this side the process begins earlier, besides going farther. It begins in the first generation after the breakdown; and it passes from curiosity through devoutness into superstition.

The earliness of the first infusion of a religious tinge is attested, in the classical Hellenic case, in the *mise-en-scène* of Plato's *Republic*. The scene is laid in the Peiraeus—the oldest crucible of social *pammixia* in the Hellenic World—before the fatal end of the Atheno-Peloponnesian War; the master of the house in which the dialogue is supposed to take place is a resident alien; and the alleged narrator, Socrates, begins by telling us that he has walked down to the port from the city of Athens 'in order to pay' his 'respects to the Thracian goddess Bendis, and out of curiosity to observe how they are going to keep the festival that is being celebrated in her honour at the Peiraeus for the first time on this occasion'. Thus religion is 'in the air' as a setting for this masterpiece of Hellenic philosophy—religion, too, of an alien and exotic character. Here, surely, is an introduction which prepares us for the sequel described by a modern Western scholar in the following words:

'The extraordinary thing . . . is that, despite the alien source of the new [i.e. the Christian] myth, the theology and philosophy of the Greek Fathers should have turned out in essential matters so thoroughly Platonic or, more accurately expressed, could have been adopted from Plato with so few modifications. Such a coalescence may lead us to conjecture that the mythology which Plato sought to substitute for the old tales of the Gods was not so much antagonistic to the faith of Christianity as imperfectly Christian. . . . From hints here and there it could even be surmised that Plato himself was dimly aware of a theophany to come, of which his allegories were a prophecy. Socrates in the *Apology* had warned the Athenians of other witnesses to the soul who should appear after him and avenge his death; and elsewhere he had admitted that, for all the reasoning and high imaginings of philosophy, the full truth could not be known until revealed to man by the grace of God.'[1]

Our historical record of this metamorphosis of philosophy into religion is ample enough in the Hellenic case to enable us to follow the process through its successive stages.

The cool intellectual curiosity which is the Platonic Socrates' attitude towards the Thracian religion of Bendis is also the mood of the historical Socrates' contemporary, Herodotus, in his incidental disquisitions on the comparative study of religion. His interest in such matters is essentially scientific. However, theological problems came to be a matter of somewhat greater practical concern to the dominant minority after the overthrow of the Achaemenian Empire by Alexander the Great, when the Hellenic rulers of the successor-states had to make some ritual provision for the

---

[1] More, P. E.: *Christ the Word*, pp. 6–7.

religious needs of their mixed populations. At the same time the founders and propagators of the Stoic and Epicurean schools of philosophy were providing a ration of spiritual comfort for individual souls which found themselves forlornly astray in a spiritual wilderness. If, however, we take as our gauge of the prevalent tendency of Hellenic philosophy in this age the tone and temper of the School of Plato, we shall find his disciples during the two centuries after Alexander pushing ever farther along the path of scepticism.

The decisive turn of the tide comes with the Syrian Greek Stoic philosopher Posidonius of Apamea (*circa* 135–51 B.C.), who opened wide the gates of the Stoa for the reception of popular religious beliefs. Less than two centuries later, the leadership in the Stoic school had passed to Seneca, the brother of Gallio and the contemporary of Saint Paul. There are passages in Seneca's philosophical works that are so arrestingly reminiscent of passages in the Pauline epistles that some of the less critical-minded Christian theologians of a later age have allowed themselves to imagine that the Roman philosopher was in correspondence with the Christian missionary. Such conjectures are as superfluous as they are improbable; for, after all, there is nothing to surprise us in these harmonies of tone between two pieces of spiritual music created in the same age under the inspiration of the same social experience.

In our study of the relations between the military guardians of the frontier of a disintegrating civilization and the barbarian warlords beyond it, we have seen how, in the first chapter, the two parties approximate towards one another to a point of virtual indistinguishability; and how, in the second chapter, they meet and mingle on a dead level of barbarism. In the parallel story of the *rapprochement* between the philosophers of the dominant minority and the devotees of a proletarian religion, the approximation, on a lofty plane, between Seneca and Saint Paul marks the conclusion of the first chapter. In the second chapter, philosophy, succumbing to less edifying religious influences, descends from devoutness into superstition.

Such is the miserable end of the philosophies of the dominant minority, and this even when they have striven with all their might to win their way on to that kindlier proletarian spiritual soil that is the seed-bed of the higher religions. It profits these philosophies nothing that they, too, have at last broken into flower, when this tardy and reluctant flowering revenges itself upon them by degenerating into an unwholesome luxuriance. In the last act of the dissolution of a civilization the philosophies die while the higher religions live on and stake out their claims upon the future.

Christianity survived, crowding out the Neoplatonic philosophy, which found no elixir of life in its discarding of rationality. In fact, when philosophies and religions meet, the religions must increase while the philosophies must decrease; and we cannot turn away from our study of the encounter between them without pausing to look into the question why it is that this defeat of the philosophies is a foregone conclusion.

What, then, are the weaknesses that doom philosophy to discomfiture when it enters the lists as the rival of religion? The fatal and fundamental weakness, from which all the rest derive, is a lack of spiritual vitality. This lack of *élan* lames philosophy in two ways. It diminishes its attractiveness for the masses and it discourages those who feel its attractions from throwing themselves into missionary work on its behalf. Indeed philosophy affects a preference for an intellectual *élite*, the 'fit though few', like the high-brow poet who regards the smallness of his circulation as evidence of the excellence of his verse. In the pre-Senecan generation Horace felt no incongruity in prefacing the philosophico-patriotic appeal of his 'Roman Odes' with:

> Avaunt, ye herd profane!
> Silence! let no unhallow'd tongue
> Disturb the sacred rites of song,
> Whilst I, the High Priest of the Nine,
> For youths and maids alone entwine
> A new and loftier strain.[1]

It is a far cry from this to the parable of Jesus:

'Go ye out into the highways and hedges and compel them to come in, that my house may be filled.'

Thus philosophy could never emulate the strength of religion at its best; it could only imitate, and parody, the weaknesses of its inferior devotees. The breath of religion which had momentarily animated the clear-cut marble of the Hellenic intellect in the generation of Seneca and Epictetus rapidly staled, after the generation of Marcus Aurelius, into a stuffy religiosity, and the heirs of the philosophic tradition fell between two stools. They discarded the appeal to the intellect without finding a way to the heart. In ceasing to be sages they became, not saints but cranks. The Emperor Julian turned from Socrates to Diogenes for his model of philosophy—the legendary Diogenes from whom, rather than from Christ, the 'Christian' asceticism of St. Simeon Stylites and his fellow-ascetics is derived. Indeed, in this tragi-comic last act, the epigoni of Plato and Zeno confessed the inadequacy of

[1] Horace: *Odes*, Bk. III, Ode i, ll. 1–4 (*Odi profanum vulgus*, &c.), Sir Stephen de Vere's translation.

their own great masters and ensamples by abandoning themselves to an imitation of the internal proletariat which was in very truth the sincerest flattery of the *profanum vulgus* that Horace had excluded from his audience. The last Neoplatonists, Iamblichus and Proclus, are not so much philosophers as priests of an imaginary and non-existent religion. Julian, with his zeal for priestcraft and ritual, was the would-be executor of their schemes, and the immediate collapse, on the news of his death, of his state-supported ecclesiastical establishment proves the truth of the judgement of the founder of a school of modern psychology:

'Great innovations never come from above; they invariably come from below . . . [from] the much-derided silent folk of the land—those who are less infected with academic prejudices than great celebrities are wont to be.'[1]

(e) CUIUS REGIO EIUS RELIGIO?[2]

We noticed, at the end of the preceding chapter, that Julian, as emperor, failed to force upon his subjects the pseudo-religion to which, as a philosopher, he was addicted. This raises the general question whether in any more favourable circumstances dominant minorities are able to make up for their spiritual weakness by bringing their physical strength into play and forcing a philosophy or a religion on their subjects by means of a political pressure which might be none the less effective for being illegitimate; and, although this question is off the main line of the argument of this part of our Study, we propose to seek for the answer to it before proceeding farther.

If we examine the historical evidence on this head we shall find that in general such attempts prove failures, at any rate in the long run—a finding which flatly contradicts one of the sociological theories of the Enlightenment during the Hellenic time of troubles; for, according to this theory, the deliberate imposition of religious practices from above downwards, so far from being impossible or even unusual, has actually been the normal origin of religious institutions in societies in process of civilization. This theory has been applied to the religious life of Rome in the following celebrated passage of Polybius (*circa* 206–131 B.C.):

---

[1] Jung, C. G.: *Modern Man in Search of a Soul*, pp. 243–4.

[2] The formula *cuius regio eius religio* (the ruler determines the religion) is the traditional summary of the principal provision of the Treaty of Augsburg of A.D. 1555, by which the ruler of each parochial German state was recognized as being entitled to opt for either the Catholic or the Lutheran form of Christianity and then, if he wished, to insist on his subjects conforming to the religion established by himself. The treaty followed the first inconclusive bout of religious wars in Germany.

'The point in which the Roman constitution excels others most conspicuously is to be found, in my opinion, in its handling of religion. In my opinion the Romans have managed to forge the main bond of their social order out of something which the rest of the world execrates: I mean, out of superstition. In dramatizing their superstition theatrically and introducing it into private as well as into public life, the Romans have gone to the most extreme lengths conceivable; and to many observers this will appear extraordinary. In my opinion, however, the Romans have done it with an eye to the masses. If it were possible to have an electorate that was composed exclusively of sages, this chicanery might perhaps be unnecessary; but, as a matter of fact, the masses are always unstable and always full of lawless passions, irrational temper and violent rage; so there is nothing for it but to control them by "the fear of the unknown" and play-acting of that sort. I fancy that this was the reason why our forefathers introduced among the masses those theological beliefs and those notions about Hell that have now become traditional; and I also fancy that, in doing this, our ancestors were not working at random but knew just what they were about. It might be more pertinent to charge our contemporaries with lack of sense and lapse from responsibility for trying to eradicate religion, as we actually see them doing.'[1]

This theory of the origins of religion is about as remote from the truth as the social contract theory of the origin of states. If we now proceed to examine the evidence we shall find that, while political power is not completely impotent to produce effects upon spiritual life, its ability to act in this field is dependent on special combinations of circumstances, and that, even then, its range of action is narrowly circumscribed. Successes are exceptional and failures the rule.

To take the exceptions first, we may observe that political potentates do sometimes succeed in establishing a cult when this cult is the expression, not of any genuine religious feeling, but of some political sentiment masquerading in a religious disguise: for example, a pseudo-religious ritual expressing the thirst for political unity in a society that has drunk to the dregs the bitter cup of a time of troubles. In these circumstances a ruler who has already won a hold over his subjects' hearts as their human saviour may succeed in establishing a cult in which his own office and person and dynasty are the objects of worship.

The classic example of this *tour de force* is the deification of the Roman emperors. Yet Caesar-worship proved a fair-weather cult, the precise opposite of the 'present help in time of trouble' which is what a real religion proves to be. It did not survive the first collapse of the Roman Empire at the turn of the second and third

[1] Polybius: *Historiae*, Bk. VI, ch. 56.

centuries; and the warrior emperors of the rally which followed began to cast about for some supernatural sanction behind and beyond their own discredited Imperial Genius. Aurelian and Constantius Chlorus enlisted under the standard of an abstract and oecumenical Sol Invictus, and, a generation later, Constantine the Great (A.D. 306–37) transferred his allegiance to that God of the internal proletariat who had proved himself more potent than either Sol or Caesar.

If we turn from the Hellenic to the Sumeric World, we shall observe an analogue of Caesar-worship in the cult of his own human person which was instituted—not by the founder of the Sumeric universal state, Ur-Engur, but by his successor, Dungi (*circa* 2280–2223 B.C.); but this also appears to have proved a fair-weather contrivance. At any rate, the Amorite Hammurabi, who occupies in Sumeric history a position analogous to that of Constantine in the history of the Roman Empire, ruled not as a god incarnate but as the servant of the transcendental deity Marduk-Bel.

An examination of such traces of 'Caesar-worship' as may be found in other universal states, Andean, Egyptiac and Sinic, confirms our impression of the congenital feebleness of cults propagated by political potentates from above downwards. Even when such cults are political in essence and religious only in form, and even when they correspond with a genuine popular sentiment, they show little capacity for surviving storms.

There is another class of cases in which a political potentate attempts to impose a cult which is no mere political institution in a religious guise but is of a genuinely religious character; and in this field, too, we can point to instances in which the experiment has secured some degree of success. It appears, however, to be a condition of success in such cases that the religion imposed in this fashion should be a 'going concern'—at any rate in the souls of a minority of its political patron's subjects—and, even when this condition is fulfilled and success attained, the price that has to be paid turns out to be a prohibitive one. For a religion which, by an exertion of political authority, is successfully imposed upon all the souls whose bodies are subject to the ruler who is imposing it, is apt to gain this fraction of the world at the price of forfeiting any prospects it may once have had of becoming, or remaining, a universal church.

For example, when the Maccabees changed, before the close of the second century B.C., from being militant champions of the Jewish religion against a forcible Hellenization into being the founders and rulers of one of the successor-states of the Seleucid

Empire, these violent resisters of persecution became persecutors in their turn, and set themselves to impose Judaism on the non-Jewish peoples whom they had conquered. This policy succeeded in extending the domain of Judaism over Idumaea and over 'Galilee of the Gentiles' and over a narrow Transjordanian Peraea. Even so, this triumph of force was narrowly circumscribed; for it failed to overcome either the particularism of the Samaritans or the civic pride of the two rows of Hellenized city-states which flanked the Maccabees' dominions on both sides, one row along the Mediterranean coast of Palestine and the other along its desert border in the Decapolis. In fact, the gain through force of arms was inconsiderable, and, as it turned out, it was to cost the Jewish religion the whole of its spiritual future. For it is the supreme irony of Jewish history that the new ground captured for Judaism by Alexander Jannaeus (102–76 B.C.) brought to birth, within a hundred years, a Galilaean Jewish prophet whose message was the consummation of all previous Jewish religious experience, and that this inspired Jewish scion of forcibly converted Galilaean Gentiles was then rejected by the Judaean leaders of the Jewry of his own age. Thereby Judaism not only stultified its past but forfeited its future.

If we now turn to the religious map of modern Europe we are naturally prompted to inquire how far the present boundaries between the domains of Catholicism and Protestantism have been determined by the arms or diplomacy of the parochial successor-states of the medieval *Respublica Christiana*. No doubt the influence of external military and political factors on the outcome of the religious conflict of the sixteenth and seventeenth centuries ought not to be rated too high; for, to take two extreme cases, it is difficult to imagine that the action of any secular authority could have retained the Baltic countries within the fold of the Catholic Church or brought the Mediterranean countries over into the Protestant camp. At the same time there was an inter-mediate and debatable zone in which the play of military and political forces was certainly influential; and this zone embraces. Germany, the Low Countries, France and England. It was in Germany, in particular, that the classical formula, *cuius regio eius religio*, was invented and applied; and we may take it that in Central Europe, at least, the secular princes did successfully use their power to force down the throats of their subjects whichever of the competing varieties of Western Christianity the local potentate happened to favour. We can also take the measure of the damage which our Western Christianity, Catholic and Protestant alike, has suffered in the sequel as a penalty for having thus allowed itself to become dependent on political patronage and consequently subservient to *raison d'état*.

One of the first instalments of the price that had to be paid was the loss of the Catholic Church's mission-field in Japan; for the seedlings of Catholic Christianity which had been planted there by Jesuit missionaries in the sixteenth century were uprooted before the middle of the seventeenth century by the deliberate action of the rulers of the newly founded Japanese universal state because these statesmen had come to the conclusion that the Catholic Church was an instrument of the imperial ambitions of the Spanish Crown. This forfeiture of a promising mission-field must be estimated, however, as a trifling loss by comparison with the spiritual impoverishment which the policy of *cuius regio eius religio* was to inflict upon Western Christianity at home. The readiness of all the competing factions of Western Christianity in the age of the Wars of Religion to seek a short cut to victory by condoning, or even demanding, the imposition of their own doctrines upon the adherents of rival faiths by the application of political force was a spectacle which sapped the foundations of all belief in the souls for whose allegiance the warring churches were competing. Louis XIV's methods of barbarism eradicated Protestantism from the spiritual soil of France only to clear the ground for an alternative crop of scepticism. The revocation of the Edict of Nantes was followed within nine years by the birth of Voltaire. In England, too, we can see the same sceptical temper setting in as a reaction from the religious militancy of the Puritan Revolution. A new Enlightenment arose of a temper akin to that displayed in the quotation from Polybius at the opening of this chapter of our Study, a school of thought which treated religion itself as an object of ridicule; so that, by 1736, Bishop Butler could write in the Preface to his *Analogy of Religion, Natural and Revealed, to the Constitution and Course of Nature*:

'It is come, I know not how, to be taken for granted by many persons that Christianity is not so much as a subject of inquiry, but that it is now at length discovered to be fictitious. And accordingly they treat it as if in the present age this were an agreed point among all people of discernment, and nothing remained but to set it up as a principal subject of mirth and ridicule, as it were by way of reprisals for its having so long interrupted the pleasures of the world.'

This attitude of mind, which sterilized fanaticism at the cost of extinguishing faith, has lasted from the seventeenth century into the twentieth, and has been carried to such lengths in all parts of our Westernized 'Great Society' that it is beginning at last to be recognized for what it is. It is being recognized, that is to say, as the supreme danger to the spiritual health and even to the material existence of the Western body social—a deadlier danger, by far, than any of our hotly canvassed and loudly advertised political and economic maladies. This spiritual evil is now too flagrant to be ignored; but it is easier to diagnose the disease than to prescribe the remedy, for faith is not like a standard article of commerce that can be procured on demand. It will be hard indeed to refill the spiritual vacuum which has been hollowed in our Western hearts by the progressive decay of religious belief that has been going on for some two-and-a-half centuries. We are still reacting against a subordination of religion to politics which was the crime of our sixteenth- and seventeenth-century ancestors.

If we take a synoptic view of the several surviving forms of Western Christianity in their present state and compare them in respect of their relative vitality, we shall find that this varies inversely with the degree to which each of these sects has succumbed to secular control. Unquestionably Catholicism is the form of Western Christianity that is showing the most vigorous signs of life to-day; and the Catholic Church—in spite of the lengths to which modern Catholic princes have gone, in certain countries and at certain times, towards asserting their own secular control over the life of the Church within their frontiers—has never lost the inestimable advantage of being united in a single communion under the presidency of a single supreme ecclesiastical authority. Next to the Catholic Church in order of vitality we shall probably place those 'free churches' of the Protestant persuasion which have extricated themselves from the control of secular governments. And we shall certainly place at the bottom of the list the Protestant 'established' churches which still remain tied to the body politic of this or that modern parochial state. Finally, if we were to venture to draw distinctions of relative vitality between the different shades of religious thought and practice within so widely ramifying and Protean an established church as the Church of England, we should unhesitatingly assign the palm of superior vitality to the Anglo-Catholic variety of Anglicanism which, ever since the Act of 1874, designed to put down 'mass in masquerade', has treated the secular law with contemptuous indifference.

The moral of this odious comparison seems plain. This diversity of the fortunes of the several fractions of the Western Christian Church in modern times would appear to complete our proof of the proposition that religion stands to lose, in the long run, far more than it can ever hope to gain by asking for, or submitting to, the patronage of the civil power. There is, however, one conspicuous exception to this apparent rule which will have to be accounted for before the rule can be allowed to pass muster; and this exception is the case of Islam. For Islam did succeed in becoming the universal church of a dissolving Syriac Society in spite of having been politically compromised at an earlier stage and in an apparently more decisive way than any of the religions that we have passed in review up to this point. Indeed, Islam was politically compromised within the lifetime of its founder by the action of no less a person than the founder himself.

The public career of the Prophet Muhammed falls into two sharply distinct and seemingly contradictory chapters. In the first he is occupied in preaching a religious revelation by methods of pacific evangelization; in the second chapter he is occupied in building up a political and military power and in using this power in the very way which, in other cases, has turned out disastrous for a religion that takes to it. In this Medinese chapter Muhammed used his new-found material power for the purpose of enforcing conformity with at any rate the outward observances of the religion which he had founded in the previous chapter of his career, before his momentous withdrawal from Mecca to Medina. On this showing, the *Hijrah* ought to mark the date of the ruin of Islam and not the date since consecrated as that of its foundation. How are we to explain the hard fact that a religion which was launched on the world as the militant faith of a barbarian war-band should have succeeded in becoming a universal church, in spite of having started under a spiritual handicap that might have been expected, on all analogies, to prove prohibitive?

When we set out the problem in these terms, we shall find several partial explanations which, taken together, may perhaps amount to a solution.

In the first place we can discount the tendency—which has been popular in Christendom—to over-estimate the extent of the use of force in the propagation of Islam. The show of adherence to the new religion exacted by the Prophet's successors was limited to the performance of a small number of not very onerous external observances, and even this much was not attempted beyond the limits of the primitive pagan communities of the Arabian no-man's-land in which Islam took its rise. In the conquered provinces of the Roman and Sasanian Empires the alternatives offered were not 'Islam or death' but 'Islam or a super-tax'—a policy traditionally praised for its enlightenment when pursued long afterwards in England by a Laodicean Queen Elizabeth. Nor was this option made invidious for the non-Muslim subjects of the Arab Caliphate under the Umayyad régime, for the Umayyads (with the exception of a single representative of the line, who reigned for only three years) were Laodiceans to a man. In fact the Umayyads were personally crypto-pagans who were indifferent, or even positively hostile, to the propagation of the Islamic faith of which they enjoyed the titular leadership.

Under these singular conditions Islam had to make its way among the non-Arab subjects of the Caliphate on its own religious merits. Its spread was slow but sure; and, in the hearts of ex-Christians and ex-Zoroastrians who embraced the new religion in face of the indifference, if not in the teeth of the displeasure, of their nominally Muslim Umayyad masters, Islam became a very different faith from what it had formerly been on the sleeves of Arab warriors who had worn it as the denominational badge of a privileged political status. The new non-Arab converts adapted it to their own intellectual outlook, translating the crude and casual assertions of the Prophet into the subtle and consistent terms of Christian theology and Hellenic philosophy; and it was in this clothing that Islam was able to become the unifying religion of a Syriac World which had been reunited hitherto only on the superficial plane of politics by the sweep of the Arab military conquest.

Within a hundred years of Mu'āwīyah's rise to political power the non-Arab Muslim subjects of the Caliphate had become strong enough to put down the Laodicean Umayyads from their seat and to enthrone in their place a dynasty whose devoutness reflected the religious temper of their supporters. In A.D. 750, when the favour of the non-Arab Muslims gave the 'Abbasids their victory over the Umayyads, it is possible that the numerical strength of the religious faction which thus turned the scales was still as small in proportion to the total population of the Arab Empire as were the numbers of the Christians in the Roman Empire at the time when Constantine overthrew Maxentius, a number estimated by Dr. N. H. Baynes at about ten per cent.[1] The mass conversions of the subjects of the Caliphate to Islam probably did not begin before the ninth century of the Christian Era or reach their term until the dissolution of the 'Abbasid Empire in the thirteenth century, and it can confidently be said of these belated harvests in the Islamic mission-field that they were the outcome of a spontaneous popular movement and not of political pressure; for the Islamic counterparts of a Theodosius and a Justinian, who misused their political power in the supposed interests of their religion, are few and far between in a list of the 'Abbasid Caliphs which stretches through five centuries.

These facts may be considered to account satisfactorily for the

[1] Baynes, N. H.: *Constantine the Great and the Christian Church*, p. 4.

exception which Islam *prima facie* presents to our rule that, while it is not impossible for a secular power to obtain some measure of success in forcibly imposing upon its subjects a religion which is already a 'going concern', the price to be paid for such political support far more than counterbalances, in the long run, any immediate advantage to the religion thus politically patronized.

The same penalty seems to be incurred even when the political patronage secures no immediate returns at all. Among the more notorious cases in which a religion has received the compromising support of the secular arm and suffered unmitigated loss we may reckon the failure of Justinian to impose his own Catholic Ortho-doxy on his Monophysite subjects beyond the Taurus; the failure of Leo Syrus and Constantine V to impose their Iconoclasm on their Iconodule subjects in Greece and Italy; the failure of the British Crown to impose its Protestantism on its Catholic subjects in Ireland; and the failure of the Mughal Emperor Awrangzīb to impose his own Islam on his Hindu subjects. And, if such is the case where the religion to be imposed is a 'going concern', it is still less likely that the political arm will succeed in imposing a philosophy of the dominant minority. We have already mentioned the failure of the Emperor Julian, which was in fact the starting-point of this inquiry. Equally complete was the failure of the Emperor Açoka to impose his Hinayanian Buddhism on his Indic subjects, though the Buddhist philosophy of his day was in its intellectual and moral prime, and is thus comparable with the Stoicism of Marcus Aurelius rather than with the Neoplatonism of Julian.

There remain to be considered the cases in which a ruler or ruling class has sought to impose not a religion which is already a 'going concern' nor a philosophy of the dominant minority but a newfangled 'fancy religion' of his or its own devising. In view of the failures already recorded where the purpose was to impose a religion or a philosophy already possessing inherent vitality, we might feel ourselves justified in assuming, without hearing the evidence, that this latter undertaking would prove a failure whenever and wherever it was attempted; and such proves indeed to be the case. However, these 'fancy religions' are among the curiosities of history and for this reason, if for no other, may now be rapidly reviewed.

The most extreme case of the kind on record is perhaps that of the Isma'īlī Shī'ī dissident Caliph al-Hākim (A.D. 996–1020); for, whatever its borrowings from external sources, the distinctive dogma of the so-called Druse theology is the deification of al-Hākim himself as the last and most perfect of ten successive incarnations of God: a divine and immortal Messiah who is to return in triumph to a world from which he has mysteriously withdrawn after a brief first epiphany. The solitary success of the missionaries of this new faith was the conversion by the apostle Darazi, in A.D. 1016, of one tiny community in the Syrian district of Wādi'l-Taym, at the foot of Mount Hermon. Fifteen years later the mission of converting the world to the new faith was explicitly abandoned, and since that date the Druse community has neither admitted converts nor tolerated apostates but has remained a closed hereditary religious corporation whose members bear the name, not of the god incarnate whom they worship, but of the missionary who first introduced them to al-Hākim's strange gospel. Ensconced in the highlands of Hermon and the Lebanon, the Druse church universal *manquée* has become a perfect example of a 'fossil in a fastness'; and by the same token al-Hākim's 'fancy religion' has proved a fiasco.

Al-Hākim's religion at least survives as a 'fossil', but nothing at all resulted from the almost equally presumptuous attempt of the Syrian pervert Varius Avitus Bassianus to install as the high god of the official pantheon of the Roman Empire, not indeed his own person, but his own parochial divinity the Emesan Sun-God Elagabalus, whose hereditary high priest he was, and whose name he continued to bear by choice after a stroke of fortune had placed him, in A.D. 218, on the Roman Imperial throne. His assassination four years later brought his religious experiment to an abrupt and final close.

While it may not be surprising to see an Elagabalus and a Hākim meet with utter failure in their endeavours to make their political authority minister to their religious caprice, we shall perhaps more clearly appreciate the difficulty of propagating creeds and rites by political action from above downwards when we observe the equally striking ill-success of other rulers who have attempted to take advantage of their political power for the promotion of some religious cause in which they have been interested from more serious motives than the desire to gratify a personal whim. There are rulers who have tried and failed to propagate a 'fancy religion' for reasons of state which may have been irreligious but have certainly not been discreditable or unworthy of high statesmanship; and there have been others who have tried and failed to propagate a 'fancy religion' in which they themselves devoutly believed and which they felt themselves on that account entitled or even in duty bound to communicate by all means at their command to their fellow men, in order to lighten their darkness and to guide their feet into the way of peace.

The classic example of the calculated manufacture of a new religion for the service of a political end is the invention of the figure and cult of Serapis by Ptolemy Soter, the founder of the Hellenic successor-state of the Achaemenian Empire in Egypt. His object was to bridge by means of a common religion the gulf between his Egyptiac and his Hellenic subjects, and he enlisted a phalanx of experts to carry out his plans. The new synthetic religion secured a considerable following from among both the communities for which it was designed, but it failed entirely to bridge the gulf between them. Each went its own way in the worship of Serapis as in everything else. The spiritual gulf between the two communities within the Ptolemaic Empire was bridged at last by another religion which arose spontaneously out of the bosom of the proletariat in the *ci-devant* Ptolemaic province of Coele-Syria a whole generation after the extinction of the last shadow of the Ptolemaic Power.

More than a thousand years before the reign of Ptolemy Soter another ruler of Egypt, the Pharaoh Ikhnaton, had set himself to substitute for the orthodox Egyptiac pantheon the worship of an etherial and only true God who made his godhead manifest to human eyes in the Aton or solar disk, and, so far as can be seen, his attempt was not prompted by any Machiavellian considerations, such as animated Ptolemy Soter, nor by a semi-insane megalomania which we may take to have been the driving power behind the enterprises of al-Hākim and Elagabalus. He appears to have been inspired by an exalted religious faith which, like Açoka's philosophic convictions, translated itself into evangelical works. The religious motive by which Ikhnaton was inspired was disinterested and single-minded. It may be said that he deserved to succeed, and yet his failure was complete; and this failure must be attributed to the fact that his programme was an attempt on the part of a political potentate to propagate a 'fancy religion' from above downwards. He incurred the bitter hostility of the dominant minority within his realm without succeeding in reaching and touching the hearts of the proletariat.

The failure of Orphism may be similarly explained if it is true, as there seems reason to believe, that the propagation of Orphism received its first impulse from the Athenian despots of the House of Peisistratus. Such modest success as Orphism did eventually achieve was posterior to the breakdown of the Hellenic Civilization and to the invasion of Hellenic souls by that sense of promiscuity which kept pace with the material expansion of the Hellenic World at the expense of alien societies.

It is hard to know whether to class with the Machiavellianism of Ptolemy Soter or with the idealism of Ikhnaton the wellnigh undecipherable mixture of motives which led the Timurid Mughal Emperor Akbar (A.D. 1554–1605) into his attempt to establish within his Empire his 'fancy religion', the Dīn Ilāhī; for this extraordinary man appears to have been simultaneously a great practical statesman and a transcendental mystic. In any case his religion never took root and was swept out of existence immediately after its author's death. Indeed the last word on this vain dream of autocrats had already been uttered, presumably within Akbar's knowledge, by one of the councillors of Akbar's own predecessor and ensample, Sultan 'Alā-ad-Dīn Khiljī, at a privy council meeting at which 'Alā-ad-Dīn had divulged his intention of committing the very act of folly which Akbar committed three hundred years later.

'Religion and law and creeds', declared the prince's councillor on this occasion, 'ought never to be made subjects of discussion by Your Majesty, for these are the concerns of prophets, not the business of kings. Religion and law spring from heavenly revélation; they are never established by the plans and designs of man. From the days of Adam till now they have been the mission of prophets and apostles, as rule and government have been the duty of kings. The prophetic office has never appertained to kings—and never will, so long as the World lasts—though some prophets have discharged the functions of royalty. My advice is that Your Majesty should never talk about these matters.'[1]

We have not as yet drawn from the history of our modern Western Society any examples of the abortive attempts of political rulers to impose 'fancy religions' on their subjects, but the history of the French Revolution offers a group of illustrations. Successive waves of French Revolutionists in the hectic decade which closed the eighteenth century failed to make any headway with any of the religious fantasies by which they proposed to replace a supposedly outmoded Catholic Church—whether it were the democratized Christian hierarchy of the Civil Constitution of 1791 or the cult of Robespierre's *Être Suprême* in 1794 or the Theophilanthropy of the Director Larevellière-Lépaux. We are told that on one occasion this Director read a long paper explaining his religious system to his ministerial colleagues. After most of them had offered their congratulations, the Minister for Foreign Affairs, Talleyrand, remarked: 'For my part I have only one observation to make. Jesus Christ, in order to found His religion, was crucified and rose again. You should have tried to do some-

---

[1] Smith, V. A.: *Akbar, the Great Mogul*, p. 210.

thing of the kind.' In this monumental gibe at the expense of the fatuous Theophilanthropist, Talleyrand merely repeated in gross terms the advice of the councillor of 'Alā-ad-Dīn. If Larevellière-Lépaux was to succeed in propagating a religion, he must leave the ranks of the Directors and take up a new career as a proletarian prophet.

It only remained for the First Consul Bonaparte to discover that France was, after all, Catholic and that therefore it would be both simpler and more politic to aim, not at imposing a new religion on France, but at enlisting her old religion on the side of her new ruler.

This last example may be left not only to complete our demonstration that *cuius regio eius religio* is on the whole a snare and a delusion, but also to point the way to a counter-proposition which contains a large element of truth, which we may express in the formula *religio regionis religio regis*. Rulers who have adopted the religion favoured by the most numerous, or at any rate the most vigorous, section of their subjects have generally prospered, whether actuated by religious sincerity or by political cynicism, like Henri Quatre with his 'Paris is worth a mass'. The list of such conformist rulers would include the Roman Emperor Constantine who embraced Christianity and the Sinic Emperor Han Wuti who embraced Confucianism; it would include Clovis, Henri Quatre and Napoleon; but its most remarkable illustration would be found in a quaint provision of the British Constitution, in virtue of which the sovereign of the United Kingdom is an Episcopalian in England and a Presbyterian on the Scottish side of the Border. The ecclesiastical status of the Crown that has resulted from the politico-ecclesiastical settlement achieved between 1689 and 1707 has indeed been the palladium of the constitution of the United Kingdom ever since; for the formal equality at law between the respective ecclesiastical establishments of the two kingdoms has been symbolized, in a fashion that can be 'understanded of the people' on both sides of the Border, in the visible fact that, on both sides alike, the King professes a religion which is the officially established religion of the land; and this palpably assured sense of ecclesiastical equality, so conspicuously absent during the century which intervened between the union of the crowns and the union of the parliaments (1603–1707), has provided the psychological foundation for a free and equal political union between two kingdoms which had previously been alienated from one another by a long tradition of hostility and which have never ceased to be differentiated by a wide disparity in population and wealth.

(6) THE SENSE OF UNITY

In our preliminary survey of the relations between the several alternative ways of behaviour, feeling and life in which human souls react to the ordeal of social disintegration, we observed that the sense of promiscuity, which we have just been studying in a variety of manifestations, is a psychological response to a blurring and blending of the sharp individual outlines that are assumed by a civilization while it is still in growth, and we also observed that the same experience may alternatively evoke another response— an awakening to a sense of unity—which is not only distinct from the sense of promiscuity but is its exact antithesis. The painfully perturbing dissolution of familiar forms, which suggests to weaker spirits that the ultimate reality is nothing but a chaos, may reveal to a steadier and more spiritual vision the truth that the flickering film of the phenomenal world is an illusion which cannot obscure the eternal unity that lies behind it.

This spiritual truth, like other truths of the kind, is apt to be apprehended first by analogy from some outward and visible sign; and the portent in the external world which gives the first intima-tion of a unity which is spiritual and ultimate is the unification of a society into a universal state. Indeed, neither the Roman Empire nor any other universal state could have established or maintained itself if it had not been led on to fortune upon a tide of desire for political unity which had mounted to its flood as a time of troubles approached its climax. In Hellenic history this longing—or, rather, the sense of relief at its belated satisfaction— breathes through the Latin poetry of the Augustan Age; and we children of the Western Society in its present phase are aware from our own experience how poignant this longing for a 'world order' may be in an age when the unity of mankind is being striven for unavailingly.

Alexander the Great's vision of *Homonoia* or Concord never faded out of the Hellenic World so long as a vestige of Hellenism survived, and, three hundred years after Alexander's death, we find Augustus putting Alexander's head on his Roman signet-ring as an acknowledgement of the source from which he was seeking inspiration for his arduous task of establishing the *Pax Romana*. Plutarch reports as one of Alexander's sayings: 'God is the common father of all men, but he makes the best ones peculiarly his own.' If this 'logion' is authentic, it tells us that Alexander realized that the brotherhood of Man presupposes the fatherhood of God— a truth which involves the converse proposition that, if the divine father of the human family is left out of the reckoning, there is no possibility of forging any alternative bond of purely human texture which will avail by itself to hold mankind together. The only society that is capable of embracing the whole of mankind is a superhuman *Civitas Dei*; and the conception of a society which embraces mankind and nothing but mankind is an academic chimaera. The Stoic Epictetus was as well aware of this supreme truth as the Christian Apostle Paul, but, whereas Epictetus stated the fact as a conclusion of philosophy, St. Paul preached it as the gospel of a new revelation made by God to man through the life and death of Christ.

In the Sinic time of troubles, also, the craving for unity was never confined to the terrestrial plane.

'To the Chinese of this period the word One (unity, singleness, etc.) had an intensely emotional connotation, reflected equally in political theory and in Taoist metaphysics. And, indeed, the longing—or more accurately, the psychological need—for a fixed standard of belief was profounder, more urgent and more insistent than the longing for governmental unity. In the long run man cannot exist without an orthodoxy, without a fixed pattern of fundamental belief.'[1]

If this comprehensive Sinic way of pursuing the quest for unity may be taken as the norm, and our modern Western cult of an arbitrarily insulated Humanity may be written off as something exceptional or even pathological, then we should expect to see the practical unification of mankind and the ideal unification of the Universe accomplished *pari passu* by a spiritual effort which would not cease to be one and indivisible because it manifested itself simultaneously in diverse fields. As a matter of fact, we have already observed that the fusion of parochial communities into a universal state is apt to be accompanied by an incorporation of parochial divinities into a single pantheon in which one composite divinity—an Amon-Re of Thebes or a Marduk-Bel of Babylon—emerges as the spiritual equivalent of the earthly king of kings and lord of lords.

It will be seen, however, that the condition of human affairs which finds its superhuman reflection in a pantheon of this kind is the situation immediately after the genesis of a universal state and not the constitution into which a polity of this type eventually settles down; for the ultimate constitution of a universal state is not a hierarchy which preserves its constituent parts intact and merely converts their former equality as sovereign states into a hegemony of one of them over the rest. It solidifies in course of time into a unitary empire. In fact, in a fully seasoned universal state there are two salient features which dominate, between them,

[1] Waley, A.: *The Way and its Power*, Introduction, pp. 69–70.

the entire social landscape: a supreme personal monarch and a supreme impersonal law. And in a world of men that is governed on this plan the Universe as a whole is likely to be pictured on a corresponding pattern. If the human ruler of the universal state is at once so powerful and so beneficent that his subjects are easily persuaded to worship him as a god incarnate, then *a fortiori* they will be prone to see in him the terrestrial likeness of a heavenly ruler likewise supreme and omnipotent—a god who is no mere God of Gods like Amon-Re or Marduk-Bel, but one who reigns alone as the One True God. Again, the law in which the human emperor's will is translated into action is an irresistible and ubiquitous force which suggests, by analogy, the idea of an impersonal Law of Nature: a law which governs not only the material universe but also the impenetrably mysterious distribution of joy and sorrow, good and evil, and reward and punishment on those deeper levels of human life where Caesar's writ ceases to run.

This pair of concepts—a ubiquitous and irresistible law and a unique and omnipotent deity—will be found at the heart of almost every representation of the Universe that has ever taken shape in human minds in the social environment of a universal state; but a survey of these cosmologies will show that they tend to approximate to one or other of two distinct types. There is one type in which Law is exalted at the expense of God and another in which God is exalted at the expense of Law; and we shall find that the emphasis on Law is characteristic of the philosophies of the dominant minority, while the religions of the internal proletariat incline to subordinate the majesty of the Law to the omnipotence of God. However, the distinction is only a matter of emphasis; in all these cosmologies both concepts are to be found, co-existing and interwoven, whatever their respective proportions may be.

Having placed this reservation upon the distinction that we are seeking to establish, we may now survey, in succession, those representations of the unity of the Universe in which Law has been exalted at the expense of God and then those other representations in which God overshadows the Law which He promulgates.

In the systems in which 'Law is king of all'[1] we can watch the personality of God growing fainter as the law that governs the Universe comes into sharper focus. In our own Western World, for example, the Triune God of the Athanasian Creed has faded by stages, in an ever-increasing number of Western minds, as physical science has extended the frontiers of its intellectual

---

[1] Herodotus, Bk. III, ch. 38, quoting Pindar.

empire over one field of existence after another—until at last, in our own day, when science is laying claim to the whole of the spiritual as well as the material universe, we see God the Mathematician fading right out into God the Vacuum. This modern Western process of evicting God to make room for Law was anticipated in the Babylonic World in the eighth century B.C., when the discovery of the periodicities in the motions of the stellar cosmos inveigled the Chaldaean *mathematici*, in their enthusiasm for the new science of astrology, into transferring their allegiance from Marduk-Bel to the Seven Planets. In the Indic World, again, when the Buddhist school of philosophy worked out to their extreme conclusions the logical consequences of the psychological law of *Karma*, the divinities of the Vedic pantheon were the most signal victims of this aggressive system of 'totalitarian' spiritual determinism. These barbaric gods of a barbarian war-band were now made to pay dearly, in their unromantic middle age, for the all too human wantonness of a turbulent youth. In a Buddhist universe in which all consciousness and desire and purpose was reduced to a succession of atomic psychological states which by definition were incapable of coalescing into anything in the nature of a continuous or stable personality, the Gods were automatically reduced to the spiritual stature of human beings on a common level of nonentity. Indeed, such difference as there was between the status of gods and of men in the Buddhist system of philosophy was all to the advantage of the latter; for a human being could at least become a Buddhist monk if he could stand the ascetic ordeal, and for this renunciation of the vulgar pleasures there was offered the compensation of a release from the Wheel of Existence and an entry into the oblivion of Nirvāna.

In the Hellenic World the Gods of Olympus fared better than they deserved if their deserts are to be measured by the punishment meted out by Buddhist justice to their Vedic cousins; for when the Hellenic philosophers came to conceive of the Universe as a 'Great Society' of supra-terrestrial dimensions whose members' relations with one another were regulated by Law and inspired by Homonoia or Concord, Zeus, who had started life as the disreputable war-lord of the Olympian war-band, was morally reclaimed and handsomely pensioned off by being elected to the presidency of the *Cosmopolis* with a status not unlike that of some latter-day constitutional monarch who 'reigns but does not govern' —a king who meekly countersigns the decrees of Fate and obligingly lends his name to the operations of Nature.[1]

[1] But was Zeus really there at all? Would it not be nearer the facts to say that the impersonal receivers installed by the philosophers to replace the

Our survey has shown that the Law which eclipses the Godhead may take various forms. It is a mathematical law that has enslaved the Babylonic astrologer and the modern Western man of science; a psychological law that has captivated the Buddhist ascetic; and a social law that has won the allegiance of the Hellenic philosopher. In the Sinic World, where the concept of Law has not found favour, we find the Godhead being, none the less, eclipsed by an Order which presents itself to the Sinic mind as a kind of magical congruence or sympathy between the behaviour of man and that of his environment. While the action of the environment upon man is recognized and manipulated in the Sinic art of geomancy, the converse action of man upon the environment is controlled and directed by means of a ritual and etiquette as elaborate and momentous as the structure of the Universe which these rites mirror and sometimes modify. The human master of the ceremonies who makes the world go round is the monarch of the Sinic universal state; and, in virtue of the superhuman scope of his function, the Emperor is officially styled the Son of Heaven; yet this Heaven who, in the Sinic scheme, is the adoptive father of the magician-in-chief is as pale and impersonal as the frosty winter skies of Northern China. Indeed the complete erasure of any conception of Divine Personality from the Chinese mind presented the Jesuit missionaries with a difficult problem when they tried to translate the word *Deus* into Chinese.

We will now pass to the consideration of those other representations of the Universe in which the unity presents itself as the work of an omnipotent Godhead, while the Law is regarded as a manifestation of God's will instead of being conceived of as the sovereign unifying force which regulates the actions of gods and men alike.

We have observed already that this concept of a unity of all things through God, as well as the alternative concept of a unity of all things through Law, is conceived by human minds through

bankrupt Olympian establishment made use, for business purposes, of the name of the defunct senior partner in that concern? In any case, Mr. Toynbee elsewhere in his work quotes a passage from Marcus Aurelius and comments: 'In these tragic cries we seem to hear the voice of a devoted citizen of the *Cosmopolis* who has suddenly awoken to find that Zeus has absconded from his presidential post. . . . But Marcus's Christian readers ought not to be too hard on Marcus's Zeus; for Zeus, after all, had never asked to be elected president of a cosmic republic; he had started life as the disreputable war-lord of a barbarian war-band and all that we know about him goes to show that this was the life that he enjoyed. If a Zeus whom the philosophers had belatedly caught and caged was unable to endure an eternity of enforced respectability as the senior inmate of a Stoic reformatory, have we the heart to blame the poor old fellow for proving incorrigible?' But perhaps, like Scrooge's partner Marley, he deserves neither blame nor sympathy, having 'died a long time before'.—EDITOR.

an analogy from the constitution which a universal state is apt to assume as it gradually crystallizes into its final shape. In this process the human ruler, who is originally a King of Kings, eliminates the client princes who were once his peers and becomes a 'monarch' in the strict sense of the term. If we now examine what happens simultaneously to the gods of the diverse peoples and lands which the universal state has absorbed, we shall find an analogous change. In place of a pantheon in which a high god exercises suzerainty over a community of gods, once his peers, who have not lost their divinity in losing their independence, we see emerging a single God whose uniqueness is His essence.

This religious revolution generally begins with a change in the relations between divinities and their worshippers. Within the framework of a universal state divinities tend to divest themselves of the bonds which have hitherto bound each of them to some particular local community. The divinity who started life as the patron of some particular tribe or city or mountain or river now enters a wider field of action by learning to appeal on the one hand to the souls of individuals and on the other hand to mankind as a whole. In this latter capacity the once local divinity, hitherto a celestial counterpart of the local chieftain, takes on characteristics borrowed from the rulers of the universal state in which the local community has been engulfed. We can observe, for example, the influence of the Achaemenian monarchy, overshadowing Judaea politically, upon the Jewish conception of the God of Israel. This new conception of Yahweh had worked itself out to completion by 166–164 B.C., which appears to have been the approximate date of the writing of the apocalyptic part of the Book of Daniel.

'I beheld till the thrones were cast down, and the Ancient of Days did sit, whose garment was white as snow, and the hair of his head was like the pure wool; his throne was like the fiery flame and his wheel as burning fire. A fiery stream issued and came forth from before him; thousand thousands ministered unto him, and ten thousand times ten thousand stood before him; the judgement was set and the books were opened.'[1]

Thus a number of previously parochial divinities assume the insignia of the newly established terrestrial monarch and then compete with one another for the sole and exclusive dominion which these insignia imply, until at length one of the competitors annihilates his rivals and establishes his title to be worshipped as the One True God. There is, however, one vital point on which the analogy between the 'Battle of the Gods' and the otherwise analogous competition between the 'princes of This World' does not hold good.

[1] Daniel vii. 9–10.

In the constitutional evolution of a universal state the universal monarch whom we find enthroned in solitary sovereignty at the end of the story is usually the direct successor, in an unbroken constitutional sequence, of the Pādishāh, or overlord of client princes, under whose auspices the story opens. When an Augustus, who has been content to make his authority felt in Cappadocia or Palestine by maintaining a general superintendence over local kings or tetrarchs (corresponding to the rulers of the 'Indian States' of the British Indian Empire), is succeeded in due course by a Hadrian who administers these former principalities as provinces under his own direct rule, there is no break in the continuity of the dominant power. But in the corresponding religious change continuity, so far from being the rule, is a theoretically possible exception which it might be difficult to illustrate by a single historical example. The writer of this Study cannot call to mind a single case in which the high god of a pantheon has ever served as the medium for an epiphany of God as the unique and omnipotent master and maker of all things. Neither the Theban Amon-Re nor the Babylonian Marduk-Bel nor the Olympian Zeus has ever revealed the countenance of the One True God beneath his own Protean mask. And even in the Syriac universal state, where the god who was worshipped by the imperial dynasty was not a divinity of this synthetic kind nor a product of *raison d'état*, the deity through whose lineaments the existence and the nature of a One True God became apparent to mankind was not the Zoroastrian Ahuramazda, the god of the Achaemenidae; it was Yahweh, the god of the Achaemenidae's insignificant Jewish subjects.

This contrast between the ultimate destinies of rival divinities and the momentary fortunes of their respective followers makes it evident that the religious life and experience of generations born and bred under the political aegis of a universal state is a field of historical study which offers striking examples of *peripeteia* or the 'reversal of roles'—the theme of innumerable folk-tales of the type of Cinderella. At the same time, lowly and obscure origins are not the only features characteristic of the divinities that attain to universality.

When we look into the character of Yahweh as portrayed in the Old Testament, two other features immediately strike the eye. On the one hand Yahweh is in origin a local divinity—in the literal sense *glebae adscriptus* if we are to believe that he first came within the Israelites' ken as the *jinn* inhabiting and animating a volcano in North-West Arabia, and in any case a divinity who struck root in the soil of a particular parish, and in the hearts of a particular parochial community, after he had been carried into the hill country of Ephraim and Judah as the patron of the barbarian war-bands who broke into the Palestinian domain of 'the New Empire' of Egypt in the fourteenth century B.C. On the other hand Yahweh is 'a jealous god', whose first commandment to his worshipper is 'Thou shalt have none other gods but me'. It is not, of course, surprising to find these two traits of provincialism and exclusiveness displayed by Yahweh simultaneously; a god who keeps to his own domain may be expected to warn other gods off it. What is surprising—and even repellent, at any rate at first sight—is to see Yahweh continuing to exhibit an unabated intolerance towards the rivals with whom he courts a conflict when, after the overthrow of the kingdoms of Israel and Judah and the establishment of the Syriac universal state, this *ci-devant* god of two highland principalities steps out into the wider world and aspires, like his neighbours, to win for himself the worship of all mankind. In this oecumenical phase of Syriac history the persistence of Yahweh in maintaining the intolerant attitude that was a legacy from his parochial past was an anachronism which was undoubtedly out of tune with the temper prevalent in that age among the host of *ci-devant* local deities of Yahweh's kind. This unamiable anachronism was nevertheless one of the elements in his character that helped him to his astonishing triumph.

It may be instructive to look at these traits of provincialism and exclusiveness more closely, taking the provincialism first.

The choice of a provincial divinity to be the vehicle for the epiphany of a God who is omnipresent and unique might seem at first sight to be an inexplicable paradox; for while the Jewish, Christian and Islamic conception of God has indisputably been derived, as a matter of historical fact, from a tribal Yahweh, it is equally indisputable that the theological content, as opposed to the historical origin, of the idea of God common to these three religions is immeasurably different from the primitive conception of Yahweh and bears a much closer resemblance to a number of other conceptions to which, as a matter of historical fact, the Islamic-Christian-Jewish conception is indebted either much less deeply or not at all. In point of universality the Islamic-Christian-Jewish conception of God has less in common with the primitive representation of Yahweh than with the idea of the high god of a pantheon—an Amon-Re or a Marduk-Bel—who reigns in some sense over the whole Universe. Or again, if we take spirituality as our standard, the Islamic-Christian-Jewish conception has more in common with the abstractions of the philosophic schools: a Stoic Zeus or a Neoplatonic Helios. Why then is it that, in the mystery play which has for its plot the revelation of God to man, the supreme role has been allotted, not to an etherial Helios or an imperial Amon-Re but to a barbaric and provincial Yahweh whose qualifications for playing this tremendous part might seem, on our present showing, to be so conspicuously inferior to those of some of his unsuccessful competitors?

The answer is to be found in calling to mind one element in the Jewish-Christian-Islamic conception which we have not yet mentioned. We have dwelt on the qualities of omnipresence and uniqueness. Yet, for all their sublimity, these attributes of the Divine Nature are no more than conclusions of the human understanding; they are not experiences of the human heart. For mankind in the mass, God's essence is that he is a living God with whom a living human being can enter into a relationship that is recognizably akin to the spiritual relationships into which he enters with other living human beings. This fact of being alive is the essence of God's nature for human souls that are seeking to enter into communion with Him; and this quality of being a person, which is the essence of God as Jews and Christians and Muslims worship Him to-day, is likewise the essence of Yahweh as he makes his appearance in the Old Testament. 'For who is there of all flesh that hath heard the voice of the living god speaking out of the midst of the fire, as we have, and lived?'[1] is the boast of Yahweh's Chosen People. When this living God of Israel encounters in turn the various abstractions of the philosophers, it becomes manifest that, in the words of the Odyssey, 'he alone breathes and the rest are shadows'. For the primitive figure of Yahweh has grown into the Christian conception of God by annexing intellectual attributes from these abstractions without deigning to acknowledge the debt or scrupling to suppress their names.

If this persistent quality of being alive is the obverse of Yahweh's primitive provincialism, we may find that the exclusiveness which is an enduring as well as a primitive trait in Yahweh's character has also some value which is indispensable for the historic role which the God of Israel has played in the revelation of the Divine Nature to mankind.

This value becomes apparent as soon as we consider the significance of the contrast between the ultimate triumph of this 'jealous god' and the ultimate fiasco of the high gods of the pantheons of the two neighbouring societies which, between them, ground the political structure of the Syriac World to pieces. In respect of being rooted in the soil and of flowing with the visible and tangible sap of life, both Amon-Re and Marduk-Bel could measure themselves against Yahweh on equal terms, while they

[1] Deuteronomy v. 26.

had the advantage over him of being associated, in the minds of their worshippers, with the colossal worldly success of their native Thebes and Babylon, whereas Yahweh's people had been left, in their abasement and captivity, to solve as best they could the problem of vindicating the virtues of a tribal divinity who had apparently abandoned his tribesmen in their hour of need. If, in spite of this telling point in their favour, Amon-Re and Marduk-Bel were ultimately worsted in 'the Battle of the Gods', we can hardly avoid ascribing their failure to their innocence of Yahweh's jealous vein. A freedom—for good or ill—from the spirit of exclusiveness is implicit in the hyphen which links the two parts of the names of these synthetic divinities. No wonder that Amon-Re and Marduk-Bel were as tolerant of polytheism beyond the bounds of their own loose-knit personalities as they were tolerant of the disunity in their own Protean selves. Both of them alike were born—or, more accurately, put together—to be content with their primal state of suzerainty over a host of other beings no less divine, if rather less potent, than themselves; and this congenital lack of ambition doomed them both to drop out of the competition for a monopoly of divinity when Yahweh's devouring jealousy would as surely spur him on to run to the end this race that had been set before them all.

The same relentless intolerance of any rival was also manifestly one of the qualities which enabled the God of Israel, after he had become the God of the Christian Church, to outrun all his competitors once again in the later 'Battle of the Gods' fought out within the Roman Empire. His rivals—a Syriac Mithras, an Egyptiac Isis, a Hittite Cybele—were ready to enter into any compromise with each other and with any other cult that they severally encountered. This easy-going, compromising spirit was fatal to the rivals of the God of Tertullian, when they had to face an adversary who could be content with nothing less than 'total' victory, because anything less would be, for Him, a denial of His very essence.

The most impressive testimony to the value of the jealous vein in Yahweh's ethos is perhaps afforded by a piece of negative evidence from the Indic World. Here, as elsewhere, the process of social disintegration was accompanied by the development of a sense of unity on the religious plane. In response to an ever more insistent craving in Indic souls to apprehend the unity of God, the myriad divinities of the Indic internal proletariat gradually coalesced and dissolved into one or other of the two mighty figures of Shiva and Vishnu. This penultimate stage on the road towards the apprehension of the unity of God was attained by Hinduism at least one thousand five hundred years ago; and yet, in all the time that has elapsed since then, Hinduism has never taken the final step that was taken by the Syriac religion when Yahweh—intolerant of even a single peer—disposed of Ahuramazda by swallowing him whole. In Hinduism the concept of an Almighty God, instead of being unified, has been polarized round the mutually complementary and antithetic figures of two equally matched candidates who have persistently refrained from settling accounts with one another.

In face of this strange situation we are bound to ask ourselves why Hinduism has accepted, as a solution for the problem of the unity of God, a compromise which is no solution at all, inasmuch as it is impossible to conceive of a godhead that is omnipresent and omnipotent—as Vishnu and Shiva each claim to be—unless it is at the same time unique. The answer is that Vishnu and Shiva are not 'jealous' of one another. They have been content to go shares, and it may be surmised that they have survived—unlike Mithras and Isis and Cybele, their equivalents in the Hellenic World—only because there has not been a Yahweh in the field against them. We reach the conclusion that a divinity credited by his worshippers with a spirit of uncompromising exclusiveness proves to be the only medium through which the profound and elusive truth of the unity of God has been firmly grasped hitherto by human souls.

(7) ARCHAISM

Having now taken stock of the alternative ways of behaviour and feeling that present themselves to souls born into a socially disintegrating world, we may pass on to the alternative ways of life that lie open to be followed in the same challenging circumstances, beginning with the alternative which in our preliminary survey we labelled 'archaism' and defined as an attempt to get back to one of those happier states which, in times of troubles, are regretted the more poignantly—and perhaps idealized the more unhistorically—the farther they are left behind.

> O how I long to travel back,
> And tread again that ancient track!
> That I might once more reach that plain
> Where first I left my glorious train;
> From whence the enlighten'd spirit sees
> That shady City of Palm-trees.
>
> . . . .
>
> Some men a forward motion love,
> But I by backward steps would move.

In these lines the seventeenth-century poet Henry Vaughan is expressing the grown man's nostalgia for childhood, otherwise expressed by those Mr. Bultitudes who, with whatever degree of sincerity, tell a younger generation that 'your schooldays are the happiest time of your life'. The lines may equally serve to describe the emotions of the archaist who seeks to recapture an earlier phase in the life of his society.

In making a survey of examples of archaism we will divide the field as we divided it when discussing the sense of promiscuity, and take in turn the four fields of conduct, art, language and religion. The sense of promiscuity, however, is a spontaneous, unselfconscious feeling, whereas archaism is a deliberate self-conscious policy of attempting to swim against the stream of life, in fact a *tour de force*; and accordingly we shall find that in the field of conduct archaism expresses itself in formal institutions and formulated ideas rather than in unselfconscious manners, and in the linguistic field in points of style and theme.

If we now begin our survey with institutions and ideas, our best plan will be to start with examples of institutional archaism in matters of detail and then to follow the spread of the archaistic state of mind over a wider area until we arrive at an ideological archaism which is pervasive because it is an archaism-on-principle.

For example, in Plutarch's day, which was the heyday of the Hellenic universal state, the ceremony of scourging Spartiate boys at the altar of Artemis Orthia—an ordeal which, in Sparta's prime, had been taken over from a primitive fertility cult and incorporated into the Lycurgean *agogê*—was being practised once again with a pathological exaggeration which is one of the characteristic notes of archaism. Similarly in A.D. 248, when the Roman Empire was enjoying a temporary breathing-space in the midst of a bout of anarchy that was bringing it to its ruin, the Emperor Philip was inspired to celebrate once again the *Ludi Saeculares* instituted by Augustus, and two years later the ancient office of the censorship was re-established. In our own day the 'Corporative State' established by the Italian Fascists claimed to be a restoration of a political and economic régime in force in the medieval city-states of Italy. In the same country in the second century B.C. the Gracchi claimed to be exercising the office of the Tribunate of the Plebs in the fashion originally intended at the time of its establishment two hundred years earlier. A more successful example of constitutional archaism was the respectful treatment accorded by Augustus, the founder of the Roman Empire, to his nominal partner but actual predecessor in the government of the Roman dominions, the Senate. It is comparable with the treatment, in Great Britain, of the Crown by a victorious Parliament. In both cases there was a real transfer of authority, in the Roman case from oligarchy to monarchy, in the British case from monarchy to oligarchy, and in both cases the change was masked by archaistic formalities.

If we turn to the disintegrating Sinic World we shall observe here the emergence of a constitutional archaism of a more comprehensive scope, extending from public into private life. The challenge of the Sinic time of troubles produced a spiritual ferment in Sinic minds which displayed itself both in the Confucian humanism of the fifth century B.C. and in the later and more radical schools of the 'Politicians', the 'Sophists' and the 'Legists'; but this burst of spiritual activity was ephemeral. It was followed by a revulsion towards the past, which can be seen at its clearest in the fate which overtook the Confucian humanism. It degenerated from a study of human nature into a system of ritualized etiquette. In the administrative sphere it became a tradition that every administrative act required the sanction of historical precedent.

Another example of archaism-on-principle in a different sphere is the cult of a largely fictitious Teutonism which has been one of the provincial products of the general archaistic movement of Romanticism in the modern Western World. After having afforded a harmless gratification to some nineteenth-century English historians and instilled a perhaps more tiresome racial conceit into some American ethnologists, this cult of the imaginary virtues of the Primitive Teutons developed teeth and claws as the gospel of the National-Socialist movement in the German Reich. We are here confronted with an exhibition of archaism which would have been pathetic if it had not been so sinister. A great modern Western nation was brought, by the spiritual malady of the Modern Age, within an ace of irretrievable national collapse, and, in a desperate effort to escape from the trap into which the recent course of history had inveigled it, it doubled back upon the supposedly glorious barbarism of an imaginary historical past.

Another and earlier form of this reversion to barbarism in the West was Rousseau's gospel of the 'return to nature' and the exaltation of 'the noble savage'. The eighteenth-century Western archaists were innocent of the sanguinary designs which appear unashamedly in the pages of *Mein Kampf*, but their innocence did not render them innocuous in so far as Rousseau was a 'cause' of the French Revolution and the wars to which it gave rise.

The vogue of archaism in art is something so familiar to modern

Western man that he is apt to take it for granted; for the most conspicuous of the arts is architecture, and our nineteenth-century architecture was desolated by an archaistic 'Gothic revival'—a movement which, starting as the fad of landed proprietors who put up sham 'ruins' in their parks and built mammoth residences in styles supposed to reproduce the effect of medieval abbeys, soon spread to church building and church restoration, where it secured a potent ally in the likewise archaistic Oxford Movement and finally found riotous expression in hotels, factories, hospitals and schools. But architectural archaism is not an invention of modern Western man. If the Londoner travels to Constantinople and watches the pageant of the sun setting over the ridge of Stamboul, he will see, silhouetted against the skyline, dome after dome of the mosques which, under the Ottoman régime, have been constructed with a profoundly archaistic servility upon the pattern of the Big and the Little Haghia Sophia: the two Byzantine churches whose audacious defiance of the fundamental canons of the classical Hellenic order of architecture had once proclaimed in stone the emergence of an infant Orthodox Christian Civilization out of the wreckage of a dead Hellenic World. Finally, if we turn to the 'Indian summer' of the Hellenic Society, we find the cultivated Emperor Hadrian furnishing his suburban villa with expertly manufactured copies of the masterpieces of Hellenic sculpture of the archaic period—that is to say, the seventh and sixth centuries B.C.; for the connoisseurs of Hadrian's day were 'Pre-Raphaelites', too highly refined to appreciate the masterly maturity of the art of Pheidias and Praxiteles.

When the spirit of archaism is moved to express itself in the field of language and literature, the supreme *tour de force* to which it can address itself is to bring a dead language back to life by putting it back into circulation as a living vernacular; and such an attempt is being made to-day in several parts of our Westernized World. The impulse towards this perverse undertaking has come from the nationalistic craze for distinctiveness and cultural self-sufficiency. The would-be self-sufficient nations that have found themselves destitute of natural linguistic resources have all taken the road of archaism as the readiest way of obtaining a supply of the linguistic commodity of which they are in search. At the present moment there are at least five nations engaged in producing a distinctive national language of their own by putting back into circulation some language which has long ceased to be current in any but an academic sphere. These are the Norwegians, the Irish, the Ottoman Turks, the Greeks and the Zionist Jews; and it will be noticed that none of them is a chip of the original block of Western Christendom. The Norwegians and the Irish are respectively remnants of an abortive Scandinavian and an abortive Far Western Christian Civilization. The Ottoman Turks and the Greeks are much more recently Westernized contingents of the Iranic and the Orthodox Christian societies, and the Zionist Jews are a fragment of a fossil of the Syriac Society which has been embedded in the body of Western Christendom since its pre-natal days.

The need which the Norwegians feel to-day for the production of a national language is the historical consequence of a political eclipse of the Kingdom of Norway from A.D. 1397, when it was united with Denmark, down to A.D. 1905, when, in parting company with Sweden, it at length recovered complete independence and once more acquired a king of its own who, abandoning his modern Western baptismal name of Charles, adopted the archaistic throne-name of Haakon, which had been borne by four Norwegian monarchs in the abortive Scandinavian Society between the tenth and the thirteenth centuries of the Christian Era. In the course of the five centuries of Norway's eclipse the old Norse literature had given place to a version of modern Western literature which was written in Danish, though its pronunciation was modified to accord with that of the Norse vernacular. Thus, when the Norwegians set themselves, soon after the transfer of their country from Denmark to Sweden in 1814, to fit themselves out with a national culture of their own, they found themselves without any literary medium except one of foreign mintage, and without any mother-tongue except a *patois* which had long ceased to be a medium for literature. Confronted with this awkward gap in the linguistic department of their national outfit, they have been trying to produce a native language which will serve peasant and towns-man alike by being both indigenous and cultivated.

The problem confronting the Irish nationalists is far more difficult. In Ireland the British Crown has played the political role of the Danish Crown in Norway with linguistic results that have been similar up to a point. The English language became the language of Irish literature, but, perhaps because the linguistic gulf between the English and Irish languages, unlike the com-paratively fine shades of difference between Danish and Norse, is unbridgeable, the Irish language became virtually extinct. The Irish devotees of linguistic archaism are engaged, not in civilizing a living *patois*, but in re-creating an almost extinct language, and the results of their efforts are said to be incomprehensible to the scattered groups of peasantry in the west of Eire who still speak Gaelic as learnt at their mother's knee.

The linguistic archaism in which the Ottoman Turks have been indulging under the late President Mustafā Kemāl Atatürk's régime is of a different character. The ancestors of the modern Turks, like the ancestors of the modern English, were barbarians who trespassed on, and squatted in, the derelict domain of a broken-down civilization, and descendants of both sets of barbarians have made the same use of the vehicle of language as a means of acquiring civilization. Just as the English have enriched their meagre Teutonic vocabulary by loading it with a wealth of borrowed French and Latin and Greek words and phrases, so the 'Osmanlis have encrusted their plain Turkish with innumerable jewels of Persian and Arabic speech. The purpose of the Turkish nationalist archaizing linguistic movement is to get rid of these jewels, and, when it is realized that the Turkish borrowings from foreign sources have been quite as extensive as our own, it will be apparent that the task is no light one. However, the Turkish hero's method of setting about his task was as drastic as that which he had previously employed in ridding his native country of the alien elements in the population. In that graver crisis Kemāl had evicted from Turkey an old-established and apparently indispensable Greek and Armenian middle class on the calculation that, when once the social vacuum had been produced, sheer necessity would compel the Turks to fill it by taking on their own shoulders social tasks which they had hitherto lazily left to others. On the same principle the Ghāzi afterwards evicted the Persian and Arabic words from the Ottoman Turkish vocabulary, and by this drastic measure demonstrated what an astonishing intellectual stimulus can be given to mentally sluggish peoples when they find their mouths and ears remorselessly deprived of the simplest verbal necessities of life. In these dire straits the Turks have latterly been ransacking Cuman glossaries, Orkhon inscriptions, Uighur sutras and Chinese dynastic histories in order to find—or fake—a genuine Turkish substitute for this or that sternly prohibited Persian or Arabic household word.

For an English spectator these frantic lexicographical labours are an awe-inspiring spectacle; for they give him an inkling of the tribulations that the future may hold in store for English-speakers too, if ever the day should come when 'pure English' is required of us by some masterful saviour of our society. Indeed, some slight preparation for this event has already been made by a perhaps far-sighted amateur. Some thirty years ago, one calling himself 'C. L. D.' published a *Word-Book of the English Tongue* for the guidance of those who long 'to shake off the Norman yoke' which lies so heavy on our speech. 'What many speakers and writers, even to-day', he writes, 'call English is no English at all but sheer French.' Following 'C. L. D.' we should call a perambulator a childwain and an omnibus a folkwain; and these might be improvements. But when he seeks to get rid of resident aliens whose domicile is of more ancient date he is less happy. When he proposes to replace 'disapprove' by 'hiss', 'boo' or 'hoot' he hardly hits the nail on the head and he hits it much too hard; and 'redecraft', 'backjaw' and 'outganger' are unconvincing substitutes for 'logic,' 'retort' and 'emigrant'.[1]

The Greek case obviously resembles the Norwegian and the Irish, with the Ottoman Turkish Empire in the role played in these other cases by the Danish and British Crowns. When the Greeks became nationally self-conscious they found themselves, like the Norwegians, equipped linguistically with nothing better than a peasant *patois*, and they set out, like the Irish a hundred years later, to recondition their *patois* for the exacting tasks ahead of it by grouting it with injections of the antique form of the language. But, in making their experiment, the Greeks had to wrestle with a difficulty which was the antithesis of that confronting the Irish; for, whereas the material of Ancient Gaelic was embarrassingly scanty, the material of Classical Greek was embarrassingly abundant. In fact, the besetting snare in the path of the modern Greek linguistic archaists has been the temptation to draw upon the resources of Ancient Attic too prodigally, and thus provoke a modernist 'low-brow' reaction. Modern Greek is a battle-ground between 'the language of the purists' (ἡ καθαρεύουσα) and 'the popular language' (ἡ δημοτική).

Our fifth example, the conversion of Hebrew into a vernacular language of every-day life on the lips of the Zionist Jews of the Diaspora settled in Palestine, is the most remarkable of all; for, whereas neither Norwegian nor Greek nor even Irish had ever ceased to be spoken as a *patois*, Hebrew had been a dead language in Palestine for twenty-three centuries, since its replacement there by Aramaic before the time of Nehemiah. For all this length of time, until within living memory, Hebrew survived only as the language of the liturgy of the Jewish Church and of the scholarship that concerned itself with the Jewish Law. And then, in the course of a single generation, this 'dead language' has been brought out of the synagogue and converted into a vehicle for conveying modern Western culture—first in a newspaper press in the so-called 'Jewish Pale' in Eastern Europe and now in the schools and homes of the Jewish community in Palestine, where the children of Yiddish-speaking immigrants from Europe and

[1] Squire, J. C.: *Books in General*, p. 246, contains a review of 'C. L. D.'s' book.

English-speaking immigrants from America and Arabic-speaking immigrants from the Yaman and Persian-speaking immigrants from Bokhara are all growing up together to speak, as their common language, an ancient tongue that had 'died' five centuries before the generation of Jesus.

If we now turn to the Hellenic World, we shall find that here linguistic archaism was no mere adjunct of parochial nationalism but was something more pervasive.

If you examine a book-case filled with a complete collection of the books written in Ancient Greek before the seventh century of the Christian Era that have survived until the present day, you will notice two things: first that the overwhelmingly greater part of this collection is written in Attic Greek, and secondly that, if this Attic library is arranged chronologically, it falls apart into two distinct groups. In the first place there is an original Attic literature written at Athens in the fifth and fourth centuries B.C. by Athenians who were writing their natural language. In the second place there is an archaistic Attic literature produced over a period of some six or seven centuries—from the last century B.C. to the sixth century of the Christian Era—by authors who neither lived at Athens nor spoke Attic as their native tongue. Indeed, the geographical range of these neo-Attic writers is as wide as the domain of the Hellenic universal state, for among them are Josephus of Jerusalem, Aelian of Praeneste, Marcus Aurelius of Rome, Lucian of Samosata and Procopius of Caesarea. Yet, in spite of this wide diversity of origin, the neo-Atticists display an extraordinary uniformity of vocabulary, syntax and style; for these are, one and all, frank, shameless and servile imitators of the Attic of 'the best period'.

Their archaism has ensured their preservation; for when, on the eve of the final dissolution of the Hellenic Society, the question 'to be or not to be' was being decided for each and every Ancient Greek author by the prevailing literary taste of the day, the test question for copyists was not 'Is it great literature?' but 'Is it pure Attic?' In consequence we possess volumes of mediocre neo-Attic stuff which we would gladly exchange for a fraction of that amount of the lost non-Attic literature of the third and second centuries B.C.

The Atticism which triumphed in the archaistic age of Hellenic literature was not the only literary exercise of its kind. There is also the neo-Homeric poetry cultivated by a long line of antiquarians from Apollonius Rhodius in the second century B.C. to Nonnus Panopolitanus in the fifth or sixth century of the Christian Era. Our extant specimens of non-archaistic post-

Alexandrine Greek literature are substantially confined to two sets of works: the bucolic poetry of the third and second centuries B.C., preserved for the sake of its precious Doric, and the Christian and Jewish Scriptures.

The archaistic resuscitation of Attic Greek has an exact parallel in Indic history in the resuscitation of Sanskrit. The original Sanskrit had been the vernacular of the Eurasian Nomad horde of the Aryas, who had broken out of the Steppes and had flooded over Northern India, as well as over South-Western Asia and Northern Egypt, in the second millennium B.C.; and on Indian ground this language had been preserved in the Vedas, a corpus of religious literature which had become one of the cultural foundations of the Indic Civilization. By the time, however, when this Indic Civilization had broken down and entered upon the path of disintegration, Sanskrit had passed out of current usage and had become a 'classical' language, studied because of the enduring prestige of the literature enshrined in it. As a medium of communication in everyday life Sanskrit had by this time been replaced by a number of local vernaculars, all derived from Sanskrit but sufficiently differentiated to be regarded as separate languages. One of these prākrits—the Pali of Ceylon—was employed as the vehicle of the Hinayanian Buddhist Scriptures, and several others were employed by the Emperor Açoka (273–232 B.C.) as vehicles for his edicts. Nevertheless, soon after—or even before—Açoka's death an artificial revival of Sanskrit began and extended its range until, in the sixth century of the Christian Era, the triumph of the neo-Sanskrit language over the prākrits was complete on the Indian mainland—leaving Pali to survive as a literary curiosity in the island fastness of Ceylon. Thus our extant corpus of Sanskrit, like our extant corpus of Attic Greek, falls into two distinct portions: an older portion which is original and a younger which is imitative and archaistic.

In the field of religion, as in the fields of language and art and institutions, it is possible for the modern Western observer to watch archaism at work within the limits of his own social environment. The British Anglo-Catholic movement, for example, is based on the conviction that the sixteenth-century 'Reformation', even in its modified Anglican version, went a great deal too far, and the purpose of the movement is to bring back into currency medieval ideas and ceremonies which were abandoned and abolished—on this view inconsiderately—four hundred years ago.

In Hellenic history we find an example in the religious policy of Augustus.

'The revival of the State religion by Augustus is at once the most remarkable event in the history of the Roman religion, and one almost unique in religious history. . . . The belief in the efficacy of the old cults had passed away among the educated classes . . . the mongrel city populace had long been accustomed to scoff at the old deities, and . . . the outward practice of religion had been allowed to decay. To us, then, it may seem almost impossible that the practice, and to some extent also the belief, should be capable of resuscitation at the will of a single individual. . . . For it is impossible to deny that this resuscitation was real; that both *pax deorum* and *ius divinum* became once more terms of force and meaning. . . . The old religion continued to exist for at least three centuries in outward form, and to some extent in popular belief.'[1]

If we turn from the Hellenic World to the Japanese offshoot of the Far Eastern Society, we shall find, in the latter-day Japanese attempt to revive the native Japanese variety of primitive paganism called Shinto, another essay in religious archaism which has points in common with the policy of Augustus and also with the modern German attempt to revive a Teutonic paganism. The undertaking resembles the German rather than the Roman *tour de force*, for the Roman paganism which Augustus revived was still a going concern, though far gone in decay, whereas the Japanese, like the German, paganism had been for a thousand years supplanted, or ab- sorbed, by a higher religion—in the Japanese case, the Mahayanian variety of Buddhism. The first phase of the movement was academic; for the resuscitation of Shinto was first put in train by a Buddhist monk named Keichū (A.D. 1640–1701) whose interest in the subject seems to have been primarily philological. Others, however, followed up his work, and Hirata Atsutané (A.D. 1776– 1843) launched an attack on both the Mahāyāna and the Con- fucian philosophy as alien importations.

It will be seen that this Shinto revival, like the Augustan revival, was put in hand almost immediately after Japan had passed out of its time of troubles into its universal state, and that the neo- Shinto movement had just reached its militant stage by the time when the Japanese universal state was prematurely shattered by the impact of an aggressively expanding Western Civilization. When, upon the revolution of 1867–8, Japan entered upon her modern policy of holding her own in a semi-Westernized 'Great Society' by modernizing herself on Western nationalistic lines, the neo-Shinto movement appeared to provide just what was needed for asserting Japan's national individuality in her new international circumstances. The first step taken by the new government in regard to religion was an attempt to establish Shinto

[1] Warde-Fowler, W.: *The Religious Experience of the Roman People*, pp. 428–9.

as the religion of the state, and at one time it seemed as if Buddhism would be exterminated by persecution. But, not for the first or for the last time in history, a 'higher religion' surprised its enemies by its obstinate vitality. Buddhism and Shintoism had to agree to tolerate one another.

An air of failure or, where there is not positive failure, futility surrounds practically all the examples of archaism that we have been examining; and the reason is not far to seek. The archaist is condemned, by the very nature of his enterprise, to be for ever trying to reconcile past and present, and the incompatibility of their competing claims is the weakness of archaism as a way of life. The archaist is on the horns of a dilemma which is likely to impale him, whichever way he may turn. If he tries to restore the past without taking the present into consideration, then the impetus of life ever moving onward will shatter his brittle construction into fragments. If, on the other hand, he consents to subordinate his whim of resuscitating the past to the task of making the present workable, then his archaism will prove a sham. In either alternative the archaist will find, at the end of his labours, that he has unwittingly been playing the futurist's game. In labouring to perpetuate an anachronism he will in fact have been opening the door to some ruthless innovation that has been lying in wait outside for this very opportunity of forcing an entry.

(8) FUTURISM

Futurism and archaism are both attempts to break away from an irksome present by taking a flying leap out of it into another reach of the stream of time without abandoning the plane of mundane life on Earth. And these two alternative ways of attempting to escape from the present but not from the time-dimension also resemble one another in being *tours de force* which prove, on trial, to have been forlorn hopes. They differ from each other merely in the direction—up or down the time-stream—in which they make their two equally desperate sorties from a position of present discomfort. At the same time futurism goes more against the grain of human nature than archaism; for, while it is all too human to seek refuge from a disagreeable present by retreating into a familiar past, human nature is prone to cling to a disagreeable present rather than strike out into an unknown future. Hence in futurism the psychological *tour de force* is keyed to a distinctly higher pitch than in the archaistic alternative, and futuristic spasms are often the next reaction of souls at bay who have tried the way of archaism and have been disappointed. Disappointment is courted, *a fortiori*, by futurism too. The failure of futurism is, nevertheless, sometimes rewarded with a very different outcome; futurism sometimes transcends itself and rises into transfiguration.

If we may liken the catastrophe of archaism to the crash of a motor-car which skids right round on its tracks and then rushes to destruction in the opposite direction, the happier experience of futurism may be likened to that of a passenger on board a motor-driven vehicle who believes himself to be travelling in a terrestrial omnibus and observes, with deepening dismay, the ever-increasing roughness of the *terrain* over which he is being carried forward, until suddenly—when an accident seems immediately inevitable—the vehicle rises from the ground and soars over crags and chasms in its own element.

The futuristic, like the archaistic, way of breaking with the present can be studied in a number of different fields of social activity. In the field of manners the first gesture of the futurist is often an exchange of a traditional for an outlandish costume; and in the ubiquitously—though still no more than superficially—Westernized World of the present day we see a host of non-Western societies abandoning a hereditary and distinctive dress and conforming to a drably exotic Western fashion as an outward sign of their voluntary or involuntary enrolment in the Western internal proletariat.

The most famous, and perhaps the earliest, example of a forcible process of external Westernization is the shaving of beards and banning of kaftans in Muscovy by the order of Peter the Great. In the third quarter of the nineteenth century this Muscovite revolution in costume was emulated in Japan, and similar circumstances have evoked similar acts of tyranny in a number of non-Western countries since the General War of 1914–18. There is, for example, the Turkish law of 1925 which made it compulsory for all male Turkish citizens to wear hats with brims, and the corresponding decrees of Rizā Shāh Pehlevī of Iran and of King Amānallāh of Afghanistan in 1928.

The Islamic World in the twentieth century of the Christian Era is not, however, the only arena in which a hat with a brim has been adopted as the battle-crest of a militant futurism. In the Syriac World of 170–160 B.C. the High Priest Joshua, the leader of a Hellenizing party among the Jews, was not content to advertise his programme by the verbal gesture of transposing his name into Jason. The positive act which provoked the reaction of the Maccabees was the adoption, by the younger priests, of a broad-brimmed felt hat which was the distinctive headgear of the pagan dominant minority in the Achaemenian Empire's Hellenic successor-states. The ultimate outcome of this Jewish essay in futurism was not a triumph like Peter the Great's but a fiasco like Amānallāh's; for the Seleucid Power's frontal attack upon the Jewish religion evoked a Jewish reaction of a violence with which Antiochus Ephiphanes and his successors were unable to cope. But the fact that this particular futurist enterprise was abortive does not make it the less instructive as an example. The ethos of futurism is essentially totalitarian, and this truth was recognized by both Jason and his adversaries. The Jew who wears the Greek *petasus* will soon frequent the Greek *palaestra* and will come to regard an observance of the rules of his religion as contemptibly old-fashioned and unenlightened.

In the political sphere, futurism may express itself either geographically in the deliberate obliteration of existing landmarks and boundaries or socially in the forcible dissolution of existing corporations, parties or sects or in the 'liquidation' of whole classes of society. The classical example of the systematic obliteration of landmarks and boundaries for the express purpose of producing a breach of political continuity is the redrawing of the map of Attica by the successful revolutionary, Cleisthenes, in about 507 B.C. Cleisthenes' aim was to transform a loosely knit polity, in which claims of kinship had hitherto usually prevailed over claims of community, into a unitary state in which the obligations of citizenship would in future prevail over all lesser loyalties. His drastic policy proved remarkably successful, and this Hellenic precedent was followed in the Western World by the makers of the French Revolution—whether consciously as a result of their cult of Hellenism or because they lighted independently on the same means for compassing an identical end. Aiming at the political unification of France as Cleisthenes aimed at the political unification of Attica, they abolished the old feudal provinces and levelled the old internal customs barriers in order to turn France into a unitary fiscal area, subdivided for administrative convenience into eighty-three departments whose monotonous uniformity and strict subordination were intended to efface the memory of local diversities and loyalties. The obliteration of old boundaries outside France by the re-mapping of non-French territories temporarily incorporated in the Napoleonic Empire into departments on the French model no doubt paved the way for the creation of unitary states in Italy and Germany.

In our own day Stalin has given characteristic expression to the Bolshevik ethos in the geographical field by carrying to completion a far more radical re-articulation of the internal divisions of the Soviet Union, as becomes apparent when the new administrative map of this region of the world is superimposed upon the old administrative map of the Russian Empire. In pursuing an identical aim, however, Stalin has acted with a subtlety in which he is perhaps a pioneer. Whereas his predecessors have sought to attain their purpose by weakening the existing parochial loyalties, Stalin has pursued the contrary policy of satisfying, and even anticipating, the cravings of parochialism on the shrewd calculation that an appetite is more likely to be stifled by satiety than it is to be extinguished by starvation. In this connexion it is worth remembering that Stalin is himself a Georgian, and that in 1919 a deputation of Menshevik Georgians presented themselves at the Peace Conference in Paris demanding recognition as a distinct non-Russian nationality. They based their claims in part on the distinctiveness of the Georgian language and brought with them an interpreter whose function was supposed to be to translate their outlandish native tongue into French. It was observed, however, on one occasion, by an English journalist who happened (unknown to these Georgians) to be acquainted with the Russian language, that they and their interpreter were actually talking Russian among themselves. The inference was that a Georgian of the present day, whatever his political aspirations, would spontaneously and unconsciously do his political talking in Russian so long as the use of Russian was not being forcibly imposed upon him.

In the field of secular culture the classic expression of futurism is the symbolic act of the Burning of the Books. In the Sinic World the Emperor Ts'in She Hwang-ti, who was the revolutionary first founder of the Sinic universal state, is said to have confiscated and burnt the literary remains of the philosophers who had flourished during the Sinic time of troubles for fear that the transmission of this 'dangerous thought' might thwart his own design of inaugurating a brand-new order of society. In the Syriac Society the Caliph 'Umar, who reconstituted the Syriac universal state after it had been in abeyance for one thousand years of Hellenic intrusion, is reported to have written, in reply to an inquiry from a general who had just received the surrender of the city of Alexandria and had asked for instructions as to how he was to dispose of the famous library:

'If these writings of the Greeks agree with the Book of God, they are useless and need not be preserved; if they disagree, they are pernicious and ought to be destroyed.'

According to the legend, the contents of a library which had been accumulating for more than nine hundred years were thereupon condemned to be consumed as fuel for the heating of the public baths.

In our own day Hitler has done what he can in the way of book-burning—though the advent of printing has made the achievement of 'total' results much more difficult for tyrants who have recourse to this measure in our world. Hitler's contemporary Mustafā Kemāl Atatürk hit upon a more subtle device. The Turkish dictator's aim was nothing less than to wrench his fellow-countrymen's minds out of their inherited Iranic cultural setting and to force them into a Western cultural mould; and instead of burning the books he contented himself with changing the Alphabet. From 1929 onwards all books and newspapers were to be printed and all legally valid documents composed in the Latin Alphabet. The passage and enforcement of this law made it unnecessary for the Turkish Ghāzi to imitate the Sinic Emperor or the Arab Caliph. The classics of Persian, Arabic and Turkish literature had now been effectively placed beyond the reach of the rising generation. There was no longer any necessity to burn books when the Alphabet that was the key to them had been put out of currency. They could be safely left to rot on their shelves in the confidence that they would never be disturbed except by a negligible handful of antiquarians.

Thought and literature are not, of course, the only provinces of secular culture in which the heritage of the present from the past is exposed to futurist attack. There are other worlds for futurism to conquer in the visual and aural arts. It is in fact the workers in the field of visual art who have coined the name 'Futurism' to describe their revolutionary masterpieces. But there is one notorious form of futurism in the field of the visual arts which stands on common ground between the two spheres of secular culture and religion, namely Iconoclasm. The Iconoclast resembles the modern champion of cubist painting in his repudiation of a traditional style of art, but he is peculiar in confining his hostile attentions to art in association with religion and in being moved to his hostility by motives that are not aesthetic but theological. The essence of Iconoclasm is an objection to a visual representation of the Godhead or of any creature, lower than God, whose image might become an object of idolatrous worship; but there have been differences in the degree of rigour with which this principle has been applied. The most celebrated school of Iconoclasm is the 'totalitarian' one that is represented by Judaism and, in imitation of Judaism, by Islam, and that is expressed in the second of the Mosaic Commandments:

'Thou shalt not make unto thee a graven image or any likeness of anything that is in heaven above or that is in the earth beneath or that is in the water under the earth.'[1]

[1] In Islamic art this prohibition of the copying of objects of nature drove the

On the other hand, the Iconoclastic movements which have arisen within the Christian Church have accommodated themselves to a distinction which Christianity seems to have accepted from its earliest days. Though the eighth-century outbreak of Iconoclasm in Orthodox Christendom and the sixteenth-century outbreak in Western Christendom may have been inspired, at any rate in part, by the examples of Islam in the eighth century and Judaism in the sixteenth, they neither of them attempted to ban the visual arts altogether. They did not carry their offensive into the secular field, and even in the religious field the Orthodox Iconoclasts eventually acquiesced in a curious compromise. Three-dimensional representations of objects of religious adoration were to be banned on the tacit understanding that two-dimensional representations would be tolerated.

(9) THE SELF-TRANSCENDENCE OF FUTURISM

While success may sometimes have been achieved by futuristic devices in the political field, futurism as a way of life leads those who seek to follow it into a barren quest of a goal which is intrinsically unattainable. Yet though the quest is barren and may be tragic, it need not be without value; for it may guide the baffled seeker's feet into a way of peace. Futurism in its primitive nakedness is a counsel of despair which, even as such, is a *pis aller*; for the first recourse of a soul which has despaired of the present without having lost its appetite for life on the mundane level is an attempt to take a flying leap up the time-stream into the past; and it is only when this archaistic line of escape has been tried in vain or rejected as intrinsically impossible that the soul will nerve itself to take the less natural line of futurism.

The nature of this pure—and by the same token purely mundane—futurism can be best illustrated by citing some of the classic examples.

In the Hellenic World, for instance, in the second century B.C., thousands of Syrians and other highly cultivated Orientals were deprived of their freedom, uprooted from their homes, separated from their families and shipped overseas to Sicily and Italy to serve as slaves on plantations and cattle-ranches in areas devastated by the Hannibalic War. For these expatriated slaves, whose need of a way of escape from the present was extreme, there was no possibility of an archaistic retreat into the past. Not only was it impossible for them physically to make their way back to their homelands, but all that had made those homelands congenial to

artists to content themselves with the construction of non-representational patterns. Hence our word 'arabesques'.

them had irretrievably perished. They could not go back; they could only go forward; and so, when their oppression became intolerable, they were goaded into physical revolt. The desperate purpose of the great slave insurrections was to establish a kind of inverted Roman Commonwealth in which the present slaves would be masters and the present masters slaves.

In an earlier chapter of Syriac history the Jews had reacted in a similar way to the destruction of their sovereign independent kingdom of Judah. After they had been swallowed up in the neo-Babylonian and Achaemenian Empires and had been scattered abroad among the Gentiles, they could not hope with any conviction for an archaistic return to the pre-exilic dispensation in which Judah had lived a life of parochial independence. A hope that was to be convincing could not be conceived in terms of a state of affairs that had passed away beyond recall; and, since they could not live without a lively hope of extricating themselves from a present to which they could not be reconciled, the post-exilic Jews were driven into looking forward to the future establishment of a Davidic Kingdom in a shape which had no precedent in Judah's political past, a kingdom of the only type now conceivable in a world of great empires. If the new David was to reunite all Jewry under his rule—and what but this could be his mission?—he must wrest the sceptre of empire from the hands of its present holder and must make Jerusalem to-morrow what Babylon or Susa was to-day, the centre of the World. Why should not a Zerubbabel have as good a chance of world dominion as a Darius, or a Judas Maccabaeus as an Antiochus, or a Bar-Kōkabā as a Hadrian?

A similar dream once captivated the imaginations of 'the Old Believers' in Russia. In the eyes of these Raskolniki the Tsar Peter's version of Orthodoxy was no Orthodoxy at all, and at the same time it was impossible to imagine the old ecclesiastical order triumphantly reasserting itself in the teeth of a secular order that was omnipotent as well as Satanic. The Raskolniki were therefore driven to hope for something without precedent, for the epiphany of a Tsar-Messiah who would be able as well as willing to restore the Orthodox Faith in its pristine purity.

The significant common feature of these examples of pure futurism is that the hopes in which the futurists have sought refuge have all been set upon a purely matter-of-fact fulfilment in the ordinary mundane way; and this feature is conspicuous in the futurism of the Jews, which has left ample documentary evidence of its history. After the destruction of their kingdom by Nebuchadnezzar the Jews again and again put their treasure in the hope of establishing a new Jewish state, whenever the play of oecumenical politics gave them the slightest encouragement. The brief bout of anarchy through which the Achaemenian Empire passed between the death of Cambyses and the rise of Darius saw Zerubbabel's attempt (*circa* 522 B.C.) to re-establish a Davidic Kingdom. In a later chapter of history the longer interregnum between the decline of the Seleucid Power and the arrival of the Roman legions in the Levant was mistaken by the Jews for a triumph of the Maccabees; and a majority of the Palestinian Jews were so heedlessly carried away by this mirage of mundane success that they were willing—as 'Deutero-Isaiah' had been, four hundred years earlier—to throw overboard the now long consecrated tradition that the founder of the new state must be a descendant of David.

Whatever might have been possible against the senile Seleucids, how could the Jews hope to measure themselves against the mighty power of Rome in its heyday? The answer to this question was as clear as day to the Idumaean dictator Herod. He never forgot that he was ruler of Palestine by the grace of Rome, and so long as he reigned he contrived to save his subjects from the nemesis of their own folly. Yet, instead of being grateful to Herod for teaching them so salutary a political lesson, the Jews could not forgive him for being right; and as soon as his masterful hand was removed they took the bit between their teeth and bolted down their futuristic path to the inevitable catastrophe. Even then a single demonstration of Rome's omnipotence did not suffice. The appalling experience of A.D. 66–70 did not deter the Jews from courting and winning disaster again in A.D. 115–17 and yet again in A.D. 132–5. Bar Kōkabā in A.D. 132–5 was pursuing the same end by the same means as Zerubbabel in 522 B.C. It took the Jews more than six centuries to learn that futurism of this sort would not work.

If this were the whole Jewish story it would not be an interesting one; but it is, of course, only half the story, and the less important half. The whole story is that, while some Jewish souls 'learnt nothing and forgot nothing', like the Bourbons, other Jewish souls—or even some of the same Jewish souls in a different mood and through a different spiritual faculty—were gradually taught by bitter experience to put their treasure elsewhere. In the process of discovering the bankruptcy of futurism the Jews made the further tremendous discovery of the existence of the Kingdom of God; and century by century these two progressive revelations, the one negative and the other positive, were being unfolded simultaneously. The expected founder of the new Jewish mundane commonwealth was conceived of, appropriately enough, as a king of flesh and blood who would found a hereditary dynasty. Yet the title under which this empire-builder was predicted, and under which every successive pretender to the role, from Zerubbabel to Bar Kōkabā, was acclaimed, was not *melek* (king) but Messiah—'the Anointed of the Lord'. Thus, even if only in the background, the god of the Jews was associated with the hope of the Jews from the beginning; and, as the mundane hope inexorably faded away, the divine figure loomed ever larger till it filled the whole horizon.

To call a god in aid is not, of course, in itself an unusual procedure. It is probably as old a practice as religion itself for a people embarking on some formidable enterprise to invoke the protection of their tutelary deity. The new departure lay not in the claim, expressed in the title 'Messiah', that the people's human champion had the sanction of a god behind him; what was new, and also momentous, was the conception of the patron deity's nature and function and power. For, while Yahweh did not cease to be thought of as the parochial god of Jewry in a certain sense, it was in another and wider aspect that he was pictured as the patron of the Lord's Anointed. The Jewish futurists of the Post-Captivity Age were, after all, engaged on no ordinary political enterprise. They had set their hearts on a task which was, humanly speaking, impossible; for, when they had failed to preserve even their petty local independence, how could they hope to make themselves masters of the World? To succeed in this task they must have for their divine protector no mere parochial god but one commensurate with their futuristic ambitions.

Once this has been realized, a drama which, up to this point, has been 'common form' in the history of religions is transposed into a higher spiritual dimension. The human champion sinks to a subordinate role while the Divinity dominates the scene. A human Messiah is not enough. God Himself must condescend to play the part of Saviour. The champion of His people on the terrestrial plane must be Himself the Son of God.

By this time any modern Western psychoanalyst who is reading these lines will be raising his eyebrows. 'What you have proclaimed as a sublime spiritual discovery turns out', he will interject, 'to be nothing but a surrender to that infantile desire to escape from reality which is one of the besetting temptations of the human psyche. You have described how some unhappy people who have foolishly set their hearts on an unattainable aim attempt to shift the intolerable burden of being saddled with an impossible task from their own shoulders to those of a series of intended substitutes. First they conscript a merely human champion; then, when he cannot avail, a human champion reinforced by an imaginary divine backing; and finally the fools, in desperation, signal S.O.S. to an imaginary divine being who is to do the job himself. For the psychological practitioner this rake's progress in escapism is a familiar story and a melancholy one.'

In reply to this criticism we shall readily agree that it is childish to call upon a supernatural power to carry out a mundane task that we have chosen for ourselves and find ourselves unable to perform. The prayer '*My* will be done' stands self-convicted of futility. In the Jewish case in point there were schools of Jewish futurists who did persuade themselves that Yahweh would take upon himself his worshippers' self-chosen mundane task, and these Jewish futurists did, as we have already seen, come to a bad end. There was the melodramatic suicide of the Zealots who faced hopeless military odds in the delusion that the Lord of Hosts would be a host in Himself on the day of battle; and there were the Quietists who argued from the same erroneous premisses to exactly the opposite, but not less hopeless, conclusion that they should abstain from taking any action of their own in a mundane cause which they had decided to register as God's affair. But there were other responses—the response of the school of Johanan ben Zakkai and the response of the Christian Church; and, while these two responses resemble Quietism in the negative feature of being non-violent, they differ from both Quietism and Zealotism in the more important positive point that they have ceased to set their heart on the old mundane purpose of futurism and have put their treasure in a purpose which is not Man's but God's, and which therefore can only be pursued in a spiritual field in which God is not an ally but the director of operations.

This point is of capital importance because it disposes, in these cases, of the criticism which our psycho-analyst can direct with such deadly effect against both the Zealots and the Quietists. To call in God cannot be denounced as infantile escapism if, at the same time, the human actor withdraws his *libido* from his previous mundane aim. And, conversely, if the act of invocation does produce so great and so good a spiritual effect as this in the human soul that performs it, that would appear, *prima facie*, to give ground for a belief that the Power which has been invoked is not a mere figment of the human imagination. We shall allow ourselves to hold that this spiritual reorientation was a discovery of the One True God, and that a human make-believe about the future of This World had given place to a divine revelation of an Other World. Through the disappointment of a mundane hope we have been admitted to an apocalypse of a reality which had been there all the time behind the scenes of a narrow man-made stage. The veil of the Temple has been rent in twain.

It remains for us to note some of the principal stages in the accomplishment of this immense feat of spiritual reorientation. Its essence is that a mundane scene which was once looked on as a stage for human actors, with or without superhuman backers, is now regarded as a field for the progressive realization of the Kingdom of God. At first, however, as might be expected, the new idea largely clothes itself in imagery derived from the old futurist conception. Against this background 'Deutero-Isaiah' draws the lineaments of a Kingdom of God which transcends, but also includes, the idea of a mundane kingdom, an Achaemenian Empire in which his saviour-hero Cyrus has taken Jerusalem instead of Susa as his capital and the Jews instead of the Persians as his ruling race, because Yahweh has revealed to him that it is he (and not Ahuramazda) who has enabled Cyrus to conquer the World. In this day-dream 'Deutero-Isaiah' is exposing himself, with a vengeance, to the strictures of our psychoanalyst. This prophet's conception transcends the mundane futurist idea only on the point that both Man and Nature are depicted as experiencing a miraculous beatification. His Kingdom of God is really nothing but an Earthly Paradise, a Garden of Eden brought up to date.

The next stage comes when this Earthly Paradise is thought of as only a transitory state which may last perhaps for a thousand years[1] but is destined to pass away, at the end of its allotted term, with the passing of This World itself. But if This World must pass in order to give place to an Other World beyond it, then it is in that Other World that the true Kingdom of God must lie; for the King who is to reign during the Millennium is not yet God himself but merely his deputy or Messiah. It is manifest, however, that the conception of a miraculous Millennium in This World, pending the replacement of This World by an Other, is an untenable attempt at a compromise between ideas that are not only distinct but in the last resort are mutually incompatible. The first of these ideas, Deutero-Isaiah's idea, is the hope of a futurist mundane kingdom with miraculous 'improvements'. The second idea is that of a Kingdom of God which is not in Time at all but is in a different spiritual dimension, and which, just by virtue of this difference of dimension, is able to penetrate our mundane life and to transfigure it. For making the arduous spiritual ascent to the vision of transfiguration from the mirage of futurism, the

---

[1] Hence the popular use of the word 'Millennium' to signify a future 'Golden Age'.

eschatological scheme of the Millennium may have proved an indispensable mental ladder, but when once the height has been scaled the ladder can be allowed to fall away.

'The Pharisaic pietist had already learnt under the Hasmonaeans to turn away from This World to Heaven, to the future; and now, under Herod, all the current of national feeling which had been set running during the last generations in such strength beat against a blind wall, and itself found no outlet except through the channels opened by the Pharisee. It was among the people bent down beneath that iron necessity that the transcendental beliefs, the Messianic hopes, nurtured in the Pharisaic schools, spread and propagated themselves with a new vitality. The few books of Pharisaic piety that have come down to us—*Enoch*, the *Psalms of Solomon*, the *Assumption of Moses* and others—show us indeed what ideas occupied the minds of writers, but they could not have shown us what we learn from our Gospels: how ideas of this order had permeated the people through and through; how the figure of the Coming King, "the Anointed One", "the Son of David", how definite conceptions of the Resurrection, of the Other World, were part of the ordinary mental furniture of that common people which hung upon the words of the Lord. . . . But . . . the Christ whom the Christian worshipped was not the embodiment of any single one of those forms which had risen upon prophetic thought; in Him all the hopes and ideals of the past met and blended.'[1]

(10) DETACHMENT AND TRANSFIGURATION

Our inquiries into the nature of futurism and archaism have led us to the conclusion that both fail because they seek to escape from the present without rising above the mundane time-stream. We have seen how a realization of the bankruptcy of futurism may lead—and indeed, in a supreme historic example, has led—to an apprehension of the mystery that we have called transfiguration. But the bankruptcy of archaism may also bear fruit in a spiritual discovery. The recognition of the truth that archaism is not enough is a challenge which may, as we have seen, send the baffled archaist off in the opposite direction down the Gadarene slope of futurism, but alternatively he may respond to the challenge by taking some new spiritual departure; and his line of least resistance is to convert a flying leap that is heading for disaster into a flight that will evade the problem of landing by taking permanent leave of the ground. This is the philosophy of detachment of which we have already observed, without much comment, an example afforded by the Jewish Quietists.

To a Western inquirer, the most familiar expositions of this philosophy are those 'Leaves from a Stoic Philosopher's Note-

[1] Bevan, E.: *Jerusalem under the High Priests*, pp. 158 and 162.

Book' that have been bequeathed to us by Epictetus and Marcus Aurelius. But if we follow the path of detachment far enough we shall find ourselves sooner or later turning from a Hellenic to an Indic guide, for, far though the disciples of Zeno may go, it is the disciples of Gautama that have had the courage to pursue detachment all the way to its logical goal of self-annihilation. As an intellectual achievement this is imposing; as a moral achievement it is overwhelming; but it has a disconcerting moral corollary; for perfect detachment casts out pity, and therefore also love, as inexorably as it purges away all the evil passions.

'The man whose every motion is void of love and purpose, whose works are burned away by the fire of knowledge, the enlightened call "learned". The learned grieve not for them whose lives are fled nor for them whose lives are not fled.'[1]

To the Indic sage's mind, this heartlessness is the adamantine core of philosophy, and the same conclusion was reached by the Hellenic philosophers independently. Epictetus admonishes his disciples:

'If you are kissing a child of yours . . . never put your imagination unreservedly into the act and never give your emotion free rein. . . . Indeed, there is no harm in accompanying the act of kissing the child by whispering over him: "To-morrow you will die".'[2]

And Seneca does not hesitate to declare that

'Pity is a mental illness induced by the spectacle of other people's miseries, or alternatively it may be defined as an infection of low spirits caught from other people's troubles when the patient believes that those troubles are undeserved. The sage does not succumb to such-like mental diseases.'[3]

In pressing its way to a conclusion which is logically inevitable and at the same time morally intolerable, the philosophy of detachment ultimately defeats itself by moving us to revolt. It does not, after all, provide a solution for the problem which it sets out to solve, for in consulting only the head and ignoring the heart it is arbitrarily putting asunder what God has joined together. This philosophy of detachment has to be eclipsed by the mystery of transfiguration.

As we gird up our loins to take this fourth and last turning from the open road of disintegration, a clamour of disapproving and derisive voices assails our ears; but we need not be intimidated, for they come from the philosophers and the futurists—the 'high-brows' of detachment and the zealots of political and

---

[1] Baghavadgītā, iv, 19, and ii, 11 (Barnett's translation).
[2] Epictetus: *Dissertations*, Bk. iii, ch. 24, §§ 85-8.
[3] Seneca: *De clementia*, Bk. II, ch. 5, §§ 4-5.

economic materialism—and we have already found that, whoever may be right, they at any rate are wrong.

'God hath chosen the foolish things of the World to confound the wise; and God hath chosen the weak things of the World to confound the things which are mighty.'[1]

This truth which we can verify empirically is also known to us intuitively. And in the light and the strength of it we may brave the disapproval of futurists and philosophers alike by stepping boldly out in the footprints of a guide who is neither Bar Kōkabā nor Gautama.

'The Jews require a sign and the Greeks seek after wisdom; but we preach Christ Crucified—unto the Jews a stumbling-block and unto the Greeks foolishness.'[2]

Why is Christ Crucified a stumbling-block to futurists who have never succeeded in eliciting a sign of divine support for their mundane undertakings? And why is He foolishness to philosophers who have never found the wisdom for which they seek?

Christ Crucified is foolishness to the philosopher because the philosopher's aim is detachment, and he cannot comprehend how any reasonable being who has once attained that forbidding goal can be so perverse as deliberately to relinquish what he has so hardly won. What is the sense of withdrawing simply in order to return? And *a fortiori* the philosopher must be nonplussed at the notion of a God who has not even had to take the trouble to withdraw from an unsatisfactory World, because He is completely independent of it by virtue of His divinity, but who nevertheless deliberately enters into the World, and subjects Himself there to the utmost agony that God or man can undergo, for the sake of a race of beings of an order immeasurably inferior to His own divine nature. 'God so loved the World that He gave His only begotten son'? That is the last word in folly from the standpoint of the seeker after detachment.

'If the supreme end is tranquillity, of what use would it be to set the Wise Man's heart free from disturbance by cutting off the fear and desire which made him dependent upon outside things, if one immediately opened a hundred channels by which the World's pain and unrest could flow into his heart through the fibres, created by Love and Pity, connecting his heart with the fevered hearts of men all round? A hundred fibres!—one aperture would suffice to let in enough of the bitter surge to fill his heart full. Leave one small hole in a ship's side, and you let in the sea. The Stoics, I think, saw with perfect truth that if you were going to allow any least entrance of Love and Pity into the breast, you admitted something whose measure you could not control,

---

[1] 1 Cor. i. 27.   [2] 1 Cor. i. 22–3.

and might just as well give up the idea of inner tranquillity at once. . . .
The Christian's Ideal Figure could never be accepted by the Stoic as an
example of his typical Wise Man.'[1]

The Crucifixion is as great a stumbling-block in the way of
futurism because the death on the Cross confirms the saying of
Jesus that His Kingdom is not of This World. The sign which
the futurist requires is the announcement of a kingdom which will
be bereft of all meaning if it is not to be a mundane success. The
Messiah's task on his showing is the task assigned by Deutero-
Isaiah to Cyrus and by a succession of later Jewish futurists to the
Judas or Theudas of the hour: a Zerubbabel or a Simon Maccabaeus or a Simon bar Kōkabā.

'Thus saith the Lord to His Anointed, to Cyrus, whose right hand
I have holden . . . : "I will go before thee and make the crooked places
straight; I will break in pieces the gates of brass and cut in sunder
the bars of iron; and I will give thee the treasures of darkness and
hidden riches of secret places." '[2]

How was this authentically futurist conception of a Messiah
to be reconciled with the words of the prisoner who answered
Pilate 'Thou sayest that I am a King', and then went on to give
so fantastic an account of the royal mission on which He claimed
that God had sent Him?

'To this end was I born, and for this cause came I into the World,
that I should bear witness unto the truth.'

The disconcerting words might perhaps be ignored, but the
malefactor's death could neither be undone nor be explained
away; and Peter's ordeal shows how grievous this stumbling-
block was.

The Kingdom of God, of which Christ is King, is incommen-
surable with any kingdom that could be founded by a Messiah
envisaged as an Achaemenian world-conqueror turned into a Jew
and projected into the future. So far as this *Civitas Dei* enters
into the time-dimension at all, it is not as a dream of the future
but as a spiritual reality interpenetrating the present. If we ask
how, in fact, God's will can be done on Earth as it is in Heaven,
the answer, given in the technical language of theology, is that
the omnipresence of God involves His immanence in This World
and in every living soul in it, as well as His transcendent existence
on supra-mundane planes. In the Christian conception of the
Godhead His transcendent aspect (or 'person') is displayed in
God the Father and His immanent aspect in God the Holy Ghost;
but the distinctive and crucial feature of the Christian Faith is

[1] Bevan, E. R.: *Stoics and Sceptics*, pp. 69-70.
[2] Isaiah xlv. 1-3.

that God is not a Duality but a Trinity in Unity, and that in His
aspect as God the Son the other two aspects are unified in a
Person who, in virtue of this mystery, is as accessible to the human
heart as is He incomprehensible to the human understanding. In
the Person of Christ Jesus—Very God yet also Very Man—the
divine society and the mundane society have a common member
who in This World is born into the ranks of the proletariat and
dies the death of a malefactor, while in the Other World He is
the King of God's Kingdom, a King who is God Himself.

But how can two natures—one divine and the other human—
be both present at once in a single person? Answers, cast in the
form of creeds, have been worked out by Christian Fathers in
terms of the technical vocabulary of the Hellenic philosophers;
but this metaphysical line of approach is perhaps not the only one
open to us. We may find an alternative starting-point in the
postulate that the divine nature, in so far as it is accessible to us,
must have something in common with our own; and, if we look
for one particular spiritual faculty which we are conscious of
possessing and which we also can attribute with absolute confidence to God—because God would be spiritually inferior to man
(*quod est absurdum*) if this faculty were not in Him but were
nevertheless in us—then the faculty which we shall think of first
as being common to man and God will be one which the philosophers wish to mortify; and that is the faculty of Love. This stone
which both Zeno and Gautama have so obstinately rejected is
become the head of the corner of the temple of the New Testament.

(11) PALINGENESIA

We have now completed our survey of four experimental ways
of life which are so many exploratory attempts to find a practicable
alternative to a familiar habit of living and moving at ease in a
growing civilization. When this comfortable road has been remorselessly closed by the catastrophe of a social breakdown, these
four ways present themselves as alternative possible by-passes;
and we have found that three of them are *culs-de-sac*, and that
only one, which we have called transfiguration, and illustrated by
the light of Christianity, leads right onward. Returning now to a
concept which we employed in an earlier part of this Study, we
may say that both transfiguration and detachment—in contrast
to both futurism and archaism—are examples of that 'transference
of the field of action' from the macrocosm to the microcosm which
manifests itself in the spiritual phenomenon of 'etherialization'.
If we are right in believing that transference and etherialization

are symptoms of growth, and that every example of human growth will be found to have a social as well as an individual aspect, and if we are also bound to assume *ex hypothesi* that the society to whose growth the movements of detachment and transfiguration bear witness cannot be any society of the species we have called civilizations—considering that a disintegrating society of that species is the City of Destruction from which either movement is an endeavour to escape—then we can only conclude that the movements of detachment and transfiguration bear witness to the growth of a society or societies of some other kind or kinds.

Is the singular or the dual the right number to use in referring to the social medium in which our two movements take place? The best way to approach this question may be to ask ourselves another: What is the difference between detachment and transfiguration in terms of social growth? The answer clearly is that, while detachment is a simple movement of sheer withdrawal, transfiguration is a compound movement of withdrawal followed by return. This compound movement is illustrated in the life of Jesus by His withdrawal into the wilderness before His ministry in Galilee, and in the life of Saint Paul by his three years' sojourn in Arabia before the momentous missionary journeys which carried the new religion from its provincial Syriac seed-bed into the heart of the Hellenic World. If the Founder of the Christian religion and His apostle-missionary had been addicts to the philosophy of detachment they would have remained in their wildernesses for the rest of their lives on Earth. The limitation of the philosophy of detachment is its failure to see that its Nirvāna is not the terminus of the Soul's journey but merely a station on its route. The terminus is the Kingdom of God; and this omnipresent Kingdom calls for service from its citizens on Earth here and now.

In the Sinic terms which we employed near the beginning of this Study, the disintegration of a civilization discharges itself in a full cycle of the alternating rhythm of Yin-and-Yang. In the first beat of the rhythm a destructive Yang-movement (the disintegration) passes over into a Yin-state (detachment) which is also a peace of exhaustion; but the rhythm is not arrested at the dead point; it passes over into a creative Yang-movement (transfiguration). This double beat of the movement of Yin-and-Yang is that particular form of the general movement of withdrawal-and-return on which we stumbled near the beginning of our study of disintegration and which we then called Schism-and-Palingenesia.

The literal meaning of the Greek word 'palingenesia' is 'recurrence of birth', and the term has in it an element of ambiguity.

Do we mean the birth again of something which has been born before: for instance, the replacement of an irretrievably damaged civilization by another of the same species? That cannot be what we mean, for that is the aim, not of transfiguration, but of a movement confined within the time-stream—neither archaism nor futurism as we have hitherto used these terms but another movement of the same order. Palingenesia in this sense would be the Wheel of Existence, which the Buddhist philosophy takes for granted and seeks to break by a withdrawal into Nirvāna. Yet palingenesia cannot mean the attainment of Nirvāna, for the process by which this state of negativity is reached cannot be conceived of as a 'birth.'

But if palingenesia does not mean the attainment of Nirvāna either, it can only mean the attainment of another supra-mundane state to which the image of birth can be illuminatingly applied because this other state is a positive state of life—though one in a higher spiritual dimension than the life of This World. That is the palingenesia of which Jesus speaks to Nicodemus:

'Except a man be born again he cannot see the Kingdom of God';

and which He proclaims elsewhere as the sovereign aim of His own birth in the flesh:

'I am come that they might have life, and that they might have it more abundantly.'

The theogony which the Muses had once recited to Hesiod, the shepherd of Ascra, at the moment when a growing Hellenic Civilization had been bursting into flower, finds its antiphony in another theogony which was sung to shepherds of Bethlehem by angels at a moment when a disintegrating Hellenic Society was suffering the last agonies of its time of troubles and was falling into the coma of a universal state. The birth of which the angels then sang was not a rebirth of Hellas nor a new birth of other societies of the Hellenic species. It was the birth in the flesh of the King of the Kingdom of God.

XX. THE RELATION BETWEEN DISINTEGRATING SOCIETIES AND INDIVIDUALS

(1) THE CREATIVE GENIUS AS A SAVIOUR

THE problem of the relation between civilizations and individuals has already engaged our attention in an earlier part of this Study, and we concluded that the institution which we call a society consists in the common ground between the respective fields of action of a number of individual souls; that the source of action is never the society itself but always an individual; that the action which is an act of creation is always performed by a soul which is in some sense a superhuman genius; that the genius expresses himself, like every living soul, through action upon his fellows; that in any society the creative personalities are always a small minority; and that the action of the genius upon souls of common clay operates occasionally through the perfect method of direct illumination but usually through the second-best expedient of a kind of social drill which enlists the faculty of mimesis (or imitation) in the souls of the uncreative rank and file and thereby enables them to perform 'mechanically' an evolution which they could not have performed on their own initiative. These conclusions were reached in the course of our analysis of growth, and in general they must clearly be true of the interaction of individuals and societies in all stages of a society's history. What differences of detail are to be detected in these interactions when the society that we are considering has suffered its breakdown and is in process of disintegration?

The creative minority, out of which the creative individuals had emerged in the growth stage, has ceased to be creative and has sunk into being merely 'dominant', but the secession of the proletariat, which is the essential feature of disintegration, has itself been achieved under the leadership of creative personalities for whose activity there is now no scope except in the organization of opposition to the incubus of the uncreative 'powers that be'. Thus the change from growth to disintegration is not accompanied by any extinction of the creative spark. Creative personalities continue to arise and to take the lead in virtue of their creative power, but they now find themselves compelled to do their old work from a new *locus standi*. In a growing civilization the creator is called upon to play the part of a conqueror who replies to a challenge with a victorious response; in a disintegrating civilization he is called upon to play the part of a saviour who comes to the rescue of a society that has failed to respond because the challenge has worsted a minority that has ceased to be creative.

Such saviours will be of diverse types, according to the nature of the remedy that they seek to apply to the social disease. There will be would-be saviours *of* a disintegrating society who will refuse to despair of the present and will lead forlorn hopes in an endeavour to convert the rout into a fresh advance. These would-be saviours will be men of the dominant minority, and their common characteristic will be their ultimate failure to save. But there will also be saviours *from* a disintegrating society who will seek salvation along one or other of the four alternative possible ways of escape which we have reconnoitred already. The saviours who belong to these other four schools will agree in ruling out the idea of trying to save the present situation. The saviour-archaist will try to reconstruct an imaginary past; the saviour-futurist will attempt a leap into an imagined future. The saviour who points the way to detachment will present himself as a philosopher taking cover behind the mask of a king; the saviour who points the way to transfiguration will appear as a god incarnate in a man.

(2) THE SAVIOUR WITH THE SWORD

The would-be saviour *of* a disintegrating society is necessarily a saviour with a sword, but the sword may be either drawn or sheathed. He may be laying about him with his naked weapon or he may be sitting in state with his blade out of sight in its scabbard as a victor who has 'put all his enemies under his feet'. He may be a Heracles or a Zeus, a David or a Solomon; and though a David or a Heracles who never rests from his labours and dies in harness may be a more romantic figure than a Solomon in all his glory or a Zeus in all his majesty, the labours of Heracles and the wars of David would be aimless exertions if the serenity of Zeus and the prosperity of Solomon were not their objectives. The sword is only wielded in the hope that it may be used to such good purpose that eventually it will have no more work to do; but this hope is an illusion; 'All they that take the sword shall perish with the sword'; and the verdict of a Saviour who proclaimed a kingdom not of This World received the rueful assent of one of the most cynical realists among nineteenth-century Western statesmen when, translating the Gospel into the idiom of his own time and place, he observed that 'the one thing which you cannot do with bayonets is to sit on them'. The man of violence cannot both genuinely repent of his violence and permanently profit by it.

The classic saviours with the sword have been the captains and the princes who have striven to found, or succeeded in founding, or succeeded in rehabilitating, universal states; and although the passage from a time of troubles to a universal state is apt to bring with it so great an immediate relief that the successful founders of such states have often been worshipped as gods, universal states are at best ephemeral and if, by a *tour de force*, they obstinately outlive their normal span, they have to pay for this unnatural longevity by degenerating into social enormities which are as pernicious in their way as either the times of troubles which precede them or the interregna which follow their break-up.

The truth seems to be that a sword which has once drunk blood cannot be permanently restrained from drinking blood again any more than a tiger which has once tasted human flesh can be prevented from becoming a man-eater from that time onwards. The man-eating tiger is, no doubt, a tiger doomed to death; if he escapes the bullet he will die of the mange; yet, even if the tiger could foresee his doom, he would probably be unable to subdue his devouring appetite; and so it is with a society which has once sought salvation through the sword. Its leaders may repent of their butcher's work; they may show mercy to their enemies, like Caesar, or demobilize their armies, like Augustus; and, as they ruefully hide the sword away, they may resolve in complete good faith that they will never draw it again except for the assuredly beneficent and therefore legitimate purpose of preserving peace against criminals still at large within their borders or against barbarians still recalcitrant in the outer darkness; yet, though their fair-seeming *Pax Oecumenica* may stand steady on its grim foundations of buried sword-blades for a hundred or two hundred years, time sooner or later will bring their work to naught.

Can the Jovian ruler of a universal state succeed in curbing that insatiable lust for more and more conquests which was fatal to Cyrus? And, if he cannot resist the temptation *debellare superbos*, can he at any rate bring himself to act on the Virgilian counsel *parcere subjectis*? When we apply this pair of tests to his performance we shall find that he seldom succeeds for long in living up to his own good resolutions.

If we choose to deal first with the conflict between the alternative policies of expansion and non-aggression in the relations of a universal state with the peoples beyond its pale, we may begin with the Sinic example, for there could be no more impressive declaration of a determination to sheathe the sword than Ts'in

She Hwang-ti's building of the Great Wall along the border line of the Eurasian Steppe. Yet his good resolution to refrain from stirring up the Eurasian hornets' nest was broken less than a hundred years after his death by the 'forward policy' of his Han successor Wuti. In the history of the Hellenic universal state the policy of moderation laid down by Augustus was broken by Trajan's attempt to conquer the Parthian Empire. The price of a momentary advance from the Euphrates to the foot of Zagros and the head of the Persian Gulf was the imposition of an intolerable strain upon the Roman Empire's resources, and it took all the prudence and ability of Trajan's successor Hadrian to liquidate the formidable legacy which Trajan's sword had bequeathed to him. Hadrian promptly evacuated all his predecessor's conquests; yet he was able to restore only the territorial, not the political, *status quo ante bellum*.

In the history of the Ottoman Empire Mehmed the Conqueror (A.D. 1451–81) deliberately limited his ambitions to the enterprise of making his *Pax Ottomanica* conterminous with the historic domain of Orthodox Christendom, exclusive of Russia, and resisted all temptations to encroach on the adjoining domains of Western Christendom and Iran. But his successor Selīm the Grim (A.D. 1512–20) broke Mehmed's self-denying ordinance in Asia, while Selīm's successor Suleymān (A.D. 1520–66) committed the further and more disastrous error of breaking the same self-denying ordinance in Europe as well. In consequence the Ottoman Power was henceforth worn down by the grinding friction of a perpetual warfare on two fronts against adversaries whom the 'Osmanli could repeatedly defeat in the field but could never put out of action. And this perversity came to be so deeply ingrained in the statecraft of the Sublime Porte that even the collapse that followed Suleymān's death did not produce any lasting revulsion in favour of Mehmed's moderation. The squandered strength of the Ottoman Empire had no sooner been recruited by the statesmanship of the Köprülüs than it was expended by Qāra Mustafā on a new war of aggression against the Franks which was intended to carry the Ottoman frontier to the Rhine. Though he never came within sight of this objective, Qāra Mustafā did emulate Suleymān's feat of laying siege to Vienna. But in A.D. 1682–3, as in A.D. 1529, the boss of the Danubian carapace of Western Christendom proved to be too hard a nut for Ottoman arms to crack; and on this second occasion the 'Osmanlis did not fail before Vienna with impunity. The second Ottoman siege evoked a Western counter-attack which continued, with no serious check, from 1683 to 1922, by which date the 'Osmanlis had been bereft of the whole of their empire and confined once more to their Anatolian homelands.

In thus wantonly stirring up a hornets' nest in Western Christendom Qāra Mustafā, like Suleymān before him, was committing the classic error of Xerxes when the successor of Darius launched his war of aggression against Continental European Greece and thereby provoked the Hellenic counter-attack which immediately tore away from the Achaemenian Empire the Greek fringe of its dominions in Asia and which ultimately led to the destruction of the Empire itself, when the work begun by Themistocles the Athenian was completed by Alexander of Macedon. In the history of the Hindu World the Mughal Rāj produced its Xerxes in the person of Awrangzīb (A.D. 1659–1707), whose unsuccessful efforts to assert his authority over the Mahārāshtra by force of arms provoked a Marāthā counter-attack which ultimately destroyed the authority of Awrangzīb's successors in their metropolitan provinces on the plains of Hindustan.

It will be seen that, on the first of our two tests of ability to sheathe the sword, the rulers of universal states do not make a very good showing; and, if we now pass from the test of non-aggression against people beyond the pale to our second test of toleration towards people within it, we shall find that such rulers fare hardly better in this second ordeal.

The Roman Imperial Government, for example, made up its mind to tolerate Judaism and abode by this resolution in the face of severe and repeated Jewish provocations; but its forbearance was not equal to the more difficult moral feat of extending this tolerance to the Jewish heresy that had set itself to convert the Hellenic World. The element in Christianity which was intolerable to the Imperial Government was the Christians' refusal to accept the Government's claim that it was entitled to compel its subjects to act against their consciences. The Christians disputed the sword's prerogative, and the eventual victory of the Christian martyr's spirit over the Roman ruler's sword bore out Tertullian's triumphantly defiant boast that Christian blood was Christian seed.

The Achaemenian Government, like the Roman, set itself in principle to rule with the consent of the governed and was likewise only partially successful in living up to this policy. It succeeded in winning the allegiance of the Phoenicians and the Jews, but it failed in the long run to conciliate either the Egyptians or the Babylonians. The 'Osmanlis had no better success in conciliating their ra'īyeh, notwithstanding the wideness of the scope of the cultural, and even civil, autonomy that they conceded to them in the *millet* system. But the theoretical liberality of the system was marred by the high-handedness with which it was applied. The perilously practical fashion in which the ra'īyeh displayed their disloyalty as soon as a series of Ottoman reverses afforded an opening for treachery gave the successors of Selīm the Grim some reason to regret that this ruthless man of action had been deterred (if the tale be true) by the joint exertions of his Grand Vizier and his Sheykh-al-Islām from carrying out a plan to exterminate the Orthodox Christian majority of his subjects— as he did in fact exterminate an Imāmī Shī'ī minority. Again, in the history of the Mughal Rāj in India, Awrangzīb departed from the policy of toleration towards Hinduism which Akbar had bequeathed to his successors as the most important of their *arcana imperii*, and this departure was swiftly requited by the downfall of the Empire.

These examples may suffice to reinforce the conclusion that the Saviour with the Sword fails to save.

(3) THE SAVIOUR WITH THE TIME MACHINE

The Time Machine is the title of one of the early quasi-scientific romances of Mr. H. G. Wells. The conception of time as a fourth dimension was by then already familiar. The hero of Mr. Wells's romance invents a kind of motor-car—these were also a novelty at the time—in which he can travel forwards and backwards through space-time at will, and he uses his invention to pay a succession of visits to far-distant stages of the world's history, from all of which, except the last, he safely returns to tell his traveller's tale. The Wellsian fairy-story is a parable of the historic *tours de force* of those archaist and futurist saviours who, regarding the present condition and prospects of their societies as irreparable, seek salvation in a return to an idealized past or in a plunge into an idealized future. We need not linger long over this spectacle, for we have already analysed and exposed the futility and destructiveness of both archaism and futurism. In a word, these time-machines—conceived not as Wellsian cars for solitary explorers but as 'omnibuses ' (in a sense more exact than the popular usage) for whole societies—invariably fail to work, and this failure goads the would-be saviour into casting aside his time-machine, taking to the sword, and thereby condemning himself to the frustration that lies in wait for the undisguised 'saviour with the sword' whose case we have already examined. This tragic transformation from an idealist into a man of violence overtakes both the saviour-archaist and the saviour-futurist.

In the Western World in the eighteenth century of the Christian

Era the fundamental gospel of archaism was condensed into a sentence in the opening of Rousseau's *Le Contrat Social*: 'Man is born free and everywhere he is in chains.' Rousseau's most famous disciple was Robespierre, popularly accounted the principal author of the French 'Reign of Terror' of A.D. 1793–4. The harmless professorial cranks who spent the nineteenth century of the Christian Era in idealizing the primitive pagan 'Nordic' race cannot entirely disclaim responsibility for the Nazi terror of our own day. We have seen already how the pacific exponent of an archaizing movement may defeat his own intentions by preparing the way for an aggressive and violent successor, as Tiberius Gracchus proved the harbinger of his brother Gaius and thereby ushered in a century of revolution.

The difference between archaism and futurism might be expected to be as plain as the difference between yesterday and to-morrow, but it is often difficult to decide in which category a given movement or a given saviour should be placed, since it is in the nature of archaism to defeat itself by breaking down into futurism in pursuing its delusion that there can be an 'as you were' in history. There cannot, of course, be any such thing, for the mere fact that you had gone on and then returned would make the place to which you had returned—if you could return—a different place. The disciples of Rousseau might precipitate their revolution by idealizing the 'state of nature', admiring 'the noble savage' and deploring 'the arts and sciences', but the consciously futurist revolutionaries—a Condorcet, for example, who drew his inspiration from a doctrine of 'progress'—were assuredly more clear-sighted. The outcome of a would-be archaist movement will always be a new departure. In all such movements the archaist element is merely the coating of an essentially futurist pill, whether it be laid on innocently by 'wishful thinkers' or artfully by adepts in propaganda. In any case the pill is more readily swallowed if the coating is there; for the naked future presents all the terrors of the unknown, whereas the past can be represented as a long-lost cosy home from which the disintegrating society has strayed into the wilderness of the present. Thus, in the inter-war years, the British advocates of a certain kind of socialism came forward as archaistically minded idealizers of the Middle Ages and presented their programme under the title of Guild Socialism, with the suggestion that what was required was a revival of something like the medieval guild system. Yet we may be sure that, if the programme had been carried out, the results would have astonished any time-machine traveller from the Western Christendom of the thirteenth century.

It is evident that the archaist-futurist saviours fail as signally as the saviours with the sword to 'deliver the goods'. There is no more salvation in mundane revolutionary utopias than there is in universal states.

(4) THE PHILOSOPHER MASKED BY A KING

A means of salvation that does not invoke the aid of either a 'time machine' or a sword was propounded in the first generation of the Hellenic time of troubles by the earliest and greatest of Hellenic adepts in the art of detachment.

'There is no hope of a cessation of evils for the states [of Hellas]—and, in my opinion, none for mankind—except through a personal union between political power and philosophy and a forcible disqualification of those common natures that now follow one of these two pursuits to the exclusion of the other. The union may be achieved in either of two ways. Either the philosophers must become kings in our states or else the people who are now called kings and potentates must take—genuinely and thoroughly—to philosophy.'[1]

In suggesting this cure, Plato is at pains to disarm, by forestalling, the plain man's criticism. He introduces his proposal as a paradox which is likely to provoke the ridicule of the unphilosophic. Yet if Plato's prescription is a hard saying for laymen—be these kings or commoners—it is an even harder saying for philosophers. Is not the very aim of philosophy a detachment from life? and are not the pursuits of individual detachment and social salvation incompatible to the point of being mutually exclusive? How can one set oneself to salvage a City of Destruction from which one is rightly struggling to be free?

In the sight of the philosopher the incarnation of self-sacrifice—Christ Crucified—is a personification of folly. Yet few philosophers have had the courage to avow this conviction and fewer still to act upon it. For the adept in the art of detachment has to start as a man encumbered with the common human feelings. He cannot ignore in his neighbour a distress of which his own heart gives the measure, or pretend that a way of salvation which is commended by his own experience would not be equally valuable to his neighbour if only it were pointed out to him. Is our philosopher, then, to handicap himself by giving his neighbour a helping hand? In this moral dilemma it is vain for him to take refuge in the Indic doctrine that pity and love are vices or in the Plotinian doctrine that 'action is a weakened form of contemplation'. Nor can he be content to stand convicted of the intellectual and moral inconsistencies of which the Stoic fathers are roundly

---

[1] Plato: *Republic*, 473 D.

accused by Plutarch, who quotes texts in which Chrysippus condemns the life of academic leisure in one sentence and recommends it in another within the limits of a single treatise.[1] Plato himself decreed that the adepts who had mastered the art of detachment should not be permitted to enjoy for ever afterwards the sunlight into which they had so hardly fought their way. With a heavy heart he condemned his philosophers to redescend into the Cave for the sake of helping their unfortunate fellow-men who were still sitting 'fast bound in misery and iron'; and it is impressive to see this Platonic commandment being dutifully obeyed by Epicurus.

The Hellenic philosopher whose ideal was a state of unruffled imperturbability (ἀταραξία) was apparently the one and only private individual before Jesus of Nazareth to acquire the Greek title of Saviour (σωτήρ). That honour was normally a monopoly of princes and a reward for political and military services. Epicurus's unprecedented distinction was the unsought consequence of the cool-headed philosopher's good-humoured obedience to an irresistible call of the heart, and the fervour of the gratitude and admiration with which Epicurus's work of salvation is extolled in the poetry of Lucretius makes it clear that, in this case at least, the title was no empty formality but was the expression of a deep and lively feeling which must have been communicated to the Latin poet through a chain of tradition descending from Epicurus's own contemporaries who had known him and adored him in the flesh.

The paradoxical history of Epicurus brings out the grievousness of the burden which the philosophers have to take upon their shoulders if, in setting themselves to carry out Plato's prescription, they follow the alternative of themselves becoming kings; and it is therefore not surprising to find that Plato's other alternative—of turning kings into philosophers—has proved highly attractive to every philosopher with a social conscience, beginning with Plato himself. No less than three times in his life Plato voluntarily, though reluctantly, emerged from his Attic retreat and crossed the sea to Syracuse in the hope of converting a Sicilian despot to an Athenian philosopher's conception of a prince's duty. The results composed a curious but, we must regretfully admit, entirely unimportant chapter in Hellenic history. There have been a variety of historic sovereigns who have occupied their spare time, more or less seriously, in taking counsel with philosophers, the examples most familiar to the Western student of history being the so-called 'Enlightened Despots' of an eighteenth-

[1] Plutarch: De Stoicorum Repugnantiis, chs. 2 and 20.

century Western World who amused themselves by alternately pampering and quarrelling with a miscellaneous company of French *philosophes* ranging from Voltaire downwards. But we shall hardly find a satisfactory saviour in Frederick II of Prussia or in Catherine II of Russia.

There are also cases of notable rulers who have acquired a very genuine philosophy from teachers who had died generations earlier. Marcus Aurelius proclaims his debt to his tutors Rusticus and Sextus, but there can be little doubt that these otherwise unknown schoolmasters were merely vehicles of the philosophy of the great Stoics of the past and more particularly of Panaetius, who lived in the second century B.C., three hundred years before Marcus's day. The Indic Emperor Açoka was the disciple of the Buddha, who had died two hundred years before his accession. The state of the Indic World under Açoka and of the Hellenic World under Marcus might be held to bear out Plato's contention that 'social life is happiest and most harmonious when those who have to rule are the last people in the world who would choose to be rulers'. But their achievement perished with them. Marcus himself brought his philosophic labours to naught by selecting as his successor the son of his loins, in breach of a constitutional practice of adoption which Marcus's predecessors had followed faithfully, with unfailing success, for almost a century. As for the personal holiness of Açoka, this did not save the Mauryan Empire in the next generation from collapsing at a blow from the fist of the usurper Pushyamitra.

Thus the philosopher-king turns out to be incapable of saving his fellow-men from the shipwreck of a disintegrating society. The facts speak for themselves; but we have still to ask whether they provide their own explanation. If we look a little farther, we shall find that they do.

The explanation is, indeed, implicit in the passage of *The Republic* in which Plato introduces the figure of the prince who is a born philosopher. After putting forward his postulate that, some time and somewhere, at any rate one such philosopher-prince will live to ascend his father's throne and will there make it his business to translate his own philosophical principles into political practice, Plato eagerly jumps to the conclusion that 'a single one such ruler would suffice—if he could count on the consent of the governed—to carry out in full a programme that looks quite impracticable under existing conditions'. And the conductor of the argument then goes on to explain the grounds of his optimism. 'Supposing', he continues, 'that a ruler were to enact our ideal laws and introduce our ideal social conventions, it would assuredly not be beyond the bounds of possibility that his subjects should consent to act in accordance with their ruler's wishes.'[1]

These final propositions are evidently essential to the success of Plato's scheme, but they are no less manifestly dependent upon the enlistment of the faculty of mimesis; and we have already observed that this resort to a kind of social drill is a short cut which is apt to bring those who take it to destruction instead of expediting their journey towards their goal. The inclusion of any element of coercion—mental or physical—in the social strategy of the philosopher-king would therefore perhaps suffice of itself to account for his failure to bring to pass the salvation which he professes to offer; and, if we examine his strategy more closely from this standpoint, we shall find that his use of coercion is peculiarly gross. For, though Plato is at pains to give his philosopher-king's government the benefit of the consent of the governed, it is evident that there would be no purpose in the philosopher's surprising personal union with the potentate who is to be an absolute monarch unless the despot's power of physical coercion is to be held in readiness for use in case of necessity; and the case in point is as likely to arise as it is obvious to foresee.

'The nature of the peoples is inconstant, and it is easy to persuade them of a thing, but difficult to hold them to that persuasion. Accordingly it is expedient to be so equipped that, when their belief gives out, one will have it in one's power to make them believe by force.'[2]

In these wholesomely brutal words Machiavelli brings out a sinister feature in the strategy of the philosopher-king which Plato discreetly keeps in the background. If the philosopher-king finds that he cannot get his way by charm, he will throw away his philosophy and take to the sword. Even Marcus Aurelius resorted to this weapon against the Christians. Once again we are presented with the shocking spectacle of Orpheus transformed into a drill-sergeant. In fact, the philosopher-king is doomed to fail because he is attempting to unite two contradictory natures in a single person. The philosopher stultifies himself by trespassing on the king's field of coercion, while conversely the king stultifies himself by trespassing on the philosopher's field of passionless contemplation. Like the saviour with the 'time machine', who in his pure form is likewise a political idealist, the philosopher-king is driven into proclaiming his own failure by drawing a weapon which convicts him too of being a 'saviour with the sword' in disguise.

[1] Plato: *Republic*, 502 A–B.
[2] Machiavelli: *The Prince*, ch. 6.

(5) THE GOD INCARNATE IN A MAN

We have now examined three different epiphanies of the creative genius who is born into a disintegrating society and who bends his powers and energies to the task of coping with the challenge of social disintegration, and we have found that in each case the supposed way of salvation leads only to disaster, immediate or ultimate. What conclusion are we to draw from this series of disillusionments? Do they signify that any and every attempt to bring salvation to a disintegrating society is doomed to end in destruction if the would-be saviour is merely a human being? Let us remind ourselves of the context of the classic statement of the truth that we have so far been empirically verifying. 'All they that take the sword shall perish with the sword' are the words of a saviour who gives this as his reason for commanding one of his followers to sheathe again a sword which this henchman has just drawn and used. Jesus of Nazareth first heals the wound which Peter's sword has inflicted and then voluntarily delivers his own person up to suffer the last extremes of insult and torment. Moreover his motive for refusing to take the sword is not any practical calculation that, in the particular circumstances, his own force is no match for his adversaries'. He believes, as he afterwards tells his judge, that, if he did take the sword, he could be certain of winning, with 'twelve legions of angels', all the victory that swordsmanship can procure. Yet, believing this, he still refuses to use the weapon. Rather than conquer with the sword he will die on the Cross.

In choosing this alternative in the hour of crisis, Jesus is breaking right away from the conventional line of action taken by the other would-be saviours whose conduct we have studied. What inspires the Nazarene saviour to take this tremendous new departure? We may answer this question by asking, in turn, what distinguishes him from those other saviours who have refuted their own pretensions by turning swordsmen. The answer is that these others knew themselves to be no more than men, whereas Jesus was a man who believed himself to be the Son of God. Are we to conclude, with the psalmist, that 'salvation belongeth unto the Lord', and that, without being in some sense divine, a would-be saviour of mankind will always be impotent to execute his mission? Now that we have weighed and found wanting those *soi-disant* saviours who have avowedly been mere men, let us turn, as our last recourse, to the saviours who have presented themselves as gods.

To pass in review a procession of saviour-gods, with an eye to appraising their claims to be what they profess to be and to do what they profess to do, might seem an unprecedently presumptuous application of our habitual method of empirical study. That, however, will not prove to be our difficulty in practice. For we shall find that all but one of the figures in our procession, whatever their claims to godhead, can make only the most dubious claims to manhood. We shall move among shadows and abstractions, Berkleian unrealities whose only *esse* is *percipi*, 'persons' on whom must be passed the sentence which modern research has passed on that 'Lycurgus, king of Sparta' whom our ancestors deemed as solid and datable a reality as Solon of Athens —that he was 'not a man; only a god'. However, let us proceed. Let us start at the lower end of the scale with the *deus ex machina* and try to ascend from this perhaps infra-human level towards the ineffable height of the *deus cruci fixus*. If dying on the Cross is the utmost extreme to which it is possible for a man to go in testifying to the truth of his claim to divinity, appearing on the stage is perhaps the least trouble that an acknowledged god can take in support of his claim to be also a saviour.

On the Attic stage in the century which saw the breakdown of the Hellenic Civilization the *deus ex machina* was a veritable godsend to embarrassed playwrights who, in an already enlightened age, were still constrained by convention to take their plots from the traditional corpus of Hellenic mythology. If the action of the play had in consequence become caught, before the natural close, in some insoluble tangle of moral enormities or practical improbabilities, the author could extricate himself from the toils in which he had become involved through one of the conventions of his art by resorting to another of them. He could produce a god 'in a machine', suspended aloft or wheeled upon the stage, to effect a denouement. This trick of the Attic dramatist's trade has given scandal to scholars, for the solutions of human problems propounded by these Olympian interventionists neither convince the human mind nor appeal to the human heart. Euripides is a particularly gross offender in these respects, and it has been suggested by one modern Western scholar that Euripides never brings on a *deus ex machina* without having his tongue in his cheek. According to Verrall, Euripides 'the Rationalist' (as he calls him) has made this traditional convention serve his own purposes by using it as a screen for sallies of irony and blasphemy upon which he could hardly have ventured with impunity if he had come out into the open. This screen is ideal in texture, since it is impervious to the hostile shafts of the poet's 'low-brow' adversaries, while it is transparent to the knowing eyes of his fellow-sceptics.

'It is not too much to say that on the Euripidean stage whatever is said by a divinity is to be regarded, in general, as *ipso facto* discredited. It is in all cases objectionable from the author's point of view, and almost always a lie. "By representing the deities he persuaded men that they did not exist." '[1]

Less remote from the grandeur and misery of the human lot, and far more worthy of admiration, are the demigods born of human mothers by a superhuman sire—a Heracles, an Asklepios, an Orpheus, to mention only Greek examples. These half-divine beings in human flesh seek by their labours in various ways to lighten the lot of man, and in the punishments inflicted on them by jealous gods they share the sufferings of the mortals whom they serve. The demigod—and this is his glory—is subject, like man, to death, and behind the figure of the dying demigod there looms the greater figure of a very god who dies for different worlds under diverse names—for a Minoan World as Zagreus, for a Sumeric World as Tammuz, for a Hittite World as Attis, for a Scandinavian World as Balder, for a Syriac World as Adonis, for a Shī'ī World as Husayn, for a Christian World as Christ.

Who is this god of many epiphanies but only one Passion? Though he makes his appearance on our mundane stage under a dozen different masks, his identity is invariably revealed in the last act of the tragedy by his suffering and death. And if we take up the anthropologist's divining-rod we can trace this never varying drama back to its historical origins. 'He shall grow up before him as a tender plant, and as a root out of the dry ground.'[2] The Dying God's oldest appearance is in the role of the ἐνιαυτὸς δαίμων, the spirit of the vegetation that is born for man in the spring to die for man in the autumn. Man profits by the nature-god's death and would perish if his benefactor did not die for him perpetually.[3] 'He was wounded for our transgressions; he was bruised for our iniquities; the chastisement of our peace was upon him and with his stripes we are healed.'[4] But an outward achievement, however imposing and however dearly paid for, cannot reveal the mystery at the heart of a tragedy. If we are to read the secret, we must look beyond the human beneficiary's profit and the divine protagonist's loss. The god's death and the man's gain are not the whole story. We cannot know the meaning of the play without also knowing the protagonist's circumstances and

---

[1] Verrall, A. W.: *Euripides the Rationalist*, p. 138. The quotation in the last sentence of the passage is from Aristophanes: *Thesmophoriazusae*, ll. 450–1.
[2] Isa. liii. 2.
[3] In fact man ensures that the god shall die by taking his life in order that man himself may live. The spirit of the pagan vegetation cult is caught in Robert Burns's poem *John Barleycorn* perhaps better than in any other piece of English literature.   [4] Isa. liii. 5.

feelings and motives. Does the Dying God die by compulsion or by choice? With generosity or with bitterness? Out of love or in despair? Till we have learnt the answers to these questions about the spirit of the saviour-god, we can hardly judge whether this salvation will be merely a profit for a man through a god's equivalent loss or whether it will be a spiritual communion in which man will repay, by acquiring ('like a light caught from a leaping flame'),[1] a divine love and pity that have been shown to man by God in an act of pure self-sacrifice.

In what spirit does the Dying God go to his death? If, with this question on our lips, we address ourselves once more to our array of tragic masks, we shall see the perfect separating itself from the imperfect sacrifice. Even in Calliope's lovely lamentation for the death of Orpheus there is a jarring note of bitterness which strikes, and shocks, a Christian ear.

'Why do we mortals make lament over the deaths of our sons, seeing that the Gods themselves have not power to keep Death from laying his hand upon their children?'[2]

What a moral to read into the Dying God's story! So the goddess who was Orpheus' mother would never have let Orpheus die if she could have helped it. Like a cloud that veils the Sun, the Hellenic poet's admission takes the light out of Orpheus' death. But Antipater's poem is answered in another and greater masterpiece:

'For God so loved the World that he gave his only begotten Son, that whosoever believeth in Him should not perish but have everlasting life.'

When the Gospel thus answers the elegy, it delivers an oracle. 'The One remains, the many change and pass.'[3] And this is in truth the final result of our survey of saviours. When we set out on this quest we found ourselves moving in the midst of a mighty host, but, as we have pressed forward, the marchers, company by company, have fallen out of the race. The first to fail were the swordsmen, the next the archaists and futurists, the next the philosophers, until only gods were left in the running. At the final ordeal of death, few, even of these would-be saviour gods, have dared to put their title to the test by plunging into the icy river. And now, as we stand and gaze with our eyes fixed upon the farther shore, a single figure rises from the flood and straightway fills the whole horizon. There is the Saviour; 'and the pleasure of the Lord shall prosper in his hand; he shall see of the travail of his soul and shall be satisfied.'[4]

---

[1] Plato's *Letters*, VII, 341 C–D.
[2] Elegy on the Death of Orpheus by Antipater of Sidon (*circa* 90 B.C.).
[3] Shelley: *Adonais*, lii.   [4] Isa. liii. 10–11.

XXI. THE RHYTHM OF DISINTEGRATION

IN the last chapter we sought, and found, a parallel—which involved also an inevitable contrast—between the roles of creative personalities in growing and in disintegrating societies. We are now to pursue a similar line of investigation in a different part of our subject and to look for a parallel—which will presumably again involve a contrast—between what may be called the rhythm of growth and the rhythm of disintegration. The underlying formula in each case is one with which we are already very familiar, since it has accompanied us all through this Study; it is the formula of challenge-and-response. In a growing civilization a challenge meets with a successful response which proceeds to generate another and a different challenge which meets with another successful response. There is no term to this process of growth unless and until a challenge arises which the civilization in question fails to meet—a tragic event which means a cessation of growth and what we have called a breakdown. Here the correlative rhythm begins. The challenge has not been met, but it none the less continues to present itself. A second convulsive effort is made to meet it, and, if this succeeds, growth will of course be resumed. But we will assume that, after a partial and temporary success, this response likewise fails. There will then be a further relapse, and perhaps, after an interval, a further attempt at a response which will in time achieve a temporary and partial success in meeting what is still the same inexorable challenge. This again will be followed by a further failure, which may or may not prove final and involve the dissolution of the society. In military language the rhythm may be expressed as rout–rally–rout–rally–rout . . . .

If we revert to the technical terms which we devised early in this Study and have so constantly used, it is at once apparent that the time of troubles following a breakdown is a rout; the establishment of the universal state, a rally; and the interregnum which follows the break-up of the universal state, the final rout. But we have already noticed in the history of one universal state, the Hellenic, a relapse into anarchy following the death of Marcus Aurelius in A.D. 180 and a recovery under Diocletian. There might prove to be more than one relapse and recovery in the history of any particular universal state. Indeed the number of such relapses and recoveries might be found to depend on the power of the lens that we applied to the object under examination.

There was, for instance, a brief, but startling, relapse in A.D. 69, the 'year of four emperors', but we are concerned here with salient features only. There might also be a period of partial recovery in the middle of the time of troubles. If we allow for one signal recovery during the time of troubles and one signal relapse during the lifetime of the universal state, that will give us the formula: rout–rally–rout–rally–rout–rally–rout, which we may describe as three-and-a-half 'beats' of our rout–rally rhythm. There is, of course, no special virtue in the number three-and-a-half. A particular instance of disintegration might show two-and-a-half, or four-and-a-half, or five-and-a-half without failing to conform in essentials to the general rhythm of the disintegration process. Actually, however, three-and-a-half beats seems to be the pattern which fits the histories of a number of disintegrating societies, and we will pass a few of them in rapid review by way of illustration.

The breakdown of the Hellenic Society can be dated with peculiar exactness at 431 B.C. and the establishment of its universal state by Augustus at 31 B.C., four hundred years later. Can we discern a movement of rally-and-relapse anywhere in the course of these four centuries? Undoubtedly we can. One of its symptoms is the social gospel of Homonoia or Concord preached by Timoleon at Syracuse and in a far wider sphere by Alexander the Great, both in the second half of the fourth century B.C. Another symptom is the conception of the Cosmopolis or World Commonwealth, popularized by the philosophers Zeno and Epicurus and their disciples. A third is the crop of constitutional experiments—the Seleucid Empire, the Achaean and Aetolian Confederacies and the Roman Republic—which were all of them attempts to transcend the traditional sovereignty of the city-state. Other symptoms might be quoted, but these are enough to give our surmised rally some substance and an approximate location in time. It was a rally which failed, mainly because the new enlarged political units, though they did successfully transcend the limits of the individual city-state, proved as intolerant and uncooperative in their relations with one another as had been the city-states themselves in fifth-century Greece, when they inaugurated the Hellenic breakdown by starting the Atheno-Peloponnesian War. We may date this second relapse or (what is the same thing) failure of the first rally at the opening of the Hannibalic War in 218 B.C. We have already located a century-long relapse followed by a recovery in the course of the history of the Roman Empire, and that gives us our three-and-a-half beats.

If we turn next to the disintegration of the Sinic Society we shall identify the moment of breakdown with the disastrous collision between the two Powers Tsin and Ch'u in 634 B.C., and the moment of the establishment of the Sinic *Pax Oecumenica* with the overthrow, in 221 B.C., of Ts'i by Ts'in. If these are the two terminal dates of the Sinic time of troubles, are there any traces of a movement of rally-and-relapse in the intervening period? The answer is in the affirmative, for there is a perceptible rally in the Sinic time of troubles round about the generation of Confucius (*circa* 551–479 B.C.), inaugurated by the ultimately abortive disarmament conference of 546 B.C. Further, if we look at the history of the Sinic universal state, we find a notorious relapse and recovery in the interregnum, during the early years of the first century of the Christian Era, between the dynasties of the Prior and the Posterior Han. Again we find our three-and-a-half beats, the Sinic dates regularly occurring about two hundred years earlier than their Hellenic equivalents.

In Sumeric history we shall register the same reading; for in the course of the Sumeric time of troubles a beat of rally-and-rout is distinctly perceptible, while the life-span of the Sumeric universal state is punctuated by a counter-beat of rout-and-rally which is unusually emphatic. If we date the beginning of the time of troubles from the career of the militarist Lugalzaggisi of Erech (*circa* 2677–2653 B.C.) and equate its end with the establishment of the Sumeric universal state by Ur-Engur of Ur (*circa* 2298–2281 B.C.), at least one symptom of an intervening rally is to be found in a notable advance in visual art which had been achieved by the time of Naramsin (*circa* 2572–2517 B.C.). The time-span of the *Pax Sumerica* extends from Ur-Engur's accession to the death of Hammurabi (*circa* 1905 B.C.), but this peace turns out, on inspection, to be a thin shell encasing a wide welter of anarchy. A century after the accession of Ur-Engur his 'Empire of the Four Quarters' was broken into fragments, and in fragments it remained for over two hundred years until Hammurabi re-created this universal state on the eve of its final dissolution.

The now familiar pattern reappears in the history of the disintegration of the main body of Orthodox Christendom. We have already identified the breakdown of this civilization with the outbreak of the great Romano-Bulgarian War of A.D. 977–1019, and the eventual re-establishment of a *Pax Oecumenica* may be dated from the Ottoman conquest of Macedonia in A.D. 1371–2. In between these two termini of an Orthodox Christian time of troubles we can discern a rally led by the East Roman Emperor Alexius Comnenus (A.D. 1081–1118) which lasted for a century. The subsequent *Pax Ottomanica* eventually collapsed under the shock of defeat in the Russo-Turkish war of A.D. 1768–74; but, while this collapse marked the decisive breakdown of the Ottoman régime, the Ottoman annals present plain evidence of an earlier relapse which is retrieved by a rally. The relapse is to be discerned in the rapid decay of the Pādishāh's slave-household after the death of Suleymān the Magnificent in A.D. 1566 and the rally is heralded by the subsequent experiment of taking the Pādishāh's Orthodox Christian ra'īyeh into partnership with the free Muslim citizens—who had now seized the reins of power—without any longer insisting that the ra'īyeh should become renegades as the price of their admission to a share in the government of the state. This revolutionary innovation, which was the work of the Köprülü viziers, gave the Ottoman Empire a breathing-space which is still wistfully remembered by the 'Osmanlis of a later day as 'the Tulip Period'.

In the history of the disintegration of the Hindu Society the final half-beat is not yet quite due, since the second instalment of the Hindu universal state, as provided by the British Rāj, is not yet over and done with. On the other hand the three earlier beats of rout-and-rally have all left their record. The third rout is represented by the century of anarchy between the collapse of the Mughal Rāj and the establishment of its British successor. The rally stroke of the second beat is equally clearly represented by the establishment of the Mughal Rāj in the reign of Akbar (A.D. 1566–1602). The foregoing rout stroke is not so clear, but, if we peer into the history of the Hindu time of troubles which begins in the latter part of the twelfth century of the Christian Era with an outbreak of fratricidal wars between the Hindu parochial states, we shall notice, in between the tribulations inflicted by Hindu rulers and Muslim invaders in the twelfth and thirteenth centuries and those inflicted by the later swarms of Muslim invaders, including Akbar's own ancestors, in the fifteenth and sixteenth centuries, some signs of a temporary relief in the fourteenth century, marked by the reigns of 'Alā-ad-Dīn and Fīrūz.

We might subject the disintegrations of our other civilizations to a similar analysis in all cases where we possess sufficient evidence to make such examination remunerative. In some cases we should find that the full quota of 'beats' is lacking simply because the civilization in question was swallowed alive by one of its neighbours before it had worked its passage to the haven of natural death. We have, however, already adduced enough evidence of the rhythm of disintegration to apply this rhythm-pattern to the history of our own Western Civilization in order to see if it throws any light upon a question which we have several times asked and never yet professed to answer: the question whether our own civilization has suffered a breakdown, and, if so, what stage it has now reached in its disintegration.

One fact is plain: we have not yet experienced the establishment of a universal state, in spite of two desperate efforts by the Germans to impose one upon us in the first half of the present century and an equally desperate attempt by Napoleonic France a hundred years earlier. Another fact is equally plain: there is among us a profound and heartfelt aspiration for the establishment, not of a universal state, but of some form of world order, akin perhaps to the Homonoia or Concord preached in vain by certain Hellenic statesmen and philosophers during the Hellenic time of troubles, which will secure the blessings of a universal state without its deadly curse. The curse of a universal state is that it is the result of a successful knock-out blow delivered by one sole surviving member of a group of contending military Powers. It is a product of that 'salvation by the sword' which we have seen to be no salvation at all. What we are looking for is a free consent of free peoples to dwell together in unity, and to make, uncoerced, the far-reaching adjustments and concessions without which this ideal cannot be realized in practice. There is no need to enlarge upon this theme, which is the commonplace of thousands of contemporary disquisitions. The astonishing prestige enjoyed by the American President Wilson in Europe—though not in his own country—during the few short months preceding and following the armistice of November 1918 was a measure of the aspirations of our world. President Wilson was addressed for the most part in prose; the best-known surviving testimonials to Augustus are in the verses of Virgil and Horace. But, prose or verse, the spirit animating these two outpourings of faith, hope and thanksgiving was manifestly the same. The outcome, however, was different. Augustus succeeded in providing his world with a universal state; Wilson failed to provide his with something better.

> That low man goes on adding one to one;
>   His hundred's soon hit.
> This high man, aiming at a million,
>   Misses a unit.[1]

These considerations and comparisons suggest that we are already far advanced in our time of troubles; and, if we ask what has been our most conspicuous and specific trouble in the recent past, the answer clearly is: nationalistic internecine warfare, re-

[1] Browning, R.: *A Grammarian's Funeral*.

inforced, as has been pointed out in an earlier part of this Study, by the combined 'drive' of energies generated by the recently released forces of Democracy and Industrialism. We may date the incidence of this scourge from the outbreak of the French Revolutionary wars at the end of the eighteenth century. But, when we examined this subject before, we were confronted by the fact that, in the modern chapter of our Western history, this bout of violent warfare was not the first but the second of its kind. The earlier bout is represented by the so-called Wars of Religion which devastated Western Christendom from the middle of the sixteenth to the middle of the seventeenth century, and we found that between these two bouts of violent warfare there intervenes a century in which warfare was a comparatively mild disease, a 'sport of kings', not exacerbated by fanaticism in either the religious sectarian or the democratic national vein. Thus, in our own history too, we find what we have come to recognize as the typical pattern of a time of troubles: a breakdown, a rally and a second relapse.

We can discern why the eighteenth-century rally in the course of our time of troubles was abortive and ephemeral; it was because the toleration achieved by 'the Enlightenment' was a toleration based not on the Christian virtues of faith, hope and charity but on the Mephistophelian maladies of disillusionment, apprehension and cynicism. It was not an arduous achievement of religious fervour but a facile by-product of its abatement.

Can we at all foresee the outcome of the second and still more violent bout of warfare into which our Western World has fallen in consequence of the spiritual inadequacy of its eighteenth-century Enlightenment? If we are to try to look into our future, we may begin by reminding ourselves that, though all the other civilizations whose history is known to us may be either dead or dying, a civilization is not like an animal organism, condemned by an inexorable destiny to die after traversing a predetermined life-curve. Even if all other civilizations that have come into existence so far were to prove in fact to have followed this path, there is no known law of historical determinism that compels us to leap out of the intolerable frying-pan of our time of troubles into the slow and steady fire of a universal state where we shall in due course be reduced to dust and ashes. At the same time, such precedents from the histories of other civilizations and from the life-course of nature are bound to appear formidable in the sinister light of our present situation. This chapter itself was written on the eve of the outbreak of the General War of 1939–45 for readers who had already lived through the General War of 1914–18, and it was recast for re-publication on the morrow of the ending of the second of these two world wars within one lifetime by the invention and employment of a bomb in which a newly contrived release of atomic energy has been directed by man to the destruction of human life and works on an unprecedented scale. This swift succession of catastrophic events on a steeply mounting gradient inevitably inspires a dark doubt about our future, and this doubt threatens to undermine our faith and hope at a critical eleventh hour which calls for the utmost exertion of these saving spiritual faculties. Here is a challenge which we cannot evade, and our destiny depends on our response.

'I dreamed, and behold I saw a man cloathed with rags, standing in a certain place, with his face from his own house, a book in his hand and a great burden upon his back. I looked, and saw him open the book and read therein; and as he read he wept and trembled; and, not being able longer to contain, he broke out with a lamentable cry saying "What shall I do?" '

It was not without cause that Bunyan's 'Christian' was so greatly distressed.

'I am for certain informed [said he] that this our city will be burned with fire from Heaven—in which fearful overthrow both myself with thee my wife and you my sweet babes shall miserably come to ruine, except (the which yet I see not) some way of escape can be found, whereby we may be delivered.'

What response to this challenge is Christian going to make? Is he going to look this way and that as if he would run, yet stand still because he cannot tell which way to go? Or will he begin to run—and run on crying 'Life! Life! Eternal Life!'—with his eye set on a shining light and his feet bound for a distant wicket-gate? If the answer to this question depended on nobody but Christian himself, our knowledge of the uniformity of human nature might incline us to predict that Christian's imminent destiny was Death in his City of Destruction. But in the classic version of the myth we are told that the human protagonist was not left entirely to his own resources in the decisive hour. According to John Bunyan, Christian was saved by his encounter with Evangelist. And, inasmuch as it cannot be supposed that God's nature is less constant than Man's, we may and must pray that a reprieve which God has granted to our society once will not be refused if we ask for it again in a humble spirit and with a contrite heart.

XXII. STANDARDIZATION THROUGH DISINTEGRATION

WE have now arrived at the close of our inquiry into the process of the disintegrations of civilizations, but before we leave the subject there is one more question to be considered. We must ask whether, as we look back over the ground we have traversed, we can discern any master-tendency at work, and we do in fact unmistakably descry a tendency towards standardization and uniformity: a tendency which is the correlative and opposite of the tendency towards differentiation and diversity which we have found to be the mark of the growth stage of civilizations. We have recently noted, on a superficial plane, the tendency towards a uniformity of three-and-a-half beats in the rhythm of disintegration. A much more significant symptom of uniformity is the uniform schism of a disintegrating society into three sharply divided classes and the uniform works of creation performed by each of them. We have seen dominant minorities uniformly working out philosophies and producing universal states; internal proletariats uniformly discovering 'higher religions' which aim at embodying themselves in universal churches; and external proletariats uniformly mustering war-bands which find vent in 'heroic ages'. The uniformity with which these several institutions are generated is indeed so far-reaching that we are able to present this aspect of the disintegration-process in the tabular form in which it is displayed at the conclusion of this chapter. Even more remarkable is the uniformity of ways of behaviour, feeling and life that is revealed by the study of schism in the Soul.

This contrast between the diversity of growth and the uniformity of disintegration is what we might have expected from the consideration of simple analogies, such as the parable of Penelope's web. When the faithful wife of the absent Odysseus had promised her importunate suitors that she would give herself in marriage to one of them so soon as she had finished weaving a winding-sheet for old Laertes, she used to weave away at her loom in the day-time day by day and then spend the night watches night by night in unpicking her last day's work. When the webster set up her warp and began to weave her weft each morning she had at her command an unlimited choice of patterns, and might, if she chose, weave a different pattern every day. But her night-work was monotonously uniform, for, when it came to unravelling the web, the pattern made no difference. However complicated the set of movements employed during the day, the night task could be no other than the simple movement of drawing out the threads.

For this inevitable monotony of her night-work Penelope is assuredly to be pitied. If its dullness had led nowhere the drudgery would have been unbearable. What inspired her was a song in her soul: 'With Him will I be reunited.' She was living and working in hope; and her hope was not disappointed. The hero returned to find the heroine still his, and the Odyssey ends with their reunion.

If then, as it turns out, even Penelope has not drawn her threads in vain, what of the mightier weaver whose work is our study, and whose song finds human expression in the verse of Goethe?

> In currents of life, in tempests of motion,
> In fervour of act, in the fire, in the storm,
>> Hither and thither,
>> Over and under,
>> Wend I and wander:
>> Birth and the grave,
>> Limitless ocean,
>> Where the restless wave
>> Undulates ever,
>> Under and over
>> Their seething strife
>> Heaving and weaving
>> The changes of life.
> At the whirring loom of Time unawed
> I work the living mantle of God.[1]

The work of the Spirit of the Earth, as he weaves and draws his threads on the Loom of Time, is the temporal history of man as this manifests itself in the geneses and growths and breakdowns and disintegrations of human societies; and in all this welter of life and tempest of action we can hear the beat of an elemental rhythm whose variations we have learnt to know as challenge-and-response, withdrawal-and-return, rout-and-rally, apparentation-and-affiliation, schism-and-palingenesia. This elemental rhythm is the alternating beat of Yin and Yang; and in listening to it we have recognized that, though strophe may be answered by antistrophe, victory by defeat, creation by destruction, birth by death, the movement that this rhythm beats out is neither the fluctuation of an indecisive battle nor the cycle of a treadmill. The perpetual turning of a wheel is not a vain repetition if, at each revolution, it is carrying the vehicle that much nearer to its goal; and, if palingenesia signifies the birth of something new and not just the

---

[1] Goethe: *Faust*, ll. 501–9 (R. Anstell's translation).

rebirth of something that has lived and died before, then the Wheel of Existence is not just a devilish engine for inflicting everlasting torment on a damned Ixion. On this showing the music that the rhythm of Yin and Yang beats out is the song of creation; and we shall not be misled into fancying ourselves mistaken because, as we give ear, we can catch the note of creation alternating with the note of destruction. So far from convicting the song of being a diabolic counterfeit, this duality of note is a warrant of authenticity. If we listen well we shall perceive that, when the two notes collide, they produce not a discord but a harmony. Creation would not be creative if it did not swallow up all things in itself, including its own opposite.

But what of the living garment that the Earth Spirit weaves? Is it laid up in Heaven as fast as it is woven, or can we, here on Earth, catch glimpses at any rate of patches of its etherial web? What are we to think of those tissues that lie at the foot of the loom when the weaver has been at work unravelling? In the disintegration of a civilization we have found that, though the pageant may have been insubstantial, it does not fade without leaving a wrack behind. When civilizations pass into dissolution they regularly leave behind them a deposit of universal states and universal churches and barbarian war-bands. What are we to make of these objects? Are they mere waste products, or will these debris prove, if we pick them up, to be fresh masterpieces of the weaver's art which he has woven, by an unnoticed sleight of hand, on some more etherial instrument than the roaring loom that has been apparently occupying all his attention?

If, with this new question in mind, we cast our thoughts back over the results of our previous inquiries, we shall find reason to believe that these objects of study are something more than by-products of a social disintegration; for we came across them first as tokens of apparentation-and-affiliation; and this is a relation between one civilization and another. Evidently these three institutions cannot be entirely explained in terms of the history of any single civilization; their existence involves a relation between one civilization and another, and in virtue of this they claim study as independent entities. But how far does their independence carry them? In dealing with universal states we have found already that the peace which they bring is as ephemeral as it is imposing; and in dealing with barbarian war-bands we have found again that these maggots in the carcass of a dead civilization cannot hope to live longer than it takes the putrefying corpse to dissolve into its clean elements. Yet, though the war-bands may be doomed to the premature death of Achilles, the barbarian's short life leaves at least an echo behind it in the epic poetry that commemorates an heroic age. And what is the destiny of the universal church in which every higher religion seeks to embody itself?

It will be seen that we are not in a position at present to answer our new question off-hand, and it is clear that we cannot afford to ignore it, for this question holds the key to the meaning of the weaver's work. Our Study is not yet at an end; but we have arrived at the verge of the last of our fields of inquiry.

EDITOR'S NOTE

THE first four of these tables are reproduced as they stand in Mr. Toynbee's original work. They give a conspectus of the mighty works that are the by-products of social disintegration. The fifth table is reprinted from *Theology To-day*, volume i, Number 3, by the kind permission of the Editor, Dr. John A. Mackay, and of Dr. Edward D. Myers, by whom this table was compiled to illustrate an article by him, in this number, on 'Some Leading Ideas from Toynbee's *A Study of History*'. Dr. Myers's table gives a bird's-eye view of the whole field of Mr. Toynbee's first six volumes.

The reader of this abridged edition will find in these tables a number of names and facts to which he has not here been introduced. The reason is, of course, that the editor of this abridgement has, naturally and inevitably, been compelled to discard a large number of the historical illustrations presented in the original work and to prune away a large amount of detail from other illustrations that could only be retained at the price of being abbreviated. The tables, therefore, here serve not only their proper purpose of recapitulating some of the results of the author's inquiry, but also the secondary purpose of reminding the reader of this abridgement how much he has missed by taking the easier road and following a shortened course.

TABLE I. *Universal States*

Civilization	'Time of Troubles'	Universal State	Pax Oecumenica	Provenance of Empire-builders
Sumeric	c. 2677–2298 B.C.	The Empire of Sumer and Akkad ('The Realm of the Four Quarters')	c. 2298–1905 B.C.	Founders metropolitans (from Ur); restorers marchmen (Amorites)
Babylonic	–610 B.C.	The Neo-Babylonic Empire	610–539 B.C.	Founders metropolitans [?][1] (Chaldaeans); successors barbarians (Achaemenidae) and aliens (Seleucidae)
Indic	–322 B.C.	The Mauryan Empire	322–185 B.C.	Founders metropolitans [?][2] (from Magadha)
		The Guptan Empire	A.D. 390–c. 475	Founders metropolitans (from Magadha)
Sinic	634–221 B.C.	The Ts'in and Han Empire	221 B.C.–c. A.D. 172	Founders marchmen (from Ts'in); successors metropolitans (Prior and Posterior Han)
Hellenic	431–31 B.C.	The Roman Empire	31 B.C.–A.D. 378	Founders marchmen (Romans); restorers marchmen (Illyrians)
Egyptiac	c. 2424–2070/60 B.C.	The Middle Empire	c. 2070/60–1660 B.C.	Marchmen (from Thebes)
		The New Empire	c. 1580–1175 B.C.	Marchmen (from Thebes)
Orthodox Christian (in Russia)	c. A.D. 1075–1478	The Muscovite Empire	A.D. 1478–1881	Marchmen (from Moscow)
Far Eastern (in Japan)	A.D. 1185–1597	Hideyoshi's dictatorship and the Tokugawa Shogunate	A.D. 1597–1868	Marchmen (from the Kwanto)
Western (medieval cosmos of city-states)	c. A.D. 1378–1797	The Napoleonic Empire	A.D. 1797–1814	Marchmen (from France)
Western (carapace of assaults against 'Osmanlis')	c. A.D. 1128[3]–1526	The Danubian Hapsburg Monarchy	A.D. 1526–1918	Marchmen (from Austria)
Andean	–c. A.D. 1430	The Incaic Empire ('The Realm of the Four Quarters')	c. A.D. 1430–1533	Founders marchmen (from Cuzco); successors aliens (Spaniards)
Syriac	c. 937–525 B.C.	The Achaemenian Empire	c. 525–332 B.C.	Barbaro-marchmen (from Iran)
		The Arab Caliphate	c. A.D. 640–969	Barbarians (from Arabia)
		The Mongol Empire	A.D. 1280–1351	Barbaro-aliens (Mongols)
Far Eastern (main body)	A.D. 878–1280	The Manchu Empire	A.D. 1644–1853[4]	Barbaro-marchmen (Manchus)
Central American	–A.D. 1521	The Spanish Viceroyalty of New Spain	A.D. 1521–1821	Forerunners barbaro-marchmen (Aztecs); founders aliens (Spaniards)
Orthodox Christian (main body)	A.D. 977–1372	The Ottoman Empire	A.D. 1372–1768	Aliens ('Osmanlis')
Hindu	c. A.D. 1175–1572	The Mughal Rāj	A.D. 1572–1707	Aliens (Mughals)
		The British Rāj	A.D. 1818–	Aliens (British)
Minoan	–c. 1750 B.C.	'The Thalassocracy of Minos'	c. 1750–1400 B.C.	No evidence
Mayan	–c. A.D. 300	'The First Empire' of the Mayas	c. A.D. 300–690	No evidence

[1] The Chaldaeans in Babylonia might be classified either as metropolitans or as marchmen.
[2] Magadha might be regarded either as part of the interior of the Indic World or else as the eastern march of the Indic World in those ages.
[3] The date of the outbreak of the first of the wars between Hungary and the 'Osmanlis' East Roman forerunners the Comneni.
[4] The date of the capture of Nanking by the T'ai'ping insurgents.

TABLE II. *Philosophies*

Civilization	Philosophy
Egyptiac	Atonism (abortive)
Andean	Viracochaism (abortive)
Sinic	Confucianism
	Moism
	Taoism
Syriac	Zervanism (abortive)
Indic	Hinayanian Buddhism
	Jainism
Western	Cartesianism
	Hegelianism[1]
Hellenic	Platonism
	Stoicism
	Epicureanism
	Pyrrhonism
Babylonic	Astrology

[1] Hegelianism confined to the field of social affairs = Marxism; Marxism transplanted from the Western World to Russia = Leninism.

TABLE III. *Higher Religions*

Civilization	Higher religion	Source of inspiration
Sumeric	Tammuz-worship	indigenous
Egyptiac	Osiris-worship	alien [?] (Sumeric [?])
Sinic	The Mahāyāna	alien (Indo-Helleno-Syriac)
	Neotaoism	indigenous but imitative (of the Mahāyāna)
Indic	Hinduism	indigenous
Syriac	Islam	indigenous
Hellenic	Christianity	alien (Syriac)
	Mithraism	alien (Syriac)
	Manichaeism	alien (Syriac)
	The Mahāyāna	alien (Indic)
	Isis-worship	alien (Egyptiac)
	Cybele-worship	alien (Hittite)
	Neoplatonism	indigenous (*ci-devant* philosophy)
Babylonic	Judaism	alien (Syriac)
	Zoroastrianism	alien (Syriac)
Western	Bahaism	alien (Iranic)
	The Ahmadīyah	alien (Iranic)
Orthodox Christian (main body)	Imāmī Shiʿism	alien (Iranic)
	Bedreddīnism	semi-alien (Iranic tincture)
Orthodox Christian (in Russia)	Sectarianism	indigenous
	Revivalist Protestantism	alien (Western)
Far Eastern (main body)	Catholicism	alien (Western)
	T'aip'ing	semi-alien (Western tincture)
Far Eastern (in Japan)	Jōdo	semi-alien (from Far Eastern, main body)
	Jōdo Shinshū	indigenous (from Jōdo)
	Nichirenism	indigenous
	Zen	semi-alien (from Far Eastern, main body)
Hindu	Kabirism and Sikhism	semi-alien (Islamic tincture)
	Brahmō Samāj	semi-alien (Western tincture)

TABLE IV. *Barbarian War-Bands*

Civilization	Universal State	Frontier	Barbarians	Poetry	Religion
Sumeric	The Empire of Sumer and Akkad	NE.	Gutaeans		
Babylonic	The Neo-Babylonian Empire	NW. NE.	Eurasian Nomads (Aryas) Kassites Hittites Eurasian Nomads (Scyths) Medes and Persians	The Sanskrit Epic	The Vedic Pantheon The Hittite Pantheon Zoroastrianism
Indic	The Mauryan Empire The Guptan Empire	NW. NW.	Sakas Huns Gurjaras	The Sanskrit Epic (recultivated)	
Sinic	The Ts'in and Han Empire	NW.	Eurasian Nomads {(Hiongnu)(To Pa)(Juan Juan)} Eurasian Nomads (Sienpi)		
Hellenic	The Roman Empire	NE. NW. N.	Insular Celts Continental Teutons Eurasian Nomads {(Sarmatians)(Huns)}	The Irish Epic The Teutonic Epic	Far Western Christianity First the Continental Teutonic Pantheon, then Arianism
Egyptiac	The Middle Empire The New Empire	NE. SE. SW. S. NE. N. NW. E.	Arabs Berbers Nubians Hyksos Achaeans Libyans Hebrews and Aramaeans	The Pre-Islamic Arabic Poetry The Homeric Epic	Islam Set-worship The Olympian Pantheon Yahweh-worship
Orthodox Christian (in Russia)	The Muscovite Empire	SE.	Eurasian Nomads {(Tatars)(Torgut Calmucks)}		Islam Lamaistic Mahayanian Buddhism
Far Eastern	The Tokugawa Shogunate	NE.	Ainu		
Western	In Europe	NW. N. NE. E. SE.	Insular Celts Scandinavians Continental Saxons Wends Lithuanians Eurasian Nomads (Magyars) Bosniaks	The Irish Epic The Icelandic Sagas The Muslim Jugoslav 'heroic' ballads	Far Western Christianity The Scandinavian Pantheon First Bogomilism, then Islam
Andean	In North America The Incaic Empire	W. E. S.	Red Indians Amazonians Araucanians		Non-violent 'Zealotism'

Civilization	Universal State	Frontier	Barbarians	Poetry	Religion
Syriac	The Achaemenian Empire	NW.	Macedonians	The Alexander Romance	
	The Arab Caliphate	NE.	Parthians	The Iranian Epic	
			Sakas		
		NW.	Franks	The French Epic	Catholicism
		SW.	East Roman 'Borderers'	The Byzantine Greek Epic	Orthodox Christianity
		SE.	Berbers		Ismāʿīlī Shīʿism
		N.	Arabs		Ismāʿīlī Shīʿism
		NE.	Eurasian Nomads {(Khazars)(Turks)}		Judaism
			Eurasian Nomads {(Mongols)(Khitan)}		{Manichaeism / Nestorianism}
Far Eastern (main body)	['Time of Troubles']	NE.	Eurasian Nomads {(Kin)(Mongols)}		
	The Manchu Empire	NE.	Eurasian Nomads (Mongols)		Lamaistic Mahayanian Buddhism
Central American	The Spanish Viceroyalty of New Spain	NW.	Eurasian Nomads (Zungar Calmucks)		
		N.	Chichimecs		
Orthodox Christian (main body)	The Ottoman Empire	NW.	Serbs	The Orthodox Christian Jugoslav 'heroic' ballads	Bektashi Sunnism
			Albanians	The Albanian 'heroic' poetry	
			Rumeliot Greeks	The Rumeliot Greek Armatole and Klephtic ballads	
		NE.	Lazes		
		SE.	Kurds		
		S.	Arabs		Najdi Wahhabism
					Kordofani Mahdism
Hindu	The Mughal Rāj	NW.	Uzbegs		
			Afghans		
	The British Rāj	N.	Afghans		
Minoan	'The Thalassocracy of Minos'	N.	Achaeans	The Homeric Epic	The Olympian Pantheon
		E.	Hebrews and Aramaeans		Yahweh-worship
Iranic	['Time of Troubles']	NE.	Uzbegs		
			Afghans		
Hittite		NW.	Gagas		
		SW.	Phrygians	The Homeric Epic	The Olympian Pantheon
		NW.	Achaeans		
			Bastarnae		
Eurasian Nomadism	The Royal Scythian Horde	E.	Sarmatians		
	The Khazar Horde	NW.	Varangians	The Russian 'heroic' ballads	Orthodox Christianity
		E.	Pechenegs		
	The Golden Horde	NW.	Cossacks		
		NE.	Kirghiz Qāzāqs	The Kirghiz Qāzāq 'heroic' ballads	

TABLE V

Civilization	*Relations*	*Time and Place of Origin*	*Challenge*	*Time of Troubles*	*Universal State*	*Universal Peace*	*Philosophies*	*Religion*	*Source of Inspiration of Religion*
1. Egyptiac	wholly unrelated	Nile River Valley; before 4000 B.C.	physical: desiccation	c. 2424–2070/60 B.C.	Middle Empire New Empire	c. 2070/60–1660 B.C. c. 1580–1175 B.C.	Atonism (abortive)	Osiris-worship Atonism	alien ?—Sumeric ?
2. Andean	wholly unrelated	Andean coast and plateau; c. beginning of Christian Era	physical: coastal desert; bleak climate on almost soilless plateau	?–c. A.D. 1430	Incaic Empire (followed by Spanish Viceroyalty of Peru)	A.D. 1430–1533	Viracochaism (abortive)		
3. Sinic	unrelated to earlier; apparented to the Far Eastern	lower valley of the Yellow River; c. 1500 B.C.	physical: marsh and floods and extremes of temperature	634–221 B.C.	Ts'in and Han Empire	221 B.C.–A.D. 172	Moism; Taoism; Confucianism	Mahāyāna Buddhism Neotaoism	alien (Indo-Helleno-Syriac) indigenous but imitative
4. Minoan	unrelated to earlier; apparented (loosely) to the Hellenic and the Syriac	Aegean Islands before 3000 B.C.	physical: the sea	?–1750 B.C.	'Thalassocracy of Minos'	c. 1750–1400 B.C.			
5. Sumeric	unrelated to earlier; ? apparented to the Babylonic and ? the Hittite	lower Tigris-Euphrates valley; before c. 3500 B.C.	physical: desiccation	c. 2677–2298 B.C.	Empire of Sumer and Akkad	c. 2298–1905 B.C.	Tammuz-worship—but there is nothing created by the Sumeric Society that can be called a new religion.		
6. Mayan	unrelated to earlier; apparented to the Yucatec and the Mexic	Central American tropical forest; before c. 500 B.C.	physical: the luxuriance of the tropical forest	?–c. A.D. 300	'First Empire' of the Mayas	c. A.D. 300–690	The Mayan, Hittite, Babylonic and Indic societies all seem, as they disintegrate, to be reverting to the ethos of primitive man in their apparent insensibility to the gulf between the abandoned sexualism of their religion and the exaggerated asceticism of their philosophy; they show an awakening to a sense of sin through the shock of seeing an ancient social structure collapse.		
7. Yucatec } fused to produce: 8. Mexic } Central American	both affiliated to the Mayan	waterless, treeless limestone shelf of Yucatan peninsula; after A.D. 629	physical: barren peninsula; social: the disintegrating Mayan Society	?–A.D. 1521	Spanish Viceroyalty of New Spain (the Aztecs were on the verge of founding a universal state when the Spaniards came)	A.D. 1521–1821			
9. Hittite	possibly loosely affiliated to the Sumeric but with a non-Sumeric religion	Cappadocia just beyond Sumeric frontiers; before 1500 B.C.	social: the disintegrating Sumeric Society	predominant in its own world by 15th century B.C.; wars with Egypt after 1352 until peace in 1278 B.C.; overwhelmed by a wave of migration c. 1200–1190 B.C.					
10. Syriac	loosely affiliated to the Minoan; apparented to the Iranic and the Arabic	Syria; before 1100 B.C.	social: the disintegrating Minoan Society	c. 937–525 B.C.	Achaemenian Empire Arab Caliphate	c. 525–332 B.C. c. A.D. 640–969	Zervanism (abortive)	Islam	indigenous indigenous
11. Babylonic	closely affiliated to the Sumeric	'Iraq; before 1500 B.C.	social: the disintegrating Sumeric Society	?–610 B.C.	Neo-Babylonic Empire	610–539 B.C.	Astrology	Judaism Zoroastrianism	alien—Syriac alien—Syriac
12. Iranic } fused to produce: 13. Arabic } Islamic	both affiliated to the Syriac and, after A.D. 1516, fused to form the Islamic Society	Anatolia, Iran, Oxus-Jaxartes; before A.D. 1300 Arabia, 'Iraq, Syria, North Africa; before A.D. 1300	social: the disintegrating Syriac Society social: the disintegrating Syriac Society						
14. Far Eastern—Main Body	affiliated to the Sinic with an offshoot in Japan	China; before A.D. 500	social: the disintegrating Sinic Society	A.D. 878–1280	Mongol Empire Manchu Empire	A.D. 1280–1351 A.D. 1644–1853		Catholicism T'aip'ing	alien—Western semi-alien—Western tincture
15. Far Eastern—Japanese Offshoot	offshoot of the main body of the Far Eastern	Japanese Archipelago; after A.D. 500	physical: new ground; social: contact with the main body	A.D. 1185–1597	Hideyoshi's dictatorship and Tokugawa Shogunate	A.D. 1597–1863		Jōdo Jōdo Shinshū Nichirenism Zen	semi-alien—from main body indigenous indigenous semi-alien—from main body
16. Indic	unrelated to earlier; apparented to the Hindu	Indus and Ganges River Valleys; c. 1500 B.C.	physical: the luxuriance of the tropical forest	?–322 B.C.	Mauryan Empire Guptan Empire	322–185 B.C. A.D. 390–c. 475	Hīnayāna Buddhism; Jainism	Hinduism	indigenous indigenous
17. Hindu	affiliated to the Indic	North India; before A.D. 800	social: the disintegrating Indic Society	c. A.D. 1175–1572	Mughal Rāj British Rāj	c. A.D. 1572–1707 c. A.D. 1818–		Kabirism; Sikhism Brahmō Samāj	semi-alien—Islamic semi-alien—Western tincture
18. Hellenic	loosely affiliated to the Minoan; apparented to the Western and to the Orthodox Christian	coasts and islands of the Aegean; before 1100 B.C.	physical: barren land and the sea; social: the disintegrating Minoan Society	431–31 B.C.	Roman Empire	31 B.C.–A.D. 378	Platonism Stoicism Epicureanism Pyrrhonism	Christianity Mithraism Manichaeism Isis-worship Mahāyāna Buddhism Cybele-worship Neoplatonism	alien—Syriac alien—Syriac alien—Syriac alien—Egyptiac alien—Indic alien—Hittite indigenous
19. Orthodox Christian—Main Body	affiliated to the Hellenic with an offshoot in Russia	Anatolia; before A.D. 700 (final rupture with the West in 11th century)	social: the disintegrating Hellenic Society	A.D. 977–1372	Ottoman Empire	A.D. 1372–1768		Imāmī Sh'ism Bedreddinism	alien—Iranic semi-alien—Iranic tincture
20. Orthodox Christian—Russian Offshoot	offshoot of the main body of the Orthodox Christian	Russia; 10th century of the Christian Era	physical: new ground; social: contact with the main body	A.D. 1075–1478	Muscovite Empire	A.D. 1478–1881		Sectarianism Revivalistic Protestantism	indigenous alien—Western
21. Western	affiliated to the Hellenic	Western Europe; before A.D. 700	physical: new ground; social: the disintegrating Hellenic Society						

The *ABORTIVE CIVILIZATIONS*: The embryos of these civilizations were rendered abortive by the strain of having to respond to a series of challenges which were excessive in their severity. The Abortive Civilizations are: the *FAR WESTERN CHRISTIAN*, the *FAR EASTERN CHRISTIAN* and the *SCANDINAVIAN*.

The *FAR WESTERN CHRISTIAN CIVILIZATION* arose in the 'Celtic Fringe', mainly in Ireland, after c. A.D. 375, as a response to the physical challenge of new ground and the double social challenge of the disintegrating Hellenic Society and the nascent Western Society. The period of segregation was from c. 450 to c. 600. The Celts moulded Christianity to fit their own barbarian social heritage; by the sixth century Ireland was definitely the centre of gravity of Christianity in the West; its originality is manifested in church organization and in literature and art. The final blows against this civilization were delivered by the Vikings in the ninth to the eleventh centuries and by the ecclesiastical authority of Rome and the political authority of England in the twelfth century.

The *FAR EASTERN CHRISTIAN CIVILIZATION* arose within the chrysalis of Nestorian Christianity in the Oxus-Jaxartes Basin and perished when this region was annexed to the Arab Empire in A.D. 737–41 after it had been politically and culturally divorced from the rest of the Syriac World for the better part of nine centuries. This embryonic civilization was the product of nine centuries of Central Asian history in which this basin had been living a life of its own with special functions resulting from its place athwart the great trade routes and its large number of Greek colonists.

The *SCANDINAVIAN CIVILIZATION* emerged within the ambit of the Hellenic External Proletariat after the break-up of the Roman Empire; the Scandinavians were isolated from Roman Christendom before the end of the sixth century by the interposition of the pagan Slavs. They began to develop their own civilization only after contact with the West had been re-established, and this civilization was eventually annihilated as a result of the conversion of the Icelanders to Christianity. The ethos of the civilization was aesthetic and it bears a remarkable resemblance to the Greek culture.

The *ARRESTED CIVILIZATIONS* include the *POLYNESIANS*, the *ESKIMOS*, the *NOMADS*, the *SPARTANS*, the *'OSMANLIS*. These were all immobilized in consequence of having attempted and achieved a *tour de force*: they were all responses to challenges on the very border-line between a degree that still affords some stimulus and a degree that brings into operation the law of diminishing returns. With the Spartans and the 'Osmanlis the superlative challenge was human, with the others it was physical. The two characteristics common to them all are caste and specialization. They all performed miracles of human will-power and ingenuity but at the price of a systematic repudiation of the characteristically human quality of versatile adaptability. They all set their feet on the path of retrogression from humanity to animality.

The *ESKIMOS*: the stimulus of economic advantage impelled them to the *tour de force* of staying at or on the sea ice during the winter and hunting seals; this demands so much of their energies that none is left over to apply to further advances. They pay the penalty of the rigid conformation of their life to the Arctic climatic cycle.

The *'OSMANLIS*: their superlative challenge was the geographical transference of a nomadic community to an alien environment where the novel problem was to exercise dominion over alien communities of human beings instead of over animals. Their *tour de force* was the Ottoman slave-household: i.e. the picking and training of human watch-dogs to keep the Pādishāh's human cattle in order. They achieved their astonishing triumphs by putting off their human nature as far as possible and assuming an animal nature instead by limiting their minds to the 'single-track' action of instinct.

The *NOMADS*: the physical challenge of the Steppe was brought on by the same desiccation that evoked the Egyptiac and Sumeric civilizations. The mastery of the Steppe demands so much of the Nomads' energies that none is left over. Nomadism is superior to agriculture in several ways: in the domestication of animals and in the development of economic techniques, in which it is comparable with industrialism rather than with agriculture. Thus nomadism demands a rigorously high standard of character and behaviour: the 'good shepherd' is the symbol of the highest Christian ideal.

The *SPARTANS*: the physical challenge of over-population confronted the whole Hellenic World in the eighth century B.C., and the Spartans met it by the great *tour de force* of forcing all their energies into a rigid and 'single-track' military training with—as in the Ottoman system—a total disregard for human nature. There are many striking similarities between the Spartan and the Ottoman systems, and these are attributable to a natural conformity between the responses which were made to a virtually identic challenge by two different communities acting independently of and unknown to one another.

The *POLYNESIANS*: to the physical challenge of the sea they responded with the *tour de force* of Oceanic voyaging; their skill was to perform these stupendous voyages in frail open canoes and their penalty has been to remain in exact equilibrium with the Pacific—they were just able to cross its vast open spaces, but never with any margin of security or ease, until at last the intolerable tension has found its own relief by going slack. The megalithic statues on Easter Island are witnesses to the great past of their makers, for the art of sculpture must have been brought there by the pioneers and lost by their descendants, as the latter lost also the art of navigation.

ARGUMENT

I. INTRODUCTION

I. THE UNIT OF HISTORICAL STUDY

THE intelligible units of historical study are not nations or periods but 'societies'. An examination of English history, chapter by chapter, shows that it is not intelligible as a thing-in-itself but only as a part of a larger whole. This whole contains parts (e.g. England, France, the Netherlands) that are subject to identical stimuli or challenges but react to them in different ways. An example from Hellenic history is introduced to illustrate this. The 'whole', or 'society', to which England belongs is identified as Western Christendom; its extension in space at different dates is measured, and its origins in time. It is found to be older, but only slightly older, than the articulation of its parts. Exploration of its beginnings reveals the existence of another society which is now dead, namely the Graeco-Roman or Hellenic Society, to which ours is 'affiliated'. It is also obvious that there are a number of other living societies—the Orthodox Christian, the Islamic, the Hindu and the Far Eastern societies—and also certain 'fossilized' relics of, at this stage, unidentified societies such as the Jews and the Parsees.

II. THE COMPARATIVE STUDY OF CIVILIZATIONS

The purpose of this chapter is to identify, define and name all the societies—or, rather, civilizations, for there are also primitive or non-'civilized' societies—which have come into existence so far. The first method of search to employ is to take the existing civilizations already identified, examine their origins and see if we can find civilizations now extinct to which these are affiliated as Western Christendom has been found to be affiliated to the Hellenic Civilization. The marks of this relationship are (a) a universal state (e.g. the Roman Empire), itself the outcome of a time of troubles, followed by (b) an interregnum, in which appear (c) a Church and (d) a Völkerwanderung of barbarians in an heroic age. The Church and the Völkerwanderung are the products, respectively, of the internal and external 'proletariats' of a dying civilization. Employing these clues we find that:

The Orthodox Christian Society is, like our own Western Society, affiliated to the Hellenic Society.

Tracing the Islamic Society back to its origins we find that it is itself a fusion of two originally distinct societies, the Iranic and the Arabic. Tracing these back to their origin we find, behind a thousand years of 'Hellenic intrusion', an extinct society, to be called the Syriac Society.

Behind the Hindu Society we find an Indic Society.

Behind the Far Eastern Society, we find a Sinic Society.

The 'fossils' are found to be survivals from one or other of the extinct societies already identified.

Behind the Hellenic Society we find the Minoan Society, but we observe that the Hellenic Society, unlike the other affiliated societies so far identified, did not take over a religion discovered by the internal proletariat of its predecessor. It might therefore be regarded as being not strictly affiliated to it.

Behind the Indic Society we find a Sumeric Society.

As offspring of the Sumeric Society (in addition to the Indic Society) we find two more societies, a Hittite and a Babylonic.

The Egyptiac Society had no predecessor and no successor.

In the New World we can identify four societies: the Andean, the Yucatec, the Mexic and the Mayan.

Thus we have in all nineteen specimens of 'civilizations'; and, if we divide the Orthodox Christian Society into Orthodox-Byzantine (in Anatolia and the Balkans) and Orthodox-Russian, and the Far Eastern into Chinese and Japanese-Korean, we have twenty-one.

III. THE COMPARABILITY OF SOCIETIES

(1) *Civilizations and Primitive Societies*

Civilizations have at any rate one point in common, that they are a separate class from primitive societies. These latter are very much more numerous but also very much smaller individually.

(2) *The Misconception of 'the Unity of Civilization'*

The erroneous idea that there is only one civilization, namely our own, is examined and dismissed; also the 'Diffusionist' theory that all civilization had its origin in Egypt.

(3) *The Case for the Comparability of Civilizations*

Civilizations are, relatively speaking, a very recent phenomenon in human history, the earliest of them having originated no more than six thousand years ago. It is proposed to treat them as 'philosophically contemporaneous' members of a single 'species'. The half-truth 'History does not repeat itself' is exposed as constituting no valid objection to the procedure proposed.

(4) *History, Science and Fiction*

These are 'three different methods of viewing and presenting the objects of our thought and, among them, the phenomena of human life'. The differences between these three techniques are examined and the uses of Science and Fiction in the presentation of the theme of History are discussed.

II. THE GENESES OF CIVILIZATIONS

IV. THE PROBLEM AND HOW NOT TO SOLVE IT

(1) *The Problem Stated*

Of our twenty-one 'civilized' societies fifteen are affiliated to previous civilizations but six have emerged direct from primitive life. Primitive societies existing to-day are static, but it is clear that they must originally have been dynamically progressive. Social life is older than the human race itself; it is found among insects and animals, and it must have been under the aegis of primitive societies that sub-man rose to the level of man—a greater advance than any civilization has as yet achieved. However, primitive societies as we know them are static. The problem is: why and how was this primitive 'cake of custom' broken?

(2) *Race*

The factor we are looking for must be either some special quality in the human beings who started civilizations or some special features of their environment at the time or some interaction between the two. The first of these views, namely that there is some innately superior race, e.g. the Nordic Race, in the world, which is responsible for the creation of civilizations, is examined and rejected.

(3) *Environment*

The view that certain environments, presenting easy and comfortable conditions of life, provide the key to an explanation of the origin of civilizations is examined and rejected.

V. CHALLENGE AND RESPONSE

(1) *The Mythological Clue*

The fallacy in the two views already examined and rejected is that they apply the procedure of material sciences, biology and geology, to a problem that is really spiritual. A survey of the great myths in which the wisdom of the human race is enshrined suggests the possibility that man achieves civilization, not as a result of superior biological endowment or geographical environment, but as a response to a challenge in a situation of special difficulty which rouses him to make a hitherto unprecedented effort.

(2) *The Myth applied to the Problem*

Before the dawn of civilization the Afrasian Steppe (the Sahara and the Arabian Desert) was a well-watered grassland. The prolonged and progressive desiccation of this grassland presented its inhabitants with a challenge to which they responded in various ways. Some stood their ground and changed their habits, thus evolving the Nomadic manner of life. Others shifted their ground southwards, following the retreating grassland to the tropics, and thus preserved their primitive way of life—which they are still living to-day. Others entered the marshes and jungles of the Nile Delta and—faced with the challenge it presented—set to work to drain it, and they evolved the Egyptiac Civilization.

The Sumeric Civilization originated in the same way and from the same causes in the Tigris-Euphrates Delta.

The Sinic Civilization originated in the Yellow River Valley. The nature of the challenge which started it is unknown but it is clear that the conditions were severe rather than easy.

The Mayan Civilization originated from the challenge of a tropical forest; the Andean from that of a bleak plateau.

The Minoan Civilization originated from the challenge of the sea. Its founders were refugees from the desiccating coasts of Africa who took to the water and settled in Crete and other Aegean islands. They did not, in the first instance, come from the nearer mainlands of Asia or Europe.

In the cases of the affiliated civilizations the challenge that brought them into existence must have come primarily not from geographical factors but from their human environment, i.e. from the 'dominant minorities' of the societies to which they are affiliated. A dominant minority is, by definition, a ruling class that has ceased to lead and has become oppressive. To this challenge the internal and external proletariats of the failing civilization respond by seceding from it and thereby laying the foundations of a new civilization.

VI. THE VIRTUES OF ADVERSITY

The explanation of the geneses of civilizations given in the last chapter rests on the hypothesis that it is difficult rather than easy conditions that produce these achievements. This hypothesis is now brought nearer to proof by illustrations taken from localities where civilization once flourished but subsequently failed and where the land has reverted to its original condition.

What was once the scene of the Mayan Civilization is now again tropical forest.

The Indic Civilization in Ceylon flourished in the rainless half of the island. This is now entirely barren, though the ruins of the Indic irrigation system remain as evidence of the civilization that once flourished here.

The ruins of Petra and Palmyra stand on small oases in the Arabian Desert.

Easter Island, one of the remotest spots in the Pacific, is proved by its statues to have been once a centre of the Polynesian Civilization.

New England, whose European colonists have played a predominant part in the history of North America, is one of the bleakest and most barren parts of that continent.

The Latin townships of the Roman Campagna, till recently a malarial wilderness, made a great contribution to the rise of the Roman Power. Contrast the favourable situation and poor performance of Capua. Illustrations are also drawn from Herodotus, the Odyssey and the Book of Exodus.

The natives of Nyasaland, where life is easy, remained primitive savages down to the advent of invaders from a distant and inclement Europe.

VII. THE CHALLENGE OF THE ENVIRONMENT

(1) *The Stimulus of Hard Countries*

A series of pairs of contiguous environments is adduced. In each case the former is the 'harder' country and has also had the more brilliant record as an originator of one form or other of civilization: the Yellow River Valley and the Yangtse Valley; Attica and Boeotia; Byzantium and Calchedon; Israel, Phoenicia, Philistia; Brandenburg and the Rhineland; Scotland and England; the various groups of European colonists in North America.

(2) *The Stimulus of New Ground*

We find that 'virgin soil' produces more vigorous responses than land which has already been broken in and thus rendered 'easier' by previous 'civilized' occupants. Thus, if we take each of the affiliated civilizations, we find that it has produced its most striking early manifestations in places outside the area occupied by the 'parent' civilization. The superiority of the response

evoked by new ground is most strikingly illustrated when the
new ground has to be reached by a sea-passage. Reasons for this
fact are given, and also for the phenomenon that the epic develops
in homelands and drama in overseas settlements.

(3) *The Stimulus of Blows*

Various examples from Hellenic and Western history are given
to illustrate the point that a sudden crushing defeat is apt to stimulate the defeated party to set its house in order and prepare to
make a victorious response.

(4) *The Stimulus of Pressures*

Various examples show that peoples occupying frontier positions,
exposed to constant attack, achieve a more brilliant development
than their neighbours in more sheltered positions. Thus the
'Osmanlis, thrust up against the frontier of the East Roman Empire,
fared better than the Qaramanlis to the east of them; Austria had
a more brilliant career than Bavaria thanks to being exposed to
the prolonged assault of the Ottoman Turks. The situation and
fortunes of the various communities in Britain between the fall of
Rome and the Norman Conquest is examined from this point of
view.

(5) *The Stimulus of Penalizations*

Certain classes and races have suffered for centuries from various
forms of penalization imposed upon them by other classes or races
who have had the mastery over them. Penalized classes or races
generally respond to this challenge of being excluded from certain
opportunities and privileges by putting forth exceptional energy
and showing exceptional capacity in such directions as are left
open to them—much as the blind develop exceptional sensitiveness
of hearing. Slavery is perhaps the heaviest of penalizations, but out
of the hordes of slaves imported into Italy from the Eastern
Mediterranean during the last two centuries B.C. arose a 'freedmen'
class which proved alarmingly powerful. From this slave world,
too, came the new religions of the internal proletariat, among them
Christianity.

The fortunes of various groups of conquered Christian peoples
under 'Osmanli rule are examined from the same standpoint—
particularly the case of the Phanariots. This example and that
of the Jews are used to prove that so-called racial characteristics
are not really racial at all but are due to the historical experiences
of the communities in question.

(1) *Enough and Too Much*

Can we say simply: the sterner the challenge the finer the response? Or is there such a thing as a challenge too severe to evoke a response? Certainly some challenges which have defeated one or more parties that have encountered them have ultimately provoked a victorious response. For example, the challenge of expanding Hellenism proved too much for the Celts but was victoriously answered by their successors the Teutons. The 'Hellenic intrusion' into the Syriac World evoked a series of unsuccessful Syriac responses—the Zoroastrian, the Jewish (Maccabaean), the Nestorian and the Monophysite—but the fifth response, that of Islam, was successful.

(2) *Comparisons in Three Terms*

None the less, it can be proved that challenges can be too severe: i.e. the *maximum* challenge will not always produce the *optimum* response. The Viking emigrants from Norway responded splendidly to the severe challenge of Iceland but collapsed before the severer challenge of Greenland. Massachusetts presented European colonists with a severer challenge than 'Dixie' and evoked a better response, but Labrador, presenting a severer challenge still, proved too much for them. Other examples follow: e.g. the stimulus of blows can be too severe, especially if prolonged, as in the effect of the Hannibalic War on Italy. The Chinese are stimulated by the social challenge involved in emigrating to Malaya but are defeated by the severer social challenge of a white man's country, e.g. California. Finally, varying degrees of challenge presented by civilizations to neighbouring barbarians are reviewed.

(3) *Two Abortive Civilizations*

This section is a continuation of the argument of the last example in the preceding section. Two groups of barbarians on the frontiers of Western Christendom in the first chapter of its history were so stimulated that they began to evolve rival civilizations of their own which were, however, nipped in the bud, namely the Far Western Celtic Christians (in Ireland and Iona) and the Scandinavian Vikings. These two cases are considered and the consequences that might have ensued if these rivals had not been swallowed and absorbed by the Christian civilization radiating from Rome and the Rhineland.

(4) *The Impact of Islam on the Christendoms*

On Western Christendom the effect of this impact was wholly good, and Western culture in the Middle Ages owed much to Muslim Iberia. On Byzantine Christendom the impact was excessive and evoked a crushing re-erection of the Roman Empire under Leo the Syrian. The case of Abyssinia, a Christian 'fossil' in a fastness encircled by the Muslim World, is also noticed.

III. THE GROWTHS OF CIVILIZATIONS

IX. THE ARRESTED CIVILIZATIONS

(1) *Polynesians, Eskimos and Nomads*

It might seem that, once a civilization had been brought into existence, its growth would be a matter of course; but this is not so, as is proved by the record of certain civilizations which have achieved existence but then failed to grow. The fate of these arrested civilizations has been to encounter a challenge on the border-line between the degree of severity which evokes a successful response and the greater degree which entails defeat. Three cases present themselves in which a challenge of this kind has come from the physical environment. The result in each case has been a *tour de force* on the part of the respondents which has so engrossed the whole of their energies that they have had none left over for further development.

The Polynesians achieved the *tour de force* of inter-insular voyaging between Pacific islands. It eventually defeated them and they relapsed into primitive life on their several now isolated islands.

The Eskimos achieved an extraordinarily skilled and specialized annual cycle adapted to life on the shores of the Arctic.

The Nomads achieved a similar annual cycle as herdsmen on the semi-desert Steppe. The ocean with its islands and the desert with its oases have many points in common. The evolution of Nomadism during periods of desiccation is analysed. It is noted that hunters become agriculturists before taking the further step of becoming Nomads. Cain and Abel are types of the agriculturist and the Nomad. Nomad incursions into the domains of civilizations are always due either to increased desiccation 'pushing' the Nomad off the Steppe or to the breakdown of a civilization creating a vacuum which 'pulls' the Nomad in as a participant in a Völkerwanderung.

(2) *The 'Osmanlis*

The challenge to which the Ottoman system was a response was the transference of a Nomad community to an environment in which they had to rule sedentary communities. They solved their problem by treating their new subjects as human flocks and herds, evolving human equivalents of the sheep-dogs of the Nomad in the form of a slave 'household' of administrators and soldiers. Other examples of similar Nomad empires are mentioned, the Mamlūks for instance; but the 'Osmanli system surpassed all others in efficiency and duration. It suffered, however, like Nomadism itself, from a fatal rigidity.

(3) *The Spartans*

The Spartan response to the challenge of over-population in the Hellenic World was to evolve a *tour de force* which in many respects resembles that of the 'Osmanlis, with the difference that in the Spartan case the military caste was the Spartan aristocracy itself; but they too were 'slaves', enslaved to the duty they had imposed upon themselves of holding down permanently a population of fellow-Greeks.

(4) *General Characteristics*

Eskimos and Nomads, 'Osmanlis and Spartans have two features in common: specialization and caste. (In the former pair, dogs, reindeer, horses and cattle supply the place of the human slave castes of the 'Osmanlis.) In all these societies the human beings are degraded by specialization as boat-men, horse-men or warrior-men to a subhuman level in comparison with the all-round men, the ideal of Pericles' funeral speech, who alone are capable of achieving growth in civilization. These arrested societies resemble the societies of bees and ants, which have been stationary since before the dawn of human life on Earth. They also resemble the societies portrayed in 'Utopias'. A discussion of 'Utopias' follows, in which it is shown that 'Utopias' are generally the products of civilizations in decline and are attempts, in so far as they have a practical programme, to arrest the decline by pegging the society at its actual level at the moment.

X. THE NATURE OF THE GROWTHS OF CIVILIZATIONS

(1) *Two False Trails*

Growth occurs when the response to a particular challenge is not only successful in itself but provokes a further challenge which again meets with a successful response. How are we to measure such growth? Is it to be measured by an increasing control over the society's external environment? Such an increasing control can be of two kinds: increasing control over the human environment, which normally takes the form of conquest of neighbouring peoples, and increasing control over the physical environment, which is expressed in improvements in material technique. Examples are then adduced to show that neither of these phenomena—neither political and military expansion nor improvement in technique—is a satisfactory criterion of real growth. Military expansion is normally a result of militarism, which is itself a symptom of decline. Improvements in technique, agricultural or industrial, show little or no correlation with real growth. In fact technique may well be improving at a time when real civilization is declining, and vice versa.

(2) *Progress towards Self-determination*

Real progress is found to consist in a process defined as 'etherialization', an overcoming of material obstacles which releases the energies of the society to make responses to challenges which henceforth are internal rather than external, spiritual rather than material. The nature of this etherialization is illustrated by examples from Hellenic and modern Western history.

XI. AN ANALYSIS OF GROWTH

(1) *Society and the Individual*

Two traditional views are current as to the relation of society to the individual: one represents a society as simply an aggregate of 'atomic' individuals, and the other regards the society as an organism and the individuals as parts of it, inconceivable except as members or 'cells' of the society to which they belong. Both these views are shown to be unsatisfactory, and the true view is that a society is a system of relations between individuals. Human beings cannot be themselves without interacting with their fellows, and a society is a field of action common to a number of human beings. But the 'source of action' is in the individuals. All growth originates with creative individuals or small minorities of individuals, and their task is twofold: first the achievement of their inspiration or discovery, whatever it may be, and secondly the conversion of the society to which they belong to this new way of life. This conversion could, theoretically, come about in one or other of two ways: either by the mass undergoing the actual experience which has transformed the creative individuals, or by their imitation of its externals—in other words, by *mimesis*. In practice the latter is the only alternative open in the case of all but a small minority of mankind. Mimesis is 'a short cut', but it is a route by which the rank and file, *en masse*, can follow the leaders.

(2) *Withdrawal and Return: Individuals*

The action of the creative individual may be described as a twofold motion of withdrawal-and-return: withdrawal for the purpose of his personal enlightenment, return for the task of enlightening his fellow men. This is illustrated from Plato's parable of the Cave, from Saint Paul's analogy of the seed, from the Gospel story and from elsewhere. It is then shown in practical action in the lives of great pioneers: Saint Paul, Saint Benedict, Saint Gregory the Great, the Buddha, Muhammad, Machiavelli, Dante.

(3) *Withdrawal and Return: Creative Minorities*

Withdrawal followed by Return is also characteristic of the sub-societies which form the constituent parts of 'societies' in the proper sense. The period in which such sub-societies make their contributions to the growth of the societies to which they belong is preceded by a period in which they are markedly withdrawn from the general life of their society: for example, Athens in the second chapter of the growth of the Hellenic Society; Italy in the second chapter of the growth of the Western Society; and England in its third chapter. The possibility that Russia may be going to play a similar role in the fourth chapter is considered.

XII. DIFFERENTIATION THROUGH GROWTH

Growth as described in the foregoing chapter clearly involves differentiation between the parts of a growing society. At each stage some parts will make an original and successful response; some will succeed in following their lead by mimesis; some will fail to achieve either originality or mimesis, and succumb. There will also be increasing differentiation between the histories of different societies, and it is obvious that different societies have different predominating characteristics, some excelling in art, some in religion, others in industrial inventiveness. But the fundamental similarity in the purposes of all civilizations is not to be forgotten. Each seed has its own destiny, but the seeds are all of one kind, sown by the same Sower, in the hope of the same harvest.

IV. THE BREAKDOWNS OF CIVILIZATIONS

XIII. THE NATURE OF THE PROBLEM

Of the twenty-six civilizations we have identified (including the arrested civilizations in the list) sixteen are dead and nine of the remaining ten—all, in fact, except our own—are shown to have already broken down. The nature of a breakdown can be summed up in three points: a failure of creative power in the creative minority, which henceforth becomes a merely 'dominant' minority; an answering withdrawal of allegiance and mimesis on the part of the majority; a consequent loss of social unity in the society as a whole. Our next task is to discover the causes of such breakdowns.

XIV. DETERMINISTIC SOLUTIONS

Some schools of thought have maintained that the breakdowns of civilizations are due to factors outside human control.

(i) During the decline of the Hellenic Civilization writers, both pagan and Christian, held that the decay of their society was due to 'cosmic senescence'; but modern physicists have relegated cosmic senescence to an unbelievably distant future, which means that it can have had no effect on any past or present civilizations.

(ii) Spengler and others have maintained that societies are organisms, with natural transitions from youth and maturity to decay, like other living creatures; but a society is not an organism.

(iii) Others have held that there is something inevitably dysgenic in the influence of civilization on human nature, and that after a period of civilization the race can only be restored by an infusion of barbaric 'new blood'. This view is examined and dismissed.

(iv) There remains the cyclic theory of history, as found in Plato's *Timaeus*, Virgil's Fourth Eclogue and elsewhere. This probably originated in Chaldaean discoveries concerning our own solar system, and the vastly wider vision of modern astronomy has deprived the theory of its astronomical basis. There is no evidence for the theory and much against it.

XV. LOSS OF COMMAND OVER THE ENVIRONMENT

The argument of this chapter is the converse of that in chapter X (1), where it was shown that an increase in control over the physical environment, as measured by improvement in technique, and an increase in control over the human environment, as measured by geographical expansion or military conquest, are not the criteria or causes of growth. Here it is shown that the decline of technique and the geographical contraction caused by military aggression from outside are not the criteria or causes of break-downs.

(1) *The Physical Environment*

Several examples are adduced to show that the decay of technical achievement has been a result, not a cause, of breakdown. The abandonment of the Roman roads and of the Mesopotamian irrigation system was a result, not a cause, of the breakdowns of the civilizations that had formerly maintained them. The oncoming of malaria which is said to have caused breakdowns of civilizations is shown to have been a result of the breakdowns.

(2) *The Human Environment*

Gibbon's thesis that 'the Decline and Fall of the Roman Empire' was due to 'Barbarism and Religion' (i.e. Christianity) is examined and rejected. These manifestations of the external and internal proletariats of the Hellenic Society were consequences of a break-down of the Hellenic Society that had already taken place. Gibbon does not begin his story far enough back; he mistakes the Antonine period for a 'golden age' when it was really an 'Indian summer'. Various examples of successful aggression against civilizations are passed in review and it is shown that in every case the successful aggression occurred *after* the breakdown.

(3) *A Negative Verdict*

Aggression against a society still in process of growth normally stimulates it to greater effort. Even when a society is already in decline, aggression against it may galvanize it into activity and give it a further lease of life. (The editor adds a note on the meaning of 'breakdown' as a technical term used in this Study.)

XVI. FAILURE OF SELF-DETERMINATION

(1) *The Mechanicalness of Mimesis*

The only way in which the uncreative majority can follow the leadership of the creative leaders is by mimesis, which is a species of 'drill', a mechanical and superficial imitation of the great and inspired originals. This unavoidable 'short cut' to progress entails obvious dangers. The leaders may become infected with the mechanicalness of their followers, and the result will be an arrested civilization; or they may impatiently exchange the Pied Piper's pipe of persuasion for the whip of compulsion. In that case the creative minority will become a 'dominant' minority and the 'disciples' will become a reluctant and alienated 'proletariat'.

When this happens the society enters on the road to disintegration. The society loses capacity for self-determination. The following sections illustrate ways in which this comes about.

(2) *New Wine in Old Bottles*

Ideally each new social force released by creative minorities should beget new institutions through which it can work. Actually it works more often than not through old institutions designed for other purposes. But the old institutions often prove unsuitable and intractable. One of two results may follow: either the break-up of the institutions (a revolution) or their survival and the consequent perversion of the new forces working through them (an 'enormity'). A revolution may be defined as a delayed and consequently explosive act of mimesis; an enormity as a frustration of mimesis. If the adjustment of institutions to forces is har-monious, growth will continue; if it results in a revolution, growth becomes hazardous; if it results in an enormity, breakdown may be diagnosed. Then follow a series of examples of the impact of new forces upon old institutions, the first group being impacts of the two great new forces at work in the modern Western Society:

the impact of Industrialism on slavery, e.g. in the Southern States of the U.S.A.;

the impact of Democracy and Industrialism on war, i.e. the intensification of warfare since the French Revolution;

the impact of Democracy and Industrialism on the parochial state, as shown in the hypertrophy of nationalism and the failure of the free trade movement;

the impact of Industrialism on private property, as illustrated by the rise of Capitalism and Communism;

the impact of Democracy on education, as illustrated by the rise of the Yellow Press and of Fascist dictatorships;

the impact of Italian efficiency on Transalpine governments, as illustrated (except in England) by the emergence of despotic monarchies;

the impact of the Solonian revolution on the Hellenic city-states, as illustrated by the phenomena of *tyrannis, stasis* and *hegemony*;

the impact of Parochialism on the Western Christian Church, as illustrated by the Protestant Revolution, the 'Divine Right of Kings' and the eclipse of Christianity by patriotism;

the impact of the Sense of Unity on Religion, as illustrated by the rise of bigotry and persecution;

the impact of Religion on Caste, as shown in the Hindu Civilization;

the impact of Civilization on the Division of Labour, showing itself as esotericism in the leaders (who become ἰδιῶται) and lop-sidedness in the followers (who become βάναυσοι). The latter defect is illustrated from cases of penalized minorities, e.g. the Jews, and from aberrations of modern athleticism; the impact of Civilization on Mimesis, which is directed no longer, as in primitive societies, towards the traditions of the tribe, but towards pioneers. Too often the pioneers selected for imitation are not creative leaders but commercial exploiters or political demagogues.

(3) *The Nemesis of Creativity: Idolization of an Ephemeral Self*

History shows that the group which successfully responds to one challenge is rarely the successful respondent to the next. Various examples are given, and it is shown that this phenomenon corresponds with certain fundamental postulates of both Greek and Hebrew thought. Those who have succeeded once are apt, on the next occasion, to be found 'resting on their oars'. The Jews, having responded to the challenges of the Old Testament, are worsted by the challenge of the New. The Athens of Pericles dwindles into the Athens of Saint Paul. In the Italian *Risorgimento* the centres which have responded in the Renaissance prove ineffective, and the lead is taken by Piedmont, which has had no part in previous Italian glories. South Carolina and Virginia, leading states of the U.S.A. in the first and second quarters of the nineteenth century, have failed to make a recovery from the Civil War comparable with that of the previously undistinguished North Carolina.

(4) *The Nemesis of Creativity: Idolization of an Ephemeral Institution*

Idolization of the city-state proved, in the later stages of Hellenic history, a snare into which the Greeks fell but not the Romans. A 'ghost' of the Roman Empire caused the breakdown of the Orthodox Christian Society. Illustrations are also given of the hampering effects of the idolization of kings, parliaments and ruling castes, whether bureaucracies or priesthoods.

(5) *The Nemesis of Creativity: Idolization of an Ephemeral Technique*

Illustrations from biological evolution show that perfect 'technique' or perfect adaptation to an environment often proves an evolutionary 'cul de sac', and that the less specialized and more 'tentative' organisms prove their survival power. The amphibians are contrasted favourably with the fishes, and the rat-like ancestors of man with their contemporaries, the giant reptiles. In the industrial sphere the success of a particular community in the first stages of a new technique, e.g. in the invention of the paddle-steamer, makes that community slower than others to adopt the more efficient screw-propeller. A brief review of the history of the art of war from David and Goliath to the present day shows that, at each stage, the inventors and beneficiaries of one innovation proceed to rest on their oars and allow the next innovation to be made by their enemies.

(6) *The Suicidalness of Militarism*

The three previous sections have presented illustrations of 'resting on one's oars', which is the passive way of succumbing to the nemesis of creativity. We now pass on to the active form of aberration, summarized in the Greek formula κόρος, ὕβρις, ἄτη (surfeit, outrageous behaviour and destruction). Militarism is an obvious example. The reason why the Assyrians brought ruin on themselves was not because, like the victors reviewed at the end of the previous chapter, they allowed their armour to 'rust'. From a military standpoint they were continuously and progressively efficient. Their ruin came because their aggressiveness exhausted them—besides rendering them intolerable to their neighbours. The Assyrians are an example of a military frontier province turning its arms against the interior provinces of its society. The similar cases of the Austrasian Franks and Timur Lenk are also examined, and other examples are cited.

(7) *The Intoxication of Victory*

A theme similar to that of the preceding paragraph is illustrated from a non-military sphere by the example of the Hildebrandine Papacy, an institution which failed after raising itself and Christendom from the depths to the heights. It failed because, intoxicated by its own success, it was tempted to make illegitimate use of political weapons in pursuit of inordinate aims. The controversy over Investiture is examined from this standpoint.

V. THE DISINTEGRATIONS OF CIVILIZATIONS

XVII. THE NATURE OF DISINTEGRATION

(1) *A General Survey*

Is disintegration a necessary and invariable consequence of breakdown? Egyptiac and Far Eastern history show that there is an alternative, namely petrifaction, which was also nearly the fate of the Hellenic Civilization and may be the fate of our own. The outstanding criterion of disintegration is the schism of the body social into three fractions: dominant minority, internal proletariat and external proletariat. What has already been said about these fractions is recapitulated, and the plan of the following chapters is indicated.

(2) Schism and Palingenesia

The apocalyptic philosophy of Karl Marx proclaims that the class war will be followed, after the Dictatorship of the Proletariat, by a new order of society. Apart from Marx's particular application of the idea, this is what actually happens when a society falls into the tripartite schism already noticed. Each of the fractions achieves a characteristic work of creation: the dominant minority a universal state, the internal proletariat a universal church, and the external proletariat barbarian war-bands.

XVIII. SCHISM IN THE BODY SOCIAL

(1) Dominant Minorities

Though militarists and exploiters are conspicuous among the characteristic types in dominant minorities, there are also nobler types: the legists and administrators who maintain the universal states, and the philosophic inquirers who endow societies in decline with their characteristic philosophies, e.g. the long chain of Hellenic philosophers from Socrates to Plotinus. Examples are cited from various other civilizations.

(2) Internal Proletariats

The history of the Hellenic Society shows an internal proletariat recruited from three sources: citizens of the Hellenic states disinherited and ruined by political or economic upheavals; conquered peoples; victims of the slave-trade. All alike are proletarians in feeling themselves 'in' but not 'of' the society. Their first reactions are violent, but these are followed by 'gentle' reactions culminating in the discovery of 'higher religions' such as Christianity. This religion, like Mithraism and its other rivals in the Hellenic world, originated in one of the other 'civilized' societies conquered by Hellenic arms. The internal proletariats of other societies are examined and similar phenomena observed: e.g. the origins of Judaism and Zoroastrianism in the internal proletariat of the Babylonic Society were similar to those of Christianity and Mithraism in the Hellenic Society, though, for reasons given, their later development was different. The transformation of the primitive

Buddhist philosophy into the Mahāyāna provided a 'higher religion' for the Sinic internal proletariat.

(3) *The Internal Proletariat of the Western World*

Abundant evidence can be adduced of the existence of an internal proletariat here—among other things, the existence of an 'intelligentsia' recruited from the proletariat as an agent of the dominant minority. The characteristics of an intelligentsia are discussed. The internal proletariat of the modern Western Society has, however, shown itself markedly unfertile in the production of new 'higher religions', and it is suggested that this is due to the continued vitality of the Christian Church from which Western Christendom was born.

(4) *External Proletariats*

So long as a civilization is growing, its cultural influence radiates into and permeates its primitive neighbours to an indefinite distance. They become a part of the 'uncreative majority' which follows the creative minority's lead. But when a civilization has broken down the charm ceases to act, the barbarians become hostile and a military frontier establishes itself which may be pushed far afield but ultimately becomes stationary. When this stage has been reached, time works on the side of the barbarians. These facts are illustrated from Hellenic history. Violent and gentle responses by the external proletariat are pointed out. The pressure of a hostile civilization transforms primitive fertility religions of the external proletariat into religions of the Olympian 'divine war-band' type. The characteristic product of triumphant external proletariats is epic poetry.

(5) *External Proletariats of the Western World*

Their history is reviewed and violent and gentle responses of the external proletariats are illustrated. Owing to the overwhelming material efficiency of the modern Western Society, barbarism of the historic type has almost disappeared. In two of its remaining strongholds, Afghanistan and Sa'udi Arabia, native rulers are protecting themselves by adopting imitations of Western culture. However, a new and more atrocious barbarism has become rampant in the ancient centres of Western Christendom itself.

(6) *Alien and Indigenous Inspirations*

Dominant minorities and external proletariats are handicapped if they have an alien inspiration. For example, universal states founded by alien dominant minorities (such as British India) are less successful in making themselves acceptable than indigenous universal states like the Roman Empire. Barbarian war-bands provoke much more stubborn and passionate opposition if, like the Hyksos in Egypt and the Mongols in China, their barbarism is tinged by the influence of an alien civilization. On the other hand the 'higher religions' produced by internal proletariats generally owe their attractiveness to an alien inspiration. Nearly all the 'higher religions' illustrate this fact.

The fact that the history of a 'higher religion' cannot be understood unless two civilizations are taken into account—the civilization from which it has derived its inspiration and the civilization in which it has taken root—shows that the assumption on which this Study has hitherto been based—the assumption that civilizations, taken in isolation, are 'intelligible fields of study'—begins at this point to break down.

XIX. SCHISM IN THE SOUL

(1) *Alternative Ways of Behaviour, Feeling and Life*

When a society begins to disintegrate, the various ways of behaviour, feeling and life characteristic of individuals during the growth stage are replaced by alternative substitutes, one (the former in each pair) passive, the other (the latter) active

Abandon and self-control are alternative substitutes for creativity; truancy and martyrdom for the discipleship of mimesis.

The sense of drift and the sense of sin are alternative substitutes for the *élan* which accompanies growth; the sense of promiscuity and the sense of unity for the 'sense of style' which is the subjective counterpart of the objective process of differentiation which accompanies growth.

On the plane of life there are two pairs of alternative variations upon the movement towards a transfer of the field of action from the macrocosm to the microcosm which underlies the process previously described as etherialization. The first pair of alternatives—archaism and futurism—fail to achieve this transfer and breed violence. The second pair—detachment and transfiguration—succeed in making the transfer and are characterized by gentleness. Archaism is an attempt to 'put back the clock', futurism an attempt at a short cut to an impossible millennium on Earth. Detachment, which is a spiritualization of archaism, is a withdrawal into the fortress of the soul, an abandonment of 'the world'. Transfiguration, which is a spiritualization of futurism, is the action of the soul which produces the 'higher religions'. Examples of all four ways of life and of their relations to each other are given. Finally it is shown that some of these ways of feeling and life are primarily characteristic of souls in dominant minorities, others of souls in proletariats.

(2) '*Abandon*' *and Self-control* are defined, with examples.

(3) *Truancy and Martyrdom* are defined, with examples.

(4) *The Sense of Drift and the Sense of Sin.*

The sense of drift is due to a feeling that the whole world is ruled by Chance—or Necessity, which is shown to be the same thing. The wide range of the belief is illustrated. Certain predestinarian religions, e.g. Calvinism, are productive of remarkable energy and confidence, and the cause of this, at first sight, curious fact is considered.

Whereas the Sense of Drift normally acts as an opiate, the Sense of Sin should be a stimulus. The doctrines of *Karma* and 'Original Sin' (which combine the ideas of sin and determinism) are discussed. The Hebrew Prophets furnish the classic case of the recognition of sin as being the true, though not the obvious, cause of national misfortunes. The teaching of the Prophets was taken over by the Christian Church and was thus introduced to a Hellenic World which for many centuries had been unconsciously preparing itself to receive it. The Western Society, though inheriting the Christian tradition, seems to have discarded the sense of sin, which is an essential part of that tradition.

(5) *The Sense of Promiscuity*

This is a passive substitute for the sense of style characteristic of civilizations in course of growth. It manifests itself in various ways. (*a*) *Vulgarity and Barbarism in Manners.* The dominant minority shows itself prone to 'proletarianization', adopting the vulgarities of the internal and the barbarisms of the external proletariat, until, in the final stage of dissolution, its way of life has become indistinguishable from theirs. (*b*) *Vulgarity and Barbarism in Art* is the price commonly paid for the abnormally wide diffusion of the art of a disintegrating civilization. (*c*) *Lingue Franche.* The intermingling of peoples leads to confusion and mutual competition of languages; some of them spread as 'lingue franche', and in every case their expansion entails a corresponding debasement. Many examples are examined as illustrations. (*d*) *Syncretism in Religion.* Three movements are to be distinguished: the amalgamations of separate schools of philosophy; the amalgamations of separate religions, e.g. the dilution of the religion of Israel by combination with the neighbouring cults, which was opposed with ultimate success by the Hebrew Prophets; and the amalgamation or syncretism of philosophies and religions with one another. Since philosophies are a product of dominant minorities and 'higher religions' a product of internal proletariats, the interaction here is comparable with that illustrated in (*a*) above. Here, as there, though the proletarians move some way towards the position of the dominant minority, the dominant minority moves a far greater distance towards the position of the internal proletariat. For example, the Christian religion employs for its theological exegesis the apparatus of Hellenic philosophy, but this is a small concession compared with the transformation undergone by Greek philosophy between the ages of Plato and of Julian. (*e*) *Cuius regio eius religio?* This section is a digression arising out of the case of the philosopher-emperor Julian considered at the end of the previous section. Can dominant minorities make up for their spiritual weakness by using political force to impose the religion or philosophy of their choice? The answer is that, subject to certain exceptions, they will fail, and the religion which seeks the support of force will grievously injure itself thereby. The one apparently striking exception is the case of the spread of Islam, and this is examined and shown to be not really as much of an exception as it at first appears to be. An opposite formula, *religio regionis religio regis*, is nearer the truth: a ruler who, from cynicism or conviction, adopts the religion of his subjects prospers thereby.

(6) *The Sense of Unity*

This is the 'active' antithesis of the passive feeling of promiscuity. It expresses itself materially in the creation of universal states, and the same spirit inspires the concepts of an omnipotent law or an omnipresent godhead pervading and ruling the Universe. These two concepts are examined and illustrated. In the latter connexion the career of Yahweh, the 'jealous god' of the Hebrews, is traced from his beginnings as the 'jinn' of a Sinaitic volcano to his eventual sublimation as the historic vehicle for a purified and exalted conception of the One True God who is worshipped by the Christian Church, and an explanation is offered of his triumph over all his rivals.

(7) *Archaism*

This is an attempt to escape from an intolerable present by reconstructing an earlier phase in the life of a disintegrating society. Ancient and modern examples are given, the modern including the Gothic Revival and the artificial revival, for nationalistic reasons, of a variety of more or less extinct languages. Archaizing movements generally either prove sterile or transform themselves into their opposite, namely:

(8) *Futurism*

This is an attempt to escape the present by a leap into the darkness of an unknown future. It involves a scrapping of the traditional links with the past, and is in fact revolutionism. In art it expresses itself as iconoclasm.

(9) *The Self-transcendence of Futurism*

As archaism may fall into the gulf of futurism, so futurism may rise to the heights of transfiguration. In other words, it may abandon the forlorn attempt to find its Utopia on the terrestrial plane and may seek it in the life of the soul, untrammelled by time and space. In this connexion the history of the post-Captivity Jews is examined. Futurism expressed itself in a series of suicidal attempts to create a Jewish Empire on Earth, from Zerubbabel to Bar Kōkabā; transfiguration in the establishment of the Christian religion.

(10) *Detachment and Transfiguration*

Detachment is an attitude which finds its most uncompromising and exalted expression in a philosophy professing to represent the teaching of the Buddha. Its logical conclusion is suicide, for real detachment is possible only for a god. The Christian religion, on the other hand, proclaims a God who has voluntarily abandoned a detachment which it was clearly within His power to enjoy. 'God so loved the World . . . .'

(11) *Palingenesia*

Of the four ways of life here examined, transfiguration is the only one which presents a thoroughfare, and it does so by a transference of the field of action from the macrocosm to the microcosm. This is true also of detachment, but, whereas detachment is only a withdrawal, transfiguration is a withdrawal and return: a palingenesia, not in the sense of a rebirth of another example of an old species but in the sense of a birth of a new species of society.

XX. THE RELATION BETWEEN DISINTEGRATING SOCIETIES AND INDIVIDUALS

(1) *The Creative Genius as a Saviour*

In the growth stage creative individuals lead successful responses to successive challenges. In the disintegration stage they appear as saviours *of* or *from* the disintegrating society.

(2) The Saviour with the Sword

These are the founders and maintainers of universal states, but all the works of the sword prove ephemeral.

(3) The Saviour with the Time Machine

These are the archaists and futurists. These, too, take to the sword and suffer the swordsman's fate.

(4) The Philosopher masked by a King

This is Plato's famous remedy. It fails on account of the incompatibility between the detachment of a philosopher and the coercive methods of political potentates.

(5) The God incarnate in a Man

Various imperfect approximations fall by the way and Jesus of Nazareth alone conquers death.

XXI. THE RHYTHM OF DISINTEGRATION

Disintegration proceeds not uniformly but by an alternation of routs and rallies. For example the establishment of a universal state is a rally after the rout of a time of troubles, and the dissolution of a universal state is the final rout. As there is found to be usually one rally followed by a rout in the course of a time of troubles and one rout followed by a rally in the course of a universal state, the normal rhythm seems to be rout–rally–rout–rally–rout–rally–rout: three-and-a-half beats. This pattern is exemplified in the histories of several extinct societies, and then applied to the history of our own Western Christendom with a view to ascertaining what stage in its development our society has reached.

XXII. STANDARDIZATION THROUGH DISINTEGRATION

As differentiation is the mark of growth, so standardization is the mark of disintegration. The chapter concludes with an indication of the problems standing over for examination in the forthcoming volumes.

INDEX